"Composed in the style of the great medieval *catenae,* this new anthology of patristic commentary on Holy Scripture, conveniently arranged by chapter and verse, will be a valuable resource for prayer, study and proclamation. By calling attention to the rich Christian heritage preceding the separations between East and West and between Protestant and Catholic, this series will perform a major service to the cause of ecumenism."

AVERY DULLES, S.J.
Laurence J. McGinley Professor of Religion and Society
Fordham University

"The initial cry of the Reformation was *ad fontes*—back to the sources! The Ancient Christian Commentary on Scripture is a marvelous tool for the recovery of biblical wisdom in today's church. Not just another scholarly project, the ACCS is a major resource for the renewal of preaching, theology and Christian devotion."

TIMOTHY GEORGE
Dean, Beeson Divinity School, Samford University

"Modern church members often do not realize that they are participants in the vast company of the communion of saints that reaches far back into the past and that will continue into the future, until the kingdom comes. This Commentary should help them begin to see themselves as participants in that redeemed community."

ELIZABETH ACHTEMEIER
Union Professor Emerita of Bible and Homiletics
Union Theological Seminary in Virginia

"Contemporary pastors do not stand alone. We are not the first generation of preachers to wrestle with the challenges of communicating the gospel. The Ancient Christian Commentary on Scripture puts us in conversation with our colleagues from the past, that great cloud of witnesses who preceded us in this vocation. This Commentary enables us to receive their deep spiritual insights, their encouragement and guidance for present-day interpretation and preaching of the Word. What a wonderful addition to any pastor's library!"

WILLIAM H. WILLIMON
Dean of the Chapel and Professor of Christian Ministry
Duke University

"Here is a nonpareil series which reclaims the Bible as the book of the church, by making accessible to earnest readers of the twenty-first century the classrooms of Clement of Alexandria and Didymus the Blind, the study and lecture hall of Origen, the cathedrae of Chrysostom and Augustine, the scriptorium of Jerome in his Bethlehem monastery."

GEORGE LAWLESS
Augustinian Patristic Institute and Gregorian University, Rome

"We are pleased to witness publication of the
Ancient Christian Commentary on Scripture. It is most beneficial for us to learn
how the ancient Christians, especially the saints of the church
who proved through their lives their devotion to God and his Word, interpreted
Scripture. Let us heed the witness of those who have gone before us in the faith."

METROPOLITAN THEODOSIUS
Primate, Orthodox Church in America

"As we approach the advent of a new millennium there has emerged across Christendom a
widespread interest in early Christianity, both at the popular and scholarly level....
Christians of all traditions stand to benefit from this project, especially clergy
and those who study the Bible. Moreover, it will allow us to see how our traditions are
both rooted in the scriptural interpretations of the church fathers while at
the same time seeing how we have developed new perspectives."

ALBERTO FERREIRO
Professor of History, Seattle Pacific University

"The Ancient Christian Commentary on Scripture fills a long overdue need for scholars
and students of the church fathers.... Such information will be of immeasurable
worth to those of us who have felt inundated by contemporary interpreters and novel theories
of the biblical text. We welcome some 'new' insight from the
ancient authors in the early centuries of the church."

H. WAYNE HOUSE
Professor of Theology and Law
Trinity University School of Law

Chronological snobbery—the assumption that our ancestors working without benefit of
computers have nothing to teach us—is exposed as nonsense by this magnificent
new series. Surfeited with knowledge but starved of wisdom, many of us are
more than ready to sit at table with our ancestors and listen to their holy
conversations on Scripture. I know I am.

EUGENE H. PETERSON
James Houston Professor of Spiritual Theology
Regent College

ANCIENT CHRISTIAN
COMMENTARY ON SCRIPTURE

NEW TESTAMENT

IX

COLOSSIANS,
1-2 THESSALONIANS,
1-2 TIMOTHY,
TITUS,
PHILEMON

EDITED BY

PETER GORDAY

GENERAL EDITOR
THOMAS C. ODEN

FITZROY DEARBORN PUBLISHERS
CHICAGO · LONDON

For information write to:

FITZROY DEARBORN PUBLISHERS
919 North Michigan Avenue
Chicago, Illinois 60611
USA

or

FITZROY DEARBORN PUBLISHERS
310 Regent Street
London W1R 5AJ
England

The Scripture quotations contained herein are from the Revised Standard Version of the Bible, copyrighted, 1946, 1952, 1971 by the Division of Christian Education of the National Council of the Churches of Christ in the United States of America, and are used by permission. All rights reserved.

Selected excerpts from Ancient Christian Writers: The Works of the Fathers in Translation. Copyright 1946-. Used by permission of Paulist Press.

Selected excerpts from Fathers of the Church: A New Translation. Copyright 1947-. Used by permission of the Catholic University of America Press.

Selected excerpts from The Works of St. Augustine: A Translation for the 21st Century. Used by permission of the Augustinian Heritage Institute.

Cover photograph: Scala/Art Resource, New York. View of the apse. S. Vitale, Ravenna, Italy.

ISBN 1-57958-134-X

Printed in the United States of America ∞

First published in the USA and UK 2000

27	26	25	24	23	22	21	20	19	18	17	16	15	14	13	12	11	10	9	8	7	6	5	4	3	2	1
24	23	22	21	20	19	18	17	16	15	14	13	12	11	10	09	08	07	06	05	04	03	02	01	00		

ANCIENT CHRISTIAN COMMENTARY PROJECT RESEARCH TEAM

GENERAL EDITOR
Thomas C. Oden

ASSOCIATE EDITOR
Christopher A. Hall

TRANSLATIONS PROJECTS DIRECTOR
Joel Scandrett

RESEARCH DIRECTOR
Michael Glerup

EDITORIAL SERVICES DIRECTOR
J. Sergius Halvorsen

GRADUATE RESEARCH ASSISTANTS

Chris Branstetter	Konstantin Gavrilkin
Jill Burnett	Susan Kipper
Meesaeng Lee Choi	Sergey Kozin
Joel Elowsky	Calhoun Robertson
Jeffrey Finch	Robert Seesengood
David Fox	Christian T. Collins Winn

ADMINISTRATIVE ASSISTANTS
Åsa Nausner
Colleen Van De Walle

CONTENTS

General Introduction

The Ancient Christian Commentary on Scripture has as its goal the revitalization of Christian teaching based on classical Christian exegesis, the intensified study of Scripture by lay persons who wish to think with the early church about the canonical text, and the stimulation of Christian historical, biblical, theological and pastoral scholars toward further inquiry into scriptural interpretation by ancient Christian writers.

The time frame of these documents spans seven centuries of exegesis, from Clement of Rome to John of Damascus, from the end of the New Testament era to A.D. 750, including the Venerable Bede.

Lay readers are asking how they might study sacred texts under the instruction of the great minds of the ancient church. This commentary has been intentionally prepared for a general lay audience of non-professionals who study the Bible regularly and who earnestly wish to have classic Christian observation on the text readily available to them. The series is targeted to anyone who wants to reflect and meditate with the early church about the plain sense, theological wisdom and moral meaning of particular Scripture texts.

A commentary dedicated to allowing ancient Christian exegetes to speak for themselves will refrain from the temptation to fixate endlessly upon contemporary criticism. Rather, it will stand ready to provide textual resources from a distinguished history of exegesis which has remained massively inaccessible and shockingly disregarded during the last century. We seek to make available to our present-day audiences the multicultural, multilingual, transgenerational resources of the early ecumenical Christian tradition.

Preaching at the end of the first millennium focused primarily on the text of Scripture as understood by the earlier esteemed tradition of comment, largely converging on those writers that best reflected classic Christian consensual thinking. Preaching at the end of the second millennium has reversed that pattern. It has so forgotten most of these classic comments that they are vexing to find anywhere, and even when located they are often available only in archaic editions and inadequate translations. The preached word in our time has remained largely bereft of previously influential patristic inspiration. Recent scholarship has so focused attention upon post-Enlightenment historical and literary methods that it has left this longing largely unattended and unserviced.

This series provides the pastor, exegete, student and lay reader with convenient means to see what Athanasius or John Chrysostom or the desert fathers and mothers had to say about a particular text for preaching, for study and for meditation. There is an emerging awareness among Catholic, Protestant and Orthodox laity that vital biblical preaching and spiritual formation need deeper grounding beyond the scope of the historical-critical orientations that have governed biblical studies in our day.

Hence this work is directed toward a much broader audience than the highly technical and specialized scholarly field of patristic studies. The audience is not limited to the university scholar concentrating on the study of the history of the transmission of the text or to those with highly focused philological interests in textual morphology or historical-critical issues. Though these are crucial concerns for specialists, they are not the paramount interest of this series.

This work is a Christian Talmud. The Talmud is a Jewish collection of rabbinic arguments and comments on the Mishnah, which epitomized the laws of the Torah. The Talmud originated in approximately the same period that the patristic writers were commenting on texts of the Christian tradition. Christians from the late patristic age through the medieval period had documents analogous to the Jewish Talmud and Midrash (Jewish commentaries) available to them in the *glossa ordinaria* and catena traditions, two forms of compiling extracts of patristic exegesis. In Talmudic fashion the sacred text of Christian Scripture was thus clarified and interpreted by the classic commentators.

The Ancient Christian Commentary on Scripture has venerable antecedents in medieval exegesis of both eastern and western traditions, as well as in the Reformation tradition. It offers for the first time in this century the earliest Christian comments and reflections on the Old and New Testaments to a modern audience. Intrinsically an ecumenical project, this series is designed to serve Protestant, Catholic and Orthodox lay, pastoral and scholarly audiences.

In cases where Greek, Latin, Syriac and Coptic texts have remained untranslated into English, we provide new translations. Wherever current English translations are already well rendered, they will be utilized, but if necessary their language will be brought up to date. We seek to present fresh dynamic equivalency translations of long-neglected texts which historically have been regarded as authoritative models of biblical interpretation.

These foundational sources are finding their way into many public libraries and into the core book collections of many pastors and lay persons. It is our intent and the publisher's commitment to keep the whole series in print for many years to come.

Thomas C. Oden
General Editor

A Guide to Using This Commentary

Several features have been incorporated into the design of this commentary. The following comments are intended to assist readers in making full use of this volume.

Pericopes of Scripture

The scriptural text has been divided into pericopes, or passages, usually several verses in length. Each of these pericopes is given a heading, which appears at the beginning of the pericope. For example, the first pericope in the Commentary on Colossians is "1:1-8, Salutation and Thanksgiving." This heading is followed by the Scripture passage quoted in the Revised Standard Version (RSV) across the full width of the page. The Scripture passage is provided for the convenience of readers, but it is also in keeping with medieval patristic commentaries, in which the citations of the Fathers were arranged around the text of Scripture.

Overviews

Following each pericope is an overview of the patristic comments on that pericope. The format of this overview varies within the volumes of this series, depending on the requirements of the specific book of Scripture. The function of the overview is to provide a brief summary of all the comments to follow. It tracks a reasonably cohesive thread of argument among patristic comments, even though they are derived from diverse sources and generations. Thus the summaries do not proceed chronologically or by verse sequence. Rather they seek to rehearse the overall course of the patristic comment on that pericope.

We do not assume that the commentators themselves anticipated or expressed a formally received cohesive argument but rather that the various arguments tend to flow in a plausible, recognizable pattern. The modern reader can thus glimpse aspects of continuity in the flow of diverse exegetical traditions representing various generations and geographical locations.

Topical Headings

An abundance of varied patristic comment is available for each pericope. For this reason we have broken the pericopes into two levels. First is the verse with its topical heading. The patristic comments are then focused on aspects of each verse, with topical headings summarizing the essence of the patristic comment by evoking a key phrase, metaphor or idea. This feature provides a bridge by which modern readers can enter into the heart of the patristic comment.

Identifying the Patristic Texts

Following the topical heading of each section of comment, the name of the patristic commentator is given. An English translation of the patristic comment is then provided. This is immediately followed by the title of the patristic work and the textual reference. In many cases we have provided the reference number for the book, chapter and section (and subsection where necessary). Some selections, however, are taken from complete patristic commentaries on the text (such as those by Theodoret and Augustine), which in modern editions are organized sequentially on a verse-by-verse basis. In these cases no numerical reference is given following the title of the work.

Many of these commentaries have not been translated into English, and we have translated for this volume only the portions relevant to our editorial premises. It is assumed that anyone who has access to the original will have only to look up the specific chapter and verse of the commentary in question.

The Footnotes

Readers who wish to pursue a deeper investigation of the patristic works cited in this commentary will find the footnotes especially valuable. A footnote number directs the reader to the notes at the bottom of the right-hand column, where in addition to other notations (clarifications or biblical crossreferences) one will find information on English translations (where available) and standard original-language editions of the work cited. An abbreviated citation (normally citing the book, volume and page number) of the work in a modern edition is provided. A key to the abbreviations is provided at the front of this volume. Where there is any serious ambiguity or textual problem in the selection, we have tried to reflect the best available textual tradition. In some cases previous English translations have been adopted in this commentary, but in such a case the English has been updated or otherwise amended for easier reading.

For the convenience of computer database users the digital database references are provided to either the Thesaurus Lingua Grecae (Greek texts) or to the Cetedoc (Latin texts) in the appendix found on page 319.

Abbreviations

ACCS	T. C. Oden, ed. Ancient Christian Commentary on Scripture. Downers Grove, Ill.: InterVarsity Press, 1998-.
ACD	St. Augustine. *On Christian Doctrine.* Translated by D. W. Robertson Jr. Library of Liberal Arts. Indianapolis: Bobbs-Merrill, 1958.
ACW	Ancient Christian Writers: The Works of the Fathers in Translation. Mahwah, N.J.: Paulist, 1946-.
AHSIS	Dana Miller, ed. *The Ascetical Homilies of Saint Isaac the Syrian.* Boston: Holy Transfiguration Monastery, 1984.
ANF	A. Roberts and J. Donaldson, eds. Ante-Nicene Fathers. 10 vols. Buffalo, N.Y.: Christian Literature, 1885-1896. Reprint, Grand Rapids, Mich.: Eerdmans, 1951-1956. Reprint, Peabody, Mass.: Hendrickson, 1994.
ARL	St. Athanasius. *The Resurrection Letters.* Paraphrased and introduced by Jack N. Sparks. Nashville: Thomas Nelson, 1979.
CG	St. Augustine. *The City of God.* Translated by Henry Bettenson. London: Penguin, 1972.
CMFL	St. John Chrysostom. *On Marriage and Family Life.* Translated by Catharine P. Roth and David Anderson. Crestwood, N.Y.: St. Vladimir's Seminary Press, 1986.
COP	St. John Chrysostom. *Six Books on the Priesthood.* Translated by Graham Neville. Crestwood, N.Y.: St. Vladimir's Seminary Press, 1984.
COV	John Chrysostom. *On Virginity, Against Remarriage.* Translated by Sally Rieger Shore. Studies in Women and Religion 9. New York and Toronto: Edwin Mellen Press, 1983.
CSEL	Corpus Scriptorum Ecclesiasticorum Latinorum. Vienna: 1866-.
CWS	Classics of Western Spirituality. A Library of the Great Spiritual Masters. Mahwah, N.J.: Paulist, 1978-.
DC	D. J. Chitty. *The Desert a City.* Oxford: Blackwell, 1966.
DDCH	Kurt Niederwimmer, trans. *The Didache.* Hermeneia: A Critical and Historical Commentary on the Bible. Minneapolis: Fortress, 1998.
FC	R. J. Deferrari, ed. Fathers of the Church: A New Translation. Washington, D.C.: Catholic University of America Press, 1947-.
FGFR	*Faith Gives Fullness to Reasoning: The Five Theological Orations of Gregory Nazianzen.* Introduction and commentary by F. W. Norris. Leiden and New York: E. J. Brill, 1991.
HOG	Bede the Venerable. *Homilies on the Gospels.* Translated by L. T. Martin and D. Hurst. 2 vols. Kalamazoo, Mich.: Cistercian Publications, 1991.
JCC	John Cassian. *Conferences.* Translated by Colm Luibheid. Classics of Western Spirituality. Mahwah, N.J.: Paulist, 1985.
JDBI	St. John Damascene. *Barlaam and Ioasaph.* Translated by G. R. Woodward et al. Loeb Classical

Library 34. London: Heinemann; Cambridge, Mass.: Harvard University Press, 1967.

JDDI   St. John of Damascus. *On the Divine Images.* Translated by David Anderson. Crestwood N.Y.: St. Vladimir's Seminary Press, 1980.

JMD   R. P. C. Hanson, trans. *Selections from Justin Martyr's Dialogue with Trypho, a Jew.* World Christian Books 49, third series. London: Lutterworth, 1963.

JSL   F. A. Wright, trans. *Select Letters of St. Jerome.* Loeb Classical Library. London: Heinemann; Cambridge, Mass.: Harvard University Press, 1963.

JSSS 2   C. McCarthy, trans. and ed. *Saint Ephrem's Commentary on Tatian's Diatessaron: An English Translation of Chester Beatty Syriac MS 709.* Journal of Semitic Studies Supplement 2. Oxford: Oxford University Press for the University of Manchester, 1993.

LCC   J. Baillie et al., eds. The Library of Christian Classics. 26 vols. Philadelphia: Westminster, 1953-1966.

LCP   Eduard Lohse. *A Commentary on the Epistles to the Colossians and to Philemon.* Hermeneia: A Critical and Historical Commentary on the Bible. Philadelphia: Fortress, 1971.

NPNF   P. Schaff et al., eds. *A Select Library of the Nicene and Post-Nicene Fathers of the Christian Church,* series 1 and 2 (14 vols. each). Buffalo, N.Y.: Christian Literature, 1887-1894. Reprint, Edinburgh, T & T Clark; Grand Rapids, Mich.: Eerdmans, 1952-1956.

NTA 15   K. Staab, ed. *Pauluskommentare aus der griechischen Kirche: Aus Katenenhandschriften gesammelt und herausgegeben* (Pauline Commentary from the Greek Church: Collected and Edited Catena Writings). NT Abhandlungen 15. Münster in Westfalen: Aschendorff, 1933.

OAC   Origen. *Contra Celsum.* Translated and edited by Henry Chadwick. Cambridge: Cambridge University Press, 1953.

OAL   St. Isaac of Nineveh. *On Ascetical Life.* Translated by Mary Hansbury. Crestwood, N.Y.: St. Vladimir's Seminary Press, 1989.

OFP   Origen. *On First Principles.* Translated by G. W. Butterworth. London: SPCK, 1936. Reprint, Gloucester, Mass.: Peter Smith, 1973.

OHS   Basil of Caesarea. *On the Holy Spirit.* Translated by David Anderson. Crestwood, N.Y.: St. Vladimir's Seminary Press, 1980.

OSW   Rowan A. Greer, trans. *Origen: Selected Writings.* Classics of Western Spirituality. Mahwah, N.J.: Paulist, 1979.

OUC   St. Cyril of Alexandria. *On the Unity of Christ.* Translated by John Anthony McGuckin. Crestwood, N.Y.: St. Vladimir's Seminary Press, 1995.

OWP   St. John Chrysostom. *On Wealth and Poverty.* Translated by Catharine Roth. Crestwood, N.Y.: St. Vladimir's Seminary Press, 1984.

PETE   A. Souter, ed. *Pelagius's Expositions of Thirteen Epistles of St. Paul.* Texts and Studies 9.1-3. Cambridge: Cambridge University Press, 1922-1931.

PG   J.-P. Migne, ed. Patrologia Graeca. 166 vols. Paris: Migne, 1857-1886.

PK   *Pachomian Koinonia.* Vol. 1: *The Life of Saint Pachomius and His Disciples.* Vol. 2: *Pachomian Chronicle and Rules.* Vol. 3: *Instructions, Letters and Other Writings of Saint Pachomius and His Disciples.* Translated by Armand Veilleux. Cistercian Publications 45, 46 and 47. Kalamazoo, Mich.: Cistercian Publications, 1980, 1981, 1982.

PL   J.-P. Migne, ed. Patrologia Latina. 221 vols. Paris: Migne, 1844-1864.

POG   Eusebius. *The Proof of the Gospel.* Translated by W. J. Ferrar. London: SPCK, 1920. Reprint, Grand Rapids, Mich.: Baker, 1981.

PSD   Colm Luibheid et al., trans. *Pseudo-Dionysius: The Complete Works.* Classics of Western Spirituality. Mahwah, N.J.: Paulist, 1987.

SDF   Benedicta Ward, trans. *The Desert Christian: The Sayings of the Desert Fathers.* New York: Macmillan, 1975.

SFPSL   Sebastian Brock, trans. *The Syriac Fathers on Prayer and the Spiritual Life.* Cistercian Studies Series 101. Kalamazoo, Mich.: Cistercian Publications, 1987.

TEM   H. B. Swete, ed. *Theodori episcopi Mopsuesteni: In epistolas b. Pauli commentarii.* 2 vols. Cambridge: Cambridge University Press, 1880, 1882.

WSA   J. E. Rotelle, ed.; Edmund Hill, O.P., trans. *The Works of St. Augustine: A Translation for the Twenty-first Century.* Vols. 1-11. Brooklyn: New City Press, 1991.

INTRODUCTION TO THE SHORTER EPISTLES

The shorter epistles of Paul covered in this volume of the Ancient Christian Commentary on Scripture series received their due share of exposition and interpretation from the Fathers of the early church. While the quantity of their commentary is not so great as that on the major epistles, certain passages in these briefer compositions were, as will be evident, particularly important in the doctrinal and disciplinary disputes of the times. Pauline authorship was assumed for all of the letters, including the Pastorals (i.e., the letters to Timothy and Titus). The value of all of these letters for Christian edification, Philemon excepted, was taken for granted. In the case of Philemon, Jerome, in his preface to that letter, indicates that there was some question, because of its strictly occasional character, as to its real usefulness for teaching. Jerome's own opinion, however, as is indicated in the comments on that letter included below, was that its occasional character only increased in a particular way its status as a means for edification. All of the letters included here thus formed an indubitable part of the proclamation and instruction of the divine apostle, the great missionary to the Gentiles, as this applied to all of the churches in all times and places.[1]

With the passage of the centuries, the two greatest expositors of St. Paul's thought have turned out in the judgment of the church, as this may be determined by the abundant survival and constant use of their work, to be John Chrysostom and Augustine. In Chrysostom's case this judgment reflects the extensiveness, eloquence, spiritual richness and unquestioned orthodoxy of his homilies on each of the epistles, along with his position as one of the great spiritual masters of the Eastern church. For Augustine the mass of his writing, the importance of his dogmatic synthesis, his position of preeminence at the rise of medieval Christianity in the West and his ultimate centrality to all later doctrinal debates assured his overwhelming influence. His understanding of Paul would come to dominate not only the Latin church of the Middle Ages and beyond but also the Reformation and modern Protestantism. The exposition of Paul from the pens of these two exegetes—along with the issues they formulated on grace and free will, on the nature of divine providence, on the authority of the church and on the character and import of faithful living and discipleship—thus occupies a major place in what follows.

Alongside these two, moreover, comes a mass of exposition from Latin, Greek, Coptic and Syriac writers who found inspiration and guidance from Paul on dogmatic and practical issues, as they wove scriptural texts into the body of their preaching, teaching, meditation, theological reflection and letters. The excerpts that follow contain a broad selection from these works of what seems most important for modern students of Scripture, as well as most representative of the mind of the greatest thinkers of the

---

[1]The best general introduction is still M. F. Wiles, *The Divine Apostle: The Interpretation of St. Paul's Epistles in the Early Church* (Cambridge: Cambridge University Press, 1967). For a general introduction to the spirituality and mindset of patristic exegesis, I recommend the excerpt from Henri de Lubac's work translated as "Spiritual Understanding," in *The Theological Interpretation of Scripture: Classic and Contemporary Readings*, ed. Stephen Fowl (Oxford: Blackwell, 1997), pp. 3-25.

early church, as they pondered Paul's meaning.

By way of introduction, some consideration of the nature of the sources, as well as of the historical context and principal themes of this early commentary and of the nature of the translations presented here, will be helpful.

Sources

Greek Sources. We are particularly fortunate in having the complete commentaries in Greek of John Chrysostom and Theodoret of Cyr, as well as extensive fragments from the running commentary of Theodore of Mopsuestia and Severian of Gabala, on the entire body of Pauline epistles. These writers are all close in time in their work of composition—from the end of the fourth to the middle of the fifth centuries—and are closely interrelated theologically and in terms of literary dependence as products of the Syrian-Antiochene church.[2]

Chrysostom's commentary is in the form of homilies preached mostly in Antioch in Syria, when he was bishop there, in the years before A.D. 397, though some, like those on Colossians, belong to the later years, when he was archbishop of Constantinople.[3] Probably edited by him at a later time, each collection on a particular epistle has an introduction in which the setting and themes of the letter are discussed. There are twelve homilies on Colossians, eleven on 1 Thessalonians, five on 2 Thessalonians, eighteen on 1 Timothy, ten on 2 Timothy, six on Titus and three on Philemon. These are clearly sermons in their tone and mode of address and yet are remarkably thorough in their attention to detailed problems of interpretation. In his method of presentation Chrysostom clearly expected his audience to think through with him the continuity and structure of the apostle's argument in each epistle.

Indeed, Chrysostom has always been rightly praised for his pastoral insight and shrewd, generous empathy with the apostle and his declamatory style of expression, and for his wisdom in nurturing others in the stresses and strains of faithful Christian living. Those abilities are much in evidence in this group of homilies, where Paul was preoccupied with pastoral work and thus with the needs, human sensibilities, vulnerabilities and struggles of his readers. Central to Chrysostom's exposition, not only in the homilies but also in a great deal of other exposition of Paul found throughout his writings, are the themes of the great humility of the apostle, the balance of parental strength and tenderness with which he deals with those Christians under his care and the ringing call to virtue and patient suffering as the greatest means of witnessing to others. No greater virtue exists in Chrysostom's opinion than the rejection of wealth and its allurements in favor of compassion for the poor and an identification with their struggles.

---

[2]There are many general treatments of the subject of patristic exegesis, in which it is customary to contrast the literal-historical exegesis of the fourth-century Antiochene church, beginning with the work of Diodore of Tarsus, with the allegorical methods of the Alexandrian church, as practiced preeminently by Origen and those later inspired by him. Aside from the oversimplification contained in this contrast, which now makes it outdated, it is the case that all patristic interpretation of Scripture operates in another thought world from the historicist assumptions of modern exegesis. However, as a matter of later development, it happens that the exegesis of the Antiochene church, particularly as represented by John Chrysostom, became normative in the Eastern church, with the Alexandrian tradition as a more minor and dissenting, yet powerful, voice.

[3]For discussion and a general introduction to Chrysostom, see J. N. D. Kelly, *Golden Mouth: The Story of John Chrysostom—Ascetic, Preacher, Bishop* (Ithaca, N.Y.: Cornell University Press, 1995), especially pp. 90-103 on his interpretation of Paul.

Chrysostom seems likewise convinced that a steady adherence to the faith handed down from an admired teacher to devoted students in a father-son relationship, as with Timothy and Titus, is the surest safeguard of orthodoxy. Paul's ability as a "many-faceted man" to become "everything which was needed for the preaching and salvation of people"[4] comes through in Chrysostom's remarkable ability to attribute tone and motive to Paul's words, to catch a nuance and purpose even in what seems offhand. Though his view of Paul may be an idealization in which no faults or weaknesses are allowed, as is often noted, Chrysostom's attunement to Paul as the representative of Christ for those committed to his care allows us to get a deeper sense of the meaning of the apostle's words for all time and all pastoral relationships. "In spite of the fact that he unavoidably speaks the language of the past and his works read as topical for an age long gone, his vivid imagery, together with his love and understanding of the Bible and of the erring hearts of men, gives his work an abiding quality and relevance. Christianity is not simply a set of disputed doctrines, but a way of life, and Chrysostom never lets this be forgotten."[5]

The commentary of Theodoret of Cyr on St. Paul, strongly dependent on that of Chrysostom, has been preserved for us in its entirety in a continuous tradition from the time of the early church, probably because Theodoret was viewed as a kind of synthesis or high point of Greek exegesis by later generations.[6] Composed in the decades immediately preceding the Council of Chalcedon, that is, between A.D. 420 and 450, it is dry, scholarly and periphrastic. He is the archrepresentative of Antiochene exegesis with its emphasis on a literal, rather than allegorical, interpretation of the biblical salvation history and with the use of typological figurative explanations of passages in order to link the Testaments in a scheme of prophecy and fulfillment. In addition, he maintained a strict diophysitism, or two-nature christology, in the battle with the Nestorian separation and seeming compartmentalization of the human nature and divine nature of Christ. Often he repeated Chrysostom's views, but just as often he added to or enriched them, as excerpts below will suggest. He demonstrated a remarkable concern for sorting out the chronological course of Paul's work. Each commentary on one of the epistles is preceded by a preface that discusses its setting and unifying themes.

The work of Severian of Gabala (d. after 408) is known only from extensive fragments preserved in the medieval Greek catenas. Although he was a contemporary and an enemy of Chrysostom, we know little about him apart from his shadowy participation in Chrysostom's condemnation at the Synod of the Oak in 403. As an exegete, Severian is particularly noteworthy for his strong insistence that the letter to the Colossians makes the most sense when interpreted as Paul's steady argument for the all-sufficient lordship of Christ against the veneration of divine, angelic beings.

Preserved in two catenas are a more modest number of fragments in Greek of the commentary on the ten minor epistles of Paul by Theodore of Mopsuestia (d. 428). These may be supplemented by the Latin

---

[4]Margaret M. Mitchell, "'A Variable and Many-Sorted Man': John Chrysostom's Treatment of Pauline Inconsistency," *Journal of Early Christian Studies* 6:1 (1998): 93-111, citation p. 106.

[5]Frances M. Young, *From Nicaea to Chalcedon: A Guide to the Literature and Its Background* (Philadelphia: Fortress, 1983), pp. 158-59.

[6]Jean-Noël Guinot, *L'Exégèse de Théodoret de Cyr*, Théologie Historique 100 (Paris: Beauchesne, 1995), pp. 71-76. An excellent introduction in English to Theodoret's exegesis is Jean-Noël Guinot, "Theodoret of Cyrus: Bishop and Exegete," in *The Bible in Greek Christian Antiquity*, ed. Paul M. Blowers (Notre Dame, Ind.: University of Notre Dame Press, 1997), pp. 163-93.

renderings, produced in the ninth and tenth centuries, of the entire text of the commentary and transmitted under the supposed authorship of Ambrose of Milan. These texts, composed in a rough, obtuse
Latin, do provide us with a tolerable and sometimes quite interesting understanding, as comparison
with the Greek fragments suggests, of Theodore's thinking about Paul's meaning. He shows a genuine
concern for understanding the structure and rhetorical arrangement of each of the epistles. He evinces a
real sense for how Paul moves from dogmatic assertions to practical applications. Often, like Theodoret,
he is in complete agreement with Chrysostom, but sometimes his particular christological perspectives,
as well as his attempts to clear up obscurities in interpretation, come through clearly enough to be of real
value, and so I have reproduced a number of them below.[7]

In addition, moreover, to these close line-by-line commentaries on the letters of Paul, there is a rich
harvest of exposition to be found throughout the Greek tradition. While much early work is no longer
extant, such as the commentaries of Origen on the two Thessalonian letters, Titus and Philemon, which
were known to Jerome (Epistle 119.8-10), the surviving material is vast. This ranges from the very early
writings of the apostolic fathers, such as Ignatius of Antioch (c. 35-c. 107) and Justin Martyr (c. 100-c.
165), through the work of anti-Gnostic authors such as Irenaeus of Lyons (c. 130-c. 200), Clement of
Alexandria (c. 150-c. 215), Origen of Alexandria (c. 185-c. 254) and Methodius of Olympus (d. c. 311).
The history continues with the anti-Arian and anti-Apollinarian authors of the fourth and fifth centuries, such as Athanasius of Alexandria (c. 295-373), Cyril of Jerusalem (c. 315-386), the Cappadocians
Basil the Great (c. 330-379), Gregory of Nazianzus (329-389) and Gregory of Nyssa (c. 330-c. 395), and
the forerunners of Chalcedonian orthodoxy, such as Theodoret of Cyr (c. 393-c. 466) and Cyril of Alexandria (d. 444). This tradition of dogmatic reflection culminated in the work of the Byzantine-era theologians John of Damascus (c. 675-c. 749), Pseudo-Dionysius (sixth century) and Maximus Confessor (c.
580-662).

Alongside the more explicitly theological writings, from the fourth century on a rich stream of ascetical teaching and exposition developed from the monastic communities of Egypt and the Near East.
These works, such as the Rule and teachings of the founder of Egyptian coenobitism, Pachomius,
together with many compositions originally in Coptic or Syriac but later rendered into Greek or Latin,
form a tradition of the wisdom of the desert fathers.[8]

Frequently, as will be seen, the vast amount of Pauline exposition contained in the writings of these
Eastern church fathers is embedded in a complex context of discussion that is only hinted at in the
extracts reproduced here. The meaning of the Pauline text is frequently only incidental to the main
theme under discussion by the particular author but yet contributes to our enhanced appreciation of the
theological and moral implications of the text, as well as to certain possible ways of construing the inter-

---

[7]The best introduction to Theodore's exegesis is still Rowan A. Greer, *Theodore of Mopsuestia: Exegete and Theologian* (London: Faith Press,
1961).

[8]For a brief introduction to desert monasticism and the "Sayings of the Fathers" tradition, see Derwas Chitty, *The Desert a City: An Introduction
to the Study of Egyptian and Palestinian Monasticism Under the Christian Empire* (Crestwood, N.Y.: St. Vladimir's Seminary Press, 1966), and for an
introduction to their biblical interpretation, Douglas Burton-Christie, "Oral Culture, Biblical Interpretation and Spirituality in Early Christian Monasticism," in *The Bible in Christian Greek Antiquity*, ed. Paul E. Blowers (Notre Dame, Ind.: University of Notre Dame Press, 1997), pp.
415-40.

pretation. In each case I have tried to include enough of the surrounding train of thought to make the selected passage intelligible in its own right and helpful in illuminating Paul. In other cases, however, the cited passage is a direct comment on the scriptural material and is intended to offer an opinion on its correct understanding, thus serving as a direct supplement to the exegesis of the formal commentaries themselves.

Latin Sources. A similar pattern of formal commentaries and less formal incidental comment through a great variety of writings exists here as well. The full commentaries are those of Ambrosiaster and Pelagius, along with Jerome's work on Titus and Philemon. First, however, we must give consideration to Augustine of Hippo as the dominant Latin expositor of Paul.

Augustine (c. 354-430) produced a considerable body of writing in the exposition of Scripture, notably on the Psalter, the Gospel and epistles of John and, in the case of the Pauline letters, on Romans and Galatians.[9] For our portion of the shorter letters, however, we must comb the sermons, tractates, epistles and topical essays of his life's work, particularly the anti-Pelagian writings, including the massive *City of God,* for significant interpretation. In his work directed against the teachings of Caelestius, Pelagius and Julian of Eclanum, beginning with the appearance of *On the Merits and Remission of Sins,*[10] and until the end of his life, Augustine sharpened three principal doctrines. These are the absolute gratuity and priority of unmerited divine grace in salvation, the corruption and bondage of human willing as manifested in the dynamics of original sin and the inscrutable but just and dependable divine decrees by which some persons are elected to salvation and others not.

These later teachings must be set, however, against the emphases of his earlier periods. Augustine had contended first against the Gnostic Manichaeans and their identification of evil with the material world and the God of the Old Testament, this debate being contained primarily in his writing against the popular Manichaean teacher Faustus. Then he debated the Donatist schismatics who, in his opinion, had rejected the unity in charity that is the hallmark of the true Christian church in favor of a mistaken and prideful search for purity of faith and practice. This latter focus is contained in certain polemical writings on the sacraments and in commentary on the Gospel and epistles of John. In his final phase, represented by a whole host of writings but monumentally by the *City of God,* he combated the various Pelagian theological interpretations of Scripture and tradition, in which he believed that the nature and consequences of sin had been grossly misunderstood and underestimated.

For our purposes, it is important that Augustine produced a great deal of interpretation of Paul that is scattered through these works and in a lifetime of communication through sermons and letters and that is constantly construed in terms of his overriding theological agenda. With Paul as a principal support, he argues against the Manichaeans that evil originates not in matter but in disordered human willing. Against the Donatists, he argues that the purity of faith and practice is found only in the maintenance of

---

[9]The best introduction to Augustine as a theologian and exegete remains Eugene TeSelle, *Augustine the Theologian* (New York: Herder & Herder, 1970).
[10]A.D. 411-412.

charity within the body of Christ, leaving the separation of the elect and nonelect finally only to God. Against the Pelagians, he took the position that the corruption of sin makes us absolutely, not only relatively, dependent on unmerited grace for salvation.

Augustine knew the commentaries of Ambrosiaster and Pelagius. The work of the former, handed down through the Middle Ages under the name of Ambrose, has for various reasons been long thought by modern scholars to be the production of an unknown writer designated Ambrosiaster, that is, "Ambrose-like" or "attributed to Ambrose," by Erasmus in the sixteenth century. He probably wrote around Rome during 363 to 384 and took the position throughout his work that Paul's message is best understood in terms of the battle with Judaism and the Jewish understanding of salvation history. The Jews make the law and its faithful observance the climax of God's saving work, while, for Ambrosiaster, the redemption in Christ has essentially changed that. Now it is revealed against rabbinic teaching as well as the Sabellian heresy of monarchianism in the Godhead that God is trinitarian Father, Son and Spirit, each in a distinct personhood and yet one. It is now clear that the law must be understood primarily as a foreshadowing of Christ who brings salvation that reaches back to an undoing of the devil's work in paradise. Finally, true obedience to God may be understood to require a differentiated interpretation of the law and its mandates for living, particularly as this understanding is reflected in and mediated by the teaching authority of the Catholic church.

These views are set out repeatedly in Ambrosiaster's often subtle and nuanced exposition of Paul. They have led to much speculation about his knowledge of Judaism and his relationship to the papacy of the time. Augustine was almost certainly inspired to some of his understanding of original sin by his reading of Ambrosiaster.

Augustine also knew the work of Pelagius, whose commentaries on Paul appeared between 400 and 410, eventually to be transmitted for centuries under the name of Jerome and only to be recovered and properly identified in the modern period. For the portion of the commentaries that pertains to the epistles included here the comments are generally brief and often stated in the form of two or three equally acceptable alternatives. Pelagius's concern is preeminently with the practical, existential bearing of Paul's message, particularly as it pertains to the exercise of free will and moral seriousness in the life of faith. The implication often is that God does not require more from us than we can truly do, so long as we receive divine assistance in the form of baptism, forgiveness and guidance through the law.

Pelagius holds up a view of the Christian life as rigorously demanding, oriented toward virtue as its goal and ascetic in its particular disciplines. In these respects there is a certain common ground that has often been remarked between him and the Greek exegetes, because of their shared concern with free will and moral endeavor. What distinguishes them, however, is the emphasis laid by the Greek fathers on the all-encompassing and cosmic mediation of grace in the lives of believers. Consequently, however much they may emphasize freely willed virtue, salvation for them is always viewed in relation to grace and is always subsumed into the divinely empowered external economy of universal salvation history and the transformation of all things. Pelagius thus comes to represent not only the asceticism of the early church in its biblical interpretation but also the Latin tendency toward a narrow and legalistic humanism, against which Augustine inveighed.[11]

The combination of monastic asceticism with an Eastern flavor and Latin culture is also seen in the work of Jerome of Stridon on Titus and Philemon, produced at Bethlehem in Palestine, probably in 387-388.[12] In a tradition inherited partly from the lost commentaries of Origen, Jerome concerned himself with matters of historical detail, but even more of linguistic detail, in his exposition of these letters. In the prologues he defended their Pauline authorship and canonical status and value against critics, and in the commentaries themselves he explored a wide range of etymological meanings and issues of historical development.

As elsewhere in his work Jerome reveals a constant concern for the *hebraica veritas*, for the background in Hebrew and Jewish language and culture, as the key to understanding some obscurity in Paul's statements. He also has a fine sense for the various qualifications and nuanced modulations that Paul introduces into arguments. Unlike Chrysostom, who tends to see these as equivocations that protect the feelings and sensibilities of his readers, Jerome sees them as the balancing tools of a good scholar who wishes to state his arguments with dialectical precision. In the fashion of the Greek exegetes on whom Jerome modeled himself, he saw his exegetical work in terms of the removal of obscurities and the deft balancing of various interpretative options inherited from his predecessors, so that the reader might make judicious and informed decisions.

The Latin tradition of Pauline interpretation apart from the commentaries and the work of Augustine is as rich as that of the Greek church and through their shared history in these early centuries parallels it in many ways. There are the second- to third-century anti-Gnostic writers Hippolytus of Rome (c. 170-c. 236) and Tertullian of Carthage (c. 160-c. 225), and along with them the guardians of ecclesiastical order, Novatian of Rome (d. 257 or 258) and Cyprian of Carthage (d. 258). The fourth century is dominated by the anti-Arian theologians Hilary of Poitiers (c. 315-367), Marius Victorinus (b. c. 280-285), Nicetas of Remesiana (d. c. 414) and especially Ambrose of Milan (c. 340-397). Toward the end of the fourth century, Jerome, Rufinus of Aquileia (c. 345-410) in his exposition of the Apostles' Creed and the young Augustine are the most important writers.

In the fifth century, there is Augustine himself, but then the consolidators of orthodoxy—Leo I, the Great, of Rome (d. 461), Vincent of Lérins (d. before 450) and Maximus of Turin (d. 408/423). The ascetical writer John Cassian (c. 360-435) is especially significant in that he combines a retrieval of the

---

[11]Though Pelagius was officially a heretic, his commentaries were widely read and preserved for future generations under other names. They were repeatedly edited for orthodoxy and recycled, so that what we have today may be regarded as representative of much patristic thought and exegesis, excluding, of course, that which is ecumenically censured as "Pelagianism." It has to be remembered that the text of Pelagius on Paul as we now have it was preserved in the corpus of Jerome and probably reworked in the sixth century by Primasius or Cassiodorus or both. Pelagius's original text was in specific ways presumably explicitly heretical, but what we have now is largely unexceptional, even if it is still possible to detect points of disagreement with Augustine.

The corpus of Pelagius is highly controverted. Until 1934 all we had was a corrupted text of his Pauline commentary and fragments quoted by Augustine. R. F. Evans argues that the Pauline commentary was the original work of Pelagius. Since the Pelagian corpus has been so corrupted by a history of redactors, the reader is well advised not too quickly to equate the fourth century Pelagius with later standard stereotypes of the arch-heresy of Pelagianism. Cf. Adalbert Hamman, Supplementum to PL 1, 1959, cols. 1101-1570.

[12]The best introduction is J. N. D. Kelly, *Jerome: His Life, Writings and Controversies* (New York: Harper & Row, 1975), especially pp. 145-49 for discussion of his Pauline commentary.

traditions of the desert fathers with the rise of Western-style monasticism. Toward the end of the fifth century and beginning of the sixth the sermons of Fulgentius of Ruspe (c. 467-532) in North Africa and of Caesarius of Arles (c. 470-542) in Gaul are important witnesses to a strongly Augustinian view of Paul. The rich and important sermons of Gregory the Great (c. 540-604) in Rome as well as his great work on pastoral care, along with the commentaries composed at the Vivarium in southern Italy by Cassiodorus (c. 470-c. 540), round out the sixth century. The only later Latin writer included here from the seventh through eighth centuries is the Venerable Bede (c. 673-735), whose use of Pauline texts is often striking and fresh. With Bede the period covered in this anthology is complete for the Latin church.

The process of extracting passages from the works of these Latin writers is the same as that described for the Greek fathers. An interesting contrast, however, lies in the fact that there is a much larger volume of purely homiletical literature in the Latin tradition, while the Greek tradition inclines more to dogmatic, sometimes mystical, writings. This comparison is particularly true from the fifth century onward, when the Eastern church becomes consumed in the post-Chalcedonian debates while the West seems more preoccupied with the pastoral care of newly converted and barely civilized non-Roman populations. This latter literature is somewhat richer in the use of Pauline texts from the shorter epistles, perhaps because of their predominantly pastoral nature.

Syriac and Coptic Sources. There is some representation in the selections gathered here of passages from the ascetical and devotional writings of the Syrian and Egyptian churches, this literature being far more modest in scope than that of the Greek and Latin Christians of antiquity. From the fourth century onward we have from Syriac Christianity the homiletic work of Aphrahat (early fourth century), and then the exegetical and dogmatic discourses of Ephrem the Syrian (c. 306-373), followed by texts from the ascetical homilies of Isaac of Nineveh (died c. 700). Among the early Monophysites, there are selections here from Philoxenus of Mabbug (c. 440-523). Included as well are teachings on spiritual discipline from the fourth-century *Book of Steps*, from the *Letter to Cyriacus* of the sixth-century Babai the Great and from the letters of John the Elder in the eighth century.

Material from the writing of the Coptic Egyptian church takes the form of teachings from the desert fathers gathered into the *Apophthegmata Patrum*, or "sayings" tradition, derived from various monastic spiritual masters from the fourth century onward. Included as well is the tradition of Pachomian *Koinonia*, in which the wisdom of various early teachers is gathered in the form of short aphorisms. Preeminent in this literature is a focus on the life of prayer, of the practice of simple humility and self-denial and on the fundamental importance of the charitable sharing of one's possessions with all who are in need. Thus we are not surprised to discover a considerable use of Pauline texts, particularly those from the practical sections of 1 Thessalonians and the Pastoral Epistles, where there are many exhortations to the cultivation of vigilance, prayer, calm and simple compassion and self-denial.

Issues and Themes

What were the particular unifying themes that formed the principal concerns of the Fathers in the interpretation of these letters of Paul? What were the particular problems of interpretation that occupied their minds in developing these themes? And which passages were central in the exposition?

Dogmatic themes. The attributes and praise of the Godhead were celebrated in commentary on two passages in 1 Timothy 1:17 and 6:15-16. The focus was on the absolute, sovereign and transcendent lordship of the Father-Creator of all things, and also on the sharing of this divinity with the Son and the Spirit. While both passages allowed the anti-Arian Fathers to highlight the inability of created intelligence to grasp the mystery of God, they also served to emphasize, by juxtaposition with other texts, how this same mystery has been communicated to humankind in the divine operations through the Son and the Spirit. The challenge thus was to construe passages that testify to the transcendent majesty of God with other passages where the work of redemption through the Son and the Spirit are mentioned, in order to avoid the Arian or Eunomian contention that only the Father properly possesses the full divine attributes.[13]

This exposition of the dogma of the Trinity then led on to the most commented-upon christological passage from these epistles, Colossians 1:15-20, where a number of terms and phrases relative to the divine status and work of Jesus Christ drew careful attention. As "the image of the invisible God" (Col 1:15), Christ as the Logos-Son of God shares, some argued, in the invisibility and full divinity of the Father. Others interpreted the "image" as a reference to his visibility in the incarnation and thus his representation of God to the physical creation.

Christ's status as the "firstborn of all creation" (Col 1:15) was interpreted with reference again to his full divinity, but questions emerged as to whether the primary reference was to the entire creation or to the new creation in the church. "Firstborn" could be taken in purely temporal terms or as a title of majesty and preeminence. Some wondered whether "first" implied that others were to follow and had difficulty reconciling this implication with the use of "only-begotten" to describe the Son. Further, the "all things" in Colossians 1:16 could be taken as a reference to the entire cosmos or to the new creation in Christ.

In Colossians 1:17, where Christ is described as "before all things" and the claim is made that "in him all things hold together," the Fathers saw a strong statement of the Son's role as the Father's instrument in both creation and providence. Interpreters then split as to whether the description of the Son in Colossians 1:18 as the "beginning" applied to his work in all of creation, or specifically to his role in the new creation, especially in light of the following "firstborn from the dead." The same division appeared in the interpretation of "fullness of God" in Colossians 1:19, where the phrase could be taken of the Father's full divinity, or as a reference to the church. This latter view reflected the sense that the church as the body of the Christ manifests the fullness of God as this came to expression in the union of the heavenly and earthly spheres in the incarnation.

Paul's clear statement in Colossians 1:20 and the verses that follow of God's reconciling work in the cross of Christ could also be taken as supporting this ecclesial view, as it were, of the "fullness of God" in the preceding verse. We see thus a consistent tension that ran through the patristic exegesis of Colos-

---

[13]For general background and synthesis, one may consult Bertrand de Margerie, *An Introduction to the History of Exegesis,* 1: *The Greek Fathers* (Petersham, Mass.: St. Bede's Publications, 1993); 2: *The Latin Fathers* (Petersham, Mass.: St. Bede's Publications, 1995); 3: *Saint Augustine* (Petersham, Mass.: St. Bede's Publications, 1991). There is a fourth volume in French, *Introduction à L'Histoire de L'Exégèse,* 4: *L'Occident Latin de Leon Le Grand à Bernard de Clairvaux* (Paris: Éditions du Cerf, 1990).

sians 1:15-20 as to the central referent of the statements—cosmic creation or new creation in the incarnation. A similar polarity existed in the interpretation of "fullness" in Colossians 2:9.

Implicated in this divergence of interpretation of the christological passages in Colossians was the contrast of the anti-Arian need to argue for the full divinity of the Son from before all creation with the anti-Gnostic need to argue for the powerful and full involvement of the Son in the origination, unfolding and renewal of the material universe. This last emphasis led to concern for the nature of the incarnation and the church as a true union of both the spiritual and material realms, so that the transmission of saving grace and power would be understood as real and efficacious. Redemption itself, the Fathers argued, depends on the full assumption of human flesh by the fully divine Logos, although the precise import of this insistence remained elusive, as can be seen in the varying interpretations of Colossians 2:14-15.

Different views of the nature of the "bond," the chirograph, nailed to the cross in Christ's suffering and death, and different views of the means of cancellation of this bond may be observed in the commentary. The interpretation of the verb translated in the RSV "disarmed" in Colossians 2:15 as "stripped off" was popular and led to the idea that by his death Christ divested himself and thus all persons of the sinful flesh, or alternatively, of the vulnerability to sinful powers inherent in corporeality and mortality. Others saw here the "putting off" of the disguise of the flesh in the full revealing of divinity and divine power, so that the evil powers are exposed in their impotent ugliness, as well as in their unjust condemnation of the sinless One. Another view was that the faithfulness of Christ on the cross was the means of redemption, since this virtuous faithfulness was a full realization of the potential contained in the original creation of human beings.

There is a rich accumulation of commentary on 1 Timothy 2:5-6, where the mediatorial activity of Christ is related by the Fathers to the full union of humanity and divinity in the one redeemer, "the one mediator between God and men, the man Christ Jesus." Especially important here was the assertion of full humanity in the sense of both a real body (anti-Gnostic) and a real soul (anti-Apollinarian) for the Son. The implication was that nothing less than Jesus' complete taking up of the burden of humanity could serve as an adequate ransom in the working out of redemption. The important passage Titus 2:11-14 was then seen as a statement in miniature of the history of salvation in Christ. It begins with the first coming, "the grace of God has appeared" (Tit 2:11), and concludes with his coming again, "our blessed hope, the appearing of the glory of our great God and Savior Jesus Christ" (Tit 2:13). The patristic theme of the economy and mystery of salvation, the intentional unfolding of a cosmic and all-inclusive history of salvation, then comes to expression in many comments, such as those on Colossians 1:26-28, Colossians 2:2 and especially 1 Timothy 3:16. Particularly important in the latter is its emphasis on the cosmic dominion of Christ.

A profound concern with the theme of the return of Christ occurs naturally around the passages 1 Thessalonians 4:13-17 and 2 Thessalonians 2:1-12, where again a diversity of opinion on details existed. The phrase in 1 Thessalonians 4:13 "that you may not grieve as others do who have no hope" led to insightful reflection on what kind of sadness is appropriate and what kind is not for the faithful Christian at the time of death. Indeed, death is seen as a "sleeping," which betokens the final awakening signified in Christ's resurrection (1 Thess 4:14), for when Christ returns, the physical and mortal cosmos will be transformed.

The scenario of the rising of the dead, then the living, to embrace the Lord (1 Thess 4:15-17), is combined with Paul's insistence that the timing of these events must remain hidden for various reasons (2 Thess 2:1-2). The "rebellion" or "apostasy" on the part of the son of perdition (2 Thess 2:3) is variously assigned to the figure of Satan, to heretics and nonbelievers in the present or to the antichrist of Revelation 20. His being seated in "the temple of God" (Rev 2:4) is understood to refer to the Jerusalem temple or to all Christian churches. That which restrains the lawless one or son of perdition in 2 Thessalonians 2:8 is generally seen as the Roman Empire, but alternatively as the Holy Spirit or Nero or even, in a famous interpretation by Theodoret, as God's own decree. All of the Fathers agree that Christ in his second coming will rescue all who believe but will sit in judgment on all who resist and deny him.

Several passages from these letters served to strengthen the argument of the Fathers that the appropriation of Christ's saving work by believers requires a real union in faith with his death and resurrection. Colossians 3:1-4 was used to underline the point that faith requires the willingness to see through the veil of earthly things, particularly suffering, in order to grasp with the mind and heart the greater reality of heaven (Col 3:1-2). The combination of Paul's claim that the life of Christians is "hid" (Col 3:3) with Christ in God, along with Colossians 2:2-3, "the knowledge of God's mystery, of Christ, in whom are hid all the treasures of wisdom and knowledge," and the claim in 2 Timothy 2:11-13 that we have died with Christ and must endure, led to a variety of reflections. These included the baptismal character of Christian living.

Within this view of Christian living we find moral struggle, the lack of earthly compensation and yearning for perfection without being able to attain it in the present. All these are to be embraced without reservation. This embrace is possible because there is the sure belief that God will finally reveal what is hidden and perfect what is flawed, so long as we have faith and continue to strive. The conviction that union with Christ is made possible by baptism and registers the form of baptism in dying and suffering is present everywhere in the Fathers' interpretation of Paul. Particularly important is the commentary on Titus 3:5-7, Colossians 1:13-14, Colossians 2:11-13, and the references to the "deposit of faith" in 1 Timothy (6:20) and 2 Timothy (1:14), where that which has been entrusted may be understood as the creed of articles of belief given at baptism.

Further, the question of the extent or scope of Christ's saving work arose in connection with two famous passages. The first was 1 Timothy 2:4, where Paul enjoins prayer for all persons, because God desires "all" to be saved. The question had arisen about the appropriateness of Christian prayer for non-Christians, and various views were expressed as to the nature of the cooperation of the divine will with human willing. Clearly there was a general conviction that God's will to save does not override human resistance, but there was also the clear understanding that God's will and intentions are more powerful and more effective than those of humankind. Thus a quandary was created by Paul's statement in this verse. A related dilemma arose with the interpretation of 2 Timothy 2:20 and the theme of the great house, where various vessels are intended for various uses. Some Fathers interpreted the house as the world, some as the church, but the point was that God's creative and saving power works in different lives in different ways, always mysteriously and always beyond the full grasp of human understanding.

This mystery of God's saving work leads in the Fathers' commentary on these epistles to their consideration of the figure of Paul himself, who by his own presentation in the letters is the greatest of sinners, who yet by God's mercy in Christ has been saved. The Greek fathers tend to focus on the humility and virtue that resulted from Paul's conversion, as in their comments on 1 Timothy 1:12-14 and by implication on such verses as 2 Timothy 1:9 that deal with the calling of all Christians. The Latins, particularly Augustine, highlight the gratuitous grace of God in his life and the universal bondage to sin in the lives of the unconverted. The fact of God's call to Paul—mentioned often in these epistles, as at Colossians 1:25, 1 Thessalonians 2:4, 1 Timothy 2:7 and 2 Timothy 1:11—to become a preacher and apostle to the Gentiles underlined the amazing mercy and grace of God in Christ but also served to emphasize the persecution and chains, the suffering, that inevitably accompanies faithful discipleship and that, for Paul, also testified to the power of his witness.

There are many reflections on the exemplary role of Paul as the one who sets the standard for discipleship. Most notable here would be the commentary on 1 Thessalonians 1:5, 1 Thessalonians 2:5 and 2 Timothy 3:10-13, and the remarkable Colossians 1:24, with St. Paul's claim, "Now I rejoice in my sufferings for your sake, and in my flesh I complete what is lacking in Christ's afflictions," and 2 Timothy 4:6, "For I am already on the point of being sacrificed." The former verse led to some difference of opinion as to whether it is Paul personally (the Greek view) or whether it is the church as a whole (the Latin view) that completes Christ's work of redemption. The latter verse, followed by 2 Timothy 4:7-8, stirred questions, as did many passages of Scripture, on the role of the martyr as one who by extraordinary faithfulness refracts the atoning power of Christ's own sacrifice.

Practical themes. The ethical and moral teaching of these epistles, as the Fathers understood them, arises from their reflection on the personal character of Paul and thus on the Christian life as a spiritual discipline. The large amount of commentary on 2 Timothy 2:1-7, especially on the themes of the Christian soldier and athlete in 2 Timothy 2:3-5, focuses this perspective very nicely. Faithful Christian living is a matter of following the rules, enabled by the grace of Christ, as these have been laid down in Scripture and tradition. Questions of interpretation usually turned on the issue of how literally and how rigorously to take such injunctions, especially when they were applied to life in society as well as to life in monastic communities. This tension cut across a number of practical concerns.

One particular complication in this matter of formulating moral teaching was the fact, well recognized by the Fathers, that at various points Paul engages in polemic against the ascetic doctrines of heretics. Patristic commentary on Colossians 2:16-23 is especially rich in illustrating the difficulties involved in catching the nuances of this debate. On the one hand expositors recognized that Paul's intention is to rescue the Colossians from adherence to the rites, regulations and superstitions, either of pagan or Jewish practitioners, but on the other hand they recognized that appropriate disciplines of self-control and self-denial belong to authentic Christian discipleship as well. The question is one of being sure that such discipline is grounded in Christ and therefore is humble (emphasized by the Greek, Coptic and Syriac fathers) and truly reflects its reliance on grace and not on human achievement (emphasized by the Latins).

One interesting example of the complications involved concerned the interpretation of Colossians 2:21, "Do not handle, Do not taste, Do not touch," where the prohibitions could be viewed as Paul's ironic dismissal of heretical scrupulosity or as his qualified approval of such mandates. At stake was the sense that so long as they reflect Christian and not merely human belief, such teachings may be embraced. The theological issue was one of honoring the goodness of creation, the material creation, in an anti-Gnostic manner but also one of affirming the lordship of Christ over all things, including the most mundane, and of avoiding the spiritual pitfalls that are the perennial danger of ascetical practice.

The same concerns surface in the comments on 1 Timothy 4:1-5 and the prohibitions on foods and marriage taught by some heretics, as well as in the exposition of the various passages where Paul warns his readers against the lies of unbelievers. These would include the "philosophy and empty deceit . . . [and] human tradition" (Col 2:8), the "self-abasement and worship of angels" (Col 2:18), the preoccupation with "the times and the seasons" (1 Thess 5:1), the "myths and endless genealogies" (1 Tim 1:4), the "godless and silly myths" (1 Tim 4:7), the "godless chatter [and] gangrene" (2 Tim 2:16-17), the "myths" (2 Tim 4:4), the "Jewish myths [and] commands of men" (Tit 1:14) and the "stupid controversies, genealogies, dissensions and quarrels" (Tit 3:9) of heretical and blasphemous teachers, who are a constant temptation for Christians. Virtually every form of heresy known to the Fathers is included in their interpretation of these references, but a common theme is the pride, vainglory and self-exalting illusion exhibited by heretics in their exaggerated reliance on human capacities for knowledge or virtue.

Consequently, the Fathers strongly affirm the many passages in these epistles where Paul emphasizes the high moral calling of Christians to a correctly understood and practiced asceticism. The Old Testament law is validated as a timeless guide to the ethical uprightness of believers (1 Tim 1:8), even if it speaks as a disciplinarian to a certain immaturity of moral practice, precisely in order to make way for the spiritual living of the more mature. Frequent injunctions against worldliness stress the dangers of the desire for wealth, of the inclination to physical pleasure in domestic relations or in sexual license, of the craving for human approval and recognition through worldly success.

The Christian Stoicism often attributed by modern scholarship to John Chrysostom is found throughout patristic literature, as the Fathers hammer away at the need for self-sufficient virtue, for inner freedom from the sensual passions and for the joy of ordered lives directed to the purposes of God. There is a constant emphasis in their commentary on the simplicity and humility of godly living, as in their views on the warnings about money in 1 Timothy 6:6-10 or on the injunction to work in 2 Thessalonians 3:6-11. There are numerous calls to self-effacing righteousness, both in the catalogs of vices and virtues (Col 3:5-17; 1 Thess 5:1-11; 1 Tim 6:11-19; 2 Tim 3; Tit 2:1-8; 3:1-11) and in the encouragement to active piety, especially in the practice of prayer (Col 4:2-3; 1 Thess 5:16-18; 1 Tim 2:1-2, 8) and the study of Scripture (1 Tim 4:13; 2 Tim 3:16).

On specifics, one preeminent concern in these letters is the matter of proper discipline for those holding ecclesiastical office and, in analogous fashion, with the differentiated roles of men and women and with the management of households. The descriptions of the qualities of character and life required for bishops (presbyters being included as well) in 1 Timothy 3:1-8 and Titus 1:5-9 stimulated substantial reflection by the Fathers on a number of questions. Should they desire this office? (It depends!) What kind of moral impeccability could be legitimately demanded of such a person? (Opinions varied.) How is one to understand precisely the requirement of "only one wife"? What degree of control should the bishop be expected to exercise over his own family? How much emphasis should be placed on his longevity as a Christian as an important criterion in judging his suitability for office? What role should be played by the good will and approval of the secular community toward any individual being considered?

The moral expectations for deacons, 1 Timothy 3:8-13, were considered to be essentially the same, this teaching being a reflection for "the household of God" (1 Tim 3:15) of the kind of obedience and mutual regard fitting for all groups in the social hierarchy toward one another. Wives, husbands and children are to be properly submissive to authority and to play their traditional roles as ordained by God (Col 3:18-21; 1 Tim 2:9-15; 3:1; Tit 2:4-8), just as all are to live quietly under the just rule of the civil government (1 Tim 2:1-2; Tit 3:1-2), so long as this authority does not require anything that directly contradicts the will of God. Finally, slaves and masters are to live in genuine love and respect for one another, particularly if both happen to be Christian, and, where this is not the case, as a form of evangelism on the part of the believing slave or master toward the unbeliever (Col 3:22—4:1; 1 Tim 6:1-2; Tit 2:9-10). With regard to the institution of slavery and as a part of their counsel for Christians who are slaves, the Fathers emphasized that true equality is spiritual, rather than social or economic, while true slavery is always an inner state totally apart from external circumstances.

Two closely related concerns that were intensely discussed may round out this survey. These were the matters of the work and behavior expected of widows in the community and more generally the exalted status of virginity and the place in the church of those vowed to this state. Paul's discussion of widows in 1 Timothy 5:3-16 elicited a great deal of commentary because there were many widows, often destitute and dependent on charity, within the congregations of the early church and because widows exercised important ministries of service and prayer. The question of who was eligible to be enrolled officially among the widows was actively debated, as was the importance of maintaining good discipline with a group who (apparently) easily became undisciplined.

The matter of whether or not a widow under vows of some sort should be allowed to remarry and thus be a potential source of scandal, stirred controversy and a number of glowing descriptions of the virtues of the single and unmarried state. The many treatises on virginity and celibacy uniformly accord the highest honors to the individual who is free of the sexual entanglements, as well as the financial and domestic burdens, of family life. The descriptions of the happy virgin or celibate drew upon a well-established classical repertoire of criticism and satire aimed at the woes of marriage and the miseries and enslavement of disordered sexual passions. Also raised, however, were fundamental questions for the nature of Christian ethics and, as already suggested, for a properly Christian asceticism.

One question involved the matter of the relative good of marriage and family and the order of human procreation ordained by God, especially in the debates with extreme practitioners either of domestic bliss or of ascetic flagellation and fanaticism. Another issue was that of an external legalism versus the inwardness expected of an authentically spiritual relationship with God. John Chrysostom is a good example of those Fathers who warned repeatedly that true virginity and true celibacy are of the heart and mind and must never be a matter of mere conformity to a set of rules for conduct and comportment. Latin, Greek, Syriac and Coptic fathers, whatever their differences of emphasis and formulation, all taught that the qualities of character that arise from a contrite and humbled spirit are ultimately the essence of the Christian way.

The Selection Process, Overviews and Citations

Following the format of ACCS, I have organized the commentary that follows on several principles. Each of the epistles is broken down into passages or pericopes that more or less follow the modern topical subdivision of the letters. The Revised Standard Version of Scripture is used for the English text of the letters. At the beginning of each letter is a summary of the *argumentum* or *hypothesis* that precedes each of the epistles in the line-by-line commentaries of John Chrysostom, Theodore of Mopsuestia, Theodoret of Cyr, Severian of Gabala, Ambrosiaster, Pelagius and Jerome (for Titus and Philemon). The translations of these passages, as well as all of the excerpts from these commentaries, are my own, with the exception of that of John Chrysostom. Then come the individual passages of the letter, each passage being followed by an overview section and specific comments on individual verses or part-verses from that section.

In this volume of the ACCS, I have used the overview sections in a very particular way. Since I head the exposition of each letter with a summary of comments from the argument sections, or *hypothesis*, that begin each of the ancient line-by-line commentaries, I then use the overview sections to continue this kind of summary in my own words. Thus the general perspective adopted by these commentators on that particular passage of the letter at hand is carried from section to section of the present anthology through the overview. My hope is that the modern reader will gain a sense of how the Fathers read an epistle as a connected whole.[14] In this way the overview section performs a slightly different function in this volume as compared with the other ACCS volumes.

All of the comments that follow on individual verses under the topical or thematic headings and that are cited in the Fathers' own words enrich, expand upon and fill out in many different directions the possible implications for preaching and life of each verse. These citations come from the breadth of patristic literature, as well as from the line-by-line commentaries, and are introduced with a phrase that is an attempt to capture the sense of the particular Father's exposition. Sometimes I have clustered different pieces of exposition under one heading, if they seem to share a common emphasis. Sometimes I have organized the comments under contrasting headings if I have discerned a debate or difference of opinion on how a verse or phrase should be understood. I try to avoid idiosyncrasy and look instead for what seems to unify or focus a line of interpretation. The relative amount of commentary presented here on a verse may be taken as a fair indication of how much commentary that text of Scripture elicited from the Fathers and thus how important it was for them.

The method of citation is as follows. Each excerpt is headed by the name of the author and followed by the name in English of the work and the book, chapter and subdivision numbers of the text as appropriate. The translations of the line-by-line commentaries of Theodoret of Cyr, Theodore of Mopsuestia, Severian of Gabala, Ambrosiaster, Pelagius and Jerome are my own, and the locations of the original

---

[14]On the theme of narrative or argumentative coherence, as this was important to patristic exegesis, especially of the Antiochene school but for others as well, see Frances Young, *Biblical Exegesis and the Formation of Christian Culture* (Cambridge: Cambridge University Press, 1997), especially chaps. 4, 8 and 9.

texts in the Migne collections or the critical editions are indicated in the notes. Otherwise, and for the most part, the excerpted passages are drawn from the various available English translations whose sources I indicate with standard abbreviations. Sometimes I have made use of particular contemporary translations of individual works, but typically I have relied on the major series of patristic translations. These are The Fathers of the Church (Catholic University Press), Ancient Christian Writers (Newman Press); Library of Christian Classics (Westminster Press), Classics of Western Spirituality (Paulist), but, most of all, The Ante-Nicene Fathers and A Select Library of the Nicene and Post-Nicene Fathers (Eerdmans). The last two call for some comment because of the nineteenth-century milieu in which they were composed.

Produced during the Victorian period, either in the British Isles or in the United States, the volumes that made up the series of Ante-Nicene Fathers and the two series of Nicene and Post-Nicene Fathers in some cases included reprints from the earlier Oxford Library of the Fathers. This latter was a particular expression of the patristic scholarship of the Tractarian controversialists within the Church of England.[15] Scholarly notes, introductory matter and the English renderings themselves are rooted in the doctrinal and literary predilections of the time. In general, the earlier the translation is, the more archaic and affected the English phraseology. I have somewhat modernized these older translations, particularly that of the homilies of John Chrysostom on Paul, as indicated by an asterisk in the citations.

Anyone who has been as immersed in the writings of the Fathers as I have been in preparing this commentary becomes transfixed by their theological and devotional energy. It is no wonder that they repeatedly enable and inspire spiritual renewal in all who read them. May it be so for you, the reader.

My great thanks go to the staff and assistants of the office of ACCS at Drew University, especially the diligent Joel Scandrett and Michael Glerup, the encouraging Susan Kipper and a number of graduate helpers who assembled a large array of computerized and photocopied material for me. Under the direction and inspiration of the general editor, Dr. Thomas Oden, they have truly made a landmark contribution to the dissemination of patristic wisdom to modern students of Scripture.

Peter Gorday

---

[15]The production of these translations is itself a fascinating episode in the history of the appropriation and retrieval of the spirituality of the Fathers for the modern age. See the essays by Richard W. Pfaff, "The Library of the Fathers: The Tractarians as Patristic Translators," *Studies in Philology* 70 (1973): 329-44, and "Anglo-American Patristic Translations 1866-1900," *Journal of Ecclesiastical History* 28 (1977): 39-55.

THE EPISTLE
TO THE COLOSSIANS

ARGUMENT: With Onesimus as his faithful traveling companion, Paul has written this epistle, sometime after Romans and before the letters to Timothy, in order to strengthen the Colossian church in its time of adversity. Specifically, he urges the Colossians to understand that our approach to God is only through Christ and not through angels. Therefore, in adversity we can know that he is with us through the Spirit, just as he, Paul, is always spiritually, if not physically, present with them (CHRYSOSTOM).

Paul wishes to preserve the Gentile believers in Colossae, whom he has not seen, in order to prevent any submission to the Jewish law as necessary for salvation. His further purpose is to make a clear distinction for them between those things that are necessary to salvation and those that are not (THEODORE). Paul recognizes that believers are vulnerable to temptations from both converted Jews and converted Greeks who acknowledge, for different reasons, the power of angels to confer grace and blessing on humankind (SEVERIAN). Paul wishes to show that the greatest danger to Christian discipleship resides in the fact that believers of Jewish background are convincing Gentiles that they should keep the mandates of the law, when in reality Christ the Lord is the giver of salvation through the mystery of the incarnation (THEODORET). Paul has written to the Colossians in order to overturn the efforts of false apostles, who were teaching them to accept the notion of the divine powers in nature, by which life is supposedly governed, and thus he urges them to accept nothing beyond Christ himself (AMBROSIASTER). Having praised their beginnings in faith, Paul issues a warning that the Colossians not be seduced by philosophy or ceremonies of the law (PELAGIUS).

1:1-8 SALUTATION AND THANKSGIVING

¹Paul, an apostle of Christ Jesus by the will of God, and Timothy our brother,
²To the saints and faithful brethren in Christ at Colossae:

Grace to you and peace from God our Father.
³We always thank God, the Father of our Lord Jesus Christ, when we pray for you, ⁴because we have heard of your faith in Christ Jesus and of the love which you have for all the saints, ⁵because of the hope laid up for you in heaven. Of this you have heard before in the word of the truth, the gospel ⁶which has come to you, as indeed in the whole world it is bearing fruit and growing—so among yourselves, from the day you heard and understood the grace of God in truth, ⁷as you learned it from Epaphras our beloved fellow servant. He is a faithful minister of Christ on our^a behalf ⁸and has made known to us your love in the Spirit.

a Other ancient authorities read *your*

OVERVIEW: From the outset it is clear that Paul is emphasizing the sovereign and trustworthy will of God in all that happens for our salvation (CHRYSOSTOM). That will unfolds through the saving activity in Jesus Christ and not from any other means (SEVERIAN). This activity produces in us a steadfast assurance of final salvation and thus a real sharing in the eternal life of the kingdom (THEODORE). For pastoral reasons, these remarks are couched in the form of praise so that the Colossians will be strengthened in the midst of affliction for the exhortation to follow (THEODORET). Most remarkable is the central focus placed by Paul on Christ himself as the sole means of salvation, such that we must look only to him in giving thanks (AMBROSIASTER). Our focus must be on eternal life as a gift from God and not as the fruit of human praise (PELAGIUS).

1:1 By the Will of God

NOT THROUGH ANGELS. CHRYSOSTOM: It would be wise to explain how we have discovered the occasion and subject of this epistle as we have considered it. What, then, are they? The Colossians used to approach God through angels; they followed many Jewish and Grecian observances. Paul is correcting these practices. HOMILIES ON COLOSSIANS I.[1]

1:2 Grace to You and Peace from God Our Father

ONLY FROM GOD. CHRYSOSTOM: What is the source of grace for you? And peace? "From God our Father," Paul writes. In this place Paul does not mention the name of Christ. I will ask those who speak disparagingly of the Spirit, in what way is God the Father of servants? Who wrought these mighty achievements? Who made you a saint? Who faithful? Who a son of God? He who made you worthy to be trusted is the same who caused you to be entrusted with all. HOMILIES ON COLOSSIANS I.[2]

1:5 The Hope Laid Up for You in Heaven

A SECURE HOPE. CHRYSOSTOM: [Paul] speaks of the good things to come. He has in view their temptations. They should not seek their rest here.... "Because of the hope," he says, "which is laid up." He shows how secure this hope is. HOMILIES ON COLOSSIANS I.[3]

THEODORE OF MOPSUESTIA: So that you may pursue the good things of heaven, a firm hope for these very things is maintained, provided that all that comes from you is consistent with them. COMMENTARY ON COLOSSIANS.[4]

SEVERIAN OF GABALA: Paul shows them that the governance of angels does not fulfill the

---

[1]NPNF 1 13:258*. [2]NPNF 1 13:258*. [3]NPNF 1 13:258*. [4]*TEM* 1:255*.

2

hope laid before us of the resurrection and the kingdom. These happen by the appearing of our Lord Jesus Christ. PAULINE COMMENTARY FROM THE GREEK CHURCH.[5]

THEODORET OF CYR: We already see heaven with the eyes of faith, even as we prepare for it in the present with an eager spirit. INTERPRETATION OF THE LETTER TO THE COLOSSIANS.[6]

THE GROUNDING OF HOPE. ISAAC OF NINEVEH: Bodily discipline performed in stillness purifies the body of the matter within it. But the discipline of the mind humbles the soul, filters out her crass notions of things that perish and draws her from the state where the thoughts are passionately engrossed and toward the state where they are moved by her divine vision.... This divine, contemplative vision of heavenly things comes to us precisely when, engaged in bodily and mental discipline, we are the recipients of an unutterably pristine glory that separates [us] from this world and our thoughts of it. By this we are thoroughly convinced of our hope which is laid up for us and we stand in full assurance of its state. HOMILIES 43.[7]

1:6a *The Gospel That Has Come to You*

COME TO STAY. CHRYSOSTOM: Paul speaks metaphorically when he writes, "is come." He means, it did not come and go away, but that it remained and was there. Many doctrines are most strongly confirmed if they are held in common with many. Therefore Paul added, "As also it is in all the world." The gospel is present everywhere, everywhere victorious, everywhere established. HOMILIES ON COLOSSIANS 1.[8]

1:6b *In the Whole World It Is Bearing Fruit and Growing*

AS A PLANT GROWS. CHRYSOSTOM: "Bearing fruit." In works. "Increasing." By the coming to

faith of many, by becoming firmer; for plants then begin to thicken when they have become firm. HOMILIES ON COLOSSIANS 1.[9]

THEODORE OF MOPSUESTIA: Not only is the faith known throughout the world, but it grows daily ... and just as it grows daily in extent, it also grows in depth among you. COMMENTARY ON COLOSSIANS.[10]

SEVERIAN OF GABALA: The gospel has come not only to the Colossians, but to the whole world, where it is powerful and grows by means of the preached word. PAULINE COMMENTARY FROM THE GREEK CHURCH.[11]

THEODORET OF CYR: The "fruit of the gospel" refers to those who hear the gospel and respond with a praiseworthy life. The "growth" is the increase in the number of believers. INTERPRETATION OF THE LETTER TO THE COLOSSIANS.[12]

ESCHATOLOGICAL GROWTH. AUGUSTINE: It is much less surprising that he [Paul] used his verbs in the present tense in that passage which, as you remarked, he repeated again and again: "For the hope which is laid up for you in heaven, which you have heard before in the word of the truth of the gospel, which is come to you as also it is in the whole world, and brings forth fruit and grows." Although the gospel did not yet embrace the whole world, he said that it brings forth fruit and grows in the whole world, in order to show how far it would extend in bearing fruit and growing. If, then, it is hidden from us when the whole world will be filled by the church bringing forth fruit and growing, undoubtedly it is hidden from us when the end will be, but it certainly will not be before that. LETTERS 199.12-51.[13]

---

[5]NTA 15:316. [6]PG 82:593D/594D. [7]*AHSIS* 213*. [8]NPNF 1 13:259*. [9]NPNF 1 13:259. [10]*TEM* 1:256-57. [11]NTA 15:317. [12]PG 82:595A/596A. [13]FC 30:398*. See also Augustine *Letters* 198 (FC 30:354-55).

THE TRUE CHURCH IS UNIVERSAL. TERTUL-LIAN: I am accustomed in my prescription against all heresies to fix my concise and comprehensive criterion [of truth] in the testimony of time, claiming priority therein as our rule and alleging lateness to be the characteristic of every heresy. This shall be proved even by the apostle, when he says: "For the hope which is laid up for you in heaven, which you have heard before in the word of the truth of the gospel; which has come to you, as it has to the whole world." For if, even at that time, the tradition of the gospel had spread everywhere, how much more now! Now, if it is our gospel which has spread everywhere, rather than any heretical gospel, much less Marcion's, which only dates from the reign of Antoninus, then ours will be the gospel of the apostles. AGAINST MARCION 5.19.[14]

AUGUSTINE: "The gospel has come to you, as it is in all the world, and brings forth fruit." The Son of God said with his own mouth, "You shall be witnesses to me, both in Jerusalem, and in all Judea, and in Samaria, and even to the uttermost part of the earth."[15] Caecilianus, the bishop of the church of Carthage, is accused with human contentiousness; the church of Christ, established among all nations, is recommended by the voice of God. LETTERS 185.1-5.[16]

AUGUSTINE: There are both good and bad in the Catholic church, which has spread not in Africa alone, as the Donatist sect has done, but through all nations,[17] as it was promised, and which extends throughout the whole world, as the apostle says, bringing forth fruit and increasing. LETTERS 208.1-6.[18]

AUGUSTINE: Honor, love and praise the holy church, your mother, the heavenly Jerusalem, the holy City of God. It is she who, in this faith which you have received, bears fruit and spreads throughout the world. She is the "church of the living God, the pillar and mainstay of truth,"[19] who, in dispensing the sacraments, tolerates the wicked who are eventually to be separated and whom, meanwhile, disparity of customs keeps at a distance. For the sake of the grain now growing amid the chaff, at the final sifting of which the harvest destined for the granary will be revealed, the church has received the keys of the kingdom of heaven. SERMONS 214.11.[20]

1:7-8 Love in the Spirit

AUTHENTIC CHRISTIAN LOVE. CHRYSOSTOM: Don't doubt, Paul says, the hope which is to come: you see that the world is being converted. And why do we need to refer to the cases of others? What happened in your own case is independently a sufficient ground for belief, for "you knew the grace of God in truth": that is, in works. So that these two things, viz. The belief of all, and your own too, confirm the things that are to come. Nor was the fact one thing, and what Epaphras said, another. . . . If this man be the minister of Christ, how do you say that you approach God by angels? "He has made known to us your love in the Spirit." For this love is wonderful and steadfast. All other love has but the name. . . . For nothing, nothing is so strong as the bond of the Spirit. HOMILIES ON COLOSSIANS 1.[21]

---

[14]ANF 3:470*. [15]Acts 1:8. [16]NPNF 1 4:635*. [17]Gen 22:18. [18]FC 32:27. [19]1 Tim 3:15. [20]FC 38:141. [21]NPNF 1 13:259*.

1:9-14 INTERCESSION THROUGH CHRIST

⁹*And so, from the day we heard of it, we have not ceased to pray for you, asking that you may be filled with the knowledge of his will in all spiritual wisdom and understanding,* ¹⁰*to lead a life worthy of the Lord, fully pleasing to him, bearing fruit in every good work and increasing in the knowledge of God.* ¹¹*May you be strengthened with all power, according to his glorious might, for all endurance and patience with joy,* ¹²*giving thanks to the Father, who has qualified us*ᵇ *to share in the inheritance of the saints in light.* ¹³*He has delivered us from the dominion of darkness and transferred us to the kingdom of his beloved Son,* ¹⁴*in whom we have redemption, the forgiveness of sins.*

b Other ancient authorities read *you*

OVERVIEW: Paul's intention here is to encourage the Colossian Christians in the special knowledge and virtue that are necessary parts of faithfulness and that are possible only as we cling to Christ and not the angels (SEVERIAN. AUGUSTINE). By declaring his desire to pray for them Paul means to strengthen the Colossians in their continued growth in faith and their already realized participation in Christ's kingdom (CHRYSOSTOM, THEODORE). What is most important is that the Colossians know that this saving grace is only through Christ (SEVERIAN), this fact constituting the higher knowledge that is the antidote to heresy (THEODORET). Paul's prayer suggests that there is a "higher knowledge" yet to come, as the Colossians mature in faith (CLEMENT OF ALEXANDRIA) and come to know Jesus not only as crucified but also as risen (ORIGEN).

God's saving work in Christ on our behalf operates on the basis of pure love, which God essentially is (AMBROSE). This love is given to us through the Spirit as a pure gift, unmerited and impossible to attain by our own efforts. Therefore, it is shown that all are subject to sin, infants included (AUGUSTINE).

1:9a *We Have Not Ceased to Pray for You*

A GENTLE HINT. CHRYSOSTOM: Not for one day do we pray for you, nor yet for two, nor three. By this Paul both shows his love and gives them a gentle hint that they had not yet arrived at the end. For the words "that you may be filled" signify this. . . . He says, "that you may be filled," rather than "that you may receive," because in fact they had already received. "That you may be filled" refers to what they were still lacking. Thus Paul rebukes without giving offense and praises without producing laziness in them, as though they were already complete. HOMILIES ON COLOSSIANS 2.[1]

THEODORE OF MOPSUESTIA: Paul's prayer is his way of building on the fundamentals of belief already taught to the Colossians, so that faith will be extended to practice, to right actions. COMMENTARY ON COLOSSIANS.[2]

1:9b *The Knowledge of His Will*

WHAT IS THAT WILL? SEVERIAN OF GABALA: It is God's will, that we acknowledge him and know that it is not possible to be saved by angels but only through Jesus Christ. How then can we

[1]NPNF 1 13:264*. [2]*TEM* 1:258.

know this? Through spiritual, not worldly, wisdom. PAULINE COMMENTARY FROM THE GREEK CHURCH.[3]

BY THE HOLY SPIRIT. AMBROSE: What, then, is more divine than the working of the Holy Spirit, since God himself testifies that the Holy Spirit presides over his blessings? . . . For no blessing can be full except through the inspiration of the Holy Spirit. Wherefore, too, the apostle found nothing better to wish us than this, as he himself said: "We cease not to pray and make request for you that you may be filled with the knowledge of his will, in all wisdom and spiritual understanding walking worthily of God." He taught that this was the will of God: that by walking in good works and words and affections, we should be filled with God's will, who puts his Holy Spirit into our hearts. OF THE HOLY SPIRIT 1.7.89.[4]

1:10a To Lead a Life Worthy of the Lord

ALWAYS VIRTUE. CHRYSOSTOM: Here he speaks of life and its works, for so he does also everywhere: with faith Paul always couples conduct. . . . Summarily, Paul states, we pray that you may lead a life of virtue, worthy of your citizenship, and may stand firmly, being strengthened as it is reasonable to be strengthened by God. For this reason Paul does not yet focus upon doctrines, but dwells upon life. HOMILIES ON COLOSSIANS 2.[5]

ONLY BY GRACE. AUGUSTINE: We are commanded to do good when it says: "Decline from evil and do good,"[6] but we pray to do good when it says: "We cease not to pray for you, asking," and among other things that Paul asks he mentions: "That you may walk worthy of God in all things pleasing, in every good work and good word." As then we acknowledge the part played by the will when these commands are given, so let him acknowledge the part played by grace when these petitions are offered. LETTERS 177.1.5.[7]

1:10b Bearing Fruit

BY FREE CHOICE. PELAGIUS: That man walks worthily of God who pleases him in all things: that is, that he may bear fruit in good work with the knowledge of God. At the same time Paul has expressed something here that is obscure elsewhere, namely, how God gives the power to will and helps and strengthens us by teaching wisdom and granting the grace of understanding, and not by taking away freedom of choice. This is why he prays that they may be filled with the knowledge of God's will in all wisdom and spiritual knowledge, so that they may walk worthily of God in all things. PELAGIUS'S COMMENTARY ON COLOSSIANS.[8]

1:10c And Increasing in the Knowledge of God

A HIGHER KNOWLEDGE. CLEMENT OF ALEXANDRIA: For there is an instruction of the perfect, concerning which Paul writes to the Colossians: "We don't stop praying for you, asking that you may be filled with the knowledge of his will in all wisdom and spiritual understanding." . . . On the one hand, there are the mysteries which were hid till the time of the apostles and were delivered by them as they received from the Lord; these, concealed in the Old Testament, were manifested to the saints. And, on the other hand, there is "the riches of the glory of the mystery in the Gentiles," which is faith and hope in Christ; which in another place he has called the "foundation."[9] STROMATA 5.10.[10]

1:12a Giving Thanks to the Father Who Has Qualified Us

QUALIFIED BY GOD TO RECEIVE. CHRYSOSTOM: By saying, "who has qualified us," Paul

---

[3]NTA 15:317. [4]NPNF 2 10:105*. [5]NPNF 1 13:264*. [6]Ps 36:27. [7]FC 30:98*. [8]*PETE* 452-53. [9]Col 1:27. [10]ANF 2:458-59*.

emphasizes an important point. For example, if a person of low rank were to become a king, he would have the power to make any person he wishes governor; and this is the extent of his power, namely, that he can give such a dignity. He cannot, however, make the person he has chosen fit for the office, and often the honor thus conferred makes a person ridiculous. If, however, he has both conferred the honor, and made the person worthy of it, and capable of exercising it, then a very great honor has indeed been conferred. This is what Paul says here: that God not only has given the honor but also made us strong enough to receive it. HOMILIES ON COLOSSIANS 2.[11]

VESSELS MADE PERFECT. BASIL THE GREAT: For he himself has bound the strong man and stolen his goods,[12] that is, humanity itself, whom our enemy had abused in every evil activity. God has created "vessels fit for the Master's use,"[13] that is, us who have been perfected for every work through the preparation of that part of us which is in our own control. Thus we gained our approach to the Father through him, being translated from "the power of darkness to be partakers of the inheritance of the saints in light." ON THE SPIRIT 8.18.[14]

AUGUSTINE: How can the apostle say: "Giving thanks to God the Father, who makes us suitable for a share of the lot of the saints in light, who has snatched us from the power of darkness and transferred us to the kingdom of his beloved son," unless the will that liberates us is not ours but his? LETTERS 217.1.3.[15]

1:12b To Share in the Inheritance of the Saints in Light

THE HEAVENLY SPECTATORS. ORIGEN: A great theater is filled with spectators to watch your contests and your summons to martyrdom, just as if we were to speak of a great crowd gathered to watch the contests of athletes supposed to be

champions. . . . Thus, the whole world and all of the angels of the right and the left, and all men, those from God's portion[16] and those from the other portions, will serve as spectators when we contest for Christianity. Indeed, either the angels in heaven will cheer us on, and the floods will clap their hands together . . . or, may it not happen, the powers from below, which rejoice in evil, will cheer. EXHORTATION TO MARTYRDOM 18.[17]

ONLY HIS FREE GIFT. CHRYSOSTOM: But why does he call it an inheritance (or lot)? To show that by his own achievements no one obtains the kingdom, but as a lot is rather the result of good luck, so in truth it is the same principle here. For no one leads a life so good as to be counted worthy of the kingdom, but the whole is his free gift. HOMILIES ON COLOSSIANS 2.[18]

ONLY THE ELECT. AUGUSTINE: The lament in the Psalms, indeed, is absolutely true: "Behold in iniquity was I conceived, and in sins did my mother nourish me in her womb."[19] Again, there is what is written, that there is none clean in God's sight, not even an infant whose life has lasted but a day on the earth. So these are the exception, and it is to exceed our limited human measure to wish to inquire about the rank they may deserve in that "lot of the saints in light" which is promised for the future. SERMONS 351.2.[20]

AUGUSTINE: See, then, how it can come to pass that a man may have the baptism of Christ and still not have the faith or the love of Christ; how it is that he may have the sacrament of holiness and still not be reckoned in the lot of the holy. With regard to the mere sacrament itself, it makes no difference whether someone receives

[11]NPNF 1 13:266*. [12]Mt 12:29. [13]2 Tim 2:21. [14]NPNF 2 8:12*. [15]FC 32:80. [16]Deut 32:9, as well as Col 1:12. [17]OSW 53-54*. [18]NPNF 1 13:266*. [19]Ps 51:5. [20]WSA 3/10:120.

the baptism of Christ where the unity of Christ is not. SERMONS 8.2.[21]

SHARING IN THE LOG OF THE SAINTS. CASSIODORUS: Moreover in writing to the Thessalonians he says: "Giving thanks to God the Father, who has made us worthy to be partakers of the lot of the saints in light."[22] Since we read that many things in the Old and New Testaments were divided by lots, none has dared to deny that the lot has been God's way of manifesting what devoted hearts sought with prayerful petition. EXPLANATION OF THE PSALMS 21.19.[23]

1:13-14 He Has Delivered and Transferred Us

FROM HIM AND THEN FROM US. CHRYSOSTOM: The whole is from him, the giving both of these things and of those; for no achievement finds its source in us. . . . Not then so as to deliver man from darkness only did he show his love toward him. It is a great thing indeed to have been delivered from darkness; but to have been brought into a kingdom too is far greater. HOMILIES ON COLOSSIANS 2.[24]

THEODORE OF MOPSUESTIA: Because we share a likeness of nature with the man whom Christ assumed in the incarnation, we also share in his kingdom of love when we do good works as his adopted sons. COMMENTARY ON COLOSSIANS.[25]

NOT THROUGH ANGELS. SEVERIAN OF GABALA: Before the law and in the law the angels served God for our salvation, but God did not bring us to the kingdom through them. But now through our Lord, his only begotten Son, the kingdom is given to you. PAULINE COMMENTARY FROM THE GREEK CHURCH.[26]

ONLY THROUGH CHRIST. THEODORET OF CYR: It was not the law but Christ the Lord, who bore the law, that has given us redemption through a saving baptism. When Paul said this, he also made a statement about God and showed him to

be the maker of all things. INTERPRETATION OF THE LETTER TO THE COLOSSIANS.[27]

AMBROSIASTER: Freed thus from the condition of darkness, that is, plucked from the infernal place, in which we were held by the devil both because of our own and because of Adam's transgression, who is the father of sinners, we were translated by faith into the heavenly kingdom of the Son of God. This was so that he might show us by what love God loved us, when, raising us from deepest hell, he led us into heaven with his true Son. COMMENTARY ON COLOSSIANS.[28]

FROM SIN TO GRACE. AUGUSTINE: From this power of evil angels nothing delivers man but the grace of God, of which the apostle speaks, "Who has delivered us from the power of darkness, and has translated us into the kingdom of the Son of his love." Israel's own story illustrates this figure, when they were delivered from the power of the Egyptians and translated into the kingdom of the land of promise flowing with milk and honey, which signifies the sweetness of grace. ON THE PSALMS 77.30.[29]

AUGUSTINE: Because in Greek "to suffer" is *paschein*, for this reason Pascha has been thought of as a passion, as though this name has been derived from "suffering." But in its own language, that is, in Hebrew, Pascha means a "passing over." For this reason the people of God celebrated the Pascha for the first time when, fleeing from Egypt, they passed over the Red Sea. . . . And we effect a most salutary passing over when we pass over from the devil to Christ, and from this tottering world to his most solidly established kingdom. And therefore we pass

---

[21]FC 11:333-34; see FC 11:307 n. 1 for sermon numbering. [22]Cassiodorus erred in attributing this verse to one of the Thessalonian letters. [23]ACW 51:227. [24]NPNF 1 13:266*. [25]*TEM* 1:260 (Greek). [26]NTA 15:317-18*. [27]PG 82:597B/598B. [28]CSEL 81 3:170. [29]NPNF 1 8:377*.

over to God who endures so that we may not pass over with the passing world. Concerning this grace conferred upon us, the apostle, praising God, says, "Who has rescued us from the power of darkness and has brought us over into the kingdom of the Son of his love." TRACTATES ON JOHN 55.1.[30]

AUGUSTINE: "And he threw him," says John, "into the abyss,"[31] meaning, clearly, that he cast the devil into the abyss, and the "abyss" symbolizes the innumerable multitude of the impious, in whose hearts there is a great depth of malignity against the church of God. . . . Now because he is bound and shut up by this ban, the devil is prohibited and inhibited from leading astray the nations which belonged to Christ but were in time past led astray by him or held in his grip. For God chose those nations before the foundation of the world, to "rescue them from the power of darkness and transfer them to the kingdom of his beloved Son," as the apostle says. CITY OF GOD 20.7.3.[32]

LIVE YOUR BAPTISM! LEO THE GREAT: "Snatched from the powers of darkness" at such a great "price,"[33] and by so great a "mystery,"[34] and loosed from the chains of the ancient captivity, make sure, dearly beloved, that the devil does not destroy the integrity of your souls with any stratagem. Whatever is forced on you contrary to the Christian faith, whatever is presented to you contrary to the commandments of God, it comes from the deceptions of the one who tries with many wiles to divert you from eternal life, and, by seizing certain occasions of human weakness, leads careless and negligent souls again into his snares of death. Let all those reborn through water and the Holy Spirit consider the one whom they have renounced. SERMONS 57.5.1-2.[35]

---

[30]FC 90:3-4. [31]Rev 20:3. [32]CG 908-9. [33]1 Cor 6:20. [34]1 Tim 3:16. [35]FC 93:247.

1:15-23 THE PERSON AND WORK OF CHRIST

[15]*He is the image of the invisible God, the first-born of all creation;* [16]*for in him all things were created, in heaven and on earth, visible and invisible, whether thrones or dominions or principalities or authorities—all things were created through him and for him.* [17]*He is before all things, and in him all things hold together.* [18]*He is the head of the body, the church; he is the beginning, the first-born from the dead, that in everything he might be pre-eminent.* [19]*For in him all the fulness of God was pleased to dwell,* [20]*and through him to reconcile to himself all things, whether on earth or in heaven, making peace by the blood of his cross.*

[21]*And you, who once were estranged and hostile in mind, doing evil deeds,* [22]*he has now reconciled in his body of flesh by his death, in order to present you holy and blameless and irreproachable before him,* [23]*provided that you continue in the faith, stable and steadfast, not shifting from the hope of the gospel which you heard, which has been preached to every creature under heaven, and of which I, Paul, became a minister.*

OVERVIEW: Paul must now discourse on the dignity of the Son, in order to demonstrate that confidence in angels is senseless (CHRYSOSTOM, SEVERIAN). In this discourse Paul is careful to show that in Christ the invisible and eternal God truly assumed human flesh for our salvation (THEODORE). Here Paul proceeds to discuss the revealed aspects of Christ, on the understanding that "he who sees me sees the Father" (THEODORET). What is at stake throughout this description of the dignity of the Son is the incorporeal nature of his generation from the Father (ORIGEN), and thus his invisibility (PSEUDO-DIONYSIUS). In the whole work of divine creation of the universe Christ as the eternal Son has the primacy (THEODORET, CYRIL OF ALEXANDRIA). The whole creation derives its very being from its generation by and participation in the eternal Word of God, who is the Christ (ATHANASIUS). The thrust of the passage is to refute the Marcionite claim that the Father of Jesus was another God from that of the Old Testament, for we see here that Jesus was the pre-existent Son who was in all creation from the beginning (TERTULLIAN). Jesus was with the Father as his image at the beginning of all creation (AMBROSE, LEO THE GREAT). What is at stake throughout the following is the equality of the Son with the Father (AMBROSIASTER). We see here that the whole Trinity is involved from the beginning in the generating and ordering of the universe (AUGUSTINE).

1:15a *The Image of the Invisible God*

"IMAGE" IMPLIES INVISIBILITY. ORIGEN: Let us now see what we ought to understand by the expression "image of the invisible God," in order that we may learn from this expression how God can rightly be called the Father of his Son; and let us first of all consider what things are called images in ordinary human speech. Sometimes the term *image* is applied to an object painted or carved on some material, such as wood or stone. Sometimes a child is said to be an image of the parent, when the likeness of the parent's features is in every respect faithfully reproduced in the child. . . . In regard to the Son of God, of whom we are now speaking, the image may be compared to our second illustration for this reason, that he is the invisible image of the invisible God, just as according to the Scripture narrative we say that the image of Adam was his son Seth. ON FIRST PRINCIPLES 1.2.6.[1]

ORIGEN: We may inquire whether there exists any substance in which we can discern neither color nor shape nor possibility of touch nor size, a substance perceptible to the mind alone, which anyone can call whatever he pleases. The Greeks speak of this substance as *asōmaton,* or incorporeal; but the divine Scriptures call it "invisible"; for the apostle declares that God is invisible, when he says that Christ is the "image of the invisible God." ON FIRST PRINCIPLES 4.3.15.[2]

CHRYSOSTOM: Whose image then will you have him be? God's? Then he is exactly like the one to whom you assign him. If you compare him to a human image, say so, and I'll be done with you as a madman. . . . "The image of the invisible" is itself also invisible, and invisible in the same way, for otherwise it would not be an image. For an image, so far as it is an image, even on a human level, ought to be exactly similar, as, for example, in respect of the features and the likeness. But here indeed among us, this is by no means possible; for human art fails in many respects, or rather fails in all, if you make a careful examination. But where God is, there is no

---

[1]*OFP* 18-19*. Compare 2.4.3, where Origen argues that "seeing" the Father in the Son is a matter of spiritual perception and knowledge, not of corporeal vision. See also 2.6.3, where he claims that as the image of the invisible God, Christ "granted invisibly to all rational creatures whatsoever a participation in himself, in such a way that each obtained a degree of participation proportionate to the loving affection with which he clung to him" (*OFP* 110). [2]*OFP* 312.

error, no failure. HOMILIES ON COLOSSIANS 3.[3]

ATHANASIUS: But though he is Word, he is not, as we said, comparable to human words, composed of syllables; but he is the unchanging image of his own Father. For men, composed of parts and made out of nothing, speak in a composite and divisible fashion. But God possesses true existence and is not composite; hence his Word also has true existence and is not made of different parts or syllables. He is the one and only-begotten God, who proceeds in his goodness from the Father as from a good Fountain, and orders all things and holds them together. AGAINST THE PAGANS 41.[4]

THEODORET OF CYR: The term *image* signifies that one living being shares the same substance with another being. However, and by contrast, inanimate images, precisely because they are inanimate and have no soul, do not possess the substance of that of which they are images [i.e., they are mere outward copies]. INTERPRETATION OF THE LETTER TO THE COLOSSIANS.[5]

GREGORY OF NAZIANZUS: He is called "image" because he is of one substance with the Father; he stems from the Father and not the Father from him, it being the nature of an image to copy the original and to be named after it. But there is more to it than this. The ordinary image is a motionless copy of a moving being. Here we have a living image of a living being, indistinguishable from its original to a higher degree than Seth from Adam[6] and any earthly offspring from its parents. Beings with no complexity to their nature have no points of likeness or unlikeness. They are exact replicas, identical rather than like. ORATIONS 30.20.[7]

BASIL THE GREAT: Consider the following words also: "In our image."[8] What do you say to this? Surely, the image of God and of the angels is not the same. Now it is absolutely necessary for the form of the Son and of the Father to be

the same, the form being understood, of course, as becomes the divine, not in a bodily shape, but in the special properties of the Godhead. . . . To whom does he say: "In our image"? To whom else, I say, than to the "brightness of his glory and the image of his substance,"[9] who is "the image of the invisible God"? HOMILIES ON THE HEXAMERON 9.6.[10]

CYRIL OF ALEXANDRIA: For the Son remained the Word of God, although he became man, being the Father in form,[11] according to his spiritual image,[12] I mean, and being in every way unchangeable. LETTERS 55.27.[13]

AUGUSTINE: In parents and children there would be found an image and an equality and a likeness if the age difference were lacking. For the child's likeness has been derived from the parent, so that the likeness may rightly be called an image. . . . In God, however, the conditions of time do not obtain, for God cannot be thought of as having begotten in time the Son through whom he has created the times. Hence it follows that not only is [the Son] his image, because he is from [God], and the likeness, because the image, but also the equality is so great that there is not even a temporal distinction standing in the way between them. EIGHTY-THREE DIFFERENT QUESTIONS 74.[14]

"IMAGE" MEANS VISIBLE. TERTULLIAN: It is fortunate that in another passage [the apostle] calls Christ "the image of the invisible God." For does it not follow with equal force from that passage that Christ is not truly God, because the apostle describes him as *the image* of God? This is true, if (as Marcion contends) he is not truly man because he has taken on *the form* or *image* of

---

[3]NPNF 1 13:270*. Cf. *Homilies on John* 15 (FC 33:144). [4]NPNF 2 4:26*. [5]PG 82:597BC/598BC. [6]Gen 4:25. [7]FGFR 276. [8]Gen 1:26. [9]Heb 1:3. [10]FC 46:148-49. [11]Phil 2:6. [12]See also 2 Cor 4:4. [13]FC 77:25. [14]FC 70:191.

a man. For in both cases the true substance will have to be excluded, if *image* (or "fashion") and *likeness* and *form* are descriptions of a phantom. But since he is truly God as the Son of the Father, in his fashion and image, he has been already by the force of this conclusion determined to be truly man, as the Son of man, "found in the fashion" and image "of a man." Against Marcion 20.[15]

Novatian: Please note that the same Moses says in another passage that God appeared to Abraham.[16] Yet the same Moses hears from God that no man can see God and live.[17] If God cannot be seen, how did God appear? If he appeared, how is it that he cannot be seen? . . . This can only mean that it was not the Father, who never has been seen, that was seen, but the Son, who is apt both to descend and to be seen, for the simple reason that he has descended. In fact, he is "the image of the invisible God," that our limited human nature and frailty might in time grow accustomed to see God the Father in him who is the Image of God, that is, in the Son of God. On the Trinity 18.1-3.[18]

Theodore of Mopsuestia: He calls Christ the invisible image, not because God becomes visible in him but rather because the greatness of God is shown forth in him. In a way we do see the invisible nature of God in Christ as the image, in the sense that he was begotten by God the Word and will judge the whole earth when he appears in his proper nature at the time of his second coming. Thus, he holds for us the status of "image," which is visible and belongs to Jesus' earthly, human state, for the very reason that we are able to infer from this "image" [in its earthly appearance] to his divine nature. . . . I am astounded at those who attribute his status as the "image" to his divine nature univocally . . . since the term *image* would never have been applied to human beings (i.e., as some have done) if it had been a term exclusively proper to divine nature. Commentary on Colossians.[19]

Hilary of Poitiers: The Lord has declared: "If I do not perform the works of my Father do not believe me."[20] Hence, he teaches that the Father is seen in him because he performs his works so that the power of the nature that was perceived would reveal the nature of the power that was perceived, wherefore the apostle, indicating that this is the image of God, says: "Who is the image of the invisible God . . . that through him he should reconcile all things to himself." Accordingly, he is the image of God by the power of these works. On the Trinity 8.49.[21]

Ambrose: Be like the image on the coin, unchangeable, keeping the same habits every day. When you see the coin, see the image; when you see the law, see Christ, the image of God, in the law. And because he himself is the image of the invisible and incorruptible God, let him shine for you as in the mirror of the law. Confess him in the law that you may acknowledge him in the gospel. Letters 20.[22]

1:15b *The Firstborn of All Creation*

First in Honor Primarily. Origen: Now it is clear that the principle of the life which is pure and unmixed with anything else is properly in the firstborn of all creation. The participants in Christ truly live because they receive their life from this life, while just as those who are thought to live without him do not have the true light, so neither do they live the true life. Commentary on John 1.188.[23]

Origen: And perhaps for this reason the holy prophecies proclaim him here as servant, and there as son. He is called servant because of the "form of a servant,"[24] and because he is "of the

---

[15]ANF 3:473*. [16]Gen 12:7; 18:1. [17]Ex 33:20. [18]FC 67:67*. [19]*TEM* 1:261-62. Swete notes (262 n. 18) that a similar view is found in the work of Marcellus of Ancyra, as cited in Eusebius of Caesarea *Against Marcellum* 2. [20]Jn 10:37. [21]FC 25:313-14. [22]FC 26:114. [23]FC 80:71. [24]Phil 2:7.

seed of David,"[25] but son in accordance with his power as firstborn.[26] So it is true to say that he is man and that he is not man. He is man insofar as he is capable of death; not man insofar as he is more divine than man. COMMENTARY ON JOHN 10.23.[27]

ORIGEN: But when he said to the Pharisees, "Although I testify of myself, my testimony is true, because I know whence I came and where I go,"[28] he was speaking about his divine nature and, as one might say, on the basis of which he was the firstborn of all creation. COMMENTARY ON JOHN 19.10.[29]

ATHANASIUS: Not then because he was from the Father was he called "Firstborn," but because in him the creation came to be; and as before the creation he was the Son, through whom was the creation, so also before he was called the Firstborn of the whole creation, the Word himself was with God and the Word was God.[30] . . . If then the Word also were one of the creatures, Scripture would have said of him also that he was Firstborn of other creatures; but in fact, the saints' saying that he is "Firstborn of the whole creation" demonstrates that the Son of God is other than the whole creation and not a creature. . . . He is called "Firstborn among many brothers" because of the relationship of the flesh, and "Firstborn from the dead" because the resurrection of the dead is from him and after him. DISCOURSES AGAINST THE ARIANS 2.63.[31]

AMBROSE: The apostle says that Christ is the image of the Father—for he calls him the image of the invisible God, the firstborn of all creation. Firstborn, mark you, not first created, in order that he may be believed to be both begotten, in virtue of his nature, and the first in virtue of his eternity. OF THE CHRISTIAN FAITH 1.7.48.[32]

AUGUSTINE: For according to the form of God he is "the beginning who also speaks to us,"[33] in which beginning God "made the heavens and the earth,"[34] but according to the form of a slave he is "the bridegroom coming out of his chamber."[35] According to the form of God he is "the firstborn of every creature, and he himself is before all creatures, and in him all things hold together," and according to the form of a slave he is "the head of the body, the church." ON THE TRINITY 1.12.24.[36]

FIRST IN TIME PRIMARILY. CHRYSOSTOM: For the word *firstborn* is not expressive of dignity and honor, nor of anything else, but of time only. . . . Indeed, so that people will not suppose that he has a more recent origin in time—since in the past the approach to the Father was through angels, but is now through Christ—he shows first that these angels had no power (otherwise Christ could not have been born "out of darkness" [v. 13]), Paul shows next that Christ is also before them. HOMILIES ON COLOSSIANS 3.[37]

THEODORE OF MOPSUESTIA: Those who argue that the phrase "image of the invisible God" refers to Christ's divine nature also take the position that "firstborn" cannot apply to his human nature. They should take note of the fact that this latter term cannot, however, be applied to the divine nature. If, indeed, he were the firstborn as a creature, he would be described as the first-created . . . but since he is called "firstborn," he is so of those who must be saved in his likeness. The apostle shows this, when he says to the Romans, "Since those whom he foreknew, he also foreordained, to be conformed to the image of his Son, who is the firstborn among many brothers,"[38] and thus he calls him the firstborn brother. . . . How then, they ask, can the term *firstborn* as describing the assumed human nature be applied to the whole creation, since he

[25]Rom 1:3. [26]See also Rom 1:4. [27]FC 80:260. [28]Jn 8:14. [29]FC 89:168. [30]Jn 1:1. [31]NPNF 2 4:382-83*. [32]NPNF 2 10:208*. [33]Jn 8:25. [34]Gen 1:1. [35]Ps 18:6. [36]FC 45:36. [37]NPNF 1 13:270. [38]Rom 8:29.

did not exist in this way before every creature but has come only in recent times? They do not understand that "firstborn" is not spoken in a temporal sense only but in the sense of preeminence as well, for it refers to Christ's status with regard to those who were born after him. COMMENTARY ON COLOSSIANS.[39]

SEVERIAN OF GABALA: Paul wishes to say and show that Christ is before all. For if he is not before all, how could all things be created in him? In him, Paul says, all things were created, so that denying that our hope is in angels, we may put our hope in Christ. PAULINE COMMENTARY FROM THE GREEK CHURCH.[40]

FIRSTBORN AND ONLY-BEGOTTEN. THEODORET OF CYR: If he is the only-begotten, how is he the firstborn? If firstborn, how is he the only-begotten? For he is called in the holy Gospels "only-begotten." Thus, he is the firstborn of creation: not because he has a created sibling but because he was begotten before every creature. How could that be done, so that he was both brother of a creature and its maker? . . . The apostle does not call him first-created, but first-begotten, that is, prior to all others. INTERPRETATION OF THE LETTER TO THE ROMANS.[41]

GREGORY OF NYSSA: The meaning of the "creation," of which he is firstborn, is not unknown to us. For we recognize a twofold creation of our nature, the first that of our conception and birth, the second that of our new creation. But there would have been no need for the second creation had we not crippled the first by our disobedience. Accordingly, when the first creation had grown old and vanished away, it was necessary that there should be a new creation in Christ . . . for the maker of human nature at the first and afterwards is one and the same. *Then* he took dust from the earth and formed man: again he took dust from the Virgin and did not merely form man, but formed man about himself: *then* he created; afterwards, he was created:

then the Word made flesh; afterwards, the Word became flesh, that he might change our flesh to spirit, through becoming a partaker with us in flesh and blood. Of this new creation therefore in Christ, which he himself began, he was called the firstborn. AGAINST EUNOMIUS 4.3.[42]

LEO THE GREAT: Let those then "who were born not from blood, nor from the will of the flesh, but from God"[43] offer concord to God as peace-loving children. Let all the adopted members join together into that "firstborn" of new "creation"[44] who came "not to do his own will, but that of the one who sent him."[45] SERMONS 26.5.1.[46]

JOHN OF DAMASCUS: He who has been born first is firstborn, whether he is the only child or has preceded other brothers. So, if the Son of God were called "firstborn" without being called "only-begotten," then we should understand him to be firstborn of creatures as being a creature. Since, however, he is called both firstborn and only-begotten, we must maintain both of these as applying to him. Thus, we say that he is "the firstborn of every creature," since he is from God, and creation is also from God. . . . For this very reason, that he shared flesh and blood along with us and then, also, that we were made sons of God through him by being adopted through baptism. He who is by nature Son of God has become firstborn among us who have by adoption and grace become sons of God and are accounted as his brothers. ORTHODOX FAITH 4.8.[47]

1:16 *All Things Created Through Him and for Him*

"ALL THINGS" REFERS PRIMARILY TO THE ENTIRE COSMOS. IRENAEUS: "All things were

[39]*TEM* 1:263. [40]NTA 15:319. [41]PG 82:597CD/598CD. [42]NPNF 2 5:157-58*. See also Gregory of Nyssa *On Perfection* (FC 58:113-14). [43]Jn 1:13. [44]See also Rom 8:29; Gal 6:15; 2 Cor 5:17. [45]Jn 6:38. [46]FC 93:108-9. [47]FC 37:342-43*.

made through him and without him was made not a thing."[48] From this "all" nothing is exempt. Now, it is the Father who made all things through him, whether visible or invisible, whether sensible or intelligible, whether temporal for the sake of some dispensation or eternal. These he did not make through angels or some powers that were separated from his thought. AGAINST THE HERESIES 22.1.[49]

ORIGEN: Now that we have briefly repeated our account of the Trinity, we must go on in the same way to remind the reader that through the Son "all things" are said to be "created, in heaven and on earth, visible and invisible, whether thrones or dominions or principalities or powers—all things were created through him and in him he is before all things; in him who is the head all things hold together." The "all things" includes the various supernatural powers that are specified in the remainder of the verse. Paul insists these are subordinate to Christ's power and authority. ON FIRST PRINCIPLES 4.4.3.[50]

CYRIL OF JERUSALEM: Therefore Christ is the Only-begotten Son of God and Maker of the World, for "he was in the world, and the world was made through him,"[51] and "he came unto his own,"[52] as the Gospel teaches us. But Christ is the Maker, at the bidding of the Father, not only of things visible but also things invisible. For, according to the apostle: "In him were created all things in the heavens or on the earth, things visible and things invisible, whether thrones, or dominations, or principalities, or powers. All things have been created through him and unto him, and he is before all creatures, and in him all things hold together." Though you mention the worlds, Jesus Christ, at the bidding of the Father, is Maker of these too. CATECHETICAL LECTURES 12.24.[53]

ATHANASIUS: For the Word of God was not made for us but rather we for him, and "in him all things were created." For even if it had

seemed good to God not to make things of determinate origin, still the Word would have been no less with God, and the Father in him. At the same time, things of determinate origin could not without the Word be brought to be; hence they were made through him—and with meaning and purpose. For since the Word is the Son of God by nature proper to his essence and is from him, as he said himself, the creatures could not have come to be, except through him. DISCOURSES AGAINST THE ARIANS 2.18.31.[54]

CHRYSOSTOM: "All things," he says, "have been created through him, and to him." Indeed, "in him" is "through him," for having said "in him," Paul added, "through him." But what does "to him" mean? It is this: the subsistence of all things depends on him. HOMILIES ON COLOSSIANS 3.[55]

AMBROSE: So then, he himself who calls the Son of God the maker even of heavenly things has also plainly said that all things were made in the Son, that in the renewal of his works he might by no means separate the Son from the Father but unite him to the Father. Paul, too, says: "For in him were all things created in the heavens and in the earth, visible and invisible." OF THE HOLY SPIRIT 3.11.84.[56]

AMBROSE: If the Son, then, is not begotten within limits of time, we are free to judge that nothing can have existed before the Son, whose being is not confined by time. If, indeed, there was anything in existence before the Son, then it instantly follows that all things in heaven and

---

[48]Jn 1:3. [49]ACW 55:80-81. [50]*OSW* 207*. For similar comments from Origen, see *On First Principles* 1.5.1 (*OFP* 44), 1.7.1 (*OFP* 59) and 2.9.5 (*OFP* 133), as well as *Homilies on Exodus* 8.2 (FC 71:319) and *Commentary on John* 1.213-19 (FC 80:76-77). [51]Jn 1:10. [52]Jn 1:11. [53]FC 61:225-26. [54]NPNF 2 4:364*. See also Athanasius *Against the Pagans* 46.7 (NPNF 2 4:291). [55]NPNF 1 13:271*. [56]NPNF 2 10:147.

earth were not created in him, and the apostle is shown to have erred in so setting it down in his epistle. However, if nothing existed before he was begotten, I fail to see how he—who was begotten before all things—should be said to be after any other thing. OF THE CHRISTIAN FAITH 4.100.[57]

HILARY OF POITIERS: There is no doubt that all things are through the Son, since, according to the apostle, "All things are through him and in him." If all things are through him, and all things are from nothing, and nothing is except through him, I ask in what way does he lack the true nature of God, since he is not lacking either in the nature or the power of God? For he used the power of his nature that these things should exist which had no existence, and that these things should exist which pleased him. ON THE TRINITY 5.4.[58]

AUGUSTINE: "Before Abraham I am"[59]; that's what he said himself, the Gospel speaks. Listen to it, or read it. But that's little enough, being the creator before Abraham; he's the creator before Adam, creator before heaven and earth, before all the angels, and the whole spiritual creation, "thrones, dominions, principalities and powers," creator before all things whatsoever. SERMONS 290.2.[60]

THE NEW CREATION IN CHRIST. THEODORE OF MOPSUESTIA: He did not say, "through him," but "in him." Thus Paul is not speaking of the first creation but rather of the repair of the creation in him, according to which what was once dissolved is now brought back into a harmonious whole. COMMENTARY ON COLOSSIANS.[61]

THEODORET OF CYR: "Created through him" refers to the first creation, while "created in him" refers to what has been accomplished through his incarnation. INTERPRETATION OF THE LETTER TO THE COLOSSIANS.[62]

AMBROSIASTER: Before all things came to be, he was born. But Paul also says that all things were created "in him." He is saying that the potency of all things may be believed to be in him, and since in fact all things came into existence through him. This last means that he is the head of every creature, since they began to exist only by virtue of existing with respect to him. COMMENTARY ON THE LETTER TO THE COLOSSIANS.[63]

1:17 He Is Before All Things

THE AGENT OF THE FATHER'S PROVIDENCE. THEODORET OF CYR: Paul did not say, "he was made before all things," but "he is before all things." He is not only the maker of all, but also he manages the care of what he has made and governs the creature, which exists by his wisdom and power. INTERPRETATION OF THE LETTER TO THE ROMANS.[64]

ATHANASIUS: For after making mention of the creation, he naturally speaks of the Framer's power as seen in it, which power, I say, is the Word of God, by whom all things have been made. If indeed the creation is sufficient of itself alone, without the Son, to make God known, see that you don't err in thinking that without the Son it has come to be. For if through the Son it has come to be, and "in him all things consist," it must follow that he who contemplates the creation rightly is contemplating also the Word who framed it, and through him begins to apprehend the Father. DISCOURSES AGAINST THE ARIANS 1.4.12.[65]

AMBROSE: Now we come to that laughable method, attempted by some, of showing a dif-

---

[57]NPNF 2 10:275*. See also Ambrose *Flight from the World* 3.13 (FC 65:290). [58]FC 25:137*. [59]Jn 8:58. [60]*WSA* 3/8:126*. See also Augustine *Sermons* 212.1 (*WSA* 3/6:137) and *Tractates on John* 105.2 (FC 90:258). [61]*TEM* 1:267 (Greek). [62]PG 82:599B/600B. [63]CSEL 81 3:172. [64]PG 82:599C/600C. [65]NPNF 2 4:313*.

ference of power to subsist between Father and Son. . . . It is urged that no small difference in degree of divine majesty is signified in the affirmation that all things are "of" the Father and "through" the Son. Whereas nothing is clearer than that here a plain reason is given of the omnipotence of the Son, inasmuch as while all things are "of" the Father, nonetheless are they all "through" the Son. The Father is not "among" all things, for to him it is confessed that "all things serve Thee."[66] Nor is the Son reckoned "among" all things, for "all things were made by him,"[67] and "all things exist together in him, and he is above all the heavens." The Son, therefore, exists not "among" but *above* all things. Indeed, after the flesh, he is of the people, the Jews. Yet at the same time he is God over all, blessed forever,[68] having a name which is above every name,[69] it being said of him, "You have put all things in subjection under his feet."[70] OF THE CHRISTIAN FAITH 4.11.139-40.[71]

PSEUDO-DIONYSIUS: Hence, with regard to the supra-essential being of God—transcendent goodness transcendently there—no lover of the truth which is above all truth will seek to praise it as word or power or mind or life or being. No. It is at a total remove from every condition, movement, life, imagination, conjecture, name, discourse, thought, conception, being rest, dwelling, unity, limit, infinity, the totality of existence. And yet, since it is the underpinning of goodness and by merely being there is the cause of everything, to praise this divinely beneficent Providence you must turn to all of creation. It is there at the center of everything, and everything has it for a destiny. It is there "before all things, and in it all things hold together." THE DIVINE NAMES 1.5.[72]

1:18a Head of the Body, the Church

THE WORK OF HIS HUMANITY. CHRYSOSTOM: Then having spoken of his dignity, [Paul] also proceeds to speak of his love for humanity. "He is," he says, "the head of the body, the church." He did not say "of the fullness" of the universe, (although this too is signified) out of a wish to show his great friendliness to us, in that he who is thus above, and above all, connected himself with those below. HOMILIES ON COLOSSIANS 3.[73]

THEODORE OF MOPSUESTIA: As the one in whom all things were created, he is described here as the head of the church, which is made into his body through spiritual rebirth and which has the form of the future resurrection, which we hope to share with him as partakers of immortality when we are baptized. COMMENTARY ON COLOSSIANS.[74]

THEODORET OF CYR: Christ is head of the church and firstborn from the dead through his humanity, Paul having passed here from discourse about divinity to reflection on the economy of salvation. INTERPRETATION OF THE LETTER TO THE COLOSSIANS.[75]

AMBROSIASTER: Christ is the head of the church, if things heavenly and earthly live together in him, such that if the whole body is ever deprived of its head, that is, separated from its Creator, there would be an insane and empty chaos. COMMENTARY ON THE LETTER TO THE COLOSSIANS.[76]

FOR THE UNIFYING OF HUMANKIND WITH GOD. AUGUSTINE: For the resurrection we Christians know already has come to pass in our head, and in the members it is yet to be. The head of the church is Christ, the members of Christ are the church. That which has preceded in the head will follow in the body. This is our hope; for this we believe, for this we endure and

---

[66]Ps 119:91. [67]Jn 1:3. [68]Cf. Rom 9:5. [69]Cf. Phil 2:9. [70]Ps 8:6. [71]NPNF 2 10:280*. [72]PSD 54. [73]NPNF 1 13:271*. [74]TEM 1:273. [75]PG 82:599D/600D. [76]CSEL 81 3:173.

persevere amid so great perverseness of this world, hope comforting us, before that hope becomes reality. COMMENTARY ON THE PSALMS 66.1.[77]

AUGUSTINE: This is also what is meant when it said, "he emptied himself,"[78] because he did not appear to men in that dignity which he had with the Father, but took into account the weakness of those who did not yet have a clean heart whereby they might see the Word in the beginning with the Father.[79] What then do the words "he left the Father" mean? He left [the Father] to appear to men as he is with the Father. He likewise left his mother, that is, the old and carnal observance of the synagogue, which was a mother to him from the seed of David according to the flesh. And he clung to his wife, that is, the church, so that they might be two in one flesh.[80] For the apostle says that he is the head of the church and the church is his body. ON GENESIS AGAINST THE MANICHAEANS 2.24.57.[81]

AUGUSTINE: "If the spirit of him," he says, "that raised up Christ from the dead dwell in you, he that raised up Christ from the dead shall quicken your mortal bodies, because of the spirit that dwells in you."[82] Therefore, the universal church, which is now in the pilgrimage of mortal life, awaits at the end of time what was first shown in the body of our Lord Jesus Christ, who is "the firstborn from the dead," because the church is his body, of which he is the head. LETTERS 55.2.3.[83]

1:18b *The Beginning, the Firstborn from the Dead*

FIRST IN THE BEGINNING, FIRST IN THE NEW BEGINNING. ORIGEN: And if we should carefully consider all the concepts applied to him, he is the beginning only insofar as he is wisdom. He is not even the beginning insofar as he is the Word, since "the Word" was "in the beginning,"[84] so that someone might say boldly that wisdom is

older than all the concepts in the names of the firstborn of all creation. God, therefore, is altogether one and simple. Our Savior, however, is many things. . . . And for this reason he becomes the light of men when men, darkened by evil, need the light which shines in the darkness and is not grasped by darkness.[85] He would not have become the light of men if men had not been in darkness. And it is possible to perceive a similar thing also in the case of him being the firstborn [from] the dead. For if, by way of supposition, the woman had not been deceived and Adam had not fallen into sin, but the man created for incorruption had grasped incorruption, he would have neither descended "into the dust of death"[86] nor died since there would have been no sin for which he had to die because of his love for men. And if he had not done these things, he would not have become the "firstborn from the dead." COMMENTARY ON JOHN 1.118-21.[87]

CHRYSOSTOM: So that also in generation he is first. And this is what Paul is chiefly endeavoring to show. For if in fact he is the firstborn, that he was before all the angels, then there is brought in along with it this also as a consequence, that the work done by angels was really commanded by him. And what is indeed wonderful, Paul makes a point of showing that Christ is first, though he was actually born in human form at a relatively later time. Although elsewhere Paul calls Adam first,[88] as in truth he is, he here takes the church for the whole race of mankind. For he is first of the church, and first of men after the flesh, like as of the creation. And therefore Paul here uses the word *firstborn*. HOMILIES ON COLOSSIANS 3.[89]

THEODORE OF MOPSUESTIA: When Paul says "firstborn from the dead," it is clear that he is

---

[77]NPNF 1 8:274*. [78]Phil 2:7. [79]Cf. Mt 5:8; Jn 1:1. [80]Cf. Gen 2:24. [81]FC 84:133*. [82]Rom 8:10-11. [83]FC 12:263. [84]Jn 1:1. [85]Jn 1:5. [86]Ps 21:16. [87]FC 80:58-59. [88]1 Cor 15:45. [89]NPNF 1 13:271*.

referring to the assumed humanity of Christ. COMMENTARY ON COLOSSIANS.[90]

SEVERIAN OF GABALA: "Firstborn of all creation" applied to his status before the emergence of the created order, whereas "firstborn from the dead" refers to the fact that he was raised first of all the brothers who will share in salvation. PAULINE COMMENTARY FROM THE GREEK CHURCH.[91]

THEODORET OF CYR: The blessed Paul called the Christ "the firstborn of the dead." I suppose the firstborn has the same nature as they of whom he is called firstborn. As man then he is firstborn of the dead, for he first destroyed the pangs of death and gave to all the sweet hope of another life. As he rose, so he suffered. As man then he suffered, but as awful God he remained impassible. DEMON-STRATIONS BY SYLLOGISMS, "PROOF THAT THE DIVINITY OF THE SAVIOR IS IMPASSIBLE."[92]

GREGORY OF NYSSA: And he is also a "begin-ning." . . . But what benefits do we derive from believing that he is the beginning? We become ourselves what we believe our beginning to be. ON PERFECTION.[93]

RUFINUS OF AQUILEIA: This also confirms the truth of this confession of ours that, while it is the actual natural flesh and no other which will rise, yet it will rise purged from its faults and hav-ing laid aside its corruption, so that the saying of the apostle is true: "It is sown in corruption; it will be raised in incorruption; it is sown in dis-honor, it will be raised in glory; it is sown a natu-ral body, it will be raised a spiritual body."[94] Inasmuch then as it is a spiritual body, and glori-ous, and incorruptible, it will be furnished and adorned with its own proper members, not with members taken from elsewhere, according to that glorious image of which Christ is set forth as the perpetual type. . . . [indeed] in reference to our hope of the resurrection, Christ is set forth all through as the archetype, since he is the firstborn of those who rise, and since he is the head of

every creature. APOLOGY FOR ORIGEN 1.6-7.[95]

1:19 In Him the Fullness of God Dwells

WHAT IS THE FULLNESS? ORIGEN: The Word of God, by condescending to us and being hum-bled, as it were, in regard to his own worth, when he is present with men, is said to change places when he goes from this world to the Father. The result is that we then see him in his perfection, returning from the emptying with which he emptied himself[96] alongside us to his own [proper and divine] fullness.[97] And we, too, using him as a guide, are fulfilled and delivered from all emptiness. . . . If we understand the ascent of the Son to the Father with holy insight and in a way suitable to God, we shall realize that it is the ascent of mind rather than of body. ON PRAYER 23.2.[98]

CHRYSOSTOM: By the term *fullness* some speak of the Godhead, like as John said, "Of his fullness have we all received."[99] That is, whatever was the Son, the whole Son dwelt there, not a sort of energy, but a Substance. HOMILIES ON COLOS-SIANS 3.[100]

THEODORE OF MOPSUESTIA: He calls the church the "fullness of God." COMMENTARY ON COLOS-SIANS.[101]

THEODORET OF CYR: In the epistle to the Ephe-

---

[90]*TEM* 1:274. [91]NTA 15:319. [92]NPNF 2 3:248*. [93]FC 58:118. [94]1 Cor 15:42-44. [95]NPNF 2 3:437. [96]Cf. Phil 2:7. [97]See also Col 2:9; Eph 1:23. [98]*OSW* 126*. Origen is here commenting on the phrase from the Lord's Prayer, "Our Father in heaven," in order to make the point that God is not corporeal and does not dwell in a place that would bind him. To think, therefore, of Christ as ascend-ing, we must not envision a literal going from one place to another but rather of a change in state or status as the Son moves from his incarnate and earthly existence to the purely spiritual, incorporeal condition that is his eternal reality as the Word. So must we do, *mutatis mutandis*, as his followers. In Origen's theology the divine fullness is that of a pure incorporeality. [99]Jn 1:16. [100]NPNF 1 13:272. [101]*TEM* 1:275.

sians Paul calls the church the "fullness," because it is filled with divine gifts. By God's care it dwells in Christ, is joined to him, is under his rule, follows his laws. INTERPRETATION OF THE LETTER TO THE COLOSSIANS.[102]

AMBROSE: With regard to his Godhead, therefore, the Son of God so possesses his own glory that the glory of Father and Son is one: he is not, therefore, inferior in splendor, for the glory is one, nor lower in Godhead, for the fullness of the Godhead is in Christ. OF THE CHRISTIAN FAITH 2.9.82.[103]

AMBROSIASTER: The fullness is in him and remains in him. This means that he surpasses all things and cannot be surpassed, that he may fashion, refashion, restore the fallen, raise the dead. Thus he says, "Just as the Father has life in himself; so he gives it to the Son to have life in himself."[104] COMMENTARY ON THE LETTER TO THE COLOSSIANS.[105]

1:20 To Reconcile to Himself All Things

DESCEND AND ASCEND. ORIGEN: Therefore, for that reason, it was necessary for my Lord and Savior not only to be born a man among men but also to descend to hell that as a "prepared man" he could lead away "the lot of the scapegoat into the wilderness" of hell. And returning from that place, his work completed, he could ascend to the Father and be more fully purified at the heavenly altar so that he could give a pledge of our flesh, which he had taken with him, in perpetual purity. This, therefore, is the real day of atonement when God is propitiated for men; just as the apostle also says, "Since God was in Christ reconciling the world to himself."[106] And in another place, he says about Christ, "Making peace through the blood of his cross whether with things in heaven or things on earth." HOMILIES ON LEVITICUS 9.4.[107]

EPHREM THE SYRIAN: Thus, as peace began to

be [established], the angels proclaimed, "Glory in the highest and peace on earth."[108] When lower beings received [peace] from superior beings, "they cried, Glory on earth and peace in the heavens."[109] At that time when the divinity came down [and] was clothed in humanity, the angels cried, "Peace on earth." And at the time when that humanity ascended in order to be absorbed into the divinity and sit on the right—"Peace in heaven"—the infants were crying forth before him, "Hosanna in the highest."[110] Hence, the apostle also learned that one should say, "He made peace by the blood of his cross [for] that which is in heaven and on earth." COMMENTARY ON TATIAN'S DIATESSARON 14.[111]

ON EARTH AND IN HEAVEN, BETWEEN EARTH AND HEAVEN. ORIGEN: I believe that, when our Lord the Savior came, Abraham, Isaac and Jacob were blessed with God's mercy. Previously they had seen his day and rejoiced.[112] It is not believable that they did not profit from it later, when he came and was born of a virgin. And why do I speak of the patriarchs? I shall boldly follow the authority of the Scriptures to higher planes, for the presence of the Lord Jesus and his work benefitted not only what is earthly but also what is heavenly. Hence the apostle too says, "Establishing peace through the blood of his cross, both on earth and in heaven." HOMILIES ON LUKE 10.3.[113]

CHRYSOSTOM: But what are "things in the heav-

---

[102]PG 82:601A/602A. [103]NPNF 2 10:234*. [104]Jn 5:26. [105]CSEL 81 3:174. [106]2 Cor 5:19. [107]FC 83:185. Origen is comparing Christ in his descent at the incarnation into the mortality and suffering of human flesh (as well as in his descent from the cross into hell between Good Friday and Easter) to the scapegoat of the Jewish Day of Atonement ritual. This animal, after being prepared and led by a man who is "in readiness" (Lev 16:20-22), "carries away" the sins of the people by wandering off into the wilderness as, in effect, an exile (presumably to starve and die). [108]Lk 2:14. [109]Lk 19:38. [110]Mt 21:9. [111]JSSS 2:66. [112]Jn 8:56. [113]FC 94:41. See also Origen Homilies on Luke 13.3 (FC 94:53); Fragments on Luke 164 (FC 94:190); Homilies on Leviticus 1.3.2 (FC 83:34); 4.4.3 (FC 83:74).

ens"? . . . The earth was divided from heaven, the angels had become enemies to men, through seeing the Lord insulted. . . . What Christ did on the cross was to translate up into heaven sinful humankind still in bondage to the evil one. Thus he, in effect, brought up to the angels the enemy, the hated one. Not only did he make the things on earth to be at peace, but he brought up to them the one who was their enemy and foe. Here was peace profound. Angels again appeared on the earth thereafter, because humankind from its side had appeared in heaven. HOMILIES ON COLOSSIANS 3.[114]

THEODORE OF MOPSUESTIA: He reconciled all things (he says) in his death (that is, by his blood and his cross) and joined things on earth and in heaven for a common purpose, because he died and rose again. By rising he truly made available to all the common promise of resurrection and immortality. COMMENTARY ON COLOSSIANS.[115]

BASIL THE GREAT: For the true peace is above. Yet, as long as we were bound to the flesh, we were yoked to many things which troubled us. Seek, then, after peace, a release from the troubles of this world. Possess a calm mind, a tranquil and unconfused state of soul, which is neither agitated by the passions nor drawn aside by false doctrines that challenge by their persuasiveness to an assent, in order that you may obtain "the peace of God which surpasses all understanding and guards your heart."[116] He who seeks after peace, seeks Christ, because "he himself is our peace," who has made two men into one new man,[117] making peace, and "making peace through the blood of his cross, whether on earth or in the heavens." HOMILIES 16.10.[118]

CYRIL OF JERUSALEM: The Savior endured all this, "making peace through the blood of the cross, for all things whether in the heavens or on the earth." For we were enemies of God through sin, and God had decreed the death of the sin-

ner. One of two things, therefore, was necessary, either that God, in his truth, should destroy all men, or that in his loving-kindness, he should remit the sentence. But see the wisdom of God; he preserved the truth of his sentence and the exercise of his loving-kindness. Christ took our sins "in his body upon the tree; that we, having died to sin," by his death "might live to justice."[119] He who died for us was of no small worth; he was no material sheep; he was no mere man. He was more than an angel, he was God made man. The iniquity of sinners was not as great as the justice of him who died for them. The sins we committed were not as great as the justice he wrought, who laid down his life for us. He laid it down when he willed, and he took it up again when he willed. CATECHETICAL LECTURES 13.33.[120]

PELAGIUS: Beings on earth and beings in heaven were separated by antitheses in their way of life. Thus, we pray that God's will may be done on earth as in heaven. PELAGIUS'S COMMENTARY ON THE LETTER TO THE COLOSSIANS.[121]

1:21 You Who Once Were Estranged and Hostile

BY FREE WILL. CHRYSOSTOM: But nevertheless, he says, you that do not act against your wills, nor from compulsion, but with your wills and wishes sprang away from him, you he has reconciled, though you were unworthy of it. And seeing that he had made mention of the "things in the heavens," he shows that all the enmity had its origin from our side, not from the inhabitants of heaven. For they indeed were long ago desirous, and God also, but you were not willing. And throughout he is showing that the angels had no power during the course of human history, to the extent that human beings

---

[114]NPNF 1 13:272. [115]TEM 1:276*. [116]Phil 4:7. [117]Eph 2:14. [118]FC 46:266-67*. [119]1 Pet 2:24. [120]FC 64:26-27. [121]PETE 455.

chose to continue as enemies. The angels could neither persuade them, nor, even if they had persuaded, could they deliver humankind from the devil. HOMILIES ON COLOSSIANS 4.[122]

AMBROSIASTER: As he recalls God's gift to the Gentiles, Paul shows by how much more they are debtors with respect to God's grace. For they were enemies of his counsel, by which he had decided to visit the human race through his servant Moses. They did not receive his teaching and power but worshiped their own idols, even the evil works. They adored the works which they themselves had fabricated. COMMENTARY ON THE LETTER TO THE COLOSSIANS.[123]

1:22a He Has Reconciled in His Body of Flesh

REAL FLESH, REAL BODY. JEROME: The apostle, in his epistle to the Colossians, wishing to show that the body of Christ was made of flesh and was not spiritual and made of some gossamer, ethereal substance, said significantly, "And you, when you were sometime alienated from Christ and enemies of his spirit in evil works, he has reconciled in the body of his flesh through death." And again in the same epistle: "In whom you were circumcised with a circumcision made without hands in the putting off of the body of the flesh."[124] If by *body* is meant flesh only, and the word is not ambiguous nor capable of diverse significations, it was quite superfluous to use both expressions—bodily and of flesh—as though body did not imply flesh. LETTER TO PAMMACHIUS AGAINST JOHN OF JERUSALEM 27.[125]

ONE FLESH, ONE SON. CYRIL OF ALEXANDRIA: Note how he says that it was "his own body" and "his own flesh" which was given up for us. We must not say, then, that the flesh and blood was that of another son apart from him, understood as separate and honored as a mere conjunction, having an alien glory, someone who did not have

preeminence substantially, but only as if the name of sonship and that of Godhead which is above every name were thrown over him like a mask or a cloak. ON THE UNITY OF CHRIST 128-29.[126]

1:22b To Present You Holy and Blameless

PERFECTION POSSIBLE? THEODORE OF MOPSUESTIA: In a similar fashion to his treatment of the subject in the letter to the Ephesians, Paul speaks here of the primacy in Christ, such that there is a joining of the church to that which has already been accomplished in him.... The effect is that there is in Christ a bearing away of our mortality in the gift of immortality ... so that every uprighting act which is worked by him is contained in the promises, which foresaw the future renewal in a future time. COMMENTARY ON COLOSSIANS.[127]

PELAGIUS: [With regard to 1:22-23] you should observe that Paul does not know or teach anything that he believes to be impossible for human beings to do. PELAGIUS'S COMMENTARY ON THE LETTER TO THE COLOSSIANS.[128]

---

[122]NPNF 1 13:275*. [123]CSEL 81 3:175. [124]Col 2:11. [125]NPNF 2 6:438*. Jerome is here on a strong anti-Origenist crusade, as he polemicizes against any notion that the resurrection body of Christians could be made of a "spiritual" flesh that would be essentially different from the flesh that constitutes the means of our earthly existence. Origen was often criticized for seeming to have taught such a notion and thus to be contradicting the real physical nature of the incarnation and the dignity of the human body. Jerome's point is that by using the phrase "body of his flesh" Paul means to say "the body that is his flesh," thereby removing any possibility that one could interpret "body" as meaning something nonphysical. [126]OUC 128-29. Cyril is here attacking the supposed teaching of Nestorius. This latter was alleged to have taught that the human and divine persons of Christ are separate, each with its proper attributes and only "conjoined" by the miracle of the incarnation. The result Cyril believed was that we end up with two Sons. His point is that sonship belongs properly to the human nature as well as the divine nature of Christ, so that Christ's human attributes may not be separated (be alien) from his divinity. Cyril is thus a step away from what came to be called monophysitism, that is, that Christ has only one nature as well as one person. [127]TEM 1:277-78. [128]PETE 455.

AUGUSTINE: He, however, is not unreasonably said to walk blamelessly, not who has already reached the end of his journey but who is passing on towards the end in a blameless manner, free from damnable sins, and at the same time not neglecting to cleanse by almsgiving such sins as are venial.[129] For the way in which we walk, that is, the road by which we reach perfection, is cleansed by clean prayer. That, however, is a clean prayer in which we say in truth, "Forgive us, as we ourselves forgive."[130] So that, as there is nothing censured when blame is not imputed, we may hold on our course to perfection without censure, in a word, blamelessly. ON MAN'S PERFECTION IN RIGHTEOUSNESS 9.20.[131]

---

[129]By "damnable" sins Augustine clearly means those that would cause us by their very nature to lose our salvation. Apostasy and renunciation of baptism would be an example. By "venial" sins he means those that may be confessed, repented of and cleansed as part of the normal progress in sanctification of any Christian, and struggle with which is a lifetime process. [130]Mt 6:10. [131]NPNF 1 5:166.

1:24—2:5 PAUL'S WORK

[24]Now I rejoice in my sufferings for your sake, and in my flesh I complete what is lacking in Christ's afflictions for the sake of his body, that is, the church, [25]of which I became a minister according to the divine office which was given to me for you, to make the word of God fully known, [26]the mystery hidden for ages and generations[c] but now made manifest to his saints. [27]To them God chose to make known how great among the Gentiles are the riches of the glory of this mystery, which is Christ in you, the hope of glory. [28]Him we proclaim, warning every man and teaching every man in all wisdom, that we may present every man mature in Christ. [29]For this I toil, striving with all the energy which he mightily inspires within me.

2 For I want you to know how greatly I strive for you, and for those at Laodicea, and for all who have not seen my face, [2]that their hearts may be encouraged as they are knit together in love, to have all the riches of assured understanding and the knowledge of God's mystery, of Christ, [3]in whom are hid all the treasures of wisdom and knowledge. [4]I say this in order that no one may delude you with beguiling speech. [5]For though I am absent in body, yet I am with you in spirit, rejoicing to see your good order and the firmness of your faith in Christ.

c Or from angels and men

OVERVIEW: The apostle Paul in his suffering and preaching continues the reconciling work of Christ (CHRYSOSTOM, THEODORE, SEVERIAN, THEODORET, AMBROSIASTER). Paul represents all Christians, and ultimately the church itself, as a corporate continuation of the reconciling work of Christ (AUGUSTINE). The special responsibility of Paul is to make known the mysterious unfolding of God's plan in salvation history (CHRYSOSTOM, AMBROSIASTER), a mystery hidden in Scripture (ORIGEN), in the divine nature of Christ (AMBROSE) and in the working of grace

(AUGUSTINE). Indeed, the gospel is a treasure that God employs on many levels for our benefit, even if some aspects remain hidden by divine design (JEROME) or remain ineffable (JOHN OF DAMASCUS).

1:24 *In My Flesh I Complete What Is Lacking in Christ's Afflictions*

WHAT IS LACKING? ORIGEN: And the contest must be waged not only to escape denial of our faith but also to escape feeling the first inclination to shame when we are thought by those alien to God to be suffering what deserves shame. This is especially true of you, holy Ambrose, who have been honored and welcomed by a great many cities, if now, as it were, you go in procession bearing the cross of Jesus and following him. . . . His purpose is to go with you and to give you speech and wisdom—and to you, Protoctetus, his fellow contestant, and to you others who suffer martyrdom with them and complete what is lacking in Christ's afflictions. EXHORTATION TO MARTYRDOM 36.[1]

CHRYSOSTOM: It seems indeed to be a great thing Paul has said, but it is not based on arrogance, far be it. Rather, Paul's words come from his deep love towards Christ. For he will not have the sufferings to be his own, but his, through the desire to reconcile these persons to him. And what things I suffer, I suffer, he says, on his account. Therefore, don't thank me, but express your gratitude to Christ, for it is he himself who suffers. HOMILIES ON COLOSSIANS 4.[2]

THEODORE OF MOPSUESTIA: As you learn those things that are right for you, you have received the promise that goes with them. None of this can happen without labor and tribulation. For these reasons I, Paul, suffer in my traveling and in my preaching to all about what must be corrected . . . for these things I have functioned as a servant of the gospel. COMMENTARY ON COLOSSIANS.[3]

SEVERIAN OF GABALA: I fulfill what is lacking in the tribulations of Christ through my suffering, which is on your behalf. How so? Because in order to preach to you, I have had to suffer. Since Christ is the head of the body, tribulation will be generated through the word of truth for those who are in the church. These are naturally called the sufferings of Christ. PAULINE COMMENTARY FROM THE GREEK CHURCH.[4]

THEODORET OF CYR: Paul fills up the sufferings of Christ in the sense that he endures sufferings in order to preach salvation to the nations. INTERPRETATION OF THE LETTER TO THE ROMANS.[5]

AMBROSIASTER: Paul confesses that he rejoices in the tribulations which he suffers, because he sees growth in the faith of believers. Thus his suffering is not empty, when by what he suffers he adds to his life. He claims that these sufferings are joined to those of Christ, whose teaching they follow. COMMENTARY ON THE LETTER TO THE COLOSSIANS.[6]

AUGUSTINE: In regard to this is that which in another place the very same apostle says: "I now rejoice in sufferings for you, and I fill up those things which are wanting of the afflictions of Christ in my flesh." He did not say "of the afflictions of me" but "of Christ," because he was a member of Christ and in his persecutions, such as it was necessary for Christ to suffer in his whole body, even Paul was filling up Christ's afflictions in Paul's own portion. TRACTATES ON JOHN 108.5.1.[7]

AUGUSTINE: And when as a preacher of Christ he was now suffering from others what he had done himself as a persecutor, "that I may fill up," he said, "in my flesh what is lacking from the

---

[1]*OSW* 67. The Ambrose mentioned here is not Ambrose of Milan. [2]NPNF 1 13:276*. [3]*TEM* 1:279-80 (Greek). [4]NTA 15:321. [5]PG 82:603B/604B. [6]CSEL 81 3:175-76. [7]FC 90:281-82*.

afflictions of Christ"; thus showing that what he was suffering was part and parcel of the afflictions of Christ. That can't be understood of the head, which now in heaven is not suffering any such thing; but of the body, that is, the church; the body, which with its head is the one Christ. SERMONS 341.10.[8]

1:25 According to the Divine Office Given to Me

THE OFFICE AND ECONOMY GIVEN TO PAUL. CHRYSOSTOM: Either he means that Christ's will was that after his departure we should step up to our special place in the dispensation,[9] in order that we might not feel so deserted (since it is Christ himself who plays the necessary part of the one who suffers and is the ambassador from heaven). Or he means this, namely, for this end that he permitted me to be persecuted, that in my preaching I might gain belief. Or by "dispensation" he means that he required not deeds, nor actions, nor good works but faith and baptism. For you would not otherwise have received the word. "For you," he says, "to fulfill the word of God." He speaks of the Gentiles . . . for that the cast-away Gentiles should have been able to receive such lofty doctrines was not ultimately Paul's personal doing but proceeded from the dispensation of God. HOMILIES ON COLOSSIANS 4.[10]

1:26 The Mystery Hidden for Ages

HIDDEN, BUT REVEALED. CHRYSOSTOM: And with reason he calls that a mystery, which none knew except God. And where hid? In Christ; as he says in the Epistle to the Ephesians.[11] . . . But now it has been manifested, he says, "to his saints." So we know that it is altogether of the dispensation[12] of God. "But now has been manifested," he says. He does not say "is come to pass" but "has been manifested to his saints." So that it is even now still hid, since it has been manifested to his saints alone. HOMILIES ON COLOSSIANS 5.[13]

THEODORET OF CYR: He calls the mystery the preaching of the dispensation, so that what was once completely unknown may be learned only from God. . . . Through this Paul shows the antiquity of the gospel, and that before the law, before the very constituting of the world, God had formed this economy for the whole universe. INTERPRETATION OF THE LETTER TO THE COLOSSIANS.[14]

1:27 The Riches of the Glory of This Mystery

TO THE DIGNITY OF ANGELS. CHRYSOSTOM: For the great glory of this mystery is apparent among others also, but much more among these [i.e., among the Gentiles]. For, all of a sudden, to have brought men more senseless than stones to the dignity of angels, simply through bare words and faith alone, without any great labor or effort, shows indeed the glory and riches of mystery. It is as though one were to take a dog, quite consumed with hunger and the mange, foul and loathsome to see, and not so much as able to move but lying deserted, and were to make him all at once into a man, and to display him upon the royal throne. They were accustomed to worship stones and the earth; but they learned that they themselves are better both than the heaven and the sun and that the whole world serves them. They were captives and prisoners of the devil. Suddenly they are placed above his head and lay commands on him and punish him. From

---

[8] *WSA* 3/10:27. [9] The term *dispensation*, or *economy*, is an extraordinarily rich and polyvalent one for the Fathers. Chrysostom believes that Paul in his work somehow carries forward, becomes an instrument of, embodies a new phase of all that God has been doing providentially in the whole work of creation and redemption. The notion of dispensation covers, therefore, the idea of divine ordering, purpose and provision in an unfolding, guided process that is internally consistent and subject in all of its details to the wisdom of God's governance. In his comments on this passage, Chrysostom illustrates neatly, moreover, that the implications of the term can cut in many different directions. [10] NPNF 1 13:277*. [11] Eph 3:9. [12] See n. 9 above. [13] NPNF 1 13:279*. [14] PG 82:603CD/604CD.

being captives and slaves to demons, they have become the body of the Master of the angels and archangels. From not knowing even what God is, they have suddenly become sharers even in God's throne. . . . The mystery entails all these things; all come from the presence of Christ in the Colossian believers. "If Christ is in you," Paul asks, "why do you seek angels?" COMMENTARY ON COLOSSIANS 5.[15]

AMBROSIASTER: The mystery which has been hidden from the ages, he asserts, has now been revealed, that is, shown forth in the time of the apostles: that the Gentiles have been admitted without circumcision to the faith of Christ, which was promised to the Jews. COMMENTARY ON THE LETTER TO THE COLOSSIANS.[16]

PELAGIUS: The mystery is Christ himself, that God gives this wealth to all who call upon him. PELAGIUS'S COMMENTARY ON THE LETTER TO THE COLOSSIANS.[17]

2:3 All the Treasures of Wisdom and Knowledge

SCRIPTURAL TREASURE. ORIGEN: We have also taken the following text in this way; "But we have this treasure in earthen vessels, that the excellency may be of the power of God and not of us,"[18] since "treasure" is used elsewhere of the treasure of knowledge and secret wisdom, and "earthen vessels" of the text of the Scriptures which is simple and easily despised by the Greeks, in which the excellency of God's power truly appears. COMMENTARY ON JOHN 4.2.[19]

THE DIVINE LARGENESS. CHRYSOSTOM: "In whom are all the treasures." Christ himself knows all things. "Hid," for don't think that you truly and already have all things. These are hidden also even from angels, not from you only; so that you ought to ask all things from him. He himself gives wisdom and knowledge. Now by

saying "treasures," he shows their magnificence, by saying "all," that he is ignorant of nothing, by "hid," that he alone knows. HOMILIES ON COLOSSIANS 5.[20]

THE DIVINE NATURE OF CHRIST. AMBROSE: On consideration, your Majesty, of the reason for which many have so far gone astray, or that many—alas!—should follow diverse ways of belief concerning the Son of God, the marvel seems to be not at all that human knowledge has been baffled in dealing with superhuman things, but that it has not submitted to the authority of the Scriptures. What reason, indeed, is there to wonder, if by their worldly wisdom men failed to comprehend the mystery of God the Father and the Lord Jesus Christ, in whom all the treasures of wisdom and knowledge are hidden, that mystery of which not even angels have been able to obtain knowledge, except by revelation? OF THE CHRISTIAN FAITH 4.1.1-2.[21]

THE WORTH OF GRACE. AUGUSTINE: Herein is all the worth of grace, by which he saves those who believe, containing in itself deep treasures of wisdom and knowledge and steeping in faith the minds which it draws to the eternal contemplation of unchangeable truth. Suppose the omnipotent had created his humanity by forming it otherwise than in a mother's womb and had presented himself suddenly to our sight. Suppose he had not passed through the stages from childhood to youth, had taken no food, no sleep: would he not have given ground for the erroneous opinion which believed that he had not really become a human being? And by doing everything miraculously, would he not have obscured the effect of his mercy? But now he has appeared as Mediator between God and men, in such a way as to join both natures in the unity of

---

[15]NPNF 1 13:280*. [16]CSEL 81 3:177. [17]PETE 456. [18]2 Cor 4:7. [19]FC 80:159. See also OFP 306. [20]NPNF 1 13:281*. [21]NPNF 2 10:262*. Ambrose here addresses the Roman emperor.

one Person. He has both raised the common-place to the heights of the uncommon and brought down the uncommon to the common-place. LETTERS 137.1.3.[22]

AUGUSTINE: Pay attention, dearly beloved, and see how sound the apostle's advice is, when he says, "As therefore you received Christ Jesus our Lord, so walk in him, rooted and built up in him and confirmed in the faith."[23] What we have to do, after all, is to abide firmly in him through the simplicity and assurance of this faith, so that he may open up to us, as faithful believers, the treasure that is hidden in him. The same apostle says, "In him are all the treasures of wisdom and knowledge hidden." He didn't hide them in order to deny them to us but to rouse our desire for what is hidden. That is the value of secrets. SERMONS 51.5.[24]

THE KNOWLEDGE HIDDEN FOR OUR BENEFIT. JEROME: Can the workman be ignorant of his work? We read of Christ in St. Paul: "In whom are hidden all treasures of wisdom and knowl-edge." Note: "all treasures of wisdom and knowl-edge." Not that some are and some are not in him but that they are hidden. That which is in him, therefore, is not lacking to him, even though it be hidden to us. If, moreover, the trea-sures of wisdom and knowledge are hidden in Christ, we must find out why they are hidden. If we men were to know the day of judgment, that, for example, it would not be for two thousand years, and if we knew it so long ahead of time, we would be more careless on that account. We would say, for instance, What is it to me if the day of judgment will not be here for two thou-sand years? Scripture says, therefore, for our benefit, that "the Son does not know the day of judgment," because we do not know when the day of judgment will be upon us; and further: "Take heed, watch and pray, for you do not know when the time is."[25] Not "we do not know" but "you do not know." HOMILIES ON MARK 84(x).[26]

HE KNOWS ALL. JOHN OF DAMASCUS: For, although he was impassible, he became subject to the experience of human passions[27] and was made minister of our salvation. Now, they who say that he is a servant divide the one Christ into two, just as Nestorius did.[28] But we say that he is Lord and Master of all creation, the one Christ, the same being at once God and man, and that he knows all things, "for in him are hid all the treasures of wisdom and knowledge." ORTHODOX FAITH 3.21.[29]

JOHN'S INTIMATE KNOWLEDGE. THE VENERA-BLE BEDE: The disciple's leaning upon the mas-ter's breast was a sign not only of present love but also of future mystery. Already at that time it was prefigured that the Gospel which this same disciple was going to write would include the hidden mysteries of divine majesty more copiously and profoundly than the rest of the pages of sacred Scripture. For because in Jesus' breast "are hidden all the treasures of wisdom and knowledge," it was fitting that the one who leaned upon his breast was the one to whom he had granted a larger gift of unique wisdom and knowledge than to the rest. HOMILIES ON THE GOSPELS 1.9.[30]

2:5 The Firmness of Your Faith in Christ

THE CEMENTING WORK OF LOVE. CHRYSOS-TOM: Not only, Paul says, have you not fallen, but no one has so much as thrown you into dis-order. Paul has set himself over them that they may fear him as if he were present. Thus Paul

---

[22]FC 20:25*. [23]Col 2:6-7. [24]*WSA* 3/3:23*. [25]Mk 13:32-33. [26]FC 57:186-87. [27]In the ancient and classical view inherited by the Fathers from Greek philosophy, divine nature and the experience of change involved in "passions" of any kind were viewed as radically incompatible with one another. [28]See p. 22 n. 126 above with regard to Nestorius and his teaching. By the time of John of Damascus it had long been customary to associate any teaching that seemed to threaten the unity of the humanity and divinity of Christ with Nestorianism. [29]FC 37:326. [30]*HOG* 1:88.

has his own particular way of preserving order. He takes the view that from solidness follows firmness. Solidness is produced, as in the case of a wall, when having brought many things together, you shall cement them compactly and inseparably. In another sense such solidness is the peculiar work of love; for those who were isolated, when love has closely cemented and knit them together, it makes them solid. And faith, again, does the same thing, when it does not allow the fruitless posing of unanswerable questions to intrude themselves. For as such queries divide and shake loose, so faith produces solidity and compactness. HOMILIES ON COLOSSIANS 5.[31]

THE FIRMNESS OF GOD'S LOVE. FULGENTIUS OF RUSPE: This love, which is from God and is God, cannot be separated from the being of God, because God and love are one. For since love, itself inseparable from its source, not only possesses human beings who can be separated from one another, but from many hearts and souls makes one heart and one soul, what madness is it to say that love which is accustomed to join separated minds in an inseparable love can be separated from the human beings who express it? Hence it is that Paul said, "For even if I am absent in the flesh, yet I am with you in spirit, rejoicing as I observe your good order." And in the Acts of the Apostles, it is written that the "community of believers was of one heart and mind"[32] . . . something that was not brought about except by the Spirit of faith and love. LETTER TO VICTOR 9.5-6.[33]

---

[31]NPNF 1 13:281-82*. [32]Acts 4:32. [33]FC 95:398*.

2:6-15 CONSIDER THE MEANS OF SALVATION

[6]*As therefore you received Christ Jesus the Lord, so live in him, [7]rooted and built up in him and established in the faith, just as you were taught, abounding in thanksgiving.*

[8]*See to it that no one makes a prey of you by philosophy and empty deceit, according to human tradition, according to the elemental spirits of the universe, and not according to Christ. [9]For in him the whole fulness of deity dwells bodily, [10]and you have come to fulness of life in him, who is the head of all rule and authority. [11]In him also you were circumcised with a circumcision made without hands, by putting off the body of flesh in the circumcision of Christ; [12]and you were buried with him in baptism, in which you were also raised with him through faith in the working of God, who raised him from the dead. [13]And you, who were dead in trespasses and the uncircumcision of your flesh, God made alive together with him, having forgiven us all our trespasses, [14]having canceled the bond which stood against us with its legal demands; this he set aside, nailing it to the cross. [15]He disarmed the principalities and powers and made a public example of them, triumphing over them in him.[d]*

d Or *in it* (that is, the cross)

OVERVIEW: At the center of Paul's admonitions is the importance of tradition, of remaining faithful to what has been taught and received. Christ is the way to the Father; by no means may angels play that role (CHRYSOSTOM). The Colossians are to stand firm, not yielding to any observances other than what they have been taught by Epaphras. They are to recognize that in Christ and through baptism, mortality has been "put off" and the life of immortality embraced (THEODORE). In Christ there has been a reversal of the history of sin and bondage contained in the Old Testament history (CHRYSOSTOM, THEODORE, THEODORET, SEVERIAN) and that it is specifically in the full divinity and full humanity of the Son, particularly in his cross and death, that this reversal takes place (CYRIL OF JERUSALEM, AMBROSE, CYRIL OF ALEXANDRIA). Since there will be many corrupters to lead the Colossians astray, they must remain firm on the foundation of faith in the triune God (AMBROSIASTER). The gracious gift of salvation in Christ is always by means of the divine initiative, freely willed as an expression of the divine sovereignty (AUGUSTINE).

2:8 Empty Deceit

ORTHODOXY AND ORTHOPRAXY. CYRIL OF JERUSALEM: True religion consists of these two elements: pious doctrines and virtuous actions. Neither does God accept doctrines apart from works, nor are works, when divorced from godly doctrine, accepted by God. . . . The knowledge of doctrines is a precious possession. There is need of a vigilant soul, since there are many who would deceive you by philosophy and vain deceit. CATECHETICAL LECTURES 4.2.[1]

"VAIN" DECEIT. CHRYSOSTOM: Then because the term *philosophy* has an appearance of dignity, Paul added, "And vain deceit." For there can also be a pious deceit, such as many have been deceived by, that one should not consider a gen-

uine deception. Jeremiah notes that even God can seem to deceive. "O Lord, you have deceived me, and I was deceived"[2]; in this example we have nothing we can describe as deceit. For Jacob also deceived his father, but that was not finally a deceit but the proper way to act in the situation.[3] HOMILIES ON COLOSSIANS 6.[4]

HUMAN CONTRIVANCE. THEODORET OF CYR: "Philosophy" is smooth argumentation that persuades. "Empty deceit" refers to superfluous and noxious human tradition, that is, not the divine law itself but its intemperate and skewed observance. "Elements of the world" are the observation of cultic days. INTERPRETATION OF THE LETTER TO THE COLOSSIANS.[5]

AMBROSIASTER: He calls that philosophy worldly by which men who desire to be wise in earthly terms are seduced. COMMENTARY ON THE LETTER TO THE COLOSSIANS.[6]

PELAGIUS: The enemy here is philosophy that believes that the power of God rises from natural things, that nothing can be made from nothing, that the soul cannot have a beginning or be mortal, that a virgin cannot conceive, or God be born of a man or die and rise again. PELAGIUS'S COMMENTARY ON THE LETTER TO THE COLOSSIANS.[7]

2:9 In Him the Whole Fullness of Deity Dwells Bodily

IN CHRIST IS THE FULLNESS. CHRYSOSTOM: "For in him dwells," that is, for God dwells in him. But that you may not think him enclosed, as in a body, Paul writes, "All the fullness of the Godhead bodily: and you are made full in him." Others say that Paul means the church filled by his Godhead, as he elsewhere says, "of him that

---

[1]FC 61:119-20*. [2]Jer 20:7. [3]Gen 27. [4]NPNF 1 13:284*. [5]PG 82:607B/608B. [6]CSEL 81 3:181. [7]PETE 459.

fills all in all,"[8] and that he employs the term *bodily* here, as the body in the head. But if this interpretation is true, why did he not add "which is the church"? HOMILIES ON COLOSSIANS 6.[9]

THEODORE OF MOPSUESTIA: This "fullness" is said of the whole creation restored by him, for, in the sense that has been established earlier, all creation dwells in him, that is, is joined to him, so that he contains it in a bodily way. COMMENTARY ON COLOSSIANS.[10]

THEODORET OF CYR: Some teachers say that Christ is here being called the church, since the fullness of his divinity dwells in it. I am unsure, however, whether this interpretation suits the term *bodily*. I think that since he calls Christ the head of the church, it is clear that this refers to his humanity, by which he is our head, and that this is said about his human nature, which contained complete divinity within itself. INTERPRETATION OF THE LETTER TO THE COLOSSIANS.[11]

ATHANASIUS: In the past Christ the Word was accustomed to come to the saints individually and to sanctify those who rightly received him. But neither, when these individuals were first born did people assert that he had become man in any of them, nor when they suffered, did anyone say that God himself suffered in them. But then he came among us from Mary once at the end of the ages for the abolition of sin (for so it was pleasing to the Father to send his own Son "made of a woman, made under the law"). And then it was said, that he took flesh and became man. It was in that flesh he suffered for us. His intention was to show, so that all might believe, that whereas he was ever God, and sanctified those to whom he came, and ordered all things according to the Father's will, afterwards for our sakes he became man, and "bodily," as the apostle says, the Godhead dwelt in the flesh. This was as much as to say, "Being God, he had his own body, and using this as an instrument, he

became man for our sakes." DISCOURSES AGAINST THE ARIANS 3.26.31.[12]

GREGORY OF NYSSA: Since then it was impossible that our life, which had been estranged from God, should of itself return to the high and heavenly place, for this reason, as the apostle says, he who knew no sin is made sin for us[13] and frees us from the curse by taking on him our curse as his own.[14] Having taken up and, in the language of the apostle, "slain" in himself "the enmity"[15] which by means of sin had come between us and God (in fact sin was the "enmity") and having become what we were, he through himself again united humanity to God. For having by purity brought into closest relationship with the Father of our nature that new man which is created after God,[16] in whom dwelled all the fullness of the Godhead bodily, he drew with him into the same grace all the nature that partakes of his body and is akin to him. AGAINST EUNOMIUS 12.1.[17]

CYRIL OF ALEXANDRIA: Neither do we say that the Word of God dwelled, as in an ordinary man, in the one born of the holy Virgin, in order that Christ might not be thought to be a man bearing God. For even if the Word both "dwelt among us,"[18] and it is said that in Christ "dwells all the fullness of the Godhead bodily," we do not think that, being made flesh, the Word is said to dwell in him just as in those who are

---

[8]Eph 1:23. [9]*NPNF* 1 13:285*. [10]*TEM* 1:286. Theodore operates here with his theology of the *homo assumptus* in the incarnation. He teaches that in the man Jesus, assumed by God the Word in the incarnation, the whole physical creation comes to be included within, that is, "dwells in," the Godhead. [11]PG 82:607C/608C. Theodoret seems to be saying that the fullness of God dwells in Christ *bodily* in Christ's capacity as head of the church. This would be a different slant from Theodore's claim (see the preceding note) that the bodily indwelling happens within the assumed human nature of Christ. Thus, Theodoret takes "body" as referring to the church as the body of Christ, while Theodore takes it as referring to the human body of Jesus. [12]*NPNF* 2 4:410*. [13]2 Cor 5:21. [14]Gal 5:13. [15]Eph 2:16. [16]Eph 4:24. [17]*NPNF* 2 5:241*. [18]Jn 1:14.

holy, and we do not define the indwelling in him to be the same. But united *kata phusin*, and not changed into flesh, the Word produced an indwelling such as the soul of man might be said to have in its own body. LETTERS 17.9.[19]

AMBROSE: The law has proved God's oneness.[20] It speaks of one God, as also the apostle when he says of Christ: "In whom dwells all the fullness of the Godhead bodily." For if, as the apostle says, all the fullness of the Godhead, bodily, is in Christ, then must the Father and the Son be confessed to be of one Godhead. Or if one desired to sunder the Godhead of the Son from the Godhead of the Father, as long as the Son possesses all the fullness of the Godhead bodily, what is supposed to be further reserved, seeing that nothing remains over and above the fullness of perfection? Therefore the Godhead is one. OF THE CHRISTIAN FAITH 3.12.102.[21]

AMBROSIASTER: All that the Father has, he has given to the Son when he begot him bodily in the fullness of divinity, so that as he is the head, the creation is his body.[22] Therefore, whatever can be supposed to be a heavenly creature must be seen as fully subordinate to Christ, so that no lesser being may be thought worthy of worship. COMMENTARY ON THE LETTER TO THE COLOSSIANS.[23]

AUGUSTINE: Speaking of him as our Head, the apostle says: "For in him dwells all the fullness of the Godhead corporally." He does not say "corporally" because God is corporeal, but he either uses the word in a derived sense as if he dwells in a temple made by hands, not corporally but symbolically, that is, under prefiguring signs . . . or else the word *corporally* is certainly used because God dwells, as in his temple, in the body of Christ which he took from the Virgin. LETTERS 187.39.[24]

LEO THE GREAT: Embracing then, dearly beloved, the sole pledge of the Christian hope, let us not be torn from our faithful bonding to the body of Christ, in whom, as the apostle says, "dwells the fullness of divinity in bodily manner, and you have been filled out in him." Since the substance of God is incorporeal, how does it dwell in bodily manner in Christ unless the flesh of our race has been made the flesh of the divinity? We filled out in that God in whom we have been crucified, in whom we have been buried, in whom we have been even raised up. SERMONS 66.5.[25]

IN THE CHURCH IS THE FULLNESS. SEVERIAN OF GABALA: He calls the church that which is filled with the Father's divinity. The church is full by dwelling bodily in Christ, that is, as the body is completed in the head, he says that Christ is everywhere the head of the church. And you are fulfilled in him, fulfilled for his sake and through him. PAULINE COMMENTARY FROM THE GREEK CHURCH.[26]

2:11-13 *Circumcised, Buried and Made Alive*

THE NEW LIFE IN CHRIST AND THROUGH BAPTISM. CHRYSOSTOM: Circumcision is no

---

[19]FC 76:83-84. This is one of many passages where Cyril struggles to define a teaching about the union of the human and divine natures in Christ that will avoid the Nestorian error of juxtaposing these two without offering an adequate account of their perfect conjunction. What he claims here is that the union is "according to nature," that is, a merging of the two natures into one in the way that body and soul form one human nature in every individual man or woman. Only in this way, he claims, is the true import of the idea of "bodily indwelling" honored in the interpretation of Colossians 2:9. [20]Deut 6:4. [21]NPNF 2 10:257*. [22]Ambrosiaster is probably bringing in here a reference to such a passage as Ephesians 1:22-23, where Christ is described as "the head over all things for the church, which is his body, the fullness of him who fills all in all." The idea would seem to be that as Christ is the head of the church, which is his body, in an analogous sense he is the head of the whole creation, since he is the Word through which that creation came to be in the first place. What Ambrosiaster was trying to avoid was the panpsychism of Stoicism, in which the whole universe is identical with spirit, which in turn is identical with God. [23]CSEL 81 3:182. [24]FC 30:252-53. [25]FC 93:285*. [26]NTA 15:322.

longer performed with a knife, Paul says, but in Christ himself; for no human hand circumcises . . . but the Spirit. The Spirit circumcises the whole man, not simply a part. . . . When and where? In baptism. And what Paul calls circumcision, he again calls burial. . . . But it is not burial only: for notice what he says, "Wherein you were also raised with him, through faith in the working of God, who raised him from the dead." HOMILIES ON COLOSSIANS 6.[27]

THEODORE OF MOPSUESTIA: "Circumcision" refers to the life of immortality embraced through baptism, just as "uncircumcision" is the old life of mortality. COMMENTARY ON COLOSSIANS.[28]

SEVERIAN OF GABALA: Through baptism comes the stripping away and circumcision of sins. . . . Those being baptized in the blood of Christ confess that they share in his death through baptism and that following this they enjoy the resurrection. Resurrection is used here in a twofold sense, the one spiritual and the other physical. All persons will rise through the resurrection of Christ from the dead. Those, however, who have not been baptized in Christ but have died without faith will share in the general resurrection. However, they will not enjoy the promise of redemption. . . . As many as were baptized into Christ, these have freely benefitted before the general resurrection from the spiritual resurrection, for they have already risen from the death of sins. Thus, Paul also says: "in whom you were raised," not "in whom you will be raised." PAULINE COMMENTARY FROM THE GREEK CHURCH.[29]

AMBROSE: This, too, is plain, that in him who is baptized the Son of God is crucified. Indeed, our flesh could not eliminate sin unless it were crucified in Jesus Christ. . . . And to the Colossians he says, "Buried with him by baptism, wherein you also rose again with him." This was written with the intent that we should believe

that he is crucified in us, that our sins may be purged through him, that he, who alone can forgive sins, may nail to his cross the handwriting which was against us. CONCERNING REPENTANCE 2.2.9.[30]

AMBROSE: Therefore, the Lord permitted mortality to steal in [as an atonement], that guilt might cease. But so that the end set by nature might not also be in death, there was granted a resurrection from the dead, that the guilt might fail through death but the nature be continued through resurrection. And so death is a passage for all men, but you must pass with virtuous steadfastness—a passage from corruption to incorruption, from mortality to immortality, from disquiet to tranquillity. . . . What indeed is this death but the burial of vices and the awakening of virtues? For this reason "may my soul depart among the souls of the righteous," that is, "may it be buried together with them,"[31] that it may lay down its sins and take up the grace of the just, who "bear about the dying of Christ in their body"[32] and soul. DEATH AS A GOOD 4.14.[33]

AMBROSIASTER: [Paul] says that the Gentiles were dead, because they refused to receive the law, which had been given as a witness to the Creator, and then as a means of condemning vice. With Christ has come the forgiveness of sin, since freedom from sin is impossible without this gift, which saves us from the "penalty of death." COMMENTARY ON THE LETTER TO THE COLOSSIANS.[34]

---

[27]NPNF 1 13:285*. [28]TEM 1:287. [29]NTA 15:322-23. [30]NPNF 2 10:346*. [31]Num 23:10 (LXX). [32]2 Cor 4:10. [33]FC 65:81-82. As the title of this work of Ambrose suggests, he is working out a theodicy by trying to show how death is both a punishment for human sin but also a means to virtue. Just as physical death takes us by divine appointment through a profound experience of deserved suffering but also of release into larger resurrection life, so every act of renouncing sin in order to embrace virtue is a death-and-resurrection experience. [34]CSEL 81 3:184.

AUGUSTINE: After all, if we find these passing days, in which we recall Christ's passion and resurrection with special devotion and solemnity, so exhilarating, how blessed and blissful will that eternal day make us, when we shall actually see him and stay with him, the one we now rejoice in merely by desiring and hoping for him! What exultant joy God will give to his church, from which as it is born again through Christ he has after a fashion removed the foreskin of its fleshly nature, that is, the reproach of its natural birth! That is why it says, "And you, while you were dead in transgressions and the foreskin of your flesh, he made alive in him, forgiving us all our debts." SERMONS 229D.2.[35]

2:14 Canceling the Bond, Nailing It to the Cross

THE NATURE OF THE BOND AND THE MEANS OF RELEASE. CHRYSOSTOM: What bond? He means either that which they said to Moses, namely, "All that God has said will we do, and be obedient,"[36] or, if not that, this, that we owe to God obedience; or if not this, he means that the devil held possession of it, the bond which God made for Adam, saying, "In the day you eat of the tree, you shall die."[37] This bond then the devil held in his possession. And Christ did not give it to us, but himself tore it in two, the action of one who joyfully remits what we owe. HOMILIES ON COLOSSIANS 6.[38]

CHRYSOSTOM: See to it that we do not again become debtors to the old contract. Christ came once; he found the certificate of our ancestral indebtedness which Adam wrote and signed. Adam contracted the debt; by our subsequent sins we increased the amount owed. In this contract are written a curse, and sin, and death and the condemnation of the law. Christ took all these away and pardoned them. St. Paul cries out and says: "The decree of our sins which was against us, he has taken it completely away, nailing it to the cross." He did not say "erasing the decree," nor did he say "blotting it out," but "nailing it to the cross," so that no trace of it might remain. This is why he did not erase it but tore it to pieces. BAPTISMAL INSTRUCTIONS 3.21.[39]

THEODORE OF MOPSUESTIA: The decree, or bond, was the demand contained in the old law that we fulfill all of its provisions. Since, however, not to sin is impossible, punishment is necessitated. Thus the law's bond was against us in not allowing us to pursue righteousness because of its detailed demands. . . . Only in the resurrected life are we freed from sin, and then the law becomes superfluous. When Christ nails it to the cross, he makes death the end of this life and its domination by sin. In the resurrection, therefore, to which we pass through baptism, the law is not needed. COMMENTARY ON COLOSSIANS.[40]

SEVERIAN OF GABALA: When the law was given as a curse on transgressors, all the people of Israel stood crying aloud. For there was deposited with what was said a bond that bound them, as they received these things. This "bond" was the binding character of the law, which Christ transcended in his teachings, when he decreed against the observances of the law. . . . Retroactively he abolished the punishments of the law against sinners through the forgiveness of sins and repentance for salvation. PAULINE COMMENTARY FROM THE GREEK CHURCH.[41]

THEODORET OF CYR: This decree or bond may be understood, some say, as the law, but it is better to equate it with the human body, since it is here that every evil action is conceived. Thus, it is the senses and their tendency to sin that are nailed to the cross, when God the Word assumes

---

[35]WSA 3/6:279*. [36]Ex 24:3. [37]Gen 2:17. [38]NPNF 1 13:286*. [39]ACW 31:63. [40]TEM 1:290*. [41]NTA 15:323-24.

our human nature. INTERPRETATION OF THE LETTER TO THE COLOSSIANS.[42]

AMBROSE: But Christ was sold because he took our condition upon himself, not our sins themselves; he is not held to the price of sin, because he himself did not commit sin.[43] And so he made a contract at a price for our debt, not for money for himself; he took away the debtor's bond, set aside the moneylender, freed the debtor. He alone paid what was owed by all. We ourselves were not permitted to escape from bondage. He undertook this on our behalf, so that he might drive away the slavery of the world, restore the liberty of paradise and grant new grace through the honor we received by his sharing of our nature. This is by way of mystery. JOSEPH 4.19.[44]

AMBROSIASTER: Paul expounds here the nature of God's gracious care through its various sources. He recalls the many deeds by which God has brought rescue to the human race, so that he has not only remitted our transgressions but also lifted that sin, which from Adam's disobedience (which he calls the signed bond) did not allow us to rise from the dead. . . . Because death came from sin, when sin in fact was overcome, the resurrection of the dead became a reality. Indeed this could not have been done, if he had not nailed it to the cross. While the Savior conquers sin by not sinning, he holds man to be culpable and, being innocent, is killed by him: thus he crucifies sin. Sin being overcome is said to be put to death; the cross is not the death of the Savior, but of sin. COMMENTARY ON THE LETTER TO THE COLOSSIANS.[45]

PELAGIUS: Some say that the bond was, as it were, a written memorial before God of sins. This, then, was destroyed on the cross, when, sins being forgiven, the memorial of transgressions was abolished. PELAGIUS'S COMMENTARY ON THE LETTER TO THE COLOSSIANS.[46]

AUGUSTINE: She [i.e., his mother, Monica] did not ask for such things but simply requested that remembrance be made for her at Thy altar, which she had attended without missing a single day. She knew that on it the Holy Victim is offered; by means of which "the decree against us, which was hostile to us" is canceled; by means of which the Enemy, adding up our offenses and seeking something to charge against us, and finding nothing in him in whom we conquer, was overcome. CONFESSIONS 9.13.36.[47]

AUGUSTINE: With good reason do we celebrate the Passover wherein the blood of the Lord was poured out, by which we are cleansed of every offense. Let us be assured; the devil was holding the bond of slavery against us, but it was blotted out by the blood of Christ. HOMILIES ON 1 JOHN 1.5.3.[48]

AUGUSTINE: This is the whole scheme of our salvation, by which the one who as God had made man himself became man, for the sake of finding lost man. This is the whole matter of Christ shedding for the forgiveness of our sins true, not false, blood, and with his blood, "obliterating the bond of our sins." All this these damnable heretics strive to drain of all meaning. All this, so the Manichaeans believe, as it appeared to human eyes, was spirit and not flesh. SERMONS 237.1.[49]

EPHREM THE SYRIAN: At the birth of the Son the King was enrolling all men for the tribute money,

---

[42]PG 82:611AB/612AB. [43]Cf. 2 Cor 5:21. [44]FC 65:201. [45]CSEL 81 3:186-87. [46]PETE 460. [47]FC 21:261. [48]FC 92:127-28*. [49]WSA 3/7:51. In the teaching of the Manichaean sect, of which Augustine had once been an adherent and then repudiated, Jesus suffers on the cross as a symbol of the particles of divine light that have been trapped in gross human materiality. Thus the true meaning of the cross is not in the suffering humanity truly assumed by the Son in the incarnation but rather in the divine nature of the spirit temporarily housed in a human container and soon to be freed when death comes. See Kurt Rudolf, *Gnosis: The Nature and History of Gnoticism*, trans. Robert McLachlan Wilson (New York: Harper & Row, 1983), p. 339.

that they might be debtors to him: the King came forth to us who blotted out our bills and wrote another bill in his own name that he might be our debtor. HYMNS ON THE NATIVITY 4.[50]

2:15 Disarming Principalities and Powers

STRIPPING OFF THE DEMONIC POWERS. ORIGEN: Although Jesus was one, he had several aspects; and to those who saw him he did not appear alike to all. . . . Moreover, that his appearance was not just the same to those who saw him, but varied according to their individual capacity will be clear to people who carefully consider why, when about to be transfigured on the high mountain, he did not take all the apostles but only Peter, James, and John. . . . Accordingly, as we hold that Jesus was such a wonderful person, not only as to the divinity within him which was hidden from the multitude, but also as to his body which was transfigured when he wished and before whom he wished, we affirm that everyone had the capacity to see Jesus prior to the time when he had not "put off the principalities and powers" and had not yet died to sin. But after he put off principalities and powers, all those who formerly saw him could not look upon him, as he no longer had anything about him that could be seen by the multitude. AGAINST CELSUS 2.64.[51]

CHRYSOSTOM: "Having put off from himself the principalities and the powers." He means the diabolical powers; because human nature had arrayed itself in these, or because they had, as it were, a hold on human nature. When he became man he put away from himself that hold. What is the meaning of "he made a show of them"? Paul speaks well in these words. Never yet was the devil in so shameful a plight. For while expecting to have him, he lost even those he had; and when Christ's body was nailed to the cross, the dead arose. At the cross death received his wound, having met his death stroke from a dead body. And as an athlete, when he thinks he

has hit his adversary, himself is caught in a fatal grasp, so truly does Christ also show, that to die with arrogance is the devil's shame. HOMILIES ON COLOSSIANS 6.[52]

THEODORE OF MOPSUESTIA: It is in the putting off of mortality that the demonic powers are overcome. COMMENTARY ON COLOSSIANS.[53]

SEVERIAN OF GABALA: Through the exposing and putting off of the flesh Christ subdued the opposing powers. . . . For until his cross and death it was not clearly known that Christ was their Lord, that he was both God and Son of God. This was because he exercised his wonder-working powers in a way that was hidden in his body. This is why Satan made an attempt on him, wishing to learn if he was truly the one proclaimed by the prophets. This was with the intention that if it was so, Satan might hinder the outworking of salvation [i.e., the "economy"]. But the evil one accomplished nothing, nor was he able to learn anything; for a while the Christ escaped his notice. But when Christ was beaten and died and was buried and rose, God's plan of salvation was completed, his being unnoticed was over, his divinity became visible and was seen in his head and body. PAULINE COMMENTARY FROM THE GREEK CHURCH.[54]

THEODORET OF CYR: Since through the bodily affections the demons have power over us, he, clothed with the body, was more powerful than

---

[50]NPNF 2 13:235*. [51]OAC 115-16*. Origen, as did a number of other expositors, interprets the disarming of the powers (RSV) on the cross as a stripping away of their dominion over Jesus. This dominion was exercised through the human limitations of a fleshly body, a body visible to the crowds who lacked the capacity, believed Origen, to see *through* the body to the spirit within. The event of the transfiguration was an anticipation of the death on the cross, for it allowed the disciples and others to see the reality of Christ, no longer shrouded by the body and the ability of the demonic powers to use the body to hide God from human perception. It is precisely the nature of faith that it penetrates this veil in the present. [52]NPNF 1 13:286*. [53]*TEM* 1:291. [54]NTA 15:324.

sin, and he overturned the power of the adversaries. He made their stupidity known to all, since through his body the victory was given to all of us against them. INTERPRETATION OF THE LETTER TO THE COLOSSIANS.[55]

ATHANASIUS: But if a man is gone down even to Hades and stands in awe of the heroes who have descended there, regarding them as gods, yet he may see the fact of Christ's resurrection and victory over death. He may infer that among them also Christ alone is true God and Lord. For the Lord touched all parts of creation and freed and undeceived all of them from every illusion. As Paul says, "Having put off from himself the principalities and the powers, he triumphed on the cross"; that no one might by any possibility be any longer deceived but everywhere might find the true Word of God. ON THE INCARNATION 45.[56]

AUGUSTINE: And where the devil could do something, there he met with defeat on every side. While from the cross he received the power to slay the Lord's body outwardly, it was also from the cross that the inward power, by which he held us fast, was put to death. For it came to pass that the chains of many sins in many deaths were broken by the one death of the One who himself had no previous sin that would merit death. And, therefore, for our sake the Lord paid the tribute to death which was not his due, in order that the death which was due might not injure us. For he was not stripped of the flesh by any obligation to any power whatsoever, but he willed his own death, for he who could not die unless he willed doubtless died because he willed; and therefore he openly exposed the principalities and the powers, confidently triumphing over them in himself. ON THE TRINITY 4.13.17.[57]

PELAGIUS: He triumphed not by killing but by dying, not by bringing force to bear on people but by providing them with sustaining power, so that, for us, all pride having been broken, he might give an example of true conquest. PELAGIUS'S COMMENTARY ON THE LETTER TO THE COLOSSIANS.[58]

THE CROSS A POWERFUL DISPLAY. CYRIL OF JERUSALEM: Let us not be ashamed to confess the Crucified. Let the cross, as our seal, be boldly made with our fingers upon our brow, and on all occasions; over the bread we eat, over the cups we drink; in our comings and in our goings; before sleep; on lying down and rising up; when we are on the way and when we are still. It is a powerful safeguard; it is without price, for the sake of the poor; without toil, because of the sick; for it is a grace from God, a badge of the faithful, and a terror to devils; for "he displayed them openly, leading them away in triumph by force of it." For when they see the cross, they are reminded of the Crucified. CATECHETICAL LECTURES 13.36.[59]

LEO THE GREAT: As renowned victor over the devil and most powerful conqueror of hostile spirits, in an admirable spectacle, he carried the trophy of his "victory." On the shoulders of his unconquered endurance, he bore the sign of salvation to be worshiped in every kingdom. Even then he encouraged all his imitators by the sight of his labor, saying, "Any who do not take up their cross and follow me do not deserve me."[60] SERMONS 59.4.[61]

---

[55]PG 82:611C/612C. [56]LCC 3:100*. [57]FC 45:152*. [58]*PETE* 461. [59]FC 64:28. [60]Mt 10:38. [61]FC 93:256.

2:16-23 THE DANGER OF FALSE OBSERVANCE

[16]*Therefore let no one pass judgment on you in questions of food and drink or with regard to a festival or a new moon or a sabbath.* [17]*These are only a shadow of what is to come; but the substance belongs to Christ.* [18]*Let no one disqualify you, insisting on self-abasement and worship of angels, taking his stand on visions, puffed up without reason by his sensuous mind,* [19]*and not holding fast to the Head, from whom the whole body, nourished and knit together through its joints and ligaments, grows with a growth that is from God.*

[20]*If with Christ you died to the elemental spirits of the universe, why do you live as if you still belonged to the world? Why do you submit to regulations,* [21]*"Do not handle, Do not taste, Do not touch"* [22]*(referring to things which all perish as they are used), according to human precepts and doctrines?* [23]*These have indeed an appearance of wisdom in promoting rigor of devotion and self-abasement and severity to the body, but they are of no value in checking the indulgence of the flesh.*[e]

e Or are of no value, serving only to indulge the flesh

OVERVIEW: In living the Christian life one must not be deceived by false and outward appearances, being led to embrace these, either in understanding or in behavior, rather than the true reality of Christ (ORIGEN, EUSEBIUS, CHRYSOSTOM, SEVERIAN, BASIL). Indeed, Christians are bound, in practicing the disciplines and observances of their religion, to be sure that these are understood only from the perspective of Christ, so that then they may be pursued in the right spirit and with right discrimination (AMBROSE, AUGUSTINE). The temptation to become absorbed in the worship of angels is a lure to superstition and bondage to the law once again (ORIGEN, CHRYSOSTOM, THEODORE, SEVERIAN, THEODORET, AMBROSIASTER), while it also raises the question of false claims and a prideful spirituality (PELAGIUS, AUGUSTINE). The prohibitions articulated by the heretics serve to lure believers into the worship of angels and into a neglect of spiritual truth and of the goodness of God's world (CLEMENT OF ALEXANDRIA, ORIGEN, NOVATIAN, THEODORE, THEODORET, CHRYSOSTOM, JOHN CASSIAN, AUGUSTINE). However, these prohibitions may be considered as having some value only if they are securely grounded in the lordship of Christ (AMBROSE, AMBROSIASTER).

2:16-17 The Substance Belongs to Christ

LET NO ONE JUDGE YOU. ORIGEN: "They drank from a spiritual rock which followed; and that rock was Christ."[1] Paul says this, "A Hebrew of Hebrews, according to the law, a Pharisee,"[2] "educated at the feet of Gamaliel,"[3] who would never dare to speak of "spiritual food" and "spiritual drink" unless he had learned that this is the meaning of the Lawgiver through the knowledge of the truest doctrine handed down to him. For this reason, he adds, as he is bold and certain about the meaning of clean or unclean foods, that it must be observed not according to the letter but spiritually. He says, "Therefore, let no one judge you in food or in drink or in participa-

---

[1]1 Cor 10:4. [2]Phil 3:5. [3]Acts 22:3.

tion of the feast days or new moons or sabbaths which are a shadow of the future." Homilies on Leviticus 7.2.[4]

Eusebius of Caesarea: "Let no man, therefore, judge you regarding food or drink, or with respect to a holy day, or the new moon, or sabbath days, which are a shadow of things to come." For if the laws relating to the difference of foods, and the holy days and the sabbath, like shadowy things, preserved a copy of other things that were mystically true, you will not say without reason that the high priest also represented the symbol of another High Priest, and that he was called Christ, as the pattern of that other, the only real Christ. The Proof of the Gospel 4.16-17.[5]

Basil the Great: There is, however, a certain other life, to which these words call us; and, although at present our days are evil, yet some others are good, which night does not interrupt; for God will be their everlasting light, shining upon them with the light of his glory.[6] Consequently, when you hear of the good days, do not think that it is your life here that is set forth in the promises. In fact, these present days are the destructible days, which the sensible sun produces; but nothing destructible could suitably be a gift for the indestructible. "This world as we see it is passing away."[7] Therefore, since the law has some shadow of the good things to come, consider I pray, present sabbaths to be pleasant and holy, as they have been brought from the eternal days, and new moons, and festivals. But look upon them, I pray you, in a manner proper to the spiritual law. Homilies 16.[8]

FIXATION ON WHAT IS UNIMPORTANT. Chrysostom: Do you see how he depreciates what the Colossians think important? If you have obtained such things [i.e., grace and wisdom through Christ], Paul asks, why make yourself accountable for these petty matters? And he makes light of them. . . . Don't put up with those

who judge you in these trivial considerations. Homilies on Colossians 7.[9]

Severian of Gabala: Paul teaches that the law is abolished, Christ having passed over the "bond" against us. He teaches that the evil one has fallen, Christ having exposed and made a parade of the evil powers. Thus, we are no longer to obey what has been abolished, and we are to reject Jews who would urge us to keep the law. . . . This law was the mere shadow of Christ, lacking the substance. Further, we are not to obey Greeks who would encourage us to worship angels or worldly elements. Pauline Commentary from the Greek Church.[10]

PROPER PERSPECTIVE, THEN PROPER OBSERVANCE. Ambrose: Shall we, then, think of festival days in terms of eating and drinking? On the contrary, let no one call us to account with respect to eating, "For we know that the law is spiritual."[11] "Let no one, therefore, call you to account for what you eat or drink or in regard to a new festival or a new moon or sabbath. These are a shadow of things to come, but the body is of Christ." So let us seek the body of Christ which the voice of the Father from heaven, the last trumpet, as it were, showed to you on that occasion when the Jews said that it thundered for him.[12] . . . Wherever the body of Christ is, there will be the truth. On the Death of His Brother Satyrus 2.108.[13]

Augustine: Whoever seeks to be a stranger to that carnal . . . Judaism which is justly repudi-

---

[4]FC 83:142. [5]*POG* 1:215. The point is that as "shadows" and "copies" truly represent the reality itself they are entitled to share in the name of that reality and, as such, to be honored. Thus the high priest in the Old Testament may be called the Christ, that is, the anointed one, since he is a real type and anticipation of Christ himself. [6]Rev 22:5. [7]1 Cor 7:31. [8]FC 46:264-65. [9]NPNF 1 13:288*. [10]NTA 15:324-25. [11]Rom 7:14. [12]Cf. Jn 12:28-29, when upon Jesus' saying "Father, glorify your name," a voice came from heaven to confirm it. [13]FC 22:246-47*.

ated and condemned must first consider as alien to himself those ancient observances which have clearly ceased to be necessary. This is so because the New Testament has been revealed, and the things which were prefigured by those others have come to pass. A person is not to be judged "in meat or drink or in respect of a festival day, or of the new moon or of the sabbaths, which are a shadow of things to come." On the other hand, he must receive, embrace and observe, without any reserve, those commandments in the law which help to form the character of the faithful . . . [and] whatever progress he makes in them he must not attribute to himself but to "the grace of God by Jesus Christ our Lord." LETTERS 196.2.8.[14]

2:18a Let No One Disqualify You

UNFAIRNESS OR HOSTILITY? CHRYSOSTOM: The term meaning "to rob you of your prize" is employed when one person is victorious, but the prize of victory is given to another, when though a victor, you are robbed of the victor's prize. HOMILIES ON COLOSSIANS 7.[15]

THEODORET OF CYR: The verb translated "disqualify" means "to judge a victory unfairly." Whoever mixes legal observances with the gospel leads people from better things to worse. INTERPRETATION OF THE LETTER TO THE COLOSSIANS.[16]

2:18b Insisting on Self-Abasement and Worship of Angels

ANGEL WORSHIP A JEWISH APOSTASY. ORIGEN: You will find particularly in Jeremiah that the word of God through the prophet finds fault with Israel because they worship these [i.e., angels] and sacrifice to the queen of heaven and to all the host of heaven.[17] . . . Paul, who received a meticulous education in Jewish doctrines and later became a Christian as a result of a miraculous appearance of Jesus, says these words in the epistle to the Colossians: "Let no man rob you." AGAINST CELSUS 5.8.[18]

THE HEART OF THE MATTER. CHRYSOSTOM: But what is the general drift of Paul's words? There are some who maintain that we must be brought near by angels, not by Christ; for Christ to do so would seem too great an act on our behalf. Paul continually emphasizes what has been done by Christ. HOMILIES ON COLOSSIANS 7.[19]

THEODORE OF MOPSUESTIA: Because it was said that the law had been given through angels— since it was by these ministers that the law was given at that time—the blessed Paul himself had said, "For if the message declared by angels was valid."[20] They, therefore, who were arguing with them to keep the law were also taking the position that the angels were angered if the law were not being kept. COMMENTARY ON COLOSSIANS.[21]

THEODORET OF CYR: Those who defend the law lead persons to worship angels, since they say that the law was given through them. This vice persisted for a long time in Phrygia and Pisidia, such that a synod gathered at Laodicea in Phrygia laid down a law that angels should not be invoked.[22] INTERPRETATION OF THE LETTER TO THE COLOSSIANS.[23]

SEVERIAN OF GABALA: What is self-abasement? Saying that we are self-abased [can only mean] that God is great and far above any service we can render to him. Since, then, we cannot get near him, it is through his angels that propitia-

---

[14]FC 30:337-38*. [15]NPNF 1 13:288*. [16]PG 82:613A/614A. [17]Jer 51:17; 7:17-18; 19:13. Origen here is taking advantage of Jeremiah's criticism of the people of Israel for their faithless embrace of some of the fertility deities of the Canaanites. The queen of heaven is the Canaanite deity Astarte, called Ishtar by the Babylonians and Assyrians in the sixth century B.C. [18]OAC 269-70. [19]NPNF 1 13:288*. [20]Heb 2:2. [21]TEM 1:294 (Greek). [22]Theodoret refers to canon 35 of the Council of Laodicea. [23]PG 82:613AB/614AB.

tion comes and we may draw near him. For this reason he spoke earlier of one "who is the head of every power and principality." And now he says, "Why do you come to elements and angels, having renounced their head, who is Christ?"[24] PAULINE COMMENTARY FROM THE GREEK CHURCH.[25]

FALSE CLAIMS. AUGUSTINE: There is another even more obscure passage about which I ask you to pull me up out of deep water and set me in the shallows. In the epistle to the Colossians, I simply cannot see the connection where he says: "Let no man seduce you into taking pleasure in the humility and religion of angels, walking in the things which he has not seen; in vain puffed up by the sense of his flesh and not holding the head." What angels does he mean? If he means the rebel and wicked angels, what is their religion or their humility, or who is the master of this seduction, who under cover of some angelic religion or other would teach what he does not see as something seen or experienced? Doubtless, the heretics, who follow the teachings of demons, who think up false systems under the impulse of their spirit, who give out that they have seen visions which they have not seen and by their deadly arguments sow their seed in foolish and credulous hearts—doubtless, these are the ones who do not hold the head, namely, Christ, the source of truth. LETTERS 121.2.1.[26]

2:18c *Taking His Stand on Visions*

SPIRITUAL BLINDNESS. ORIGEN: There is a corporeal eye, by which we see those earthly things, an eye according to the sense of the flesh. Scripture says of it, "He walks in vain, puffed up by the sense of the flesh." We have another eye, opposed to this one. It is better and perceives divine things. But it was a blind eye in us. Jesus came to enable it to see, so that those who were blind might see and those who saw might become blind. HOMILIES ON LUKE 16.8.[27]

SPIRITUAL ARROGANCE. CHRYSOSTOM: For [this man] has not seen angels and yet acts as though he had. Therefore Paul says, "vainly puffed up by his carnal mind," not about any true fact. About this doctrine, he is puffed up and puts forward a false humility. He acts and thinks carnally, not spiritually. His reasoning is simply human reason alone. HOMILIES ON COLOSSIANS 7.[28]

AMBROSIASTER: It happens that persons become bound up with the worship of earthly things under the form of philosophy, so that, held by these, they do not rise. . . . They end up simulating true religion. They become inflated by watching the movements of the stars, which Paul calls angels, not by divine authority but by human superstition, which brings nothing but damnation. COMMENTARY ON THE LETTER TO THE COLOSSIANS.[29]

PELAGIUS: Let no one, haughty with feigned humility and telling the lie that he sees angels, vainly exalt himself above other men; these voice their "visions" from the heart. Let the man who only seems to be humble and religious not be imitated. PELAGIUS'S COMMENTARY ON THE LETTER TO THE COLOSSIANS.[30]

2:19 *Holding Fast to the Head*

THE ESSENCE. SEVERIAN OF GABALA: The purpose and view of the epistle is here, as Paul mentions, to respond to the emphasis on angels urged by some. Christ is the head of all, just as the soul is the head of the body. Christ is head of all the cosmic elements. It makes no sense to be

---

[24]Severian's point is that the angels and their power are real but that all of this is subordinate to Christ, to whom the angels bow in submission even as we bow to them, to Christ and to the Father in self-abasement. [25]NTA 15:325. [26]FC 18:326*. [27]FC 94:68-69. [28]NPNF 1 13:289*. [29]CSEL 81 3:189. [30]*PETE* 189*. Just as one would not imitate a blind angel, so one should not imitate a person who falsely claims to see angels.

in submission to anything else. PAULINE COMMENTARY FROM THE GREEK CHURCH.[31]

2:20-23 Elemental Spirits, Human Precepts and Doctrines

THE SUBTLE CHALLENGE OF FALSE ASCETICISM. CLEMENT OF ALEXANDRIA: It follows that celibacy is not particularly praiseworthy unless it arises through love of God. The blessed Paul says of those who show a distaste for marriage: "In the last times people will abandon the faith, attaching themselves to deceitful spirits and the teachings of demonic powers that they should abstain from food, at the same time forbidding marriage."[32] Again he says, "Do not let anyone disqualify you in forced piety of self-mortification and severity to the body." STROMATA 3.51.1-3.[33]

ORIGEN: To have one's feet washed by Jesus was expedient in order to have a part with him. But Peter, because he did not understand that this was expedient, first objected, as it were, and said, so as to put himself to shame, "Lord, are you going to wash my feet?" and a second time, "You shall never wash my feet."[34] If what he said was a hindrance to the act that would cause him to have a part with the Savior, it is clear that although he said this to the teacher with a sound and reverent intention, he spoke in a way harmful to himself. Now life is full of errors of this kind, of people who intend what they believe to be best but out of ignorance say, or even do, things which take them in the opposite direction. Such indeed are those who declare, "Touch not, taste not, handle not," concerning everything that is meant for destruction and human consumption, based on some teaching which generally falls far below the divine statement, "You shall die as men."[35] COMMENTARY ON JOHN 32.57-59.[36]

NOVATIAN: God delights only in our faith, our innocence, our truthfulness, those virtues of ours which dwell in the soul, not the stomach. Fear of God and heavenly awe, not earthly perishable food, obtain these virtues for us. With reason does the apostle rebuke those who are slaves to the superstitions pertaining to angels, "inflated with their fleshly outlook, not clinging to Christ, who is the head, by whom the whole body is fitted together by joints, and fastened together and united by mutual members in the bond of love to reach full growth in the Lord." They prefer to follow the admonition: "Do not touch nor handle" things that indeed seem to have a show of religion because the body is treated severely. Yet there is in them no increase at all of righteousness in that we are recalled by a self-imposed slavery to the rudiments to which we are dead through baptism. JEWISH FOODS 5.17-18.[37]

CHRYSOSTOM: You are not in the world, Paul says. How is it you are subject to its elements? And note how he pokes fun at them, "touch not, handle not, taste not," as though they were cowards and keeping themselves clear of some great matters, "all which things are to perish with the using." . . . So that even though they appear to be wise, let us turn away from them. For one may seem to be a religious person, and modest, and to have a contempt for the body. . . . They dishonor the flesh, Paul writes, depriving it and stripping it of its liberty, not allowing them to rule it with their will. But God has honored the flesh. HOMILIES ON COLOSSIANS 7.[38]

SEVERIAN OF GABALA: These prohibitions about eating and drinking that you hear from the Greeks are based on their mistaken conviction that you should not partake of anything living. But all this has been given for consumption and nourishment. So, don't pay attention to what has been given in accordance with their teaching. PAULINE COMMENTARY IN THE GREEK CHURCH.[39]

---

[31]NTA 15:325*. [32]1 Tim 4:13. [33]FC 85:288. [34]Jn 13:6-8. [35]Ps 8:17. [36]FC 89:352-53. [37]FC 67:153. [38]NPNF 1 13:289*. [39]NTA 15:326*.

Theodoret of Cyr: When these intemperate teachers bring in their own ideas, they do not follow the purpose of the law. Instead, they deceive with spurious words, they call observance of the law humility, they say that one must not transgress that which was given by God and that the body is not to be spared, that, indeed, all things are not to be used freely. This is just plain slavery and the abrogation of an honor given to us. Abstinence must be freely chosen, not because created things are repulsive but precisely because they are pleasing. Interpretation of the Letter to the Colossians.[40]

John Cassian: This is what the apostle said: "You make observations of the months and of the times and of the years."[41] Or again: "Do not touch, do not taste, do not pick up." And there is no doubt that this is said about the superstitions of the law. To plunge into them is to be an adulterer from Christ. Conferences 14.11.[42]

When to Tolerate False Asceticism. Chrysostom: To be a virgin it is not enough just to be unmarried. There must be spiritual chastity, and I mean by chastity not only the absence of wicked and shameful desire, the absence of ornaments and superfluous cares, but also being unsoiled by life's cares. Without that, what good is there in physical purity? . . . [Those who do not understand this belong] to the very weak who crawl along the earth. It was impossible to uplift souls so disposed all at once to the argument on behalf of virginity. One who has been so excited by worldly things and so admiring of the present life will think . . . that what is worthy of heaven and close to the angelic state [the call to virginity] is deserving of disgrace. How would such a one tolerate advice promoting this course? And then is it surprising if Paul has adopted the same strategy of argument in the case of something that has been permitted when he does the same thing in the case of what has been forbidden and is contrary to law? For instance: dietary laws, the acceptance of some foods while rejecting others, were a Jewish weakness. Nevertheless, there were among the Romans those who shared this weakness. Paul has not only vehemently denounced them, but he does something more than this. He disregards the wrongdoers and censures those who attempted to prevent them with the words, "But you, how can you sit in judgment on your brother?"[43] Yet he did not do this when he wrote to the Colossians; rather, with great authority he rebukes them and treats the matter philosophically: "No one is free . . . to pass judgment on you in terms of what you eat or drink." And again: "If with Christ you have died to cosmic forces, why should you be bound to rules that say, 'Do not handle! Do not taste! Do not touch!' as though you were still living a life bounded by this world? Such prescriptions deal with things that perish in their uses." Why ever does he do this? Because the Colossians were strong, but the Romans still required much accommodation. On Virginity 77.2-78.3.[44]

Correct Prohibitions Must Be Correctly Understood. Tertullian: When Paul blames those who claim to have had visions of angels, on the basis of which they teach that people are to abstain from meat . . . he does not mean to criticize the mandates of the Jewish law, as if he had been speaking at the instigation of superstitious angels. His intention, rather, is only to condemn those who do not accept Christ as the One who has true authority over all such things. Against Marcion 5.19.[45]

Ambrose: Indeed, we are often deceived by sight, and we see things for the most part other than they really are. We are deceived by hearing too. And so, if we do not wish to be deceived, let us contemplate not what is seen but what is

---

[40]PG 82:615AB/616/AB. [41]Gal 4:10. [42]JCC 166. [43]Rom 14:10. [44]COV 115-17*. [45]ANF 3:472*.

unseen. . . . On this account the apostle also cries out: "Do not touch, nor taste, nor handle, things which must all perish"; for things which are for the body's indulgence are also for its corruption. DEATH AS A GOOD 3.10.[46]

AMBROSE: With the knowledge of what Paul had seen and heard in paradise, he cried out saying: "Why, as if still viewing the world do you lay down rules: 'Do not touch; nor handle; nor taste!'—things which must all perish in their very use!" He wished us to be in the world in figure, not in actual possession and use of it. We are to use the world as if we did not use it, as if we were but passing through,[47] not residing in it, walking through as in a dream, not with desire, so that with the speed of thought we might pass through the shadow of this world. LETTERS 79.[48]

AMBROSIASTER: The problem is that the Colossians worship worldly things, put their hope in them, and not in Christ alone . . . so that these rules have been cut off from the head, who is Christ, and thus have become the basis of a pseudo-religion and a sacrilege. COMMENTARY ON THE LETTER TO THE COLOSSIANS.[49]

AUGUSTINE: What is so praiseworthy as a show of wisdom, and what so detestable as the superstition of error? Humility, also, both pleasing to God and eminently praiseworthy in true religion, is given with a show of wisdom to those of whose teachings and actions we are told: "Touch not, taste not, handle not, which are unto destruction," because they are not of God, and "all that is not of faith, is sin."[50] . . . I wish to know what this humility is and this show of wisdom which he says is in their superstition, which comes from the doctrines of men. . . . I think he is speaking of a pretended and useless abstinence such as heretics usually strive after . . . because they put on the appearance of a holy

work, but, as they do not practice it in the fold of truth, they gain neither honor nor the reward of glory. LETTERS 121.2.13.[51]

AUGUSTINE: As to the words "Touch not, taste not, handle not," they are not to be considered as a commandment of the apostle forbidding us to touch, taste or handle something or other. It is just the opposite, if I am not deluded by the obscurity of the passage. Surely he used these words in mockery of those by whom he did not want his followers to be deceived and led astray. They were the ones who made a distinction of foods according to the worship of angels and issued decrees for this life, saying: "Touch not, taste not, handle not," although "all things are clean to the clean."[52] "For every creature of God is good,"[53] as he assures us in another place. LETTERS 149.2.23.[54]

PAUL A STRICT TEACHER. AMBROSE: [Some] say that Paul was a teacher of wantonness. Pray, who will be a teacher of sobriety if he taught wantonness, for he chastised his body and brought it to subjection[55] and by many fasts said that he had rendered the worship which is due to Christ. He did so not to praise himself and his deeds but to teach us what example we must follow. Did he give us instruction in wantonness when he said: " 'Do not touch; nor handle; nor taste!' things that must all perish in their use"? And he also said that we must live "Not in indulgence of the body, not in any honor to the satisfying and love of the flesh, not in the lusts of error; but in the Spirit by whom we are renewed."[56] LETTERS 44.[57]

---

[46]FC 65:77*. [47]1 Cor 7:31. [48]FC 26:443. [49]CSEL 81 3:191. [50]Rom 14:23. [51]FC 18:327. [52]Tit 1:5. [53]1 Tim 4:4. [54]FC 20:256-57. [55]Cf. 1 Cor 9:27. [56]Tit 3:3-5. [57]FC 26:229. For the difference of opinion between Ambrose and Augustine on the matter of who speaks in Colossians 2:21, see the discussion in the introduction to this volume of ACCS.

3:1-17 PRINCIPLES OF THE NEW LIFE

¹*If then you have been raised with Christ, seek the things that are above, where Christ is, seated at the right hand of God. ²Set your minds on things that are above, not on things that are on earth. ³For you have died, and your life is hid with Christ in God. ⁴When Christ who is our life appears, then you also will appear with him in glory.*

⁵*Put to death therefore what is earthly in you: fornication, impurity, passion, evil desire, and covetousness, which is idolatry. ⁶On account of these the wrath of God is coming.ᶠ ⁷In these you once walked, when you lived in them. ⁸But now put them all away: anger, wrath, malice, slander, and foul talk from your mouth. ⁹Do not lie to one another, seeing that you have put off the old nature with its practices ¹⁰and have put on the new nature, which is being renewed in knowledge after the image of its creator. ¹¹Here there cannot be Greek and Jew, circumcised and uncircumcised, barbarian, Scythian, slave, free man, but Christ is all, and in all.*

¹²*Put on then, as God's chosen ones, holy and beloved, compassion, kindness, lowliness, meekness, and patience, ¹³forbearing one another and, if one has a complaint against another, forgiving each other; as the Lord has forgiven you, so you also must forgive. ¹⁴And above all these put on love, which binds everything together in perfect harmony. ¹⁵And let the peace of Christ rule in your hearts, to which indeed you were called in the one body. And be thankful. ¹⁶Let the word of Christ dwell in you richly, teach and admonish one another in all wisdom, and sing psalms and hymns and spiritual songs with thankfulness in your hearts to God. ¹⁷And whatever you do, in word or deed, do everything in the name of the Lord Jesus, giving thanks to God the Father through him.*

f Other ancient authorities add *upon the sons of disobedience*

OVERVIEW: Paul's purpose now is to describe the new life incumbent on those who have been baptized. We are to live under Christ and for Christ as the one focus of our striving, manifesting this new life by our attention to heavenly things and to the practical work of love (CHRYSOSTOM, SEVERIAN). We share in the resurrection of Christ (ISAAC OF NINEVEH). In what follows we see how glorious is the Christian life compared with the wretchedness of the life under the law (ORIGEN, THEODORET). The new life about to be described is the life of the baptized (CYRIL OF JERUSALEM), who contemplate heavenly things in order to rise to that place where Christ is, seated at the right hand of the Father (AMBROSIASTER). Paul reminds us that the new life in Christ is always a matter of new perceptions, of seeing through earthly things to heavenly things (ORIGEN, BASIL, ATHANASIUS, AMBROSE, APHRAHAT, BABAI). In the new life in Christ, the creation is restored and reason is back in control of the human mind (GREGORY OF NYSSA). Renewal in Christ happens in the inner person, such that, while the struggle with sin always continues, progress in virtue is possible (AUGUSTINE), looking toward full responsiveness to grace (GREGORY OF NAZIANSUS, GREGORY OF NYSSA).

3:1 Seek the Things That Are Above

STRIVE FOR PERFECTION. ORIGEN: But he who keeps the commandments not in perfect love, but in dread of future torment and in fear of punishments is indeed also himself a son of Abraham; he too receives gifts, that is, the reward of his work . . . nevertheless he is inferior to that person who is perfected not in slavish fear, but in the freedom of love. . . . "Leaving the word of the first principles of Christ,"[1] he is borne to perfection. "Seeking the things that are above, where Christ is sitting at the right hand of God, not the things that are on the earth," he "looks not at the things which are seen, but at the things which are not seen."[2] In the divine Scriptures he does not follow "the letter which kills" but "the spirit which quickens."[3] From those things he will doubtless be one who does not receive "the spirit of bondage again in fear, but the spirit of adoption, whereby they cry, Abba, Father."[4] HOMILIES ON GENESIS 7.4.[5]

LIVE ON THE HEIGHTS. CHRYSOSTOM: See the wisdom of our teacher and to what a height he immediately raises those who listen to him. He cut a path through the midst of all the angels, archangels, thrones, dominations, principalities, virtues, all those invisible powers, the cherubim and seraphim and set the thoughts of the faithful right before the very throne of the King. By his teaching he has persuaded those who walk the earth to sever the bonds of the body, to take flight and to stand in spirit by the side of him who is the Lord of all. BAPTISMAL INSTRUCTIONS 7.20.[6]

LOOK AT HEAVENLY THINGS. APHRAHAT: Let us think upon the things that are above, on the heavenly things, and meditate on them, where Christ has been lifted up and exalted. But let us forsake the world which is not ours, that we may arrive at the place to which we have been invited. Let us raise up our eyes on high, that we may see the splendor which shall be revealed. SELECT DEMONSTRATIONS 6.1.[7]

ISAAC OF NINEVEH: What is the resurrection of the soul, of which the apostle speaks, saying, "If then you have been raised with Christ"? When the apostle said, "God who commanded the light to shine out of darkness, has shined into our hearts,"[8] he showed this resurrection to be the exodus from the old state which in the likeness of Sheol incarcerates a man so that the light of the gospel will not shine mystically upon him. This is a breath of life through hope in the resurrection, and by it the dawning of divine wisdom shines in his heart, so that a man should become new, having nothing of the old man. Then the image of Christ is formed in us through the Spirit of wisdom and revelation of the knowledge of him. ASCETICAL HOMILIES 37.[9]

INWARD RENEWAL. AUGUSTINE: Because the inner man, too, if he is certainly renewed from day to day,[10] is surely old before he is renewed. For that is done inwardly, which the same apostle says: "Put off the old man and put on the new man." And he offers an explanation of this in the words that follow: "Wherefore putting away lying, speak the truth."[11] But where is lying put away, except inwardly, in order that he may dwell in the holy mountain of God who speaks the truth in his heart."[12] . . . And the words of the apostle are in keeping with this mystery [i.e., of inner resurrection]: "But if you have risen with Christ, seek the things that are above, where Christ is seated at the right hand of God; mind the things that are above." ON THE TRINITY 4.3.6.[13]

3:2 Set Your Mind on Things That Are Above

THE BAPTISMAL CHARGE. CHRYSOSTOM: It was not idly or without purpose that I anticipated the event and instructed your loving

---

[1]Heb 6:1. [2]2 Cor 4:18. [3]2 Cor 3:6. [4]Rom 8:15. [5]FC 71:132-33. [6]ACW 31:112*. [7]NPNF 2 13:363. [8]2 Cor 4:6. [9]*AHSIS* 175. [10]2 Cor 4:16. [11]Eph 4:22-25. [12]Ps 14:1, 3. [13]FC 45:137.

assembly in all these matters, but I did so that you might be carried on by the wings of hope and enjoy the pleasure before you enjoyed the actual benefit. I did it, too, that you might adopt a purpose worthy of the rite, and as blessed Paul has exhorted, you might "mind the things that are above" and change your thoughts from earth to heaven, from visible things to those that are unseen. And we see the objects of bodily sight more clearly with the eyes of the spirit. BAPTISMAL INSTRUCTIONS 2.28.[14]

PUT REASON IN CHARGE. GREGORY OF NYSSA: So . . . if reason instead assumes sway over such emotions, each of them is transmuted to a form of virtue. For anger produces courage, terror caution, fear obedience, hatred aversion from vice, the power of love the desire for what is truly beautiful. High spirit in our character raises our thought above the passions and keeps it from bondage to what is base. Indeed, even the great apostle praises such a form of mental elevation when he bids us constantly to "think those things that are above." So we find that every such motion, when elevated by loftiness of mind, is conformed to the beauty of the divine image. ON THE MAKING OF MAN 18.5.[15]

A MATTER OF FOCUS. BABAI: You should realize that you are walking on the edge of a sharp sword, that you are standing on the edge of a precipice with a ravine on either side. Do not let your thoughts be upset by things here on earth, but keep your mind's gaze on "Jerusalem which is above."[16] "Think of what is above, and not of what is on earth." Ensure that you let go of everything which belongs to this world. LETTER TO CYRIACUS 55.[17]

3:3 Your Life Is Hid with Christ in God

A SOBERING REMINDER. CHRYSOSTOM: This is to prepare the way for drawing them off from pleasure and ease . . . so that, now, you do not appear. See how Paul has transferred them into

heaven itself. For, as I said, he is always bent on showing that they have the very same things that Christ has. Through all his epistles the tenor is this, to show that in all things they are partakers with him. Therefore, he uses the terms *head* and *body* and does everything to convey this to them. HOMILIES ON COLOSSIANS 7.[18]

SEVERIAN OF GABALA: Our life is hidden until the blessing of eternal life shall be revealed to all, when the glory of Christ shall appear in his second coming. PAULINE COMMENTARY FROM THE GREEK CHURCH.[19]

BETWEEN HEAVEN AND EARTH. AMBROSE: We should be aware of the fact, therefore, that where God has planted a tree of life he has also planted a tree of life in the midst of paradise. It is understood that he planted it in the middle. Therefore, in the middle of paradise there was both a tree of life and a cause for death. Keep in mind that man did not create life. By carrying out and observing the precepts of God it was possible for man to find life. This was the life mentioned by the apostle: "Your life is hidden with Christ in God." Man, therefore, was, figuratively speaking, either in the shadow of life—because our life on earth is but a shadow—or man had life, as it were, in pledge, for he had been breathed on by God. PARADISE 29.[20]

AMBROSE: For this is the meaning of flight: to know your goal, to unburden oneself of the world, to unburden oneself of the body. . . . This is the meaning of flight from here—to die to the elements of this world, to hide one's life in God, to turn aside from corruptions, not to defile oneself with the objects of desire and to be ignorant of the things of this world. FLIGHT FROM THE WORLD 7.38.[21]

---

[14]ACW 31:53-54. [15]NPNF 2 5:408*. [16]Gal 4:26. [17]SFPSL 154-55. [18]NPNF 1 13:289-90*. [19]NTA 15:327. [20]FC 42:306-7. [21]FC 65:310.

TO BE HIDDEN IS TO LOVE TRULY. AUGUSTINE: For when God will be all in all, then nothing will be lacking to their desire.[22] Such an end does not have an end. There no one dies, where no one comes unless he should die to this world, not by the death of all in which the body is abandoned by the soul but by the death of the elect in which, even when one still remains in mortal flesh, the heart is set on high. About this kind of death the apostle said, "For you are dead, and your life is hidden with Christ in God." Perhaps about this it was said, "Strong as death is love."[23] For by this love it comes to pass that, dwelling in this still corruptible body, we die to this world and our life is hidden with Christ in God, nay rather, love itself is our death to the world and our life with God. TRACTATES ON JOHN 65.1.[24]

3:4 You Will Appear with Him

SOLID ENCOURAGEMENT. AUGUSTINE: But what did he go on to say? "When Christ appears, your life, then you also will appear with him in glory." So now is the time for groaning, then it will be for rejoicing; now for desiring, then for embracing. What we desire now is not present; but let us not falter in desire; let long, continuous desire be our daily exercise, because the one who made the promise doesn't cheat us. SERMONS 350A.4.[25]

3:5a Put to Death What Is Earthly in You

POSTBAPTISMAL SIN. CHRYSOSTOM: Does Paul write as though these things were in us? There is no contradiction. It is similar to one who has scoured a statue that was filthy, recast it, and displayed it new and bright, explaining that the rust was eaten off and destroyed. Yet he recommends diligence in clearing away the future rust. He does not contradict himself, for it is not that rust which he scoured off that he recommends should be cleared away but that which grew afterwards. So it is not that former putting to

death he speaks of here, nor those fornications, but those which afterward grow. HOMILIES ON COLOSSIANS 8.[26]

THE PRACTICE OF VIRTUE. ATHANASIUS: But the saints, and they who truly practice virtue, "mortify their members" and as the result of this, are pure and without spot, confiding in the promise of our Savior, who said, "Blessed are the pure in heart, for they shall see God."[27] These, having become dead to the world, who have renounced the merchandise of the world, gain an honorable death. FESTAL LETTERS 7.3.[28]

SINFUL DESIRE STILL PRESENT IN THE BAPTIZED. AUGUSTINE: Thus, in movements acother movements of itself according to the flesh. Conversely, in movements according to the flesh, it opposes others which it has according to the spirit, and this is why we say the flesh lusts against the spirit and the spirit lusts against the flesh. But this is also why "it is being renewed day by day,"[29] for the soul does not fail to make progress in virtue as it gradually diminishes the carnal desires to which it does not consent. It is to those already baptized that the apostle says, "Mortify your members, which are on the earth." AGAINST JULIAN 6.14.41.[30]

3:5b Covetousness Is Idolatry

ALL SIN IS IDOLATRY. JEROME: In a general way all that is of the devil is characterized by hatred for God. What is of the devil is idolatry, since all idols are subject to him. Yet Paul elsewhere lays down the law in express terms, saying: "Mortify your members." Idolatry is not confined to casting incense upon an altar with finger and thumb or to pouring libations of wine out of a cup into a bowl. LETTERS 14.5.[31]

---

[22]1 Cor 15:28. [23]Song 8:6. [24]FC 90:51. [25]*WSA* 3/10:112. [26]NPNF 1 13:294*. [27]Mt 5:8. [28]NPNF 2 4:524*. [29]2 Cor 4:16. [30]FC 35:348. [31]LCC 5:295*.

3:9-10 Put Off the Old Nature, Put On the New Nature

MORAL CHOICE, NOT PHYSICAL SUBSTANCE.
CHRYSOSTOM: Moral choice rather than human nature is the determining factor and rather constitutes "the human condition" than the natural determinants. For human nature itself does not cast one into hell, nor does it lead one into the kingdom, but this happens by men themselves. We neither love nor hate anyone so far as he is man, but so far as he is such or such a man. If then our real essence as human beings is the body, which in any case cannot be accountable, how can one say that the body is evil? But what does Paul say? "With his doings." He means freedom of choice, with its accompanying acts. HOMILIES ON COLOSSIANS 8.[32]

STRIPPING OFF THE OLD. BASIL THE GREAT: Seek nothing with exterior gold and bodily adornment; but consider the garment as one worthy to adorn him who is according to the image of his Creator, as the apostle says: "Stripping off the old man, and putting on the new, one that is being renewed unto perfect knowledge 'according to the image of his Creator.'" And he who has put on "the heart of mercy, kindness, humility, patience and meekness" is clothed within and has adorned the inner man. HOMILIES 17.11.[33]

RECLAIM THE IMAGE. AMBROSE: Therefore, as upon the cross it was not the fullness of the Godhead but our weakness that was brought into subjection, so also will the Son hereafter become subject to the Father in his participation in our nature. This is so that when the lusts of the flesh are brought into subjection the heart may have no concern for riches or ambition or pleasures. The intention is that God may be all to us, if we live after his image and likeness, as far as we can attain to it, through all. The benefit has passed, then, from the individual to the community; for in his flesh he has tamed the nature of all human flesh. . . . Therefore, "laying aside all these," that is those things we read of: "anger, malice, blasphemy, filthy communication"; as he also says below: "Let us, having put off the old man with his deeds, put on the new man, which is renewed in knowledge after the image of him that created him." OF THE CHRISTIAN FAITH 5.14.175-76.[34]

RESTORE THE CREATION. GREGORY OF NYSSA: And even so we say that the true and perfect soul is the human soul, as is clear from the very nature of its operations in both sensory power and intellect. Anything else that shares in life, because it possesses the power of growth, we call animate by a sort of customary misuse of language, because in these cases the soul does not exist in a perfect condition. . . . Thus Paul, advising those who were able to hear him to lay hold on perfection, indicates also the mode in which they may attain that object. He tells them that they must "put off the old man" and put on the man "which is renewed after the image of him that created him." Now may we all return to that divine grace in which God at the first created man, when he said, "Let us make man in our image and likeness."[35] ON THE MAKING OF MAN 30.33-34.[36]

IN THE MIND, THE INNER PERSON. AUGUSTINE: The renewal and reforming of the mind takes place "after God," or "after God's image": it is said to be "after God," to exclude one thinking it to be after some other creature; and "after God's image," to make it plain that the renewal is effected in the place where God's image is, that is, in the mind. ON THE TRINITY 14.16.22.[37]

3:11 Christ Is All and in All

THE FINAL PERFECTION. GREGORY OF NAZ-

---

[32]NPNF 1 13:294-95*. [33]FC 46:293. [34]NPNF 2 10:306*. [35]Gen 1:28. [36]NPNF 2 5:427*. [37]LCC 8:121*.

IANZUS: But God will be all in all[38] in the time of restitution; not in the sense that the Father alone will be, and the Son be wholly resolved into him, like a torch into a great pyre, from which it was pulled away for a short time and then put back . . . when we shall be no longer divided (as we are now by movements and passions) and containing nothing at all of God, or very little, but then we shall be entirely like God, ready to receive into our hearts the whole God and him alone. This is the perfection to which we press on. Paul himself indeed bears witness to this. ORATIONS 30.6.[39]

3:14 Love Binds Everything in Perfect Harmony

WITHOUT LOVE, NOTHING IS POSSIBLE. CHRYSOSTOM: Now what Paul wishes to say is that there is no benefit in those things, for all those things fall apart, unless they are done with love. This is the love that binds them all together. Whatever good thing it is that you mention, if love be absent, it is nothing, it melts away. The analogy is like a ship; though its rigging be large, yet if it lacks girding ropes, it is of no service. Or it is similar to a house; if there are no tie beams, of what use is the house? Think of a body. Though its bones be large, if it lacks ligaments, the bones cannot support the body. In the same way, whatever good our deeds possess will vanish completely if they lack love. HOMILIES ON COLOSSIANS 8.[40]

SEVERIAN OF GABALA: When love does not lead, there is no completion of what is lacking; but, where love is present we abstain from doing evil to one another. Indeed we put our minds in the service of doing good, when we love one another. PAULINE COMMENTARY FROM THE GREEK CHURCH.[41]

AMBROSIASTER: When love is in command, the way of the law is followed: when the full mind does the operation, it is done with love. COM-MENTARY ON THE LETTER TO THE COLOS-SIANS.[42]

3:16 Teach and Admonish One Another

THE CHRISTIAN SAGE. CHRYSOSTOM: Nothing is wiser than the person who lives virtuously. Observe how wise he is, says one. He gives what he owns, he is compassionate, he is loving to all. He has understood well that he shares a common human nature with others. He has thought through how to use his wealth wisely. He realizes the position of wealth makes him no one special. He knows that the bodies of his relatives are more valuable than his wealth. The one who despises glory is wholly wise, for he understands human affairs. This is genuine philosophy, the knowledge of things divine and human. So then he comprehends what things are divine and what are human. From the one he keeps himself, and to the other he devotes his labors. And he also knows how to thank God in all things. He considers the present life as nothing; therefore he is neither delighted with prosperity nor grieved with the opposite condition. HOMILIES ON COLOSSIANS 9.[43]

3:17 Giving Thanks to God the Father

NOTHING UNCLEAN. CHRYSOSTOM: For if we act this way, there will be nothing polluted, nothing unclean, wherever Christ is called on. If you eat, if you drink, if you marry, if you travel, do all in the name of God, that is, calling him to help you: in everything first pray, then conduct your business. HOMILIES ON COLOS-SIANS 9.[44]

THEODORET OF CYR: It is because the Colossians were being directed to worship angels that Paul felt compelled to teach what we read

---

[38]1 Cor 15:28. [39]LCC 3:181*. [40]NPNF 1 13:295*. [41]NTA 15:328. [42]CSEL 81 3:198. [43]NPNF 1 13:300*. [44]NPNF 1 13:302*.

here. This is that they should adorn their words and deeds with the remembrance of Christ the Lord, that is, they should offer to God the Father the activity of grace through Christ, not through angels. INTERPRETATION of the Letter to the Colossians.[45]

[45]PG 82:619D/620D.

3:18 — 4:1 SOCIAL DUTIES

[18]*Wives, be subject to your husbands, as is fitting in the Lord.* [19]*Husbands, love your wives, and do not be harsh with them.* [20]*Children, obey your parents in everything, for this pleases the Lord.* [21]*Fathers, do not provoke your children, lest they become discouraged.* [22]*Slaves, obey in everything those who are your earthly masters, not with eyeservice, as men-pleasers, but in singleness of heart, fearing the Lord.* [23]*Whatever your task, work heartily, as serving the Lord and not men,* [24]*knowing that from the Lord you will receive the inheritance as your reward; you are serving the Lord Christ.* [25]*For the wrongdoer will be paid back for the wrong he has done, and there is no partiality.*

4 *Masters, treat your slaves justly and fairly, knowing that you also have a Master in heaven.*

OVERVIEW: Paul turns to practical matters in this part of Colossians, as well as in Ephesians and the letters to Timothy and Titus, because these churches were at peace and were already well-grounded in basic doctrine. The relations of wives, husbands, children, servants and masters are to be grounded in the love that God has for each, as well as in the social order that God has commanded (CHRYSOSTOM, THEODORET). Love is to be properly spiritual in nature; there is no license here for lustful or self-serving relations (AUGUSTINE). Those in authority are to operate with great humility and forbearance, those under authority with great respect and eagerness to serve (CYRIL OF JERUSALEM, AMBROSE, GREGORY THE GREAT).

3:18 Wives Subject to Husbands

FOR GOD'S GLORY. CHRYSOSTOM: That is, be subject for God's sake, because this adorns you, Paul says, not them. For I mean not that subjection which is due to a master nor yet that alone which is of nature but that offered for God's sake. HOMILIES ON COLOSSIANS 10.[1]

THEODORET OF CYR: Paul is particularly concerned here with believing women who are married to unbelieving men: thus, their subjection is in service to the Lord, that is, as the Lord commands. INTERPRETATION OF THE LETTER TO THE COLOSSIANS.[2]

THE NATURAL ORDER. AUGUSTINE: Nor can it

[1]NPNF 1 13:304*. [2]PG 82:621A/622A.

be doubted that it is more consonant with the order of nature that men should bear rule over women than women over men. It is with this principle in view that the apostle says, "The head of the woman is the man"[3]; and, "Wives, submit yourselves to your own husbands." ON MARRIAGE AND CONCUPISCENCE 1.9.10.[4]

3:19 Husbands, Love Your Wives

RECIPROCITY THE KEY. CHRYSOSTOM: Observe again that Paul has exhorted husbands and wives to reciprocity. As with wives toward husbands, here too he enjoins fear and love. For it is possible for one who loves to be bitter. What Paul says then is this. Don't fight; for nothing is more bitter than fighting in marriage, when it takes place on the part of the husband toward the wife. For disputes between people who love another are bitter. These arise from great bitterness, when, Paul says, any one disagrees with his own member. To love, therefore, is the husband's part, to yield pertains to the other side. If, then, each one contributes his own part, all stand firm. From being loved, the wife too becomes loving; and from her being submissive, the husband learns to yield. HOMILIES ON COLOSSIANS 10.[5]

PROCREATION IMPOSSIBLE ALONE. CHRYSOSTOM: See again a mystery of love! If the two don't become one, so long as they continue two, they have no children, but when they come together, many children result. What do we learn from this? That the power of union is great. At the beginning God's wise counsel divided the one into two; and yet even after this division God desired to show that humanity was still one. To do so he determined that human procreation could not be accomplished by only one person. . . . For man and wife are not two men, but one humanity. . . . If he is the head, and she the body, how are they two? . . . Moreover, from the very fashioning of her body, one may see that they are one, for she was made from his

side, and they are, as it were, two halves. . . . The child is a sort of bridge, so that the three become one flesh, the child connecting on either side, each to the other. For just as two cities divided by a river can be united by a bridge, so it is in this case; and the reality is more than the analogy; the very bridge in this case is formed from the substance of each. HOMILIES ON COLOSSIANS 12.[6]

LOVE SHOULD BE SPIRITUAL. AUGUSTINE: God forbid that a man who possesses faith should, when he hears the apostle bid men "love their wives," love that disordered sexual desire in his wife which he ought not to love even in himself. He may know this if he listens to the words of another apostle: "Love not the world, neither the things that are in the world."[7] ON MARRIAGE AND CONCUPISCENCE 1.18.20.[8]

3:20 Children, Obey Your Parents

FOR GOD'S GLORY. CHRYSOSTOM: Again Paul has written, "in the Lord," at once laying down the laws of obedience, producing shame in them. For this, he says, is well-pleasing to the Lord. See how Paul would have us live not only according to natural principles but, prior to this, according to what is pleasing to God. In this way we also gain a reward. HOMILIES ON COLOSSIANS 10.[9]

TRUE LOVE OF GOD AND OF ONE'S PARENTS NOT INCOMPATIBLE. CYRIL OF JERUSALEM: But while honoring our heavenly Father, let us also honor the "fathers of our flesh,"[10] since the Lord in the Law and the Prophets has clearly laid this down, saying: "Honor your mother and your father, that it may be well with you, and that you may have a long life in the land."[11]

---

[3]1 Cor 11:3. [4]NPNF 1 5:267*. [5]NPNF 1 13:304*. [6]NPNF 1 13:318-19*. [7]1 Jn 2:15. [8]NPNF 1 5:272*. [9]NPNF 1 13:304*. [10]Heb 12:9. [11]Ex 20:12; Deut 5:16.

Let those present who have mothers and fathers pay attention to this command. "Children, obey your parents in all things, for this is pleasing to the Lord." For our Lord did not say: "He who loves father or mother is not worthy of me," else what was well written you might interpret falsely out of ignorance, but he added "more than me."[12] CATECHETICAL LECTURES 7.15.[13]

3:21 *Fathers, Do Not Provoke Your Children*

RECIPROCITY AGAIN. CHRYSOSTOM: Again here Paul mentions submission and love. And he did not say, "Love your children," for this would have been unnecessary, seeing that nature itself causes us to do so. Rather he corrected what needed correction; that the love shown in this case should be much stronger, because the obedience commanded is greater. Here Paul does not use the example of a husband and wife. Instead, hear the prophet saying, "Like a father pities his children, so the Lord pitied those that fear him."[14] HOMILIES ON COLOSSIANS 10.[15]

A MESSAGE IMPLANTED BY NATURE, PERVERTED BY CULTURE. AMBROSE: We have here the message of the Scriptures which declares: "Children, love your fathers; parents, do not provoke your children to anger." Nature has implanted in beasts the instinct to love their own brood and hold dear their own progeny. But the beasts know nothing of relations-in-law. Here, parents do not become estranged from their offspring by the act of changing their mates. They know nothing of preferences given to children of a later union to the neglect of those of a former marriage. They are conscious of the value of their pledges and are unacquainted with distinctions in respect to love, to incentives due to hate and to discriminations in acts that involve wrongdoing. Wild creatures have a nature that is simple and one which has no concern in the perversion of truth. And so the Lord has ordained that those creatures to

whom he has bestowed a minimum of reason are endowed with the maximum of feeling. SIX DAYS OF CREATION 6.22.[16]

THE WISE EXERCISE OF ADMONISHMENT. GREGORY THE GREAT: Subjects are to be admonished in one way, superiors in another, but the former in such a way that subjection may not crush them; the latter, that their exalted position may not lift them up; the former; that they should not do less than is ordered; the latter, that they should not command more than is just; the former, that they submit with humility; the latter, that they be moderate in the exercise of their superiority. For it is said to the former, and this can be understood figuratively: "Children, obey your parents in the Lord." But superiors are commanded: "Fathers, do not provoke your children to anger." Let the former learn to order their interior dispositions before the eyes of the hidden Judge; the others, how to set outwardly the example of a good life to those committed to them. PASTORAL CARE 3.4.[17]

3:22—4:1 *Slaves and Masters*

RECIPROCITY YET AGAIN. ANONYMOUS: But as for servants, what can we say more than that the slave act with good will toward his master, with the fear of God, though his master be impious and wicked; yet the servant should not comply

---

[12]Mt 10:37. [13]FC 61:178*. [14]Ps 103:13 (LXX). [15]NPNF 1 13:304*. [16]FC 42:240-41*. The modern reader ought not to be put off by Ambrose's argument here, for it is valuable. What he contends is that we human beings, richly endowed with reason but dulled in our natural sympathies and empathies, use our sophisticated level of culture, particularly the structure of law, as a means of doing cruel harm to one another, all in the name of legality. Ambrose suggests that if we got in touch with more of our natural feeling, we would not resort to legal arguments quite so quickly in order to gain selfish advantage in family relationships. Though his thinking is an example of the idealism attached to primitive states (i.e., the harmony of nature) in ancient philosophy, it is still worth pondering. [17]ACW 11:96-97*.

with requests or commands to worship other gods. And the master should love his servant, although he be his superior. Let him observe in what ways they are equal, even as he is a man. And let him who has a believing master love him both as his master, and as of the same faith, and as a father, but still with the preservation of his authority as a master. . . . In like manner, let a master who has a believing servant love him as a son or as a brother, on account of their communion in the faith, but still preserving the difference in status between the two. CONSTITUTIONS OF THE HOLY APOSTLES 4.12.[18]

LOVE THAT EMERGES FROM OBEDIENCE. CHRYSOSTOM: There is also a certain kind of love that does not proceed from nature, as in Paul's earlier examples, but from habit, and from the nature of authority itself. . . . In these relationships love's sphere is narrowed while that of obedience is widened. HOMILIES ON COLOSSIANS 10.[19]

"SLAVERY" ALWAYS A RELATIVE TERM. THEODORET OF CYR: Paul shows that the soul is always free, that it is only the body that is subjected to servitude. INTERPRETATION OF THE LETTER TO THE COLOSSIANS.[20]

AMBROSIASTER: Paul implies that God has created all persons to be freeborn and says this to keep masters from arrogance. Slavery is itself a sign of iniquity in the world, of the curse of Cain. In fact, the wise person is always free, though a slave outwardly, while it is foolish sinners who are the true slaves. COMMENTARY ON THE LETTER TO THE COLOSSIANS.[21]

ULTIMATELY EQUALS. GREGORY THE GREAT: Slaves are to be admonished in one way, masters in another. That is, slaves are to be admonished to consider always the lowliness of their condition; masters, ever to bear in mind their own nature, namely, that they have been created equal to their slaves. Slaves are to be admonished not to despise their masters, lest they offend God by their proud opposition to his ordinance. Masters are also to be admonished that they offend God by priding themselves on his gift to them, without realizing that they who are held in subjection by reason of their state of life are their equals in virtue of their common humanity. PASTORAL CARE 3.5.[22]

---

[18]ANF 7:436*. [19]NPNF 1 13:305*. [20]PG 82:621B/622B. [21]CSEL 81 3:202*. [22]ACW 11:101*.

4:2-18 ADMONITIONS AND FINAL GREETINGS

[2]*Continue steadfastly in prayer, being watchful in it with thanksgiving;* [3]*and pray for us also, that God may open to us a door for the word, to declare the mystery of Christ, on account of which I am in prison,* [4]*that I may make it clear, as I ought to speak.*

[5]*Conduct yourselves wisely toward outsiders, making the most of the time.* [6]*Let your speech always be gracious, seasoned with salt, so that you may know how you ought to answer every one.*

[7]*Tychicus will tell you all about my affairs; he is a beloved brother and faithful minister and fellow servant in the Lord.* [8]*I have sent him to you for this very purpose, that you may know*

how we are and that he may encourage your hearts, ⁹and with him Onesimus, the faithful and beloved brother, who is one of yourselves. They will tell you of everything that has taken place here.

¹⁰Aristarchus my fellow prisoner greets you, and Mark the cousin of Barnabas (concerning whom you have received instructions—if he comes to you, receive him), ¹¹and Jesus who is called Justus. These are the only men of the circumcision among my fellow workers for the kingdom of God, and they have been a comfort to me. ¹²Epaphras, who is one of yourselves, a servantᵍ of Christ Jesus, greets you, always remembering you earnestly in his prayers, that you may stand mature and fully assured in all the will of God. ¹³For I bear him witness that he has worked hard for you and for those in Laodicea and in Hierapolis. ¹⁴Luke the beloved physician and Demas greet you. ¹⁵Give my greetings to the brethren at Laodicea, and to Nympha and the church in her house. ¹⁶And when this letter has been read among you, have it read also in the church of the Laodiceans; and see that you read also the letter from Laodicea. ¹⁷And say to Archippus, "See that you fulfil the ministry which you have received in the Lord."

¹⁸I, Paul, write this greeting with my own hand. Remember my fetters. Grace be with you.

g Or *slave*

OVERVIEW: These concluding admonitions must be placed in the context of Paul's imprisonment, since he does not seek to be freed from this but to exercise his discipleship within it. He urges the Colossians to watchfulness in prayer, to pray for him and his ministry, to be wise in evangelism and to receive his messengers, always remembering the glory of his suffering for them (CHRYSOSTOM). Paul calls us to watchfulness, charity and pure hearts, humbly seeking their support in prayer even as he prays for them (AUGUSTINE). Prayer is the strongest weapon available to a Christian in the battle for righteousness (CAESARIUS OF ARLES), even as it is the principal means of spiritual support for all spiritual leaders (PACHOMIUS). In practical discipleship we are to be shrewd and sensitive as to when and how we proclaim the word (CHRYSOSTOM, AMBROSIASTER), always observing that fundamental humility that is key to effective proclamation (SAYINGS OF THE FATHERS). In the final urging of the Colossians to receive his messengers and to remember his chains, Paul again encourages them by his love and spiritual beauty (CHRYSOSTOM).

4:2 Steadfast in Prayer

WATCHFULNESS THE KEY. CHRYSOSTOM: Paul realizes that continuing in prayer can frequently produce restlessness. Therefore he writes, "watching," that is, be sober, avoid wandering. For the devil knows, yes he knows, how great a good prayer is. Hence, he presses heavily on us as we pray. And Paul also knows how careless many are when they pray. Thus he says "continue" in prayer, as something that takes hard work, "watching therein with thanksgiving." For let this, Paul says, be your work, to give thanks in your prayers both for the seen and the unseen, for his benefits to the willing and the unwilling, for the kingdom, for hell, for tribulation and for refreshment. This is how the saints normally pray, giving thanks for the benefits shared by all. HOMILIES ON COLOSSIANS 10.[1]

THE WATCHFULNESS OF FAITH. AUGUSTINE: When the blessed apostle was reminding us of

[1]NPNF 1 13:305*.

the importance of prayer, he also reminded us at the same time about being watchful: "Be persistent in prayer," he said, "being watchful in it." Impure love, brothers and sisters, compels those who are possessed by it to keep awake; the shameless person watches, in order to seduce; the evildoer, in order to harm; the drunkard, to drink; the bandit, to slay; the self-indulgent, to spend; the miser, to hoard; the thief, to steal; the robber, to smash and grab. How much more, therefore, ought love to remain awake in holy and harmless people, if iniquity can extort wakefulness from the criminal and the corrupt? SER-MONS 223J.[2]

VICTORY THROUGH PRAYER. CAESARIUS OF ARLES: This seems to indicate that the people of God did not fight with the hand or weapons so much as with the voice and tongue, that is, they poured forth prayer to God, and thus overcame their adversaries. Therefore, you, too, if you want to be victorious, listen to the apostle say, "Be assiduous in prayer, being wakeful." This is the most glorious fight of the Christian, not to presume upon his own strength but always to implore the assistance of God. SER-MONS 103.5.[3]

4:3 And Pray for Us Also

PAUL, HUMAN AND A SINNER. AUGUSTINE: Schisms arise when men say, we are righteous; when they say, we sanctify the unclean, we justify the wicked, we ask, we obtain. But what did John say? "If any man sin, we have an advocate with the Father, Jesus Christ the righteous."[4] You will say, But may not holy men ask on our behalf? May not bishops and rulers ask on behalf of the people? Look at the Scripture, and you will find rulers commending themselves to the people's prayers. The apostle says to his people, "Praying also for us." The apostle prays for the people and the people for the apostle. We pray for you, my brothers, but you should also pray for us. Let all the members pray for one

another, and let the Head intercede for all. HOMILIES ON 1 JOHN 1.8.2.[5]

PRAY FOR OUR SPIRITUAL LEADERS. ANONY-MOUS: Again, he prayed for the clergy of the Catholic church, saying, "Although they are my fathers, it is nevertheless a duty for me to remember them and to pray for them, because the holy apostle invites us to do so, saying, Brothers, pray for us as well, so that God may open for us the door for the Word." Such was the way he used to pray for all. THE BOHAIRIC LIFE OF PACHOMIUS 101.[6]

4:5 Conduct Yourselves Wisely Toward Outsiders

WISE AS SERPENTS. CHRYSOSTOM: "Redeeming," he says, "the time": that is, the present time is short. Now Paul said this because he did not want them to be crafty, nor hypocrites (for this is not a part of wisdom, but of senselessness). What then? In matters where outsiders are not harming you, don't give them an opportunity. . . . If you are going to experience conflict with the outside world, Paul writes, let the conflict have its origin in your preaching—and not in any other source. HOMILIES ON COLOSSIANS 11.[7]

AMBROSIASTER: Since we must live among unbelievers and mix with them in worldly business, Paul urges us to be wise about the possibility of creating a stir, lest we give these folk an opportunity for blaspheming God or engaging in persecution. Why then should you carry on business with anyone that you know to be a source of contention and trouble? Thus, Paul admonishes us to use religious speech opportunely both as to time and place. But if anyone is difficult, be silent. Different courses of action are suitable for dealing with powerful people,

[2]*WSA* 3/6:238*. [3]FC 47:112*. [4]Jn 2:1. [5]LCC 8:265*. [6]*PK* 1:140. [7]NPNF 1 13:309*.

with people of middle or lower stations in life. One deals one way with gentle persons, another way with those who are filled with anger. This is what it means to redeem the time. COMMENTARY ON THE LETTER TO THE COLOSSIANS.[8]

PELAGIUS: Paul enjoins the Colossians to make a good time from a bad time by means of their prudence. PELAGIUS'S COMMENTARY ON THE LETTER TO THE COLOSSIANS.[9]

4:6 Gracious Speech, Seasoned with Salt

REQUIREMENTS OF THE EFFECTIVE PREACHER. CHRYSOSTOM: Here, too, a man needs a loftiness of mind far beyond my own littleness of spirit, if he is to correct this disorderly and unprofitable delight that ordinary people enjoy. He must try to divert their attention to something more useful, so that church people will follow and defer to him. He should not be governed by their desires. It is impossible to acquire this power except by these two qualities: contempt of praise and the force of eloquence. If either is lacking, the one left is made useless by the divorce from the other. If a preacher despises praise yet does not produce the kind of teaching which is "with grace, seasoned with salt," he is despised by the people, and his sublime words accomplish nothing. And if he is eloquent but is a slave to the sound of applause, again an equal damage threatens both him and the people, because through his passion for praise he aims to speak more for the pleasure than the profit of his hearers. ON THE PRIESTHOOD 5.2.[10]

DEPENDENT UPON CHRIST. ANONYMOUS: An old man said to a brother: Do not measure your heart against your brother, saying that you are more serious or more continent or more understanding than he. But be obedient to the grace of God, in the spirit of poverty and in genuine love. The efforts of a man swollen with vanity are futile. It is written, "Let the one who thinks he stands be careful lest he fall."[11] Be in your spirit

seasoned with salt—and so dependent upon Christ. SAYINGS OF THE FATHERS 15.55.[12]

4:7 Tychicus a Messenger

PAUL'S STRATEGY. CHRYSOSTOM: Admirable! How great is the wisdom of Paul! Observe, he does not put everything into his epistles, but only things necessary and urgent. In the first place, he doesn't want his letters to be unnecessarily long. Second, his messenger will be more respected if he too has something personal to relate. Third, in this way Paul demonstrates his affection for Tychicus; if he did not feel this way, he would not have entrusted him with the news of his affairs. In addition, there are some things that are best not mentioned in writing. HOMILIES ON COLOSSIANS 11.[13]

THEODORET OF CYR: Paul would have been reluctant to send Onesimus to the Colossians on his own, since he was an escaped slave and thus perhaps offensive to them; thus Tychicus was more suitable for teaching and instruction. INTERPRETATION OF THE LETTER TO THE COLOSSIANS.[14]

AMBROSIASTER: However much Paul insists that he is present with them in spirit and sees them, he nonetheless still makes use of a messenger for reporting. COMMENTARY ON THE LETTER TO THE COLOSSIANS.[15]

4:9 Onesimus, Faithful and Beloved

THE LETTER TO THE COLOSSIANS LATE? CHRYSOSTOM: Holy, indeed, are all Paul's letters. But those he writes behind bars are especially advantageous for the reader. Those include, for instance, the letters to the Ephesians

---

[8]CSEL 81 3:203-4. [9]PETE 471. [10]COP 128*. [11]1 Cor 10:12. [12]CC 12:168-69*. [13]NPNF 1 13:309*. [14]PG 82:623C/624C. [15]CSEL 81 3:204.

and Philemon, that to Timothy, that to the Philippians and the one before us. For Colossians was written while Paul was imprisoned, since he writes in it: "for which I am also in bonds: that I may make it manifest as I ought to speak." But this epistle appears to have been written after that to the Romans. For he wrote to the Romans before he had seen them, but this letter later, near upon the close of his preaching. And it is evident from this that in the epistle to Philemon he says, "Being such a one as Paul the aged,"[16] and makes request for Onesimus. But in the Colossian letter Paul sends Onesimus himself, as he says, "With Onesimus the faithful and beloved brother." HOMILIES ON COLOSSIANS 1.[17]

4:12-13 Epaphras Has Worked Hard

"STRIVING" IN PRAYER FOR YOU. CHRYSOSTOM: And he says, "always striving for you in prayers." He did not write simply "praying," but "striving," trembling and fearing. "For I bear him witness," Paul says, "that he has much zeal for you." HOMILIES ON COLOSSIANS 12.[18]

ANONYMOUS: Paul said to the brothers in the Lord: "Epaphras wrestles for your sakes in his prayer." This is the prayer which our Lord gasped out forcefully when "he was in anguish in prayer, and his sweat was like drops of blood,"[19] and he shed many tears. BOOK OF STEPS 18.3.[20]

4:18 Remember My Fetters

THE CHRISTIAN WAY. CHRYSOSTOM: Hear Paul's chains, and you will understand that to be in affliction is no proof of being forsaken. Would you wear silken robes? Remember Paul's chains, and these fine clothes will appear to you more worthless than the rags of a menstruating woman. Would you array yourself with gold trinkets? Listen in your mind to Paul's chains, and trinkets will seem to you no better than a withered bulrush.... Would you daub yourself with pastes and pigments and similar things? Think of Paul's tears: for three years, night and day, he continued to weep.... What fountain will you compare to these tears? HOMILIES ON COLOSSIANS 12.[21]

---

[16]Philem 9. [17]NPNF 1 13:257*. [18]NPNF 1 13:314. [19]Lk 22:43. [20]SFPSL 56-57*. [21]NPNF 1 13:315-16*.

THE FIRST EPISTLE
TO THE THESSALONIANS

ARGUMENT: After leaving the Christians of Thessalonica, Paul had sent Timothy back to them from Athens. He now writes to praise them for their firmness of faith, as well as to exhort them to look for the resurrection of the dead (THEODORET). Paul wrote this letter to the Thessalonians in order to praise them for their steadfastness in faith and to give them further instruction (THEODORE). Here Paul encourages the Thessalonian Christians, who have endured a great deal of persecution and who remain vulnerable to pagan Greek influences. Central to Paul's encouragement is his teaching about the resurrection of the dead, since grief at the death of fellow believers is an especially heavy burden for the Thessalonians (SEVERIAN). They must not be too curious about the exact time of the Lord's coming (THEODORET). Paul praises the Thessalonians as an example of faith but also presses them to push on toward perfection. He wishes them to have such a measure of the Spirit that in the hope of what is to come they might continue to suffer persecution for the name of Christ (AMBROSIASTER).

1:1-10 GREETINGS AND PRAISE

¹*Paul, Silvanus, and Timothy,*
To the church of the Thessalonians in God the Father and the Lord Jesus Christ:
Grace to you and peace.
²*We give thanks to God always for you all, constantly mentioning you in our prayers,*
³*remembering before our God and Father your work of faith and labor of love and steadfastness of hope in our Lord Jesus Christ.* ⁴*For we know, brethren beloved by God, that he has cho-*

sen you; *[5]for our gospel came to you not only in word, but also in power and in the Holy Spirit and with full conviction. You know what kind of men we proved to be among you for your sake.* *[6]And you became imitators of us and of the Lord, for you received the word in much affliction, with joy inspired by the Holy Spirit;* *[7]so that you became an example to all the believers in Macedonia and in Achaia.* *[8]For not only has the word of the Lord sounded forth from you in Macedonia and Achaia, but your faith in God has gone forth everywhere, so that we need not say anything.* *[9]For they themselves report concerning us what a welcome we had among you, and how you turned to God from idols, to serve a living and true God,* *[10]and to wait for his Son from heaven, whom he raised from the dead, Jesus who delivers us from the wrath to come.*

OVERVIEW: Paul's intention in this opening section is to come before the Thessalonians in all humility, eschewing all titles, magnifying the work of his associates and praising the Thessalonians for their great faith and their hard work during persecution (CHRYSOSTOM). The very nature of true faith is that it arouses believers to good work, for love produces steadfastness in laboring, and hope produces endurance with patience. Paul gives thanks for all of the progress that the Thessalonians have made, holding them up to the other churches and praying for their continued growth (AMBROSIASTER). Paul shows here that the believer who has perfect love, whose faith is whole, is able to bear all things patiently for the sake of the future hope (PELAGIUS).

1:1 *Paul, Silvanus and Timothy*

WITHOUT TITLE. CHRYSOSTOM: Here Paul gives himself no title. He refers to himself neither as "an apostle" nor as "a servant." Paul avoids such titles, I suppose, because the Thessalonians were newly instructed and still didn't know Paul well. His preaching ministry to this church was just beginning. HOMILIES ON 1 THESSALONIANS 1.[1]

A DIVINE HARMONY. ORIGEN: Two made a symphony, Paul and Sosthenes, when writing the first epistle to the Corinthians. After this

Paul and Timothy sang in harmony when they wrote their second letter to the same church. And even three made a symphony when Paul and Silvanus and Timothy gave instruction by letter to the Thessalonians. COMMENTARY ON MATTHEW 14.1.[2]

1:2 *We Give Thanks to God Always for You*

OPENING ENCOURAGEMENT. CHRYSOSTOM: For to give thanks to God for them is the act of one testifying to how they have advanced in the faith. Not only are the Thessalonians praised by Paul, but Paul thanks God for them, as though God himself had accomplished everything. Paul also teaches them to be moderate in their self-estimation, all but saying that all their growth is from the power of God. HOMILIES ON 1 THESSALONIANS 1.[3]

1:5 *In Power and in the Holy Spirit*

YOUR CONVERSION FROM GOD. THEODORE OF MOPSUESTIA: For you know, he says, how you came to be chosen (that is, how you arrived at faith), for you did not believe solely by means of our words. Indeed, we not only spoke but also showed wonders, great and glorious and worked by the Spirit, by which you were strengthened

---

[1]NPNF 1 13:323*. [2]ANF 9:495*. [3]NPNF 1 13:324.

with regard to the things we had spoken to you. Hold on tightly to what you have learned, and don't be deflected from your course by the external things that happen to you. COMMENTARY ON 1 THESSALONIANS.[4]

RECEIVING THE SPIRIT. GREGORY OF NYSSA: Thus, the obedient and responsive soul gives itself over to the virtuous life. This life is freedom itself, on the one hand, from the chains of this life, separating itself from the slavery of base and empty pursuits. On the other hand, this soul devotes itself to faith and the life of God alone, because it sees clearly that where there is faith, reverence and a blameless life, there is present the power of Christ, there is flight from all evil and from death which robs us of life. For shameful things do not have in themselves sufficient power to compete with the power of the Lord. It is their nature to develop from disobedience to his commands. This was experienced in ancient times by the first man, but now it is experienced by all of us when we imitate Adam's disobedience through stubborn choice. However, those who approach the Spirit with honest intent, unfeigned faith and an undefiled conscience, are cleansed by the Spirit according to the one who says, "for our gospel was not delivered to you in word only, but in power also; and in the Holy Spirit and in much fullness, as you know." ON THE CHRISTIAN MODE OF LIFE.[5]

PAUL'S HUMILITY. AMBROSIASTER: In order to indicate that he showed all humility among the Thessalonians and in order to adopt a gentle approach in dealing with them, Paul makes it clear that none of the powerful means by which they have been brought to faith is lacking. His preaching was accompanied by signs and wonders and was empowered by the Holy Spirit. It embodied the fullness of truth rather than fantasy. This could be seen in the teaching of grace, in the quality of discourse among them and in the healing of the sick. By these they could be

seen to be the true heirs of the gift of God in the promises to Abraham. COMMENTARY ON THE FIRST LETTER TO THE THESSALONIANS.[6]

THE NATURE OF SPIRITUAL POWER. PELAGIUS: The reception of the gospel by the Thessalonians "in power" may mean that Paul's preaching was accompanied by miraculous signs, but it may also mean that it strengthened the Thessalonians for much endurance in suffering. PELAGIUS'S COMMENTARY ON THE FIRST LETTER TO THE THESSALONIANS.[7]

1:6 In Much Affliction, with Joy

THE JOY OF THE SPIRIT. CHRYSOSTOM: "With joy inspired by the Holy Spirit," Paul says. So that no one can say, "How can you speak of affliction and of joy in the same breath?" he adds, "inspired by the Holy Spirit." The affliction pertains to the body, and the joy to things spiritual. But how? The things that happened to them were burdensome, but not so the things that sprang up out of them, for the Spirit does not allow it. So then, it is possible for one who suffers not to rejoice when he is suffering for his sins but nevertheless to experience pleasure when he is being beaten and suffers for Christ's sake. For such is the joy of the Spirit. In return for the things which seem to be burdensome, the Spirit brings delight. They have afflicted you, he says, and persecuted you, but the Spirit did not forsake you even in those circumstances. HOMILIES ON 1 THESSALONIANS 1.[8]

TRUE IMITATION. AMBROSIASTER: Those who, eager to believe, suffer insults and injuries from their fellows, are precisely those who may be called imitators of the apostles and of the Lord himself. He suffered the same things from the Jews, as did the apostles who endured persecu-

---

[4]*TEM* 2:4. [5]FC 58:129*. [6]CSEL 81 3:212-13. [7]*PETE* 418. [8]NPNF 1 13:325*.

tion as they pursued their faith in God. COM-
MENTARY ON THE FIRST LETTER TO THE THES-
SALONIANS.[9]

1:7 An Example to All the Believers

GRACE REQUIRES COOPERATION. CHRYSOS-
TOM: Do you see what a great thing zeal is? It
does not ask for more time or delay or procrasti-
nate. It is sufficient simply to offer one's self,
and all is fulfilled. . . . Why then do I say this?
Because if we are awake we shall not need the
help of others. If we sleep, the help of others
accomplishes nothing for us, but even with their
aid we perish. . . . You say that your prayers
accomplish little? They accomplish much when
we combine them with our acts. . . . But if you
remain idle, you will receive no benefit. HOMI-
LIES ON 1 THESSALONIANS 1.[10]

1:9 How You Turned to God from Idols

THE FOUNDATION OF BELIEF. BASIL THE
GREAT: By what means do we become Christians? Through our faith would be the universal
answer. And in what way are we saved? Plainly
because we were regenerated through the grace

given to us in our baptism. How else could we
be? And after recognizing that this salvation is
established through the Father and the Son and
the Holy Spirit, shall we fling away "that form of
doctrine"[11] which we received? Would it not
rather be grounds for great groaning if we are
found now further off from our salvation "than
when we first believed,"[12] and deny now what we
then received? . . . What if one does not always
and everywhere keep to his initial confession
and cling to it as a sure protection? . . . What if
one, having been delivered "from the idols," to
the "living God," now constitutes himself a
"stranger" from the "promises"[13] of God? He
fights against his own handwriting, which he
put on record when he professed the faith. To
me my baptism was the beginning of life and
that day of regeneration the first of days. It is
plain that the utterance confessed in the grace of
adoption is the most honorable of all. ON THE
HOLY SPIRIT 10.26.[14]

---

[9]CSEL 81 3:213. [10]NPNF 1 13:325-26*. [11]Rom 6:17. [12]Rom
13:11. [13]Eph 2:12. [14]NPNF 2 8:17*.

2:1-12 PAUL'S SOLICITOUS CARE

[1]*For you yourselves know, brethren, that our visit to you was not in vain;* [2]*but though we
had already suffered and been shamefully treated at Philippi, as you know, we had courage in
our God to declare to you the gospel of God in the face of great opposition.* [3]*For our appeal
does not spring from error or uncleanness, nor is it made with guile;* [4]*but just as we have been
approved by God to be entrusted with the gospel, so we speak, not to please men, but to please
God who tests our hearts.* [5]*For we never used either words of flattery, as you know, or a cloak
for greed, as God is witness;* [6]*nor did we seek glory from men, whether from you or from others, though we might have made demands as apostles of Christ.* [7]*But we were gentle[a] among
you, like a nurse taking care of her children.* [8]*So, being affectionately desirous of you, we were*

ready to share with you not only the gospel of God but also our own selves, because you had become very dear to us.

⁹For you remember our labor and toil, brethren; we worked night and day, that we might not burden any of you, while we preached to you the gospel of God. ¹⁰You are witnesses, and God also, how holy and righteous and blameless was our behavior to you believers; ¹¹for you know how, like a father with his children, we exhorted each one of you and encouraged you and charged you ¹²to lead a life worthy of God, who calls you into his own kingdom and glory.

a Other ancient authorities read *babes*

Overview: In this passage Paul chooses to emphasize his weakness, in order then to highlight the great power of God working through him (Chrysostom). Paul's visit to the Thessalonians was clearly a matter of divine intention and divine leading, not a matter of human wisdom or of mere chance (Theodore). Paul shows here that his sufferings are a demonstration of the truth and power of his preaching, that such sufferings intensified his eagerness and zeal (Ignatius, Caesarius of Arles, Theodoret, Gregory the Great). Paul teaches that the boldness of his preaching was sustained by the hope of future reward, by the promise of a crown (Ambrosiaster). Do not make another's praise your motive for doing right (Augustine, Fulgentius). Be gentle as a nurse caring for children (Clement of Alexandria, Origen, Augustine).

2:1 Our Visit Was Not in Vain

Frost and Fire. Gregory the Great: I beg you, in all this recall to your mind what I believe you must never forget: "All who would live godly in Christ suffer persecution."[1] And with regard to this I confidently say that you would live less godly if you suffered less persecution. For let us hear what else the same teacher of the Gentiles says to his disciples. "You yourselves know, brothers, how we came to you; we did not come in vain, for we had already suffered and been shamefully treated." My most sweet son, the holy preacher declared that his coming to the Thessalonians would have accomplished nothing if he had not been shamefully treated. . . . On the basis of Paul's example be even more disciplined in the midst of adverse circumstances. In this way adversity itself may increase significantly your desire for the love of God and your earnestness in good works. Similarly, the seeds planted for a future harvest germinate more fruitfully if they are covered over with frost. Likewise fire is increased by blowing on it that it may grow greater. Letters 30.[2]

2:3, 5 Not from Error or Uncleanness

The Source of Success. Chrysostom: For Paul's work found its source in power, mighty power, power that surpassed mere human diligence. For Paul brought three qualifications to the preaching of the word: a fervent and adventurous zeal, a soul ready to undergo any possible hardship and the combination of knowledge and wisdom. Even with Paul's love of the difficult task, his blameless life would have accomplished little had he not also received the power of the Spirit. Examine the matter from Paul's own words: "That our ministry not be blamed."[3] And again, "For our exhortation is not founded on error, nor uncleanness, nor guile nor hidden under a cloke of covetousness." Thus you have seen his blamelessness. And again, "For we aim

---

[1]2 Tim 3:12.   [2]NPNF 2 12:223*.   [3]2 Cor 6:3.

at what is honorable, not only in the sight of the Lord but also in the sight of men."[4] . . . Without this, Paul's work would have been impossible. People were not converted because of Paul's miracles; no, it was not the miracles that produced faith, nor did Paul base his high calling upon the miraculous but upon other grounds: a man must be irreproachable in conduct, prudent and discreet in his dealings with others, regardless of the dangers involved, and apt to teach. These were the qualifications that enabled Paul to reach his goal. HOMILIES ON EPHESIANS 6.[5]

2:4 Not to Please People but to Please God

THE COMPOSURE OF THE TRUE MARTYR.
IGNATIUS: Since God has answered my prayer to see you godly people, I have proceeded to ask for more. I mean, it is as a prisoner for Christ Jesus that I hope to greet you, if indeed it be [God's] will that I should deserve to meet my end. Things are off to a good start. May I have the good fortune to meet my fate without interference! What I fear is your generosity which may prove detrimental to me. For you can easily do what you want to, whereas it is hard for me to get to God unless you leave me alone. I do not want you to please men but to please God, just as you are doing. For I shall never again have such a chance to get to God, nor can you, if you keep quiet, get credit for a finer deed. For if you quietly let me alone, people will see in me God's word. But if you are enamored of my mere bodily presence, I shall, on the contrary, be a meaningless noise. Grant me no more than to be a sacrifice for God while there is an altar at hand. TO THE ROMANS 1.1—2.2.[6]

NOT SEEKING PRAISE. AUGUSTINE: Therefore, our good Master has taught us by his apostle not to live right and to do right in order to be praised by men,[7] that is, not to make the praise of men our motive for doing right, yet for the sake of men we are to seek what is worthy of

praise. Even when good men are praised, the benefit falls more on those who praise than on those who are praised. For, as far as the latter are concerned, it is enough for them that they are good. But the former, whose advantage it is to imitate the good, are to praise the good because they give evidence that those whom they praise sincerely are pleasing to them. Thus the apostle says in a certain passage: "If I pleased men, I should not be the servant of Christ."[8] In another passage he says: "Please all men in all things as I also in all things please all men," but he gives the reason: "not seeking that which is profitable to myself but to many that they may be saved."[9] LETTERS 231.1.4.[10]

MOTIVATION THE KEY. FULGENTIUS OF RUSPE:
In all good works, be careful lest you be stirred by desire for human praise. You ought to be praised in your good works, but insofar as you do them, you ought not to expect human praises. The human tongue may praise you, but desire praise from God alone. And thus it may come about that while you do not seek human praise, God may be praised in your deeds. Recall how much the Lord forbids us to do our righteous works to garner human praise, saying, "take care not to perform righteous deeds in order that people may see them; otherwise, you will have no recompense from your heavenly Father."[11] Therefore, when he says that we should look out lest we do our righteous deeds before human beings, that we may be seen by them, and again he commands that our light shine before human beings,[12] is he not com-

---

[4]2 Cor 8:21. [5]NPNF 1 13:77*. [6]LCC 1:103. Apparently having been arrested during a general persecution of the church in Antioch in Syria, about A.D. 115, the bishop Ignatius here anticipates his martyrdom in the city of Rome. As with the apostle Paul in the Acts of the Apostles, Ignatius is being taken to the capital city of the empire for his trial, and thus he is writing ahead to the congregation in that city. It is noteworthy that he asks the Christians there not to interfere in any way with what he foresees as his martyrdom. [7]See also Mt 5:16. [8]Gal 1:10. [9]1 Cor 10:33. [10]FC 32:160-61. [11]Mt 6:1. [12]Mt 5:16.

manding contrary things? Certainly not, but he commands that good deeds be done in such a way that we wish, not that we ourselves but that God be praised in our works. For the apostle too avoided human glory in his works but sought God's glory. So he says, writing to the Thessalonians, "Nor, indeed, did we ever appear with flattering speech, as you know, or with a pretext for greed—God is witness—nor did we seek praise from human beings, either from you or from others." LETTERS 2.35.[13]

2:7 We Were Gentle Among You

LIKE A NURSE. AUGUSTINE: But there is no greater proof of charity in Christ's church than when the very honor which seems so important on a human level is despised. This is why Solomon's wise attempt to prevent the limbs of the infant being cut in two is like our efforts to prevent Christian infirmity from being torn to shreds by the break-up of unity.[14] The apostle says that he had shown himself like a mother to the little ones among whom he had done the good work of the gospel, not he but the grace of God in him. The harlot could call nothing her own but her sins, whereas her ability to bear children came from God. And the Lord says beautifully about a harlot, "she to whom much is forgiven loves much."[15] So the apostle Paul says, "I became a little one[16] among you, like a nurse fondling her children." But when it comes to the danger of the little one being cut in two, when the insincere woman claims for herself a spurious dignity of motherhood and is prepared to break up unity, the mother despises her proper dignity provided she may see her son whole and preserve him alive. She is afraid that if she insists too obstinately on the dignity due to her motherhood, she may give insincerity a chance to divide the feeble limbs with the sword of schism. So indeed let mother Charity say "Give her the boy." SERMONS 10.8.[17]

ALL DISCIPLES ARE CHILDREN. CLEMENT OF

ALEXANDRIA: We ought now to be in a position to understand that the name "little one" is not used in the sense of lacking intelligence. The notion of childishness has that pejorative meaning, but the term "little one" really means "one newly become gentle," just as the word gentle means being mild-mannered.[18] So, a "little one" means one just recently become gentle and meek of disposition. St. Paul obviously suggests this when he says: "Although as the apostle of Christ we could have claimed a position of honor among you, still while in your midst we were children, as if a nurse were cherishing her own children." A little one is gentle and for that reason decidedly amenable, mild and simple, without deceit or pretense, direct and upright of mind. Childlikeness is the foundation for simplicity and truthfulness. CHRIST THE EDUCATOR 1.5.19.[19]

THE LITTLENESS OF CHRISTIAN PERFECTION. ORIGEN: But another might say that the perfect man is here called little, applying the word, "For he that is least among you all, the same is great."[20] He will affirm that he who humbles himself and

---

[13]FC 95:308. [14]In this striking passage Augustine is using the account contained in 1 Kings 3:16-28 as an allegory of the disputes that threaten to tear apart the church. In the Old Testament passage two women stand before wise King Solomon in order to ask a judgment as to which of the two of them is the true mother of a particular child. Paradoxically, Solomon decides to tear the child in two in order to give half to each contender. At that point the true mother is revealed by her grief, the false one by her complaisance. For Augustine, Paul is likened to the true mother of the church, while his opponents are the false mothers (the "harlots"), little caring what damage their contentiousness might do to the church. [15]Lk 7:47. [16]Augustine cites the Old Latin form of 1 Thessalonians 2:7, in which the Latin parvulus ("little one") had come to correspond to the Greek nepios ("little one"), itself a corruption of epios ("gentle," "mild"). [17]WSA 3/1:288*. [18]Clement seems to be aware here of the confusion in the Greek text, where the Alexandrian tradition has the Greek word for "gentle" (the reading chosen in RSV), while the tradition that we know from the early papyrus fragments of Paul has the reading "like infants." It is as if Clement, in his discourse about childishness and childlikeness, combines the two of these here by arguing that Paul was a "gentle little one" in the way he came among the Thessalonians and that, by implication, all Christians are to be this way. [19]FC 23:19-20. [20]Lk 9:48.

becomes a child in the midst of all that believe, though he be an apostle or a bishop, and becomes such "as when a nurse cherishes her own children," is the little one pointed out by Jesus. He will also affirm that the angel of such a person is worthy to behold the face of God.[21] The little are here called perfect, according to the passage "He that is least among you all, the same is great."[22] Paul said, "Unto me who am less than the least of all saints was this grace given."[23] These are in harmony with the saying, "Whoever shall cause one of these little ones to stumble,"[24] and "So it is not the will of my Father in heaven that one of these little ones should perish."[25] Commentary on Matthew 13.29.[26]

The Faithful Mother. Augustine: While Scripture is spiritual in itself, nonetheless it often, so to say, adapts itself to carnal, materialistic people in a carnal, materialistic way. But it doesn't want them to remain carnal and materialistic. A mother, too, loves to nurse her infant, but she doesn't love it so that it will always remain a baby. She holds it in her bosom, she cuddles it with her hands, she comforts it with caresses, she feeds it with her milk. She does all this for the baby, but she wants it to grow, so that she won't be doing this sort of thing forever. Now look at the apostle. We can fix our eyes on him all the more suitably because he wasn't above calling himself a mother. He writes "I became like a baby in your midst, like a nurse fondling her children."[27] There are of course nurses who fondle babies that are not their own children. And on the other hand there are mothers who give their children to nurses and don't fondle them themselves. The apostle, however, full of genuine, juicy feelings of love, takes on the role both of nurse when he says "fondling" and of mother when he completes it with "her children." Sermons 23.3.[28]

Paul's Tender, Solicitous Care. Augustine: There you are then; persecution had increased so much, and tribulation so much,

that the psalmist was even weary of living. See how fear and trembling had come upon him and darkness had covered him, as you heard when it was said in the psalm. It's the voice, you see, of the body of Christ, the voice of Christ's members. Do you want to recognize your own voice there? Be a member of Christ. "Fear," it says, "and trembling fell upon me, and darkness covered me. And I said, Who will give me wings like a dove's, and I will fly away and take my rest?"[29] ... The psalmist felt weariness, after a fashion, from the earthly heaviness and decay of the flesh, when he wanted to fly away to Christ; a plethora of tribulations was infesting the way but not blocking it altogether. He was weary of living but not of the eternal life about which he says, "For me to live is Christ, and to die is gain." But because he was held down here by charity, how does he go on? "If, though, to live in the flesh here is the fruit of my work—and which I should choose I do not know. But I am being torn both ways, having a longing to cast off and be with Christ."[30] ... "But to remain in the flesh is necessary on your account."[31] He had given in to the cheepings of his chicks. He was covering them with the spread of his wings, cherishing his chicks, as he says himself: "I became a little one in your midst, like a nurse cherishing her children." Sermons 305A.5.[32]

Paul's Loving Condescension. Augus-

---

[21]Origen refers here to his belief that each of us has a guardian angel, as well as to his more idiosyncratic conviction that our angels exist in heaven in a hierarchy of virtue or perfection, as we do on earth, relative to each one's state of personal growth at that time. [22]Lk 9:48. [23]Eph 3:8. [24]Mt 18:6. [25]Mt 18:14. [26]ANF 9:492*. As with Clement above, this selection from the writings of the Alexandrian theologian is included to illustrate the preoccupation with virtue, understood as lowliness and humility, that marked these thinkers. They see in Paul the personification of this meaning of virtue, and they seize on every opportunity to make the point. In a somewhat analogous way many modern commentators have been much fascinated with the feminine side of the image of the nurse used by Paul. [27]Cf. p. 65 n. 14. This translation, reflected in the Latin text, appears repeatedly in Augustine. [28]WSA 3/2:57*. [29]Ps 55:5-6. [30]Phil 1:22-23. [31]Phil 1:24. [32]WSA 3/8:328*.

tine: See Paul ascending: "I know a man in Christ who fourteen years ago (whether in the body or out of the body I do not know, God knows) was caught up to the third heaven and heard unutterable words which it is not granted to man to speak."[33] You heard him ascending; hear him descending: "I could not speak to you as spiritual men but only as carnal, as to little ones in Christ. I gave you milk to drink, not solid food."[34] Look, he who had ascended descended. Seek where he had ascended: "Up to the third heaven." Seek where he had descended: To giving milk to little ones. Hear that he descended: "I became a little one," he says, "in your midst, as if a nurse were fondling her own children." For we see both nurses and mothers descend to little ones; and though they know how to speak Latin, they clip their words and somehow switch their speech so that they may be able to communicate their desires through simple language; for if they should speak in a mature, grammatically correct fashion, the in-fant does not hear with understanding. Neither does he benefit. And some eloquent father, though he be a great orator, thundering with his tongue and rattling the magistrates' platforms, if he should have a son, when he returns home, he puts aside the legal eloquence by which he had ascended and with childish language he de-scends to his little one. TRACTATES ON JOHN 7.23.4.[35]

FLESHLY CHARITY AND SPIRITUAL CHARITY.
AUGUSTINE: Can we not see, even in dumb, unreasoning creatures, where there is no spiritual charity but only that which belongs to their nature as animals, with what eager insistence the mother's milk is demanded by her little ones? Yet, however rough be the nursing calf's mouth upon the udder, the mother likes it better than if there were no sucking, no demanding of the debt that charity admits. Indeed, we often see the bigger calf butting with its head at the cow's udders, and the mother's body forced upward by the pressure; yet she will never kick her calf away, but if the young one not be there

to suck, she will low for him to come. Of spiritual charity, the apostle says: "I have become little among you, like a nurse cherishing her children." If such charity be in us, we cannot but love you when you press your demand upon us. We do not love backwardness in you. It makes us fearful that your strength is failing. HOMILIES ON 1 JOHN 9.1.[36]

2:9 *You Remember Our Labor and Toil*

THE BALANCE OF WORK AND PRAYER. CAESARIUS OF ARLES: Perhaps someone says: Who can always be thinking of God and eternal bliss, since all men must be concerned for food, clothing and the management of their household? God does not bid us be free from all anxiety over the present life, for he instructs us through his apostle: "If any man will not work, neither let him eat."[37] The same apostle repeats the idea with reference to himself when he says: "We worked night and day so that we might not burden any of you." Since God especially advises reasonable thought of food and clothing, so long as avarice and ambition which usually serve dissipation are not linked with it, any action or thought is most rightly considered holy. The only provision is that those preoccupations should not be so excessive that they do not allow us to have time for God, according to the words: "The burdens of the world have made them miserable."[38] SERMONS 45.1.[39]

CHRYSOSTOM: "The sleep of a working man is sweet, whether he eats little or much."[40] Why does he add, "whether he eat little or much"? Both these things usually bring sleeplessness, namely, poverty and abundance; . . . . But the effect of hard work is such that neither poverty nor excess disrupt this servant's sleep. Though

---

[33]2 Cor 12:2-4. [34]1 Cor 3:1-2. [35]FC 78:176-77*. [36]LCC 8:329. [37]2 Thess 3:10. [38]The source of this quotation is unknown. [39]FC 31:226-27*. [40]Eccles 5:12.

throughout the whole day they are running about everywhere, ministering to their masters, being knocked about and hard pressed, having little time to catch their breath, they receive a sufficient recompense for their toils and labors in the pleasure of sleeping. And thus it has happened through the goodness of God toward humanity, that these pleasures are not to be purchased with gold and silver but with labor, with hard toil, with necessity and every kind of discipline. Not so with the rich. On the contrary, while lying on their beds, they are frequently without sleep throughout the night. Though they devise many schemes, they do not obtain much pleasure. . . . For this reason also, from the beginning, God tied the man to labor, not for the purpose of punishing or chastising but for amendment and education. When Adam lived in idle leisure, he fell from para- dise, but when the apostle labored abundantly and toiled hard, writing, "In labor and travail, working night and day," then he was taken up into paradise and ascended to the third heaven! HOMILIES CONCERNING THE STATUES 2.8.[41]

2:11 *Like a Father with His Children*

THEN A NURSE, NOW A FATHER. PELAGIUS: Just as a nurse cherishes small children, now also as a father Paul instructs the Thessalonians to increase their abilities and effectiveness as Christians. PELAGIUS'S COMMENTARY ON THE FIRST LETTER TO THE THESSALONIANS.[42]

---

[41]NPNF 1 9:352-53*. [42]PETE 423*.

2:13-20 THE INTEGRITY OF THE PREACHER

[13]*And we also thank God constantly for this, that when you received the word of God which you heard from us, you accepted it not as the word of men but as what it really is, the word of God, which is at work in you believers.* [14]*For you, brethren, became imitators of the churches of God in Christ Jesus which are in Judea; for you suffered the same things from your own countrymen as they did from the Jews,* [15]*who killed both the Lord Jesus and the prophets, and drove us out, and displease God and oppose all men* [16]*by hindering us from speaking to the Gentiles that they may be saved—so as always to fill up the measure of their sins. But God's wrath has come upon them at last!*[b]

[17]*But since we were bereft of you, brethren, for a short time, in person not in heart, we endeavored the more eagerly and with great desire to see you face to face;* [18]*because we wanted to come to you—I, Paul, again and again—but Satan hindered us.* [19]*For what is our hope or joy or crown of boasting before our Lord Jesus at his coming? Is it not you?* [20]*For you are our glory and joy.*

b Or *completely*, or *for ever*

OVERVIEW: Paul intends here to make it clear that because his preaching contained no flattery or vanity, the Thessalonians received it gladly and have been properly fortified for the suffering that belongs to discipleship (CHRYSOSTOM, AUGUSTINE). Paul shows that it is not just great eloquence but faithful deeds that prove the truth of the gospel (Chrysostom). Both Paul's extraordinary gifts and his endurance of great hardship demonstrated to the Thessalonians that his words were inspired (Augustine). The glory and delight of preachers arise from the readiness and eagerness of their listeners to believe and to endure suffering (Origen, Athanasius, Jerome).

2:13 Not as the Word of Men but the Word of God

The Word of God Incarnate in the Words of Men. Augustine: We may compare the manner in which our own word is made as it were the speech produced by our body, through assuming that speech as a means of displaying itself to human senses, with the assumption of flesh by the Word of God as a means of displaying himself to human senses. Even as our human words are human thoughts not yet not changed into speech, so the Word of God was made flesh, but most assuredly not changed into flesh. Our words become vocalized. So the divine Word becomes flesh by an assumption of the outward form and not by a transformation of one thing into another. He, therefore, who desires to arrive at some sort of likeness— unlike as it must be at many points—of the Word of God, should not regard as final the human word that sounds upon the ear, either in its vocal utterance or in the unspoken thinking of it. The words of every audible language may also be the subject of thought without being vocalized. Poems may be repeated mentally, while the bodily mouth remains silent. Not only the series of syllables but the notes of tunes, material as they are, and addressed to the material sense which we call hearing, may be presented through their material images to the thinking mind which rehearses them all in silence. We must go beyond all this to arrive at the human word which may furnish some small measure of likeness for comprehending, as in an enigma, the Word of God. We speak here not of that word which came to one or another of the prophets, of which it is said that "the word of God grew and multiplied"[1]; or again that "faith comes of hearing, and hearing through the word of Christ"[2]; or again: "when you received from us the word of the hearing of God, you received it not as the word of men but as it is in truth, the word of God." There are numberless instances in the Scriptures where similar statements are made about the word of God, which is scattered in the sounds of many different languages through the hearts and minds of men. But it is called the word of God, therefore, because a divine and not a human doctrine is handed down. On the Trinity 15.11.20.[3]

Faith Begins Only When God Elects. Augustine: Is it not apparently the beginning of the Thessalonians' faith for which this same apostle thanks God, when he says, "Therefore, we also give thanks to God without ceasing, because when you had received the word which you heard from us, you received it not as the word of men, but (as it truly is) the word of God, which works in you, in which you have believed"? Why does he give thanks here to God? Certainly, it would be vain and meaningless if the person to whom he gives thanks for something is not the person who did it. But since this is not vain and meaningless, then certainly God, to whom he gives thanks for this work, is the one who brought it about that the Thessalonians, when they had received from the apostle the word by hearing it, received it not as the word of men but, as it truly is, as the word of God. Therefore, God works in the hearts of men, by that calling which is according to his purpose and of which we have said much, so that they would not hear the gospel in vain. On the Predestination of the Saints 19.39.[4]

---

[1]Acts 6:7. [2]Rom 10:17. [3]FC 45:477-78*. [4]FC 86:266*.

2:14 For You Suffered the Same Things

THE SUFFERING OF ALL PROPHETS. ORIGEN: "But Jesus said unto them, A prophet is not without honor, save in his own country."[5] We must inquire whether the expression has the same force when applied universally to every prophet (as if all prophets are dishonored in their own country). Or, it may be the case that because the expression "a prophet" is in the singular, these things were said only about one. If, then, these words are spoken about one person, these things which have been said suffice, if we refer that which was written to the Savior. But if it is a general principle in view, it is not historically true; for Elijah was not dishonored in Tishbeth of Gilead, nor Elisha in Abelmeholah, nor Samuel in Ramathaim, nor Jeremiah in Anathoth. But figuratively interpreted, it is absolutely true; for we must think of Judea as their country and Israel as their kindred and perhaps of the body as the house.[6] For all suffered dishonor in Judea from the Israel which is according to the flesh, while they were yet in the body. Thus it is written in the Acts of the Apostles, as Stephen censured the people, "Which of the prophets did not your fathers persecute, who appeared before of the coming of the Righteous One?"[7] And Paul says similar things in his first letter to the Thessalonians: "For you brethren became imitators of the churches of God which are in Judaea in Christ Jesus, for you also suffered the same things of your own countrymen even as they did of the Jews, who both killed the Lord Jesus and the prophets, and drove us out, and please not God, and are contrary to all men." COMMENTARY ON MATTHEW 10.18.[8]

THE NEED TO TAKE CHANCES. CHRYSOSTOM: Are we worthy, then, so much as even to mention the name of Paul? He had, in addition, the help of grace, yet did not presume that grace eliminated the need to take chances. We, on the other hand, who are destitute of the confidence grace brings, on what basis, tell me, do we expect either to preserve those who are committed to our charge or to gain those who have not come to the fold? We, indeed, are those who have been making a study of self-indulgence, who are searching the world over for ease and who are unable or rather unwilling to endure the slightest hint of danger. We are as far distant from Paul's wisdom as earth is from heaven. So it is, too, that they who are under us fall so far short of the men of those days. The reason is that the disciples of those days were better than the teachers of the present, isolated as they were in the midst of the populace, tyrants, surrounded by enemies on all sides, and yet not in the slightest degree dragged down or giving up. Hear at least what Paul says to the Philippians[9]: "Because to you it has been granted in the behalf of Christ, not only to believe on him but also to suffer in his behalf." And again to the Thessalonians, "For you, brethren, became imitators of the churches of God which are in Judea." . . . And you see them too, all employed in doing good. And so in those days grace worked effectually, and they also lived in good works. HOMILIES ON EPHESIANS 6.[10]

CHRIST AS THE MODEL FOR FAITHFUL ENDURANCE. CHRYSOSTOM: There is something more in the statement "as they also did in Judea." It shows that everywhere they rejoiced when they contended nobly for the faith. Paul says therefore, "that you also suffered the same things." And again, what wonder is it if you receive the same abuse when they dared to do the same things to the Lord himself? Do you see

---

[5]Mt 13:57. [6]That is, Origen is saying that the region from which we come, the nation to which we belong and even the physical body in which we dwell constitute together "our native country." It is in this context that every prophet experiences dishonor and that the Scripture cited at the beginning of the passage has universal application. The reference to the physical body is part of Origen's sense, shared by many of the Fathers, that life in the body is our native habitat, so to speak, but also a kind of alienation and exile from our true home and thus a place where dishonor is bound to happen once a person becomes a prophet, that is, speaks out against the "flesh." [7]Acts 7:52. [8]ANF 9:425*. [9]Phil 1:29. [10]NPNF 1 13:78*.

how Paul introduces this truth as containing great consolation? And how constantly he focuses our attention on it. Upon a close examination one may find it in nearly all his letters, how variously, upon all occasions of temptation, Paul brings forward Christ. Observe accordingly, that here also, when accusing the Jews, Paul puts them in mind of the Lord and of the sufferings of the Lord. Well does he know that this is a matter of the greatest consolation. Homilies on 1 Thessalonians 3.[11]

2:18 But Satan Hindered Us

Hardship Permitted for the Sake of Future Reward. Chrysostom: You, too, when you are about to perform any duty for God, expect manifold dangers, punishments, deaths. Don't be surprised or disturbed if such things happen. For it is said, "My Son, if you come to serve the Lord, prepare your soul for temptation."[12] For surely no one choosing to fight, expects to carry off the crown without wounds! And you, therefore, who have decided to wage full combat with the devil, don't think to pursue such a life without danger, expecting luxury instead! God has not pledged to you his recompense and promise for this life. These splendid things await you in the future life! Be glad and rejoice then, if when you have yourself done any good action, you receive evil in return . . . inasmuch as your suffering is the source of a higher recompense! . . . We see Paul in prison, yes, even in chains, instructing and initiating. He does the very same in a court of justice, in shipwreck, in tempest and in a thousand dangers. You also imitate these saints, and as long as you are able continue in your good works. Although you see the devil thwarting you ten thousand times, never fall back! Perhaps you have lost your wealth in a shipwreck. Remember Paul, carrying God's word, a message far more precious than all material wealth, was traveling to Rome and was wrecked, and sustained innumerable hardships. And this principle he himself signified when he said, "Many times we desired to come to you, but Satan hindered us." And God permitted it, thus revealing more abundantly his power. Homilies on the Statues 1.30.[13]

The Thorn in the Flesh. Jerome: Paul, the chosen vessel, chastised his body and brought it into subjection, lest after preaching to others he himself should be found a reprobate. He relates that there was given to him "a thorn in the flesh, a messenger of Satan to buffet him."[14] And to the Corinthians he writes: "But I am afraid that as the serpent deceived Eve by his cunning, your thoughts will be led astray from a sincere and pure devotion to Christ."[15] And elsewhere he says, "Any one whom you forgive, I also forgive. What I have forgiven, if I have forgiven anything, has been for your sake in the presence of Christ, to keep Satan from gaining the advantage over us, for we are not ignorant of his designs."[16] And again, "No temptation has overtaken you that is not common to man, but God is faithful, and he will not let you be tempted beyond your strength; but with the temptation will also provide the way of escape, that you may be able to endure it."[17] And "Let anyone who thinks that he stands take heed lest he fall."[18] And to the Galatians, "You were running well; who hindered you from obeying the truth?"[19] And elsewhere: "We greatly desired to have come unto you, I Paul once and again; and Satan hindered us." Against Jovinian 2.3.[20]

2:19 Our Hope or Joy or Crown

The Basis of Paul's Zeal. Athanasius: For we ought to walk by the standard of the saints and the fathers, and imitate them, and to be sure that if we depart from them we put ourselves also out of their fellowship. Whom then do they

---

[11]NPNF 1 13:333*. [12]Eccles 2:1. [13]NPNF 1 9:342-43*. [14]2 Cor 12:7. [15]2 Cor 11:3. [16]2 Cor 2:10-11. [17]1 Cor 10:13. [18]1 Cor 10:12. [19]Gal 5:7. [20]NPNF 2 6:388-89*. The point here is to show how persistently Satan hinders us.

wish you to imitate? The one who hesitated, and while wishing to follow, delayed the decision and took counsel because of his family?[21] Or blessed Paul, who, the moment the stewardship was entrusted to him, "did not immediately consult with flesh and blood"? For although he said, "I am not worthy to be called an apostle,"[22] yet, knowing what he had received and fully aware of the giver, he wrote, "For woe is me if I do not preach the gospel."[23] But, as it was "woe to me" if he did not preach, so, in teaching and preaching the gospel, he had his converts as his joy and crown. This explains why the saint was zealous to preach as far as Illyricum and did not shrink from proceeding to Rome[24] or even going as far as the Spains,[25] in order that the more he labored, he might receive so much the greater reward for his labor. He boasted then that he had fought the good fight and was confident that he should receive the great crown.[26] LETTERS TO DRACONTIUS 49.4.[27]

THE WELL-BEING OF THE NEIGHBOR OUR TRUE CROWN. CHRYSOSTOM: He who will not seek in the well-being of his neighbor his own benefit will not attain to the crown for this reason: God himself has so decided that human beings should be mutually bound together. When one awakens a sleeping child and asks him to follow his brother, left to himself he is often unwilling. If, however, we place in his brother's hand an object the child desires, he will pursue his brother to obtain what he desires. It is the same case here. God has placed our benefit in the hand of our neighbor so that we will pursue one another and not be torn apart.

If you wish, apply this illustration to the one who addresses you today. For my benefit depends on you, as yours does on me. Thus, on the one hand, it is to your profit to be taught the things that please God, for these things have been entrusted to me that you might receive them from me and therefore might be compelled to run to me. On the other hand, it is to my benefit that

you should be made better: for the reward which I shall receive for this will be great. This again, however, lies in you; and therefore am I compelled to follow after you that you may improve and that I may profit from your improvement. And so also Paul says, "For what is my hope? Are not you that?" And again, "My hope and my joy, and the crown of my rejoicing." HOMILIES ON FIRST CORINTHIANS 33.3.[28]

THE GOOD TEACHER. PELAGIUS: Good teachers are accustomed to locate every hope and joy and crown in the progress of their students. PELAGIUS'S COMMENTARY ON THE FIRST LETTER TO THE THESSALONIANS.[29]

THE NEW BISHOP'S EARNEST DESIRE. LEO THE GREAT: I beg you, therefore, "by the mercy of the Lord,"[30] help with your prayers the one for whom you have voted with your desires. Pray that the "Spirit" of grace "might remain in me"[31] and that you might not begin to reconsider your decision. May the one who has instilled in you an eager longing for agreement provide for us all the shared benefit of peace. I could then be made fit for serving almighty God and for surrendering myself to you for the rest of my life, entreating the Lord with confidence, "Holy Father, keep in your name the ones you have given me."[32] While you continually make progress toward salvation, "my soul could" then "proclaim the greatness of the Lord."[33] In the compensation of the judgment that is to come, the reckoning of my priesthood could take its stand before the just Judge in such a way that, through your good works, "you" might be "a joy" to me, and "you a crown."[34] You have already given sincere testimony about the present life by your good will. SERMONS 1.2.[35]

---

[21]Lk 9:61. [22]1 Cor 15:9. [23]1 Cor 9:16. [24]Rom 1:15. [25]Rom 15:19, 28. [26]Cf. 2 Tim 4:7-8. [27]NPNF 2 4:559*. [28]NPNF 1 12:197*. [29]PETE 425. [30]Rom 12:1. [31]1 Jn 3:24. [32]Jn 17:11. [33]Lk 1:46. [34]See also Phil 4:1. [35]FC 93:18-19.

The True Pastor's Only Defense. Gregory of Nazianzus: What then is my defense? If it be false, you must convict me. But if true, you on behalf of whom and in whose presence I speak, must bear witness to it. For you are my defense, my witnesses and my crown of rejoicing, if I also may venture to boast myself a little in the apostle's language. This flock was, when it was small and poor, as far as appearances went, no, not even a flock, but only a trace and relic of a flock, without order, shepherd or boundaries, with neither the right to pasture nor the defense of a sheepfold. Instead, you were wandering upon the mountains, in caves and dens of the earth, scattered and dispersed hither and yon as each one could find shelter or pasture or could gratefully secure its own safety. . . . Such then was the condition of this flock. Now it is so healthy and well grown that if it is not yet perfect, it is advancing toward perfection by constant growth, and I prophesy that it will advance. Orations 42.2, 6.[36]

---

[36]NPNF 2 7:386, 388*.

3:1-13 PAUL'S TRAVAIL AND CONSOLATION

¹*Therefore when we could bear it no longer, we were willing to be left behind at Athens alone, ²and we sent Timothy, our brother and God's servant in the gospel of Christ, to establish you in your faith and to exhort you, ³that no one be moved by these afflictions. You yourselves know that this is to be our lot. ⁴For when we were with you, we told you beforehand that we were to suffer affliction; just as it has come to pass, and as you know. ⁵For this reason, when I could bear it no longer, I sent that I might know your faith, for fear that somehow the tempter had tempted you and that our labor would be in vain.*

⁶*But now that Timothy has come to us from you, and has brought us the good news of your faith and love and reported that you always remember us kindly and long to see us, as we long to see you—⁷for this reason, brethren, in all our distress and affliction we have been comforted about you through your faith; ⁸for now we live, if you stand fast in the Lord. ⁹For what thanksgiving can we render to God for you, for all the joy which we feel for your sake before our God, ¹⁰praying earnestly night and day that we may see you face to face and supply what is lacking in your faith?*

¹¹*Now may our God and Father himself, and our Lord Jesus, direct our way to you; ¹²and may the Lord make you increase and abound in love to one another and to all men, as we do to you, ¹³so that he may establish your hearts unblamable in holiness before our God and Father, at the coming of our Lord Jesus with all his saints.*

Overview: Paul emphasizes the intimacy and fond love of his relationship with the Thessalonians in order to draw them more deeply into the mystery of suffering and its place in Christian discipleship (Chrysostom). Paul wants the Thessalonians to know that their steadfastness in faith is life itself for him (Theodore). It is their growing or progressing in faith that is his life (Chrysostom, Theodoret). In sending Timothy to them, Paul is letting them know that there is more that they need to know, if they wish to grow toward perfection (Theodoret). The dominant note here is that of praise and thanksgiving: for the maturity which the Thessalonians manifest, for their blessing of the Lord by their steadfastness and by the example they provide for others (Augustine).

3:1 When We Could Bear It No Longer

God Permits Hardship. Chrysostom: "Therefore when we could bear it no longer, we were willing to be left at Athens alone. And Paul sent two of those who ministered to him," both to announce his coming and to make them more eager. . . . Do you see how God permits trials, and by them stirs up and awakens the disciples and makes them more energetic? Then let us not sink down under trials: for he himself will "also make the way of escape, that we may be able to bear them."[1] Nothing so makes friends and rivets them so firmly as affliction; nothing so fastens and joins the souls of believers; nothing is so timely for us teachers in order that the things said by us may be heard. For when the hearer is living an easy life, listless and indolent, those who try to teach him only annoy him. But when he is in affliction and distress, he longs to hear his teachers. For when he is distressed in his soul, he seeks comfort from all directions in his affliction. And the preaching brings no small comfort. Homilies on the Acts of the Apostles 42.[2]

3:2 We Sent Timothy

Proper Assistantship. Theodoret of Cyr: Whenever anything happens to the helmsman, either the officer in command at the bows or the seaman of highest rank takes his place, not because he becomes a self-appointed helmsman but because he looks out for the safety of the ship. So again in war, when the commander falls, the chief tribune assumes the command, not in the attempt to lay violent hands on the place of power but because he cares for his men. So too the thrice blessed Timothy when sent by the divine Paul took his place. It is, therefore, appropriate to you as a man of faith to accept the responsibilities of helmsman, of captain, of shepherd, gladly to run all risk for the sake of the sheep of Christ and not to leave his creatures abandoned and alone. Letters 78.[3]

3:3 Moved by These Afflictions

Fear for the Leader. Chrysostom: What, then, does Paul say here? The teachers' trials trouble their disciples. Paul had fallen into many tribulations. He himself also says, that "Satan hindered us."[4] Paul adds immediately "both once" and "and again I would have come to you" and was not able, words that prove the depth of his struggle. And it was reasonable that this should trouble them, for they are not so much troubled at their own trials as at those of their teachers. Neither is the soldier so much troubled at his own struggles as when he sees his general wounded. Homilies on 1 Thessalonians 3.[5]

Be Cheered by My Suffering. Chrysostom: "Therefore I ask that you not be discouraged by my tribulations for you, which are your glory."[6] How are Paul's tribulations "for them"? How are they "their glory"? It is because God so loved them that he gave even the Son for them and afflicted his servants for them. Paul was in prison so that they might attain so many blessings. Surely this comes from God's exceeding

---

[1]1 Cor 10:13. [2]NPNF 1 11:259-61*. [3]NPNF 2 3:274*. [4]1 Thess 2:19. [5]NPNF 1 13:335*. [6]Eph 3:13.

love toward them. It illustrates what God also says concerning the prophets, "I have slain them by the word of my mouth."[7] But why were they fainting through another's affliction? He means they were troubled and distressed. Paul says the same things when writing to the Thessalonians: "that no one be moved by these afflictions." For we should rejoice in afflictions rather than grieve in them. If you find consolation in being warned beforehand, we tell you that here we have tribulation. And why you ask? Because the Lord has ordered it so. HOMILIES ON EPHESIANS 7.[8]

NO GIVING IN TO PERSECUTORS. THEODORE OF MOPSUESTIA: Paul says that Timothy is coming to strengthen the Thessalonians with his words, stabilizing the thinking of the Thessalonians by his presence with them, lest they collapse under the weight of their tribulations. Paul describes this collapsing as a "commotion," being caught up in the passions of your persecutors. COMMENTARY ON 1 THESSALONIANS.[9]

SEVERIAN OF GABALA: Paul does not say that no one should occasionally grow weak with weariness but rather that no one should "stoop down" or bow to persecutors. PAULINE COMMENTARY FROM THE GREEK CHURCH.[10]

3:4 We Told You Beforehand

EXPECTING AFFLICTION. CHRYSOSTOM: You shouldn't be troubled, Paul says, for nothing strange, nothing contrary to expectation is happening. These words were sufficient to encourage them. Christ spoke to his disciples in the same way and for the same reason. For hear him saying, "Now I have told you before it came to pass, that when it has come to pass you may believe."[11] For greatly indeed, greatly does it tend to the comfort of others to have heard from their teachers what is to happen. It is the same for those who are sick. If their physicians explain what is happening and what to expect,

their anxiety is dramatically reduced. But if anything happens unexpectedly, as though beyond the physician's ability and knowledge, the patient is afflicted and troubled. It is much the same here. Paul knew beforehand and lets them know in advance that "we are about to be afflicted," "as it came to pass, and you know." He not only says that this came to pass but that he foretold many things, and they occurred as he predicted. "For we are appointed to these things." Hence, you shouldn't be troubled and disturbed about the past, nor even about the future. If any troubling thing should happen, "we are appointed for this very thing." HOMILIES ON 1 THESSALONIANS 3.[12]

3:8 For Now We Live

YOU ARE OUR LIFE. CHRYSOSTOM: Let us imagine a person occupying a place of honor in a king's court. He possesses vast wealth, great power, a birthplace excelling others, distinguished ancestors and the admiration of all people. Examine the matter. Is not this person more of a slave than all others? And let us compare him to not merely a slave but a slave's slave—for many servants have slaves. . . . But our circumstances are different. If one fares poorly, there are many to grieve with him. Should he obtain distinction, many to find pleasure with him. Not so with the apostle Paul. "For if one member suffers, all the members suffer; or if one member is honored, all the members rejoice."[13] Paul's words of admonition vary with the situation. "What is my hope or joy? Are not you it?" At another, "Now we live, if you stand fast in the Lord"; at another, "Out of much affliction and anguish of heart I wrote unto you"[14]; and "Who is weak, and I am not weak? Who is offended, and I burn not?"[15] HOMILIES ON MATTHEW 58.4-5.[16]

---

[7]Hos 6:5. [8]NPNF 1 13:81*. [9]*TEM* 2:17. [10]NTA 15:329. [11]Jn 14:29. [12]NPNF 1 13:335*. [13]1 Cor 12:26. [14]2 Cor 2:4. [15]2 Cor 11:29. [16]NPNF 1 10:362-63*.

HIS STUDENTS ARE EVERYTHING. CHRYSOSTOM: The attitude of a teacher should be such as to regard his disciples as everything. "Now we live," Paul says, "if you stand fast in the Lord." And again, "What is our hope, or joy, or crown of rejoicing? Is it not even you in the presence of our Lord Jesus Christ?"[17] You see Paul's concern in this matter, his regard for the good of his disciples, not less than for his own. For teachers ought to surpass natural parents, to be more zealous than they. And it is right for their children to show deep affection for them. For he says, "Obey those that rule over you, and submit yourselves; for they watch for your souls as they that must give account."[18] HOMILIES ON SECOND TIMOTHY 2.[19]

TOGETHER LET US BE ON GUARD. AUGUSTINE: This is why I am admonishing your graces and urging you in the Lord to think lightly, my brothers and sisters, of things present, which you can't carry with you when you die. Be on your guard against sin, on your guard against injustice of all sorts, on your guard against worldly appetites and greed. It is only then, you see, that our profit from you is undiminished and our reward full of joy in the Lord. I mean, we say what has to be said. We preach what has to be preached and absolve ourselves of our debt to the Lord in the Lord's sight. We haven't kept quiet about what we fear, and haven't kept quiet about what we love. So the sword of the Lord's vengeance, upon whomever it may fall, cannot blame the sentinel for failing at his post. Still, we don't want our reward to be assured with all of you being lost, but with all of you being found. The apostle Paul too was sure of his reward, and yet what did he say to the people? "Now we live, if you stand fast in the Lord." SERMONS 359.9.[20]

3:10 What Is Lacking in Your Faith

THE TRUTH OF FAITH PASTORALLY TAUGHT. AUGUSTINE: But every discourse on this topic,

where one's goal is that what is said may not only be believed but also understood and known, is burdensome for those still spiritually immature. These the apostle says are carnal, needing to be nourished with milk, as they do not have the strength to perceive such things and are more easily frustrated than fed. Because of this it happens that spiritual men do not in all circumstances refuse to discuss these things with the carnal, on account of the Catholic faith, which must be preached to all. Yet, having the desire to transmit some degree of truth to understandings not capable of a secure grasp, they take care to transmit these in a way that does not cause their discourse to be regarded with disdain and the truth contained therein to be completely ignored. Thus, in order to continue to nourish them despite their immaturity, [the apostle], writing to the Colossians, says, "Even if I am absent in body, in spirit I am with you, rejoicing and beholding your order and that which is lacking to your faith in Christ."[21] And to the Thessalonians, "Night and day," he says, "more abundantly praying that we may see your face and may supply the things that are lacking to your faith." TRACTATES ON JOHN 98.5.1.[22]

AN ENRICHMENT, NOT AN ADDITION. AUGUSTINE: Let the admonition of the most blessed apostle not depart from your hearts, "If anyone preaches to you a gospel besides that which you have received, let him be anathema."[23] He did not say "more than you received" but "besides that which you have received." For if he said the former, he himself would be prejudging himself, who desired to come to the Thessalonians that he might supply what things were lacking to their faith. But he who supplies adds to what was smaller, he does not

---

[17]1 Thess 2:19. [18]Heb 13:17. [19]NPNF 1 13:481*. [20]WSA 3/10:206*. [21]Col 2:5. Augustine here witnesses to a Latin text based on an underlying Greek word *hysterema* ("what is lacking") instead of *stereoma* ("steadfastness"), the accepted reading. [22]FC 90:212-13*. [23]Gal 1:9.

take away what was there. But he who goes beyond the rule of faith does not go forward in the way but goes back to the way. TRACTATES ON JOHN 98.7.4.[24]

3:11 Our God and Father and Our Lord Jesus

THEIR WORK IS ONE. AMBROSE: Again, this is said that you may know that the Father is, and the Son is, and that the work of the Father and the Son is one. Note the saying of the apostle, "Now may God himself, and our Father, and our Lord Jesus Christ direct our way to you." Both Father and Son are named, but there is unity of direction, because there is unity of power. So also in another place we read, "Now may our Lord himself, Jesus Christ, and God and our Father, who has loved us, and given us eternal consolation, and good hope in grace, console and strengthen your hearts."[25] How perfect a unity it is that the apostle presents to us, insomuch that the fountain of consolation is one fountain, not many. Let doubt be silenced, then, or if it will not be overcome by reason, let the thought of our Lord's gracious kindness incline it in the right direction. OF THE CHRISTIAN FAITH 2.10.87.[26]

THEIR GRACE IS ONE. ATHANASIUS: For one and the same grace is from the Father in the Son, as the light of the sun and the sun's radiance is one, and as the sun's illumination is effected through the radiance. So too when Paul prays for the Thessalonians, in saying, "Now God himself our Father, and the Lord Jesus Christ, may he direct our way to you," he has guarded the unity of the Father and of the Son. For he has not said, "May they direct," as if a double grace were given from two sources . . . but "May he direct," to show that the Father gives grace through the Son—at which these irreligious ones will not blush, though they well might. DISCOURSES AGAINST THE ARIANS 3.25.11.[27]

3:12 Increase and Abound in Love

THE UNRESTRAINED OVERFLOWING OF LOVE. CHRYSOSTOM: This is a proof of superabundant love, that he not only prays for them by himself but even inserts his prayer in his epistles. Paul's prayers demonstrate a fervent soul unable to restrain his love. The mention of his prayers also proves that Paul and Silvanus's failure to visit them was not voluntary nor the result of indolence. It is as though Paul said: May God himself shorten the trials that constantly distract us, so that we may come directly to you. "And the Lord make you to increase and abound." Do you see the unrestrained madness of love that is shown by these words? HOMILIES ON 1 THESSALONIANS 4.[28]

ALWAYS HIS LOVE FOR US FIRST. AUGUSTINE: Suppose we first loved him so as to merit his love in return. Then wouldn't we first choose him so as to merit our being chosen by him? But he who is Truth itself says otherwise and openly contradicts such human vanity by declaring, "You have not chosen me."[29] Consequently, if it is not you who have chosen, then it is certainly not you who have loved; for how could they choose him whom they did not love? "But it is I," he says, "who have chosen you." And how could they possibly fail to choose him afterward or fail to prefer him to all the goods of this world? It was because they were chosen that they chose him. They were not chosen because they had chosen him. There would be no merit in men's choosing him unless the action of God's grace in choosing them had gone before. That is why in imparting his blessing to the Thessalonians the apostle Paul declares, "And may the Lord make you to in-crease and abound in charity toward

---

[24]FC 90:216*. [25]2 Thess 2:15-16. [26]NPNF 2 10:235*. [27]NPNF 2 4:400*. [28]NPNF 1 13:341*. [29]Jn 15:16.

one another and toward all men." He who gave this blessing to love one another is the same who gave us the love to love one another.

Grace and Free Will 38.[30]

[30]FC 59:294.

4:1-12 EXHORTATION TO GODLY FAITH AND LOVE

[1]*Finally, brethren, we beseech and exhort you in the Lord Jesus, that as you learned from us how you ought to live and to please God, just as you are doing, you do so more and more.* [2]*For you know what instructions we gave you through the Lord Jesus.* [3]*For this is the will of God, your sanctification: that you abstain from unchastity;* [4]*that each one of you know how to take a wife for himself[x] in holiness and honor,* [5]*not in the passion of lust like heathen who do not know God;* [6]*that no man transgress, and wrong his brother in this matter,[c] because the Lord is an avenger in all these things, as we solemnly forewarned you.* [7]*For God has not called us for uncleanness, but in holiness.* [8]*Therefore whoever disregards this, disregards not man but God, who gives his Holy Spirit to you.*

[9]*But concerning love of the brethren you have no need to have any one write to you, for you yourselves have been taught by God to love one another;* [10]*and indeed you do love all the brethren throughout Macedonia. But we exhort you, brethren, to do so more and more,* [11]*to aspire to live quietly, to mind your own affairs, and to work with your hands, as we charged you;* [12]*so that you may command the respect of outsiders, and be dependent on nobody.*

x *Or how to control his own body* c *Or defraud his brother in business*

Overview: Paul emphasizes that faithful Christian discipleship is a matter of active love in which the believer goes beyond a mere avoidance of evil (Chrysostom). Paul now moves to instruction that will aid the Thessalonians in seeking the perfection of mature faith and practice, particularly in abstention from all forms of fornication (Pseudo-Cyprian, Augustine, Theodore). Though Paul has been careful to praise the Thessalonians, now he moves to warning and admonition lest they be led astray by false teaching (Chrysostom, Ambrosiaster, John Cassian). The Christian life is by its very nature a growth process analogous to the growth of the body; perfection in good habits ought to grow as faith grows (Clement of Alexandria, Ambrose).

4:1 *How You Ought to Live and to Please God*

One Proper Anxiety. Chrysostom: There is only one calamity for a Christian, this being disobedience to God. All the other things, such as loss of property, exile, peril of life, Paul does not even consider a grievance at all. And that which all dread, departure from this life to the other world—this is to him sweeter than life itself. For as when one has climbed to the top of a cliff and gazes on the sea and those who are sailing upon it, he sees some being washed by the waves, others running upon hidden rocks, some hurrying in one direction, others being driven in another, like prisoners, by the force of the gale. Many are actually in the water, some of them using their hands only in the place of a boat and a rudder, and many drifting along upon a single plank or some fragment of the vessel, others floating dead. He witnesses a scene of manifold and various disasters. Even so he who is engaged in the service of Christ draws himself out of the turmoil and stormy billows of life and takes his seat upon secure and lofty ground. For what position can be loftier or more secure than that in which a man has only one anxiety, "How he ought to please God"? Have you seen the ship-wrecks, Theodore, of those who sail upon this sea? Letters to the Fallen Theodore 2.4.[1]

4:3 The Will of God, Your Sanctification

An Educational Process. Clement of Alexandria: For the devil tempts us. He knows what we are but does not know if we will hold out. Wishing to dislodge us from the faith, he also attempts to bring us into subjection to himself. This tempting is all that God has allowed him to do, partly because it is God's will to save us from ourselves. For indeed, by the opportunity afforded by the commandment we are truly sinners.[2] But the other reason God so limits the devil is to disgrace him and show him up as a failure, thereby strengthening the church and the conscience of those who are awed at such constancy. . . . The Lord did not suffer by the will of the Father, nor are those who are per-secuted persecuted by the will of God. Indeed, either of two things is the case: persecution in consequence of the will of God is a good thing, or, those who decree and inflict suffering are guiltless. But nothing is without the will of the Lord of the universe. It remains to say that such things happen without the prevention of God. Only this way of thinking about suffering saves both the providence and the goodness of God.

We must not think therefore that he actively produces afflictions (far be it that we should think this!) . . . Providence is a disciplinary art—in the case of others for each individual's sins, and in the case of the Lord and his apostles for ours. To this point the divine apostle prays: "For this is the will of God, even your sanctifica-tion." Stromata 4.12.[3]

The Sanctity of Marriage. Pseudo-Cyprian: The cardinal principles of chastity, brothers, are ancient. How so? Because they were ordained at the same time as the human race itself. For both her own husband belongs to the woman, for the reason that she may know no other besides him, and because the woman is given to the man. This latter is in order that, when what is his own has been given to him, he should seek nothing belonging to another. . . . Christ gave this judgment when, having been questioned, he said that a wife must not be put away except because of adultery. Thus did he honor chastity. From this has come the levitical decree, "You shall not allow adulteresses to live."[4] Therefore, the apostle says, "This is the will of God, your sanctification, that you abstain from fornication." On the Discipline and Advantage of Chastity 5-6.[5]

Proper Humility. Gregory the Great: It is said through the voice of the prophet to the soul that grows proud, "You trusted in your beauty and played the harlot because of your

---

[1]NPNF 1 9:115*. [2]Clement here reproduces a phrase from Romans 7:11 that is inevitably obscure literally, "For sin, finding opportunity in the commandment, deceived me and by it killed me." [3]ANF 2:424-25*. Clement is here arguing, in anti-Gnostic fashion, against the view of the teacher Basilides that suffering and martyrdom are a kind of punishment that souls must undergo in order to be freed from the gross prisonhouse of the body. On the contrary, says Clem-ent, suffering and martyrdom are used by God, who wishes salvation for all of his creatures, as a means to their sanctification. Thus suffer-ing belongs to the goodness of a world governed by God's provi-dence, though it is not directly willed by God. [4]Lev 20:10. [5]ANF 5:589*. Traditionally but doubtfully attributed to Cyprian.

renown."[6] For a soul to trust in its beauty is to presume within itself on its righteous works. It plays the harlot on the basis of its renown when in its righteous acts it seeks the glory of its own reputation rather than the spread of its Creator's praise. . . . What then is to be done in this case but that, when the malignant spirit of pride enjoys the good things that we have done in order to exalt the mind, we should ever recall to memory our evil deeds. The goal is that we may acknowledge our sinful acts as our own and our avoidance of sin as the gift of Almighty God. And so Paul says, "For this is the will of God, even your sanctification, that you abstain from unchastity." LETTERS 122.[7]

LAWFUL MARRIAGE. AUGUSTINE: The disease of disordered desire is what the apostle refers to, when, speaking to married believers, he says, "This is the will of God, even your sanctification, that you should abstain from fornication, that everyone of you should know how to possess his vessel in sanctification and honor, not in the disease of desire, even as the Gentiles who do not know God." The married believer, therefore, must not only not use another man's vessel—which is what they do who lust after other men's wives—but he must know that even his own vessel is not to be possessed in the disease of disordered sexual desire. Paul's counsel is not to be understood as if the apostle prohibited conjugal—that is to say, lawful and honorable—cohabitation. ON MARRIAGE AND CONCUPISCENCE 1.8.9.[8]

4:4 A Wife for Himself in Holiness

THE HONORABLE VESSEL. TERTULLIAN: It is quite possible to pass decisive sentences on vessels and on instruments, to the extent that they participate in the merits of their proprietors and employers. . . . For every vessel or every instrument becomes useful by external manipulation, consisting as it does of material which is quite extraneous to the substance of the human owner or employer. However, the flesh, being conceived, formed and generated along with the soul from its earliest existence in the womb, is mixed up with the soul[9] likewise in all of its operations. For, although it is called "a vessel" by the apostle,[10] such as he commands to be treated "with honor," yet it is designated by the same apostle as "the outward man."[11] This is the clay, of course, which at first was inscribed with the title of a man, not of a cup, or a sword or any common vessel. THE RESURRECTION OF THE FLESH 16.[12]

GOOD CULTIVATION. AMBROSE: Warn the Lord's people, therefore, and beg them to abound in good works, to renounce vice, not to enkindle the fires of passion—I shall not say on the sabbath, but in every season. Let them not destroy their bodies. Let there be no immorality and uncleanness in the servants of God, because we are the servants of the unblemished Son of God.[13] Let each one know himself and possess his vessel, and when the soil of the body has been ploughed, let him wait for the fruit in due season. Let his hand not cultivate thorns and thistles.[14] Rather let him, too, say, "Our earth has yielded her fruit,"[15] and in the bodily passions that might once have been seen as being like thick and wild woods let there be seen the calm order of virtues that have been grafted onto each tree. LETTERS 15.[16]

TEMPERATE USE THE KEY. CHRYSOSTOM: We must diligently learn to avoid sexual immorality. But we "possess" our vessel, when it is pure;

---

[6]Ezek 16:15. [7]NPNF 2 13:36*. [8]NPNF 1 5:267*. [9]Tertullian here appeals to the Stoic doctrine of *krasis*, or "mixing," in which the elements that constitute a composite entity have a kind of interpenetration that allows them to share properties. Thus soul has some of the qualities of body and may be thought of as material, even though as body and soul these two, strictly speaking, are separate. Likewise, "vessels" may share in the honor of that which they contain. [10]Modern exegetes continue to be divided as to whether the Greek *skeuos* is best translated as "vessel" or "wife." [11]2 Cor 4:16. [12]ANF 3:556*. [13]Eph 5:3. [14]Gen 3:18. [15]Ps 84:13. [16]FC 26:79*.

when it is impure, sin possesses it. . . . For it does not do the things which we wish, but what sin commands. "Not in the passion of lust," Paul says. Here he shows also the manner of moderation. By moderation we should channel the passions of lust. For luxury, wealth, idleness, sloth, ease and all similar things lead to irregularity of lust within us. Homilies on 1 Thessalonians 5.[17]

Lust as Disordered Will. Augustine: There are, then, many kinds of lusts for this or that, but when the word is used by itself without specification it suggests to most people the lust for sexual excitement. Such lust does not merely invade the whole body and outward members. It takes such complete and passionate possession of the whole man, both physically and emotionally, that what results is the keenest of all pleasures on the level of sensation. And at the crisis of excitement, it practically paralyzes all power of deliberate thought.

This is so true that it creates a problem for every lover of wisdom and holy joys, who is both committed to a married life and also conscious of the apostolic ideal, that every one should "learn how to possess his vessel in holiness and honor, not in the passion of lust like the Gentiles who do not know God." Any such person would prefer, if this were possible, to beget his children without suffering disordered passion. He could wish that, just as all his other members obey his reason in the performance of their appointed tasks, so the genital organs, too, might function in obedience to the orders of will and not be inordinately excited by the ardors of lust. The City of God 14.16.[18]

4:6-7 The Lord Is an Avenger

Wronging the Brother. Chrysostom: To each man God has assigned a wife. He has set boundaries on nature and limits sexual intercourse to one person only. Therefore, intercourse with another is transgression, and taking more than belongs to one, and robbery. Or rather it is more cruel than any robbery; for we grieve less when robbed of our riches than when our marriage is invaded. Do you call him a brother and yet wrong him, and that in things which are unlawful? . . . Paul does not mean by the use of the word *brother* that we are free to sleep with the wife of an unbeliever. Paul shows God will avenge and punish such an act, not to avenge the unbeliever but to avenge himself. Why? You have insulted God. He himself called you, and you in turn have insulted him. Whether you sleep with the empress or your married handmaid, it makes no difference. The crime is the same. Why? Because he does not avenge the injured persons but himself. Homilies on 1 Thessalonians 5.[19]

4:8 Disregarding God

Grieving the Spirit. Chrysostom: "And don't grieve," he adds, "the Holy Spirit of God."[20] This is a terrible and startling matter, as he also says in the epistle to the Thessalonians. For there he uses an expression of this sort. "He that rejects, rejects not man, but God." It is the same here. If you utter a reproachful word, if you strike your brother, you are not striking him; rather you are "grieving the Holy Spirit." Homilies on Ephesians 14.[21]

4:9a You Have No Need to Have Anyone Write to You

The Wound of Spiritual Torpor. John Cassian: The blessed apostle, like a true and spiritual physician, either seeing this disease which springs from the spirit of lethargy already creeping in, or foreseeing through the Holy Spirit that it would arise among monks, is quick to anticipate it by the healing medicines of his

---

[17]NPNF 1 13:344*. [18]FC 14:388-89*. [19]NPNF 1 13:345*. [20]Eph 4:30. [21]NPNF 1 13:120*.

directions. For when he writes to the Thessalonians, he first sounds like a skillful and excellent physician, applying the soothing and gentle remedy of his words to the sickness of his patients. He begins with charity . . . that this deadly wound, having been treated with a milder remedy, might cease its angry festering and more easily bear severer treatment. He writes, "But concerning brotherly charity you have no need that I write to you, for you yourselves are taught of God to love one another. For this you do toward all the brothers in the whole of Macedonia." He first began with the soothing application of praise and made their ears submissive and ready for the remedy of the healing words. . . . At last with difficulty he breaks out into that at which he was driving before. He gave the first aim. "Take pains to be quiet." Then Paul adds a second: "Mind your own business." And a third as well: "Work with your own hands, as we commanded you." . . . [The upshot is] that one who does not dutifully and peacefully work for his daily food with his own hands is sure to view enviously another's gifts and blessings. You see what conditions, serious and shameful, may spring solely from the malady of leisure. INSTITUTES 10.7.[22]

4:9b Taught by God

GRACE FIRST. AUGUSTINE: It is through grace that we not only discover what ought to be done but also that we do what we have discovered. That is, not only that we believe what ought to be loved but also that we love what we have believed. If this grace is to be called "teaching," let it at any rate be called "teaching" in such a manner that God may be believed to infuse it, along with an ineffable sweetness, more deeply and more internally. This teaching, therefore, would be not only by their agency who plant and water from without but likewise by God also who ministers in secret his own increase. All this is in such a way that God not only exhibits truth but likewise imparts love. . . . Thus the apostle speaks to the Thessalonians, "As touching love of the brothers, you have no need that I write to you, for you yourselves have been taught by God to love one another." ON THE GRACE OF CHRIST 12.13-13.14.[23]

4:11 Work with Your Hands

THE HUMILITY OF MANUAL LABOR. BASIL THE GREAT: The Christian should not make a display of dress or shoes, as this is indeed idle ostentation.[24] He should use inexpensive clothing for his bodily needs. He should not spend anything beyond actual necessity or for mere extravagance. This is an abuse. He should not seek honor nor lay claim to the first place.[25] Each one ought to prefer all others to himself.[26] He ought not to be disobedient.[27] He who is idle, although able to work, should not eat.[28] Moreover, he who is occupied with some task which is rightly intended for the glory of Christ ought to limit himself to the pursuit of work within his ability. LETTERS 22.[29]

---

[22]NPNF 2 11:268-69*. [23]NPNF 1 5:222*. [24]Mt 6:29; Lk 12:27. [25]Cf. Mk 9:34. [26]Cf. Phil 2:3. [27]Cf. Tit 1:10. [28]Cf. 2 Thess 3:10. [29]FC 13:58*.[22]NPNF 2 11:268-69*. [23]NPNF 1 5:222*. [24]Mt 6:29; Lk 12:27. [25]Cf. Mk 9:34. [26]Cf. Phil 2:3. [27]Cf. Tit 1:10. [28]Cf. 2 Thess 3:10. [29]FC 13:58*.

4:13-18 JOY IN THE FACE OF DEATH

[13]*But we would not have you ignorant, brethren, concerning those who are asleep, that you may not grieve as others do who have no hope.* [14]*For since we believe that Jesus died and rose again, even so, through Jesus, God will bring with him those who have fallen asleep.* [15]*For this we declare to you by the word of the Lord, that we who are alive, who are left until the coming of the Lord, shall not precede those who have fallen asleep.* [16]*For the Lord himself will descend from heaven with a cry of command, with the archangel's call, and with the sound of the trumpet of God. And the dead in Christ will rise first;* [17]*then we who are alive, who are left, shall be caught up together with them in the clouds to meet the Lord in the air; and so we shall always be with the Lord.* [18]*Therefore comfort one another with these words.*

OVERVIEW: In our grieving over those who have died, God's intention is to teach us to trust in him alone, and so to cure us of earthly attachments (CHRYSOSTOM). Paul wishes the Thessalonians to know that their grieving and sadness over the dead is understandable but that it must not pass over into despondency and a lack of faith in God (THEODORE, CHRYSOSTOM, GREGORY THE GREAT). Paul's warning here is against immoderate or unbounded grief (AMBROSE, AUGUSTINE, FULGENTIUS). Christians are privileged to know that their deceased loved ones go to a blessed place, unlike the unbelieving dead, and in this fact they can rejoice (AMBROSE, JEROME).

4:13a Those Who Are Asleep

SLEEP AS METAPHOR OF DEATH. AUGUSTINE: In the Gospel it is written, "And the bridegroom tarrying, they all slept"?[1] If we understand that sleep as caused by the delay of the last judgment, to which Christ is to come to judge, and the fact that because iniquity has abounded, the charity of many grows cold,[2] how shall we put the wise virgins there, when they are rather of those of whom it is said, "But he that shall persevere to the end, he shall be saved"?[3] It says, "they all slept," because it is not only the foolish who do their good works for the sake of human

praise, but also the wise who do them that God may be glorified, who experience that death. Both kinds die. And that death is often spoken of in the Scripture as sleep, as the resurrection is called an awakening. Hence the apostle says, "But I will not have you ignorant, brothers, concerning them that are asleep," and in another place, "of whom many remain until this present, and some are fallen asleep."[4] LETTERS 140.32.76.[5]

SLEEP SIGNIFIES DEATH. CAESARIUS OF ARLES: In the Gospel passage which was read to us concerning the ten virgins, beloved brothers, it is said, "All the virgins trimmed their lamps."[6] Now the foolish virgins did not have oil ready with their lamps, "While the wise did take oil in their vessels. Then as the bridegroom was long in coming, they all became drowsy and slept. And at midnight a great cry arose, Behold the bridegroom is coming, go forth to meet him! Then all the virgins rose and trimmed their lamps."[7] When the lamps of the foolish virgins went out, they asked the others who had oil in their ves-

---

[1]Mt 25:5. Augustine and Caesarius view the sleep-as-death metaphor in relation to the parable of the Wise and Foolish Virgins (Mt 25:1-12). [2]Mt 24:12. [3]Mt 24:13. [4]1 Cor 15:6. [5]FC 20:126. [6]Mt 25:7. [7]Mt 25:4-7.

sels to give them some of theirs, but they said, "Lest there may not be enough for us and for you, go rather to those who sell it, and buy some for yourselves. Now while they were gone to buy it, the bridegroom came; and those who were ready went in with him to the marriage feast, and the door was shut. Afterwards there came the other virgins, who said, 'Sir, open the door for us!' The answer was given to them, 'I do not know where you are from.'"[8] Now what these facts signify, dearest brothers, we briefly suggest to your charity according to what we read in the exposition of the ancient fathers. They were not called five virgins because there was to be so small a number in eternal life, but because of the five senses through which death or life enters the soul. If we use them badly, we are corrupted, but if we steadfastly use them well, we preserve the purity of our soul. When it was said, "As the bridegroom was long in coming, they all became drowsy and slept,"[9] that sleep signified death. Finally, the apostle also speaks in the same way, "I would not, brothers, have you ignorant concerning those who are asleep." When a great cry arose, the middle of the night typified the day of judgment. It is called the middle of the night on account of human ignorance, since no one knows when or at what hour the day of judgment will come. SERMONS 156.1.[10]

PHILOXENUS OF MABBUG: "Brothers, I want you to know about those who sleep: you must not grieve like the rest of humanity, who have lost all hope." Our resurrection too will take place by the power of the Holy Spirit who is within us. Because the Holy Spirit is in faithful persons when they die, their death cannot be called death, but only sleep. ON THE INDWELLING OF THE HOLY SPIRIT.[11]

4:13b As Others Do Who Have No Hope

THE SIN OF EXCESSIVE GRIEF. CHRYSOSTOM: Here Paul now proceeds to start his discourse concerning the resurrection. And why? . . .

[Because] this subject of the resurrection was sufficient to comfort those who were grieving. Indeed that which Paul now teaches about the resurrection makes the resurrection eminently worthy of belief. . . . To continue to endure misery for the departed is to act like those who have no hope. Hear this, women, as many of you as are fond of wailing, as many as grieve impatiently; by doing so you act just like the heathens. Do you not grieve like a pagan when you beat yourself and tear your cheeks? Why do you lament if you believe that he will rise again, that he has not perished, that the matter is but a slumber or a sleep? You say, on account of his company, his protection, his care of our affairs, and all his other services. When, therefore, you lose a child at an untimely age, who is not yet able to do anything, on what account do you lament? Why do you seek to recall him? He was displaying, you say, good hopes, and I was expecting that he would support me financially. On this account I miss my husband, on this account my son, on this account I wail and lament, not believing the resurrection, but being left destitute of support, having lost my protector, my companion, who shared with me in all things—my comforter. . . . It is for these things that I afflict myself, for these things I wail. . . . But none of this is painful to us, if we are willing to cultivate wisdom. HOMILIES ON 1 THESSALONIANS 6.[12]

GREGORY THE GREAT: Still, lest some tribulation should still maintain itself in your soul, I exhort you to rest from sorrow, to cease to be sad. For it is unseemly to addict oneself to weary affliction for those of whom it is to be believed that they have attained to true life by dying. Those have, perhaps, just reason for long continued grief who are unaware of another life and have no trust that there is a passing from this world to a better one. We, however, who know

[8]Mt 25:9-11. [9]Mt 25:5. [10]FC 47:348-49*. [11]*SFPSL* 123**. [12]NPNF 1 13:349*.

this, who believe it and teach it, should not be too much distressed for those that depart, lest what in others demonstrates affection be to us instead a matter of blame. For it is, as it were, a kind of distrust to be tormented by sadness in opposition to what everyone preaches. It is as the apostle says, "But we would not have you ignorant, brothers, concerning those who are asleep, that you may not grieve as others do who have no hope." LETTERS 107.[13]

ON THE CONSCIOUSNESS OF THE FAITHFUL DEPARTED. AMBROSE: But if you again remind me of your grief because he departed so early from life, I certainly do not deny that he died at an untimely age, one whom we would have wished to support with time taken from our own life, that he might live out of our own years who could not complete his own. But I ask whether or not there is any consciousness after death? If there is, he is alive; no, rather, because there is, he now enjoys eternal life. For how does he not possess consciousness whose soul lives and flourishes and will return to the body, and will make that body live again when it has been reunited with it? The apostle cries out, "We would not, brothers, have you ignorant concerning those who are asleep, lest you should grieve, even as others who have no hope. For we believe that Jesus died and rose again, so with him God will bring those also who have fallen asleep through Jesus." Life, therefore, awaits them for whom resurrection awaits. CONSOLATION ON THE DEATH OF EMPEROR VALENTINIAN 43-44.[14]

FINAL REUNION. AUGUSTINE: And you should not grieve as the heathen do who have no hope, because we have hope, based on the most assured promise, that as we have not lost our dear ones who have departed from this life but have merely sent them ahead of us, so we also shall depart and shall come to that life where, more than ever, their dearness to us will be proportional to the closeness we shared on earth

and where we shall love them without fear of parting. LETTERS 92.1.1.[15]

SADNESS AND HOPE. AUGUSTINE: Paul didn't just say that you may not be saddened, but that you may not be saddened as the heathen are, who do not have any hope. It is unavoidable, after all, that you should be saddened; but when you feel sad, let hope console you. SERMONS 173.3.[16]

FULGENTIUS OF RUSPE: There must remain in our heart a distinction between a beneficial and a harmful sadness. The benefit of the distinction is that we see that a spirit given over to eternal things does not collapse because of the loss of temporal solace. Rather it is able to feel a salutary sadness concerning those things in which it considers that it acted either below, or apart from, the standard which it ought to have observed. So Paul teaches that each type of sadness is different, no less in deed than in word. Finally, he shows that in one there is progress toward salvation but in the other an ending in death, saying, "For godly sorrow produces a beneficial repentance without regret, but worldly sorrow produces death."[17] LETTERS 2.3.[18]

GOD'S GOOD PURPOSE. BASIL THE GREAT: All things are directed by the goodness of the Master. Nothing which happens to us should be received as distressful, although at present it affects our weakness. In fact, even if we are ignorant of the reasons for which each event is applied as a blessing to us from the Master, nevertheless, we ought to be convinced of this—that what happens is assuredly advantageous either for us as a reward for our patience or for the soul that was taken up, lest tarrying too long in this life it should be filled with the evil which exists in this world. For if the hope of Christians were limited to this life, for what reason would

---

[13]NPNF 2 13:27*. [14]FC 22:284-85. [15]FC 18:50*. [16]*WSA* 3/5:255*. [17]2 Cor 7:10. [18]FC 95:292*.

the premature separation from the body be considered difficult?[19] If, however, the beginning of true life for those living in God is the release of the soul from these corporeal chains, why do you grieve, even as those who have no hope? Therefore, be encouraged. Do not succumb to your afflictions, but show that you are superior and have risen above them. LETTERS 101.[20]

THE NATURAL AVERSION TO DEATH. GREGORY OF NYSSA: At the time that Basil, great among the saints, left the life of man and went to God, and a common onset of grief descended upon the churches, my sister and teacher was still alive, and I hurried to her to tell her the sad news about our brother. . . . She, however, like those who are skilled in the equestrian art, first allowed me to be swept along for a little while by the violence of my grief and, after this tried to restrain me, guiding the disorder of my soul with her own ideas as if with a bridle. She [Macrina] quoted the following apostolic saying: "It is not right to grieve for those who are asleep, since we are told that sorrow belongs only to those who have no hope." And I, with my heart still seething with pain, asked: "How is it possible for me to achieve this attitude, since there is a natural aversion to death in each person, and no one can endure the sight of others dying, and those who are dying themselves flee from it as much as they can?" ON THE SOUL AND THE RESURRECTION.[21]

4:14 God Will Bring with Him Those Who Have Fallen Asleep

ALL MUST DIE. AUGUSTINE: The apostle's words show with the utmost clarity that there will be a resurrection of the dead when Christ comes; and assuredly the purpose of his coming will be to judge the living and the dead. But it is continually being asked whether those whom Christ is to find living in this world (represented in the apostle's picture by himself and his contemporaries) are never to die at all, or whether

in that precise moment of time when they are caught up in the clouds, along with those rising again, to meet Christ in the air, they will pass with marvelous speed through death to immortality. For it must not be said that it is impossible for them to die and come to life again in that space of time when they are being carried on high through the air. . . . The apostle himself seems to demand that we should take his words in this sense; that is, we should take it that those whom the Lord will find alive here will undergo death and receive immortality in that brief space of time. He confirms this interpretation when he says, "In Christ all men will be brought to life,"[22] and by his statement in another passage, dealing directly with the resurrection of the body: "The seed you sow does not come to life unless it first dies."[23] THE CITY OF GOD 20.20.1-2.[24]

THE MEANING OF SLEEPING. AUGUSTINE: And after this he says to them, "Lazarus, our friend, is sleeping; but I am going that I may awaken him from sleep."[25] He spoke the truth. To the sisters he was dead; to the Lord he was sleeping. He was dead to men who were unable to raise him up; for the Lord roused him from the tomb with such ease as you would not rouse a sleeping person from his bed. Therefore, as regards his own power he spoke of him as sleeping; for other dead men, too, are often referred to in the Scriptures as sleeping, as the apostle says, "But I will not have you ignorant, brothers, about those who are asleep, so that you may not grieve, even as others who have no hope." And so he, too, called them sleeping, because he foretold that they would rise again. Therefore, every

---

[19]Basil seems to argue that considering how much evil one must endure in the course of an earthly life, wouldn't it be a blessing for those who do not believe in eternal life to depart from this world early? For us, however, who believe that the course of an earthly life is meant to teach many things through suffering, an early separation is a loss in terms of sanctification, even if it means, in a positive way, release from that suffering. [20]FC 13:225-26. [21]FC 58:198. [22]1 Cor 15:22. [23]1 Cor 15:36. [24]CG 935-36. [25]Jn 11:11.

dead man sleeps, both the good and the evil. Tractates on John 49.9.1-2.[26]

The Name of Death Abolished. Chrysostom: If, however, we are on the alert, these evils that came into life as a result of the sins of our forebears will in no way be able to harm us, going no further than the level of terminology, as they do. While it was the first formed human being who through the Fall brought on the punishment of death and was responsible for spending his life in pain and distress, and it was he who was the cause of servitude, Christ the Lord on the contrary came and permitted all these evils to occur only at the level of terminology, provided we are of the right mind. You see, death is now not death but only carries the name of death—or, rather, even the very name has been abolished. I mean, we no longer call it death, but sleeping and dreaming. Hence Christ himself said, "Our friend Lazarus is asleep."[27] And Paul, writing to the Thessalonians, said, "About those who are asleep, brethren, I don't want you to be ignorant." Homilies on Genesis 29.7.[28]

Jerome: Thus when we have to face the hard and cruel necessity of death, we are upheld by this consolation, that we shall shortly see again those whose absence we now mourn. For their end is not called death but a slumber and a falling asleep. Therefore the blessed apostle forbids us to feel sorrow concerning those who are asleep, telling us to believe that those whom we know to sleep now may hereafter be roused from their sleep. And when their slumber is ended, they may watch once more with the saints and sing with the angels, "Glory to God in the highest and on earth peace among men of good will."[29] Letters 75.1.[30]

4:14-15 Shall Not Precede

In His Own Order. Ambrose: All men shall rise again, but let no one lose heart, and let not the just grieve at the common lot of rising again, since he awaits the chief fruit of his virtue. All indeed shall rise again,[31] but, as says the apostle, "each in his own order." The fruit of the divine mercy is common to all, but the order of merit differs. The day gives light to all, the sun warms all, the rain fertilizes the possessions of all with genial flowers. We are all born, and we shall all rise again. But each shall be in his proper state, whether of living or living again, for grace differs and the condition differs. . . . Therefore he is aroused that he may live, that he may be like to Paul, that he may be able to say, "For we that are alive shall not precede those that are asleep." He speaks here not of the common manner of life and the breath which we all alike now enjoy but of the future merit of the resurrection. On Belief in the Resurrection 2.92-93.[32]

With the Angels. Chrysostom: And do you say, How is it possible for one that is human not to mourn? . . . Do not say then, "he is perished and shall no more be"; for these are the words of unbelievers; but say, "He sleeps and will rise again," [or] "He is gone a journey and will return with the King." Who speaks like this? He that has Christ speaking in him. "For," Paul says, "if we believe that Jesus died and rose again," and revived, "even so God will bring with him those also who sleep in Jesus." If then you seek your son, seek him where the King is, where the army of the angels is; not in the grave; not in the earth; lest while he is so highly exalted, you yourself remain groveling on the ground. Homilies on 2 Corinthians 1.6.[33]

4:16b The Dead in Christ

The Dead in Christ Arise First. Origen: We

---

[26]FC 88:246. [27]Jn 11:11. [28]FC 82:214. [29]Lk 2:14. [30]NPNF 2 6:155*. [31]1 Cor 15:23. [32]NPNF 2 10:189* (= *On the Death of His Brother, Satyrus* 2.92-93 [FC 22:237-38]). [33]NPNF 1 12:276*.

think that those who have been perfected and who no longer commit sin are alive in Christ. The dead in Christ are those who are favorably disposed to the Christian faith and who prefer to live a good life but who have not, in fact, actually succeeded, but still sin, either in ignorance of the accurate true word of justice or in weakness, because their decisions are overcome by the flesh, which lusts against the spirit.[34] And it is in conformity with these matters that Paul, conscious of himself, says, because he has already succeeded, "We who are alive." But those whom we spoke of as dead have special need of the resurrection, since not even those who are alive can be taken up in the clouds to meet the Lord in the air before the dead in Christ first rise. This is why it has been written, "The dead in Christ shall rise first, then we who are alive," etc. COMMENTARY ON JOHN 20.232-33.[35]

THE TAX OF DEATH. AMBROSE: For truly death was no necessary part of the divine operation, since for those who were placed in paradise a continual succession of all good things streamed forth. Because of transgression, however, human life, condemned to lengthened labor, began to be wretched with intolerable groaning. Thus, it was fitting that an end should be set to the evils and that death should restore what life had lost. For immortality, unless grace breathed upon it, would be rather a burden than an advantage. And if one consider accurately, it is not the death of our being but of evil, for being continues, but it is evil that perishes. . . . So we shall either pay the penalty of our sins or attain to the reward of our good deeds. For the same being will rise again, now more honorably for having paid the tax of death. And then "the dead who are in Christ shall rise first. Then we who are alive will follow," it is said, "and together with them be caught up in the clouds into the air to meet the Lord, and so we shall always be with the Lord." ON BELIEF IN THE RESURRECTION 2.47-48.[36]

4:16 *The Sound of the Trumpet*

FESTIVAL ANTICIPATION. AMBROSE: Shall we, then, think of festival days in terms of eating and drinking? On the contrary, let no one call us to account in respect to eating, "For we know that the law is spiritual."[37] "Let no one, therefore, call you to account for what you eat or drink in regard to a festival or a new moon or a sabbath. These are a shadow of things to come, but the body is of Christ."[38] So let us seek the body of Christ which is the voice of the Father from heaven, the last trumpet, as it were, showed to you on that occasion when the Jews said that it thundered for him.[39] Let us seek, I repeat, the body of Christ which the last trumpet will reveal to us, "For the Lord himself with cry of command, with voice of archangel, and with trumpet of God will descend from heaven, and the dead in Christ will rise up first." ON THE DEATH OF HIS BROTHER SATYRUS 2.108.[40]

THE REVERSAL OF HUMAN WISDOM. JEROME: Then at the sound of the trumpet the earth and its peoples shall tremble, but you shall rejoice. The world shall howl at the Lord who comes to judge it, and the tribes of the earth shall smite the breast. Once mighty kings shall tremble in their nakedness. Venus shall be exposed, and her son, too. Jupiter with his fiery bolts will be brought to trial. Plato, with his disciples, will be but a fool. Aristotle's arguments shall be of no avail. You may seem a poor man and country-bred, but then you shall exult and laugh, and say, Behold my crucified Lord, behold my judge. LETTERS 14.9.[41]

---

[34]Gal 5:17. [35]FC 89:255*. [36]NPNF 2 10:181*. [37]Rom 7:14. [38]Col 2:16-17. The argument is intricate here. With the use of Colossians 2:16-17 Ambrose is defending the church's use of festivals and outward observances by suggesting that there is an outward form, the "shadow," to these, but also an inward substance, the invisible "body," which is Christ speaking to us through the outward form. This body, or voice of Christ, will be revealed to us directly at the last trump, where outward forms that veil the inner substance will no longer be necessary. [39]Jn 12:28-29. [40]FC 22:246-47. [41]NPNF 2 6:18.

PRUDENTIUS:
When at the awful trumpet's sound
   The earth will be consumed by fire,
   And with a mighty rush the world
   Unhinged, will crash in dreadful ruin.
HYMNS 11, 105-8.[42]

FINAL BLISS. GREGORY OF NAZIANZUS: I believe the words of the wise, that every fair and God-beloved soul, when, set free from the bonds of the body, it departs hence, at once enjoys a sense and perception of the blessings which await it. This happens to the extent that whatever darkened that soul has been purged away, or laid aside—this is the only way I can express it—such that it feels a marvelous pleasure and exultation and goes rejoicing to meet its Lord. This soul has escaped, as it were, the grievous poison of life here and has shaken off the fetters which bound it and held down the wings of the mind. And so the soul enters upon the bliss laid up for it, a bliss of which it has even now some conception. . . . Why, then, be faint-hearted in my hopes? Why behave like a mere creature of the day? I await the voice of the archangel, the last trumpet, the transformation of the heavens, the transfiguration of the earth, the liberation of the elements, the renovation of the universe. Then shall I see Caesarius for myself, no longer in exile, no longer laid upon a bier, no longer the object of mourning and pity, but brilliant, glorious, heavenly, such as in my dreams I have often beheld you, dearest and most loving of brothers, pictured thus by my desire, if not by the truth itself. ON HIS BROTHER ST. CAESARIUS 21.[43]

RESURRECTION. JOHN OF DAMASCUS: Then after long seasons, Christ our God shall come to judge the world in awful glory, beyond words to tell. For fear of him the powers of heaven shall be shaken, and all the angel hosts shall stand beside him in dread. Then at the voice of the archangel, and at the trump of God, shall the dead arise and stand before his awful throne.

Now the resurrection is the reuniting of soul and body. So that very body, which decays and perishes, shall arise incorruptible. And concerning this, take care not to be overwhelmed by unbelief, for it is not impossible for him, who at the beginning formed the body out of earth, when according to its maker's judgment it had returned to earth whence it was taken, to raise the same again. BARLAAM AND IOASAPH 8.64.[44]

4:17 *To Meet the Lord in the Air*

AS WITH CHRIST, SO FOR US. GREGORY OF NYSSA: For that which has taken place in Christ's humanity is a common blessing on humanity generally. For we see in him the weight of the body, which naturally gravitates to earth, ascending through the air into the heavens. Therefore, we believe according to the words of the apostle, that we also "shall be caught up in the clouds to meet the Lord in the air." Even so, when we hear that the true God and Father has become the God and Father of Christ, precisely as the firstfruits of the general resurrection, we no longer doubt that the same God has become our God and Father too. This is true inasmuch as we have learned that we shall come to the same place where Christ has entered for us as our forerunner.[45] AGAINST EUNOMIUS 12.1.[46]

CAUGHT UP IN THE CLOUDS. RUFINUS OF AQUILEIA: That the righteous shall ever abide with Christ our Lord, we have already demonstrated. This is where we have shown that the apostle says, "Then we who are alive and remain shall be caught up together with them in the clouds to meet Christ in the air, and so shall we

---

[42]FC 52:83. [43]FC 22:22-23. Deceased in A.D. 368 or 369, St. Caesarius, brother of St. Gregory of Nazianzus, was eulogized by the latter at the funeral observance. A bachelor, he had been recently baptized, had retired from a distinguished career as a physician and public servant, and had given all of his possessions to the poor. [44]JDBI 109. [45]Heb 6:20. [46]NPNF 2 5:242*.

ever be with the Lord." And do not marvel that the flesh of the saints is to be changed into such a glorious condition at the resurrection as to be caught up to meet God, suspended in the clouds and borne in the air. Indeed, the same apostle, setting forth the great things which God bestows on them that love him, says, "Who shall change our vile body that it may be made like his glorious body."[47] It is in no way absurd, then, if the bodies of the saints are said to be raised up in the air, seeing that they are said to be renewed after the image of Christ's body, which is seated at God's right hand. A COMMENTARY ON THE APOSTLES' CREED 46.[48]

THE LIVING AND THE DEAD. EPHREM THE SYRIAN: This Jesus that gathered and carried and brought with him of the fruit was longing for the Tree of Life to taste the fruit that quickens all. For him Rahab too was looking. For when the scarlet thread in type redeemed her from wrath, in type she tasted of the Truth.[49] For him Elijah longed, and when he did not see him on earth, he, thoroughly cleansed through faith, mounted up to heaven to see him. Moses saw him and Elijah.[50] The meek man from the depth ascended, the zealous from on high descended, and in the midst beheld the Son. They figured the mystery of his advent: Moses was a type of the dead, and Elijah a type of the living, that fly to meet him at his coming. For the dead that have tasted death, them he makes to be first: and the rest that are not buried, are at last caught up to meet him. HYMNS ON THE NATIVITY 1.[51]

THE VENERABLE BEDE: By Moses and Elijah [at the transfiguration] we can rightly understand everyone who is going to reign with the Lord. By Moses, who died and was buried, [we can understand] those who at the judgment are going to be raised up from death. By Elijah, on the other hand, who has not yet paid the debt of death, [we can understand] those who are going to be found alive in the flesh at the Judge's coming. At one and the same moment, both of them,

having been caught up "in clouds to meet the Lord in the air," will be led into eternal life, as soon as the judgment is brought to completion. HOMILIES ON THE GOSPELS 1.24.[52]

THE GREAT RECEPTION. CHRYSOSTOM: If he is about to descend, on what account shall we be caught up? For the sake of honor. For when a king drives into a city, those who are in honor go out to meet him; but the condemned await the judge within. And upon the coming of an affectionate father, his children indeed, and those who are worthy to be his children, are taken out in a chariot, that they may see and kiss him; but the housekeepers who have offended him remain within. We are carried upon the chariot of our Father. For he received him up in the clouds, and "we shall be caught up in the clouds."[53] Do you see how great is the honor? And as he descends, we go forth to meet him, and, what is more blessed than all, so shall we be with him. HOMILIES ON 1 THESSALONIANS 8.[54]

TRUE LIFE. CYRIL OF JERUSALEM: Now the life that is really and truly life is God the Father, the fount of life, who pours out his heavenly gifts upon all his creatures through the Son and in the Holy Spirit, and the blessings of eternal life are faithfully promised even to us men, through his love for us. There must be no incredulity about the possibility of that. For we ought to believe, because our minds should be set on his power, not on our feebleness. For anything is possible with God, and that our eternal life is both possible and to be looked forward to by us

---

[47]Phil 3:21. [48]NPNF 2 3:562*. [49]Particularly in the Antiochene (see introduction to this volume of ACCS) tradition of biblical exegesis, in which the Syriac fathers like Ephrem share, "type" refers to the Old Testament person or event that anticipates in salvation history, or prefigures, its New Testament "antitype," or fulfillment. [50]For the story of Rahab, see Joshua 2:1-21; for the ascension of Elijah, 2 Kings 2:9-12; and for the reference to Moses' sight of Jesus and Elijah, the account of the transfiguration in Mark 9:2-13 and parallels. [51]NPNF 2 13:224. [52]HOG 1:239-40. [53]Acts 1:9. [54]NPNF 1 13:356*.

is shown when Daniel says, "the understanding . . . from among the many righteous shall shine as the stars for ever and ever."[55] And Paul says, "And so shall we be ever with the Lord." For "being ever with the Lord" means the same thing as eternal life. Catechetical Lectures 18.29.[56]

The Final Vision. Pseudo-Dionysius: In a fashion beyond words, the simplicity of Jesus became something complex, the timeless took on the duration of the temporal, and, with neither change nor confusion of what constitutes him, he came into our human nature, he who totally transcends the natural order of the world. . . . And so it is that the Transcendent is clothed in the terms of being, with shape and form on things which have neither, and numerous symbols are employed to convey the varied attributes of what is an imageless and supranatural simplicity. But in time to come, when we are incorruptible and immortal, when we have come at last to the blessed inheritance of being like Christ, then, as Scripture says, "we shall always be with the Lord." The Divine Names 1.4.[57]

---

[55]Dan 12:3 (LXX). [56]LCC 4:189. [57]PSD 52.

5:1-11 PREPARATION FOR THE LORD'S COMING

¹*But as to the times and the seasons, brethren, you have no need to have anything written to you. ²For you yourselves know well that the day of the Lord will come like a thief in the night. ³When people say, "There is peace and security," then sudden destruction will come upon them as travail comes upon a woman with child, and there will be no escape. ⁴But you are not in darkness, brethren, for that day to surprise you like a thief. ⁵For you are all sons of light and sons of the day; we are not of the night or of darkness. ⁶So then let us not sleep, as others do, but let us keep awake and be sober. ⁷For those who sleep sleep at night, and those who get drunk are drunk at night. ⁸But, since we belong to the day, let us be sober, and put on the breastplate of faith and love, and for a helmet the hope of salvation. ⁹For God has not destined us for wrath, but to obtain salvation through our Lord Jesus Christ, ¹⁰who died for us so that whether we wake or sleep we might live with him. ¹¹Therefore encourage one another and build one another up, just as you are doing.*

Overview: Paul's intention is to suppress all detailed questioning about the time of the end as essentially faithless. The point is that there is an end, and we must live well in anticipating it (Origen, Chrysostom). Serious moral preparation is required for the return of the Lord, which will come suddenly (Augustine, Isaac of Nineveh, Prudentius). We know that the end will come, but God never allows us to know when (Theodoret). The faithful Christian always lives in a state of readiness and watchfulness (Clement of Alexandria, Leo). The coming of the Lord may be painful, just like any process of repentance and transformation into new life (Chrysostom).

5:2 The Day of the Lord Will Come

The Divine Intention. Chrysostom: Do not place your confidence in your youth, nor think that you have a very fixed term of life, "For the day of the Lord comes as a thief in the night." On this account he has made our end invisible, so that we might demonstrate clearly our diligence and forethought. Do you not see men taken away prematurely day after day? On this account a certain one admonishes, "don't delay in turning to the Lord, and don't put things off from day to day,"[1] lest at any time, while you delay, you are destroyed. Let the old man keep this admonition; let the young man heed this advice. Indeed, are you in insecurity, and are you rich, and do you abound in wealth, and does no affliction happen to you? Still hear what Paul says: "when they say peace and safety, then sudden destruction comes upon them." Affairs change often. We are not masters of our end. Let us be masters of virtue. Our Master Christ is loving. The Second Homily Concerning the Power of Demons 2.[2]

You Are the Day. Augustine: So what is this day which the Lord has made? Live good lives, and you will be this day yourselves. The apostle, you see, was not talking about the day which begins with sunrise and ends with sunset, when he said, "Let us walk honorably, as in the day";[3] where he also said, "For those who get drunk are drunk at night." Nobody sees people getting drunk at the midday meal; but when this does happen, it is a matter of the night, not of the day which the Lord has made. You see, just as that day is realized in those who live godly, holy and righteous lives, marked by moderation, justice, sobriety. So too on the contrary, for those who live in an ungodly, loose-living, proud and irreligious manner—for that sort of night, the night will undoubtedly be a thief. "The day of the Lord will come just like a thief in the night." Sermons 229b.1.[4]

5:3 As Travail Comes Upon a Woman

Luxury a Sign. Chrysostom: And so that you may learn by another thing that the Lord's silence on this matter is not a sign of ignorance on his part, take note of something else in addition to what we have mentioned. "But as in the days of Noah they were eating and drinking, marrying and giving in marriage, until the day that the flood came and took everything away, so also shall the coming of the Son of Man be."[5] He said these things in order to show that he would come suddenly and unexpectedly, and precisely when a majority of people would be living luxuriously. Paul also said this when he wrote, "When they shall speak of peace and safety, then sudden destruction will come upon them," and to show how unexpectedly, he said, "as travail upon a woman with child." Homilies on Matthew 77.2.[6]

The Certainty of What Is to Come. Theodoret of Cyr: The woman who is pregnant knows that she has a fetus in the womb but does not know when birth will occur. So it is with us as we know that the Lord will come, but we do not teach the time itself with certainty. Interpretation of the First Letter to the Thessalonians.[7]

5:4 For You Are Not in Darkness

Keeping the Balance. Augustine: Therefore, not to know the times is something different from decay of morals and love of vice. For, when the apostle Paul said, "Don't allow your thinking to be shaken nor be frightened, neither by word nor by epistle as sent from us, as if the day of the Lord were at hand,"[8] he obviously did not want them to believe those who thought the coming of the Lord was already at hand, but nei-

---

[1]Sir 5:8. [2]NPNF 1 9:190*. [3]Rom 3:13. [4]*WSA* 3/6:273. [5]Mt 24:38-39. [6]NPNF 1 10:464. [7]PG 82:651A/652A. [8]2 Thess 2:2.

ther did he want them to be like the wicked servant and say, "My Lord is long in coming," and deliver themselves over to destruction by pride and riotous behavior. Thus, his desire that they should not listen to false rumors about the imminent approach of the last day was consistent with his wish that they should await the coming of their Lord fully prepared, packed for travel and with lamps burning.[9] He said to them, "But you, brothers, are not in darkness that that day should overtake you as a thief, for all you are the children of light and children of the day; we are not of the night nor of darkness." LETTERS 199.1.2.[10]

ISAAC OF NINEVEH: Now if the good God sees that a man's heart has not inclined to any of these things as David said, indicating the same, "You have tested my heart, You have visited it in the night, You have tried me by fire, and unrighteousness was not found in me,"[11] then God will help him and deliver him. Why does he say "in the night" and not "in the day"? Because the enemy's deceptions are a night, as Paul also said, "We are not children of the night but children of the day," since the Son of God is the Day, but Satan is night. THE FIRST SYRIAC EPISTLE OF SAINT MAKARIOS OF EGYPT 7.[12]

MANY KINDS OF DAYS. AUGUSTINE: On the verse: "This is the day which the Lord has made."[13] What we have sung to our Lord let us put into practice with his help. To be sure, every day has been made by the Lord, but with good reason has it been said of a particular day, "This is the day which the Lord has made." We read that when he created heaven and earth, "God said, 'Let there be light,' and there was light, and God called the light Day, and the darkness Night."[14] But there is another day, well established and definitely to be commended by us, concerning which the apostle says, "Let us walk becomingly as in the day." That day, commonly called "today," is caused by the rising and setting of the sun. There is still another day by which

the word of God shines on the hearts of the faithful and dispels the darkness, not of the eyes, but of evil habits. Let us, therefore, recognize this light; let us rejoice in it; let us pay attention to the apostle when he says, "For we are children of the light and children of the day. We are not of night nor of darkness." SERMONS 230.[15]

5:5 For You Are All Sons of Light

SUN TO THE SONS. ORIGEN: If you wish to see Jesus transfigured before those who went up on the mountain with him, behold with me the Jesus in the Gospels as more simply understood. This is Jesus, as one might say, known "according to the flesh" by those who do not go up through uplifting words and works to the holy mountain of wisdom. Behold him with me as known in his divinity by means of all of the Gospels, beheld in the form of God according to the knowledge that his companions had. For before them Jesus is transfigured, but not to any of those who are below. But when he is transfigured, his face also shines as the sun, so that he may be manifested to the children of light. These have put off the works of darkness and have put on the armor of light[16] and are no longer the children of darkness or night, but have become sons of the day and walk honestly as in the day. Being manifested, he will shine for them not only as the sun, but as the son of righteousness. COMMENTARY ON MATTHEW 12.37.[17]

5:6 Let Us Keep Awake

AFFLICTION AND WATCHFULNESS. CHRYSOSTOM: So that you may know that the prayers which are uttered in time of affliction would have the best chance of being heard, hear what the prophet says, "In my affliction I cried to the

[9]Cf. Lk 12:35-36. [10]FC 30:358. [11]Ps 16:3. [12]AHSIS 452. [13]Ps 117:24. [14]Gen 1:3-6. [15]FC 38:202-3. [16]Rom 13:13. [17]ANF 9:470*.

Lord, and he listened to me."[18] Therefore, let us stir up our conscience to fervor, let us afflict our soul with the memory of our sins, not so that it is crushed with anxiety but so that we may make it ready to be heard, so that we make it live in sobriety and watchfulness and ready to attain heaven itself. Nothing puts carelessness and negligence to flight the way grief and affliction do. They bring together our thoughts from every side and make our mind turn back to ponder itself. The man who prays in this way, in his affliction, after many a prayer, can bring joy into his own soul. ON THE INCOMPREHENSIBLE NATURE OF GOD 5.6.[19]

SLEEP HALF-AWAKE. CLEMENT OF ALEXANDRIA: We should sleep half-awake. . . . A man who is asleep is not good for anything, any more than a man who is dead. Therefore, even during the night we should rouse ourselves from sleep often and give praise to God. Blessed are they who have kept watch for him, for they make themselves like the angels whom we speak of as ever watchful. CHRIST THE EDUCATOR 2.9.79.[20]

THE FRUIT OF OUR EFFORT. LEO THE GREAT: Wherefore, let us honor this sacred day, the day on which the author of our salvation appeared. Whom the wise men revered as an infant in his crib, let us worship as all-powerful in heaven. Just as they offered to the Lord mystical kinds of gifts from their treasures, let us bring forth from our hearts things that are worthy of God. Although he himself bestows all good things, he nevertheless asks for the fruit of our effort. For the kingdom of heaven comes not to those who sleep but to those who work and watch according to the Lord's command. If we do not render his gifts ineffective, we may deserve to receive what he promised through the very things which he has given. SERMONS 32.1.[21]

DAWN'S APPROACH. PRUDENTIUS:
The winged messenger of day
Sings loud, foretelling dawn's approach,

And Christ in stirring accents calls
Our slumbering souls to life with him.
"Away," he cries, "with dull repose,
The sleep of death and sinful sloth;
With hearts now sober, just and pure,
Keep watch, for I am very near."
HYMNS 1.1-8.[22]

5:8 Let Us Be Sober

SPIRITUAL DARKNESS AND LIGHT. ORIGEN: But if we must also examine the statement, "And it was night,"[23] so that it has not been interjected to no purpose by the Evangelist, we must say that the perceptible night at that time was symbolic, an image of the night that was in Judas's soul when Satan, the darkness that lies over the abyss, entered him. "For God called the darkness night,"[24] of which night, indeed, Paul says we are not children, nor of darkness, when he says, "Therefore, brothers, we are not of the night, nor of darkness," and, "But let us who are of the day be sober." COMMENTARY ON JOHN 32.313.[25]

5:11 Build One Another Up

SEEING THE CHURCH GROW. CHRYSOSTOM: You see, I wish and pray that you would all hold fast to right order as teachers, that you would not simply be listeners to what is said by us but also transmit it to others, casting your net for those still in error so as to bring them to the way of truth—as Paul says, "Edify one another," and "With fear and trembling work out your own salvation."[26] In this way we will have the satisfaction of seeing the church grow in strength, and you will enjoy more abundant favor from above through the great care you show for your members. God, you know, does not wish Christians to be concerned only for themselves but also to edify others, not simply through their teaching

---

[18]Ps 119:1 (LXX). [19]FC 72:157. [20]FC 23:161. [21]FC 93:138. [22]FC 52:3. [23]Jn 13:30. [24]Gen 1:2. [25]FC 89:400-401*. [26]Phil 2:12.

but also through their behavior and the way they live. After all, nothing is such an attraction to the way of truth as an upright life—in other words, people pay less attention to what we say than to what we do. HOMILIES ON GENESIS 8.4-5.[27]

EDIFY ONE ANOTHER. CHRYSOSTOM: Do you see how everywhere Paul puts the health of the community into the hands of each individual? "Exhorting one another daily," he says, "while it is called today."[28] Do not then cast all of the burden on your teachers, and do not cast everything on those who have authority over you. You are able to edify one another. He says this in writing to the Thessalonians, "Edify one another, just as

you are doing." And again, "Comfort one another with these words."[29] If you are willing, you will have more success with one another than we can have. For you have been with one another a longer time. You know more about one another's affairs. You are not ignorant of one another's failings. You have more freedom of speech and love and intimacy. These are helpful for teaching. . . . You have more ability than we do to reprove and exhort. Furthermore, because I am only one person, but you are many, you will be able to be teachers to one another. HOMILIES ON HEBREWS 30.1.[30]

---

[27]FC 74:112*. [28]Heb 3:13. [29]1 Thess 4:18. [30]NPNF 1 14:504.

5:12-28 FINAL EXHORTATIONS AND GREETINGS

[12]But we beseech you, brethren, to respect those who labor among you and are over you in the Lord and admonish you, [13]and to esteem them very highly in love because of their work. Be at peace among yourselves. [14]And we exhort you, brethren, admonish the idlers, encourage the fainthearted, help the weak, be patient with them all. [15]See that none of you repays evil for evil, but always seek to do good to one another and to all. [16]Rejoice always, [17]pray constantly, [18]give thanks in all circumstances; for this is the will of God in Christ Jesus for you. [19]Do not quench the Spirit, [20]do not despise prophesying, [21]but test everything; hold fast what is good, [22]abstain from every form of evil.

[23]May the God of peace himself sanctify you wholly; and may your spirit and soul and body be kept sound and blameless at the coming of our Lord Jesus Christ. [24]He who calls you is faithful, and he will do it.

[25]Brethren, pray for us.

[26]Greet all the brethren with a holy kiss.

[27]I adjure you by the Lord that this letter be read to all the brethren.

[28]The grace of our Lord Jesus Christ be with you.

OVERVIEW: Once again, Paul makes it clear that the Thessalonians are to be faithful, joyful and upright in their dealings, particularly in the midst of affliction, and particularly as he, Paul, models these by his humility (Chrysostom). Paul describes in essence the work of sound pastoral leadership in relation to different kinds of troubles in the community (Augustine, Theodore). These troubles are described by Paul with careful attention to the spiritual malady that underlies each (Augustine, Theodoret). Paul is most concerned here with the matter of due obedience to lawful pastors, as well as the importance of carefully distinguishing false from true teaching (Ambrosiaster, Caesarius of Arles). Faithful pastors and leaders are called to discern just what remedy and form of care are required for the ills of body, soul and spirit that afflict believers (Origen, Ambrose).

5:14 Be Patient with Them All

Medicine for the Pilgrimage. Augustine: Of course, even good men can be sick, suffering from that disobedience which is the penalty of a primal disobedience which, therefore, is a wound or weakness in a nature that is good in itself. It is because of this wound that the good who are growing in grace and living by faith during their pilgrimage on earth are given the counsels, "Bear one another's burdens, and so you will fulfill the law of Christ,"[1] and elsewhere, "We exhort you, brothers, reprove the irregular, comfort the fainthearted, support the weak, be patient toward all men. See that no one renders evil for evil to any man." . . . It is in this way that citizens of the City of God are given medicine during their pilgrimage on earth while praying for the peace of their heavenly fatherland. And, of course, the Holy Spirit is operative internally to give healing power to the medicine which is applied externally, for, otherwise, no preaching of the truth is of any avail. Even though God makes use of one of his obedient creatures, as when he speaks in human guise to our ears— whether to the ears of the body or to the kind of ears we have in sleep—it is only by his interior grace that he moves and rules our mind. The City of God 15.6.[2]

Boldness to Rebuke. Augustine: Hence, as far as concerns us, who are not able to distinguish those who are predestinated from those who are not, we ought on this very account to will all humanity to be saved. Severe rebuke should be medicinally applied to all by us that they neither themselves perish nor may be the means of destroying others. It belongs to God, however, to make that rebuke useful to them whom he himself has foreknown and predestinated to be conformed to the image of his Son. We do not abstain from admonishing for fear lest by rebuke a person should perish. So why do we not also rebuke for fear that one should rather perish by our withholding admonition? For there is no greater act of compassion on our part than when the blessed apostle says, "Rebuke those that are unruly; comfort the feeble-minded; support the weak; be patient toward all men. See that none render evil for evil." On Rebuke and Grace 16.49.[3]

Responsible for One Another. Caesarius of Arles: It was to the laity and to women and not only the clergy that the apostle said, "Reprove the irregular, comfort the fainthearted, support the weak." Provided that you are willing to rebuke one another in case of sin, the Enemy will be able to take you by surprise only with difficulty or not at all. If he does take you by surprise, the evil which was done is easily amended and corrected. Then is fulfilled in you what was written, "A brother who helps his brother will be exalted,"[4] and again, "he who helps a sinner to be brought back from the misguided way will save his soul from death, and will cover a multitude of sins."[5] Sermons 74.4.[6]

Humble Compassion. Chrysostom: If we are to hate ungodly and lawless men, we shall go on also to hate sinners. Thus, in regular succession,

---

[1]Gal 6:2. [2]FC 14:422-23. [3]NPNF 1 5:491*. [4]Prov 18:19. [5]Jas 5:20. [6]FC 31:348-49.

you will find yourself cut off from most of your brothers, indeed, from all of them. There is not one of them without sin. If it is our duty to hate the enemies of God, we would have to hate not only the ungodly but backsliders[7] as well. Then we would be worse than wild beasts, shunning all and puffed up with pride, just like the Pharisee. Paul commanded us differently. "Admonish the disorderly, encourage the faint-hearted, support the weak, be long-suffering toward all." HOMILIES ON FIRST CORINTHIANS 33.5.[8]

HELP THE WEAK. THEODORET OF CYR: Let us then bravely bear the ills that befall us. It is in war that heroes are discerned; in conflicts that athletes are crowned; in the surge of the sea that the art of the helmsman is shown; in the fire that the gold is tried. And let us not, I beseech you, have concern for only ourselves, but let us rather look out for the rest, and that much more for the sick than for the whole, for it is an apostolic precept which exclaims, "Comfort the feeble-minded, support the weak." Let us, then, stretch out our hands to them that lie low, let us tend their wounds and set them at their post to fight the devil. Nothing will so vex him as to see them fighting and smiting again. LETTERS 78.[9]

5:15 Not Repaying Evil

STAGES OF PASSION. POEMEN: "What does 'See that none of you repays evil for evil' mean?" The old man said . . . 'Passions work in four stages—first, in the heart; secondly, in the face; thirdly, in words; and fourthly, it is essential not to render evil for evil in deeds. If you can purify your heart, passion will not come into your expression; but if it comes into your face, take care not to speak; but if you do speak, cut the conversation short in case you render evil for evil.'" SAYINGS OF THE FATHERS 34.[10]

5:16-18 Rejoice, Pray, Give Thanks

KEEP THE FEAST. ATHANASIUS: For no one is going to turn away from sin and start behaving righteously unless he thinks about what he is doing. Not until he has been straightened out by practicing godly behavior will he actually possess the reward of faith: the crown of righteousness that Paul possessed, having fought the good fight. That crown is laid up not just for Paul but for all who are like him in this respect. This sort of meditation and exercise in godliness should be familiar to us, as it was to the saints of old. It should be especially so in the season when the divine word calls upon us to keep the feast.[11] For what, after all, is the feast but continual worship of God, recognition of godliness and unceasing prayer all done from the heart in full agreement with each other? St. Paul, wanting us to be so inclined, urges us, "Always rejoice, pray without ceasing, give thanks in all things." FESTAL LETTERS 9.[12]

TRUE CONSTANCY. BASIL THE GREAT: Then, because he [David] had been delivered from great danger,[13] he sent up this prayer of thanksgiving to God who had rescued him. "I will bless the Lord at all times."[14] Having escaped death, as if he were setting up norms for his life, he molded his soul to an exact manner of living, so that he ceased at no time from praise but referred the beginning of affairs, great and small, to God. "I will not think," he says, "that anything was done through my diligence nor happened through spontaneous chance, but, 'I will bless the Lord at all times,' not only in prosperity of life, but also in precarious times." The apostle, learning from this, says, "Rejoice always. Pray without ceasing. In all things give thanks." HOMILIES 16.[15]

---

[7]Those among the faithful who continue to struggle with sins. [8]NPNF 1 12:199. [9]NPNF 2 3:274. [10]PG 65:332AB. [11]Athanasius refers specifically to the keeping of the Easter observance, in the light of which our rejoicing at the new life in Christ ought to be marked by special attention to purity of heart and of life. [12]ARL 157. [13]See 1 Sam 21:10-11. [14]Ps 33:2. [15]FC 46:249.

PERFECT DEVOTION. CASSIODORUS: "Sing with jubilation to God, all the earth." The prophet was troubled for the faithful people in case they believe they are to serve the Lord with gloomy anxiety, so he began at once with jubilation, for ministering to the Lord with happiness of mind constitutes the perfect devotion of the just man. As Paul warns us, "Always rejoice: pray without ceasing: in all things give thanks." COMMENTARY ON THE PSALMS 99.2.[16]

THE WAY OF SALVATION. BENJAMIN: And when Abba Benjamin was dying, he quoted a text to his disciples, "Be joyful at all times, pray without ceasing, and give thanks for all things." He told them, "Do these things and you can be saved." SAYINGS OF THE FATHERS 4.[17]

TRUE FREEDOM. JOHN CASSIAN: When the mind is freed from lust, established in tranquility and does not waver in its intention toward the one supreme good, the monk will fulfill the precept of St. Paul, "Pray without ceasing," and "In every place lifting up holy hands without wrath and controversy."[18] By purity of heart the mind is drawn away from earthly feelings and is re-formed in the likeness of an angelic spirit. Then, whatever thought the mind receives, whatever it considers, whatever it does, will be a prayer of true purity and sincerity. CONFERENCES 9.6.[19]

THE PRAYER OF THE HEART. AUGUSTINE: And who observed and noticed the cause of his [i.e., the psalmist's] groaning? "All my desire is before You."[20] For it is not before men, who cannot see the heart, but is before You that all my desire is open! Let your desire be before him, and "the Father, who sees in secret, shall reward you."[21] For it is your heart's desire that is your prayer. If your desire continues uninterrupted, your prayer continues also. For it was not without meaning, when the apostle said, "Pray without ceasing." Are we to be "without ceasing" in bending the knee and prostrating the body and lifting up our hands, such that he says, "without ceasing"? If that is what "without ceasing" means, then I do not believe it is possible. There is another kind of inward prayer without ceasing, which is the desire of the heart. COMMENTARY ON THE PSALMS 37.14.[22]

THE RECOLLECTED HEART. BASIL THE GREAT: For prayer and psalmody, however, as also, indeed, for some other duties, every hour is suitable, that, while our hands are busy at their tasks, we may praise God sometimes with the tongue (when this is possible, or, rather, when it is conducive to edification); or, if not, with the heart. . . . Thus we acquire a recollected spirit— when in every action we beg from God the success of our labors and satisfy our debt of gratitude to him who gave us the power to do the work, and when, as has been said, we keep before our minds the aim of pleasing him. If this is not the case, how can there be consistency in the words of the apostle bidding us to "pray without ceasing," with those other words, "we worked night and day."[23] THE LONG RULES Q37.R.[24]

JOHN THE ELDER: Why did Paul say, "Pray and do not grow weary"? As long as he is a servant, he indeed prays; but once born of the Spirit in the world of prayer, he is a son of God, and he has authority over riches, being an heir; thus he does not merely ask. LETTERS 5.6.[25]

5:18 *In Everything Give Thanks*

NOT ONLY IN DELIVERANCE. CHRYSOSTOM: Most appropriately have we all this day sung together, "Blessed be the Lord God of Israel,

---

[16]ACW 52:443. Cassiodorus is discussing Psalm 66:1.   [17]PG 65:145A.   [18]1 Tim 2:8.   [19]LCC 12:218*.   [20]Ps 38:9.   [21]Mt 6:6. [22]NPNF 1 8:106-7*.   [23]2 Thess 3:8.   [24]FC 9:308*.   [25]SFPSL 336.

who only does wondrous things."[26] For marvelous, and beyond all expectation, are the things which have happened. A whole city, and so great a population, when just about to be overwhelmed—to sink under the waves, and to be utterly and instantly destroyed—he has entirely rescued from shipwreck in a single moment of time! Let us give thanks, then, not only that God has calmed the tempest but that he permitted it to take place. Not only did he rescue us from shipwreck, but he allowed us to fall into such distress and permitted such an extreme peril to hang over us. Thus also Paul bids us "in every thing give thanks." But when he says, "In every thing give thanks," he means not only in our deliverance from evils but also at the time when we suffer those evils. Homilies on the Statues 17.1.[27]

5:19 Do Not Quench the Spirit

The Spirit Is Holiness of Life. Athanasius: We can thus see why Paul, not wanting the grace of the Spirit given to us to grow cold, exhorts us, "Do not quench the Spirit." The only way we can continue to be partakers of Christ is to cling until the end to the Holy Spirit, who was given to us at the beginning.[28] Paul said, "Do not quench" not because the Spirit is under the power of men but because evil and unthankful men certainly do wish to quench the Spirit. Demonstrating their impurity, they drive the Spirit away by their unholy deeds. Festal Letters 4.4.[29]

Fire and Fuel. Chrysostom: As fire requires fuel, so grace requires our prompt response, that it may be ever fervent. "I put you in remembrance that you stir up the gift of God that is in you by the putting on of my hands," that is, the grace of the Spirit, which you have received, for presiding over the church, for the working of miracles and for every service. For this grace it is in our power to kindle or extinguish. For this reason Paul elsewhere says, "Do not quench the

Spirit." Homilies on Second Timothy 1.[30]

Chrysostom: On this account Paul says, "Do not quench the Spirit," that is, the gift of grace, for it is his custom so to call the gift of the Spirit. But an impure life extinguishes the gift of grace. For as anyone who has sprinkled both water and dust upon the light of our lamp extinguishes it. . . . So it is also with the gift of grace. Homilies on 1 Thessalonians 11.[31]

Mystical Reception of the Spirit. Mark the Hermit: Learn from the apostle that we are the ones who grieve the Spirit, extinguishing him in our hearts. He says, "Do not quench the Spirit, do not despise prophecy"; and again, "Do not grieve the Holy Spirit, in whom you have been sealed for the day of redemption."[32] We introduce these testimonies not as if to suggest that every man who has been baptized and obtained grace is henceforth immutable and no longer in need of repentance, but to say that through baptism, according to Christ's gift, the complete grace of God is granted to us for the fulfillment of the commandments. Henceforth each one who receives baptism mystically and yet does not fully perform the commandments, is activated by sin in proportion to their failure—the sin not of Adam but of the one who is negligent. On Baptism, Response 5.[33]

---

[26]Ps 72:18. [27]NPNF 1 9:452*. The historical context here is that in February 387 the citizens of Chrysostom's see city of Antioch in Syria had new imperial taxes imposed on them. After an official protest was unavailing, the Antiochenes rioted and defaced effigies of the emperor. Punishment of the city was swift and harsh, though in due course the punishment was softened and peace restored. Chrysostom here gives thanks for the restoration of peace and celebrates the growth in virtue that the crisis made possible, particularly the punitive closing of the bathhouses and public entertainments, which had been favorite targets of his invective for some time. See J. N. D. Kelly, *Golden Mouth: The Story of John Chrysostom—Ascetic, Preacher, Bishop* (Ithaca, N.Y.: Cornell University Press, 1995), pp. 72-82. [28]Cf. Mt 10:22; Heb 3:6. [29]NPNF 2 4:514*. [30]NPNF 1 13:477*. [31]NPNF 1 13:370. [32]Eph 4:30. [33]PG 65:1004BC (cited in Paul M. Blowers, ed., *The Bible in Greek Christian Antiquity* [Notre Dame, Ind.: University of Notre Dame Press, 1997], p. 245).

PHILOXENUS OF MABBUG: That is to say, do not grieve him by sin, otherwise his light will be quenched from your soul—a light which, when kindled within you, gives you the possession of a power that is beyond expression; and you will be able to contend "with principalities and powers,"[34] and fight against the evil spirits under heaven, and reject all the world with its pleasures and pains. All are effected by the fervor of the Spirit within us. MEMRA ON THE INDWELLING OF THE HOLY SPIRIT.[35]

5:23 Spirit, Soul and Body

THE HUMAN COMPOSITE. AMBROSE: On this subject the Lord says, "When you come into the land to which I bring you and when you eat of the food of the land, you shall present an offering to the Lord. When you separate the firstfruits of your barn floors, you shall also give the firstfruits of your dough to the Lord."[36] We are a composite of diverse elements mixed together, cold with hot, and moist with dry. This mixture is the source of many pleasures and manifold delights of the flesh. But these are not the firstfruits of this body of ours. Since we are composed of soul and body and spirit, the first place is held by that mixture in which the apostle desires that we find sanctification.[37] "And may the God of peace himself sanctify you completely, and may your spirit and soul and body be preserved sound, blameless at the coming of our Lord Jesus Christ." CAIN AND ABEL 2.6.[38]

FULL PARTICIPATION. GREGORY OF NYSSA: This, therefore, is perfection in the Christian life in my judgment, namely, the participation of one's soul and speech and activities in all of the names by which Christ is signified, so that the perfect holiness, according to the eulogy of Paul, is taken upon oneself in "the whole body and soul and spirit," continuously safeguarded

against being mixed with evil. ON PERFECTION.[39]

ONE SANCTIFIED LUMP. ORIGEN: In another way,[40] it is possible to take the woman for the church, the leaven for the Holy Spirit and the three measures for body, spirit and soul. These three are sanctified by the leaven of the Holy Spirit, so that by the Holy Spirit they become one lump, in order that "our whole body and spirit and soul may be kept blameless in the day of our Lord Jesus Christ," as Paul says. HOMILIES ON LUKE, FRAGMENT 205.[41]

THE HARMONY OF THE THREE. ORIGEN: In the wicked sin reigns over the soul, being settled as on its own throne in the mortal body, so that the soul obeys its lusts . . . but in the case of those who have become perfected, the spirit has gained the mastery and put to death the deeds of the body. It imparts to the body of its own life and there arises a concord of the two, body and spirit, on the earth. . . . But still more blessed is it if the three [i.e., body, soul and spirit] be gathered together in the name of Jesus, that this may be fulfilled, "May God sanctify you wholly, and may your spirit and soul and body be preserved entire without blame at the coming of our Lord Jesus Christ." COMMENTARY ON MATTHEW 14.3.[42]

---

[34]Eph 6:12. [35]SFPSL 118. [36]Num 15:18-21. [37]Ambrose is constructing a parallel between the Israelites' offering of firstfruits and the sacrifice that is appropriate for a faithful Christian. The Israelites were sanctified by returning to God a representative portion of the "mixture," the composite of natural product and human labor, that constituted their food: wheat harvested from the fields, stored in barns and turned into dough. Just so are we to consecrate to God the whole "mixture" or composite of body, soul and spirit that makes up our human nature as the true firstfruits that God desires. [38]FC 42:405*. [39]FC 58:121. [40]Origen is commenting on Luke 13:21. [41]FC 94:210. [42]ANF 9:496*.

THE SECOND EPISTLE
TO THE THESSALONIANS

ARGUMENT: Since the Thessalonians have asked Paul about the "times and seasons, and since he is not able to visit in person, this is the letter that he sends instead. He wishes to refute "deceivers," who have led the Thessalonians to think that the resurrection is past, that there is no retribution yet to come. Further, believers must be strengthened not only for retribution but for vindication yet to come (CHRYSOSTOM). Paul wishes to encourage the faith of the Thessalonians, as well as to warn them against expecting the Lord's advent too soon. Antichrist must come first (THEODORE). Paul reminds them that great rewards await the righteous, as well as just punishment the unrighteous. The Thessalonians must not be led astray by false teaching about when the end will come (SEVERIAN). Central to Paul's intention is the need to console the Thessalonians with the conviction that enemies of Christ must come, so that finally Christ our God and Savior will appear (THEODORET). In his discussion of the Lord's final appearance and the resurrection of the dead, Paul speaks obscurely here about the end of the Roman kingdom and the person of Antichrist (AMBROSIASTER).

1:1-12 SALUTATION AND REMINDER
OF COMING JUDGMENT

¹*Paul, Silvanus, and Timothy,*
To the church of the Thessalonians in God our Father and the Lord Jesus Christ:
²*Grace to you and peace from God the Father and the Lord Jesus Christ.*
³*We are bound to give thanks to God always for you, brethren, as is fitting, because your faith is growing abundantly, and the love of every one of you for one another is increasing.* ⁴*Therefore we ourselves boast of you in the churches of God for your steadfastness and faith in all your persecutions and in the afflictions which you are enduring.*

[5]*This is evidence of the righteous judgment of God, that you may be made worthy of the kingdom of God, for which you are suffering—*[6]*since indeed God deems it just to repay with affliction those who afflict you,* [7]*and to grant rest with us to you who are afflicted, when the Lord Jesus is revealed from heaven with his mighty angels in flaming fire,* [8]*inflicting vengeance upon those who do not know God and upon those who do not obey the gospel of our Lord Jesus.* [9]*They shall suffer the punishment of eternal destruction and exclusion from the presence of the Lord and from the glory of his might,* [10]*when he comes on that day to be glorified in his saints, and to be marveled at in all who have believed, because our testimony to you was believed.* [11]*To this end we always pray for you, that our God may make you worthy of his call, and may fulfil every good resolve and work of faith by his power,* [12]*so that the name of our Lord Jesus may be glorified in you, and you in him, according to the grace of our God and the Lord Jesus Christ.*

OVERVIEW: Paul holds up the high moral standard to which Christians are called and to which they, along with all other persons, will be held accountable. It is a standard of mutual love, as well as of the patient endurance of affliction (CHRYSOSTOM). The final judgment that is to come will render justice for faithful believers who have suffered, but also torment for their persecutors (THEODORE). If it is true that the faithful will be held to a high standard and punished for their lapses, how much more true this must be for their persecutors (THEODORET)! The judgment that God exercises is truly a reflection of the righteousness that God essentially is. It is God's nature, therefore, to require retribution of those who have sinned, as well to give reward to virtue (PELAGIUS). We see the work of the whole Trinity of Father, Son and Spirit in the growth of the Thessalonians' faith (AMBROSE). The merit that accrues to believers in their spiritual growth is based on God's grace at work within them (THEODORE, AUGUSTINE). This grace works in the lives of believers through affliction (AUGUSTINE). The Lord speaks to us both gently and fiercely when reproof is in order (EPHREM).

1:2 God the Father and the Lord Jesus Christ

OF THE FATHER AS WELL. AMBROSE: For while I say that similar things are written of the Son as of the Spirit, I am rather proceeding to the following point. My claim is not that because something is written of the Son, therefore it would appear to be reverently written of the Holy Spirit. Rather, I am contending against the argument that because the same is written of the Spirit, therefore the Son's honor is lessened because of the Spirit. For they say, Is it not written of God the Father?[1] But let them learn that it is also said of God the Father, "In the Lord I will praise the word,"[2] and elsewhere, "In God we will do mighty deeds,"[3] "My remembrance shall be ever in Thee,"[4] and "In Thy name will we rejoice,"[5] and again in another place, "That his deeds may be manifested, that they are wrought in God,"[6] and by Paul, "In God, who created all things,"[7] and again, "Paul and Silvanus and Timothy to the church of the Thessalonians in God the Father and the Lord Jesus Christ." OF THE HOLY SPIRIT 2.8.75-76.[8]

---

[1]In other words, because something in Scripture is said with reference to God the Father, can it not also be said to apply to the Spirit without detracting glory from the Father, just as something said of the *ousia* of the Father can also be applied to the Son equally? Ambrose here argues for the full divinity of the Holy Spirit with the same logic that is applied to the divinity of the Son, namely, that honorific statements in Scripture can apply not just to two but to all three—Father, Son and Spirit—equally. His Arian opponents tend to take the position that if statements about the Father are applied to the Son or to the Spirit, somehow the majesty, or monarchy, of God is threatened. [2]Ps 56 (55):4. [3]Ps 60 (59):12. [4]Ps 71 (70):6. [5]Ps 89 (88):16. [6]Jn 3:21. [7]Eph 3:9. [8]NPNF 2 10:124*.

1:3a We Are Bound to Give Thanks

THANKSGIVING OUR BOUNDEN DUTY. THE-ODORE OF MOPSUESTIA: Paul seems to say here that the activity of grace has grown, for he does not say that "we give thanks" but that "we are bound to give thanks." In the same way we deserve to have a complaint lodged against us if we do not render to someone what is justly owed. This is the force of "as is fitting," where the point is that there has been an increase in the work of grace, such that what has happened in the Thessalonians is rightly referred to God as its source. COMMENTARY ON 2 THESSALO-NIANS.[9]

NOT OUR OWN DOING. AUGUSTINE: There could be no merit in men's choice of Christ, if it were not that God's grace precedes any faith or action on their part in his choosing them. This is why the apostle Paul pronounces to the Thessalonians this benediction, "The Lord make you to increase and abound in love toward one another, and toward all men."[10] This benediction to love one another he gave us, who had also given us a law that we should love one another. Then, in the salutation addressed to the same church where some of its members possessed the disposition which he had wished them to cultivate, Paul says, "We are bound to thank God always for you, brothers. This is quite fitting, because your faith grows robustly, and your mutual charity abounds." ON GRACE AND FREE WILL 1.18.38.[11]

1:3b Your Faith Is Growing Abundantly

HOW CAN FAITH GROW? CHRYSOSTOM: And how, you say, can faith increase? It does so when we suffer something horrible for the sake of faith. It is a great thing for faith to be solidly established and not to be carried away by some sophistry. But when the winds assail us, when the rains burst upon us, when a violent storm is raised on every side and the waves follow upon

one another, that fact that we are not shaken is a proof that faith grows, grows abundantly and becomes more exalted. HOMILIES ON 2 THESSA-LONIANS 2.[12]

1:5 That You May Be Made Worthy

NO ONE IS SPARED. AUGUSTINE: Lastly, there is the matter of Faustus' crafty insinuation, that the Old Testament misrepresents God as threatening to come with a sword which will spare neither the righteous nor the wicked. If the words were explained to the pagan, he would perhaps disagree neither with the Old Testament nor with the New; and he might see the beauty of the parable in the Gospel, which people who pretend to be Christians either misunderstand from their blindness or reject from their perversity. The vine's great farmer uses his pruning hook differently on the fruitful and in the unfruitful branches. Yet he spares neither good nor bad, pruning one and cutting off the other.[13] No one is so just that he does not need to be tried by affliction to advance or to establish or prove his virtue. Do the Manichaeans not reckon Paul as righteous, who, while confessing humbly and honestly his past sins, still gives thanks for being justified by faith in Jesus Christ? Was Paul himself then spared of suffering by God whom fools misunderstand? He says, "I will spare neither the righteous nor the sinner."[14] Hear the apostle himself, "Lest I should be exalted above measure by the abundance of the revelation, there was given to me a thorn in the flesh, a messenger of Satan to buffet

---

[9]TEM 2:42-43. Theodore's point seems to be that our thanksgiving to God is based on our observation of what we see God's grace doing in those who are sanctified; that is, we see the increase. Augustine, by contrast (see the next selection), argues that our gratitude flows from the recognition that we must be completely dependent on this free grace in the first place. Here we have something of the difference between the Greek Christian and Latin Christian emphases in the doctrine of grace. [10]1 Thess 3:12. [11]FC 59:234.* [12]NPNF 1 13:380*. [13]Jn 15:1-3. [14]Ezek 21:3-4; cf. Gen 18:23-26.

me. For this I asked the Lord three times, that he would remove it from me; and he said to me, My grace is sufficient for you, for strength is perfected in weakness."[15] . . . Paul also, besides recording his own experience, says that the afflictions and persecutions of the righteous exhibit the judgment of God. REPLY TO FAUSTUS THE MANICHAEAN 22.20.[16]

1:6 Repay with Affliction Those Who Afflict You

NOT AN OPINION BUT A DECLARATION. THEODORET OF CYR: When Paul says "since indeed," he means it as an affirmation without any shred of doubt. When we are in the habit of making an affirmation, we say "Since indeed this is true," meaning "This is to be treated as true without any question." Therefore God is said to be just, when, coming as the enforcer of the law, there is reward for us who have suffered for the faith and punishment for the godlessness of our persecutors. INTERPRETATION OF THE SECOND LETTER TO THE THESSALONIANS.[17]

PELAGIUS: "Since indeed" suggests confirmation, not doubt. It is as if Paul had said that since the source of righteousness can judge what is righteous, just as God has promised rest for those who suffer for his name, so tribulation will come for those who make tribulation for the faithful. PELAGIUS'S COMMENTARY ON THE SECOND LETTER TO THE THESSALONIANS.[18]

1:7 In Flaming Fire

GENTLE SHOWERS AND VIOLENT RAINS. EPHREM THE SYRIAN: But why instead of a stern reproof did our Lord speak a parable of persuasion to that Pharisee?[19] He spoke the parable to him tenderly, that he, though stubborn and resistant, might unawares be enticed to correct his perversities. For the waters that are frozen by the force of a cold wind, the heat of the sun gently dissolves. So our Lord did not oppose

him harshly, that he might not give occasion to the rebellious to rebel again. . . . Our Lord, then, did not employ harsh reproof, because his coming was of grace. He did not refrain from reproof, because his later coming will be of retribution. Even though he had come in humility, he nonetheless caused men to be afraid, because "it is a fearful thing to fall into his hands"[20] when he shall come "in flaming fire." But our Lord most often helped others by way of persuasion than by reproof. For the gentle shower softens the earth and penetrates all through it. But violent rain binds and hardens the face of the earth, so that it does not receive it. THREE HOMILIES 1.22.[21]

1:9 The Punishment of Eternal Destruction

ULTIMATE CONSEQUENCES. CHRYSOSTOM: But where, I ask, will be the location of hell? Somewhere, I think, far removed from this world. For as the prisons and the mines are at a great distance from royal residences, so will hell be located far from this world. We aren't interested in finding its location but in escaping it. And just because God doesn't punish everyone here, don't doubt things to come. For God is merciful and patient. That is why he issues warnings and doesn't immediately cast us into hell. For "I

---

[15]2 Cor 12:7-9. [16]NPNF 1 4:278-79*. Having himself been an argumentative member of the Manichaean sect before his conversion to the faith of the Catholic church, Augustine understood their cosmological dualism well and contended against it in a famous debate with a revered Manichaean bishop, Faustus. Considering themselves to be the true Christians, the Manichaeans took the position that the God of the Old Testament is an evil God who has imposed the suffering of gross materiality on humankind and that in the Jewish Scriptures this God is portrayed in all of his jealous, vengeful perversity. Augustine responds with the classic anti-Gnostic argument that God in the Old Testament and God in the New Testament are the same. What we see in the Old Testament is the intentional working out of God's righteous judgment in sanctifying the righteous and meting out to the unrighteous their deserved punishment. In the background of this latter argument is the unfolding of Augustine's doctrine of double election, not yet fully elaborated. [17]PG 82:659BC/660BC [18]PETE 440. [19]Lk 18:9-14, in the parable of the Pharisee and the Publican. [20]Heb 10:31. [21]NPNF 2 13:314*.

don't desire," he says, "the death of a sinner."[22] These words have no meaning, however, if sinners never die. And I know, indeed, that there is nothing less pleasant to you than these words. But to me nothing is more pleasant. . . . Let us, then, continually discuss these things. For to remember hell prevents our falling into hell. Do you not hear St. Paul saying, "Who shall suffer everlasting punishment from the face of the Lord"? Homilies on Romans 31.4-5.[23]

The Import of "Eternal." Theodore of Mopsuestia: Paul shows here just how seriousness this punishment is by his use of "eternal." Indeed the punishment of those wicked who have died is completed in a reality that transcends time itself and is forever. Commentary on 2 Thessalonians.[24]

1:11 Our God May Make You Worthy

Only by Grace. Augustine: I said, "Salvation through this religion, through which alone true salvation is promised and truly promised, has never been lacking to anyone who was worthy of it, and the one to whom it was lacking was unworthy of it." I did not mean this as though anyone were worthy according to his own merits, but as the apostle says, "God's purpose in election" does not depend on deeds but is applied according to him who calls—Rebekah was told, "The elder shall serve the younger"[25] —and he asserts that this call depends on the purpose of God. Hence Paul says, "Not according to our works, but according to his own purpose and grace."[26] Similarly, he says, "We know that for those who love God all things work together for good, for those who are called according to his purpose."[27] Concerning this call he says, "that he may consider you worthy of his calling." Retractations 2.31.[28]

---

[22]Ezek 18:32. [23]NPNF 1 11:558*. [24]TEM 2:45-46. [25]Rom 9:12. [26]2 Tim 1:9. [27]Rom 8:28. [28]FC 60:184-85*. Augustine is commenting on his *Exposition of Six Questions Against the Pagans*.

2:1-12 THE SIGNS OF THE COMING JUDGMENT

[1]Now concerning the coming of our Lord Jesus Christ and our assembling to meet him, we beg you, brethren, [2]not to be quickly shaken in mind or excited, either by spirit or by word, or by letter purporting to be from us, to the effect that the day of the Lord has come. [3]Let no one deceive you in any way; for that day will not come, unless the rebellion comes first, and the man of lawlessness[a] is revealed, the son of perdition, [4]who opposes and exalts himself against every so-called god or object of worship, so that he takes his seat in the temple of God, proclaiming himself to be God. [5]Do you not remember that when I was still with you I told you this? [6]And you know what is restraining him now so that he may be revealed in his time. [7]For the mystery of lawlessness is already at work; only he who now restrains it will do so until he is out of the way. [8]And then the lawless one will be revealed, and the Lord Jesus will slay him with the breath of his mouth and destroy him by his appearing and his coming. [9]The coming of the lawless one by the activity of Satan will be with all power and with pretended signs and wonders,

[10]*and with all wicked deception for those who are to perish, because they refused to love the truth and so be saved. [11]Therefore God sends upon them a strong delusion, to make them believe what is false, [12]so that all may be condemned who did not believe the truth but had pleasure in unrighteousness.*

a Other ancient authorities read *sin*

OVERVIEW: In laying out a description of what the future holds, Paul emphasizes that the resurrection has not yet occurred and thus much suffering and much discipline are still required. Antichrist is the man in whom Satan fully works (CHRYSOSTOM). It is essential that the Thessalonians, as they look to the future, resist false teachers and lying prophets, for they will be tempted by much superstition and heresy (AUGUSTINE). The most important thing is that the Thessalonians not be confused about the timing of things, particularly on the matter of the final appearance of the Lord (SEVERIAN). Paul is concerned to help the Thessalonians identify clearly the kinds of deceptions and lies to which they will be exposed, so that the faithful may stand fast (THEODORET). It is important to remember that the Lord warned that deceivers would come, particularly the Antichrist (CYRIL OF JERUSALEM, AUGUSTINE), who is the one who persecutes the saints (CHRYSOSTOM). Firmness in the basic precepts of the gospel is our only defense in the difficult times that are to come (JOHN OF DAMASCUS). Misunderstanding of the resurrection leads to heresy, though it is not necessary for Christians to know exactly when the general resurrection will occur (ATHANASIUS).

Disputes about such things as the keeping of the Jewish food laws and the time frame of the resurrection have existed in the church from the beginning. The figure of Antichrist represents the extreme of evil, just as Jesus represents the fullness of goodness (ORIGEN). Not to know the exact time of the Lord's coming in no way detracts from the commandment to be ready with lamps burning. The important thing is not to know the time of his coming but to be ready when he does come. Attempts to pinpoint the identity of Antichrist are quite presumptuous (AUGUSTINE), though some speculate that it might be Nero (CHRYSOSTOM) or the heretics (THEODORET). There will be much falling away from faith as the end approaches. Therefore, we must be vigilant (CYRIL OF JERUSALEM). That which restrains the coming of Antichrist is the Roman Empire (TERTULLIAN, CHRYSOSTOM). The restrainer is the Holy Spirit (SEVERIAN) or God's own decree (THEODORET). The casting out of Antichrist will be done by Father, Son and Spirit together (AMBROSE). The delusion that will come upon wicked people as the end approaches is willed by God out of the demands of his justice, as well as from his will to sanctify while there is still time (AUGUSTINE, FULGENTIUS, JOHN OF DAMASCUS).

2:1 *The Coming of Our Lord Jesus Christ*

THE TIMING OF THE RESURRECTION UNKNOWN. CHRYSOSTOM: When the resurrection will be, he has not said: "It will come in due order"; he has said: "And our assembling to meet him." This point is quite important. Observe how Paul's exhortation is accompanied by praise and encouragement, for he makes it clear that Jesus and all the saints will certainly appear at that time with us. HOMILIES ON 2 THESSALONIANS 3.[1]

A CORRECT UNDERSTANDING OF TIME.

---

[1]NPNF 1 13:386*.

ATHANASIUS: Now it is right and necessary, as in all divine Scripture, so here, faithfully to explain the time of which the apostle wrote, and the person and the point. This is so that the reader will not from ignorance miss either these or any similar particular and thus miss the true sense of the text. This was what the inquiring eunuch understood when he asked Philip, "I ask you, of whom does the prophet speak this? Of himself, or of someone else?"[2] He feared lest, having explained the lesson unsuitably to the person, he should wander from the right sense. And the disciples, wishing to learn the time of what was predicted, implored the Lord: "Tell us," they said, "when shall these things be? And what is the sign of your coming?"[3] And again, hearing from the Savior the events of the end, they desired to learn the time of it, that they might be kept from error themselves. They also wished to be able to teach others, just as, when they had learned, they set right the Thessalonians, who were going wrong.[4] When, then, one understands these points properly, knows properly these points, his understanding of the faith is right and healthy. But if he fails to understand, he immediately falls into heresy. Thus, Hymenaeus and Alexander and their followers[5] were beside the time when they said that the resurrection had already taken place. The Galatians, too, were after the time[6] in continuing to think circumcision was an important issue. DIS-COURSES AGAINST THE ARIANS 1.54.[7]

THE BENEFIT OF NOT KNOWING. ATHANA-SIUS: And further, not to know when the end is, or when the day of the end will occur, is actually a good thing. If people knew the time of the end, they might begin to ignore the present time as they waited for the end days. They might well begin to argue that they should only focus on themselves. Therefore, God has also remained silent concerning the time of our death. If people knew the day of their death, they would immediately begin to neglect themselves for the greater part of their lifetime. The Word, then, has con-

cealed both the end of all things and the time of our own death from us, for in the end of all is the end of each, and in the end of each the end of all is comprehended. This is so that, when things remain uncertain and always in prospect, we advance day by day as if summoned, reaching forward to the things before us and forgetting the things behind.[8] . . . The Lord, then, knowing what is good for us beyond ourselves, thus stabilized the disciples in a correct understanding. They, being taught, set right those of Thessalonica, who were likely to err on the very same point. DISCOURSES AGAINST THE ARIANS 3.49.[9]

THE SAME CHRIST WILL COME. THEODORET OF CYR: To what has been said it must also be added that we must not affirm that after the ascension the Lord Christ is not Christ but only the begotten Son. The divine Gospels and the history of the Acts and the epistles of the apostle himself were, as we know, written after the ascension. It is after the ascension that the divine Paul exclaims "Seeing then that we have a great high priest that is passed into the heavens, Jesus the Son of God, let us hold fast our profession."[10] . . . And again when writing to the same a second time, he says, "Now we beseech you, brothers, by the coming of our Lord Jesus Christ, and by our gathering together unto him." LETTERS 146.[11]

DISAGREEMENTS FROM THE BEGINNING. ORIGEN: At least, when the apostles were preaching and the eyewitnesses of Jesus were teaching his

---

[2]Acts 8:34. [3]Mt 24:3. [4]1 Thess 4:13. [5]2 Tim 2:17; 1 Tim 1:20. [6]These curious phrases "beside the time" and "after the time," translated literally from Athanasius, seem to be his way of getting at a statement often made in modern theology that Christians live "between the times," that is, between the time of Christ's resurrection and the general resurrection of all the dead at the end of history. His argument is that Gnosticizing heretics like Hymenaeus and Alexander act as if all of the work of redemption is now complete, while Judaizing heretics like some of the Galatians act as if the resurrection of Christ has not yet happened. [7]NPNF 2 4:338*. [8]Phil 3:13. [9]NPNF 2 4:420-21*. [10]Heb 4:14, attributed to Paul by Theodoret. [11]NPNF 2 3:321.

precepts, no minor dispute in the church took place among Jewish believers about those of the Gentiles who were converted to the faith; the question was whether they ought to keep the Jewish customs or if the burden of clean or unclean meats ought to be taken away so that it would not be a load upon those Gentiles who abandoned their traditional customs and believed in Jesus. Furthermore, in the epistles of Paul, who was contemporary with those who had seen Jesus, there are some statements to be found which concern certain disputes about the resurrection, and about the view that it had already occurred, and about the question whether the day of the Lord was already present or not. AGAINST CELSUS 3.11.[12]

2:2 Not to Be Quickly Shaken

WARNING AGAINST COMPLACENCY. AUGUS-TINE: Therefore, not to know the times is something different from moral decay and the love of vice. For when the apostle Paul said, "Don't be easily shaken in your mind nor be frightened, neither by word nor by epistle as sent from us, as if the day of the Lord were at hand," he obviously did not want them to believe those who thought the coming of the Lord was already at hand. Neither, moreover, did he want them to be like the wicked servant and say, "My Lord will not be coming for a long time," and deliver themselves over to destruction by pride and immoral behavior. Thus, Paul's desire that they should not listen to false rumors about the imminent approach of the last day was consistent with his wish that they should await the coming of their Lord fully prepared and ready for the journey, with lamps burning.[13] LETTERS 199.1.2.[14]

AUGUSTINE: All this you repeat with great piety and truth, praising the happiness of those who love the coming of the Lord. But those to whom the apostle said, "Be not easily moved from your mind as if the day of the Lord were at hand," evi-

dently loved the Lord's coming. The purpose of the doctor of the Gentiles in saying this was not to break them away from the love which burned in them. Rather, he did not want them to put their faith in those from whom they heard that the day of the Lord was at hand, lest, perhaps, when the time had passed when they thought he would come and they realized that he had not come, they might think that the other promises made to them were also false and might despair of the mercy of faith itself. Therefore, it is not the one who asserts that he is near nor the one who asserts that he is not near who loves the coming of the Lord but the one who rightly waits for him, whether he be near or far, with sincere faith, firm hope and ardent love. LETTERS 199.4.15.[15]

2:3 Let No One Deceive You

THE TWO EXTREMES. ORIGEN: As Celsus also objects to the doctrine about the figure called Antichrist, though he has read neither the passages about him in Daniel, nor those in Paul, nor the Savior's prophecies in the Gospels concerning his coming,[16] we have to say a little about this also. "Just as faces are unlike other faces, so also the hearts of men are unlike one another."[17] Obviously differences exist in the hearts of men, both among those who have inclined to goodness, since they have not all been molded and shaped equally and similarly in their propensity toward good, and among those who because of their neglect of what is good rapidly pass to the other extreme. For among the latter there also are some who have been overwhelmed by the flood of evil, while others have sunk less far. Why, then, is it absurd that among

---

[12]OAC 134-35. Origen is arguing against the pagan philosopher Celsus that differences of opinion on time among Christians have always been present and that such differences are no presumption against the truth of the gospel. [13]Lk 12:35-36. [14]FC 30:358*. [15]FC 30:367*. [16]Cf. Dan 8:23-27; 11:36; 2 Thess 2:3-4; Mt 24:27; Lk 17:24. [17]Prov 27:19.

men there should be two extremes, if I may so say, the one of goodness, the other of the opposite, so that the extreme of goodness exists in the human nature of Jesus, since from him the mighty work of conversion, healing and improvement flowed to the human race, whereas the opposite extreme exists in him who is called Antichrist? God understood all this through his foreknowledge. Seeing that there were these two extremes, he willed to tell men about these things through the prophets, in order that those who understood their words might be made lovers of what is better and be on their guard against the opposite. It was right, also, that one of the extremes, the best, should be called Son of God because of his superiority, and that the one diametrically opposed to him should be called son of the evil demon, who is Satan and the devil. AGAINST CELSUS 6.45.[18]

2:3-4 The Rebellion, the Man of Lawlessness

THE ANTICHRIST. CHRYSOSTOM: Here Paul discusses the Antichrist and reveals great mysteries. What is the "falling away"? He calls him Apostasy; soon he will destroy many and make them fall away. . . . And he calls him "the man of sin." For he shall commit numberless evils and shall cause others to do them. But Paul calls him "the son of perdition," because he is also to be destroyed. But who is he? Satan? By no means. Rather he is a man in whom Satan fully works. For he is a man. . . . For he will not introduce idolatry but will be a kind of opponent to God. He will abolish all the gods and will order men to worship him instead of God. He will be seated in the temple of God, not that in Jerusalem only, but also in every church. HOMILIES ON 2 THESSALONIANS 3.[19]

MASKED HERETICS. CYRIL OF JERUSALEM: Such is Paul's account.[20] And we have reached the "falling away." Men, that is, have fallen away from the true faith. Some proclaim the identity of Father and Son. Others dare to assert that

one should believe Christ has come into existence out of nonexistence. Formerly heretics were quite evident, but now the church is full of masked heretics. For men have deserted the truth and want to have their ears tickled.[21] Make a plausible case, and everyone is ready to listen to you. Talk of changing one's life, and everyone deserts you. The majority have fallen away from the sound doctrines and are readier to choose what is bad than to prefer what is good. So there you have the "falling away," and the coming of the enemy is to be expected next. Meanwhile, he has begun to send out his forerunners here and there, so that the spoil may be prepared for him when he comes. Therefore, brothers, look to yourselves. Watch over your souls carefully. CATECHETICAL LECTURES 15.9.[22]

A WISE CAUTION. AUGUSTINE: No one can doubt that Paul is here[23] speaking of Antichrist, telling us that the day of judgment (which he calls the day of the Lord) will not come without the prior coming of a figure whom he calls the Apostate, meaning, of course, an apostate from the Lord God. And if this appellation can rightly be attached to all the ungodly, how much more to him! There is, however, some uncertainty about the "temple" in which he is to take his seat. Is it the ruins of the temple built by King Solomon, or actually in a church? For the apostle would not say "the temple of God" if he meant the temple of some idol or demon. For that reason some people would have it that Antichrist means here not the leader himself but what we may call his whole body, the multitude, that is, of those who belong to him, together with himself, their leader. . . . For myself I am much astonished at the great pre-

---

[18]OAC 362*. Origen is arguing the position against Celsus that evil can exist only as a diminishment and distortion of good and that, therefore, even as evil it eventually serves the providential purposes of God. [19]NPNF 1 13:386*. [20]Cyril has just cited 2 Thessalonians 2:3-10. [21]Cf. 2 Tim 4:3. [22]LCC 4:154-55*. [23]Augustine has just cited 2 Thessalonians 2:1-12.

sumption of those who venture such guesses. THE CITY OF GOD 20.19.2.[24]

HIS OWN GLORY. AUGUSTINE: He who speaks on his own seeks his own glory.[25] This will be that one who is called the Antichrist, "exalting himself," as the apostle says, "above all that is called God and that is worshiped." Indeed, the Lord, announcing that he would seek his own glory, not the glory of the Father, said to the Jews, "I have come in the name of my Father, and you have not received me; another will come in his own name, this one you will receive."[26] He signified that they would receive the Antichrist, who would seek the glory of his own name, puffed up, hollow, and so not enduring but in fact ruinous. But our Lord Jesus Christ offered us a great example of humility. TRACTATES ON JOHN 29.8.[27]

THE TRIAL IS TRANSITORY. BASIL THE GREAT: In truth, both of our ears rang on learning of the shameless and inhuman heresy of those who persecuted you. They had no regard for age, nor for the labors of a life well spent, nor for the affection of the people. On the contrary, they tortured and dishonored bodies, handed them over to exile and plundered whatever property they were able to find, not fearing the censure of men nor foreseeing the fearful requital of the just Judge. . . . But, along with these considerations, there came this thought also: The Lord has not entirely abandoned his churches, has he? And this is not the last hour, is it? Is apostasy finding an entrance through them, in order that now the impious one may be revealed, "the son of perdition, who opposes and is exalted above all that is called God, or that is worshiped"? But if the trial is transitory, bear it, noble champions of Christ. . . . For if all creation is destroyed and the scheme of the world is altered, what wonder is it if we also, being a part of creation, suffer the common evils and are given over to afflictions? . . . The crowns of martyrs await you, brothers; the choirs of confessors

are ready to reach out to you their hands and to receive you into their own number. LETTERS 139.[28]

2:6-7 He Who Now Restrains It

THE ROMAN EMPIRE. TERTULLIAN: There is also another, even greater, obligation for us to pray for the emperors; yes, even for the continuance of the empire in general and for Roman interests. We realize that the tremendous force which is hanging over the whole world, and the very end of the world with its threat of dreadful afflictions, is arrested for a time by the continued existence of the Roman Empire. This event we have no desire to experience and, in praying that it may be deferred, we favor the continuance of Rome. APOLOGY 32.[29]

CHRYSOSTOM: One may naturally inquire what is that which restrains the man of lawlessness, and in addition, why Paul expresses it so obscurely. What then is it that holds back, that is, that hinders the revealing of, the Antichrist? Some indeed say, the grace of the Spirit, but others the Roman Empire. I agree with the latter position. Why? Because if Paul meant to say the Spirit, he would not have spoken obscurely but plainly, that even now the grace of the Spirit, that is the gifts, hold back the Antichrist. If not, he should have come by now, if his coming was to occur with the cessation of the gifts of the Spirit; for they have long since ceased.[30] But because Paul said this of the Roman Empire, he merely touched the topic, understandably speaking covertly and darkly. For he had no need to create unnecessary enemies and useless dangers.

---

[24]CG 932-33. [25]Cf. Jn 5:30-31; 2 Cor 10:18. [26]Jn 5:43. [27]FC 88:19-20*. [28]FC 13:284-85*. Basil here writes to the Alexandrians. [29]FC 10:88. [30]This means not that all gifts of the Spirit have ceased (for this Chrysostom elsewhere denies; cf. his *Homilies on 1 Corinthians 12*) but that the mightiest and most miraculous gifts given at and following Pentecost have already been given, received and had their effect.

. . . "For the mystery of lawlessness does already work." He speaks here of Nero, as if he were the type of the Antichrist. HOMILIES ON 2 THESSALONIANS 4.[31]

THE HOLY SPIRIT. SEVERIAN OF GABALA: That which restrains and prevents the coming of the lawless one is the Holy Spirit. Paul says this to show that the mystery of iniquity is already beginning in the heresies that have arisen since apostolic times. The Manichaeans say that the devil is the God of the law, and the Marcionites say that the father of Christ is not the God of the law. PAULINE COMMENTARY FROM THE GREEK CHURCH.[32]

GOD'S OWN DECREE. THEODORET OF CYR: Indeed, the God of the universe has decreed that this figure shall himself appear during the time of consummation, and thus it is God's own decree that actually detains him until that appearance. What this means is as follows. When the divine apostle taught that the Lord had instructed him to preach the gospel among all the Gentiles, and then the end would come, and when he saw the worship of idols flourishing in connection with this, he spoke in obedience to the Lord's teaching. He said that superstition would be openly overturned and that when divine preaching would shine forth, then the adversary of the truth would appear. . . . Some say that the mystery of iniquity is Nero, that the master of impiety has already lived. But I think that the apostle indicates the heresies that have since arisen. INTERPRETATION OF THE SECOND LETTER TO THE THESSALONIANS.[33]

DISORDER AND DISHARMONY. BASIL THE GREAT: Now, if good order with its attendant harmony is characteristic of those who look to one source of authority and are subject to one king, then universal disorder and disharmony are a sign that leadership is lacking. By the same token, if we discover in our midst such discord as I have mentioned, both with regard to one

another and with respect to the Lord's commands, it would either be an indictment or our rejection of the true king. That agrees with the scriptural saying, "only that he who now holds back does so until he is taken out of the way," or of denial of him according to the psalmist, "The fool has said in his heart: There is no God."[34] PREFACE ON THE JUDGMENT OF GOD.[35]

2:8a The Lawless One Will Be Revealed

THE NATURE OF ANTICHRIST. CYRIL OF JERUSALEM: The Antichrist just mentioned by Paul will come when the destined period of the Roman Empire has run its course and the subsequent end of the world is drawing near. Ten claimants to the empire will arise simultaneously, I suppose in different parts, but all wearing the purple at the same time. Antichrist will form an eleventh after them, having seized the imperial power by the use of magic arts. He will humble three of those who came to power before him and cause the remaining seven to be Caesars under him.[36] At first he will feign mildness and will appear to be a learned and understanding man, with pretended prudence and kindness. Then he will take in the Jews, by making them suppose him to be their expected Messiah, by false signs and wonders produced by magical trickery. And afterwards his character will be written large in evil deeds of inhumanity and lawlessness of every kind, so as to outdo all wicked and godless men that were before him. He will display a murderous, most absolute, pitiless and unstable temper toward all people, but especially toward us Christians. He will act insolently for only three and a half years. Then he will be defeated by the second glorious coming from heaven of the only-begotten Son of

---

[31]NPNF 1 13:388-89*. [32]NTA 15:334. A hallmark of both the Marcionite and Manichaean heresies was the contention that there is an evil God who has created the material world and who is represented in the Jewish Scriptures. [33]PG 82:665AB/666AB. [34]Ps 13:1. [35]FC 9:39*. [36]Cf. Dan 7:24.

God, our Lord and Savior Jesus, the true Christ. He will destroy Antichrist "with the spirit of his mouth" and commit him to the flames of hell. CATECHETICAL LECTURES 15.12.[37]

2:8b *The Lord Jesus Will Slay Him*

CHRIST AND THE SPIRIT. AMBROSE: We have heard that the Lord Jesus not only judges but also punishes in the Spirit. For neither would he punish Antichrist, whom, as we read, "the Lord Jesus shall slay with the Spirit of his mouth," unless he had already judged him as fit for punishment . . . but the unity of the divine action remains undivided, since Christ cannot be separated from the Spirit, nor the Spirit act apart from Christ. For the unity of the divine nature cannot be divided. OF THE HOLY SPIRIT 3.44.[38]

THE PROPER POWER OF GOODNESS. CHRYSOSTOM: "To the one a savor from death to death, to the other a savor from life to life."[39] For this sweet savor some so receive that they are saved, others so that they perish. If any one is lost, it is his own fault. . . . Light (as I have already observed) blinds the weak. Such is the nature of good things. They not only correct things similar to them but also destroy their opposite. In this way their power is most clearly displayed. Fire displays its unique power when it gives light and when it purifies gold. The same is true when it consumes thorns. In all these cases it demonstrates itself to be fire. Christ, too, in the same way will display his own majesty when he "shall consume" Antichrist "with the breath of his mouth and overcome him with the manifestation of his coming." HOMILIES ON SECOND CORINTHIANS 5.2.[40]

THE JUSTICE OF THE WORD. ORIGEN: Now just as it is said that the task of the Word is to judge with justice, so also the Word's task is to fight with justice, that by thus fighting the soul's enemies with reason and justice, he may dwell in the soul, justifying it when the irrational elements and injustices are destroyed. He casts out the hostile elements from that soul which, if I may speak in this way, has been taken captive by Christ for salvation. The war that the Word wages is seen even more clearly when we compare it to the war waged by he who pretends to be the Word. This one proclaims himself the truth when he is not the truth but a lie, declaring that he is the truth. For then the Word, having fully armed himself against the lie, "destroys it with the breath of his mouth and annihilates it by the appearance of his presence." COMMENTARY ON JOHN 2.54-55.[41]

2:9-10 *The Activity of Satan*

JUDGMENTS PRECEDE AND FOLLOW. AUGUSTINE: Thus it is that what is obscure in the words of the apostle has given rise to various conjectures. Yet, of one thing there is no doubt, namely, that Paul meant Christ will not come to judge the living and the dead until after his adversary, Antichrist, has come to seduce the souls of the dead. And, of course, the fact that those souls are to be seduced is already a part of God's hidden judgment. . . . There seems to be some ambiguity in the expression "pretended signs and wonders." It may be that Satan is to deceive men's senses by means of phantasms, in which they imagine they see wonders which are nonexistent. Or perhaps true miracles will lead into deception those who ought to believe that miracles can be done only by God but who mistakenly ascribe them to the devil's power, particularly at a time when Satan is to be given unheard-of power. . . . What the devil does is done with his own wicked and malign purpose, but it is permitted by God's just judgment so "that all may be judged who have not believed the truth but have preferred wickedness." Thus

---

[37]LCC 4:156-57*. [38]NPNF 2 10:141*. [39]2 Cor 2:16. [40]NPNF 1 12:302*. [41]FC 80:108*.

it comes about that judgments both precede and follow the deception. Those who are deceived are antecedently judged by these judgments of God, covertly just and justly covert, by which he has never ceased to judge even since the first sin of his rational creature. Those are deceived and subsequently judged in a last and overt judgment by Christ Jesus, who is to be the great judge of all judges as he was the victim of the most unjust of all judgments. THE CITY OF GOD 20.19.4.[42]

THE INSTRUMENT OF EVIL. CYRIL OF JERUSALEM: "And his coming is according to the working of Satan with all power and signs and lying wonders." This means that Satan will use him as his personal instrument. Realizing that his own condemnation will be no longer deferred, he will no longer wage war through his ministers in his usual way, but now openly, in person. "With all signs and lying wonders," for the father of falsehood will display his lying works and cheating fantasies, to make the people think they see a dead man raised, when he is not raised, and the lame walking, and the blind receiving sight, when there have been no such cures. CATECHETICAL LECTURES 15.14-15.[43]

2:11 God Sends Judgment Upon Them

GOD'S HIDDEN JUDGMENT. AUGUSTINE: We can recount many other events clearly showing that from a hidden judgment of God comes perversity of heart, with the result that refusal to hear the truth leads to commission of sin, and this sin is also punishment for preceding sin. For to believe a lie and not believe the truth is indeed sin, but it comes from the blindness of heart which by a hidden but just judgment of God is also punishment for sin. We see this also in what the apostle says to the Thessalonians, "For they have not received the love of truth, that they might be saved. Therefore God sends them a misleading influence that they may believe falsehood." AGAINST JULIAN 5.3.12.[44]

THE WILLINGNESS TO REPENT. CYPRIAN: Not to recognize sins lest penance follow is the wrath of God, as it is written, "And the Lord gave to them the spirit of a deep sleep,"[45] lest they actually return and be cured and healed by their lamentations and just satisfactions after their sins.[46] The apostle Paul in his epistle states and says, "For they have not received the love of truth that they might be saved. Therefore God will send them a misleading influence that they may believe falsehood, that all may be judged who have not believed the truth but have preferred wickedness." The first degree of happiness is not to sin; the second, to recognize the sins committed. LETTERS 59.13.[47]

THE HIDDEN COUNSEL OF HIS WISDOM. FULGENTIUS OF RUSPE: Sometimes by the hidden and incomprehensible judgment of God, the bad angels are permitted to make certain things to test the good and seduce the evil. Now the bad angels themselves do not create what they produce, but they are permitted to bring forth certain things, because these already exist hidden in the heart of God, things which we cannot see.[48] Similarly, the devil was not able to create serpents or frogs, although with God's permission he produced them, just as he was not the creator of the fire when, to test Job, he, with fire falling from heaven, consumed his sheep together with the shepherds. Nor was he the creator of the wind, when a wicked wind

---

[42]FC 24:300-301*. [43]FC 64:62*. [44]FC 35:254. [45]Is 29:10. [46]Cyprian's reference here is to the penitential discipline taught in the church of Carthage at the beginning of the third century. Acts of penance, done in a spirit of contrition and under the supervision of a proper confessor, "make satisfaction" for the sins of the penitent person by being joined to the one sacrifice of Christ. [47]FC 51:184-85*. [48]Fulgentius seems to be repeating in his own way the Augustinian teaching that evil has no being in the strict sense but rather is a decline or falling away from true being. Thus, to the extent that the activity of the bad angels produces anything, that something must have real being and have its origin in God. Evil always has a misguided and deluded intention of good at its core, that is, in Augustinian language, evil intends to produce something but instead reflects its own nothingness.

blowing out of the desert, struck the four corners of the house and crushed all the children of holy Job in one simultaneous ruin. The omnipotent God alone created the various natures, that is, the elements of this world. In secret and hidden places, God places certain seeds of things, hidden to us but visible to the angels. From these, as the nature of the work and its own proper time require, by the hidden counsel of his wisdom, God either commands that certain things be produced by the good angels or permits them to be shown through the bad angels. By permitting these latter things, God shows how much power he has given to the holy angels when he has given the ability to do certain things in the material creation even to the wicked angels. . . . So it is [that] the blessed apostle, speaking of the Antichrist, says, "And thus the lawless one will be revealed." LETTERS TO SCARILA 10.46.[49]

ORTHODOX CONFESSION. JOHN OF DA-

MASCUS: One should know that the Antichrist must come. Antichrist, to be sure, is everyone who does not confess that the Son of God came in the flesh, is perfect God and became perfect man while at the same time he was God. In a peculiar and special sense, however, he who is to come at the consummation of the world is called Antichrist. So, it is first necessary for the gospel to have been preached to all the Gentiles, as the Lord said,[50] and then God shall proceed to the conviction of the impious Jews. . . . "Because they refused to love the truth and so be saved. Therefore God sends upon them a strong delusion, to let them believe what is false, so that all may be condemned who did not believe the truth but had pleasure in unrighteousness." THE ORTHODOX FAITH 4.26.[51]

---

[49]FC 95:464-65*. [50]Mt 24:14. [51]FC 37:398-99*.

2:13-17 REASSURANCE

[13]*But we are bound to give thanks to God always for you, brethren beloved by the Lord, because God chose you from the beginning*[b] *to be saved, through sanctification by the Spirit*[c] *and belief in the truth.* [14]*To this he called you through our gospel, so that you may obtain the glory of our Lord Jesus Christ.* [15]*So then, brethren, stand firm and hold to the traditions which you were taught by us, either by word of mouth or by letter.*

[16]*Now may our Lord Jesus Christ himself, and God our Father, who loved us and gave us eternal comfort and good hope through grace,* [17]*comfort your hearts and establish them in every good work and word.*

b Other ancient authorities read *as the first converts*   c Or *of spirit*

OVERVIEW: Paul here describes the means of salvation: belief in the truth, loyalty to tradition and a sure hope for the future (CHRYSOSTOM). It is this steadfastness in clinging to approved tradition against all innovation and novelty, against heresy itself, that is our assurance of salvation

(AMBROSE, BASIL). Further, it is the knowledge that God has chosen us and the certainty that we are beloved of God that provide the basis for our perseverance in discipline and charity (AMBROSIASTER). Indeed, God chose us because he foreknew that we would be steadfast and true (PELAGIUS). The sanctification of Christians comes through Father, Son and Holy Spirit together (AMBROSE). The faithful traditions of the church are gathered into the creed (CYRIL OF JERUSALEM).

2:13 Sanctification by the Spirit

SANCTIFICATION IS ONE. AMBROSE: And the apostle also teaches that the Holy Spirit sanctifies. For he speaks thus, "We are bound to give thanks to God always for you, brothers dearly beloved of the Lord; because God chose you as first fruits for salvation, in sanctification of the Spirit, and belief of the truth." So, then, the Father sanctifies, the Son also sanctifies, and the Holy Spirit sanctifies; but the sanctification is one, and the grace of the sacrament is one. OF THE HOLY SPIRIT 3.4.27-28.[1]

2:14-15 The Traditions You Were Taught

THE CREED. CYRIL OF JERUSALEM: In learning and professing the faith, embrace and guard that only which is now delivered to you by the church and confirmed by all the Scriptures. For since not everyone has the education and the leisure required to read and know the Scriptures, to prevent the soul perishing from ignorance, we sum up the whole doctrine of the faith in a few lines. . . . For the present, just listen and memorize the creed as I recite it, and you will receive in due course the testimony from Scripture of each of its propositions. For the articles of faith have not been composed to please human desire, but the most important points collected from the Scriptures make up one complete teaching of the faith. And just as the mustard seed in a small grain contains in embryo many future branches, so also the creed embraces in a few words all the religious knowledge in both the Old and New Testament. Pay attention, therefore, brothers, and cling to the teachings which are now delivered to you, and "write them on the tablet of your heart."[2] CATECHETICAL LECTURES 5.12.[3]

2:15 By Word of Mouth or by Letter

UNWRITTEN TRADITION. BASIL THE GREAT: In answer to the objection that the doxology in the form "with the Spirit" has no written authority, we maintain that if there is no other instance of that which is unwritten, then this must not be received. But if the greater number of our mysteries are admitted into our constitution without written authority, then, in company with the many others, let us receive this one. For I hold it apostolic to abide also by the unwritten traditions. "I praise you," it is said, "that you remember me in all things and keep the ordinances as I delivered them to you,"[4] and "Hold fast the traditions which you have been taught whether by word or by our epistle." ON THE SPIRIT 29.71.[5]

DELIVERED WITHOUT WRITING. CHRYSOSTOM: Paul did not instruct Timothy in his duty through letters alone, but also through the spoken word. He shows this, both in many other passages, as where he says, "whether by word or our epistle," and especially here.[6] Let us not, therefore, suppose that Paul spoke anything imperfectly that was related to doctrine. For he

---

[1]NPNF 2 10:139*. [2]Prov 7:3. [3]LCC 4:124*. [4]1 Cor 11:2. [5]NPNF 2 8:44-45. In this passage Basil states in classic form a conviction held by many of the Fathers, that there is an unwritten and authoritative tradition handed down by the church along with the written authority of the Scriptures and the ecumenical councils. This unwritten tradition is embodied in the liturgical, devotional and disciplinary practices of the various Christian communities as they made claims to be handing down what was taught by the apostles themselves in their practices. Basil sees in Paul's distinction between oral and written tradition here a reference to this kind of authority. [6]Chrysostom is commenting on 2 Timothy 1:13-14.

delivered many things to Timothy without writing. He reminds him of these when he says, "Hold fast the form of sound words, which you have heard from me." After the manner of artists, I have impressed on you the image of virtue, fixing in your soul a sort of rule, model and outline of all things pleasing to God. Therefore, cling to these things, and whether you are meditating on any matter of faith or love, or of a sound mind, form your ideas from what I have taught you. It will not be necessary to consult others for examples, when all has been deposited within yourself. HOMILIES ON SECOND TIMOTHY 3.1.[7]

---

[7]NPNF 1 13:484*.

3:1-5 POWER BELONGS TO GOD

[1]*Finally, brethren, pray for us, that the word of the Lord may speed on and triumph, as it did among you,* [2]*and that we may be delivered from wicked and evil men; for not all have faith.* [3]*But the Lord is faithful; he will strengthen you and guard you from evil.*[d] [4]*And we have confidence in the Lord about you, that you are doing and will do the things which we command.* [5]*May the Lord direct your hearts to the love of God and to the steadfastness of Christ.*

d Or the evil one

OVERVIEW: Everywhere in this passage Paul emphasizes that God rather than our mutual self-confidence is the source of our strength (CHRYSOSTOM). Like a millstone, the Scriptures draw out the fine flour of a clean heart from our thoughts (MAXIMUS OF TURIN). In our prayers the Lord directs our hearts (BASIL, AUGUSTINE, CAESARIUS OF ARLES). God ceaselessly grows the faithful soul in the direction of greater spiritual embrace with himself (AMBROSE). God's word is powerful in its ever-present capacity to convert us to God (AUGUSTINE).

3:1 Speed On and Triumph

THE SOUL HASTENS. AMBROSE: Good, indeed, is prudence, but mercy is sweet. Few attain the former, whereas the latter comes to all men. "By reason of your loving-kindness, the souls renewed in the spirit love you." On this account it is also said to the soul, "Your youth shall be renewed like the eagle's."[1] For the psalmist spoke to the soul and said, "Bless the Lord, O my soul."[2] And therefore the soul hastens to the Word and asks that she be drawn to him, so that she may not, perhaps, be left behind, for "the Word of God runs and is not bound." ISAAC, OR THE SOUL 3.10.[3]

THE WORD IS POWERFUL. AUGUSTINE: He also says to the Thessalonians, "For the rest, brothers, pray for us that the word of the Lord may run and may be glorified even as among you; that we may be delivered from troublesome and evil men, for not all men have faith." How else could the word of God run and be glorified

---

[1]Eph 4:23; Ps 102 (103):5. [2]Ps 102 (103):1. [3]FC 65:17.

except by the conversion to the faith of those to whom it is preached, when Paul says to present believers, "Even as among you"? Surely he knows that this is accomplished by him to whom he wishes prayer to be made that this may be so, and also that he may be delivered through their prayers from troublesome and evil men. It is for this reason that he adds, "For not all men have faith," as if to say, "The word of God will not be glorified among all, even though you are praying" because those who were likely to believe were the ones "who were ordained to life everlasting,"[4] predestined "to the adoption of children through Jesus Christ to himself" and chosen "in him before the foundation of the world."[5] No one is so unlearned, so carnal, so slow of wit as not to see that God does what he commands us to ask him to do. Letters 217.7.27.[6]

Like Rapidly Grinding Millstones. Maximus of Turin: Through the operation of these millstones—the new and the old covenants— the holy church, then, acts with unceasing care so as to draw out the fine flour of a clean heart from hidden thoughts, once the roughness of sins has been scattered, and to produce spiritual food from their kernels when they have been cleansed by the heavenly commandments. The apostle Paul says about this food, "I gave you milk to drink, not food,"[7] and again, "Solid food is for the perfect, who have their faculties trained by habit,"[8] and so forth. Purifying our hearts from all that is human, the faithful soul strives to offer God as it were the finest wheat, as holy David says, "A broken spirit is a sacrifice to God."[9] The gospel rushes forward with such speed, however, that only the wise know of its movement. About this speed the blessed Paul says with understanding, "May the word of God speed on and be made glorious in us." But in the eyes of the foolish the gospel seems to stand still, I say, because they neglect its commands, for they do not believe that what has been written will come to pass. Sermons 20.4.[10]

The Significance of Mutual Intercessory Prayer. Augustine: With this in mind, dearly beloved, let us always look forward with longing toward our everlasting joy. Let us always pray for fortitude in our temporal labors and trials. Let us offer prayers for one another. Let my prayers be offered for you, and yours for me. And, brothers, do not think that you need my prayers, but that I have no need of yours. We have mutual need of one another's prayers, for those reciprocal prayers are enkindled by charity and—like a sacrifice offered on the altar of piety—are fragrant and pleasing to the Lord. If the apostles used to ask for prayers on their own behalf, how much more does it behoove me to do so? For I am far from being their equal, although I long to follow their footsteps as closely as possible. But I have neither the wisdom to know nor the rashness to say what progress I have made. Sermons 13.10.[11]

Pray for the Bishop. Caesarius of Arles: Just as it is expedient for us to implore God's mercy for the salvation of your souls, so you ought to pour forth prayers to the Lord on our behalf. We should not consider the apostle's actions inappropriate. To so great an extent did he long to be commended to God through prayer that he himself implored the people and said, "Pray for us." Therefore we ought to say what can both encourage ourselves and instruct you. Just as we must reflect with great fear and anxiety on how we may fulfill the office of bishop without reproach, so you should observe that you ought to strive to practice humble obedience in everything that has been commanded you. So let us pray, dearly beloved, that my episcopacy may be profitable for both you and me. Sermons 232.[12]

3:2 Not All Have Faith

[4]Acts 13:48. [5]Eph 1:4-5. [6]FC 32:93-94*. [7]1 Cor 3:2. [8]Heb 5:14. [9]Ps 51:18. [10]ACW 50:50-51*. [11]FC 11:354-55*; cf. FC 1:307 n. 1 for sermon numbering. [12]FC 66:191-92.

Two Kinds of Grace. Augustine: For a man swollen with pride in comparison to another might say, "My faith distinguishes me," or "my justice" or whatever. It is to prevent such ideas that the good teacher asks, "But what do you have that you have not received?" Did you not receive it from him who chose to distinguish you from another? It was he who chose to give you what another did not receive. "But if you have received, why do you glory as if you had not received it?"[13] Now I ask, is the apostle concerned here with anything else than that "He who glories should glory in the Lord"?[14] But nothing is so contrary to this sentiment than for anyone to glory in his own merits as if he and not the grace of God were responsible for them. I refer to that grace that distinguishes the good from the wicked, not one which is common to the good and the wicked. On this premise the grace by which we are living and rational creatures, and thus distinguished from beasts, would be enmeshed in nature. The grace by which the beautiful are distinguished from the ugly, or the intelligent from the stupid, is a grace that perceives nature. But that person whose pride the apostle was trying to restrain was not puffing himself up in comparison to the beasts, nor in comparison to the gifts of nature that might exist even in the worst of men. Rather, he was puffed up because he attributed some good thing which pertained to the morally good life to himself and not to God. Thus, he deserved to hear the rebuke, "For who distinguishes you? Or what do you have that you have not received?" For though the ability to possess faith belongs to our nature, is that also true of the actual possession of faith? "For not all men have faith," although all men have the possibility of having faith. On the Predestination of the Saints 1.5.10.[15]

He Will Come Again As Before. Augustine: Then, therefore, they afterwards marveled at the fact that they saw him ascending and they rejoiced that he went up to heaven, for the precedence of the Head is the hope of the members.[16] Moreover, they heard the angelic message, "men of Galilee, why do you stand looking up to heaven? This Jesus . . . shall come in the same way as you have seen him going up to heaven."[17] What is the significance of "he will come in the same way"? He will come in that same form, so that the Scripture may be fulfilled, "They shall look upon him whom they have pierced."[18] He shall come to men; he shall come as a Man; but he shall come as the God-Man. He shall come as true God and true Man to make men like God. He has ascended as Judge of heaven; he has expressed himself as Herald of heaven. Let us stand justified so that we may not fear the judgment that is to come. As a matter of fact, he did ascend; those who announced it to us witnessed it. The people who did not see it believed; still some incredulous persons mocked, "for not all have faith." Sermons 265.1.[19]

3:5 May the Lord Direct Your Hearts

No Human Motive. Basil the Great: We are convinced that action taken by one or two pious men is done through the counsel of the Spirit. Since there is no human motive placed before their eyes, and saintly men are moved to action not with an aim of personal advantage but after having proposed to themselves what is pleasing to God, it is evident that it is the Lord who directs their hearts. And whenever spiritual men are the initiators of plans, and the people of the Lord follow them in harmony of thought, who will doubt that the plan has been arrived at in communion with our Lord Jesus Christ, who poured out his blood for the churches? Letters 229.[20]

---

[13]1 Cor 4:7. [14]2 Cor 10:17. [15]FC 86:230*. [16]This sermon is being preached on the observance of the feast of the ascension. [17]Acts 1:11. [18]Jn 19:37; Zech 12:10. [19]FC 38:409*. [20]FC 28:151.

3:6-12 WARNING AGAINST IDLENESS

[6]*Now we command you, brethren, in the name of our Lord Jesus Christ, that you keep away from any brother who is living in idleness and not in accord with the tradition that you received from us.* [7]*For you yourselves know how you ought to imitate us; we were not idle when we were with you,* [8]*we did not eat any one's bread without paying, but with toil and labor we worked night and day, that we might not burden any of you.* [9]*It was not because we have not that right, but to give you in our conduct an example to imitate.* [10]*For even when we were with you, we gave you this command: If any one will not work, let him not eat.* [11]*For we hear that some of you are living in idleness, mere busybodies, not doing any work.* [12]*Now such persons we command and exhort in the Lord Jesus Christ to do their work in quietness and to earn their own living.*

OVERVIEW: Paul strongly emphasizes, in strict words of command, the importance of labor, especially manual labor, as an accompaniment to prayer and fasting. These religious acts must never substitute for hard work (CHRYSOSTOM, AUGUSTINE). Prayer without work is a pious pretext (CYRIL OF ALEXANDRIA). There is no inconsistency between trusting God to provide and engaging in hard work in order to support ourselves and not be a burden on others (AUGUSTINE, CAESARIUS OF ARLES). Faithful and hardworking members of the congregation must be careful to make a sharp separation between themselves and those brothers and sisters who are living in a disorderly way (JOHN CASSIAN, THEODORE). Paul holds himself up as "the form of a believer," expecting the Thessalonians to see in him how one ought to live (CHRYSOSTOM, PELAGIUS). In our pursuit of faithful discipleship we are to avoid the controversy that arises from idle questioning and curiosity (BASIL). Christian bothers and sisters who depart from the discipline and charity required by faith are to be directly confronted (JOHN CASSIAN). There is the very real danger that if we consort with erring brothers and sisters, we will be infected with their wrongdoing (CYPRIAN).

AVOID CONTROVERSY, PRACTICE CHARITY. BASIL THE GREAT: "And now there remain faith, hope, charity, these three; but the greatest of these is charity."[1] In view of such declarations on the part of our Lord and the apostle, I marvel, I say, how it is that men display such zeal and such intense absorption in the pursuit of goods that will come to an end and be destroyed but have no regard for that which will remain, especially charity, the greatest of all goods, the distinguishing mark of the Christian. And not only this, but they show hostility to those who are zealous in its practice, and in fighting against them they fulfill the words of the Lord, namely, that they themselves do not enter in and those that are entering in they hinder.[2] I beg and implore you, therefore, to be content with the words of the saints and of the Lord himself. Desist from curious inquiry and unseemly controversies. Think on those things that are worthy of your heavenly calling. Live in a manner befitting the gospel of Christ, relying on the hope of eternal life and the heavenly kingdom prepared for all those who keep the commandments of God the Father, according to the gospel of Jesus Christ our Lord in the Holy

3:6 Keep Away from Any Brother

[1]1 Cor 13:13. [2]Lk 11:52.

Spirit and in truth. Concerning Faith.[3]

Basil the Great: [Paul] says, "Knowing this, that our old nature is crucified with him, that the body of sin may be destroyed to the end that we may serve sin no longer."[4] By these words we are taught that he who is baptized in Christ is baptized in his death, and is not only buried with Christ and planted together with him but is first of all crucified with him. Thus we are instructed that as he who is crucified is separated from the living, so also he who has been crucified with Christ in the likeness of his death is completely set apart from those who live according to the old nature. Hence the Lord commanded us to beware of false prophets,[5] and the apostle says, "And we command you, brothers, that you withdraw yourselves from every brother walking disorderly and not according to the tradition which they have received of us." The "old nature" mentioned by the apostle signifies all sin and defilement, taken individually and together, as if they represented his own members. Concerning Baptism.[6]

Surgical Removal. John Cassian: Lastly, those very people [the Thessalonians] whom in his first epistle Paul had treated with the gentle application of his words, he endeavors in his second epistle to heal with severer and sterner remedies, as those who had not profited from any more gentle treatment. And he no longer applies the treatment of gentle words, no mild and kindly expressions such as, "But we ask you, brothers." Rather he says, "We command you, brothers, in the name of our Lord Jesus Christ, that you withdraw from every brother that lives in a disorderly fashion." In the first letter Paul asks; in the second he commands. In the first we see the kindness of one who is persuading; in the second the sternness of one protesting and threatening. "We command you, brothers," because, when we first asked you, you scorned our words. Now at least obey our threats. Paul

renders this commandment severe, not by his bare word but by the im-precation of the name of our Lord Jesus Christ. He is concerned that they might again scorn his teaching as merely a human word, considering it of little importance. And so quite directly, like a well-skilled physician operating on infected limbs to which he could not apply the remedy of a mild treatment, Paul attempts to cure by an incision with a spiritual knife. . . . He bids them withdraw from those who will not make time for work and to cut them off like limbs tainted with the festering sores of leisure. This is so that the malady of idleness, like some deadly contagion, might not infect even the healthy portion of their limbs by the gradual advance of infection. Institutes 10.7.[7]

A Solid Unity of Body. Cyprian: The words of the apostle's testimony are, "We command you in the name of the Lord Jesus Christ that you withdraw from all brothers who are living disorderly lives and not according to the tradition which they received from us." And again he says, "Let no one deceive you with empty words; for because of these things the wrath of God comes on the children of disobedience. Don't be, therefore, partakers with them."[8] We must withdraw, indeed flee from those who fall away, lest, while one is joined with them while they walk wickedly, passing over the paths of error and crime, wandering apart from the way of the true road, he himself also be caught in a similar crime. God is one and Christ one and his church one and the faith one and the people one, all joined together by the tie of concord into a solid unity of body. The unity cannot be torn apart, nor can the one body be separated by a division of its structure, nor torn into bits by the lacerating of its entrails. Whoever departs from the root of the parent body will not be able to breathe and live apart. By

---

[3]FC 9:66-67. [4]Rom 6:6. [5]Cf. Mt 7:15. [6]FC 9:368-69*. [7]NPNF 2 11:269*. [8]Eph 5:6-7.

departing one loses the substance of health. THE UNITY OF THE CHURCH 23.[9]

3:7 You Ought to Imitate Us

THE GOOD TEACHER. CHRYSOSTOM: A teacher demonstrates great confidence if he uses his own good actions to reprove his disciples. And so Paul writes, "For yourselves know how you ought to imitate us." And he ought to be a teacher more of life than of the word. Let no one think that Paul says this because of a boastful heart. The necessity of the situation in Thessalonica drove him to speak this way, with a view to the advantage of the entire community. HOMILIES ON FIRST THESSALONIANS 5.[10]

3:8 We Worked Night and Day

ONLY BY THE GRACE OF GOD. AUGUSTINE: Perhaps someone will dare to think or say that the apostle Paul did not attain the perfection of those who, leaving all behind, followed Christ. The reason for entertaining such a thought would be because Paul procured his own substance by his own hands in order that he might not burden anyone of those to whom he was preaching the gospel. Thus the words he says, "I have labored more than all of them," have all been fulfilled, and he added, "Yet not I, but the grace of God with me."[11] We can only ascribe Paul's ability both to preach and support himself financially to the grace of God at work in his mind and body. He neither ceased from preaching the gospel nor did he, as his detractors, support himself financially from the gospel.[12] TRACTATES ON JOHN 122.3.[13]

WORK, BUT NOT ANXIOUSLY. AUGUSTINE: Of course, there are those who misunderstand the same apostle when he writes, "He who was apt to steal, let him steal no longer; but let him labor, doing good with his hands, that he may have something to give to one who has need."[14] For, when he is ordering such persons to work so efficiently with their hands that they will also have

something to bestow on others, his misinterpreters believe that he is going counter to the instruction which the Lord gives when he says, "Look at the birds of the air: they do not sow, or reap, or gather into barns. . . . Consider the lilies of the field: They neither toil nor spin."[15] Paul does not seem to have imitated the birds of the air and lilies of the field. He has repeatedly said of himself that he was working with his own hands so as not to burden anyone,[16] and it is written of him that he joined with Aquila because of the similarity of their handicraft, so that they might work together to maintain a livelihood.[17] From these and other such passages of the Scripture it is clear enough that our Lord does not reprove a man for procuring these things in the usual manner. SERMON ON THE MOUNT 2.17.57.[18]

WORK AS YOU ARE ABLE. BASIL THE GREAT: But why should we dwell upon the amount of evil there is in idleness, when the apostle clearly specifies that he who does not work should not eat. As daily sustenance is necessary for everyone, so labor in proportion to one's strength is also essential. Solomon has written effectively in praise of hard work: "And she has not eaten her bread in idleness."[19] And again, the apostle says of himself, "neither did we eat any man's bread for nothing, but in labor and in toil we worked night and day." Yet, since he was preaching the gospel, he was entitled to receive his livelihood from the gospel. . . . We have reason to fear, therefore, lest, perchance, on the day of judgment this fault also may be alleged against us, since he who has endowed us with the ability to work demands that our labor be proportioned to our capacity. For the Lord says, "To whom they have committed much, of him they will demand much."[20] THE LONG RULES, Q.37.R.[21]

---

[9]FC 36:118-19*. [10]NPNF 1 13:396*. [11]1 Cor 15:10. [12]Rom 15:20. [13]FC 92:64*. [14]Eph 4:28. [15]Mt 6:28. [16]Acts 20:34; 1 Cor 4:12; 1 Thess 2:9; 2 Thess 3:8. [17]Acts 18:3. [18]FC 11:167*. [19]Prov 31:27. [20]Lk 12:48. [21]FC 9:307*.

WORK RECOLLECTED WITH PRAYER. BASIL THE GREAT: In this way we acquire a recollected spirit—when in every action we beg from God the success of our labors and satisfy our debt of gratitude to him who gave us the power to do the work, and when, as has been said, we keep before our minds the aim of pleasing him. If this is not the case, how can there be consistency in the words of the apostle bidding us to "pray without ceasing,"[22] with those other words: "we worked night and day"? Thanksgiving at all times has been commanded even from law and has been proved necessary to our life from both reason and nature. So we should not therefore be negligent in observing those times for prayer customarily established in communities—times which have inevitably been selected because each period contains a reminder peculiar to itself of blessings received from God. THE LONG RULES, Q.37.R.[23]

THE HUMILITY OF WORK. JOHN CASSIAN: Once Abba Serapion finely mocked this sham humility.[24] A man arrived at his cell, making a great show of lowliness in his dress and speech. Serapion, as is usual, asked him to offer a prayer. The visitor refused and said that he was guilty of such crimes that he did not deserve even to breathe the same air. Refusing the mat, he sat on the ground. Still less would he allow Serapion to wash his feet. After supper it is usual to have a religious conference. So Serapion began, with kindness and gentleness, to warn him against being an idle and haphazard wanderer, especially as he was young and strong. He told him that he ought to settle in a cell, subject himself to the rules of the elders and maintain himself by his own work instead of living on the hospitality of others. Since St. Paul was working for the spread of the gospel, he might reasonably have lived on others. Yet he preferred to work day and night to get daily bread for himself and those who were ministering to him and could not work themselves. . . . You must keep true humility of heart—and true humility comes not from affectation of posture or speech but from an interior humbling of the mind. CONFERENCES 18.11.[25]

3:10 *If Anyone Will Not Work, Let Him Not Eat*

WATCH FOR THOSE WHO TRAFFIC IN CHRIST. ANONYMOUS: Let everyone who comes in the name of the Lord be received, and then, when you have taken stock of him, you will know—for you will have insight—what is right and false. If the person who comes is just passing through, help him as much as you can, but he shall not stay with you more than two or three days—if that is necessary. If he wants to settle in with you, though, and he is a craftsman, let him work and eat. If he has no craft, take care in your insight: no Christian should live with you in idleness. If he is unwilling to do what that calls for, he is using Christ to make a living. Be on your guard against people like this. THE DIDACHE 12.1-5.[26]

LOOK AT THE ANT. ANONYMOUS: Let the young persons of the church endeavor to minister diligently in all essential matters. Mind your business with all suitable seriousness, that so you may always have enough to support yourselves and those who are needy, and not burden the church of God. For we ourselves, besides our attention to the word of the gospel, do not neglect our inferior vocations. For some of us are fishermen, some tentmakers, some farmers, that so we may never be idle. So says Solomon somewhere, "Go to the ant, you sluggard; consider her ways diligently, and become wiser than she. For she, having neither field, overseer, nor ruler, prepares her food in the summer, and lays up a great store in the harvest. Or else go to the

---

[22]1 Thess 5:17. [23]FC 9:308-9*. [24]Cassian has been discussing the subject of true versus false humility. [25]LCC 12:271. [26]DDCH 183-86.

bee, and learn how laborious she is, and how valuable her work is, whose labors both kings and common men make use of for their health. The bee is desirable and glorious, though she be weak in strength, yet by honoring wisdom she is improved"[27] . . . Labor therefore continually; for the blot of the slothful is not to be healed. But "if anyone among you does not work, let not such a one eat" among you. For the Lord our God hates the lazy. For no one of those who are dedicated to God ought to be idle. Constitutions of the Holy Apostles 2.8.[28]

The Ant. Chrysostom: Therefore also the Scripture has sent the sluggard to the ant, saying, "Go to the ant, you sluggard, emulate his ways, and be wiser than he."[29] Are you unwilling, he means, to learn from the Scriptures, that it is good to labor, and that he who will not work neither should eat? Learn it from the irrational beasts! We do the same in our families, urging those who have erred—though they be older and considered superior—to observe thoughtful children. We say, "Note how earnest and watchful this child is, though he is younger than you." In the same way learn from the ant the best exhortation to hard work. Marvel at your Lord, not only because he has made heaven and the sun, but because he has also made the ant. For although the ant is small, it proves the greatness of God's wisdom. Consider, then, how prudent the ant is. Consider how God has implanted in so small a body such an unceasing desire for work! But while you learn the lesson of hard work from the ant, learn from the bee a lesson of neatness, industry and social concord! For the bee labors more for us than for herself, working every day. This is indeed a thing especially proper for a Christian, not to seek his own welfare, but the welfare of others. As, then, the bee travels across the meadows that she may prepare a banquet for another, so also O man, you do likewise. And if you have accumulated wealth, spend it on others. If you have the ability to teach, do not bury the talent, but bring it out

publicly for the sake of those who need it! Or if you have any other advantage, become useful to those who reap the benefit of your labors. Homilies Concerning the Statues 12.2.[30]

Charity, Not Anxiety. Augustine: In the first place, we must prove that the blessed apostle Paul wished the servants of God to perform manual labor which would merit a great spiritual reward, and to do this without seeking food and clothing from anybody but to procure these commodities for themselves by their own work. Secondly, we must show that those gospel precepts by which some monks justify not only laziness but even arrogance are not contrary to the direction and example of the apostle. Let us examine the statements made by the apostle prior to this one: "If any man will not work, neither let him eat," and the statements which follow it, so that the meaning which St. Paul intended may be gathered from the setting of the passage. What can be said in reply to this, since, indeed, by his own example he taught what he commanded, lest later someone might be permitted to interpret this with a view to his will and not his charity. For, the Lord had directed that apostle, as preacher of the gospel, as soldier of Christ, as planter of the vineyard, as shepherd of the flock, to live by the Gospel; nevertheless, St. Paul did not accept the payment due him in order to give example to those who wished to exact unmerited compensation. The Work of Monks 3.4.[31]

Reasonable Thought of Food and Clothing. Caesarius of Arles: We read in sacred

[27]Prov 6:6-9 (LXX). [28]ANF 7:424-25*. [29]Prov 6:6. [30]NPNF 1 9:420*. [31]FC 16:335. In this work Augustine goes to great lengths to show that the biblical teachings with regard to the bounty from divine providence and our need to trust God in the necessities of life are not inconsistent with St. Paul's admonitions to hard work and self-support. Augustine wishes to admonish a community of monks whom he regards as self-indulgent and lazy because they refuse to support themselves.

Scripture, dearly beloved, that a holy understanding should keep those who are concerned about their soul's salvation, as the divine Word puts it, "Holy understanding shall protect you."[32] If such holy understanding keeps a soul, that which is unholy not only fails to keep it but even kills it. Perhaps someone says, "Who can always be thinking of God and eternal bliss, since all men must be concerned about food, clothing and the management of their household?" God does not ask us to be free from all anxiety over the present life, for he instructs us through his apostle, "If any man will not work, neither let him eat." The same apostle repeats the idea with reference to himself when he says, "We worked night and day so that we might not burden any of you."[33] Since God especially advises reasonable concern for food and clothing, so long as avarice and ambition . . . are not linked with it, an ordinary action or thought can be most rightly considered holy. The only provision is that those preoccupations should not be so excessive that they do not allow us to have time for God, according to the words, "The burdens of the world have made them miserable."[34] SERMONS 45.1.[35]

A CAUTION ON INTRUSIVE INVESTIGATION OF THE NEEDY. CHRYSOSTOM: I do not say these things haphazardly now, but rather because many are often overly intrusive in their investigation of the needy. They examine their lineage, life, habits, vocation and the vigor of their body. They make complaints and demand immense public scrutiny for their health. For this precise reason, many of the poor simulate physical disabilities, so that by dramatizing their misfortunes they may deflect our cruelty and inhumanity. And although when it is summertime, it is terrible to make these complaints, it is not quite so dreadful. However, during the frost and the cold, for someone to become such a savage and inhuman judge and not impart any forgiveness to the unemployed, does this not involve extreme cruelty? "Therefore, what did

Paul ordain by law," they say, "when he said to the Thessalonians, 'If any one does not wish to work, neither let him eat'?" So that you, too, may also hear these things, you should discuss the words of Paul not only with the poor individual but even with yourself. For the laws of Paul are laid down not only for the poor but also for all. Let me say something burdensome and grievous. I know that you will grow angry. Nevertheless, I will say it; for I do not say it to strike you but to correct you. We criticize them for their laziness, something which is worthy of forgiveness for the most part. However, we too often do things which are even more grievous than any laziness. . . . Therefore, when you say, "What then shall we say to Paul?" converse with yourself, too, and say these things not only to the poor. Read not only the threat of punishment but also Paul's admonition to forgiveness, for the one who said, "If anyone does not wish to work, neither let him eat," added, "And you, brothers, do not lose heart in doing good." ON REPENTANCE AND ALMSGIVING 10.6.23-24.[36]

3:11 Not Doing Any Work

PIETY A PRETEXT. CYRIL OF ALEXANDRIA: There are some other men going about, as they say, pretending only to devote themselves to prayer[37] and doing no work, making piety a pretext for cowardice and a means of gaining a living, but not thinking rightly. Let them say that they are better even than the holy apostles who worked when opportunity gave them time for it, and they were exhausted for the word of God. How did they miss reading the holy Paul writing to certain people, "For I hear that some among you are living irregularly, doing no work but busy at meddling." The church does not admit

---

[32]Prov 2:11. [33]1 Thess 2:9; 2 Thess 3:8. [34]The source of this quotation is not known; cf. FC 31:227. [35]FC 31:226-27*. [36]FC 96:146-47* (*On Mercy* 6). [37]These are the so-called Euchites, or Messalians, an ascetic sect committed to the view that perfection is possible only with ceaseless prayer, since the sacraments lack ultimate efficacy.

those who do this. It is necessary without doubt that those who live a quiet life in the monasteries pray continually. But it does no harm and rather is exceedingly helpful to work so that he who accepts the labors of others for his own need may not be found to be burdensome to others. It might be possible from his labors to relieve the widow and the orphan and some of the weak ones of his brothers. LETTERS 83.7.[38]

3:12 To Do Their Work in Quietness

SERVICE TO THE NEEDY. BASIL THE GREAT: This we must also keep in mind—that he who labors ought to perform his task not for the purpose of ministering to his own needs but that he may accomplish the Lord's command, "I was hungry and you gave me to eat,"[39] and so on. To be concerned for oneself is strictly forbidden by the Lord in the words, "Be not concerned for your life, what you shall eat, nor for your body,

what you shall put on," and he adds, "for the heathens seek after all these things."[40] Everyone, therefore, in doing his work, should place before himself the aim of service to the needy and not his own satisfaction. Thus, he will escape the charge of self-love and receive the blessing for fraternal charity from the Lord, who said, "As long as you did it to one of these, the least of my brothers, you did it to me."[41] Nor should anyone think that the apostle is at variance with our rule when he says, "that working they would eat their own bread." This is addressed to the unruly and indolent, and means that it is better for each person to minister to himself at least and not be a burden to others than to live in idleness. THE LONG RULES, Q.42.R.[42]

---

[38]FC 77:111. [39]Mt 25:35. [40]Mt 6:25, 32. [41]Mt 25:40. [42]FC 9:317*.

3:13-18 FINAL EXHORTATIONS

[13]*Brethren, do not be weary in well-doing.*

[14]*If any one refuses to obey what we say in this letter, note that man, and have nothing to do with him, that he may be ashamed.* [15]*Do not look on him as an enemy, but warn him as a brother.*

[16]*Now may the Lord of peace himself give you peace at all times in all ways. The Lord be with you all.*

[17]*I, Paul, write this greeting with my own hand. This is the mark in every letter of mine; it is the way I write.* [18]*The grace of our Lord Jesus Christ be with you all.*

OVERVIEW: Paul holds up what is for him the most severe punishment of all—separation from the community, and thus from the spiritual family—for those who refuse to obey his instructions (CHRYSOSTOM). At the same time, there is the reminder always to keep in mind the welfare of the excluded brother, such that prayers are offered up for him, as for anyone who is spiritually ill (AUGUSTINE, THEODORET). It is in fact merciful to remonstrate with an erring member of the community (Augustine). To welcome back into fellowship those who have erred, when they repent, is to build up the body of Christ (Polycarp). The purpose of the superscription at the end is to make it clear that this letter is by Paul himself, for there has been counterfeiting or misrepresentation to the Thessalonians of his views about the Lord's return (Chrysostom, Theodore, Theodoret).

3:15 Warn Him as a Brother

Quarreling of Doves. Augustine: Here it is as though doves are quarreling together. The apostle said, "If anyone fails to obey our word by this letter, mark that person and do not mix with him." There's the quarrel. But notice how it's a quarrel of doves, not of wolves. He immediately added, "And do not regard him as an enemy, but rebuke him as a brother." A dove is loving even when it is beating; a wolf hates even when it is being charming. Sermons 64.3.[1]

Merciful Severity. Augustine: It is true that some take the phrase "from your midst"[2] to mean that each one is to expel the wickedness out of oneself in order to be good. But, no matter how it is interpreted, whether that the wicked in the church are checked by the severity of excommunication or whether each one by self-blame and self-discipline drives wickedness out of himself, there can be no misunderstanding of the teaching of the apostle in the passage of Scripture just quoted: we are to refrain from association with brothers who are accused of any of the vices mentioned above, that is, with those who are notoriously scandalous. With what intention and with what charity this merciful severity is to be administered is evidenced not only by his statement, "that his spirit may be saved in the day of our Lord Jesus Christ,"[3] but appears elsewhere even more clearly where he says, "if anyone does not obey our word by this letter, note that man and do

not associate with him, that he may be put to shame. Yet do not regard him as an enemy, but admonish him as a brother." Faith and Works 2-3.[4]

Love Never Fails. Chrysostom: What then does Paul mean[5] when he says, "If any one refuses to obey what we say in this letter, note that man, and have nothing to do with him"? In the first place, he says this of brothers, but with a significant limitation which is stated with gentleness. Do not disconnect what is said here from what follows, where, having said, "have nothing to do with him," he added, "do not look on him as an enemy, but warn him as a brother." Do you see how he urges us to hate the deed but love the person? For indeed it is the work of the devil to tear us apart, and he has always taken great care to destroy love, so that the means of correction will be gone, the sinner maintained in error and the way of his salvation blocked. For when the physician hates the sick man and runs from him, and the sick man turns away from the physician, when will the distempered person be restored, seeing that neither the one will call in the other's aid, nor will the other go to him? Homilies on First Corinthians 33.5.[6]

Invite Them Back. Polycarp: I have been exceedingly grieved on account of Valens, who was at one time a presbyter among you, because he forgot the office that was given him. I warn you, therefore, to refrain from the love of money and be pure and truthful. . . . I am, therefore, very grieved indeed for that man and his wife. "May the Lord grant them true repentance."[7] But you, too, must be moderate in this matter; and "do

---

[1]WSA 3/3:186*. [2]1 Cor 5:13. [3]1 Cor 5:5. [4]FC 27:224-25*. [5]Chrysostom is commenting on 1 Corinthians 13:8 and is discussing the apparent contradiction between what is said there about the unfailing nature of love and the seeming lack of love in 2 Thessalonians 3:14. [6]NPNF 1 12:199*. [7]2 Tim 2:25; 1:18.

not consider such persons as enemies" but reclaim them as suffering and straying members, in order that you may save the whole body of you. For in doing this you will edify yourselves.[8]

To the Philippians 11.1, 4.[9]

---

[8]1 Thess 5:11. [9]LCC 1:135-36.

THE FIRST EPISTLE TO TIMOTHY

ARGUMENT: Having earlier entrusted Timothy with the economy of the gospel in his instruction as a convert and disciple, Paul moves on to instruct Timothy as a pastor and teacher in the life of the church (CHRYSOSTOM). After warning against Judaizing teachers, Paul gives instructions for worship, for church government, for the selection and oversight of ministers and for episcopal duties, with the inclusion of an important section on doctrinal teaching. Paul intends these as instruction for Timothy, through whom they will go from Ephesus to all of the churches of Asia, but also for every bishop who is to be regarded as a capable overseer of the church (THEODORE). Paul's intention is to strengthen Timothy for the refutation of heresy and for the governance of the Asian churches (THEODORET). Paul instructs his own convert from Judaism in how to be an effective evangelist, especially against Judaizing heresies, as well as how to be a capable leader of the church (AMBROSIASTER).

1:1-11 SALUTATION AND CALL TO HOLD TO SOUND TEACHING

¹*Paul, an apostle of Christ Jesus by command of God our Savior and of Christ Jesus our hope,* ²*To Timothy, my true child in the faith:*
Grace, mercy, and peace from God the Father and Christ Jesus our Lord.
³*As I urged you when I was going to Macedonia, remain at Ephesus that you may charge certain persons not to teach any different doctrine,* ⁴*nor to occupy themselves with myths and endless genealogies which promote speculations rather than the divine training*ᵃ *that is in faith;* ⁵*whereas the aim of our charge is love that issues from a pure heart and a good conscience and sincere faith.* ⁶*Certain persons by swerving from these have wandered away into vain discussion,* ⁷*desiring to be teachers of the law, without understanding either what they are saying or the*

things about which they make assertions.

⁸Now we know that the law is good, if any one uses it lawfully, ⁹understanding this, that the law is not laid down for the just but for the lawless and disobedient, for the ungodly and sinners, for the unholy and profane, for murderers of fathers and murderers of mothers, for manslayers, ¹⁰immoral persons, sodomites, kidnapers, liars, perjurers, and whatever else is contrary to sound doctrine, ¹¹in accordance with the glorious gospel of the blessed God with which I have been entrusted.

a Or stewardship, or order

OVERVIEW: Paul shows the humility of one who is truly called to office in the church, in that he does not intrude himself into the office, nor does he shrink from it. In the quality of the father-son relationship between Paul and Timothy, we see a likeness of the intimacy of Father and Son in the Trinity. Always Paul exhorts Timothy to unquestioning faith as well as genuineness in action and living, for the true test of the gospel is always the lives of its adherents (CHRYSOSTOM). Paul adopts a tone that is humble and gentle with Timothy, urging him to discipline those in the church who would impose on believers more than faith truly requires (THEODORE). Paul's principal concern here is to warn Timothy against the tricks of Jewish converts to the gospel, who are persuading Gentiles, with arguments based on Jesus' Hebrew genealogy, to observe the law in all of its superfluous detail (THEODORET). The key point to grasp in Paul's warnings to Timothy about the misuse of the law is that, since the coming of Christ, the status and role of the law in salvation has been changed. Christ has separated what is eternal in the law from what is merely temporal and transitory (AMBROSIASTER). The purpose of all Christian teaching is love (CHRYSOSTOM, THEODORE, THEODORET, AMBROSIASTER, PELAGIUS).

1:1 His True Child in Faith

MY TRUE CHILD IN THE FAITH. CHRYSOSTOM: Mark well his reference to "my true child." Timothy is not the biological son of Paul. So what kind of son was he? Does it even make sense to call him a "son"? Someone might say that if he was not the son of Paul, then he must be someone else's son. What then? Was he of some other substance? Not so, for after saying "my own son," he adds: "in the faith." This shows that he was really his own son, and truly from him, there being no essential difference between father and son in the faith. The likeness he bore to him was in respect to his faith, just as in human births there is a substantive likeness. The son is like the father in human beings, but the analogy is even closer in the relation of human beings to God in faith. Though the father and the son may be of the same genetic strain, they may differ in many particulars, as in color, figure, understanding, age, bent of mind, endowments of soul and body, and in many other things they may be like or unlike. But in the relation of the divine Father and Son there is no such dissimilarity. HOMILIES ON 1 TIMOTHY 1.[1]

A TRUE SON. AMBROSIASTER: Timothy is a

---

[1] NPNF 1 13:409*. Chrysostom's contention that sonship in faith constitutes a profounder likeness between father and son than does biological kinship reflected his staunchly anti-Arian views. The Arians at times contended that Jesus' sonship was an inherent indication that he could not be coeternal with the Father; that is, they could not be alike in all things. Chrysostom's point is that spiritual sonship is in fact such a sharing of likeness and, with the divine Father and Son, even of essence.

true son in faith, for his generation is one that will not know death or sickness or pestilence or hunger or thirst, because it is based on God and the future is glorious immortality in the gift of God in the kingdom of God and Christ. Commentary on the First Letter to Timothy.[2]

A Son by Faith. Theodoret of Cyr: It is not nature but faith that has made Timothy a son. Interpretation of the First Letter to Timothy.[3]

Not by Flesh. Pelagius: Timothy is a son in faith, not in flesh. Pelagius's Commentary on the First Letter to Timothy.[4]

1:3a Remain in Ephesus

The First Bishop of Ephesus. Eusebius of Caesarea: Paul's fellow workers and fellow soldiers, as he himself called them, numbered many thousands, the majority of whom he considered worthy of an everlasting memorial, for he has made his testimony to them enduring in his own letters. Moreover, Luke also, as he lists those known to him, makes mention of them by name. So Timothy is recorded as the first one called to oversee the church of Ephesus, just as Titus was for the churches in Crete. Ecclesiastical History 3.4.[5]

1:4a Endless Myths About Genealogies

Like an Anvil. Ignatius of Antioch: You must not be panic-stricken by those who have an air of credibility but who teach heresy.[6] Stand your ground like an anvil under the hammer. A great athlete must suffer blows to conquer. And especially for God's sake must we put up with everything, so that God will put up with us. Show more enthusiasm than you do. Mark the times. Be on the alert for him who is above time, the Timeless, the Unseen, the One who became visible for our sakes, who was beyond touch and passion, yet who for our sakes became subject to

suffering and endured everything for us. Letter to Polycarp 3.[7]

About the Demiurge. Irenaeus: Certain men, rejecting the truth, are introducing among us false stories and vain genealogies, which serve rather to elicit controversies, as the apostle said, than to God's work of building up in the faith. By their craftily constructed rhetoric they lead astray the minds of the inexperienced and take them captive, corrupting the oracles of the Lord. They are evil expounders of what was first well spoken. For they upset many, leading them away by the pretense of knowledge from him who constituted and ordered the universe, as if they had something higher and greater to show them than the God who made the heaven and the earth and all that is in them. By clever language they artfully attract the simple-minded into their kind of inquiry and then crudely destroy them by developing their blasphemous and impious view about the Demiurge. Nor can their simple hearers distinguish the lie from the truth. Against the Heresies 1.1.[8]

Against Legalistic Sabbath Speculations. Origen: Moreover, the commandment, "Do not bear a burden on the sabbath day,"[9] seems to me impossible. For by these words the Jewish teachers have fallen into "endless fables," as the apostle says, by saying that it is not reckoned a "burden" if someone has shoes without nails, but that it is a "burden" if someone has gallic[10] shoes with nails. And if someone carries something on one shoulder, they judge it a "burden," but if he carries it on both shoulders, they will deny it is a burden. On First Principles 4.3.2.[11]

The Dialectic Art. Tertullian: The same

---

[2]CSEL 81 3:252. [3]PG 82:787C/788C. [4]PETE 475. [5]FC 19:142. [6]See also 1 Tim 6:3. [7]LCC 1:118-19. [8]LCC 1:358. [9]Jer 17:21. [10]From gallium, a metal with a low melting point. [11]OSW 191.

matter is turned and twisted by the heretics and the philosophers, and the same questions are involved: Whence comes evil? And what is its purpose? And whence human history? And how? And, what Valentinus has lately propounded—whence God? All of this ensues from an excessive exercise of mind and from an abortive birth. Wretched Aristotle! Who has taught them this dialectic art, cunning in building up and pulling down, using many shifts in sentence, making forced guesses at truth, stiff in arguments, busy in raising contentions, contrary even to itself, dealing backwards and forwards with every subject, so as really to deal with none! Hence, those "fables and endless genealogies," and "unprofitable questions" and "words that spread like a cancer," from which the apostle restraining us, testifies of philosophy by name, that it ought to be shunned. . . . When Paul spoke of "endless genealogies," we can now recognize the hand of Valentinus, according to whom the "aeon" generates its own grace, sense and truth. Whoever this is, it is not of one divine name but of a new name, who supposedly then produces word and life, humanity and church in the first pair of aeons. Prescriptions Against Heretics 14.7; 14.33.[12]

Vain Questioning. Chrysostom: By "fables" he does not mean the law; far from it, but inventions and forgeries and counterfeit doctrines. For, it seems that some Jewish teachers wasted their whole discourse on these unprofitable points. They numbered up their fathers and grandfathers, that they might have the reputation of historical knowledge and research. . . . Why does he call them "endless"? It is because they had no end, or none of any use, or none easy for us to apprehend. Note how he disapproves of skeptical questioning. For where faith exists there is no need of suspicion. Where there is no room for curiosity, questions are superfluous. Homilies on 1 Timothy 1.[13]

The Common Enemy. Theodore of Mopsuestia: Paul here discourses about the com-

mon theme of all of his letters written to those converted from the Gentiles. He does this to point out that often things said by converts from Judaism may undermine the genuine piety of Gentile converts. In the case of the Galatians, he found that they were observing things required by the law, including especially the rite of circumcision. He pointed out that the use of genealogies was a particularly bad practice, because it made it possible for Jews to argue that Christ was not the promised offspring of Abraham and David and thereby throw into confusion Gentiles who are not well grounded in the Scriptures. He calls these genealogies "endless" because they can be turned in a great variety of bewildering directions. They are called "myths" because they contain only narration and nothing really necessary to the understanding of salvation. Commentary on 1 Timothy.[14]

Jewish Interpretation. Theodoret of Cyr: Believers of Jewish background, taking pride in their knowledge of the Old Testament, laid certain questions before Gentile believers. They did this in order to take advantage of their ignorance of these same divine words, and in the attempt to persuade them to embrace the law as a way of life. They rehearsed with them the human genealogy of the Lord as descended from Abraham and David. Therefore, Paul instructs Timothy to block these people and to prevent them from corrupting the teaching. The others he orders not to listen. He calls their ideas "myth" because they involve the Jewish, Mishna-like exposition of the Scripture, which focuses on superfluous and useless questions, rather

---

[12]ANF 3:246, 259*. Tertullian here gives some details of his version of the Valentinian "pleroma," or divine realm of pure spirit with its hierarchical levels of "aeons," or divine beings. There is no better scholarly treatment than that of Kurt Rudolph, *Gnosis: The Nature and History of Gnosticism*, trans. Robert McLachlan Wilson (New York: Harper & Row, 1983). [13]NPNF 1 13:410*. [14]TEM 2:71-72 (Greek).

than the essential divine economy of salvation. INTERPRETATION OF THE FIRST LETTER TO TIMOTHY.[15]

NOVELTY AND INVENTION. ATHANASIUS: In this passage we note the novelty as well as the viciousness of their devices, and how they go beyond all other heresies. They support their madness by seductive arguments calculated to deceive the simple. The Greeks, as the apostle has said, make their attack with excellency and persuasiveness of speech and with fallacies that have the aura of plausibility. The Jews, departing widely from the divine Scriptures, now, as the apostle again has said, contend about "fables and endless genealogies." Meanwhile the Manichaeans and Valentinians with them, and others, corrupt the divine Scriptures, putting forth fables of their own invention. But the Arians are bolder than them all and have shown that the other heresies are but their younger sisters, whom, as I have said, they surpass in impiety, emulating them all, and especially the Jews, in their circumventions. HISTORY OF THE ARIANS 8.66.[16]

1:4b God's Salvation Is by Faith

THE FOOL'S LINE. AMBROSE: I will take the fool's line and propound some examples drawn from the things of a lower world. "I am become a fool; you have compelled me."[17] What indeed is more foolish than to debate over the majesty of God, which rather occasions questionings, than receiving godly instruction which is by faith. But to arguments let arguments reply. Let words make answer to them. Rather we will answer with love, the love which is in God, issuing of a pure heart and good conscience and faith unfeigned. OF THE CHRISTIAN FAITH 4, 5, 61.[18]

THE MISTRUST OF QUESTIONING. CHRYSOSTOM: What is enabled by faith? The reception of God's mercies that we may become better persons, to doubt and dispute of nothing, but to

repose in confidence. HOMILIES ON 1 TIMOTHY 1.[19]

1:5a Love That Issues from a Pure Heart

LACK OF LOVE LEADS TO HERESY. CHRYSOSTOM: "Because of the increase of wickedness, the love of most will grow cold."[20] It is this that has been the occasion of all heresies. For those who do not love their brothers and sisters easily come to envy those in high repute. From envying, they have become eager for power, and from a love of power have introduced heresies. On this account Paul having said, "that you might charge some that they teach no other doctrine," now shows that the manner in which this may be effected is by charity. HOMILIES ON 1 TIMOTHY 2.[21]

THE SCRIPTURES TEACH LOVE. AUGUSTINE: The end of all divine Scriptures is the love for the Being in which we should rejoice and love for the being that can rejoice with us in that love.[22] . . . Whoever . . . thinks that he understands the divine Scriptures or any part of them so that it does not build the double love of God and of our neighbor does not understand it at all. Whoever finds a lesson there useful to the building of charity, even though he has not said what the author may be shown to have intended in that place, has not been deceived. . . . But anyone who understands in the Scriptures something other than that intended by them is deceived, although they do not lie. ON CHRISTIAN DOCTRINE 1.35.39-1.36.41.[23]

THE PURPOSE OF THE LAW. AUGUSTINE: When all these things have been said and considered, I am unwilling to contend about words, for such contention is profitable for nothing but

---

[15]PG 82:789AB/790AB. [16]NPNF 2 4:294*. [17]2 Cor 12:11. [18]NPNF 2 10:269-70. [19]NPNF 1 13:410*. [20]Mt 24:12. [21]NPNF 1 13:412*. [22]Cf. Rom 13:10. [23]ACD 30-31.

the subverting of the hearer.[24] But the law is profitable for edification if one uses it lawfully. For the end of the law "is love out of a pure heart, and a good conscience and faith unfeigned." And our Master knew it well, for it was on these two commandments[25] that he hung all the law and the prophets. CONFESSIONS 12.18.[26]

1:5b A Pure Heart, a Good Conscience and Sincere Faith

LOVE BASED ON TRUTH. AUGUSTINE: Faith, hope and charity, those three virtues for whose building up is mounted all the scaffolding of the Bible, are only in the soul that believes what it does not yet see, and hopes and loves what it believes. Therefore there can be love even of One who is not known, if yet he is believed. Doubtless, we must beware lest the soul, believing what it does not see, fabricates for itself an image of that which is not and bases its hope and love upon a lie. Then there will not emerge that "charity from a pure heart and a good conscience and a faith unfeigned, which is the end of the commandment." ON THE TRINITY 8.4.6.[27]

AN UNFEIGNED FAITH. AUGUSTINE: When anyone knows the end of the commandments to be charity "from a pure heart, and a good conscience and an unfeigned faith" and has related all of his understanding of the divine Scriptures to these three, he may approach the treatment of these books with security. For when he says "charity" he adds "from a pure heart," so that nothing else would be loved except that which should be loved. And he joins with this "a good conscience" for the sake of hope, for he in whom there is the smallest taint of bad conscience despairs of attaining that which he believes in and loves. Third, he says "an unfeigned faith." If our faith involves no lie, then we do not love that which is not to be loved, and living justly, we hope for that which will in no way deceive our hope. ON CHRISTIAN DOCTRINE 1.40.44.[28]

BEHOLDING THROUGH A MIRROR. AUGUSTINE: When the promised vision, "face to face," has come, we shall behold the Trinity—that Trinity which is not only incorporeal but perfectly inseparable and truly changeless—far more clearly and surely than we now behold its image in ourselves. This present vision, through a mirror and in an enigma, as offered to us in this life, belongs not to any one who can perceive in their own mind all that we have here set out by our analysis but to those who see the mind as a reflective image. In this way they are able to relate what they see to the One whose image it is. They reach through their actual vision of the image to a presumptive vision of the original, which cannot yet be seen face to face. The apostle does not say, "We see now a mirror" but "we see now through a mirror."[29] Those who see the mind as it may be seen, and in it that Trinity of which I have attempted to give a variety of descriptions, yet without believing or understanding it to be the image of God: they are seeing as if in a mirror. But so far from seeing through the mirror him who is now to be seen only in that way, they are unaware that the mirror seen is a mirror—which is to say, an image. If they knew it, they might be conscious of the need to seek and in some measure even now to see, through this mirror, him whose mirror it is—their hearts being purified by faith unfeigned, so that he who is seen now through a mirror may at last be seen face to face. But if they despise the faith that purifies hearts, no understanding of the most subtle analysis of our mind's nature can serve but to condemn them, on the testimony of their own understanding itself. ON THE TRINITY 15.23.44-15.24.44.[30]

---

[24]2 Tim 2:14. [25]Love of God and neighbor. [26]LCC 7:284. [27]LCC 8:44. [28]ACD 33. This passage is pivotally cited by Bertrand de Margerie, *An Introduction to the History of Exegesis*, 3 vols. (Petersham, Mass.: St. Bede's Publications, 1991), 3:25. [29]1 Cor 13:12. [30]LCC 8:171-72.

The Nature of Happiness. Augustine: Now, you know, I think, not only the nature of your prayer but its object, and you have learned this, not from me but from him who has humbled himself to teach us all. Happiness is what we must seek and what we must ask of the Lord God. Many arguments have been fashioned by many men about the nature of happiness, but why should we turn to the many men or the many arguments? Brief and true is the word in the Scripture of God, "Happy is the people whose God is the Lord."[31] "The aim of our charge is love that issues from a pure heart and a good conscience and sincere faith," that we may belong to that people and that we may be able to attain to contemplation of God and to eternal life with God. Letters 130.12.24.[32]

The End of All Your Actions. Caesarius of Arles: Ascend the mountain and see the end. Christ is the mountain; come to him, and from there you will see the end of all perfection. What is the end? Ask Paul, "Now the purpose of this charge is charity, from a pure heart and a pure conscience and faith unfeigned,"[33] and in another place, "love is the fulfillment of the law."[34] . . . Therefore, whatever you do, do it for the love of Christ, and let the intention or end of all your actions look to him. Do nothing for the sake of human praise, but everything for love of God and the desire for eternal life. Sermons 137.1.[35]

1:6 Swerving into Vain Discussion

Word Juggling. Gregory of Nyssa: What is this vain juggling with words? Is he[36] aware that it is God of whom he speaks, Who was in the beginning and is in the Father, nor was there any time when he was not? He knows not what he says nor what he affirms, but he endeavors, as though he were constructing the pedigree of a mere man, to apply to the Lord of all creation the language which properly belongs to our nature here below. Against Eunomius 2.9.[37]

The Ark, the House, the Flood and Baptism. Fulgentius of Ruspe: In the ark and in the house, one and the same church was prefigured. As for those who perished outside the ark in the flood and in those who died by the sword outside that house, a twofold mystery can be considered: In the flood the baptism of Christians is prefigured. So it seems to me to apply now for the current time, and not unfittingly. Heretics, if they remain outside the church, by their baptism, deserve punishment, not life. Those who, denying Christ, leave the church catholic, will perish in eternal punishment. For blessed Peter expounds the mystery of the ark in these words, . . . "while God patiently waited in the days of Noah during the building of the ark in which a few persons, eight in all, were saved through water: this prefigured baptism, which saves you now; it is not a removal of dust from the body but an appeal to God for a clean conscience."[38] With similar intent the apostle Paul teaches, "The aim of this instruction is love from a pure heart, a good conscience and a sincere faith." On the Forgiveness of Sins 20.2.[39]

1:7 Desiring to Be Teachers of the Law

The Distortion of the Heretics. Athanasius: It is encouraging to the faithful but distressing to the heretical to see these[40] heresies overthrown. Moreover, their further question, "whether the Unoriginated be one or two,"[41] shows how false are their views, how treacherous and full of guile. It is not for the Father's honor that they say this but for the dishonor of

---

[31]Ps 143:15. [32]FC 18:394-95*. [33]1 Tim 1:5. [34]Rom 13:10. [35]FC 47:270*. [36]Eunomius, who taught that the Son was inferior to the Father. Gregory sees in the reasoning of Eunomius a case in point of what Paul spoke of when certain persons by swerving from a pure heart, good conscience and sincere faith wander away into vain discussion. [37]NPNF 2 5:116. [38]1 Pet 3:20-21. [39]FC 95:135*. [40]Arian. [41]Certain Arian teachers were claiming that God as the Unoriginated must also be one, thereby necessitating the claim that only the Father can possess this attribute.

the Word. Accordingly, if any one should answer, unaware of their craft, that "the Unoriginated is one," they immediately spurt out their own venom, saying, "'Therefore the Son is among things originated,' and well have we said, 'He was not before his generation.'" This in turn elicits all sorts of disturbances and confusions, separating the Son from the Father and reckoning the Framer of all among his works. Now first they may be convicted on this score, that, while blaming the Nicene bishops for their use of phrases not in Scripture, though these are not injurious but subversive of their irreligion, they themselves went off upon the same fault, that is, using words not in Scripture, and those that show contempt for the Lord, being "without understanding either what they are saying or the things about which they make assertions." AGAINST THE ARIANS 1.9.30.[42]

MENTAL BLINDNESS. AUGUSTINE: Two walls must adhere to the cornerstone in order to preserve "the unity of the Spirit in the bond of peace"[43]—one from the Jews and the other from the Gentiles. We mustn't let our minds be put off by the great number of reprobate Jews, among whom were the builders; those, that is, who "wished to be teachers of the law," but as the apostle says about them, "do not understand either what they are saying or the things about which they are making their assertions." It was as a result of this mental blindness, after all, that they rejected the stone which was put at the head of the corner. But it wouldn't be put at the head of the corner unless it offered to the two peoples coming from different points a peaceful joining, a coupling of grace. SERMONS 204.3.[44]

LOVING PASTORAL CARE. AUGUSTINE: Therefore, let us not love ourselves but him, and in feeding his sheep let us seek those things that are his, not those things that are ours. For in some inexplicable way whoever loves himself, not God, does not love himself; and whoever loves God, not himself, does himself love himself. For he who cannot live of himself dies, of course, by loving himself. Then he who loves himself so that he may not live does not love himself. But when he from whom comes life is loved, by not loving himself, he who does not love himself—precisely that he may love him from whom he has life—loves himself all the more. Therefore, let those who feed Christ's sheep not be "lovers of themselves," that they may not feed them as their own but as his. Let them not wish to acquire their own gains from them, as "lovers of money," or to be their lords, as "haughty," or to glory over honors which they take from them, as "proud," or to go so far as even to create heresies, as "blasphemous," or to not yield to the holy fathers, as "disobedient to parents." Let them return evils for goods to those who wish them to perish because they do not wish them to perish, as "ungrateful." Let them not kill their own souls and those of others, as "wicked." Let them not sunder the motherly bowels of the church, as "irreligious," not feel no compassion for the weak, as "without affection," not attempt to taint the reputation of the saints, as "detractors," or not fail to rein in their worst desires, as "incontinent." Let them not engage in lawsuits, as "unmerciful," or fail to know how to give help, as "without kindness." Let them not point out to the enemies of the godly the things that they have learned ought to be kept secret, as "traitors." Let them not disturb the human sense of shame by shameless pursuits, as "licentious," or fail to understand what they say or assert, as if they were "blinded." Let them not prefer carnal enjoyments to spiritual joys, as "lovers of pleasures more than of God." TRACTATES ON JOHN 123.5.[45]

SOME QUESTIONS REMAIN UNSETTLED. AU-

---

[42]NPNF 2 4:324*. Athanasius uses the same argument against the views of Asterius the Sophist in Against the Arians 3.23.2 (NPNF 2 4:394) and against George of Cappadocia in *On the Councils* 3.37 (NPNF 2 4:470). [43]Eph 4:3. [44]*WSA* 3/6:99. [45]FC 92:78-79*.

gustine: What, therefore, if the soul and spirit of a human being is given by God himself, whenever it is given; and given, too, by propagation from its own kind? Now this is a position which I neither maintain nor refute. Nevertheless, if it must be defended or confuted, I certainly recommend its being done by clear and certain proofs. Nor do I deserve to be compared with senseless cattle because I avow myself to be as yet incapable of determining the question, but rather with cautious persons, because I do not recklessly teach what I know nothing about. But I am not disposed on my own part to return railing for railing and compare this man with brutes. Rather, I warn him as a son to acknowledge that he is really ignorant of that which he knows nothing about. I warn him not to attempt to teach that which he has not yet learned, lest he should deserve to be compared with those persons whom the apostle mentions as "desiring to be teachers of the law, understanding neither what they say nor the things about which they make assertions." On the Soul and Its Origin 1.16.26.[46]

Cling to the Fathers. Cyril of Alexandria: This, therefore, is the upright and most exact faith of the holy Fathers, that is, the confession of faith. But as Paul says, "the god of this world has blinded the minds of unbelievers that they should not see the light of the gospel of the glory of Christ."[47] Accordingly some, after having ceased to go along the straight road of truth, dash themselves against the rocks, "when they understand neither what they say nor the things about which they make assertions."[48] For after attributing the glory of the sonship only to the Word begotten of God the Father, they say that another son of the seed of David and Jesse has been conjoined to him and has a share in the filiation and of the glory proper to God and of the very indwelling of the Word and has had almost everything from him but has nothing at all of his own. Letters 55.41.[49]

1:8 The Law Is Good

Using the Law Lawfully. Chrysostom: The law, he seems to say, is good, and again, not so good. What then? Suppose one uses it unlawfully, is it not good? No, even then the law itself as such remains good. What he means is this: if any one fulfills the law in his actions, it is good. For that is to "use it lawfully," as here intended. But when one trumpets the law in words but neglects it in deeds, that is using it unlawfully. For such a person uses it, but not to his own profit. Further, the law, if you use it correctly, sends you to Christ. For since its aim is to justify, when the law itself fails to justify, it sends you on to the One who can justify. Some may keep the law but only superficially. It is kept as a bridle worn only for the purpose of going through the motions of constraint, but not, in fact, for constraint itself. The bridle here does not serve the true need of the prancing horse that should be guided by it, but only exists to look good. The faithful use the law lawfully when they govern themselves in its spirit but are not constrained by the letter of it. One uses the law lawfully who is conscious that it is not needed for salvation. The faithful fulfill the law not from fear of it, but from that principle of virtue that it makes possible. The faithful use the law not as being in fear of it, but having before their eyes rather the condemnation of their own conscience than the punishment hereafter. Homilies on 1 Timothy 2.[50]

The Minimum Standard. Theodore of Mopsuestia: The purpose of the law is to prohibit all iniquity and to set a minimum standard for those in need of it. For those who have been justified and freed from sin it is superfluous. These are the baptized, who need not to be instructed to refrain from sin, but rather to be taught to conform to the pattern in which they now stand. Commentary on 1 Timothy.[51]

---

[46]NPNF 1 5:326*. [47]2 Cor 4:4. 481 Tim 1:7. [49]FC 77:34-35*. [50]NPNF 1 13:413*. [51]TEM 2:76.

THE LAW LEADS TO CHRIST. THEODORET OF CYR: To use the law appropriately is to keep its purpose, that is, to lead one to Christ the Lord. Those who refrain from the sins that Paul mentions are living in conformity with the law. INTERPRETATION OF THE FIRST LETTER TO TIMOTHY.[52]

THE LAW MAKES SIN APPARENT. AUGUSTINE: Accordingly "the law is holy and the commandment holy, just and good."[53] It commands what ought to be commanded, and prohibits what ought to be prohibited. "Was that which is good, then, made death to me? God forbid."[54] The fault lies in making a bad use of the commandment, which in itself is good. "The law is good if one uses it lawfully." But he makes a bad use of the law who does not subject himself to God in humble piety, so that, with the aid of grace, he may become able to fulfill the law. He who does not use the law lawfully receives it to no other end than that his sin, which was latent before the prohibition, should be made apparent by his transgression. TO SIMPLICIAN: ON VARIOUS QUESTIONS 1.1.6.[55]

THE BURDEN IS LIGHT. AUGUSTINE: Indeed, "the precepts are good," as Pelagius says, if we use them lawfully. And in virtue of our strong conviction "that the good and just God could not have prescribed impossibilities," we are admonished both what to do in easy things and what to ask for in difficult ones. Indeed, all things are easy for love, to which alone the burden of Christ is light,[56] or which alone is itself the burden which is light. ON NATURE AND GRACE 1.69.83.[57]

1:9a The Law Is Not Laid Down for the Just

VIRTUE ASSUMES CHOICE. CLEMENT OF ALEXANDRIA: Virtue can come only through voluntary choice. The law assumes this from the outset. Thus the commandments are not laid down for those who are already righteous. STROMATA 2.2.[58]

ENCLOSED IN THE HEART OF THE JUST. AMBROSE: I consider not wealth but virtue as liberty, for it does not bow to the wishes of the stronger, and it is laid hold of and possessed by one's own greatness of soul. The wise man is always free. He is always held in honor; he is always master of the laws. The law is not made for the just but for the unjust. The just man is a law unto himself, and he does not need to summon the law from afar, for he carries it enclosed in his heart, and it is said to him, "Drink water out of your own vessels and from the stream of your own well."[59] LETTERS 54.[60]

RIGHTEOUS USE OF THE LAW. AUGUSTINE: "The law is not made for the righteous," and yet "the law is good, if one uses it lawfully." Now by connecting together these two seemingly contrary statements, the apostle warns and urges his reader to sift the question and solve it. For how can it be that "the law is good, if one uses it lawfully," if what follows is also true: "Knowing this, that the law is not made for the righteous"? For who but a righteous man lawfully uses the law? Yet it is not for him that it is made, but for the unrighteous. . . . The unrighteous man therefore lawfully uses the law, that he may become righteous. But when he has become so, he must no longer use it as a vehicle, for he has arrived at his journey's end—or rather (that I may employ the apostle's own simile, which has been already mentioned) as a schoolmaster, seeing that he is now fully instructed.[61] ON THE SPIRIT AND THE LETTER 1.10.16.[62]

THE JUDGMENT OF HIS WILL. CAESARIUS OF ARLES: Avoid pride, into which it is natural for anyone to fall. Pursue humility, in which everyone ought to grow. Let your beloved self not be ignorant of the laws of the church, in order that

---

[52]PG 82:789D/790D. [53]Rom 7:12. [54]Rom 7:13. [55]LCC 6:378. [56]Cf. Mt 11:30. [57]FC 86:88. [58]ANF 2:525*. [59]Prov 5:15. [60]FC 26:292. [61]Cf. Gal 3:24. [62]NPNF 1 5:89.

you may keep the rights of your authority within the rules and regulations of the Fathers. To be sure, it is said "that the law is not aimed at the good man," because he fulfills the norm of the precept already by the free judgment of his will. True love holds within itself both the authority of the apostles and the moral requirements. SERMONS 230.2.[63]

BEYOND THE TITHE. JOHN CASSIAN: The righteous, upon whom no law need be imposed, spend no small part—as if a tithe—but the whole extent of their lives in spiritual works. They are free of the legal tax of tithing. If a good and holy need presents itself, they are free to relax their fasting without any scruple. For it is not a paltry tithe that is being subtracted by those who have offered their all to the Lord along with themselves. Certainly the person who offers nothing of his own will and is compelled by legal necessity, without recourse, to pay his tithes to God, cannot do this without being seriously guilty of fraud. Hence it is eminently clear that the one who is responding fully to grace cannot be a slave of the law, watching out for things that are forbidden and carrying out things that are commanded, and that the perfect are those who do not make use even of things permitted by the law. CONFERENCES 21.29.2.[64]

1:9b For the Lawless and Disobedient

GREATER HOLINESS BY THE SPIRIT. ORIGEN: If they who are weak and incapable of the deeper mystery are edified by the letter, let them understand that if "anyone neglects the teachings of the Lord and lies to his neighbor over a deposit, or by a partnership, or by robbery,"[65] he is declared guilty of a great sin. But let this be absent from the church of God.... For I say boldly concerning you that "you did not so learn Christ" nor "were you so taught."[66] Besides, the law itself does not teach these things to the saints and the faithful. Do you want to know

that these are not said about the saints and the faithful? Hear the apostle when he distinguishes between them, "The law was not laid down for the just but for the unjust and for those not subject, for the wicked and the impure, for the father-killers and for the mother-killers," and for those similar to these. Because, therefore, for such men as this the apostle says, "the law was imposed," the church of God, having left behind the letter, is built up to greater holiness by the spirit, since heaven forbid that it would ever be polluted with such misdeeds. HOMILIES ON LEVITICUS 4.2.[67]

THE LAW NO OBSTACLE TO THE GIVER OF IT. EPHREM THE SYRIAN: The Lord touched the leper[68] in order to show that the law was not an obstacle to him who had constituted the law.... The leper was afraid to touch the Lord lest he defile him. But the Lord touched the leper to show him that he would not be defiled, he, at whose rebuke the defilement fled from the defiled one.[69] ... Samson ate honey from the dead body of an impure animal,[70] and with the jawbone of a dead ass he was victorious and rescued Israel.[71] God gave him water from the dead jawbone. COMMENTARY ON TATIAN'S DIATESSARON 12.21.[72]

THE LAW AND THE OLD COVENANT. EUSEBIUS OF CAESAREA: You see here that he distinguishes two covenants, the old and the new, and says that the new would not be like the old which was given to the fathers. For the old covenant was given as a law to the Jews, when they had fallen from the religion of their forefathers, and had embraced the manners and life of the Egyptians, and had declined to the errors of polytheism and the idolatrous superstitions of the Gentiles. It was intended to raise up the

---

[63]FC 66:180. [64]ACW 57:742. [65]Lev 6:2. [66]Eph 4:20-21. [67]FC 83:71. Origen is commenting on Leviticus 5:21-22. [68]Mt 8:3-4. [69]What follows is not present in the Armenian translation. [70]Judg 14:9. [71]Judg 15:15-16. [72]JSSS 2:201.

fallen, and to set on their feet those who were lying on their faces, by suitable teaching. "For the law, it is said, is not for the righteous, but for the unjust and disorderly, for the unrighteous and sinners, and for those like them." The Proof of the Gospel 1.4.[73]

Living Water Has Driven Away Pagan Seas. John of Damascus: From the time when we were born again of water and the Spirit, we have become sons of God and members of his household. For this reason St. Paul calls the faithful "saints."[74] Therefore we do not grieve but rejoice over the death of the saints. We are not under the law but under grace,[75] having been justified by faith[76] and having seen the one true

God. For the law is not laid down for the just, nor do we serve as children, held under the law,[77] but we have reached the estate of mature manhood and are fed on solid food, not on that which leads to idolatry. The law was good, as a lamp shining in a dark place until the day dawns, and the morning star rose in our hearts.[78] The living water of divine knowledge has driven away pagan seas, and now all may know God. The old creation has passed away, and all things are made new. On Divine Images 1.21.[79]

---

[73]POG 23. [74]1 Cor 1:2. [75]Rom 6:14. [76]Rom 5:1. [77]Gal 4:1-7. [78]2 Pet 1:9. [79]JDDI 30.

1:12-20 THANKFULNESS FOR MERCY

[12]*I thank him who has given me strength for this, Christ Jesus our Lord, because he judged me faithful by appointing me to his service,* [13]*though I formerly blasphemed and persecuted and insulted him; but I received mercy because I had acted ignorantly in unbelief,* [14]*and the grace of our Lord overflowed for me with the faith and love that are in Christ Jesus.* [15]*The saying is sure and worthy of full acceptance, that Christ Jesus came into the world to save sinners. And I am the foremost of sinners;* [16]*but I received mercy for this reason, that in me, as the foremost, Jesus Christ might display his perfect patience for an example to those who were to believe in him for eternal life.* [17]*To the King of ages, immortal, invisible, the only God, be honor and glory for ever and ever.[b] Amen.*

[18]*This charge I commit to you, Timothy, my son, in accordance with the prophetic utterances which pointed to you, that inspired by them you may wage the good warfare,* [19]*holding faith and a good conscience. By rejecting conscience, certain persons have made shipwreck of their faith,* [20]*among them Hymenaeus and Alexander, whom I have delivered to Satan that they may learn not to blaspheme.*

b Greek *to the ages of ages*

Overview: With great humility Paul reminds us that his strength comes ultimately not from himself but from God, though this claim in no way invalidates the importance of his own free resolution. In fact, his moral attentiveness and zeal, even if misguided, were essential to a full reception of, and response to, God's election of him (CHRYSOSTOM). In Paul we see how a life progresses, under God, from being based on law to being based on the eternal life given in Christ, which is the form of things to come (THEODORE). In the conversion of Paul, but even more in the selection of Timothy for ordination, it is clear that moral worthiness, as well as sound faith, manifests the reality of divine election, since without these the stupidity of shipwreck is the result (THEODORET). With both Paul and Timothy, divine adoption and election preceded visible anointing, since it is clear, at least in Paul's case, that a great deal of human obtuseness had to be overcome (AUGUSTINE). Paul's culpable ignorance prevented his conversion, such that his eyes had to be opened by God about the law. God had foreseen Paul's great worthiness and, having thus preassessed him, called him to be an apostle (CHRYSOSTOM, ISAAC OF NINEVEH).

1:12a The One Who Has Given Me Strength

PAUL'S HUMILITY. CHRYSOSTOM: Consider how he abounds in the expressions of humility. For so "to me last of all he appeared,"[1] he says. He views himself alone "as one born out of due time." He himself is "the least of all the apostles," and not even worthy of this appellation. And he was not content even with these, but that he might not seem in mere words to be humble-minded, he states both reasons and proofs: of his being "one born out of due time," his seeing Jesus last; and of his being unworthy even of the name of an apostle, "his persecuting the church." For one who is simply humble-minded sets down the reasons for his contrition. To Timothy he makes mention of these same things, saying, "I thank him who has given me strength for this, Christ Jesus our Lord, because he judged me faithful by appointing me to his service, though I formerly blasphemed and persecuted and

insulted him." HOMILIES ON FIRST CORINTHIANS 38.5.[2]

1:12b He Judged Me Faithful

LET YOUR LIFE BE OPENLY EXPOSED. CHRYSOSTOM: If you have sinned and God has pardoned your sin, receive your pardon and give thanks. But do not be forgetful of your sin. It is not that you should fret over the thought of it, but that you may school your soul not to grow lax or relapse again into the same snares. This is what Paul did, not hiding his actions as a blasphemer, persecutor and injurer. It is as if he were saying: "Let the life of your servant be openly exposed, so that the loving kindness of the Lord might be all the more apparent. For although I have received the remission of sins, I do not reject the memory of those sins." And this not only made transparent the loving kindness of the Lord but made the man himself the more remarkable. For when you have learned who he was before, then you will be the more astonished at him. When you see what he came to be out of what he was, then you will commend him the more. So if you have greatly sinned, you yourself upon being changed will hope all the more by seeing him. Such an example comforts those who are in despair and causes them again to stand tall. HOMILIES CONCERNING THE STATUES 12.1.[3]

1:13a I Formerly Blasphemed, but I Received Mercy

AN APPARENT CONTRADICTION. AUGUSTINE: We heard the reading from the apostle, and perhaps some of you may be worried by what is written there, "According to the justice which is from the law, I was without reproach. Whatever was a gain for me, that I have regarded as a dead

---

[1] 1 Cor 15:10. [2] NPNF 1 12:231*. [3] NPNF 1 9:418*.

loss on account of Christ."[4] Then he went on to say, "I have reckoned it to be not only a dead loss, but even muck, that I may gain Christ and may be found in him, not having my own justice which is from the law, but the justice which is from the faith of Jesus Christ."[5] The question is, how could he consider conducting himself without reproach according to the justice which is from the law, to be so much muck and loss? After all, who gave the law? . . . But let us listen to what he says in another place, "It was not as a result of works," he says, "which we have done ourselves, but according to his own mercy that he saved us, by means of the bath of rebirth."[6] And again, "I, who was previously a blasphemer and persecutor, and an overbearing man; but I obtained mercy," and so on.[7] On the one hand he affirmed that he conducted himself without reproach; on the other he confessed he had been a sinner of such proportions that no sinners need despair of themselves, precisely because even Paul had found remission. Sermons 170.1.[8]

Free to Fall, Helpless to Rise. Augustine: From being a persecutor he was changed into "a preacher and the teacher of the nations."[9] "Previously," he says, "I was a blasphemer and persecutor and an insolent man. But the reason I obtained mercy was this, that Christ Jesus might demonstrate his forbearance first of all in me, and for the instruction of those who were going to trust him for eternal life."[10] It is by the grace of God, you see, that we are saved from our sins, in which we are languishing. God alone is the medicine that cures the soul. The soul was well able to injure itself but quite unable to cure itself. In the body, too, after all, people have it in their power to get sick, but not equally in their power to get better. I mean, if they exceed the proper limits, and live self-indulgent lives and do all the things that undermine the constitution and are injurious to health, the day comes, if that's what they want, when they fall sick. When they've so fallen, though, they don't get better. In order to fall sick, you see, they apply

themselves to self-indulgence. But in order to get better, they must apply the doctor's services to their health. . . . And so it goes with the soul. Sermons 278.1-2.[11]

Grace Given to the Unworthy as Pure Gift. Augustine: What then is this "grace for grace"?[12] By faith we first win God's favor; and for us who were not worthy to have our sins forgiven, from the very fact that, though unworthy, we received so great a gift, it is called grace. What is grace? That which is given gratuitously. That which is bestowed, not paid back. If it was owed, recompense was paid, not grace bestowed. . . . Having acquired this grace of faith, you will be just by faith. "For the just man lives by faith."[13] And you will first win God's favor from living by faith. When you have won God's favor from living by faith, you will receive as a reward immortality and everlasting life. And that is grace. . . . Paul acknowledges this grace when he says that he had before been a blasphemer and a persecutor, and insulting, "but I obtained mercy." Tractates on John 3.9-10.[14]

Mercy Heals. Peter Chrysologus: Paul introduces a new kind of admonition by exhorting others "by the mercy of God."[15] Why does he not exhort through God's might, or majesty, or glory? Why by his mercy? Because it was through that mercy alone that Paul escaped from the criminal state of a persecutor and obtained the dignity of his great apostolate. He himself tells us this, "For I formerly was a blasphemer, a persecutor and a bitter adversary; but I obtained the mercy of God."[16] . . . "I exhort you by the mercy of God." Paul asks—rather, God himself is asking through Paul—for God has greater desire to be loved than feared. God is

---

[4]Cf. Phil 3:6-7. [5]Cf. Phil 3:8-9. [6]Tit 3:5. [7]1 Tim 1:13. [8]WSA 3/5:238. [9]2 Tim 1:11. [10]1 Tim 1:13, 16. [11]WSA 3/8:50-51. [12]Jn 1:16. [13]Rom 1:7. [14]FC 78:83. [15]Rom 12:1. [16]1 Tim 1:13.

asking because he wants to be not so much a Lord as a Father. SERMONS 108.[17]

1:13b *Acting Ignorantly in Unbelief*

I ACTED IGNORANTLY. CHRYSOSTOM: Why then did other Jews not obtain mercy? Because what they did, they did not ignorantly but willfully, well knowing what they did. . . . Thus their love of power was everywhere an obstacle in their way. When they admitted that no one can forgive sins but God alone and Christ immediately did that very thing—forgive sin—which they had confessed to be a sign of divinity, this could not be a case of ignorance. But did Paul act out of such ignorance? . . . Paul did not act, as some other Jews did, from the love of power, but from zeal. For what was the motive of his journey to Damascus? He thought the doctrine pernicious and was afraid that the preaching of it would spread everywhere. . . . It is for this he condemns himself, saying, "I am not fit to be called an apostle."[18] It is for this he confesses his ignorance, which was a consequence of his disbelief. HOMILIES ON 1 TIMOTHY 3.[19]

WHY THE PERSECUTOR WAS CHOSEN TO WRITE SO MANY LETTERS. CYRIL OF JERUSALEM: At this point in my discourse I confess my amazement at the wise dispensation of the Holy Spirit, in limiting the epistles of the others to a small number but granting grace to Paul, the former persecutor, to write fourteen. For it was not as though Peter and John were less than Paul that he withheld the gift in their case—God forbid!—but that his doctrine might be beyond question, he gave the grace to the former enemy and persecutor to write more, that thus we might all be confirmed in our faith. Indeed, all were astonished at Paul and said, "Is not this he who used to make havoc" previously "and who has come here for the purpose of taking us in bonds to Jerusalem?"[20] Do not be astonished, Paul says, "I know that 'it is hard for me to kick against the goad.'[21] I know that 'I am not worthy to be called

an apostle, because I persecuted the church of God,'[22] but 'I acted ignorantly.' For I considered the preaching of Christ to be the destruction of the law, for I did not know that he came 'to fulfill the law, not to destroy it.'[23] But 'the grace of our Lord has abounded beyond measure in me.'" CATECHETICAL LECTURES 10.18.[24]

1:15a *Sure and Worthy of Full Acceptance*

WHAT THE APOSTLES RECEIVED. ATHANASIUS: What the apostles received, they passed on without change, so that the doctrine of the mysteries (the sacraments) and Christ would remain correct. The divine Word—the Son of God—wants us to be their (the apostles') disciples. It is appropriate for them to be our teachers, and it is necessary for us to submit to their teaching alone. Only from them and those who have faithfully taught their doctrine do we get, as Paul writes, "faithful words, worthy of full acceptance." FESTAL LETTERS 2.7.[25]

THE HUMAN WORD. AUGUSTINE: We heard the blessed apostle Paul saying, "The word is human[26] and worthy of total acceptance, that Christ Jesus came into the world to save sinners, of whom I am the foremost." So it's a human word, and worthy of total acceptance. Why human, and not divine? Without the slightest doubt, unless this word were also divine, it would not be worthy of total acceptance. But this word is both human and divine in the same

---

[17]FC 17:167. [18]1 Cor 9:9. [19]NPNF 1 13:417*. [20]Acts 9:21. [21]Acts 9:5. [22]1 Cor 15:9. [23]Mt 5:17. [24]FC 61:207. [25]ARL 65. [26]"The saying is sure": Augustine had before him a Latin text of 1 Timothy 1:15, in which the term *humanus* (*anthropinos* in Greek) had been substituted in some Old Latin versions for the more reliable reading *fidelis* (*pistos*). Present also in Ambrosiaster, both here and at 1 Timothy 3:1, the reason for the substitution is unclear. In the case of 1 Timothy 3:1 it serves to soften the contrast between 3:1 and what follows in 3:2, that is, a statement of the ethical requirements for the office of bishop is turned into a merely human, thus relative, tradition (*DC* 51). The reason for the variant at 1 Timothy 1:15 is puzzling, however.

sort of way that Christ himself is both man and God. So if we are right in understanding this word to be not only human but also divine, why did the apostle prefer to call it human rather than divine? . . . So the aspect he chose was the one by which Christ came into the world. He came, after all, insofar as he was man. Because insofar as he was God, he was always there. SERMONS 174.1.[27]

THE CRITIC TAKES ON THE CRITICS. JEROME: They[28] may choose to read, "It is a man's saying, and worthy of all acceptation." We are content to err with the Greeks, that is to say, with the apostle himself, who spoke Greek. Our version, therefore, is, "it is a faithful saying, and worthy of all acceptation." LETTERS 27.3.[29]

1:15b *He Came Into the World to Save Sinners*

A GREAT INVALID. AUGUSTINE: There was no reason for Christ the Lord to come, except to save sinners. Eliminate diseases, eliminate wounds, and there is no call for medicine. If a great doctor has come down from heaven, a great invalid must have been lying very sick throughout the whole wide world. This invalid is the whole human race. SERMONS 175.1.[30]

ALL WHO SIN DESERVE JUST PUNISHMENT. AUGUSTINE: "For all have sinned," either in Adam or by themselves, "and are deprived of the glory of God."[31] Consequently, the whole human mass ought to be punished, and if the deserved punishment of damnation were rendered to all, beyond all doubt it would be justly rendered. This is why those who are liberated from it by grace are not called vessels of their own merits but "vessels of mercy."[32] But whose mercy was it but him who sent Jesus Christ into this world to save sinners, whom he foreknew, predestined, called, justified and glorified?[33] Hence, who could be so advanced in foolish insanity as not to render ineffable thanks to the mercy of this

God who liberates those whom he has wished, considering that one could not in any way reproach the justice of God in condemning all entirely? ON NATURE AND GRACE 1.4.4-1.5.5.[34]

DIVINE FOREKNOWLEDGE DOES NOT DETERMINE HUMAN RESPONSES. LEO THE GREAT: What was foreknown about the malice of Jews and what was properly decreed regarding the passion of Christ were very different and quite contrary. For the will to murder did not proceed from the same place as the will to die. Nor did their heinous crime and the Redeemer's patience arise from a single spirit. Our Lord did not himself cause the wicked hands of his attackers to be laid on him, but he permitted this. He did not force what was going to happen actually to happen simply by foreknowing it. Yet it was for this purpose that he had taken on flesh, so that it might happen. Finally, so disparate were the motives of the Crucified and of those crucifying, that what was undertaken by Christ could not be abolished, what was committed by those others could indeed have been put to a halt. He who came "to save sinners" did not deny his mercy even to his own murderers,[35] but turned the evil of godless people to the good of believers.[36] SERMONS 67.2-3.[37]

1:15c *The Foremost of Sinners*

INSTRUMENTS OF THE MIRACLE OF CONVERSION. ORIGEN: Moreover, Paul says in the epistle to Timothy, even though he himself had later become an apostle of Jesus, "this is a faithful saying, that Christ Jesus came into the world to save sinners, of whom I am chief." For some unknown reason he [Celsus] forgot or did not think of saying anything about Paul, who after

---

[27]*WSA* 3/5:257. [28]Those who read from the Old Latin text rather than the Greek. [29]NPNF 2 6:44. See the preceding note. [30]*WSA* 3/5:265. [31]Rom 3:23. [32]Rom 9:23. [33]Rom 8:29-30. [34]FC 86:25-26. [35]Lk 23:34. [36]Rom 11:11-12. [37]FC 93:292.

Jesus established the churches in Christ. . . . Why then is it outrageous if Jesus, wanting to show mankind the extent of his ability to heal souls, chose infamous and most wicked men and led them on so far that they were an example of the purest moral character to those who were converted by them to the gospel of Christ? AGAINST CELSUS 1.63.[38]

TRUE HUMILITY. CHRYSOSTOM: It is no humility to think that you are a sinner when you really are a sinner. But whenever one is conscious of having done many great deeds but does not imagine that he is something great in himself, that is true humility. When a man is like Paul and can say, "I have nothing on my conscience," and then can add, "But I am not justified by this,"[39] and can say again, "Christ Jesus came to save sinners of whom I am the chief," that is true humility. That man is truly humble who does exalted deeds but, in his own mind, sees himself as lowly. ON THE INCOMPREHENSIBLE NATURE OF GOD 5.6.[40]

HOW THE FIRST? AUGUSTINE: Pay attention to the apostle Paul, "The word is faithful and worthy of total acceptance, that Christ Jesus came into the world to save sinners, of whom I am the first." He said, "of whom I am the first." How was he the first? Weren't there so many Jews who were sinners before him? Weren't there any sinners before him in the whole human race? . . . So what's the meaning of "of whom I am the first"? That I am worse than all of them. By first he meant us to understand worst. . . . Remember Saul, and you'll discover why. Isn't he the one who wasn't satisfied with only one hand to stone Stephen, and who took care of the coats of the others? Isn't he the one who persecuted the church everywhere? . . . So he it is who was the number one persecutor. There was none worse than he. SERMONS 175.6-7.[41]

GOD'S DESCENT TO HUMAN SUFFERING. CASSIODORUS: This is a short psalm,[42] but it annihi-

lates the boundless wickedness of pagans who believe that the glory of the heavenly majesty could not have descended to the humility of suffering. How foolish they are. For their thinking is confounded by the Source of the world's realization that it has been freed! As Paul says, "Christ Jesus came into the world to save sinners, of whom I am the chief." EXPLANATION OF THE PSALMS 3.9.[43]

1:16a For This Reason

THE PORT OF DIVINE CLEMENCY. TERTULLIAN: To all sins, then, committed whether by flesh or spirit, whether by deed or will, the same God who has destined penalty by means of judgment has nevertheless engaged to grant pardon by means of repentance. For he has said to the people, "Repent, and I will save you";[44] and again, "I live, says the Lord, and I will have repentance rather than death."[45] Repentance, then, is "life," since it is preferred to "death." That repentance, O sinner, like myself (nay, rather, less than myself, for preeminence in sins I acknowledge to be mine), do you so hasten to so embrace, as a shipwrecked man the protection of some plank.[46] This will draw you forth when sunk in the waves of sins and will bear you forward into the port of the divine clemency. ON REPENTANCE 4.[47]

HIS CALLING BY GRACE. CHRYSOSTOM: God indeed says that he called Paul on account of his excellent capacity, as he said to Ananias, "for he is a chosen instrument of mine to carry my name before the Gentiles and kings."[48] That is to say, he was capable of service and the accomplishment of great deeds. God gives this as the reason

---

[38]OAC 58-59. [39]1 Cor 4:4. [40]FC 72:158-59. [41]*WSA* 3/5:268-69. [42]Cassiodorus is commenting on Psalm 3. [43]ACW 51:72. [44]Ezek 18:30, 32. [45]Ezek 33:11. [46]There is a longstanding debate as to whether Tertullian's reference here is to baptism or penance. See ACW 28:20 and 149 n. 54 for discussion. [47]ANF 3:659*. [48]Acts 9:15.

for his call. But Paul himself everywhere ascribes it to grace and to God's inexpressible mercy. He says this in the words, "I received mercy for this reason, that in me, as the foremost, Jesus Christ might display his perfect patience for an example to those who were to believe in him for eternal life." COMMENTARY ON GALATIANS 1.[49]

1:16b For an Example

HIS FRANK REVELATION OF HIS SINS. CHRYSOSTOM: Paul pointed out to all the deeds he had dared to commit before. He thought that it was better for his former life to be publicized to all in order to make evident the greatness of the gift of God than to cover up his ineffable and indescribable mercy by shrinking from proclaiming his own sins to all. He therefore recounted in detail his persecutions, his plots, his fights against the church. He says, "I am not worthy to be called an apostle, because I persecuted the church of God";[50] and again, "that Jesus came to save sinners of whom I am the chief." And once more, "You have heard of my former way of life in Judaism; how beyond all measure I persecuted the church of God and ravaged it."[51] Indeed, to give, as it were, some kind of return to Christ for his long-suffering toward him, by telling plainly what sort he was and what an enemy and foe he had saved, he very frankly revealed the battle which in the beginning he had waged with consuming zeal against Christ. And because of this he held out good hope even to those who had despaired of themselves. HOMILIES ON JOHN 10.1.[52]

THE DOCTOR'S TEST CASE. AUGUSTINE: So note how this Saul, later Paul, ironically "congratulates himself" on having attained to the mercy of God, because he was found to be the first, that is the most outstanding, in sins! . . . This was so that others could all say to themselves, "if Paul was cured, why should I despair? If such a desperately sick man was cured by such

a great physician, who am I, not to fit those hands to my wounds, not to hasten to the care of those hands?" That people might be able to say that sort of thing, that's why Saul was made into an apostle out of a persecutor. When a doctor comes to a new place, he looks for someone there who's been despaired of and cures him, even if he finds he's very poor, provided he finds him a desperate case. He is not looking for a fee but displaying his skill. SERMONS 175.9.[53]

STILL MAKING A BEGINNING. ISAAC OF NINEVEH: We bring to mind how the holy apostle Paul recounts his transgressions and puts his soul in the last and nethermost place, saying, "Jesus Christ came into the world to save sinners, of whom I am chief." . . . When and at what time did he say this? After great struggles, after mighty works, after the preaching of the gospel of Christ which he proclaimed throughout the whole world, after continual deaths and manifold tribulations which he suffered from the Jews and from the heathen. Even then he saw himself as only making a beginning. He was of the opinion not merely that he had not yet attained to purity of soul but that he would not even number himself among the disciples of Christ, as was fitting. AN EPISTLE TO ABBA SYMEON OF CAESAREA.[54]

1:17 To the King of Ages

THE DOXOLOGY. CHRYSOSTOM: We must first turn our words to prayer. I say this because, sometimes, when prayer accompanies a teaching, it will serve to provide us with a demonstration of the things we are seeking to prove. . . . And Paul often does this at the beginning of his epistles. He first mentions God and then does not go on to his teaching until he pays to God the glory and praise due to him. Listen: "To the

---

[49]NPNF 1 13:11*. [50]1 Cor 15:9. [51]Gal 1:13. [52]FC 33:98. [53]WSA 3/5:269-70. [54]AHSIS 434.

King of ages, the immortal, the invisible, the only God of wisdom, be honor and glory for ever and ever! Amen." ON THE INCOMPREHENSIBLE NATURE OF GOD 3.2.[55]

DISTINGUISHABLE DIVINE ATTRIBUTES. GREGORY OF NYSSA: We know that of all the names by which Deity is indicated some are expressive of the Divine majesty, employed and understood absolutely, and some are assigned with reference to the operations over us and all creation. When the apostle says, "Now to the immortal, invisible, only wise God," and the like, by these titles he suggests conceptions which represent to us the transcendent power. In other cases, however, God is spoken of in the Scriptures as gracious, merciful, full of pity, true, good, Lord, Physician, Shepherd, Way, Bread, Fountain, King, Creator, Artificer, Protector, Who is over all and through all, Who is all in all; these and similar titles contain the declaration of the operations of the Divine loving kindness in the creation. AGAINST EUNOMIUS 2.11.[56]

THE COMMUNION OF FATHER AND SON. RUFINUS OF AQUILEIA: He is the only Son of God, our Lord. For he is born One of One, because there is one brightness of light, and there is one word of the understanding. Neither does an incorporeal generation degenerate into the plural number or suffer division. The One who is born is in no way separated from the One who gives life. He is the one and only, the unique. He is as thought is to the mind, as wisdom is to the wise, as a word is to the understanding, as valor is to the brave. As the Father is said by the apostle to be "alone wise," so likewise the Son alone is called wisdom. He is then the "only Son." In glory, everlastingness, virtue, dominion, power, he is what the Father is. Yet all these he has not unoriginately as the Father but from the Father, as the Son, without beginning and equal. Although he is the head of all things, yet the Father is the head of him. For so it is written,

"The head of Christ is God."[57] COMMENTARY ON THE APOSTLES' CREED 6.[58]

THE VISION OF GOD. AUGUSTINE: In order to attain that vision by which we see God as he is, he has warned us that our hearts must be cleansed. As objects are called visible in our fashion of speaking, so God is called invisible[59] lest he be thought to be a material body. Yet he will not deprive pure hearts of the contemplation of his essence, since this great and sublime reward is promised, on the Lord's own word, to those who worship and love God. At the time when he appeared visibly to bodily eyes, he promised that his invisible being also would be seen by the clean of heart, "He that loves me shall be loved of my Father, and I will love him and will manifest myself to him."[60] It is certain that this nature of his, which he shares with the Father, is equally as invisible as it is equally incorruptible. LETTERS 147.19.48.[61]

LIGHT UNAPPROACHABLE. JEROME: But if you think that God is seen by those who are pure in heart in this world, why did Moses, who had previously said, "I have seen the Lord face to face, and my life is preserved," afterwards plead that he might see him distinctly? And because he said that he had seen God, the Lord told him, "You cannot not see my face. For no one shall see my face and live."[62] For this reason also the apostle calls him the only invisible God, who dwells in light unapproachable, whom no man has seen nor can see. AGAINST THE PELAGIANS 3.12.[63]

UNBOUNDED ALMIGHTY. AUGUSTINE: So this faith is also a rule for salvation, to "believe in God the Father almighty," creator of all things, "king of the ages, immortal and invisible." He is

---

[55]FC 72:98-99. [56]NPNF 2 5:119*. [57]2 Cor 11:3. [58]NPNF 2 3:546*. [59]Cf. Col 1:15. [60]Jn 14:21. [61]FC 20:216-17. [62]Ex 33:20. [63]NPNF 2 6:479*.

indeed the almighty God who at the origin of the world made all things out of nothing. He is before the ages and made and governs the ages. He doesn't, after all, grow with time, or stretch out in space, nor is he shut in or bounded by any material. He abides with and in himself as full and perfect eternity, which neither human thought can comprehend nor tongue describe. SERMONS 215.2.[64]

EQUALLY INVISIBLE AND IMMORTAL. AUGUS-TINE: Let us hold firmly that Father and Son and Holy Spirit in their own proper nature, their proper substance, are together and equally invisible. We believe them to be together and equally immortal, together and equally imperishable. There is one place where the apostle states all these things simultaneously, "Now to the king of ages, immortal, invisible, imperishable, to the only God, be honor and glory for ever and ever. Amen." SERMONS 277.15.[65]

THE ESSENCE OF BEING. PSEUDO-DIONYSIUS: Now let me speak about the Good, about that which truly is and which gives being to everything else, the God who transcends everything by virtue of his power. . . . So he is called "king of the ages," for in him and around him all being is and subsists. He was not, nor will he be in a static sense. He did not come to be. He is not in the midst of becoming. He will not come to be. No. It is not that he can be defined by the word *is*, but rather he is the essence of being for the things which have being. Not only things that are but also the essence of what they are come from him who precedes the ages. THE DIVINE NAMES 5.4.[66]

1:18a *Timothy, My Son*

FATHERLY AUTHORITY. CHRYSOSTOM: When again he speaks of a charge, which implies something burdensome, he adds, "This charge I commit to you, my son Timothy." He charges him as his son, not so much with arbitrary or despotic

authority. Rather as a father, he says, "My son, Timothy." HOMILIES ON 1 TIMOTHY 5.[67]

NAMING THE SON. THEODORET OF CYR: With the name of "son," Paul gives his blessing to Timothy. INTERPRETATION OF THE LETTER TO THE ROMANS.[68]

1:18b *In Accordance with the Prophetic Utterances*

THE HOLY SPIRIT. CHRYSOSTOM: The offices of teacher and priest are of great dignity, and to bring forward one that is worthy requires God's own calling. So it was of old, and so it is now. This choice is to be made apart from human sentiments, not looking to any temporal consideration, swayed neither by friendship nor by enmity. . . . In those days the calling of a priest was "in accordance with prophecy." But what does that imply? That nothing human is to interfere with the leading of the Holy Spirit. For prophecy is not only the telling of things future but also of the present. HOMILIES ON 1 TIMOTHY 5.[69]

ENTRUSTED WITH THE WORK OF TEACHING. THEODORE OF MOPSUESTIA: It was according to divine revelation that I, Paul, laid hands on you and entrust to you the work of teaching. COMMENTARY ON 1 TIMOTHY.[70]

AFTER SIGNS OF GOD'S CALLING. THEODORET OF CYR: By recalling prophecy, Paul makes it clear that Timothy received the laying on of hands in accordance with divine revelation, and after numerous signs that he, Timothy, had been so elected. INTERPRETATION OF THE FIRST LETTER TO TIMOTHY.[71]

1:19 *Shipwreck of Their Faith*

---

[64]WSA 3/6:160-61. [65]WSA 3/8:42. [66]PSD 98*. [67]NPNF 1 13:423. [68]PG 82:795A/796A. [69]NPNF 1 13:423. [70]TEM 2:82. [71]PG 82:795B/796B.

REFUSAL OF THE PILOT. AMBROSE: The truth of the Lord encompasses him, so that he is not afraid of the terror of the night or of the thing that walks about in darkness.[72] Therefore, "Zabulon shall dwell by the sea." Thus he may look upon the shipwrecks of others while himself free from danger. He may behold others driven here and there on the sea of this world, those who are borne about by every wind of doctrine, while himself persevering on the ground of an immovable faith. THE PATRI-ARCHS 5.26-27.[73]

REJECTION OF DUALISM. ATHANASIUS: But the sectarians, who have fallen away from the teaching of the church and made shipwreck concerning the faith, wrongly think that evil has some sort of eternal existence. They arbitrarily imagine another god besides the true One, the Father of our Lord Jesus Christ. They fantasize that he is the unmade producer of evil and the head of wickedness, who is also artificer of creation. These men one can easily refute, not only from the divine Scriptures but also from the human understanding itself, the very source of these insane imaginations. AGAINST THE HEATHEN 6.3.[74]

BLUNDERS FROM ENEMIES WITHIN. BASIL THE GREAT: What storm at sea was ever so fierce and wild as this tempest[75] within the churches? In it every landmark of the Fathers has been moved. Every foundation, every bulwark of opinion has been shaken. Everything buoyed up on the unsound is dashed about and shaken down. We attack one another. We are overthrown by one another. If our enemy is not the first to strike us, we are wounded by the comrade at our side. If an enemy soldier is stricken and falls, his fellow soldier tramples him down. There is at least this bond of union between us that we hate our common foes, but no sooner has the enemy gone by than we find enemies in one another. And who could make a complete list of all the wrecks? Some have gone to the bottom on the attack of the enemy, some through the unsuspected treachery of their allies, some from the blundering of their own officers. We see, as it were, whole churches, crews and all, dashed and shattered upon the sunken reefs of deceitful teaching, while others of the enemies of the Spirit of salvation have seized the helm and made shipwreck of the faith. ON THE SPIRIT 30.77.[76]

SWAMPED BY WAVES. CHRYSOSTOM: In all circumstances, beloved, we need faith—faith, the mother of virtues, the medicine of salvation—without it we cannot grasp any teaching on sublime matters. But those who are without faith are like people trying to cross the sea without a ship. They are able to swim for a while by using hands and feet, but when they have gone farther out they are soon swamped by the waves. So, also, those who have recourse to their own reasoning before accepting any knowledge are inviting shipwreck, even as Paul speaks of those "who have made shipwreck of the faith." HOMILIES ON JOHN 33.1.[77]

PROFANE NOVELTIES. VINCENT OF LÉRINS: Innumerable are the examples we must omit, since we wish to be brief. But all of them make it sufficiently clear that the customary method of most heresies consists in rejoicing in "profane novelties," in loathing traditional knowledge, which some rejecting have made shipwreck concerning the faith.[78] Conversely, it is proper for Catholics to guard the "deposit," handed down by the holy fathers, to condemn profane novelties, and, as the apostle said, "before and now I say again," let him be anathema "if any one preach to you a gospel besides that which you have received."[79] COMMONITORIES 24.[80]

---

[72]Ps 90:4-6 (LXX; 91:4-6). [73]FC 65:256-57. [74]NPNF 2 4:6-7*. [75]The heresy that the Holy Spirit is not truly God. [76]NPNF 1 8:48-49*. [77]FC 33:322*. [78]See also 1 Tim 6:20. [79]Gal 1:9. [80]FC 7:315.

1:20a *Hymenaeus and Alexander*

THE NATURE OF THEIR ERROR. ATHANASIUS: When one knows properly these timely points,[81] his understanding of the faith is right and healthy. But if he mistakes any such points, he quickly falls into heresy. Thus Hymenaeus and Alexander and their fellows were untimely when they said that the resurrection had already been. The Galatians were untimely in the other direction in making much of circumcision now. AGAINST THE ARIANS 1.54.2.[82]

1:20b *Delivered to Satan That They May Learn*

COMPARING PAUL'S THORN TO THE SHIP-WRECKED BROTHERS. TERTULLIAN: Plainly Paul states that he delivered to Satan Hymenaeus and Alexander, "that they learn not to blaspheme," as he writes to Timothy. Nevertheless Paul himself says that a "thorn was given him, an angel of Satan,"[83] by which he was to be buffeted, lest he should exalt himself. Weren't these brothers delivered to Satan not for perdition but for giving them an opportunity to change? If so, what is the difference between blasphemy and incest and a soul entirely free from these? The free soul would be elated from no other source than the highest sanctity and all innocence. The elation of such a soul would be in the apostle's case restrained by this buffeting, by means, some say, of pain in the ear or head. Incest, however, and blasphemy would have deserved a different punishment. The person would have been delivered over to Satan himself for a possession, not to an "angel" of his. . . . If you take the assumption that the crime of Hymenaeus and Alexander—blasphemy—is irremissible in this and in the future age,[84] the apostle would not, in opposition to the clear directive of the Lord, have given to Satan, under a hope of pardon, men already irremediably sunken from the faith into blasphemy. Thus, he pronounced them "shipwrecked with regard to faith," having no longer the solace of the ship, the church. ON MODESTY 13.[85]

SEPARATED FROM THE FOLD. CHRYSOSTOM: As executioners, though themselves laden with numberless crimes, are made the correctors of others; so it is here with the evil spirit. . . . He [the offender] was then immediately expelled from the common assembly, separated from the fold. They became deserted and destitute. They were delivered to the wolf. HOMILIES ON 1 TIMOTHY 5.[86]

TOWARD PENITENCE. THEODORE OF MOPSUESTIA: The sinner is handed over to Satan, that is, is separated from the church, so that penitence may follow. COMMENTARY ON 1 TIMOTHY.[87]

THE SENTENCE REVOKED IN REPENTANCE. THEODORET OF CYR: The sinner is separated from the body of the church, stripped of divine grace, and so will be cruelly beaten by the Adversary, will fall into illnesses and painful passions and into a host of scrapes and calamities. It is understood that the sentence will be revoked when the sinner has repented. INTERPRETATION OF THE FIRST LETTER TO TIMOTHY.[88]

INCREASING CONSTRAINTS. BASIL THE GREAT: Those whom the usual penalties do not recall to their senses, and even exclusion from prayers does not lead to repentance, must be subjected to the canons given by the Lord. For it has been written, "If your brother sins, go and show him his fault, between you and him. But if he does not listen to you, take one or two others along with you. If he refuses to listen to them, tell it to the church. And if he refuses to listen even to the church, let him be to you as a Gen-

---

[81]About the events of the end. [82]NPNF 2 4:338. [83]2 Cor 12:7-10. [84]Mt 12:32. [85]ANF 4:87*. [86]NPNF 1 13:425. [87]TEM 2:84. [88]PG 82:795D/796D-797A/798A.

tile and a tax collector."[89] Now, this truly has been done in the case of this man. Once he was accused; in the presence of one or two he was convicted; a third time, in the presence of the church. Since, therefore, we have solemnly protested to him and he has not acquiesced, let him for the future be excommunicated. And let it be announced to all the village that he is not to be admitted to any participation in the ordinary relations of life, so that, by our refusal to associate with him, he may become wholly the food for the devil. LETTERS 288.[90]

CORRECTION A GOOD WORK. AUGUSTINE: Let us learn, brethren, when actions are alike, to distinguish the intentions of the actors; otherwise, if we shut our eyes to this, we might judge falsely, and we might accuse well-wishers of doing us harm. Likewise, when the same apostle says that he delivered up certain men to Satan, "that they may learn not to blaspheme," did he render evil for evil, or did he, rather, judge that it was a good work to correct evil men even by evil? LETTERS 93.2.7.[91]

OUT OF LOVE. AUGUSTINE: Out of love the apostle delivered a man up to Satan for the destruction of the flesh, that his spirit might be saved in the day of the Lord Jesus. REPLY TO FAUSTUS THE MANICHAEAN 22.79.[92]

WHO MADE THE DEVIL? AUGUSTINE: Again they say, "Who made the devil?" He made himself; for the devil was made by sinning, not by nature. "Or," they say, "God should not have made him if he knew that he would sin." On the contrary, why should he not have made him? For through his own justice and providence God corrects many as a result of the malice of the devil. Or have you perhaps not heard the apostle Paul saying, "And I handed them over to Satan so that they might learn not to blaspheme"? ON GENESIS, AGAINST THE MANICHAEANS 2.28.42.[93]

---

[89]Mt 18:15-17. [90]FC 28:276. [91]FC 18:63-64. [92]NPNF 1 4:304. [93]FC 84:139.

2:1-7 INSTRUCTIONS ON PRAYER

[1]*First of all, then, I urge that supplications, prayers, intercessions, and thanksgivings be made for all men, [2]for kings and all who are in high positions, that we may lead a quiet and peaceable life, godly and respectful in every way. [3]This is good, and it is acceptable in the sight of God our Savior, [4]who desires all men to be saved and to come to the knowledge of the truth. [5]For there is one God, and there is one mediator between God and men, the man Christ Jesus, [6]who gave himself as a ransom for all, the testimony to which was borne at the proper time. [7]For this I was appointed a preacher and apostle (I am telling the truth, I am not lying), a teacher of the Gentiles in faith and truth.*

OVERVIEW: It is in the work of prayer in its various forms that the essence of Christian living emerges, where everything must be done ultimately in the spirit of love, particularly the love of Jesus Christ. This love leads to a spirit of peaceableness and humility both within and apart from the community of faith (CHRYSOSTOM). The work of prayer lies at the center of church order and thus naturally follows Paul's earlier comments on apostolic teaching, while preceding his instructions with regard to the sexes and the ranks of ministry (THEODORE). The central purpose of prayer is the cultivation of that good order, peace and godliness that make the authentic practice of Christian faith possible, such that the peace represented in the union of united human and divine natures in Christ becomes manifest in the world (THEODORET). Paul lays down rules for prayer, true belief and the roles of the sexes, so that the medicine prescribed by the Father for sinful humankind through the redemption of Christ may take due effect (AMBROSIASTER). Paul makes it clear that the work of prayer, the discipline of a holy life and the observance of good church order are by grace not beyond the capacity of human striving, if we are willing to consent to the God who calls us in Jesus Christ (CHRYSOSTOM).

2:1a I Urge for All

PRIESTLY WORK OVERCOMES ALIENATION BY PRAYER. CHRYSOSTOM: The priest serves as the common father, as it were, of all the world. It is proper therefore that he should care for all, even as God, whom he serves cares for all. . . . From this, two advantages result. First, hatred toward those who are outside the circle is transcended, for no one can feel hatred toward those for whom he prays. Those apart are made better by the prayers that are offered for them, by losing their ferocious disposition toward us. For nothing is so apt to draw men under teaching as to love and to be loved. HOMILIES ON 1 TIMOTHY 6.[1]

GIVING THANKS FOR GENERAL PROVIDENCE. CHRYSOSTOM: Let us then exhort the saints to give thanks for us. And let us exhort one another toward gratitude. To ministers especially this good work belongs, since it is an exceeding privilege. Drawing near to God, we give thanks for the whole world and the good things we commonly share. The blessings of God are shared in common, and in this common preservation you yourselves are included. Consequently, you both owe common thanksgivings for your own peculiar blessings and for those shared in common with others, for which you rightly should offer your own special form of praise. . . . So then let us give thanks also for the faith that others have toward God. This custom is an ancient one, planted in the church from the beginning. Thus Paul also gives thanks for the Romans,[2] for the Corinthians[3] and for the whole world. HOMILIES ON SECOND CORINTHIANS 2.5.[4]

2:1b Supplications, Prayers, Intercessions, Thanksgivings

DISTINGUISHING VARIOUS TYPES OF PRAYER. ORIGEN: I think that *supplication* is a prayer offered with a special request for something a person lacks. From this is distinguished *prayer* which is more plainly offered with simple praise, not to obtain a request but simply to praise the nobility of great things. And I think that *intercession* is a petition for certain things addressed to God by someone who has some greater boldness, while *thanksgiving* is a statement of gratitude made with prayers for receiving good things from God, either when it is a great thing that is received and acknowledged with gratitude or when the greatness of the benefit is apparent only to the one who has benefited. ON PRAYER 14.2.[5]

AMBROSIASTER: "Supplications" are on behalf of secular rulers, that they may have obedient sub-

---

[1]NPNF 1 13:426*. [2]Rom 1:8. [3]1 Cor 1:4. [4]NPNF 1 12:281*. [5]OSW 109.

jects, and thus peace and tranquillity. "Prayers" are for those to whom power has been entrusted, that they may govern with justice and truth, so that all may prosper. "Intercessions" are for those in dire necessity, that they may find help. And "thanksgivings" refer to gratitude for God's daily providences. COMMENTARY ON 1 TIMOTHY.[6]

THEODORE OF MOPSUESTIA: Here *supplications* express the desire for good things from God. *Prayers* express the desire to be released from various evils. *Intercessions* ask for freedom from undeserved consequences. And *thanksgivings* express gratitude for blessings. COMMENTARY ON 1 TIMOTHY.[7]

AUGUSTINE: I prefer to understand by these words what the entire, or almost the entire, church observes: that we take as supplications those prayers which are said in celebrating the mysteries, before we begin to consecrate what lies on the table of the Lord. Prayers are said when it is blessed and sanctified and broken for distribution; and the whole church, for the most part, closes this complete petition with the Lord's Prayer. The original Greek word helps us to understand this distinction: the Scripture seldom uses the word *euche* in the sense of *oratio*, but generally and much more frequently *euchē* means *votum*; whereas *proseuchē*, the word used in the passage we are treating, is always rendered by *oratio*. . . . Now, all the things which are offered to God are vowed, especially the oblation at the holy altar, for in this sacrament we show forth that supreme offering, by which we vow to abide in Christ, even to the union of the body of Christ. The outward sign of this is that "we, being many, are one bread, one body."[8] Consequently, I think that at this consecration and this preparation for Communion the apostle fittingly wishes that *proseuchas*, that is, prayers, should be made, or, as some have unskillfully rendered it, adoration, that is, what takes place at the offering, although this is more commonly

expressed in Scripture by *euchē*. Intercessions, however, or, as your texts have it, requests, are offered while the blessing is being given to the people, for at that time, by the laying on of hands, the bishops, as intercessors, offer the members of their flock to the most merciful Power. When this is completed and all have received the holy sacrament, the whole is ended by thanksgiving, and this last is the very term called to our notice by the apostle. LETTERS 149.2.16.[9]

JOHN CASSIAN: "Supplication' is a beseeching or petition for sins. . . . "Prayers" are those by which we offer a vow to God. . . . "Intercession" is customarily offered, in moments of fervor, for other men and women—our family, the peace of the world. To use St. Paul's words, we pray "for all men, for kings and all in authority." . . . "Thanksgiving" is when the mind recollects what God has done or is doing or looks forward to the good which he has prepared for those who love him, and so offers its gratitude in an indescribable transport of spirit. Sometimes it offers still deeper prayers of this sort; when the soul contemplates in singleness of heart the reward of the saints and so is moved in its happiness to pour forth a wordless thanksgiving. CONFERENCES 9.11-14.[10]

2:2 For Kings and All in High Positions

PRAYING FOR PEACE. ORIGEN: Then Celsus next exhorts us to *help the emperor with all our power, and cooperate with him in all that is right, and fight for him, and be fellow soldiers if he presses for this, and fellow generals with him*. We may reply to this that at appropriate times we render to the emperors divine help, if I may so say, by taking up even the whole armor of God.[11] And this we do in obedience to the apostolic utterance which

---

[6]CSEL 81 3:259-60. [7]TEM 2:85. [8]1 Cor 10:17. [9]FC 20:250-51. [10]LCC 12:219-20. [11]Eph 6:11.

says, "I exhort you, therefore, first to make prayers, supplications, intercessions and thanksgivings for all men, for emperors, and all that are in authority."[12] Indeed, the more pious a man is, the more effective he is in helping the emperors—more so than the soldiers who go out into the lines and kill all the enemy troops that they can. AGAINST CELSUS 8.73.[13]

PRAYING FOR ENEMIES. TERTULLIAN: If you think that we have no interest in the emperor's welfare, look into our literature, read the Word of God. We ourselves do not keep it concealed, and in fact it is in some cases by chance handed over to outsiders. Learn from this literature that it has been enjoined upon us, that our charity may more and more abound, to pray to God even for our enemies and to beg for blessings for our persecutors. APOLOGY 31.1-2.[14]

A BULWARK OF SAFETY. CHRYSOSTOM: The soul of some Christians might be slow at hearing this and may resist this exhortation. For at the celebration of the holy mysteries it may be necessary to offer prayers for a heathen king. Paul shows them the advantage of fulfilling this duty at least to reconcile them to the advice, "that we may lead a peaceable and quiet life." . . . For God has appointed government for the public good. When therefore they use force for the common good and stand on guard for our security, isn't it reasonable that we should offer prayers for their safety in wars and dangers? Such prayers are not excessive flattery but agreeable to the rules of justice. HOMILIES ON 1 TIMOTHY 6.[15]

CHRIST THE ONLY MEDIATOR OF THOSE WHO PRAY FOR ALL. AUGUSTINE: My very special reason for saying all this was that after I had briefly defined and interpreted these terms [i.e., the terms of 1 Timothy 2:1], no one should think of overlooking the passage that follows, "for all men, for kings and for all those who are in high station, that we may lead a quiet and peaceable life in all piety and charity," and that

no one should imagine, by a common frailty of the human mind, that these prayers are not also to be made even for those at whose hands the church suffers persecution. For the members of Christ are to be gathered from every class. Hence he continues and says, "for this is good and acceptable in the sight of God our Savior, who desires all men to be saved and come to the knowledge of the truth." And that no one might say there can be a way of salvation without partaking of the body and blood of Christ but simply by living a good manner of life and worshiping one God Almighty, Paul continues: "For there is one God and one mediator of God and men, the man Christ Jesus." This makes it clear that what he had said above, "He will have all men to be saved," is to be realized only through a mediator who would not be God, as the Word is always God, but the man Christ Jesus, since "the Word was made flesh and dwelt among us."[16] LETTERS 149.2.17.[17]

MAKE USE OF THE PEACE OF BABYLON. AUGUSTINE: As the life of the body is the soul, so the "blessed life" of a man is God. As the sacred writings of the Hebrews have it, "Happy is that people whose God is the Lord."[18] Yet even such a people cherishes a peace of its own which is not to be scorned, although in the end it is not to be had because this peace, before the end, was abused. Meanwhile, it is to our advantage that there be such peace in this life. For, as long as the two cities are mingled together, we can make use of the peace of Babylon. Faith can assure our exodus from Babylon, but our pilgrim status, for the time being, makes us neighbors. All of this was in St. Paul's mind when he advised the church to pray for this world's kings and high authorities—in order that "we may lead a quiet and peaceful life in all piety and worthy behav-

---

[12]1 Tim 2:1-2. [13]OAC 509. [14]FC 10:87. [15]NPNF 1 13:426. [16]Jn 1:14. The incarnate mediator is here distinguished, but not separated, from the Godhead. [17]FC 20:252. [18]Ps 143:15.

ior." Jeremiah, too, predicting the Babylonian captivity to the Old Testament Jews, gave them orders from God to go submissively and to serve their God by such sufferings, and meanwhile to pray for Babylon. "For in the peace thereof," he said, "shall be your peace"[19]—referring, of course, to the peace of this world, which the good and bad share in common. THE CITY OF GOD 19.26.[20]

2:4a Who Desires All to Be Saved

A WHIP AND A ROD. ORIGEN: Therefore, because God is merciful and "wishes all men to be saved," he says, "I will visit their crimes with an iron rod and their sins with whips. I will not, however, remove my mercy from them."[21] . . . For "God is jealous" and does not wish that soul which he betrothed to himself in faith to remain in the defilement of sin, but wishes it immediately to be purified, wishes it swiftly to cast out all its impurities, if it has by chance been snatched away to some. HOMILIES ON EXODUS 8.6.[22]

OUR COMMON LOT. CHRYSOSTOM: Do not be afraid to pray for the Gentiles. God himself wills it. Fear only to pray against anyone. For that God does not will. And if you pray for the heathen, you ought of course to pray for heretics as well, for we are to pray for all humanity and not to persecute. And this is good also for another reason: We are partakers of the same nature. God calls us to have good will and affection toward one another. HOMILIES ON 1 TIMOTHY 7.[23]

WHETHER GOD'S DESIRE IS IMMEDIATELY EFFECTED. CHRYSOSTOM: See how great the darkness is [in discussing the nature of God], and how everywhere there is need of faith. This much is sure and solid. But let us now come to matters less sure, for example, as to the relation of the divine will and its way of working. Is God's will already immediately his working? Is

it a particular type of causality? If God is immutable, how does God's will enter into physical movement? . . . Is the movement in God's willing reducible to the familiar seven types of causality?[24] Is God's movement more like the movement of the mind? Not quite. For in many things the mind is even absurdly moved. When God wills, is he already at work or not? If to will is to work and God wills all men to be good and to be saved, why doesn't this come immediately to pass? There is here a subtler distinction between God's [primordial] willing and God's actual working within history.[25] HOMILIES ON COLOSSIANS 5.[26]

THE OPERATION OF THE FATHER'S WILL. GREGORY OF NYSSA: To those who with simplicity of heart receive the preaching of the cross and the resurrection, the same grace should be a cause of equal thankfulness to the Son and to the Father. Now, moreover, that the Son has accomplished the Father's will (and this, in the language of the apostle, is "that all men should be saved"), they ought for this gift to honor the Father and the Son alike. This is because our salvation would not have been accomplished had not the good will of the Father proceeded to actual operation for us through his own power. And we have learned from Scripture that the Son is the power of the Father. AGAINST EUNOMIUS 12.3.[27]

GOD DOES NOT COMPEL THE UNWILLING TO BE SAVED. AMBROSE: Is God not good to all, then? He is certainly good to all, because he is the Savior of all, especially the faithful. And so the Lord Jesus came that he might save what was lost;[28] he came, indeed, to take away the sin of

---

[19]Jer 29:7. [20]FC 24:245-46. [21]Ps 88:32-33. [22]FC 71:331. [23]NPNF 1 13:430*. [24]In the Aristotelian tradition. [25]There is assumed here a familiar distinction between the primordial or original will of God prior to the Fall and the consequential will of God, which works as a result of the Fall within the contingencies of history. [26]NPNF 1 13:282*. [27]NPNF 2 5:245*. [28]Cf. Lk 19:10.

the world[29] to heal our wounds. But not all desire the remedy, and many avoid it. . . . He heals those that are willing and does not compel the unwilling. The Prayer of Job and David 2.4.[30]

God Desires All to Be Saved. Ambrosiaster: That God wishes all men to be saved means that he wishes that all who freely and willingly desire it shall find salvation. Commentary on the First Letter to Timothy.[31]

No Salvation Unless God So Wills. Augustine: Accordingly. When we hear and read in sacred Scripture that God "wills that all should be saved," although we know well enough that not all are saved, we are not on that account to underrate the omnipotent will of God. Rather, we must understand the Scripture, "who will have all to be saved," as meaning that no one is saved unless God wills his salvation. It is not that there is no one whose salvation God does not will, but that no one is saved unless God wills it. Moreover, God's will should be sought in prayer, because if he wills, then what he wills must necessarily be. And, indeed, it was of prayer to God that the apostle was speaking when he made that statement. Enchiridion 103.27.[32]

God's Saving Will. John Cassian: To pray "Thy will be done in earth, as it is in heaven" is to pray that men may be like angels, that as angels fulfill God's will in heaven, men may fulfill his will, instead of their own, on earth. No one can say this sincerely except one who believes that every circumstance, favorable or unfavorable, is designed by God's providence for his good, and that he thinks and cares more for the good of his people and their salvation than we do for ourselves. It may be understood thus: the will of God is the salvation of all men, according to that text of Paul, "who wills all men to be saved and to come to the knowledge of the truth." Conferences 9.20.1.[33]

All of the Predestined Are to Be Saved. Augustine: And what is written, that "he wills all men to be saved," while yet all men are not saved, may be understood in many ways, some of which I have mentioned in other writings of mine; but here I will say one thing: "He wills all men to be saved" is so said that all the predestinated may be understood by it, because every kind of man is among them. On Rebuke and Grace 14.44.[34]

God Gives Lavishly. John of Damascus: The third kind of absolute worship is thanksgiving for all the good things he has created for us. All things owe a debt of thanks to God and must offer him ceaseless worship, because all things have their existence from him, and in him all things hold together.[35] He gives lavishly of his gifts to all, without being asked. He desires all men to be saved and to partake of his goodness. He is long-suffering with us sinners, for he makes his sun rise on the evil and on the good, and sends rain on the just and the unjust.[36] He is the Son of God, yet he became one of us for our sake and made us participants of his divine nature, so that "we shall be like him,"[37] as John the Theologian says in his catholic epistle. On Divine Images 3.30.[38]

God Wishes Our Salvation More Than We Do. John Cassian: As angels fulfill God's will in heaven, men may fulfill his will, instead of their own, on earth. No one can say this sincerely except one who believes that every circumstance, favorable or unfavorable, is designed by God's providence for good. God thinks and cares more for our good and our salvation than we do for ourselves. It may be understood thus: the will of God is the salvation of all. Conferences 9.20.1.[39]

---

[29]Jn 1:29. [30]FC 65:371. [31]CSEL 81 3:260-61. [32]LCC 7:401. [33]LCC 12:224. [34]NPNF 1 5:489. [35]Col 1:16-17. [36]Mt 5:45. [37]1 Jn 3:2. [38]JDDI 83. [39]LCC 12:224.

2:4b And Come to the Knowledge of the Truth

GOD STRENGTHENS OUR DESIRE TO KNOW THE TRUTH. JOHN CASSIAN: For God's purpose, according to which he did not make the human being to perish but to live forever, abides unchanging. When his kindness sees shining in us the slightest glimmer of good will, which he himself has sparked from the hard flint of our heart, he fosters it, stirs it up and strengthens it with his inspiration, "desiring all to be saved and to come to the knowledge of the truth." CONFERENCES 13.7.1.[40]

2:5a God Is One

FATHER AND SON ARE NOT TWO GODS. CHRYSOSTOM: He says that "there is one God," that is, not as some say, many, and that he has sent his Son as mediator, thus giving proof that he desires that all be saved. But is not the Son God? Most truly he is. Why then does he say, "One God"? To distinguish the one God from idols, not from the Son. HOMILIES ON 1 TIMOTHY 7.[41]

2:5b One Mediator Between God and Humanity

HIS BODY A SHARED BED. ORIGEN: Through his body the church has been allied to Christ and has been enabled to become a partaker in the Word of God. We know this both from the fact that he is called the "mediator of God and humanity," and from the apostle's saying that "in him we have access through faith in the hope of the glory of God."[42] COMMENTARY ON THE SONG OF SONGS 3.2.[43]

THE MEDIATOR IS TRULY GOD AND TRULY MAN. AMBROSE: But what is he who is at once the Most High and man, what but "the Mediator between God and man, the man Christ Jesus who gave himself as a ransom for us"? This text

indeed refers properly to his incarnation, for our redemption was made by his blood, our pardon comes through his power, our life is secured through his grace. He gives as the Most High; he prays as man. The one is the office of the Creator; the other of a redeemer. Be the gifts as distinct as they may, yet the Giver is one, for it was fitting that our Maker should be our Redeemer. OF THE CHRISTIAN FAITH 3.2.8.[44]

HIS MEDIATORSHIP ETERNAL. GREGORY OF NAZIANZUS: O how beautiful and mystical and kind![45] For to intercede does not imply to seek for vengeance, as is most men's way (for in that there would be something of humiliation), but it is to plead for us by reason of his mediatorship, just as the Spirit is also said to make intercession for us. For "there is one God, and one mediator between God and men, the man Christ Jesus." For he still pleads even now as man for my salvation. He continues to wear the body which he assumed, until he makes me divine by the power of his incarnation; although he is no longer known after the flesh—the same as ours, except for sin. THE THEOLOGICAL ORATIONS 4.30.14.[46]

THE MYSTERY OF GODLINESS. GREGORY OF NYSSA: By the distinction implied in the word *mediator* he reveals to us the whole aim of the mystery of godliness. Now the aim is this. Humanity once revolted through the malice of the enemy, and, brought into bondage to sin, was also alienated from the true Life. After this the Lord of the creature calls back to him his own creature and becomes Man while still remaining God, being both God and man in the entirety of the two separate natures. Thus humanity was indissolubly united to God, the man that is in Christ conducting the work of mediation, to whom, by the firstfruits assumed

---

[40]ACW 57:472. [41]NPNF 1 13:430. [42]Rom 5:2. [43]ACW 26:174. [44]NPNF 2 10:243*. [45]Gregory is commenting on Hebrews 7:25, "He always lives to make intercession for them." [46]LCC 3:187.

for us, all the lump is potentially united.[47] Against Eunomius 2.12.[48]

As Mediator Both Priest and Oblation. Augustine: Christ Jesus, himself man, is the true Mediator, for, inasmuch as he took the "form of a slave,"[49] he became "the Mediator between God and men." In his character as God, he received sacrifices in union with the Father, with whom he is one God. Yet he chose, in his character as a slave, to be himself the sacrifice rather than to receive it, lest any one might take occasion to think that sacrifice could be rendered to a creature. Thus it is that he is both the Priest who offers and the Oblation that is offered. The City of God 10.20.[50]

The Separating Middle. Augustine: But how are we reconciled unless what separates us and him is broken? For he says through the prophet, "The Lord's ear is not dull, that it cannot hear, but your sins separate you and your God."[51] Therefore, because we are not reconciled unless what is in the middle has been removed and what should be in the middle has been put there—for there is a separating middle, but over against it is a reconciling mediator. The separating middle is sin. The reconciling mediator is the Lord Jesus Christ, "For there is one God and one mediator of God and man, the man Christ Jesus." And so, in order that the separating wall which is sin may be taken away, that Mediator has come, and the Priest himself has become the sacrifice. Tractates on John 41.5.[52]

Medicine for Weak Eyes. Isaac of Nineveh: May attention to the economy of God which ministered to those of former times be reckoned by you as precious medicine for weak eyes. Let the memory of it stay with you at all times of the day. Meditate, apply your mind, and learn wisdom from it, that you may be able to receive into your soul with honor the memory of the greatness of God and find eternal life for yourself in Christ Jesus, the Mediator between

God and mankind and the Uniter in his two natures. Ascetical Homilies 3.[53]

2:5c The Man Christ Jesus

Real Flesh. Tertullian: Valentinus, indeed, on the strength of his heretical system, might consistently fantasize a spiritual flesh for Christ.[54] Any who refused to believe that that flesh was human might then pretend it to be anything he liked. This pretense characterizes all heresies. For if his flesh was not human and was not born of man, I do not see of what substance Paul himself spoke, when he said "The man Christ Jesus is the one mediator between God and man." On the Flesh of Christ 15.[55]

True Man. Ambrose: Let not the venom of Apollinaris[56] flatter itself because it is written, "And in appearance he was found as a man,"[57] for the manhood of Jesus is not thereby denied but confirmed, since elsewhere Paul himself speaks of him as "Mediator of God and men, himself man, Christ Jesus." It is the customary manner of Scripture so to express itself as we also read in the Gospel, "And we saw his glory —glory as of the only-begotten of the Father."[58] As he is there called only-begotten Son of God, so he is said to be man, and the fullness of humanity that was in him is not denied. Letters 27.[59]

Our Common Humanity. Theodore of Mopsuestia: This refers to the perfect humanity by which salvation is wrought. The fact that Jesus shares a common humanity with us is the

---

[47]Rom 11:16. [48]NPNF 2 5:122*. [49]Phil 2:7. [50]FC 14:153. [51]Is 59:1-2. [52]FC 88:140-41. [53]OAL 60-61. [54]The Valentinian Gnostics sometimes taught that Jesus possessed only a glorious, aethereal body, not a body of true flesh. See the remarks of Kurt Rudolph, *Gnosis: The Nature and History of Gnosticism*, trans. Robert McLachlan Wilson (New York: Harper & Row, 1983), pp. 166-69. [55]ANF 3:534*. [56]The followers of Apollinaris seem to have denied that Jesus had a real human soul but taught that the indwelling Word took the place of that soul. [57]Phil 2:7. [58]Jn 1:14. [59]FC 26:140.

whole key to salvation. COMMENTARY ON 1 TIM-
OTHY.[60]

JOINING WHAT HAD BEEN ALIENATED. THE-
ODORET OF CYR: There is one conciliator of
peace, who joins in himself what has been in dis-
junction. Paul calls Christ man precisely
because he is the Mediator, the one in whom
human and divine natures are joined in friendship. INTERPRETATION OF THE FIRST LETTER
TO TIMOTHY.[61]

**TRUTH PUTS ON HUMANITY WITHOUT CEAS-
ING TO BE DIVINE.** AUGUSTINE: It was in order
to make the mind able to advance more confidently toward the truth that Truth itself, the
divine Son of God, put on humanity without
putting off his divinity and built this firm path
of faith so that man, by means of the God-Man,
could find his way to man's God. I speak of the
"mediator between God and men, himself man,
Christ Jesus." For it is as man that he is the
Mediator and as man that he is the way. THE
CITY OF GOD 11.2.[62]

FEELINGS REQUIRE A HUMAN SOUL. AUGUS-
TINE: Hence we respond to this objection of
theirs,[63] which they propose from the gospel, in
a way which allows no man to be so lacking in
understanding that he thinks we are compelled
by this text to believe and confess that the mediator between God and men, the man Christ
Jesus, did not have a human soul. In the same
way I inquire how they respond to objections so
palpable as ours, whereby we show through
countless places in the Gospel writings what was
narrated of him by the Evangelists, namely, that
he was found with feelings that are impossible
without a soul. EIGHTY-THREE DIFFERENT
QUESTIONS 80.3.[64]

**MAN'S PRIDE HEALED THROUGH GOD'S
HUMILITY.** AUGUSTINE: Now, we could not be
redeemed, even through "the one mediator
between God and man, Man himself, Christ

Jesus," if he were not also God. For when Adam
was made—being made an upright man—there
was no need for a mediator. Once sin, however,
had widely separated the human race from God,
it was necessary for a mediator, who alone was
born, lived and was put to death without sin, to
reconcile us to God and provide even for our
bodies a resurrection to life eternal—and all
this in order that a man's pride might be
exposed and healed through God's humility.
ENCHIRIDION 108.28.[65]

HIDDEN AS GOD, APPARENT AS MAN. AUGUS-
TINE: Who can so organize what he does as this
man organized what he suffered?[66] But the
man, the Mediator of God and man, was the
man about whom one reads that it was foretold, "And he is a man and who will know
him?"[67] For the men through whom these
things happened did know the man of God. For
he who was hidden as God was apparent as
man. He who was apparent suffered these
things. He who was hidden is the very same
One who ordered these things. Therefore he
saw that all the things were finished which
were necessary to be done before he took the
vinegar and delivered over his spirit. TRAC-
TATES ON JOHN 119.4.[68]

HIS HUMANITY, HIS TIME. THE VENERABLE
BEDE: We have heard from the Gospel reading
[commenting on Lk 2:1-14], dearly beloved
brothers, that when the Redeemer of the world,
our Lord and God, Jesus Christ, was about to be
born into the world, an edict went out from
Caesar Augustus, who then held the highest
place with respect to worldly reigns. The edict
said that the entire world was to be enrolled. We

[60]TEM 2:88. [61]PG 82:797D/798D—799A/800A. [62]FC 14:189.
[63]That of the Apollinarians. See p. 158 n. 56. [64]FC 70:209. [65]LCC
7:404. [66]Augustine is commenting on John 19:28-30, Christ's dying
words from the cross. [67]Jer 17:9 (LXX). Augustine had before him
an Old Latin version of this verse that differed from the standard
Septuagint text. [68]FC 92:47*.

must not suppose that this happened by chance, but we must understand that it was provided through a most certain divinely arranged plan of this same Redeemer of ours. And, indeed, just as in his divinity the Mediator between God and human beings foresaw the mother of whom he willed to be born when he should so will, so also in his humanity he chose the time when he wished for his nativity. Moreover, he himself granted that this time should be such as he willed, namely, that in a calm among the storm of wars a singular tranquillity of unusual peace should cover the whole world. HOMILIES ON THE GOSPELS 1.6.[69]

2:6 A Ransom for All

OVERFLOWING KINDNESS. ANONYMOUS: And so, when he had planned everything by himself in union with his Child, he still allowed us, through the former time, to be carried away by undisciplined impulses. . . . And so, when our unrighteousness had come to its full term, and it had become perfectly plain that its recompense of punishment and death had to be expected, then the season arrived in which God had determined to show at last his goodness and power. O the overflowing kindness and love of God toward man! God did not hate us, or drive us away, or bear us ill will. Rather, he was long-suffering and forbearing. In his mercy, he took up the burden of our sins. He himself gave up his own Son as a ransom for us—the holy one for the unjust, the innocent for the guilty, the righteous one for the unrighteous, the incorruptible for the corruptible, the immortal for the mortal.[70] LETTER TO DIOGNETUS 9.1-2.[71]

THE TREE OF JESUS. CYRIL OF JERUSALEM: Do not wonder that the whole world was redeemed, for it was no mere man but the Only-begotten Son of God who died for it. The sin of one man, Adam, availed to bring death to the world; if by one man's offense death reigned for the world,

why should not life reign all the more "from the justice of the one?"[72] If Adam and Eve were cast out of paradise because of the tree from which they ate, should not believers more easily enter into paradise because of the Tree of Jesus? If the first man, fashioned out of the earth, brought universal death, shall not he who fashioned him, being the Life, bring everlasting life? If Phinees by his zeal in slaying the evildoer appeased the wrath of God, shall not Jesus, who slew no other, but "gave himself a ransom for all," take away God's wrath against man? CATECHETICAL LECTURES 13.2.[73]

2:7 A Teacher of the Gentiles in Faith and Truth

INTERPRETING THE LAW TO THE GENTILES. ORIGEN: The apostle Paul, "teacher of the Gentiles in faith and truth," taught the church which he gathered from the Gentiles how it ought to interpret the books of the law. These books were received from others and were formerly unknown to the Gentiles and were very strange. He feared that the church, receiving foreign instructions and not knowing the principle of the instructions, would be in a state of confusion about the foreign document. For that reason he gives some examples of interpretation that we might also note similar things in other passages, lest we believe that by imitation of the text and document of the Jews we be made disciples. He wishes, therefore, to distinguish disciples of Christ from disciples of the synagogue by the way they understand the law. HOMILIES ON EXODUS 5.1.[74]

THIS TRUMPET AMONG THE APOSTLES. VINCENT OF LÉRINS: Consequently, to announce to Catholic Christians a doctrine other than that which they have received was never permitted,

---

[69]HOG 1:52. [70]Cf. Mk 10:45; 1 Tim 2:6; Tit 2:14; Rom 8:32. [71]LCC 1:220. [72]Rom 5:18. [73]FC 64:4-5. [74]FC 71:275.

is nowhere permitted and never will be permitted. It was ever necessary, is everywhere necessary and ever will be necessary that those who announce a doctrine other than that which was received once and for all be anathema. If this be so, is there anyone alive so bold as to preach dogmas other than those taught by the church, or so foolish as to accept doctrines besides those accepted by the church? Crying aloud, crying aloud again and again and again, crying aloud to everyone, always and everywhere throughout his writings, Paul remains this "vessel of election,"[75] this "doctor of the Gentiles," this trumpet among the apostles, this herald of the earth, this heaven-conscious man. He is crying aloud that whoever announces a new doctrine is anathema. COMMONITORIES 9.[76]

TEACHER OF ALL CHRISTIANS OF ALL TIME. ATHANASIUS: So, then, let us celebrate this heavenly joy, together with the saints of old who kept the same feast. Yes, they keep the feast with us, and they are examples to us of life in Christ. Not only were they commissioned to preach the gospel, but if we look back at their lives, we will see that they also lived it. St. Paul wrote to the Corinthians, "You, therefore, follow me."[77] Let us follow him then, because that command has been passed down to us. The admonition originally given to the church at Corinth reaches to all Christians of all time in every place. For the apostle Paul was "a teacher of all nations in faith and truth." FESTAL LETTERS 2.[78]

PAUL EXCEPTIONALLY HONORED. CHRYSOSTOM: If the Son was born a perfect and complete king, it is also clear that he is a judge and arbiter. For it is especially the mark of a king that he makes decisions and judgments both to grant honors and to punish. And another source might help you to see that he has the power to grant heavenly honors. So we shall bring forward the man who is better than all men, and we shall show that Christ granted this man a crown. . . . Who is the one who is better than all men? Who other than that tentmaker,[79] that teacher of the entire world, the one who coursed over land and sea as if equipped with wings, the chosen instrument,[80] the attendant of Christ the bridegroom, the one who planted the church,[81] the wise builder,[82] the preacher, the one who ran the course and fought the good fight,[83] the soldier, the trainer of athletes, the one who left memorials of his own virtue everywhere in the world. ON THE INCOMPREHENSIBLE NATURE OF GOD 8.3.[84]

---

[75]Acts 9:15. [76]FC 7:283. [77]1 Cor 4:16. [78]ARL 60. [79]Acts 18:3. [80]Acts 9:15. [81]1 Cor 3:6. [82]1 Cor 3:10. [83]2 Tim 4:7. [84]FC 72:220-21.

2:8-15 PRAYING MEN AND MODEST WOMEN

[8]*I desire then that in every place the men should pray, lifting holy hands without anger or quarreling;* [9]*also that women should adorn themselves modestly and sensibly in seemly apparel, not with braided hair or gold or pearls or costly attire* [10]*but by good deeds, as befits women who profess religion.* [11]*Let a woman learn in silence with all submissiveness.* [12]*I permit no woman to teach or to have authority over men; she is to keep silent.* [13]*For Adam was formed first, then*

Eve; [14]and Adam was not deceived, but the woman was deceived and became a transgressor. [15]Yet woman will be saved through bearing children,[c] if she continues[d] in faith and love and holiness, with modesty.

c Or by the birth of the child   d Greek they continue

OVERVIEW: Men should pray in every place (ORIGEN), not in the temple only (CHRYSOSTOM), and with pure hands (TERTULLIAN) and with a good conscience (AUGUSTINE), with body, soul and spirit in tune (JEROME), praying with uplifted hands so as to bear the sign of the cross (MAXIMUS OF TURIN). Yet "every place" does not imply places designated for shameful human deeds (BASIL). Meanwhile we ought to be trying to be the kind of people whom we wish God to find when we pray (JOHN CASSIAN). We pray modestly, remembering our faults (AMBROSE).

Equally with men, women are called to approach God without anger or doubt. Modesty, however, requires something more of women—that they adorn themselves fittingly (CHRYSOSTOM, AMBROSE). Women are not by ostentation to deprive the poor. Gems do not adorn the soul (CHRYSOSTOM). In her original relation with Adam before the Fall, woman was not called into a state of submissiveness; only after the Fall did that become pertinent (CHRYSOSTOM). The prohibition in the law against a man wearing female garments refers not so much to clothing as to social manners, habits and actions, since one act is becoming to a man, another to a woman (AMBROSE). Women retain authority in the home as teachers of virtue (THEODORE). As woman was the first one in the revolt against God, she became the first witness of the resurrection that she might retrieve by her faith the overthrow caused by her disobedience (GREGORY OF NYSSA). That woman played such a decisive role in bringing forth the Redeemer must be seen as the work of divine providence (AMBROSE). Adam yielded to Eve, as husband to wife, as the only man in the world to the only woman. Eve accepted the serpent's word as true, whereas Adam refused to be separated from his partner even in a union of sin. This does not imply that Adam was any less guilty (AUGUSTINE). When Paul speaks of the salvation that comes through childbearing, he refers to the baptism and rebirth to which their children are led by the believing mother (PELAGIUS, THEODORE, AMBROSIASTER). The calling to virginity is viewed in relation to our dying in Eve and being reborn as a result of the Savior to whom Mary gave birth (GREGORY OF NYSSA). The church is united with its heavenly bridegroom Christ, desiring to be mingled with him through the Word so that she may conceive from him and be enabled to be saved through the chaste bearing of children (ORIGEN).

2:8a Men Everywhere Should Pray

WHERE SHOULD MEN PRAY? ORIGEN: Now concerning the place, let it be known that every place is suitable for prayer if a person prays well. For "in every place you offer incense to me . . . says the Lord"[1] and "I desire then that in every place men should pray," But everyone may have, if I may put it this way, a holy place set aside and chosen in his own house, if possible, for accomplishing his prayers in quiet and without distraction. ON PRAYER 4.[2]

IN EVERY PLACE? BASIL THE GREAT: Certainly, the Lord gives the authority for praying in every place, in the words: "Woman, believe me, the hour is coming when neither on this mountain nor in Jerusalem will you worship the Father."[3]

[1]Mal 1:11. [2]OSW 166. [3]Jn 4:21.

And the words of the apostle are legitimate, because the word *every* does not include places designated for human usage or for unclean or shameful human deeds, but it does take in the regions from the confines of Jerusalem to every place in the world duly appointed, in conformity with the prophecy of sacrifice,[4] that is, consecrated to God, for the celebration of the glorious mystery. CONCERNING BAPTISM.[5]

JEWISH TEMPLE WORSHIP DISTINGUISHED FROM CHRISTIAN PRAYER. CHRYSOSTOM: The object of Paul is to distinguish the Christian from the Jewish prayers. Therefore observe what he says, "In every place lifting up holy hands," this being something which was not permitted the Jews, for they were not allowed to approach God, to sacrifice and perform their services elsewhere. Rather, assembling from all parts of the world in one place, they were bound to perform all their worship in the temple. . . . Henceforth the consideration is not of the place but of the manner of the prayer. "Pray everywhere," but, "everywhere lift up holy hands." That is the thing required. And what is "holy"? Pure. And what is pure? Not washed with water, but free from covetousness, murder, rapacity, violence, "without wrath and doubting." HOMILIES ON 1 TIMOTHY 8.[6]

2:8b Lifting Holy Hands

HANDS LIFTED UP IN PURITY. TERTULLIAN: But what reason is there in going to prayer with hands indeed washed, but the spirit has become fouled?—inasmuch as to our hands themselves spiritual cleansing is necessary, that they may be "lifted up pure" from falsehood, from murder, from cruelty, from poisonings, from idolatry and all the other blemishes which, conceived by the spirit, are effected by the operation of the hands. ON PRAYER 13.[7]

HOLY HANDS. AUGUSTINE: He must be quite cognizant, certain and confident of his own innocence who stretches out and extends his

hands to God. Hence the apostle says, "I wish then that men pray everywhere, lifting up pure hands." He rightly lifts his hands to God, he pours forth prayers with a good conscience, who can say, "You know, O Lord, how holy, how innocent, how pure from every fraud, injury and plunder are the hands which I lift up to you; how unstained and free from all deceit are the lips with which I pour forth prayers to you so that you may have pity on me." Such a person deserves to be heard quickly and can obtain what he asks even before he has finished his prayer. THE CHRISTIAN LIFE 11.[8]

PRAY WITH HANDS UPLIFTED. MAXIMUS OF TURIN: But the good farmer also, when he prepares to turn the soil in order to plant life-sustaining foods, undertakes to do this by nothing other than the sign of the cross. For when he sets the share beam on the plough, attaches the earthboard and puts on the plowhandle, he imitates the form of the cross, for its very construction is a kind of likeness of the Lord's suffering. Heaven, too, is itself arranged in the form of this sign, for since it is divided into four parts—namely, east, west, south, and north—it consists in four quarters like the cross. Even a person's bearing, when he raises his hands, describes a cross; therefore we are ordered to pray with uplifted hands so that by the very stance of our body we might confess the Lord's suffering. SERMONS 38.3.[9]

2:8c Without Anger or Quarreling

IN PERFECT TUNE. JEROME: Whenever we lift up pure hands in prayer, without diverting distractions or contention, we are playing to the Lord with a ten-stringed instrument. We play,

---

[4]Mal 1:11. [5]FC 9:409. [6]NPNF 1 13:432-33*. [7]ANF 3:685. [8]FC 16:32. This tract, traditionally ascribed to Augustine, was probably written by fifth-century British Bishop Fastidius; see FC 12, preface. [9]ACW 50:93.

as the psalmist wrote: "with ten-stringed instrument and lyre, with melody upon the harp."[10] Our body and soul and spirit —our harp—are all in harmony, all their strings in tune. HOMILIES ON THE PSALMS 21.[11]

NOURISHED BY CONTINUAL CONTEMPLATION. JOHN CASSIAN: Whatever the mind has been thinking about before it prays will certainly come to it while it is praying. Therefore, before we begin to pray, we ought to be trying to be the kind of people whom we wish God to find when we pray. The mind is conditioned by its recent state. In prayer, the mind remembers recent acts or thoughts and experiences, sees them dancing before it like ghosts. And this annoys us, or depresses us, or reminds us of past lust or past worry, or makes us (I am ashamed to say) laugh like fools at some absurdity or circumstance, or go over again some recent conversation. Whatever we do *not* want to creep into our time of prayer, we must try to keep out of the heart when we are not praying. St. Paul's words were, "Pray without ceasing,"[12] and "In every place lifting up pure hands without wrath or controversy." To obey this is impossible, unless the mind is purified from sin, is given to virtue as its natural good and is continually nourished by the contemplation of God. CONFERENCES 9.3.3.[13]

2:9a Women Should Adorn Themselves Modestly and Sensibly

PARTICULARLY AT PRAYER. AMBROSE: In our prayers, too, modesty is most pleasing and gains us much grace from our God. . . . A noble thing, then, is modesty, which, though giving up its rights, seizing on nothing for itself, laying claim to nothing and in some ways somewhat retiring within the sphere of its own powers, yet is rich in the sight of God, in whose sight no one is rich. Richness is modesty, for it is the portion of God. Paul bids that prayer be offered up with modesty and sobriety. He desires that this should be first, and, as it were, lead the way of

prayers to come, so that the sinner's prayer may not be boastful but veiled, as it were, with the blush of shame. Indeed, it may merit a far greater degree of grace, in giving way to modesty at the remembrance of its fault. DUTIES OF THE CLERGY 1.18.70.[14]

ESPECIALLY FOR A WOMAN. AMBROSE: Let us then hold fast modesty and that moderation which adds to the beauty of the whole of life. For it is no light thing in every matter to preserve due measure and to bring about order, wherein that is plainly conspicuous which we call "decorum," or what is seemly. This is so closely connected with what is virtuous that one cannot separate the two. . . . This seemliness which we offer to God we may believe to be far better than other things. It befits also a woman to pray in an orderly dress, but it is especially fitting to her to pray humbly covered and to pray giving promise of purity together with wholesome conversation. DUTIES OF THE CLERGY 1.44.228-30.[15]

WHAT MORE IS REQUIRED OF WOMEN. CHRYSOSTOM: Equally with men, women are called to approach God without wrath or doubting, lifting up holy hands, not following their own desires, nor being covetous or rapacious. . . . Paul however requires something more of women, that they adorn themselves "in modest apparel, with self-effacement and sobriety" . . . such attire as covers them completely, and decently, not with superfluous ornaments, for the one is becoming, the other is not. HOMILIES ON 1 TIMOTHY 8.[16]

2:9b In Seemly Apparel

DO NOT BY YOUR OSTENTATION DEPRIVE THE POOR. CHRYSOSTOM: For what reason will you be able to state, what defense, when the

---

[10]Ps 150:3. [11]FC 48:166. [12]1 Thess 5:17. [13]LCC 12:215. [14]NPNF 2 10:13*. [15]NPNF 2 10:36-37. [16]NPNF 1 13:433.

Lord lays these pearls to your charge and brings the poor who have perished with hunger into your midst? On this account Paul said, "not with braided hair, or gold, or pearls or costly raiment." For these would be a snare.... Take off all ornament and place it in the hands of Christ through the poor. INSTRUCTIONS TO CATECHUMENS 2.4.[17]

2:10a Good Deeds Befit Women Who Profess Religion

WHAT ADORNS THE SOUL. CHRYSOSTOM: Gems and gold and costly garments and lavish, embroidered flowers of various colors and anything else perishable in nature in no way adorn souls. But the following do: fasts, holy vigils, gentleness, reasonableness, poverty, courage, humility, patience—in a word, disdain for everything passing in this life. ON VIRGINITY 63.1.[18]

2:11 Let a Woman Learn in Quietness

WOMEN RETAIN AUTHORITY IN THE HOME. THEODORE OF MOPSUESTIA: While Paul forbids women teaching in church, he very much wants them to exercise their authority in the home as the teachers of virtue. COMMENTARY ON 1 TIMOTHY.[19]

SUSTAINING THE VIRTUE OF QUIETNESS. AMBROSE: I think the prohibition in the law against a man wearing female garments refers not so much to clothing as to manners and to our habits and actions, since one act is becoming to a man, another to a woman. Therefore, the apostle, as the interpreter of the law, says, "Let your women keep silence in the churches, for it is not permitted them to speak, but to be submissive, as the law says. But if they wish to learn anything, let them ask their husbands at home."[20] And to Timothy he says, "Let a women learn in quietness[21] in all submissiveness. I permit no woman to teach or have authority over

men." How unsightly it is for a man to act like a woman! LETTERS 78.[22]

2:12 I Permit No Woman to Have Authority Over Men

HOW WOMEN EXERCISE POWER. CHRYSOSTOM: The divine law indeed has excluded women from the ministry, but they endeavor to thrust themselves into it. And since they can effect nothing of themselves, they do all through the agency of others. In this way they have become invested with so much power that they can appoint or eject priests at their will. Things in fact are turned upside down, and the proverbial saying may be seen realized—"Those being guided are leading the guides." One would wish that it were men who were giving such guidance, rather than women who have not received a commission to give instruction in church. Why do I say "give instruction"? The blessed Paul did not suffer them even to speak with authority in the church. But I have heard someone say that they have obtained such a large privilege of free speech as even to rebuke the prelates of the churches and censure them more severely than masters do their own domestics. ON THE PRIESTHOOD 3.9.[23]

GOD SAYS NOTHING ABOUT SUBMISSIVENESS PRIOR TO THE FALL. CHRYSOSTOM: For with us indeed the woman is reasonably subjected to the man, since equality of honor causes contention. And not for this cause only, but by reason also of the deceit which happened in the beginning. You see Eve was not subjected in her original condition as she was made. Nor was she called to submission when God first brought her to the man. She did not hear anything from God then about

[17]NPNF 1 9:169-70*. [18]COV 99*. [19]TEM 2:94, 96. [20]1 Cor 14:34-35. [21]Ambrose follows the traditional view that *hēsychia*, or quietness, is a special virtue of which women are particularly capable. [22]FC 26:436. [23]NPNF 1 9:49*.

submissiveness. Nor did Adam originally say any such word to her. Rather he said indeed that she was "bone of his bone, and flesh of his flesh,"[24] but of rule or subjection he mentioned nothing. This occurred only after she made an ill use of her privilege. She who had been made a helper was found to be an ensnarer. Then the original relation was ruined, and she was justly told for the future: "your turning shall be to your husband."[25] HOMILIES ON FIRST CORINTHIANS 26.2.[26]

2:13 Adam Was Formed First, Then Eve

NOT GOOD FOR MAN TO BE ALONE. AMBROSE: It was said, moreover, that it was not good for man to be alone. Yet we know that Adam did not commit sin before woman was created. However, after creation, she was the first to disobey the divine command and even allured her husband to sin. If, therefore, the woman is responsible for the sin, how then can her coming be considered a good? But, if you consider that the universe is in the care of God, then you will discover this fact, namely, that the Lord must have gained more pleasure for himself in being responsible for all creation than condemnation from us for providing the basis for sin. Accordingly, the Lord declared that it was not good for man to be alone, because the human race could not have been propagated from man alone. . . . For the sake therefore of the successive generations of men it followed that woman had to be joined to man. Thus we must interpret the very words of God when he said that it was not good for the man to be alone. If the woman was to be the first one to sin, the fact that she was the one destined to bring forth redemption must not be excluded from the operations of divine Providence. Although "Adam was not deceived, the woman was deceived and was in sin." Yet woman, we are told, "will be saved by childbearing," in the course of which Christ became born of woman. PARADISE 10.47.[27]

THE TYPE OF THE CHURCH. ORIGEN: But you should not be surprised that she [the church] who is gathered out of the dispersion of the nations and prepared to be the bride of Christ has sometimes been guilty of these faults. Remember how the first woman was seduced and was in the transgression and could find her salvation, so the Scripture says, only in bearing children, which for our present purpose means those who continue in faith and love with sanctity. The apostle, therefore, declares what is written about Adam and Eve thus, "This is a great mystery in Christ and in the church." Christ so loved her that he gave himself for her, while she was yet undutiful, even as he says, "When as yet we were ungodly according to the time, Christ died for us"; and again, "While we were yet sinners, Christ died for us."[28] COMMENTARY ON THE SONG OF SONGS 2.3.[29]

2:14a Adam Was Not Deceived

ADAM EQUALLY GUILTY. AUGUSTINE: So, too, we must believe that Adam transgressed the law of God, not because he was deceived into believing that the lie was true but because in obedience to a social compulsion he yielded to Eve, as husband to wife, as the only man in the world to the only woman. It was not without reason that the apostle wrote, "Adam was not deceived, but the woman was deceived." He means, no doubt, that Eve accepted the serpent's word as true, whereas Adam refused to be separated from his partner even in a union of sin. This does not imply that he was on that account any less guilty, since he sinned knowingly and deliberately. THE CITY OF GOD 14.11.2.[30]

2:14b But the Woman Was Deceived

---

[24]Gen 2:23. [25]Gen 3:16. [26]NPNF 1 12:150-51*. [27]FC 42:326-27. [28]Cf. Eph 5:32; Gal 2:20; Rom 5:6, 8-9. [29]ACW 26:116-17. [30]FC 14:378.

First to Behold the Resurrection.
Gregory of Nyssa: And the fact too that this
grace was revealed by means of a woman agrees
with the interpretation that we have given. For
since, as the apostle tells us, "the woman, being
deceived, was in the transgression," and was by her
disobedience foremost in the revolt from God, for
this reason she is the first witness of the resurrection. This is so that she might retrieve by her faith
in the resurrection the overthrow caused by her
disobedience. Indeed, by making herself at the
beginning a minister and advocate to her husband
of the counsels of the serpent, she brought into human life the beginning of evil and its train of consequences. Therefore, by ministering to his disciples
the words of him who slew the rebel dragon, she
might become to men the guide of faith, whereby
with good reason the first proclamation of death is
annulled. Against Eunomius 12.1.[31]

2:15a Woman Saved Through Bearing Children

The Woman Is Eve. Theodore of Mopsuestia: The claim that she will be saved by childbearing is said of all women, not just of Eve.
Commentary on 1 Timothy.[32]

To Those Reborn in Christ. Ambrosiaster: The salvation that comes to women
through childbearing applies only to the children who are reborn in Christ. Commentary
on the First Letter to Timothy.[33]

**Reborn Children Led by a Believing
Mother.** Pelagius: When Paul speaks of the
salvation that comes through childbearing, he
refers to the baptism and rebirth to which their
children are led by the believing mother.
Pelagius's Commentary on the First Letter to Timothy.[34]

2:15b Continuing in Faith, Love and Holiness

Joined to the Bridegroom by Faith. Origen: The present book of Scripture,[35] then,
speaks of this love with which the blessed soul
burns and is on fire with regard to the blessed
Word of God. And she sings this wedding song
through the Spirit, by which the church is
joined and united with its heavenly bridegroom
Christ, desiring to be mingled with him through
the Word so that she may conceive from him
and be enabled to be saved through this chaste
bearing of children. Commentary on the
Song of Songs, Prologue.[36]

Virginity a Higher Childbearing. Gregory of Nyssa: Therefore, just as the power
which destroys what is born is begotten along
with physical birth, so it is clear that the Spirit
bestows a life-giving power upon those born
through it. What, then, can be deduced from
what we have said? That separating ourselves
from life in the flesh, which death normally follows upon, we may seek a kind of life which does
not have death as its consequence. This is the
spiritual significance of the life of virginity. That
this is true will be clearer if we explain a little
further. Everyone knows that the function of
bodily union is the creation of mortal bodies.
But life and incorruptibility are born to those
who remain united in their participation in the
Spirit. It is not having children as such that is
important but this spiritual regeneration. Excellent is the apostolic saying about this, that the
mother blessed with such children "will be saved
by childbearing," just as the psalmist utters in
the divine hymns, "He establishes in her home
the barren wife as the joyful mother of children."[37] On Virginity 14.[38]

---

[31]NPNF 2 5:242*. [32]TEM 2:94, 96. [33]CSEL 81 3:264. [34]PETE 483.
[35]Song of Solomon. [36]OSW 230. [37]Ps 112:9. [38]FC 58:48*.

3:1-7 INSTRUCTIONS ON BISHOPS

[1]*The saying is sure: If any one aspires to the office of bishop, he desires a noble task.* [2]*Now a bishop must be above reproach, the husband of one wife, temperate, sensible, dignified, hospitable, an apt teacher,* [3]*no drunkard, not violent but gentle, not quarrelsome, and no lover of money.* [4]*He must manage his own household well, keeping his children submissive and respectful in every way;* [5]*for if a man does not know how to manage his own household, how can he care for God's church?* [6]*He must not be a recent convert, or he may be puffed up with conceit and fall into the condemnation of the devil;*[f] [7]*moreover he must be well thought of by outsiders, or he may fall into reproach and the snare of the devil.*[f]

f Or slanderer

OVERVIEW: Paul sets a high standard for the virtue and uprightness of bishops, but not one that is too high, lest there be insufficient persons to fill this office (CHRYSOSTOM). It is right for appropriate persons, upright and talented, to seek this office, as long as marriage, family life and personal behavior are in good order (THEODORET). Paul highlights the essential importance of the cultivation of virtue in the office of bishop (THEODORET). Being a bishop requires the living of a good life (GREGORY OF NYSSA, JEROME, AUGUSTINE). Only the most responsible persons are worthy of ordination to the priestly and episcopal offices (ORIGEN, PELAGIUS).

3:1 He Desires a Noble Task

A TERRIBLE TEMPTATION. CHRYSOSTOM: The first of all qualities that a priest or bishop ought to possess is that he must purify his soul entirely of ambition for the office.... The right course, I think, is to have so reverent an estimation of the office as to avoid its responsibility from the start.... But if anyone should cling to a position for which he is not fit, he deprives himself of all pardon and provokes God's anger the more by adding a second and more serious offense.... It is indeed a terrible temptation to covet this

honor. And in saying this, I do not contradict St. Paul but entirely agree with what he says. What are his words? "If a man seeks the office of a bishop, he desires a good work." What is terrible is to desire the absolute authority and power of the bishop but not the work itself. ON THE PRIESTHOOD 3.10-11.[1]

ADMONITION FOR THOSE TAKING ORDERS. JEROME: Should the entreaties of your brethren induce you to take orders, I shall rejoice that you are lifted up and fear lest you may be cast down. You will say, "if a man desire the office of a bishop, he desires a good work." I know that; but you should add what follows: such a one "must be blameless, the husband of one wife, sober, chaste, prudent, well-prepared, given to hospitality, apt to teach, not given to wine, no striker but patient." ... Woe to the man who goes in to the supper without a wedding garment. LETTERS 14.8.[2]

SOME MUST BE DRAGOONED. AUGUSTINE: But you think that this should not have happened to

[1]COP 80-81. [2]LCC 5:298.

you because you believe that no one should be forced to do good. See what the apostle said, "If a man desire the office of a bishop, he desires a good work," yet how many are forced against their will to undertake the episcopacy. Some are dragged in, locked up and kept under guard, suffering all this unwillingly until there arises in them a will to undertake this good work. LETTERS 173.1.2.[3]

THE BALANCE OF ACTIVITY AND CONTEMPLATION. AUGUSTINE: Consider these three temperaments: the contemplative, the active, the contemplative-active. A man can live the life of faith in any of these three and get to heaven. What is not indifferent is that he love truth and do what charity demands. No man must be so committed to contemplation as, in his contemplation, to give no thought to his neighbor's needs, nor so absorbed in action as to dispense with the contemplation of God. The attraction of leisure ought not to be empty-headed inactivity but in the quest or discovery of truth, both for his own progress and for the purpose of sharing ungrudgingly with others. Nor should the man of action love worldly position or power, for all is vanity under the sun,[4] but only what can be properly and usefully accomplished by means of such position and power . . . of contributing to the eternal salvation of those committed to one's care. Thus, as St. Paul wrote, "If any one aspires to the office of bishop, he desires good work." He wanted to make clear that the office of bishop, *episcopatus*, implies work rather than dignity. THE CITY OF GOD 19.19.[5]

WHEN A SCARECROW GUARDS THE VINEYARD. AUGUSTINE: "I want to be a bishop; oh, if only I were a bishop!" Would that you were! Are you seeking the name or the real thing? If it's the real thing you're seeking, you are setting your heart on a good work. If it's the name you're seeking, you can have it even with a bad work but with a worse punishment. So what shall we say? Are there bad bishops? Perish the thought, there aren't any; yes, I have the nerve, the gall to say there are no bad bishops; because if they are bad, they aren't bishops. You are calling me back again to the name and saying, "He is a bishop, because he is seated on the bishop's throne." And a straw scarecrow is guarding the vineyard. SERMONS 340A.6.[6]

RIGHTLY ASPIRING TO A GOOD WORK. CAESARIUS OF ARLES: The office of a bishop is a good work, dearest brethren, as the blessed apostle says, "Whoever wants to be a bishop aspires to a noble task." Now when "task" is heard, labor is understood. Therefore whoever desires the office of bishop with this understanding wants it without the arrogance of ambition. To express this more clearly, if a man wants not so much to be in authority over the people of God as to help them, he aspires to be a bishop in the true spirit. SERMONS 230.1.[7]

3:2a Above Reproach

DO NOT DESIRE AN OFFICE IF YOUR ACTIONS DISQUALIFY YOU. CHRYSOSTOM: *Blameless:* every virtue is implied in this word. If anyone is conscious to himself of any sins, he does not well to desire an office for which his own actions have disqualified him. . . . For why did no one say of the apostles that they were fornicators, unclean or covetous persons, but that they were deceivers, which relates to their preaching only? Must it not be that their lives were irreproachable? This is clear. HOMILIES ON 1 TIMOTHY 10.[8]

NOT WITHOUT CRITICS. THEODORE OF MOPSUESTIA: "Without reproach" can scarcely mean "without critics," since Paul himself had such, but blameless as to living. COMMENTARY ON 1 TIMOTHY.[9]

---

[3]FC 30:74. [4]Cf. Eccles 1:14; 2:11, 17; 4:7. [5]FC 24:230. [6]*WSA* 3/9:300. [7]FC 66:179. [8]NPNF 1 13:438*. [9]TEM 2:99 (Greek).

The Analogy of the Metalsmith. Gregory of Nyssa: When making a vessel of iron, we entrust the task not to those who know nothing about the matter but to those who are acquainted with the art of the smith. Ought we not, therefore, to entrust souls to him who is well-skilled to soften them by the fervent heat of the Holy Spirit and who by the impress of rational implements may fashion each one of you to be a chosen and useful vessel? It is thus that the inspired apostle bids us to take thought, in his epistle to Timothy, laying injunction upon all who hear, when he says that a bishop must be without reproach. Is this all that the apostle cares for, that he who is advanced to the priesthood should be irreproachable? And what is so great an advantage as that all possible qualifications should be included in one? But he knows full well that the subject is molded by the character of his superior and that the upright walk of the guide becomes that of his followers too. For what the Master is, such does he make the disciple to be. Letters 13.[10]

3:2b The Husband of One Wife

Good to Be Married. Clement of Alexandria: Some people run down the law and marriage. To them it is as if marriage were alien to the new covenant and merely a legalism. What do they say in face of this text? Especially those who have such an aversion to sex and childbirth—what have they to say in answer? Paul himself sets it down that leadership in the church should rest with "a bishop who presides successfully over his household" and that "marriage to one wife" constitutes a household with the Lord's blessing. Stromata 3.108.2.[11]

Second Marriages. Basil the Great: The canon[12] absolutely excludes from the ministry those who are twice married. Letters 188.12.[13]

Only One Wife. Chrysostom: Paul is not making a hard and fast rule that a bishop must

have a wife, but that he must not have more than one. Homilies on 1 Timothy 10.[14]

What Is Forbidden and Permitted. Theodore of Mopsuestia: For they [i.e., various interpreters] say that Paul has spoken thus, so that any man who is brought forward to be a bishop and has taken a wife will live chastely with her, being content with her alone as the recipient of his natural desires. Likewise any man who lives on after the death of his first wife may legitimately take a second wife, as long as he lives in the same way with her as with the first, and ought not be prohibited from becoming a bishop. They say that Paul has laid down a canon here. I accept this view, though I am not persuaded that he lays down a specific rule with regard to the second matter, i.e., that of the eligibility of remarried men for episcopal office.[15] Commentary on 1 Timothy.[16]

A Defense of Second Marriage. Cyril of Jerusalem: Do not let the once-married set at nought those who have come together in marriage for the second time. For continence is a fine thing and admirable. But folk may be pardoned for contracting a second marriage, lest infirmity end in fornication. Catechetical Lectures 4.26.[17]

A Mediating View. Ambrose: Therefore, the apostle laid down the law saying, "If any one is without reproach, the husband of one wife." Whoever, then, is without reproach, the husband of one wife, is included among those held

---

[10]NPNF 2 5:537*. [11]FC 85:325. [12]Probably Basil refers to generally accepted tradition among the churches, but a specific example might be Canon 17 of the Apostolic Canons: "If anyone after baptism has been joined in a second matrimony, or have a concubine, he cannot be a bishop, or a priest, or a deacon, or any of those who serve in the sacred ministry." [13]FC 28:23. [14]NPNF 1 13:438. [15]In Greek the text here reads "I accept," but in the Latin version the reading "I reject" appears. In the opinion of Swete, the Greek text was the more reliable. See TEM 2:103. [16]TEM 2:103-4 (Greek). [17]LCC 4:113.

by the law to be qualified for the priesthood, but he who entered a second marriage has not the guilt of pollution, though he is disqualified from the privilege of the priesthood. LETTERS 59.[18]

3:3a No Drunkard

REASONABLE CONTROL. JEROME: Let your breath never smell of wine, lest the philosopher's words be said to you, "Instead of offering me a kiss, you are giving me a taste of wine." Priests given to wine are both condemned by the apostle and forbidden by the old law. . . . Whatever intoxicates and disturbs the balance of the mind, avoid as you would wine. I do not say that we are to condemn what is a creature of God.[19] The Lord himself was called a "wine-bibber," and wine in moderation was allowed to Timothy because of his weak stomach.[20] I only require that drinkers should observe that limit which their age, their health or their constitution requires. LETTERS 52.11.[21]

3:3b Not Violent but Gentle

SMITING THE CONSCIENCE UNSEASONABLY. CHRYSOSTOM: "No striker." This too does not mean a striker with the hands. What does "no striker" then mean? Because there are some who unseasonably smite the consciences of their brethren, it seems to be said with reference to them. HOMILIES ON 1 TIMOTHY 10.[22]

REASONABLE CAUSE. THEODORE OF MOPSUESTIA: Not striking without reasonable cause, for sometimes this is permitted, if for a good reason and not with undue fierceness. COMMENTARY ON 1 TIMOTHY.[23]

VARIED MEANINGS. PELAGIUS: This could range widely in meaning from not delivering blows to the point of death to not striking the consciences of the weak with a bad example. PELAGIUS'S COMMENTARY ON THE FIRST LETTER TO TIMOTHY.[24]

3:4-5 Manage His Own Household

A GOOD STATESMAN. CHRYSOSTOM: The church leader must be "one that governs well his own house." Even those who are without the church have the saying that one who is a good manager of a house will be a good statesman. For the church is, as it were, a small household. In a house there are children and wife and domestic duties, and some one person has to provide order for them all. So in the church there are women, children, employees and subordinates. As a man has in his wife a partner in power, so does one who presides over the church. HOMILIES ON 1 TIMOTHY 10.[25]

GUIDANCE TO COUNTER DISBELIEF. THEODORE OF MOPSUESTIA: What is meant by good management, in the case of the children, is that the father is to guide them with wise counsel, such that, if they end up as nonbelievers, it is not his fault. COMMENTARY ON 1 TIMOTHY.[26]

TEACHING VIRTUE. THEODORET OF CYR: As a good overseer of his children, the father's task is not to abdicate to their opinion but to teach them all the virtues, even if he must act strongly to shape their wills. INTERPRETATION OF THE FIRST LETTER TO TIMOTHY.[27]

ONLY BY GOOD SELF-GOVERNANCE CAN ONE GOVERN OTHERS. PSEUDO-DIONYSIUS: Therefore how could we avoid being ashamed as we witness reason harmed by anger and desire, when we see it driven from the authority given to it by God so that in an unholy and unjust manner trouble, discord and disorder are stirred up in us? That is why our blessed and God-given lawmaker proclaimed that anyone who has not put his own house in order is unfit to hold

[18]FC 26:344. [19]1 Tim 4:4. [20]Mt 11:19; 1 Tim 5:23. [21]LCC 5:326. [22]NPNF 1 13:438. [23]TEM 2:109. [24]PETE 484. [25]NPNF 1 13:439*. [26]TEM 2:111. [27]PG 82:807A/808A.

authority in the church of God. For the one who commands himself will command another. LETTERS 8.3.[28]

3:6a Not a Recent Convert

YOUTHFULNESS NOT THE ISSUE. CHRYSOSTOM: The point is not that the bishop cannot be a young man but that he must not be a new convert. . . . For if youth only was an objection, why did he himself appoint Timothy, a young man? . . . But since there were many then who came over from heathen cultures to be baptized, Paul says, "Do not immediately advance to a station of dignity a novice, that is, one of these new converts." For, if even before he has proved himself as a disciple he is made a teacher, he will soon be lifted up into insolence. HOMILIES ON 1 TIMOTHY 10.[29]

3:6b The Condemnation of the Devil

SUBVERTING THE TYRANNY OF PRIDE. CHRYSOSTOM: Indeed, nothing so estranges from the mercy of God and gives over to the fire of hell as the tyranny of pride. . . . Therefore, let us check this puffing up of the soul, and let us cut out this tumor, if we wish to be pure and be rid of the punishment prepared for the devil. Listen to Paul declaring that the proud must suffer those very penalties: "Not a new convert, lest he be puffed up with pride and incur the condemnation passed on the devil." HOMILIES ON JOHN 9.2.[30]

LOSING THE BLESSING PROMISED TO HUMILITY. BASIL THE GREAT: His rank should not arouse feelings of pride in the superior, lest he himself lose the blessing promised to humility[31] or "lest being puffed up with pride he fall into the judgment of the devil." THE LONG RULES, Q.30.R.[32]

CONDEMNED WITH THE DEVIL. AUGUSTINE: What does Paul mean by saying "or he may be puffed up with conceit and fall into the condemnation of the devil"? It doesn't mean he is to be judged by the devil but that he is to be condemned with the devil. The devil, after all, won't be our judge. He himself fell through pride. Like him, one who has become godless on account of pride will be condemned to everlasting fire. We are to consider carefully, Paul is saying, to whom a position of eminence is given in the church, lest the person being lifted up should through pride fall into the very judgment into which the devil fell. SERMONS 340A.2.[33]

PRIDE INJURES OTHERS. JEROME: Realize how evil pride is from the very fact that there is no excuse for it. Other vices harm only those who commit them. Pride inflicts far more injury on everyone. I am saying all this lest you consider pride a trifling sin. What, in fact, does the apostle say? "Lest he incur the condemnation passed on the devil." The man who is puffed up with his own importance falls into the judgment of the devil. HOMILIES 95.[34]

3:7a Well Thought Of by Outsiders

"OUTSIDERS" MEANS CONGREGATIONAL SUPPORT. ORIGEN: Therefore let us see by what order the high priest is appointed. It says, "Moses called together the congregation and said to them, 'This is the Word that the Lord commanded.'"[35] Although the Lord had given them commands about appointing the high priest and had made his choice, the congregation was still called together. For in ordaining a priest, the presence of the people is also required that all may know and be certain that from all the people one is chosen for the priesthood who is more excellent, who is more wise, who is more holy, who is more eminent in every virtue, lest afterwards, when he stands before

---

[28]PSD 275. [29]NPNF 1 13:439. [30]FC 33:94-95. [31]Cf. Mt 5:6. [32]FC 9:293. [33]WSA 3/9:296. [34]FC 57:256. [35]Lev 8:4-5.

the people, any hesitation or any doubt should remain. This is also what the apostle taught when he spoke about the ordination of a priest: "It is necessary to have a good witness from those who are outside." Homilies on Leviticus 6.3.1.[36]

Taken into Account with Other Criteria. Chrysostom: For when St. Paul said, "Moreover he must have good testimony from them that are without," he does not do away with careful and exact scrutiny, nor does he set up this testimony as a chief sign of assurance about such men. But having listed many requirements already, he added this one afterwards, to show that we must not be content with it alone for this kind of election but only take it into account along with other considerations. For it often happens that popular report is false. On the Priesthood 2.4.[37]

The Relative Value of Popular Report. Augustine: This is not the praise given a man by a few wise and just people but popular report. Indeed, popular report bestows greatness and renown on a man, which is not desirable for its own sake but is essential to the success of good men in their endeavors to benefit their fellow men. So the apostle says that it is proper to have a good report of those that are without. For though they are not infallible, the luster of their praise and the odor of their good opinion are a great help to the efforts of those who seek to benefit them. This popular renown is not obtained by those who are highest in the church, unless they expose themselves to the toils and hazards of an active life. Reply to Faustus the Manichaean 22.56.[38]

Leave No Opportunity for Scandal. Leo the Great: The wishes of the congregation and the testimony of the populace should certainly be waited for. The opinions of the nobles and the choice of the clerics should be asked for. These are the procedures ordinarily observed in the consecrating of bishops by those who know the decrees of the Fathers. That would be to preserve in every way the requirement made by apostolic authority which demands that a bishop who is to be in charge of a church must be supported not only by the testimony of his congregation but by a good reputation among outsiders as well. No opportunity for such a scandal should be left. One who is going to be the teacher of peace is himself consecrated in peace and in harmony pleasing to God, through the common efforts of all. Letters 10.4.[39]

3:7b *The Snare of the Devil*

Falling Back. Theodore of Mopsuestia: This reason is foremost, and in no way weaker than the ones already mentioned, that it is not prudent to entrust the care of others to such a one and to offer such great power so quickly. Why? Because he has not yet given proof of his life and manners, and it is not yet certain as to whether anything is left of his former life, since the devil has many devices to use against him. These are such that he may fall back into old sins. Indeed, because it seems that he has moved away from his former and worse state, he cannot be corrected in the direction of better things, for he is now seen to have had the nurture of others entrusted to him instead. Commentary on 1 Timothy.[40]

---

[36]FC 83:120-21. [37]COP 62. [38]NPNF 1 4:294*. Augustine is offering a spiritual interpretation of Rachel's desire for the mandrakes in Genesis 30:15, in order to counter Faustus the Manichaean's view that much of the Old Testament is immoral and unworthy of the true God. [39]FC 34:42-43. [40]TEM 2:115.

3:8-13 INSTRUCTIONS ON DEACONS

[8]*Deacons likewise must be serious, not double-tongued, not addicted to much wine, not greedy for gain;* [9]*they must hold the mystery of the faith with a clear conscience.* [10]*And let them also be tested first; then if they prove themselves blameless let them serve as deacons.* [11]*The women likewise must be serious, no slanderers, but temperate, faithful in all things.* [12]*Let deacons be the husband of one wife, and let them manage their children and their households well;* [13]*for those who serve well as deacons gain a good standing for themselves and also great confidence in the faith which is in Christ Jesus.*

OVERVIEW: Paul does not include a separate discussion of the qualifications for *presbyteroi* (elders, priests), because this order is considered identical with that of the bishops (CHRYSOSTOM, THEODORE, THEODORET, AMBROSIASTER, PELAGIUS). The instructions for women are directed at female deacons (CHRYSOSTOM, THEODORE, THEODORET, PELAGIUS), though it was claimed by some that the ordination of such women was a Montanist aberration (AMBROSIASTER). Deacons serve according to God's own service to us (POLYCARP).

3:8a Deacons Likewise

SERVING AS GOD SERVED. POLYCARP: Likewise the deacons should be blameless before the Lord's righteousness, as servants of God and Christ and not of men; not slanderers, or double-tongued, not lovers of money, temperate in all matters, compassionate, careful, living according to the truth of the Lord, who became a "servant of all";[1] to whom, if we are pleasing in the present age, we shall also obtain the age to come, inasmuch as he promised to raise us from the dead. LETTER OF POLYCARP 5.2.[2]

3:8b Not Double-Tongued

NO NEW COMMANDMENT. ATHANASIUS: What Moses taught, Abraham observed. What Abraham observed, Noah and Enoch acknowledged, discriminating pure from impure and becoming acceptable to God. For Abel too in this way witnessed, knowing what he had learned from Adam. This one himself had learned from that Lord, who said, when he came at the end of the ages for the abolishment of sin, "I give no new commandment to you, but an old commandment, which you have heard from the beginning."[3] In the same way also the blessed apostle Paul, who had learned it from the Lord, when describing ecclesiastical functions, forbade that deacons, not to say bishops, should be double-tongued. In his rebuke of the Galatians, he made a broad declaration: If anyone preach any other gospel unto you than that which you have received, let him be anathema, as I have said, so say I again. DEFENSE OF THE NICENE DEFINITION 2.5.[4]

DECEIT DEBASING. CHRYSOSTOM: Not hollow, or deceitful. For nothing so debases a man as deceit, nothing is so pernicious in the church as insincerity. HOMILIES ON 1 TIMOTHY 11.[5]

NO DOUBLE TALK. THEODORET OF CYR: "Not double-tongued" means that the deacon is not to be a person who says one thing to one person

---

[1]Mk 9:35. [2]LCC 1:133. [3]1 Jn 2:7. [4]NPNF 2 4:153*. [5]NPNF 1 13:441.

and something else to another. INTERPRETA-TION OF THE FIRST LETTER TO TIMOTHY.[6]

THE PARTICULAR INTEGRITY OF DEACONS. THEODORE OF MOPSUESTIA: Since the ministry of deacons is at least as much toward the women in the community as the men, their integrity is all the more important. They are to be honorable and sincere in performing the duties assigned to them by the presbyters. COMMENTARY ON THE FIRST LETTER TO TIMOTHY.[7]

3:9 The Mystery of the Faith

TEACHING ABOUT JESUS. THEODORE OF MOPSUESTIA: The mystery of faith referred to by the apostle here is the teaching about Christ, which he is about to expound in what follows. COMMENTARY ON THE FIRST LETTER TO TIMOTHY.[8]

THE PASSION OF CHRIST. PELAGIUS: The mystery of faith is the passion of Christ, out of which comes the redeeming process by which our salvation is won. "The clear conscience" refers to the fact that the person who knows this mystery purely is not confounded by the spectacle of Christ's humiliation, or, it means that this mystery should be preached straightforwardly, piety not requiring anything beyond the statement itself. PELAGIUS'S COMMENTARY ON THE FIRST LETTER TO TIMOTHY.[9]

3:10a Let Them Also Be Tested First

APPROPRIATE CAUTION. CHRYSOSTOM: Would it not be absurd that when a new servant is not entrusted with anything in a house till he has by long trial given proofs of his character, yet that one should enter into the church of God from a state of heathenism and be at once placed in a station of preeminence? HOMILIES ON 1 TIMOTHY 11.[10]

ONE STEP AT A TIME. GREGORY THE GREAT: Orders, then, should be risen to in an orderly way; for he courts a fall who seeks to rise to the topmost heights of a place by steep ascents, disregarding the steps that lead to it. LETTERS 106.[11]

3:10b Blameless

NOT WITHOUT SIN. AUGUSTINE: None could rightly be ordained a minister in the church if the apostle had said, "If any is without sin," where he says, "If any is without crime";[12] or if he had said, "Having no sin," where he says, "Having no crime." Because many baptized believers are without crime, but I should say that no one in this life is without sin—however much the Pelagians are inflated, and burst asunder in madness against me because I say this: not because there remains anything of sin which is not remitted in baptism; but because by us who remain in the weakness of this life such sins do not cease daily to be committed, as are daily remitted to those who pray in faith and work in mercy. AGAINST TWO LETTERS OF THE PELAGIANS 1.14.28.[13]

3:11 The Women Also Must Be Serious

WOMEN DEACONS. CHRYSOSTOM: Some have thought that this is said of women generally, but it is not so, for why should he introduce anything about women to interfere with his subject? He is speaking of those who hold the rank of deaconesses. HOMILIES ON 1 TIMOTHY 11.[14]

WOMEN IN GENERAL. AMBROSIASTER: Paul does not refer here to women deacons, since

---

[6]PG 82:807C/808C. [7]TEM 2:126. [8]TEM 2:127. [9]PETE 486-87*. [10]NPNF 1 12:441*. [11]NPNF 2 13:25. [12]Tit 1:5. [13]NPNF 1 5:386. Cf. Augustine *Tractates on John* 41.3.10:"When the apostle Paul chose either priests or deacons to be ordained, and when anyone is to be ordained to take charge of a church, he does not say, If anyone is without sin. For if he were to say this, every person would be rejected, no one would be ordained" (FC 88:145). [14]NPNF 1 12:441.

these are not allowed in the church. It is heretics who have such persons. The reference here is to women in general. COMMENTARY ON THE FIRST LETTER TO TIMOTHY.[15]

3:12 The Husband of One Wife

DEACONS HELD TO THE SAME STANDARD. CHRYSOSTOM: Observe how he requires the same virtue from the deacons as from the bishops, for though they were not of equal rank, they must be equally blameless, equally pure. HOMILIES ON 1 TIMOTHY 11.[16]

3:13 A Good Standing for Themselves

DESERVED ADVANCEMENT. CHRYSOSTOM: "They that use the office of a deacon well purchase to themselves a good degree," that is, heavenly advancement, "and much boldness in the faith of Jesus Christ"; as if he would say, that those who have been found vigilant in the lower degree will soon ascend to the higher. HOMILIES ON 1 TIMOTHY 11.[17]

A HEAVENLY REWARD. THEODORE OF MOPSUESTIA: A "good reward" refers to a future, heavenly good, since earthly promotion would have required the idea of "better reward." COMMENTARY ON THE FIRST LETTER TO TIMOTHY.[18]

HELD ACCOUNTABLE. JEROME: Woe to him who, when he has received a talent, has bound it in a napkin; and while others make profits, only preserves what he has received. His angry Lord shall rebuke him in a moment. "You wicked servant," he will say. "Why then did you not put my money into the bank, and at my coming I could have collected it with interest?"[19] That is to say you should have laid before the altar what you were not able to bear. For while you, a slothful trader, keep a penny in your hands, you occupy the place of another who might double the money. Thus as one who ministers well purchases to himself a good degree, so one who approaches the cup of the Lord unworthily shall be guilty of the body and blood of the Lord. LETTERS 14.8.[20]

CAREFUL OF HIS OWN SOUL. BENEDICT OF NURSIA: The keeper of the wine cellar for the community shall be chosen out of the community, discreet, mature in his behavior and sober. If a brother chance to demand anything unreasonable of him, he is not to be contemptuous in his refusal but to refuse reasonably and humbly. He is to be careful of his own soul and remember that St. Paul says: "He that has done his duty well, gains for himself a good degree." He is to show a particular concern for the sick, children, strangers and the poor, as being accountable for them at the day of judgment. RULE 31.[21]

---

[15]CSEL 81 3:268. [16]NPNF 1 12:441. [17]NPNF 1 12:441-42*. [18]TEM 2:130. [19]Lk 19:22. [20]LCC 5:298-99*. [21]LCC 12:313*.

3:14-16 MAINTAINING THE HOUSEHOLD

[14]*I hope to come to you soon, but I am writing these instructions to you so that,* [15]*if I am delayed, you may know how one ought to behave in the household of God, which is the church of the living God, the pillar and bulwark of the truth.* [16]*Great indeed, we confess, is the mystery of our religion:*

He[h] was manifested in the flesh,
vindicated[i] in the Spirit,
    seen by angels,
preached among the nations,
believed on in the world,
    taken up in glory.

h Greek Who; *other ancient authorities read* God; *others,* Which   *i Or* justified

---

OVERVIEW: Wishing to forestall any dejection on Timothy's part at his continued delay, Paul encourages him with directions on how to preach the faith as the mystery of the incarnation and thereby nurture and maintain the community of believers (CHRYSOSTOM). Paul lays out for Timothy the central teaching of a dogmatically correct statement of the teaching about the incarnation, so that the church may be faithfully instructed (CHRYOSTOM, AUGUSTINE, THEODORE). Paul indicates that while he does not know much of what will happen in the future, he is sure that the faithful teaching of the incarnation will sustain the church (THEODORET). The mystery of the Word become flesh (GREGORY OF NYSSA, AUGUSTINE) was so powerful even in its prefigurations that those who believed it when promised attained to it no less than those who received it when actually given (AUGUSTINE, LEO). We are together in the household of God even when apart (AUGUSTINE). In this house we learn to study the Testaments old and new (ORIGEN). There is one church which is spread throughout the whole world, though many in particular expressions (FULGENTIUS).

3:15a The Household of God

A ROYAL HOUSE. ORIGEN: The spiritual interpretation, however, is not so difficult and hard to come by.[1] For the bride of the Word, the soul who abides in his royal house—that is, in the church—is taught by the Word of God, who is her Bridegroom, whatever things are stored and hidden within the royal court and in the king's chamber. In this house, which is the church of the living God, she becomes acquainted also with the cellar of that wine which is extracted from the holy wine presses, the wine that is not only new, but also old and sweet—that is, the teaching of the Law and the Prophets. COMMENTARY ON THE SONG OF SONGS 3.13.[2]

THE HOUSE IS ONE. AUGUSTINE: Therefore, beloved, with assured mind and steadfast heart, let us continue to live under so lofty a Head in so glorious a body, in which we are mutually members. Thus, even if my absence were as far as the most distant lands, we should be together in him, and we should never withdraw from the unity of his body. If we lived in one house, we should certainly be said to be together; how much more are we together when we are together in one body! LETTERS 142.1.1.[3]

3:15b The Pillar and Bulwark of the Truth

THE CORE GOSPEL. IRENAEUS: Such, then, are the first principles of the gospel. There is one God, the Maker of this universe; he who was also announced by the prophets and who by

---

[1]Origen is commenting on Song of Songs 2:10 but refers to his interpretation of the "house" prepared for the lovers. Compare the comments on 1:17, for example (ACW 26:175): "It is plain, however, that Christ is describing the church, which is a spiritual house and the house of God. So, if the church is the house of God, then—because all things that the Father has are the Son's—it follows that the church is the house of the Son of God." [2]ACW 26:231-32. [3]FC 20:147.

Moses set forth the dispensation of the law—principles which proclaim the Father of our Lord Jesus Christ and ignore any other God or Father except him. So firm is the ground upon which these Gospels rest that the very heretics themselves bear witness to them, and, starting from these documents, each one of them endeavors to establish his own peculiar doctrine.... It is not possible that the Gospels can be either more or fewer in number than they are. For there are four zones of the world in which we live, and four principal winds, while the church is scattered throughout all the world, and the "pillar and ground" of the church is the gospel and the spirit of life. Therefore, it is fitting that it should have four pillars, breathing out immortality on every side and vivifying all humanity afresh. AGAINST HERESIES 3.11.7-8.[4]

THE CHURCH, A MIXTURE OF TYPES. BASIL THE GREAT: Every one of us, indeed, who is instructed in the Holy Scripture is the administrator of some one of those gifts which, according to the gospel, have been apportioned to us. In this great household of the church not only are there vessels of every kind—gold, silver, wooden and earthen[5] —but also a great variety of vocational pursuits. The house of God, which is the church of the living God, has hunters, travelers, architects, builders, farmers, shepherds, athletes, soldiers. HOMILY ON THE WORDS: "GIVE HEED TO THYSELF."[6]

THE HOLY CATHOLIC CHURCH. CYRIL OF JERUSALEM: "For from the rising of the sun, even to its setting, my name is great among the nations."[7] It is of this holy Catholic church that Paul writes to Timothy.... He calls the church "the pillar and mainstay of the truth." CATECHETICAL LECTURES 18.25.[8]

THE CHURCH. AMBROSE: Accordingly, as Scripture says, Jacob became rich by such means and reared a very good flock for Christ.[9] He improved it with the title of faith and a diversity

of virtues, the marks of a glorious name. And so he did not consider himself poor, for he was rich with the wealth of faith.... And it is no wonder that Jacob possessed peace, for he had set up a pillar and anointed it to God,[10] and that pillar is the church. Paul calls that pillar "the bulwark of the truth." That man anoints it who pours the ointment of faith upon Christ and of compassion upon the poor. JACOB AND THE HAPPY LIFE 5.20.[11]

THE CHURCH, A MIXED BODY. AUGUSTINE: Honor the holy church as your mother. Love her, proclaim her the Jerusalem which is above, the holy city of God. She it is who, in this faith which you have heard, bears fruit and grows in the whole world, the church of the living God, the pillar and buttress of the truth. She tolerates the wicked in the communion of the sacraments, knowing that they are due to be separated from her at the end and withdrawing from them meanwhile in the dissimilarity of their morals. SERMONS 214.11.[12]

MANY CHURCHES, BUT ONE CHURCH. FULGENTIUS OF RUSPE: We know through the grace of God that the holy church is called a virgin, as the apostle says, "I betrothed you to one husband to present you as a chaste virgin to Christ,"[13] but in that one virgin herself, virgins in the plural are also named. For we read, "Virgins will be brought to the king after her."[14] Nor is there any doubt that there is one church which is spread throughout the whole world which is called by the apostle "the church of the living God, the pillar and foundation of truth." Still this is one church in such a way that in it many are called churches. LETTERS 14.7.[15]

---

[4]ANF 1:428*. [5]2 Tim 2:20. [6]FC 9:436-37. [7]Mal 1:11. [8]FC 64:134. [9]Cf. Gen 30:43. [10]Gen 35:20. [11]FC 65:157. [12]WSA 3/6:157. Augustine offers a similar interpretation of the church as a "mixed body" based on this text in *Converts and the Creed* 11 (FC 38:41). [13]2 Cor 11:2. [14]Ps 45:14. [15]FC 95:505-6.

3:16a *The Mystery of Our Religion*

THE ECONOMY OF SALVATION. CHRYSOSTOM: Here he speaks of the economy of salvation given to us. Tell me not of the bells, nor of the holy of holies, nor of the high priest. The church is the pillar of the world. Consider this mystery, and you may be struck with awe. For it is indeed a "great mystery," and a "mystery of godliness," and that is "without controversy" or question, for it is beyond all doubt. HOMILIES ON 1 TIMOTHY 11.[16]

THEODORE OF MOPSUESTIA: The "mystery" is the scriptural teaching concerning Christ. COMMENTARY ON 1 TIMOTHY.[17]

FOREORDAINED. THEODORET OF CYR: The "mystery" is the sacred object of reverence, namely, that what was foreordained from the beginning and afterward became manifest. INTERPRETATION OF THE FIRST LETTER TO TIMOTHY.[18]

FROM ALL ETERNITY. LEO THE GREAT: No, indeed, it is not that God has just recently come up with a plan for attending to human affairs, nor that it has taken him this long to show compassion. Rather, he laid down from the very "foundation of the world"[19] one and the same "cause of salvation"[20] for all. For, the grace of God—by which the entire assembly of saints has always been justified—was not initiated at the time that Christ was born but augmented. This "mystery of great compassion," with which the whole world has now been filled, was so powerful even in its prefigurations that those who believed it when promised attained to it no less than those who received it when actually given. SERMONS 23.4.[21]

3:16b *Manifested in the Flesh, Vindicated in the Spirit*

WONDERFUL IS THE MYSTERY. GREGORY OF NYSSA: We hold it necessary to honor, even as the Father is honored, the God who was manifested by the cross. They [the Eunomians] find the passion a hindrance to glorifying the Only-Begotten God equally with the Father that begat him. . . . Eunomius makes the suffering of the cross to be a sign of divergence in essence, in the sense of inferiority, considering, I know not how, the surpassing act of power, by which he was able to perform this, to be an evidence of weakness. He fails to perceive the fact that, while nothing which moves according to its own nature is looked upon as surprisingly wonderful, all things that overpass the limitations of their own nature become especially the objects of admiration. Indeed, to them every ear is turned, every mind is attentive, in wonder at the marvel. And hence it is that all who preach the word point out the wonderful character of the mystery in this respect—that "God was manifested in the flesh," that "the light shined in the darkness,"[22] "the Life tasted death"—and all such declarations which the heralds of the faith are prone to make. By these is increased the marvelous character of him who manifested the superabundance of his power by means external to his own nature. AGAINST EUNOMIUS 5.3.[23]

THE WORD BECOME FLESH. AUGUSTINE: But when the fullness of time came, Wisdom was sent in the flesh, not to fill angels[24] nor to be an angel, except insofar as she announced the Father's plan which was also her own. She was sent not to be with men and in men, for this too had been done before, both in the Fathers and in the prophets, but that the Word itself might become flesh, that is, that it might become a man. This future mystery, when revealed, would likewise be the salvation of those wise and saintly men, who had been born of women

---

[16]NPNF 1 13:442*. [17]TEM 2:134. [18]PG 82:809D/810D. [19]Eph 1:4. [20]Heb 5:9. [21]FC 93:90-91. [22]Jn 1:5. [23]NPNF 2 5:176*. [24]Wis 7:27

before he himself was born of a virgin, and ever since it has been accomplished and preached, it is the salvation of all who believe, hope and love. On the Trinity 4.20.27.[25]

3:16c Seen by Angels

To the Angels Also. Origen: Behold the Savior's greatness. It extends to all the world. . . . Go up to the heavens. See how he fills the celestial regions, "He appeared to the angels." Go down in your mind to the nether world. See that he went down there, too. . . . Ponder the Lord's power, how it has filled the world—that is, the heavens, the earth and the nether regions. Homilies on Luke, 6.9-10.[26]

Seen as Angels See. Chrysostom: "If you knew my essence and dignity, you would also know that of the Father. And henceforth you will know him, and you have seen him" (the former in future, the latter at present), that is, "through me."[27] Moreover by "sight" he meant knowledge by means of the understanding. For we can both see and fail to know persons whom we actually see, but we cannot both know and fail to know at the same time persons whom we know. That is why he declared, "And you have seen him," just as Scripture says, "as he has been seen by angels also." Even though his very essence was not, of course, seen, it said that he "has been seen," clearly meaning "seen" in such a way as it was possible for the angels to see. Homilies on John 73.2.[28]

---

[25]FC 45:166. [26]FC 94:27. [27]Cf. Jn 8:19. [28]FC 41:288.

4:1-5 FALSE TEACHING

[1]Now the Spirit expressly says that in later times some will depart from the faith by giving heed to deceitful spirits and doctrines of demons, [2]through the pretensions of liars whose consciences are seared, [3]who forbid marriage and enjoin abstinence from foods which God created to be received with thanksgiving by those who believe and know the truth. [4]For everything created by God is good, and nothing is to be rejected if it is received with thanksgiving; [5]for then it is consecrated by the word of God and prayer.

Overview: The Spirit gives authoritative guidance to the church (Cyril of Jerusalem, Nicetas). The exact span of time to the end is not for us to know (Augustine). Meanwhile false prophets and heresies with perverse intentions abound in history (Justin Martyr, Tertullian, Alexander of Alexandria, Ambrose, Athanasius, Augustine). One living with a divided, seared, dead conscience is not ready for the coming of the Lord (Chrysostom, Theodore, Theodoret, Ambrosiaster).

It is the Gnostic heretics who reject marriage and foods and other things that belong to God's creation. These things are meant to be good and available to humankind, as long as we cleanse our hearts first (Chrysostom). Heretical denial of the incarnation leads to false asceticism of the type practiced by the Marcionites, Manichaeans and Valentinians (Theodore). Not only do they reject things that God has created, but also by

---

compelling ascetic practice, which may in itself be good, they rob such discipline of the freedom of choice that is its real value (Theodoret). We are not to despise marriage (Gregory of Nyssa) or wholesome foods (Cyril of Jerusalem). Food laws may run contrary to sound doctrine (Augustine). While all things are of God, continency will reasonably seek out plainer foods and those necessary to sustain life, avoiding foods lacking nutritional value, whose sole purpose is to give delight (Basil). Christian ethics does not block access to pleasure in God's creation, but allows it in a chaste way so that the will is not subject to countless misgivings (Tertullian, Jerome, Chrysostom). What God creates is good as created (Basil). Nothing is unclean by nature, but it becomes so through willful disobedience (Chrysostom, Augustine, Leo). The intelligible and the sensible are blended in all creation. Nothing that exists is altogether deprived of some share in the divine fellowship (Gregory of Nyssa).

4:1a The Spirit Expressly Says

Authority of the Spirit. Cyril of Jerusalem: That the Holy Spirit subsists, lives, speaks and foretells I have told you repeatedly on former occasions. Paul writes clearly to Timothy, "Now the Spirit expressly says that in later times some will depart from the faith." This we see in the factions of former times and in our own day. How diverse and multiform are the errors of the heretics. Catechetical Lectures 17.33.[1]

Thus Says the Spirit. Nicetas of Remesiana: How could anyone be silent in regard to the divine authority of the Holy Spirit? The ancient prophets cried out, "These things say the Lord." When Christ came, he also used this word "say" in his own person, "But I say unto you." Listen now to what the prophets of the New Testament proclaim. Take the prophet Agabus in the Acts of the Apostles, "Thus says the Holy Spirit."[2] So, too, Paul to Timothy, "Now the Spirit expressly says . . .". Power of the Holy Spirit 15.[3]

4:1b In Later Times

The Later Times Are Getting Nearer. Augustine: Considering the signs mentioned by Gospel and prophecy which we see happening, would anyone deny that we ought to hope for the coming of the Lord? Manifestly, it is nearer and nearer every day. But the exact span of the nearness, that, as we said, "is not for you to know." Notice when the apostle said this, "For our salvation is nearer than when we believed. The night is past and the day is at hand,"[4] and look how many years have passed! Yet, what he said was not untrue. How much more probable is it to say now that the coming of the Lord is near when there has been such an increase of time toward the end! Certainly the apostle said, "The Spirit manifestly says that in the last times some shall depart from the faith." Obviously, those were not yet the times of heretics such as he describes them in the same sentence, but they have now come. According to this, we seem to be in the last times, and the heretics seem to be a warning of the end of the world. Letters 199.8.22.[5]

4:1c Some Will Depart from the Faith

True and False Prophets. Justin Martyr: There were prophets a very long time ago more ancient than these[6] who are reputed to be phi-

---

[1]FC 64:33. [2]Acts 21:11. [3]FC 7:35. [4]Rom 13:11-12. [5]FC 30:373*. [6]Justin is comparing the various Hellenistic philosophers with the Old Testament prophets and is claiming that the wisdom of the latter predates that of the former. This argument that biblical truth is older, and thus more venerable, than that of philosophy was a commonplace of early Christian apologetics and rested on the assumption generally shared in the ancient world that what is more ancient is more true. The high point of such thinking is the work *Against Celsus* by Origen.

losophers, blessed and righteous and dear to God. They spoke by a divine spirit, and they oracularly predicted future events which are now taking place. They are truly called prophets. . . . Past events and events now taking place compel us to agree with what was spoken by them. Furthermore they deserved to be believed because of the miracles which they performed, since they were glorifying God the Creator and Father of the universe and they were announcing the Christ coming from him, his Son. The false prophets who were filled with the deceitful and filthy spirit never did nor now do this. They dare to work various supposed miracles in order to impress men, and they glorify the spirits and demons of deceit. DIALOGUE WITH TRYPHO 1.7.[7]

DOCTRINES FOR ITCHING EARS. TERTULLIAN: These are "the doctrines" of men and "of demons" that produce for itching ears of the spirit this world's wisdom. This is what the Lord called "foolishness."[8] God "chose the foolish things of the world" to confound even philosophy itself. For philosophy is the material of the world's wisdom, the rash interpreter of the nature and the providence (dispensations) of God. ON PRESCRIPTION AGAINST HERETICS 7.[9]

THE ARIAN HERETICS. ALEXANDER OF ALEXANDRIA: Now concerning their blasphemous assertion who say that the Son does not perfectly know the Father, we need not wonder. Indeed, having once purposed in their mind to wage war against Christ, they impugn also these words of his, "As the Father knows Me, even so know I the Father."[10] . . . Moreover, concerning these very men, warnings are not wanting to us, for the Lord foretold, "Take heed that you are not deceived: for many shall come in My name, saying, I am Christ; and the time draws near: do not go therefore after them."[11] Paul, too, having learned these things from the Savior, wrote, "In the latter times some shall depart from the faith, giving heed to seducing spirits, and doctrines of devils which turn away from the truth." EPIS-

TLES ON THE ARIAN HERESY 2.4-5.[12]

THEIR PERVERSE INTENTIONS. AMBROSE: As for me, indeed, would that they might have a will to hear, that they might believe—to hear with true love and meekness, as men seeking what is true and not assailing all truth. For it is written that we pay no heed to "endless fables and genealogies, which do rather raise disputes than set forward the godly edification, which is in faith. But the aim of the charge is love from a pure heart, and a good conscience, and faith unfeigned, whence some have erred and betaken themselves to empty babbling. For they are desirous of being teachers of the law, without understanding the words they say, nor the things whereof they speak with assurance."[13] In another place also the same apostle says, "Avoid foolish and ignorant questionings."[14] Such men, who sow disputes—that is to say, heretics—the apostle bids us leave alone. Of them he says in yet another place that "certain shall depart from the faith, giving heed to deceitful spirits and the doctrines of devils." OF THE CHRISTIAN FAITH 2.15.133-34.[15]

THE CLOTHING OF THEIR PHRASES. ATHANASIUS: Therefore it becomes us to watch, lest some deception be conveyed under the clothing of their phrases and they lead some away from the true faith. And if they venture to advance the opinions of Arius, when they see themselves proceeding in a prosperous course, nothing remains for us but to use great boldness of speech. For we are to remember the predictions of the apostle, which he wrote to forewarn us of such heresies and which it becomes us to repeat. For we know that, as it is written, "in the latter times some shall depart from the true faith, giving heed to seducing spirits and doctrines of

---

[7]JMD 21*. [8]1 Cor 3:8, 25. Notice Tertullian's curious practice of calling a reference from Scripture "the Lord." [9]ANF 3:246. [10]Jn 10:15. [11]Lk 21:8. [12]ANF 6:298*. [13]1 Tim 1:4-7. [14]2 Tim 2:23. [15]NPNF 2 10:240-41*.

devils, that turn from the truth."[16] TO THE BISHOPS OF EGYPT 2.20.[17]

THE MANICHAEAN HERETICS. AUGUSTINE: The fulfillment of these predictions in the Manichaeans is as clear as day to all that know them and has already been proved as fully as time permits. REPLY TO FAUSTUS THE MANICHAEAN 15.10.[18]

4:2 The Pretensions of Liars

CULPABLE FALSEHOOD. CHRYSOSTOM: "Speaking lies in hypocrisy." This implies that they do not utter these falsehoods through ignorance and unknowingly but as acting a part, knowing the truth but "having their conscience seared," for they are men who live evil lives. HOMILIES ON 1 TIMOTHY 12.[19]

THE BRIDE MUST BE READY FOR THE BRIDEGROOM. CHRYSOSTOM: In what way then is she a virgin who has fallen away from the faith, who has devoted herself to the deceivers, who obeys the demons and honors falsehood? In what way is she a virgin who has a seared conscience? For the virgin must be pure not only in body but also in soul if she is going to receive the holy bridegroom. . . . Virginity is defined by holiness of body and soul. But if a woman is unholy and impure in each respect, how could she be a virgin? . . . But she shows me a pale face, wasted limbs, a shabby garment and gentle glance. . . . What is the good of all that when the eye of the soul is bold,[20] for what could be more audacious than that eye encouraging her real eyes to consider the objects of God's creation as bad? ON VIRGINITY 5.2-6.1.[21]

LACKING WHOLENESS OF CONSCIENCE. THEODORE OF MOPSUESTIA: "Having their consciences seared" means not having a whole conscience, for they live the opposite of what they teach. COMMENTARY ON 1 TIMOTHY.[22]

THE NUMBING OF CONSCIENCE. THEODORET OF CYR: "Consciences seared" refers to their final numbing, the deadening of their consciences. INTERPRETATION OF THE FIRST LETTER TO TIMOTHY.[23]

CORRUPTED BY FALSEHOOD. AMBROSIASTER: The seared conscience is a branded conscience, with the implication that they have been corrupted by falsehood which makes a mark on their consciences like a brand on skin. COMMENTARY ON THE FIRST LETTER TO TIMOTHY.[24]

4:3a Forbidding Marriage and Enjoining Abstinence from Foods

THE DANGER OF FORCED PIETY. CLEMENT OF ALEXANDRIA: It follows that celibacy is not particularly praiseworthy unless it arises through love of God. The blessed Paul says of those who show a distaste for marriage, "In the last days people will abandon the faith, attaching themselves to deceitful spirits and the teachings of demonic powers that they should abstain from food, at the same time forbidding marriage." Again he says, "Do not let anyone disqualify you in forced piety of self-mortification and severity to the body."[25] . . . Well? Did not the righteous of past days share gratefully in God's creation? Some of them married and produced children without loss of self-control. STROMATA 3.51-52.[26]

MAINTAINING VOWS. ORIGEN: The Savior then commanded, "What God has joined together, let not man put asunder."[27] But man wishes to put asunder what God has joined together. He does this when, "falling away from the sound faith, he gives heed to seducing spirits and doctrines of demons, through the hypocrisy

---

[16]See also Tit 1:14. [17]NPNF 2 4:233*. [18]NPNF 1 4:218-19*. [19]NPNF 1 13:444. [20]Cf. Plato *Republic* 7.527e, 7.533d. [21]COV 7-8. [22]TEM 2:141. [23]PG 82:811D/812D. [24]CSEL 81 3:272-73. [25]Col 2:18, 23, freely cited. [26]FC 85:288. [27]Mt 19:6.

of men who speak lies, branded in their own conscience as with a hot iron, and by forbidding" them not only to commit fornication but even "to marry." In this way he dissolves even those who before had been joined together by the providence of God. COMMENTARY ON MATTHEW 14.16.[28]

FASTING IN THE HEART. ORIGEN: Do you still want me to show you what kind of fast it is appropriate for you to practice? Fast from every sin, take no food of malice, take no feasts of passion, do not burn with any wine of luxury. Fast from evil deeds, abstain from evil words, hold yourself from the worst evil thoughts. Do not touch the secret loaves of perverse doctrine. Do not desire the deceptive foods of philosophy which seduce you from truth. Such a fast pleases God. But "to abstain from the foods which God created to be received with thanksgiving by the faithful" and to do this with those who crucified Christ cannot be acceptable to God. . . . However, we do not say this that we may loosen the restraints of Christian abstinence. HOMILIES ON LEVITICUS 10.5-6.[29]

ASCETIC BALANCE. TERTULLIAN: The apostle set a brand upon those who were inclined entirely to forbid marriage and who were determined to lay an interdict on meats which God has created. We, however, do not do away with marriage if we disavow its repetition, nor do we condemn meats if we fast oftener than others. It is one thing to regulate but another thing to do away with altogether. ON MONOGAMY 15.[30]

THE ERROR OF THE ENCRATITES. HIPPOLYTUS: Others, however, styling themselves Encratites, acknowledge some things concerning God and Christ consistently with the church. In respect, however, of their ascetic mode of life, they pass their days inflated with pride. They suppose that by their choice of foods they magnify themselves. They abstain from animal food, [and] being water drinkers, forbid to marry, devoting themselves during the remainder of life to habits of asceticism. But persons of this description are viewed more as cynics than as Christians, inasmuch as they do not attend to the words spoken against them by the apostle Paul. THE REFUTATION OF ALL HERESIES 8.13.[31]

LIVE IN THE WORLD. CHRYSOSTOM: "Well," someone says, "what do you expect us to do? To live in the mountains and become monks?" This question saddens me for this reason, that some think only monks to be truly concerned with decency and chastity. Yet surely Christ made his laws to apply to everyone. . . . Indeed, I do not "forbid marriage," nor do I mean to block your access to pleasure, but I want you to have it in a chaste way, not shamefully or in a way deserving reproach and subject to endless misgivings. I do not insist that you live in the mountains and the deserts but that you be good and moderate and chaste, while dwelling in the midst of the city. HOMILIES ON MATTHEW 7.7.[32]

DO NOT DESPISE MARRIAGE. GREGORY OF NYSSA: Let no one think . . . we are disregarding the institution of marriage. We are not ignorant of the fact that this also is not deprived of God's blessing. But since there is sufficient support for it and since the common nature of man, bestowed on all who come to birth through marriage, automatically inclines in this direction— whereas virginity somehow goes against nature —it would be superfluous to go to the trouble of writing a plea for marriage or a eulogy of it. It is pointless to emphasize its indisputable inducement, I mean pleasure, unless there should be

---

[28]ANF 9:506*. [29]FC 83:206-7. [30]ANF 4:71. Cf. Bertrand de Margerie's comment (*An Introduction to the History of Exegesis* [Petersham, Mass.: St. Bede's Publications, 1995], 2:43 n. 145) on the responses of the Fathers to Tertullian's moral rigorism. Augustine seems to have explicitly condemned Tertullian's stand on second marriages as a reflection of his heretical Montanism and a contradiction of 1 Timothy 4:3 (*De Haeresibus* 86). [31]ANF 5:124*. [32]NPNF 1 10:49*.

need of such words because of some people who tamper with the teachings of the church on marriage, whom the apostle calls "those having their conscience branded." ON VIRGINITY 7.[33]

NOT DESPISING BUT TRANSCENDING. CYRIL OF JERUSALEM: Do not abhor meats as if they were taboo. The apostle evidently knew people like that, since he says that there are those "who forbid to marry and command to abstain from meats which God has created to be received with thanksgiving by those who believe." If therefore you are abstaining from these things, let it not be as from things abominated, or your reward is lost, but as good things let them be transcended, in the quest of the fairer spiritual rewards that are set before you. CATECHETICAL LECTURES 4.27.[34]

DIFFERENT VESSELS. JEROME: Have I not, I would ask, in the very forefront of my work[35] set the following preface: "We are no disciples of Marcion or of Manichaeus, to detract from marriage. Nor are we deceived by the error of Tatian, the chief of the Encratites, into supposing all cohabitation unclean. For he condemns and reprobates not marriage only but foods also which God has created for us to enjoy. We know that in a large house there are vessels not only of silver and of gold but of wood also and of earth.[36] We know, too, that on the foundation of Christ which Paul the master builder has laid, some build up gold, silver and precious stones; others, on the contrary, hay, wood and stubble."[37] LETTERS 48.2.[38]

AGAINST THE MANICHAEANS. AUGUSTINE: The fact that the Lord was invited and came to the wedding, even without considering the mystical meaning, was meant to affirm what he himself created.[39] For there were going to be those, about whom the apostle spoke, who would forbid marriage and say that marriage is an evil and that the devil created it, although the same Lord in the Gospel, when asked whether a man is

allowed to divorce his wife for any reason, replied that he is not allowed except in the case of fornication.[40] TRACTATES ON JOHN 9.2.[41]

FOOD LAWS MAY BE CONTRARY TO SOUND DOCTRINE. AUGUSTINE: The church of God, established in the midst of much chaff and much cockle, tolerates many things, yet it does not approve or accept in silence or practice those things that are contrary to faith and good living. Therefore, what you wrote of certain brothers refraining from meat because they believe it to be unclean is very clearly against faith and sound doctrine. LETTERS 55.19.35-20.36.[42]

CONTINENCE SEEKS OUT PLAIN, WHOLESOME FOODS. BASIL THE GREAT: It should also be laid down as essential that continency is inexorably demanded of combatants for godliness, so that they may bring the body into subjection, "for every athlete exercises self-control in all things."[43] However, to avoid being classed with the enemies of God who are seared in their conscience and, therefore, abstain from food which God has made for the faithful to partake of with thanksgiving, we should taste each dish when occasion offers so as to indicate to those looking on that "all things are clean to the clean"[44] and that "every creature of God is good and nothing to be rejected that is received with thanksgiving; for it is sanctified by the word of God and prayer." The aim of continency must nevertheless be kept in mind also, to the extent that we satisfy our need with the plainer foods and those necessary to sustain life, avoiding the evil of taking our fill of them and abstaining absolutely from those foods whose sole purpose is to

---

[33]FC 58:31*. [34]LCC 4:114. [35]Jerome is citing from his work *Against Jovinian*. [36]Cf. 2 Tim 2:20. [37]1 Cor 3:10-12. [38]NPNF 2 6:67. [39]Augustine is commenting on Jesus' presence and activity at the wedding in Cana of Galilee (Jn 2:1-11). [40]Cf. Mt 19:3-9. [41]FC 78:195*. [42]FC 12:291. [43]1 Cor 9:25. [44]Tit 1:15.

give delight. The Long Rules, q.18.r.[45]

4:4-5 Everything Created by God Is Good

Clean Hearts. Chrysostom: By speaking thus of things eatable, he by anticipation impugns the heresy of those who introduce an uncreated matter and assert that these things proceed from it. . . . He lays down two positions. The first is that no creature of God is unclean. The second is that if it were to become so, you have a remedy: seal it, give thanks and glorify God, and all the uncleanness passes away. . . . So a thing is not unclean by nature but becomes so through your willful disobedience. What then, is not swine's flesh unclean? By no means, when it is received with thanksgiving and with the seal. Nor is anything else. It is your unthankful disposition to God that is unclean. **Homilies on 1 Timothy 12.**[46]

Abstinence Not Necessary. Basil the Great: This, assuredly, appeared to me to be ridiculous—to vow to abstain from pork. Therefore, teach them to refrain from foolish prayers and promises; nevertheless, allow the use to be a matter of indifference. No creature of God which is received with thanksgiving is to be rejected. Therefore, the vow is ridiculous; the abstinence is not necessary. **Letters 199.28.**[47]

Creation an Inward Harmony. Gregory of Nyssa: The whole of creation is in inward harmony, since the bond of concord is nowhere broken by the natural opposition. In the same way the divine wisdom also provides a blending and admixture of the sensible with the intelligible nature, so that all things equally participate in the good and no existing thing is deprived of a share in the higher nature. Now the sphere corresponding to the intelligible nature is a subtle and mobile essence, which by virtue of its special nature and its transcending the world has a great affinity with the intelligible. Yet, for the reason given, a superior wisdom provides a min-gling of the intelligible with the sensible creation. In that way, as the apostle says, "no part of creation is to be rejected," and no part fails to share in the divine fellowship. On this account the divine nature produces in man a blending of the intelligible and the sensible, just as the account of creation teaches. **Address on Religious Instruction 6.**[48]

Evil Is Like Rusted Steel. Gregory of Nyssa: Let it be observed that there is no such thing in the world as evil irrespective of a will. Evil is not discoverable in a substance apart from willing. Every creature of God is good, and nothing of his "to be rejected." All that God made was "very good."[49] But the habit of sinning entered as we have described, and with fatal quickness, into the life of man. From that small beginning spread into this infinitude of evil. Then that godly beauty of the soul which was an imitation of the Archetypal Beauty, like fine steel blackened with vicious rust, preserved no longer the glory of its familiar essence but was disfigured with the ugliness of sin. **On Virginity 12.**[50]

Evil Resides in Volition, Not Creation. Augustine: Because sin or iniquity is not a seeking of things evil by nature but an abandonment of the better things, this is found written in Scripture. "Every creature is good." Every tree that God planted in paradise was good. Man, therefore, did not desire anything evil by nature when he touched the forbidden tree. But by departing from what was better he himself committed an act that was evil. **The Nature of the Good 34.**[51]

Uncleanness in the Appetite. Augustine: It is not the uncleanness of meat that I fear, but

---

[45]FC 9:273-74. [46]NPNF 1 13:445. [47]FC 28:54. [48]LCC 3:278-79. [49]1 Tim 4:4, from Gen 1:31. [50]NPNF 2 5:357*. [51]LCC 6:229.

the uncleanness of an incontinent appetite. CONFESSIONS 10.31.46.[52]

CREATION GOOD BUT NOT DIVINE. AUGUSTINE: As there is an unconscious worship of idols and devils in the fanciful legends of the Manichaeans, so they knowingly serve the creature in their worship of the sun and the moon. And in what they call their service of the Creator they really serve their own fancy, and not the Creator at all. For they deny that God created those things which the apostle plainly declares to the creatures of God, when he says of food, "Every creature of God is good, and nothing to be refused, if it is received with thanksgiving." This is sound doctrine.... The apostle praises the creature of God but forbids the worship of it. And in the same way Moses gives due praise to the sun and moon, while at the same time he states the fact of their having been made by God. They have been placed by him in their

courses—the sun to rule the day, and the moon to rule the night. REPLY TO FAUSTUS THE MANICHAEAN 14.11.[53]

SELF-RESTRAINT THE GOAL. LEO THE GREAT: The first cause of sin crept in from the enjoyment of food. What more salutary gift of God does our redeemed liberty use than that the will, which once did not know how to restrain itself from forbidden things, now knows how to restrain itself from lawful things? "Every creature of God is good, and nothing ought to be rejected, which is received with the giving of thanks." We were not created to seek out all the riches of the world with a foul and shameless greed. We can restrain voluntarily from what is lawful. SERMONS 81.1.[54]

---

[52]LCC 7:229. [53]NPNF 1 4:210*. [54]FC 93:350.

4:6-16 PERSONAL DISCIPLINE FOR TIMOTHY

[6]*If you put these instructions before the brethren, you will be a good minister of Christ Jesus, nourished on the words of the faith and of the good doctrine which you have followed.* [7]*Have nothing to do with godless and silly myths. Train yourself in godliness;* [8]*for while bodily training is of some value, godliness is of value in every way, as it holds promise for the present life and also for the life to come.* [9]*The saying is sure and worthy of full acceptance.* [10]*For to this end we toil and strive,*[j] *because we have our hope set on the living God, who is the Savior of all men, especially of those who believe.*

[11]*Command and teach these things.* [12]*Let no one despise your youth, but set the believers an example in speech and conduct, in love, in faith, in purity.* [13]*Till I come, attend to the public reading of scripture, to preaching, to teaching.* [14]*Do not neglect the gift you have, which was given you by prophetic utterance when the council of elders laid their hands upon you.* [15]*Practice these duties, devote yourself to them, so that all may see your progress.* [16]*Take heed to yourself and to your teaching; hold to that, for by so doing you will save both yourself and your hearers.*

j Other ancient authorities read *suffer reproach*

Overview: Christians are called to use what is seasonable (Chrysostom) and reject what is superficial in Jewish legal and apocryphal traditions (Origen, Theodore, Theodoret). The school of righteousness attempts to bring us to maturity by first teaching easy, elementary lessons (Athanasius, Basil). That which is truly useful has eternity as its frame of reference (Ambrose, Augustine, John Cassian). The ways of life and death are entirely different (Apostolic Constitutions). All humanity stands in need of the saving work of the triune God (Gregory of Nyssa, Augustine). The goal of Christian formation is the training and purification of the soul. This training is to be exemplified in the life of the teacher (Chrysostom). It is by the exercise of spiritual disciplines that the Christian teacher remains wise and faithful in ministry (Theodore). Praiseworthy living on the part of the Christian teacher is the key to effectiveness (Theodoret). What praise pastor-teachers accept must not be for themselves (Augustine). They are is to be examples of the good life (Athanasius, Augustine) and must give no excuse for those under their guidance to think the Lord's commands impossible (Basil). The pastor brings forth from the inexhaustible Scriptures treasures old and new (Origen, Chrysostom), preserving right doctrine and sound living, as did Paul (Caesarius). In this way the soul is fed by virtue (Athanasius). Good teaching occurs best in a highly particular context, not abstractly (Chrysostom). There remain differences of opinion among the Fathers as to whether presbyters and bishops are distinguishable (Chrysostom, Jerome, Theodore).

4:6 Nourished on the Words of the Faith

Fed by Virtue. Athanasius: Virtues and vices are the food of the soul, which can feed on either one, turning to whichever one it wants to. If it is bent toward moral excellence, it will be fed by virtue—by righteousness, temperance, meekness, endurance. In other words, it's just as St. Paul says, "being nourished by the word of truth." That's the way it was with our Lord, who said, "My food is to do the will of him who sent me."[1] Festal Letters 1.5.[2]

4:7a Godless and Silly Myths

Provide Honorable Interpretations. Origen: Let the church of God, therefore, in this spiritual way[3] understand the births, in this way receive the procreations, in this way uphold the deeds of the fathers with a fitting and honorable interpretation and in this way not disgrace the words of the Holy Spirit with foolish rabbinic fables[4] but reckon them to be full of honor, full of virtue and usefulness. Homilies on Genesis 6.3.[5]

Using What Is Seasonable. Chrysostom: By these are meant Jewish traditions, and he calls them "fables," either because of their falsehood or their unseasonableness. For what is seasonable is useful, but what is unseasonable is not only useless but injurious. Homilies on 1 Timothy 12.[6]

Falsely Reading the Law. Theodoret of Cyr: "Godless wives tales" are Jewish speculations in the form of false interpretations of the law and its proper observance. Interpretation of the First Letter to Timothy.[7]

Christian Apocrypha. Theodore of Mopsuestia: Paul is here rejecting apocryphal books that profess to contain his teaching or that of other apostles but that are really misrepresentations of that teaching. Commentary on 1 Timothy.[8]

---

[1]Jn 4:34. [2]ARL 52. [3]Origen is commenting specifically on the importance of engaging in spiritual interpretation of Scripture, lest the absurdities of heretical interpretation be countenanced. [4]See also Tit 1:14. [5]FC 71:126. [6]NPNF 1 13:445. [7]PG 82:813C/814C. [8]TEM 2:145.

4:7b *Train Yourself in Godliness*

Exercise Yourself in Godliness. Athanasius: Therefore St. Paul urges us to exercise our faith in the face of troubles. Having already come through them victoriously, he said, "Therefore I take pleasure in persecutions and weaknesses."[9] In another place he said, "Exercise yourself in godliness." He knew that those who choose to live godly lives are going to be persecuted, so he wanted his disciples to be aware of the difficulties they would face. Then when the trials and afflictions did come, they would have built up enough strength to handle them easily. You yourself know that when you've been looking forward to something, even if it's hard, you experience a secret joy when it actually comes. Festal Letters 10.3.[10]

A Gradual Process. Basil the Great: Surely only an infantile mind, like a baby who can only drink milk, is ignorant of the great mystery of our salvation. Education progresses gradually. The school of righteousness attempts to bring us to maturity by first teaching us easy, elementary lessons suited for our limited intelligence. Then God, who provides us with every good thing, leads us to the truth, by gradually accustoming our darkened eyes to its great light. In the deep reaches of his wisdom and the unsearchable judgments of his intelligence, he spares our weakness and prescribes a gentle treatment. He knows our eyes are accustomed to dim shadows, so he uses these at first. On the Holy Spirit 14.33.[11]

4:8 *Godliness Is of Value in Every Way*

True Usefulness. Ambrose: Some indeed put it thus, "Incline my heart unto Thy testimonies and not to what is useful." The reference is to that kind of usefulness which is always on the watch for making gains in business and has been bent and diverted by the habits of men to the pursuit of money. For as a rule most people call that only useful which is profitable, but we are speaking of that kind of usefulness which is sought in earthly loss "that we may gain Christ,"[12] whose gain is "godliness with contentment."[13] Great, too, is the gain whereby we attain to godliness, which is rich with God, not indeed in fleeting wealth but in eternal gifts, and in which rests no uncertain trial but grace constant and unending. There is therefore a usefulness connected with the body, and also one that has to do with godliness, according to the apostle's division, "Bodily exercise profits a little, but godliness is profitable for all things." Duties of the Clergy 2.6.26-27.[14]

Trouble Is Deflected. Augustine: "Godliness," then, "which is the true worship of God, is profitable to all things," since it deflects or blunts the troubles of this life and leads to that other life, our salvation, where we shall suffer no evil and enjoy the supreme and everlasting good. I exhort you as I do myself to pursue this happiness more earnestly and to hold to it with strong constancy. Letters 155.2.17.[15]

A Future Reward. John Cassian: St. Paul is plainly referring to this when he says, "bodily exercise is profitable for a little, but godliness" (by which he surely means charity) "is profitable for all things, having the promise of the life that now is and of the life to come." What is said to be profitable for a little cannot be profitable forever and cannot (of itself) bring a man to the perfect life. The phrase "for a little" might mean one of two things. It might mean "for a short time," since these bodily exercises are not going to last as long as the man who practices them. Or it might mean "only of little profit." Corporal austerity brings the first beginnings of progress, but it does not beget that perfect charity which

---

[9]2 Cor 12:10. [10]*ARL* 168. [11]*OHS* 56. [12]Phil 3:8. [13]1 Tim 6:6. [14]NPNF 2 10:48*. [15]FC 20:317.

has the promise of this life and the life to come. CONFERENCES 1.10.[16]

4:10 *The Savior of All, Especially of Those Who Believe*

GOD'S CARE FOR ALL. ORIGEN: Our reply to this[17] is that he attributes to us statements which we do not make. For we both read and know that God "loves everything that exists and hates nothing that he has made; for he would never have made anything if he had hated it."[18] . . . He is also called "Savior of all men, especially of those who believe," and his Christ is "a propitiation for our sins, but not for ours only, but also for the whole world."[19] . . . But now, according to our preaching, Jesus who is called the Christ of God by a certain traditional usage in the Bible has come on behalf of sinners in all places, that they may forsake their sin and entrust themselves to God. AGAINST CELSUS 4.28.[20]

THE TWO WAYS. ANONYMOUS: We also, following our teacher Christ, "who is the Savior of all men, especially of those that believe." are obliged to say that there are two ways. One is the way of life, the other of death. These have no comparison one with another, for they are very different, or rather entirely separate. The way of life is that of nature, but that of death was afterwards introduced—it not being according to the mind of God but from the snares of the adversary. CONSTITUTIONS OF THE HOLY APOSTLES 7.1.[21]

ALL HAVE NEED. AUGUSTINE: But in the Lord's own very humility (in consenting to be baptized by John) there is a marvelous medicine; one was baptizing, the other healing. You see, if Christ is the Savior of all, especially of the faithful—it is the apostle's judgment, and a true one, that Christ is the Savior of all—then nobody may say, "I have no need of a savior." If you say this, you are not bowing humbly to the doctor's

orders but perishing in your disease. SERMONS 292.4.[22]

NOT THREE SAVIORS BUT THREE IN ONE. GREGORY OF NYSSA: The Savior of all, especially of believers, is spoken of by the apostle as one. Yet no one argues from this expression that the Son does not save believers or that those who share in salvation receive it apart from the Spirit. But God who is over all is the Savior of all, while the Son brings salvation to effect by the grace of the Spirit. Yet on this account Scripture does not call them three Saviors, although salvation is recognized to come from the holy Trinity. AN ANSWER TO ABLABIUS: THAT WE SHOULD NOT THINK OF SAYING THERE ARE THREE GODS.[23]

4:11 *Command and Teach These Things*

DISTINGUISHING COMMANDING FROM TEACHING. CHRYSOSTOM: In some cases it is necessary to command, in others to teach. If you command in cases where teaching is required, you will become ridiculous. Again, if you teach where you ought to command, you are exposed to the same reproach. . . . Not to profess Judaism should be a simple command, but teaching is required when you would lead people persuasively to part with their possessions, to live chastely, or when you would discourse on faith. . . . But where the salvation of others is concerned, command and interpose with authority. This is not a case for moderation but for authority, lest the common good suffer. HOMILIES ON 1 TIMOTHY 13.[24]

4:12a *Let No One Despise Your Youth*

---

[16]LCC 12:201. [17]Origen is responding to the pagan philosopher Celsus's charge that the Christian God cares only for Christians and for no one else. [18]Wis 11:25. [19]See also 1 Jn 2:8. [20]OAC 203-4. [21]ANF 7:465*. [22]WSA 3/8:140*. [23]LCC 3:264. [24]NPNF 1 13:449*.

AGE NO IMPEDIMENT. CHRYSOSTOM: For what reason then does he write only to Titus and Timothy? It is because he had already committed the care of churches to them, and certain specified places had been assigned to them, but the others were listening in to what he said to them. For so preeminent in virtue was Timothy that his youth was no impediment to his promotion; therefore he writes, "Let no man despise your youth." . . . For where there is virtue, all other things are superfluous, and there can be no impediment. HOMILIES ON 1 TIMOTHY, ARGUMENT 2.[25]

4:12b Become an Example

FOR THE BENEFIT OF UNBELIEVERS. ATHANASIUS: But the wise servants of the Lord, who have really put on the new nature created in the likeness of God,[26] listen to what he says. They apply to themselves the commandment given to Timothy, "Set an example for the believers in speech, in conduct, in love, in faith, in purity." They keep the Easter feast so properly that even unbelievers, seeing their orderliness, must say, "God is truly with them."[27] FESTAL LETTERS 2.4.[28]

TO AVOID DAMAGE TO BELIEVERS. AUGUSTINE: In what way is it said that bad shepherds kill the sheep? By leading bad lives, by setting a bad example. Was it for nothing that a servant of God was told, one prominent among the members of the supreme shepherd, "Offering yourself in all company as an example of good works";[29] and "Be a model to the faithful". You see, even a strong sheep often enough, when he notices his pastor leading a bad life, if his eyes wander from the rules of the Lord and are attracted by human considerations, begins to say to himself, "If my pastor lives like that, who am I not to behave as he does?" He has killed a strong sheep. So if he has killed a strong sheep, what must he be doing for the others, seeing that by his bad life he has slaughtered what he hadn't fattened himself, but

has found fat and sturdy? SERMONS 46.9.[30]

THE POWER OF PRACTICE. AUGUSTINE: However, the life of the speaker has greater weight in determining whether he is obediently heard than any grandness of eloquence. For he who speaks wisely and eloquently but lives wickedly may benefit many students, even though, as it is written, he "may be unprofitable to his own soul."[31] . . . And thus they benefit many by preaching what they do not practice; but many more would be benefitted if they were to do what they say. For there are many who seek a defense of their evil lives in those of their superiors and teachers, responding in their hearts or, if it breaks forth so far, with their lips, and saying, "Why do you not do what you preach that I do?" Thus it happens that they do not obediently hear one who does not hear himself, and they condemn the word of God which is preached to them along with the preacher himself. Hence, when the apostle, writing to Timothy, said, "Let no man despise thy youth," he added the reason why he was not to be despised and said, "but be an example of the faithful in word, in conduct, in charity, in faith, in chastity." ON CHRISTIAN DOCTRINE 4.27.59-60.[32]

TO ANIMATE THOSE WEAKER THAN THEMSELVES. BASIL THE GREAT: So, then, the superior guide is to be mindful of the apostle's precept, "Be an example to the faithful." He should make his life a shining model for the observance of every commandment of the Lord, so that there may be no excuse for those under his guidance to think the Lord's commands impossible or readily to be set aside. He should consider first, then, that which is first in importance. He should be, by the love of Christ, so confirmed in humility that, even if he is silent, the example of his actions may afford more effective instruction

---

[25]NPNF 1 13:407. [26]Cf. Eph 4:24. [27]1 Cor 14:25. [28]ARL 62-63. [29]Tit 2:7. [30]WSA 3/2:268. [31]Sir 37:21. [32]ACD 164-65.

than any words. If, indeed, the goal of Christianity is the imitation of Christ according to the measure of his incarnation, insofar as is conformable with the vocation of each individual, they who are entrusted with the guidance of many others are obliged to animate those still weaker than themselves, by their assistance, to the imitation of Christ. The Long Rules, Q.43.R.[33]

The Skillful Management of Worldly Honor. Augustine: There is no way of resisting the temptation[34] to pride except by instilling the fear and love of God, through frequent pondering of the sacred books. But he who does this must show himself a model of patience and humility by attributing to himself less honor than is offered, neither swallowing all nor refusing all from those who honor him. What praise and honor he accepts he must not receive for himself—for he should refer all to God and despise human things—but for the sake of those whom he could not help if he were to lose dignity by too great self-depreciation. Applicable to this is the saying, "let no man despise your youth," recalling that he who said that said in another place, "If I yet pleased men, I should not be the servant of Christ."[35] Letters 22.2.7.[36]

4:13 Public Reading of Scripture, Preaching, Teaching

Out of His Treasury Things New and Old. Origen: Now "every scribe who has been made a disciple to the kingdom of heaven is like a man that is a householder who brings forth out of his treasury things new and old."[37] Therefore, it clearly follows by "conversion of the proposition,"[38] as it is called, that every one who does not bring forth out of his treasury things new and old is not a scribe who has been made a disciple for the kingdom of heaven. We must endeavor, therefore, in every way to gather in our heart, "by giving heed to reading, to exhortation, to teaching" and by "meditating in the

law of the Lord day and night."[39] We must observe not only the new oracles of the Gospels and of the apostles and their revelation but also the old things in the law "which has the shadow of the good things to come"[40] and in the prophets who prophesied in accordance with them. Commentary on Matthew 10.15.[41]

To Preserve Right Doctrine. Caesarius of Arles: In addition, if grief and trouble, even perils and reproaches from an unlearned people are stirred up as the result of a spirit of animosity, bear them with courage and constancy. Look rather to our Lord and Savior, the true shepherd who condescended to suffer, not only tribulation but even death, for the sake of the sheep. It is necessary for you to bear many adversities, if you want to preserve right doctrine and continuously to preach the word of God as it is expedient to do. The precepts of justice are always bitter to those who lead a wicked life. For this reason I exhort you today in the sight of God and his angels, and I declare with the voice of the apostle, "Devote yourself to the reading of Scripture, to preaching and teaching." Sermons 230.4.[42]

Paul's Own Work the Example. Chrysostom: In what did St. Paul surpass the rest of the apostles? . . . Is it not because of the excellence of his epistles? By this he has helped and will help and, as long as the human race remains, will never stop helping the faithful, not only of his own time but from that day to this and those who shall believe until the coming of Christ. For his writings fortify the churches all over the world like a wall of steel. . . . His writings are not only useful to us for the refutation of false doctrine and the establishment of the true, but

---

[33]FC 9:319*. [34]To pride, since one having been honored, is the object of envy. [35]Gal 1:10. [36]FC 12:55-56. [37]Mt 13:52. [38]Applying an abstract principle concretely. [39]Ps 1:2. [40]Heb 11:1. [41]ANF 9:422-23*. [42]FC 66:181.

they help us very greatly, too, in living a good life. . . . These facts are enough to show that he took great pains over this part of his work. But listen also to what he says to his disciple in a letter, "Give heed to reading, to exhortation, to teaching." On the Priesthood 4.7.[43]

Scripture an Infinite Resource. Chrysostom: It is not possible, I say, not possible, ever to exhaust the mind of the Scriptures. It is a well which has no bottom. Homilies on the Acts of the Apostles 19.5.[44]

4:14a The Gift You Have

The Gift Is Teaching. Chrysostom: Here he calls teaching "prophecy." Homilies on 1 Timothy 13.[45]

Do Not Neglect This Gift. Chrysostom: If you are willing, you will have more success with each other than we can have. For you both are with one another for a longer time, and you know more than we of each other's affairs. Further, you are not ignorant of each other's failings, and you have more freedom of speech, and love and intimacy. These are no small advantages for teaching but great and opportune moments for it. You will be more able than we both to reprove and exhort. And not this only, but because I am but one, whereas you are many; and you will be able, however many, to be teachers. Therefore I entreat you, do not "neglect this gift." Homilies on Hebrews 30.1.[46]

4:14b The Council of Elders

Presbyters and Bishops Different.

Chrysostom: He speaks here not of presbyters but of bishops. For presbyters cannot be supposed to have ordained a bishop. Homilies on 1 Timothy 13.[47]

Presbyters and Bishops the Same. Jerome: The apostle clearly teaches that presbyters are the same as bishops. . . . Writing to Titus the apostle says, "For this cause I left you in Crete, that you should set in order the things that are wanting, and appoint presbyters in every city, as I had instructed. If any be blameless, the husband of one wife, having believing children not accused of wantonness or unruly. For a bishop must be blameless as the steward of God."[48] And to Timothy he says, "Neglect not the gift of prophecy that is in you, which was given you through the laying on of hands of the presbytery." Letters 146.1.[49]

A Mediating Position. Theodore of Mopsuestia: Those whom he calls presbyters in this passage are not those whom we now call by that name—Paul does not usually allow to presbyters as such the power of ordination by the laying on of hands. Rather he says that the gathering of the apostles was present with him when he laid hands in his ordination. He calls this the "council of presbyters" as a designation of honor. It is in accordance with this custom that at the ordination of a bishop not one, but the multitude of bishops present, implement the ordination. Commentary on 1 Timothy.[50]

---

[43]COP 123. [44]NPNF 1 11:127*. [45]NPNF 1 13:449. [46]NPNF 1 14:504*. [47]NPNF 1 13:449. [48]Tit 1:5-7. [49]LCC 5:386. [50]TEM 2:150 (Greek).

5:1-22 TREATMENT OF ELDERS, WIDOWS AND PRESBYTERS

¹Do not rebuke an older man but exhort him as you would a father; treat younger men like brothers, older women like mothers, younger women like sisters, in all purity.

³Honor widows who are real widows. ⁴If a widow has children or grandchildren, let them first learn their religious duty to their own family and make some return to their parents; for this is acceptable in the sight of God. ⁵She who is a real widow, and is left all alone, has set her hope on God and continues in supplications and prayers night and day; ⁶whereas she who is self-indulgent is dead even while she lives. ⁷Command this, so that they may be without reproach. ⁸If any one does not provide for his relatives, and especially for his own family, he has disowned the faith and is worse than an unbeliever.

⁹Let a widow be enrolled if she is not less than sixty years of age, having been the wife of one husband; ¹⁰and she must be well attested for her good deeds, as one who has brought up children, shown hospitality, washed the feet of the saints, relieved the afflicted, and devoted herself to doing good in every way. ¹¹But refuse to enrol younger widows; for when they grow wanton against Christ they desire to marry, ¹²and so they incur condemnation for having violated their first pledge. ¹³Besides that, they learn to be idlers, gadding about from house to house, and not only idlers but gossips and busybodies, saying what they should not. ¹⁴So I would have younger widows marry, bear children, rule their households, and give the enemy no occasion to revile us. ¹⁵For some have already strayed after Satan. ¹⁶If any believing woman¹ has relatives who are widows, let her assist them; let the church not be burdened, so that it may assist those who are real widows.

¹⁷Let the elders who rule well be considered worthy of double honor, especially those who labor in preaching and teaching; ¹⁸for the scripture says, "You shall not muzzle an ox when it is treading out the grain," and, "The laborer deserves his wages." ¹⁹Never admit any charge against an elder except on the evidence of two or three witnesses. ²⁰As for those who persist in sin, rebuke them in the presence of all, so that the rest may stand in fear. ²¹In the presence of God and of Christ Jesus and of the elect angels I charge you to keep these rules without favor, doing nothing from partiality. ²²Do not be hasty in the laying on of hands, nor participate in another man's sins; keep yourself pure.

l Other ancient authorities read *man or woman*; others, simply *man*

OVERVIEW: It is clear that when Paul describes the treatment of elders, he is referring not strictly to the priests of the community but to the older leaders. They are to receive respectful and sensitive care, even in the administering of discipline. It is possible to correct without offense, if done with great discretion (CHRYSOSTOM) and charity (LEO). In cases where an elder sets a ruinous example to young people, he is to be confronted more severely (Gregory the Great).

Special care is to be given to the supervision of the work of widows in the church. It is important to distinguish those widows who deserve appropriate support from those who do not and to monitor the widows who are being supported, lest their time turn to idleness and mischief (Chrysostom, Theodore, Theodoret). The true widow is chaste and patient, and if she is without children (Theodore), she deserves the church's support (Chrysostom, Theodoret).

Children are to take care of parents (Chrysostom). This is their religious duty (Theodore). The law of God and of nature is violated by those who do not provide for their own family (Chrysostom). Each one has a special responsibility for one's own household (Augustine).

Widows who have no children are free to please God and serve others all the more (Chrysostom), persisting in prayer (Ambrose), remembering past enjoyments and being called to persevere (Jerome). Insofar as every soul understands that it is poor and desolate in this world, it identifies with widowhood, with God as its only defender (Augustine). The church is rightly called a widow because it is bereft of worldly protection and has placed its hope in its heavenly Bridegroom, who has transformed its swarthiness into beauty, its error into uprightness and its frailty into total constancy (Cassiodorus).

The real widow avoids luxurious living so as to remove a thousand other evils (Chrysostom). It is an idle pretense that people can take their fill of pleasure with their faith and purity and mental uprightness unimpaired (Jerome). The compulsively pleasure-seeking body is dead on account of sin even while it is alive (Augustine). Many whose bodies are supposedly still alive are already dead and cannot praise God, while many whose bodies seem dead, bless and praise God (John Cassian). Paul admonishes

one who has professed perpetual widowhood to God but then has later married, having treated superficially her agreement with God (Chrysostom). Various writers differ on whether this instruction is addressed primarily to deaconesses or to those enrolled in the order of widows (Theodore, Pelagius). Marriage is the ordained means of procreation, the guarantee of chastity and the bond of union (Augustine). Second marriages, sometimes preferable (Chrysostom), may offer a helping hand to those who are down but not a crown to those who stand (Jerome).

With regard to the presbyters, the support of those who are worthy and effective must be generous, while discipline, in the case of accusations of wrongdoing, must be carefully and firmly administered, once due process has taken place (Chrysostom, Theodore, Theodoret).

Second marriages for church leaders are discouraged (Tertullian, Origen), although this does not make them impure (Chrysostom). The widow becomes a pattern for chastity (Ambrose, Theodoret). Hospitality is to be shown as if one were receiving Christ himself (Chrysostom).

Liberality should be neither too freely shown to those who are unsuitable, nor too sparingly bestowed upon the needy (Ambrose). Jesus did not hesitate to have a purse (Augustine). Preaching is hard work worthy of support (Chrysostom). It is the duty of the pastor to function as the common father of both the men and women of the congregation (Theodore).

There are times when to punish is to ruin but to leave unpunished may ruin even more (Augustine). A feigned kindness to the wicked is a betrayal of the truth (Basil). The hired hand is one who does not provide admonition to the fallen (Augustine). Anyone who gives the authority that arises from his office to one living in evil draws down on his own head all the fire of that man's sins (Chrysostom). The peace and order of the Lord's whole household will be shaken if what is required in the body be not found in the head (Leo).

5:1 Do Not Rebuke but Exhort

GREAT DISCRETION. CHRYSOSTOM: Admonition in its own nature tends to be offensive, particularly when it is addressed to an older man, and when it proceeds from a young man, too, there is an intensified impression of forwardness. By the manner and mildness of it, therefore, one had best soften it. For it is possible to correct without offense, if one will only make a point of this: it requires great discretion, but it may be done. HOMILIES ON 1 TIMOTHY 13.[1]

CORRECTION WITH CHARITY. LEO THE GREAT: Among our negligent and sluggish brothers there is generally something requiring correction by a sterner show of authority. But the correction should be applied so as not to destroy charity. Hence, also, the blessed apostle Paul, instructing Timothy in the government of the church, says, "Do not rebuke an elderly man, but exhort him as you would a father, and young men as brothers, elderly women as mothers, younger women as sisters in all chastity." If, by the apostle's direction, this moderation is to be shown to any members of lesser rank, how much more should it be displayed without offense toward our brothers and fellow bishops? LETTERS 14.1.[2]

A RUINOUS EXAMPLE FOR YOUTH. GREGORY THE GREAT: The preacher of almighty God, Paul the apostle, says, "Do not rebuke an older man." This rule is to be observed in cases where the fault of an older man does not draw the hearts of the younger into ruin through his example. But when an elder sets an example to the young for their ruin, he is to be confronted with severe rebuke. For of him it is written, "You are all a snare to the young."[3] LETTERS 9.1.[4]

5:3 Honor Widows Who Are Real Widows

THE WIDOW'S VIRTUE. AMBROSE: So, then, a widow is not only marked off by bodily absti-

nence but is distinguished by virtue. It is not I who give this command but the apostle. I am not the only person to do them honor, but the teacher of the Gentiles did so first, when he said, "Honor widows that are widows indeed. But if any widow has children or nephews, let her first learn to govern her own house and to take care of her parents." Thus we encourage every inclination of affection in a widow to love her children and to do her duty to her parents. So when discharging her duty to her parents she is teaching her children and is rewarded herself by her own compliance with duty, in that what she performs for others benefits herself. CONCERNING WIDOWS 2.7.[5]

INCAPABLE OF SELF-SUPPORT. JEROME: [Paul] is training a church still untaught in Christ and making provision for people of all stations but especially for the poor, the charge of whom has been committed to himself and Barnabas.[6] Thus he wishes only those to be supported by the exertions of the church who cannot labor with their own hands and who are widows indeed, approved by their years and by their lives. LETTERS 79.7.[7]

THE TRUE WIDOW. CHRYSOSTOM: In order to be a virgin, it is not enough merely to avoid sex. Many other things are necessary: blamelessness and perseverance. Similarly the loss of a husband does not constitute a true widow, but rather patience, with chastity and distance from all men. Such widows he justly bids us honor, and indeed support. For they need support, being left desolate and having no husband to stand up for them. HOMILIES ON 1 TIMOTHY 13.[8]

WIDOWS IN DEED AS WELL AS IN WORD. THEODORE OF MOPSUESTIA: Paul's intention is

---

[1]NPNF 1 13:450*. [2]FC 34:58-59. [3]Is 42:22. [4]NPNF 2 13:1*.
[5]NPNF 2 10:392. [6]Cf. Gal 2:9-10. [7]NPNF 2 6:166. [8]NPNF 1 13:450*.

precisely not to give honor to women who have given only a promise of widowhood but rather to give honor to those who have clearly fulfilled the promise by their action. COMMENTARY ON 1 TIMOTHY.[9]

CHURCHLY ASSISTANCE. THEODORET OF CYR: Those faithful widows who have no other support must have churchly assistance. INTERPRETATION OF THE FIRST LETTER TO TIMOTHY.[10]

5:4 Let Them First Learn Their Religious Duty

REPAY YOUR PARENTS? CHRYSOSTOM: Observe the discretion of Paul, how often he urges us to attend to human considerations. For he does not here lay down any great and lofty motive but one that is easy to be understood: "to requite their parents." Why? For bringing them up and educating them. It is as if he should say, you have received from them great care. They are departed. You cannot compensate them. For you did not bring them forth or nourish them. Compensate them in their descendants. Repay the debt through the children. HOMILIES ON 1 TIMOTHY 13.[11]

THE CHILDREN'S RELIGIOUS DUTY. THEODORE OF MOPSUESTIA: It is the children and grandchildren who should learn their religious duties, namely, to care for widowed forebears, and not the widows who are to learn, for it is precisely they who are worthy of assistance, partly because they have no children. COMMENTARY ON 1 TIMOTHY.[12]

5:5 She Has Set Her Hope on God

SHE IS UNENCUMBERED. CHRYSOSTOM: To whom is this said? To those who have no children, because they are more highly approved and have a greater opportunity of pleasing God, because all their chains are loosened to them. There is no one to hold them fast, no one to

compel them to drag their chains after them. You are separated from your husband but are united to God. You have not a fellow servant for your associate, but you have your Lord. HOMILIES ON 1 THESSALONIANS 6.[13]

SHE STILL HAS GOD. CHRYSOSTOM: But if any one has no children, he means, she is desolate. Her he especially consoles, saying that she is most truly a widow who has lost not only the consolation of a husband but that arising from children, yet she has God in the place of all. HOMILIES ON 1 TIMOTHY 13.[14]

PERSIST IN PRAYER. AMBROSE: And you, O widow, find those who will pray for you. If as a true widow and desolate you hope in God, continue constant in supplications. Persist in prayers. Treat your body as dying daily, that by dying you may live again. Avoid pleasures, that you, too, being sick, may be healed. CONCERNING WIDOWS 9.56.[15]

MAINTAIN PERSEVERANCE. JEROME: A widow who has ceased to have a husband to please, and who in the apostle's language is a widow indeed, needs nothing more earnestly than perseverance. Remembering past enjoyments, she knows what gave her pleasure and what she has now lost. By rigid fasting and vigils she must quench the fiery darts of the devil.[16] LETTERS 54.7.[17]

WE ARE ALL WIDOWS. AUGUSTINE: When the Lord exhorted us to pray always and not to faint,[18] he told of the widow whose continuous appeal brought a wicked and impious judge, who scorned both God and man, to hear her cause. From this it can be easily understood how widows, beyond all others, have the duty of applying

---

[9]TEM 2:155. [10]PG 82:817B/818B. [11]NPNF 1 13:450*. [12]TEM 2:155-56 (Greek). [13]NPNF 1 13:351*. [14]NPNF 1 13:450-51*. [15]NPNF 2 10:400*. [16]Eph 6:16. [17]NPNF 2 6:104-5. [18]Cf. Lk 18:1-5.

themselves to prayer, since an example was taken from widows to encourage us all to develop a love of prayer. But, in a practice of such importance, what characteristic of widows is singled out but their poverty and desolation? Therefore, insofar as every soul understands that it is poor and desolate in this world, as long as it is absent from the Lord,[19] it surely commends its widowhood, so to speak, to God its defender, with continual and most earnest prayer. LETTERS 130.15.29-30.[20]

THE CHURCH IS THE WIDOW. CASSIODORUS: The church is called Christ's widow, because she is stripped of all worldly help and places her hope solely in the Lord. Like a widow, she suffers the shameful actions of evil men, the most cruel plunderings of the wicked. Like a woman deprived of a husband's aid, she always grieves and is always worn out, yet she enjoys the unchanging steadfastness of a most chaste mind. . . . She is called a widow because she is bereft of worldly protection and has placed her hope in her heavenly Bridegroom, who has transformed her swarthiness into beauty, her error into uprightness, her cruelty into devotion and her frailty into total constancy. EXPLANATION OF THE PSALMS 131.15.[21]

5:6 Dead Even While She Lives

BEWARE OF LUXURY. CHRYSOSTOM: To live in luxury does not seem in itself to be a manifest and admitted crime. But then it brings forth in us great evils—drunkenness, violence, extortion and plunder. For the prodigal and sumptuous liver, bestowing extravagant service on the belly, is often compelled to steal, and to seize the property of others and to use extortion and violence. If, then, you avoid luxurious living, you remove the foundation of extortion, and plunder, and drunkenness, and a thousand other evils, cutting away the root of iniquity from its extremity. Hence Paul says that "she who lives in pleasure is dead while she lives." HOMILIES

CONCERNING THE STATUES 15.4.[22]

AVOID INDULGENT LIVING. CHRYSOSTOM: It is not possible, not possible at all, for those who enjoy an easy life and freedom from want in this world, who continually indulge themselves in every way, who live randomly and foolishly, to enjoy honor in the other world. For if poverty does not trouble them, still desire troubles them and they are afflicted because of this, which brings more than a little pain. If disease does not threaten them, still their temper grows hot, and it requires more than an ordinary struggle to overcome anger. If trials do not come to test them, still evil thoughts continually attack. It is no common task to bridle foolish desire, to stop vain glory, to restrain presumption, to refrain from luxury, to persevere in austerity. A person who does not do these things and others like them cannot be saved. As testimony that those who live luxuriously cannot be saved, hear what Paul says about the widow: "she who is self-indulgent is dead even while she lives." ON LAZARUS AND THE RICH MAN 3.[23]

SWIMMING IN PLEASURE. JEROME: It is difficult, or rather impossible, when we are swimming in luxury or pleasure, not to think of what we are doing. And it is an idle pretense which some put forward that they can take their fill of pleasure with their faith and purity and mental uprightness unimpaired. It is a violation of nature to revel in pleasure, and the apostle gives a caution against this very thing when he says, "She that gives herself to pleasure is dead while she lives." The bodily senses are like horses madly racing, but the soul like a charioteer holds the reins. And as the horses without a driver go at breakneck speed, so the body, if it be not governed by the reasonable soul, rushes to its own destruction. AGAINST JOVINIAN 2.9-10.[24]

---

[19]Cf. 2 Cor 5:6. [20]FC 18:400. [21]ACW 53:329. [22]NPNF 1 9:442*. [23]OWP 67. [24]NPNF 2 6:395*.

Dead While Alive. Augustine: But there is a kind of death that the apostle detests when he says of the widow, "But she that lives in pleasures is dead while she is living." Hence, the soul which was impious but has now become pious is said to have come back to life from the dead and to live on account of justification by faith. The body, on the contrary, is not only said to be about to die on account of the departure of the soul, which will come to pass, but, in a certain number of passages, it is even spoken of as already dead on account of the great weakness of flesh and blood, as where the apostle says, "The body, it is true, is dead on account of sin, the spirit is life on account of justice."[25] On the Trinity 4.3.5.[26]

Some Whose Bodies Seem Dead Praise God. John Cassian: No one—not even though he call himself a Christian or a monk a thousand times over—confesses God while he is sinning. No one remembers God while he allows what the Lord hates. It is like pretending he is a faithful servant while he takes no notice of his master's commands. St. Paul says of a widow, "She that gives herself to pleasure is dead while she lives." This is the kind of death he means. Many whose bodies are alive are dead and in hell and cannot praise God. And many whose bodies are dead bless and praise God together in the spirit. . . . In the Apocalypse the souls of the martyrs are described as praying to God as well as praising him. Conferences 1.14.3, 4.[27]

Yielding to Indulgence. Caesarius of Arles: May God avert from us the sentence which will be in hard pursuit of those who indulge in any kind of wickedness, who are adorned with the most precious ornaments for the sake of vanity and worldly pomp. Such persons seize the property of another, are filled even to the point of vomiting with many delicacies, bury themselves in excessive drinking and store up by almsgiving little or nothing for heaven. It is of these persons that the apostle says, "The soul which gives herself up to plea-sures is dead while she is still alive." Sermons 151.8.[28]

5:8 *If Any One Does Not Provide*

Nature Is Violated. Chrysostom: And what will be said, if instructing others, someone neglects his own family, though he has greater capacities and a higher obligation to benefit those near? Will it not be said: "Aha! These 'Christians' are affectionate indeed, who neglect their own relatives!" "He is worse than an infidel." So what? One who does not benefit those far away benefits even less those nearer. What is meant is this: The law of God and of nature is violated by him who does not provide for his own family. Homilies on 1 Timothy 14.[29]

The Order of Charity. Augustine: Now God, our master, teaches two chief precepts: love of God and love of neighbor. In them one finds three objects for his love: God, himself and his neighbor. One who loves God is not wrong in loving himself. It follows, therefore, that he will be concerned also that his neighbor should love God, since he is told to love his neighbor as himself. And the same is true of his concern for his wife, his children, for the members of his household, and for all others, so far as is possible. And, for the same end, he will wish his neighbor to be concerned for him, if he happens to need that concern. For this reason he will be at peace, as far as in him lies, with all. In that peace he will live in ordered harmony. The basis of this order is the observance of two rules: first, to do no harm to anyone, and, second, to help everyone whenever possible. To begin with, therefore, one has a responsibility for his own household—obviously, both in the order of nature and in the framework of human society. He has easier and more immediate contact with

---

[25]Rom 1:17. [26]FC 45:136. [27]ACW 57:53. [28]FC 47:332. [29]NPNF 1 13:453*.

them. The City of God 19.14.[30]

5:9a Let a Widow Be Enrolled

Widowhood a Spiritual Reality. Chrysostom: It is possible to be a widow and not be enrolled in the rank of widows, as when a woman has not as yet accepted this way of life. . . . Paul allows the uncommitted woman to remarry if she so desires. But he strongly admonishes the one who has professed perpetual widowhood to God but then has later gotten married, because she has treated superficially her commitment to God. On Virginity 39.2.[31]

Widows Only, or Deaconesses As Well? Theodore of Mopsuestia: What is said here applies only to the order of widows and not to deaconesses, as some believe. Commentary on 1 Timothy.[32]

Addressed to Women Considering Ordination as Deaconesses. Pelagius: What is being said here applies in particular to the women who are being considered for ordination as deaconesses. Pelagius's Commentary on the First Letter to Timothy.[33]

5:9b The Wife of One Husband

Second Marriages Forbidden the Ordained. Origen: Not only fornication but also a second marriage excludes someone from office in the church. Anyone twice married may be neither a bishop nor a presbyter nor a deacon nor a widow. Homilies on Luke 17.10.[34]

Love Continence. Tertullian: So far as we can, let us love the opportunity of continence. As soon as it offers itself, let us resolve to accept it, so that what one may not have had the strength to follow in matrimony one may now follow in widowhood. Continence in widowhood transcends the command that has previously been necessary for marriage. How detrimental to faith, how obstructive to holiness, second marriages are. The discipline of the church and the prescription of the apostle also declare this, when he does not permit men twice married to preside over a church. The same is true when he would not grant a widow admittance into an order unless she had been "the wife of one man." To His Wife 1.7.[35]

Second Marriages Discouraged. Chrysostom: But why does he discourage second marriages? Is the thing condemned? By no means. That is heretical. Only he would have her henceforth occupied in spiritual things, transferring all her care to virtue. For marriage is not an impure state but one of much occupation. He speaks of their having leisure, not of their being more pure by remaining unmarried. Homilies on 1 Timothy 14.[36]

An Encouragement to Chastity. Theodoret of Cyr: The teaching that a widow should be the wife of only one man is an encouragement to chastity within marriage, not a forbidding of second marriages. Interpretation of the First Letter to Timothy.[37]

The Virtues of the Widow. Ambrose: It is not that old age alone makes the widow. Rather the virtues of the widow may become the duties of old age. For she certainly is the more prone to virtue who represses the heat of youth and the impetuous ardor of youthful age, coveting neither the tenderness of a husband nor the abundant delights of children. She rises above one who, now worn out in body, cold in age, of ripe years, can neither grow warm with pleasures nor hope for offspring. Concerning Widows 2.9.[38]

---

[30]CG 873*. [31]COV 58. [32]TEM 2:158-59. [33]PETE 494. [34]FC 94:75. [35]ANF 4:43*. See the comment at p. 184 n. 30. [36]NPNF 1 13:454. [37]PG 82:817D/818D. [38]NPNF 2 10:392*.

5:10a *Shown Hospitality*

As If Receiving Christ Himself. Chrysostom: Observe, the hospitality here spoken of is not merely a friendly reception but one given with zeal and alacrity, with readiness, and going about it as if one were receiving Christ himself. Homilies on 1 Timothy 14.[39]

5:10b *Washed the Feet of the Saints*

A Necessity Even for the Holiest. Origen: It is possible, however, that even one who is a saint needs the washing of feet, since even the widow who is enrolled into ecclesiastical honor is examined, along with her other good works, also about this, "If she has washed the feet of saints." . . . Consequently, the faithful are obliged to do this in whatever station of life they happen to be, whether bishops and presbyters, who seem to be in ecclesiastical prominence, or even those in other positions of honor in the world. This means that the master comes to wash the feet of the believing servant, and parents the feet of their son. Commentary on John 32.131-33.[40]

The Quality of Mind. Theodoret of Cyr: In emphasizing hospitality and the care of the saints as important qualifications for the widow, Paul's goal is not to focus on a certain quantity of virtuous activity but rather on a quality of mind. Interpretation of the First Letter to Timothy.[41]

5:10c *Devoted Herself to Doing Good*

Faithful Widowhood a Title of the Greatest Honor. Chrysostom: The title of true widow is not a title of calamity but of honor, even of the greatest honor. . . . "Heavens," cried a sophist teacher [of Chrysostom as a young man], "what women there are among the Christians." So great is the admiration and praise enjoyed by widowhood not only among ourselves but also among those who are outside the church. And being aware of all this, the blessed Paul said, "Let not a widow be enrolled under threescore years of age." And even after this great qualification of age he does not permit her to be ranked in this sacred society but mentions some additional requisites. She must be "well reported of for good works, if she has brought up children, if she has lodged strangers, if she has washed the saints' feet, if she has relieved the afflicted, if she has diligently followed every good work." Heavens! What testing and scrutiny! How much virtue does he demand from the widow, and how precisely does he define it! He would not have done this had he not intended to entrust to her a position of honor and dignity. Letter to a Young Widow 2.[42]

5:11 *Refuse to Enroll Younger, Wanton Widows*

Apostolic Condemnation. Chrysostom: Paul himself has condemned women who chose widowhood but then do not desire to abide by their decision. On Virginity 36.2.[43]

Promise Keeping. Chrysostom: Why then, you ask, did Paul forbid young women to remain as widows even if they were willing? . . . Do you not see that it is not those who wish to keep their widowhood but rather those who prefer to marry after being widowed whom he forbids to remain as widows and to be appointed to that holy company? And he does so very wisely. For if you should intend to engage in second marriages, he says, do not profess widowhood. For breaking a promise is much worse than not promising at all. Against Remarriage 3.[44]

---

[39]NPNF 1 13:454. [40]FC 89:367. [41]PG 82:819A/820A. [42]NPNF 1 9:122*. [43]COV 52. [44]COV 134. Cf. Chrysostom *Homilies on 1 Corinthians* 19 (CMFL 40): "'But if you marry, you do not sin' [1 Cor 7:28]. He does not mean someone who has vowed to remain a virgin. She would be sinning if she married, because if widows incur condemnation for violating their pledge and seeking second marriage, the judgment for virgins would be even greater."

Young Widows May Marry. Augustine: When the apostle says elsewhere, "I desire that the younger widows marry, bear children, rule their households," he recommends the good of marriage with wisdom and apostolic authority. He does not impose the duty of bearing children. It is not to be treated as it were a law to be observed, at least in the case of those who have chosen the state of continence. Finally, he makes it clear why he has said this, by adding, "Give the adversary no occasion for abusing us. For already some have turned aside after Satan." By these words he wishes us to understand that for the young widows whom he thought it fitting to be married, continence would have been better than marriage, but that it was better for them to marry than to turn aside after Satan, that is, by looking back to former things after having chosen the excellent state of chastity in virginity or widowhood, to abandon it and to perish. The Excellence of Widowhood 8.11.[45]

5:12 They Incur Condemnation

The King's Highway. Jerome: The apostle, in concluding his discussion of marriage and virginity, is careful to observe a right balance in discriminating between them. Turning neither to the right hand nor to the left, he keeps to the King's highway[46] and thus fulfills the injunction, "Be not righteous overmuch."[47] . . . Do we not clearly show by this language[48] what is typified in the Holy Scriptures by the terms *right* and *left*, and also what we take to be the meaning of the words "Be not righteous overmuch"? We turn to the left if, following the lust of Jews and Gentiles, we burn for sexual intercourse. We turn to the right if, following the error of the Manichaeans, we under a pretense of chastity entangle ourselves in the meshes of unchastity. But we keep to the King's highway if we aspire to virginity yet refrain from condemning marriage. Can anyone, moreover, be so unfair in his criticism of my poor treatise as to allege that I condemn first marriages, when he reads my opinion of second

ones as follows, "The apostle, it is true, allows second marriages, but only to such women as are bent upon them, to such as cannot contain,[49] lest 'when they have begun to wax wanton against Christ they marry, having condemnation because they have rejected their first faith,' and he makes this concession because many 'are turned aside after Satan.' But they will be happier if they abide as widows." Letters 48.8.[50]

Immature Vows. Augustine: The apostle mentions evil, unmarried women who are gossipers and busybodies and says that this vice springs from idleness. "And further," he says, "being idle, they learn to go about from house to house, and are not only idle, but gossipers as well as busybodies, mentioning things they ought not." He had previously said of these, "But refuse younger widows, for when they have wantonly turned away from Christ, they wish to marry and are to be condemned because they have broken their first pledge," that is, they did not persevere in what they had first vowed. However, he does not say "They marry" but "They wish to marry," for it is not the love of their noble vow which prevents many of them from marrying but fear of outright indecency. This itself springs from pride by which human displeasure is more dreaded than the divine displeasure. Holy Virginity 33.34-34.34.[51]

5:13 They Learn to Be Idlers

Idle and Unblushing Effrontery. Jerome: Paul speaks of idle persons and busybodies, whether virgins or widows, such as go from house to house calling on married women. They display an unblushing effrontery greater than that of a stage parasite. Cast them from you as you would the plague. For "evil communications

---

[45]FC 16:291. [46]Num 20:17. [47]Eccles 7:16. [48]Jerome has quoted from his own work, *Against Jovinian* 1.14. [49]1 Cor 7:9. [50]NPNF 2 6:70*. [51]FC 27:183.

corrupt good manners,"[52] and women like these care for nothing but their lowest appetites. They will often urge you, saying, "My dear creature, make the best of your advantages, and live while life is yours," and, "Surely you are not laying up money for your children." Given to wine and wantonness, they instill all manner of mischief into people's minds and induce even the most austere to indulge in enervating pleasures. LETTERS 22.29.[53]

THE AMBIGUITY OF SECOND MARRIAGES. JEROME: It is true that in writing to Timothy the apostle from fear of fornication is forced to countenance second marriage. . . . He is offering not a crown to those who stand but a helping hand to those who are down. What must a second marriage be if it is looked on merely as an alternative to the brothel! LETTERS 79.10.[54]

MARRIAGE ITSELF IS A GOOD. AUGUSTINE: Marriage is a good in all the things which are proper to the married state. And these are three: it is the ordained means of procreation, it is the guarantee of chastity, it is the bond of union. In respect of its ordination for generation the Scripture says, "I will therefore that the younger women marry, bear children, guide the house." As regards its guaranteeing chastity, it is said of it, "The wife has not power over her own body, but the husband; and likewise also the husband has not power over his own body, but the wife."[55] And considered as the bond of union, "What God has joined together, let no one put asunder."[56] ON NATURE AND ORIGINAL SIN 39.34.[57]

5:14 I Would Have Younger Widows Marry

SECOND MARRIAGES SOMETIMES PREFERABLE. CHRYSOSTOM: It is likely that many widows at that time had lived more recklessly and arrogantly after the death of their husbands, as if freed from some constraining tyranny of their husbands over them; and so some earn a bad reputation for themselves because of their

audacity. Drawing them away from this ruinous freedom, Paul leads them back to their former yoke. He says that if a widow intends to secretly cheapen and dishonor herself, it is much better to marry and "give our enemies no occasion to speak ill of us." Thus, because he did not want to furnish opportunities for rebuke or want the widow to live the wanton life of a harlot, he permitted second marriages. AGAINST REMARRIAGE 3.[58]

5:16 Let the Church Not Be Burdened

USEFUL LIBERALITY. AMBROSE: But if it is praiseworthy to have one's soul free from this failing of greed, how much more glorious is it to gain the love of the people by liberality. This should be neither too freely shown to those who are unsuitable, nor too sparingly bestowed upon the needy. . . . There is also another kind of liberality which the apostle teaches, "If any believing woman has relatives who are widows, let her assist them. Let the church not be burdened so that it may assist those who are real widows." Useful, then, is liberality of this sort. DUTIES OF THE CLERGY 2.15.68, 72-73.[59]

THE PARADIGM FOR HANDLING MONEY. AUGUSTINE: "But none of those reclining at table understood why he said this to him. For some thought that, because Judas held the purse, Jesus says to him, 'Buy the things that we need for the feast,' or that he should give something to the poor."[60] Therefore, the Lord, too, had a purse. Keeping safe the offerings from the faithful, he distributed both to the needs of his people and to others in need. The paradigm for handling church money was thereby established: We should understand that his teaching that

---

[52]1 Cor 15:33. [53]NPNF 2 6:35*. [54]NPNF 2 6:168. [55]1 Cor 7:14. [56]Mt 19:6. [57]NPNF 1 5:251*. [58]COV 135. For his opinion on the difficulties of second marriages, see Chrysostom *On Virginity* 37 (COV 53-55). [59]NPNF 2 10:54*. [60]Jn 13:28-29.

one must not take thought of tomorrow[61] was taught for this purpose, that no money should be kept by the saints, but that God should not be served for money and that justice should not be abandoned because of a fear of need. For the apostle too, looking ahead to the future, said, "If any believing woman has widowed relatives, let her provide sufficiently for them so that the church not be burdened, in order that it can have enough for true widows." TRACTATES ON JOHN 62.5.[62]

5:17a Worthy of Double Honor

DOUBLE STATUS. TERTULLIAN: The apostle has given them "double honor" as being both brothers and officers. ON FASTING 17.[63]

LIBERAL SUPPORT. CHRYSOSTOM: The "honor" of which he here speaks is attention to them and the supply of their necessities. . . . But what is double support? Double that of the widows, or of the deacons, or simply liberal support. HOMILIES ON 1 TIMOTHY 15.[64]

EFFECTIVE ELDERS. AMBROSIASTER: Effective presbyters should be rewarded not only with sublime honor but with earthly as well, that they not be burdened with poverty. COMMENTARY ON THE FIRST LETTER TO TIMOTHY.[65]

5:17b Who Labor in Preaching and Teaching

PREACHING IS HARD WORK. CHRYSOSTOM: Preaching really entails hard work. This fact Paul made plain when he said, "Let the presbyters who rule well be held worthy of double honor, especially those who labor in the word and in teaching." But you are responsible for making this toil light or heavy. If you despise my words or, though you do not despise them, do not embody them in your deeds, my toil will be heavy, because I am laboring fruitlessly and in vain. But if you pay attention and make my words manifest in your deeds, I shall not even be aware of the perspiration, for the fruit produced by my work will not permit me to feel the laboriousness of the toil. HOMILIES ON JOHN 22.1.[66]

TEACHING AND DOING. CHRYSOSTOM: For this is the ultimate aim of their teaching: to lead their disciples, both by what they do and what they say, into the way of that blessed life which Christ commanded. Example alone is not sufficient instruction. And this statement is not mine but the Savior's. For he says, "Whoever shall do and teach, he shall be called great."[67] Now if to do were the same as to teach, the second word would be superfluous. It would have been enough to say, "Whosoever shall do." But in fact by distinguishing these two he shows that example is one thing and instruction another. Each requires the other for perfect edification. ON THE PRIESTHOOD 4.8.[68]

5:19 Any Charge Against an Elder

AN OLDER PERSON OR A PRESBYTER? CHRYSOSTOM: May we then receive an accusation against a younger man or against any one at all without witnesses? Ought we not in all cases to come to our judgments with the greatest exactness? What then does he mean? Do not do this, he means, with any, but especially in the case of an elder. For he speaks of an elder not with respect to office but to age, since the young more easily fall into sin than their elders. HOMILIES ON 1 TIMOTHY 15.[69]

CARE OF BOTH SEXES. THEODORE OF MOPSUESTIA: It is the duty of the presbyter to function as the common father of both the men and women of the congregation; because the care of both sexes involves seeing and speaking discreetly with the women, pastoral work must be

---

[61]Cf. Mt 6:34. [62]FC 90:40. [63]ANF 4:114. [64]NPNF 1 13:460. [65]CSEL 81 3:284. [66]FC 33:212. [67]Mt 5:19. [68]COP 125. [69]NPNF 1 13: 461.

done with great reverence. Furthermore, the duty of presbyters involves the administration of penitential discipline on admitted sinners and the exercise of oversight where such discipline is substandard. For both reasons the presbyters are vulnerable to charges. Commentary on 1 Timothy.[70]

No Secret Backbiting. Jerome: When a man is advanced in years, you must not be too ready to believe evil of him. His past life is itself a defense, and so also is his rank as an elder. Still, since we are human and sometimes in spite of the ripeness of our years fall into the sins of youth, if I do wrong and you wish to correct me, accuse me openly of my fault. Do not backbite me secretly. Letters 125.19.[71]

5:20 Rebuke Them in the Presence of All

Act Firmly. Chrysostom: Do not, he says, hastily cut them off, but carefully inquire into all the circumstances. When you have thoroughly informed yourself, then proceed against the offender with rigor, that others may take warning. For as it is wrong to condemn hastily and rashly, so not to punish manifest offenses is to open the way to others, and embolden them to offend. . . . Let us therefore love God with fear . . . as I have ever said, the threatenings of hell show the care of God for us no less than the promises of heaven. Homilies on 1 Timothy 15.[72]

A Dilemma. Augustine: And here is a dilemma which often occurs: If you punish a man, you may ruin him. If you leave him unpunished, you may ruin another. I admit that I make mistakes in this matter every day. Letters 95.[73]

The Hired Hand. Augustine: Who is the hired hand?[74] One who sees the wolf coming and flees. One who seeks his own things, not those of Jesus Christ. He does not dare openly to accuse the sinner. Suppose someone has sinned,

and sinned grievously. He ought to be reproached and perhaps excommunicated. But if he is excommunicated, you imagine, he will be an enemy, he will make plots, he will do harm when he can. Now consider one who seeks his own things, not those of Jesus Christ. He does not lose what he is pursuing, the advantage of a human friendship. He does not incur the distress of human enmities—he is quiet; he does not correct. Look, the wolf seizes the sheep's throat. The devil has persuaded a believer to commit adultery. You are silent; you do not scold. O hired hand, you saw the wolf coming and you fled. Tractates on John 46.8.[75]

Feigned Kindness Is Betrayal. Basil the Great: A feigned kindness to the wicked is a betrayal of the truth, an act of treachery to the community and a means of habituating oneself to indifference to evil. . . . "Them that sin, reprove before all," says the apostle, and he immediately adds the reason, saying, "that the rest also may have fear." The Long Rules, Q.27.R.[76]

5:22a Not Hasty in the Laying On of Hands

Baptism and Penance, Not Ordination. Tertullian: Baptism is not rashly to be administered. . . . Similarly, this precept is rather to be looked at carefully. . . . "Lay not hands easily on any; share not other men's sins." On Baptism 18.[77]

Entrusting a Madman with a Sword. Chrysostom: What does Paul say? If one who I

---

[70]TEM 2:170. [71]NPNF 2 6:251. [72]NPNF 1 13:461. [73]FC 18:118. [74]Jn 10:12. [75]FC 88:210-11. [76]FC 9:291. [77]ANF 3:677. In *On Penitence* 6, Tertullian carefully cautions against the "presumptuous" receiving of holy baptism, in which catechumens do not approach the sacrament with appropriate penitential fear (ACW 28:27). In *On Modesty* 18, Tertullian seems to apply 1 Timothy 5:22 and the laying on of hands to a ritual of penance preceding the Eucharist (ANF 4:94).

have ordained has sinned, do I share his blame and punishment? Yes, says he. One who authorizes evil is blameworthy. It is just as in the case of any one entrusting into the hands of a raging and insane person a sharply pointed sword, with which the madman commits murder, that one who gave the sword incurs the blame. So anyone that gives the authority that arises from this office to a man living in evil, draws down on his own head all the fire of that man's sins and audacity. Homilies on S. Ignatius and S. Babylas, Eulogion for Ignatius 2.[78]

Good Order in the Household. Leo the Great: For the peace and order of the Lord's whole household will be shaken, if what is required in the body be not found in the head. What is it to lay on hands hastily but to confer the priestly dignity on unproved men before the proper age, before there has been time to test them? Letters 12.2.[79]

5:22b Nor Participate in Another's Sins

Participation Means Consent. Augustine: If the church partakes of the sins which were forbidden by the apostle, then it must be considered to consent to them. On Baptism, Against the Donatists 7.5.9.[80]

5:22c Keep Yourself Pure

Give What You Command. Augustine: The apostle writes to Timothy: "Practice self-control." It's a command; it's an order; it has to be listened to; it has to be carried out. But unless God comes to our help, we get stuck. We try, indeed, to do it by willpower, and the will makes some effort. It shouldn't, though, rely on its ability unless it is assisted in its debility. Sermons 348a.4.[81]

---

[78]NPNF 1 9:136-37*. [79]NPNF 2 12:13. [80]NPNF 1 4:502*. [81]WSA 3/10:98.

5:23-25 FATHERLY SOLICITUDE

[23]No longer drink only water, but use a little wine for the sake of your stomach and your frequent ailments. [24]The sins of some men are conspicuous, pointing to judgment, but the sins of others appear later. [25]So also good deeds are conspicuous; and even when they are not, they cannot remain hidden.

Overview: Timothy is reminded that he is human also, being subject to disease and thus in need of the rules of medicine (Chrysostom). One ought not to drink water in order to court good opinion but should use wine moderately, trusting to the overall goodness of one's life as a vindication (Augustine, Theodore). Wine is allowed for infirmities (Ambrose, Jerome, Augustine). Some deeds point immediately to their own judgment, while others' sins remain temporarily hidden (Chrysostom, Jerome, Augustine). Temperance is in harmony with nature (Ambrose). One's care of the flesh must be viewed in relation to one's final salvation (Augustine).

5:23 Use a Little Wine

For Health, Not for Luxury. Chrysostom: If one who had practiced fasting to such an extent and used only water, so long that he had brought on "infirmities" and "frequent infirmities," is thus commanded to be chaste and does not refuse the admonition, much less ought we to be offended when we receive an admonition from anyone.... For the miracles Timothy wrought were enough to have rendered him arrogant. For this reason he is left to be subject to the rules of medicine, that he may be humbled and others may not be offended but may learn that they who performed such excellent actions were men of the same nature as themselves.... Paul does not however allow him to indulge freely in wine, but as much as was for health and not for luxury. Homilies on 1 Timothy 16.[1]

Bodily Infirmity Injures the Church. Chrysostom: But if he, the bishop, takes care of his body that he may minister to you, if he attends to his health that he may be useful, ought he for this to be accused? Do you not know that bodily infirmity no less than infirmity of soul injures both us and the church? ... For if we could practice virtue with the soul alone, we need not take care of the body. And why then were we born at all? But if this has contributed a great share, is it not the extreme of folly to neglect it? Homilies on Titus 1.[2]

The Natural Food of Temperance. Ambrose: And is not temperance in harmony with nature and that divine law which in the beginning of all things gave the springs for drink and the fruits of trees for food? After the flood, the just man found wine a source of temptation to him.[3] Let us, then, use the natural food of temperance, and would that we all could do so! But, because not all are strong, the apostle therefore says, "Use a little wine for your frequent infirmities." We must drink it not for our pleasure but for our infirmity, sparingly as a remedy, not excessively as a gratification. Letters 63.27.[4]

Wine Is Allowed for Infirmities. Jerome: Notice the reasons why wine is allowed: it is to cure pain in the stomach and to relieve a frequent infirmity and hardly then. And lest perchance we should indulge ourselves on the ground of illness, Paul recommends that but a little wine should be taken, advising rather as a physician than as an apostle—although indeed an apostle is a spiritual physician. Letters 22.8.[5]

Health Is Not to Be Despised. Augustine: Because of the necessary activities of this life, health is not to be despised until "this mortal shall put on immortality,"[6] and that is the true and perfect and unending health which is not refreshed by corruptible pleasure when it fails through earthly weakness but is maintained by heavenly strength and made young by eternal incorruptibility. The apostle himself says, "Make not provision for the flesh in its concupiscence,"[7] because our care of the flesh must be in view of the exigencies of salvation. "For no man ever hated his own flesh."[8] Letters 130.2.7.[9]

Meat and Wine Not Unclean. Augustine: Thus, many Christians do not eat meat, yet they do not superstitiously consider it unclean. And the same individuals who abstain when healthy

---

[1]NPNF 1 13:464-65. See also Chrysostom *Homilies on the Statues* 1.5 (NPNF 1 9:332), "For besides the subjects that have been mentioned, there is another about which some are no less perplexed, enquiring within themselves on what account God permitted a man possessing such confidence toward him whose bones and relics expelled demons to fall into such a state of infirmity; for it is not merely that he was sick but constantly, and for a length of time; and by these recurring and prolonged infirmities he was not permitted to have even a brief respite. Let those then attend to this, whoever they are, who being given over to a lingering sickness are querulous and dejected under it." [2]NPNF 1 13:523*. [3]Gen 9:20-21. [4]FC 26:330-31. [5]JSL 71. [6]1 Cor 15:54. [7]Rom 13:14. [8]Eph 5:29. [9]FC 18:382.

take meat without qualm when sick, if it be required as a cure. Many do not drink wine. Nevertheless, they do not think it would defile them. In fact, they show great sympathy and good judgment in seeing that it is provided for those who tend to be listless and for all who cannot maintain bodily health without it. The Way of Life of the Catholic Church 1.33.72.[10]

5:24 The Sins of Others Appear Later

Eventual Punishment. Chrysostom: Even as legislators have overlooked punishments for the guilty though they be established by law, so too our Lord Jesus Christ by punishing one or two sinners sets down like an inscription on a bronze stele their punishment and uses their experiences as a warning to all. It says that even if those who dare the same sins do not suffer a similar penalty now, they will suffer a more rigorous one in the future. On Virginity 23.[11]

Discerning Intention. Augustine: When it is clear with what intention they are committed, he calls them manifest sins, and these sins precede judgment. This means that if judgment follows them at once, it will not be rash judgment. But concealed sins follow judgment, because not even these will remain hidden in their proper time. And this is to be understood about good works as well. . . . On things that are manifest, therefore, let us pass judgment, but with regard to hidden things, let us leave the judgment to God. For, whether the works themselves be bad or good, they cannot remain hidden when the time comes for them to be revealed. Sermon on the Mount 2.18.60.[12]

5:25 Good Deeds Are Conspicuous

Some Deeds Concealed, Others Conspicuous. Jerome: The words mean this: Certain persons sin so deliberately and flagrantly that you no sooner see them than you know them at once to be sinners. But the defects of others are so cunningly concealed that we only learn them from subsequent information. Similarly the good deeds of some people are public property, while those of others we come to know only through long intimacy with them. Letters 54.8.[13]

---

[10]FC 56:56. [11]COV 32*. [12]FC 11:170-71. [13]NPNF 2 6:105.

6:1-2 THE TREATMENT OF SERVANTS

[1]*Let all who are under the yoke of slavery regard their masters as worthy of all honor, so that the name of God and the teaching may not be defamed.* [2]*Those who have believing masters must not be disrespectful on the ground that they are brethren; rather they must serve all the better since those who benefit by their service are believers and beloved.*

Overview: It is important that unbelievers see that faith does not lead to insubordination and equally important that slaves appreciate the benefits that masters provide. The fear that a servant should have toward the one to whom he is accountable is analogous to the fear we should all have of God. Since it is to be expected that slaves will exhibit a certain fear toward nonbelieving masters, how much more should they be thankful and devoted in their service to masters who are believers (Chrysostom)! Let a master who has a believing servant love him as a son (Apostolic Constitutions).

6:1-2a All Who Are Under the Yoke of Slavery

True Freedom and True Slavery. Chrysostom: Those who have believing masters must not be disrespectful on the ground that they are brothers. Rather they must serve all the better since those who benefit by their service are believers and beloved. In the epistles to the Ephesians and Colossians he commands the same. So it is obvious that Paul's intention is not to abolish slavery as a social institution. Rather, he attacks slavery in its worst form, the slavery to evil, which pays no respect to any external freedom. Homilies on First Corinthians 19.4.[1]

Of Servants and Masters. Anonymous: But as to servants, what can we say more than that the servant should bring a good will to his master, with the fear of God, although his master be impious and wicked, but yet not yield any compliance as to his worship? And let the master love his servant, although he is his supervisor. Let him reflect on the fact that each shares equally in the other's humanity. And let one who has a believing master[2] love him both as his master, and as of the same faith, and as a father, but still with the preservation of his authority as his master. . . . In like manner, let a master who has a believing servant love him as a son or as a brother, on account of their communion in the faith, but still preserving the difference of a servant. Constitutions of the Holy Apostles 4.12.[3]

---

[1]CMFL 37. [2]Cf. Col 4:1 [3]ANF 7:436.

6:2-10 CALL TO PERSONAL INTEGRITY IN TEACHING AND IN LIFE

Teach and urge these duties. [3]If any one teaches otherwise and does not agree with the sound words of our Lord Jesus Christ and the teaching which accords with godliness, [4]he is puffed up with conceit, he knows nothing; he has a morbid craving for controversy and for disputes about words, which produce envy, dissension, slander, base suspicions, [5]and wrangling among men who are depraved in mind and bereft of the truth, imagining that godliness is a means of gain. [6]There is great gain in godliness with contentment; [7]for we brought nothing into the world, and[m] we cannot take anything out of the world; [8]but if we have food and clothing, with these we shall be content. [9]But those who desire to be rich fall into temptation, into a snare, into many senseless and hurtful desires that plunge men into ruin and destruction. [10]For the love of money is the root of all evils; it is through this craving that some have wandered away from the faith and pierced their hearts with many pangs.

m Other ancient authorities insert *it is certain that*

OVERVIEW: The good pastor is instructed to teach and preach with authority and gentleness, and most of all to cultivate a genuine humility and an inner freedom from the desire for possessions (CHRYSOSTOM). The apostle played down appalling excesses in language skills (CLEMENT OF ALEXANDRIA, GREGORY OF NAZIANZUS) that give us rhetorical bellyaches (TERTULLIAN).

Learn humility from Christ (JEROME), not avarice from Judas (ORIGEN). People are happy who have everything they want but do not want anything improper (AUGUSTINE). If one does not choose to injure himself, no one else will be able to do this, for such a person is not stung by earthly losses who has learned of heaven (CHRYSOSTOM, AUGUSTINE). The believer is rich even when poor (CYRIL OF JERUSALEM), being like a wheel touching the ground only at one point but continuing to move (JEROME). We pray only for daily bread (AUGUSTINE), not letting a scrap of covetousness remain in our hearts (JOHN CASSIAN).

You cannot take worldly things with you to heaven (AUGUSTINE). Your soul is diminishing while you are afraid of your wealth diminishing (CYPRIAN). Listen to the physician of souls concerning what makes for your health (CHRYSOSTOM). Do not be so misled by one unworthy desire that you cling to many real evils (AUGUSTINE). Avarice is like a worm within the soul (VALERIAN). It dulls our moral senses (AMBROSE). Temptations would surely fail if they were not decked out with some fair color to entice to the desire of the one they are deceiving (GREGORY OF NYSSA). Do not consent to unworthy desires that lead to death (AUGUSTINE). One who possesses nothing fears nothing (CLEMENT OF ALEXANDRIA, CHRYSOSTOM). Take away the love of money, and you put an end to war, to

enmity, to strife and contention (CHRYSOSTOM). In its apostatizing pride, the beginning of sin, the soul seeks for something more than the whole, and while it is struggling to govern itself by its own laws, it is thrust into caring for a part; by desiring more, it becomes less (AUGUSTINE).

6:3-4 Sound Words of Our Lord

HUMBLY KNOWING. CHRYSOSTOM: Presumption therefore arises not from knowledge but from "knowing nothing." For he that knows the doctrine of godliness is also the most disposed to moderation. He who knows sound words is not unsound. For what inflammation is to the body, pride is to the soul. And as we do not in the first case say that the inflamed part is healthy, so neither do we say of the soul that the arrogant part is healthy. It is possible then to be knowing and yet to know nothing. HOMILIES ON 1 TIMOTHY 17.[1]

6:4-5 Disputes About Words

DANGEROUS SOPHISTRY. CLEMENT OF ALEXANDRIA: Skill in sophistry, an enthusiasm of the Greeks, is a power operating on the imagination, using arguments to implant false opinions as if they were true. It produces rhetoric for persuasion and eristic for controversy.[2] If the skills lack philosophy, then anyone at all would find them damaging. . . . So the admira-

---

[1]NPNF 1 13:467. [2]Rhetoric is smooth and pleasing, sometimes flattering and ingratiating, while eristic is polemical, antagonistic and provocative. As forms of discourse, however, both play on the seductive power of words and impressions, as opposed to substance. Cf. Plato *Sophist* 226A, 236A, 239C, 240D.

ble apostle was right to play down these appalling excesses in language skills. STROMATA 1.8.39.1—40.1.[3]

THE MORBID CRAVING FOR CONTROVERSY.

TERTULLIAN: The apostle forbids us to enter into hypothetical questions, or to lend our ears to newfangled statements or to consort with a heretic "after the first and second admonitions."[4] We do not enter into these discussions. Discussion has been inhibited in this way by designating *admonition* as the purpose of dealing with a heretic. The first reason, too, is because he is not a Christian. The instruction is given in order that he might not, after the manner of a Christian, seem to require correction again and again and "before two or three witnesses."[5] The impression could be created that he ought to be corrected, for the very reason that he is not to be disputed with. The second reason is that a controversy over the Scriptures can, clearly, produce no other effect than to upset either the stomach or the brain. PRESCRIPTION AGAINST HERETICS 16.[6]

ACTIONS RATHER THAN ELABORATE WORDS.

GREGORY OF NAZIANZUS: I shall address my words to those whose cleverness is in words. . . . "Strife of words" is the term given to all elaborate verbiage by Paul, who proclaims and confirms the "short and final account,"[7] Paul, the pupil and teacher of fishermen. These people I speak of have versatile tongues and are resourceful in attacking doctrines nobler and worthier than their own. I only wish they would display comparable energy in their actions. ORATIONS 27.1.[8]

6:5 Godliness Is a Means of Gain

THE SIN OF JUDAS. ORIGEN: In appearance Judas championed the cause of the poor and said with indignation, "This ointment might have been sold for three hundred pence and given to the poor."[9] But in reality he "was a thief, and

having the bag took away what was put in it."[10] If, then, anyone in our time who has the bag of the church speaks like Judas on behalf of the poor but takes away what is put in it, let there be assigned to him the portion along with Judas who did these same things. COMMENTARY ON MATTHEW 11.9.[11]

THE SIN OF COMMERCE IN HOLY THINGS.

JEROME: It is of all of us . . . that the apostle speaks. Christ is a pauper, let us blush with shame. Christ is lowly, let us be made lowly. Christ was crucified. He did not rule. He was crucified in order to rule. He conquered the world, not in pride but in humility. He destroyed the devil, not by derisive laughter but by weeping; he did not scourge but was scourged. He received a blow but did not give blows. Let us, therefore, imitate our Lord. HOMILIES ON MARK 83.[12]

6:6 Great Gain in Godliness

PROPER TEMPORAL DESIRE. AUGUSTINE: He,

then, is happy who has everything he wants but does not want what is not proper. . . . But, when men have attained that welfare for themselves and for those whom they love, shall we be able to say that they are now happy? They have something which it is proper to wish for, but if they have nothing else, either greater or better or more to their advantage and personal distinction, they are still far from happiness. . . . Certainly it is proper for them to wish for these things, not for the sake of the things themselves but for another reason, namely, that they may do good by providing for the welfare of those who live under them, but it is not proper to covet them out of the empty pride of self-esteem or useless ostentation or hurtful vanity. LETTERS 1305.11.[13]

---

[3]FC 85:51. [4]Tit 3:10. [5]Mt 18:16. [6]ANF 3:251*. [7]Rom 9:28, based on Is 10:23. [8]FGFR 217. [9]Mk 14:5; Jn 12:5. [10]Jn 12:6. [11]ANF 9:438-39*. [12]FC 57:184. [13]FC 18:384-85.

The Poor Also Can Abuse Resources.
Augustine: I've been wagging a finger at the rich. Poor people, you listen too. You should pay out too; you shouldn't go plundering either. You should give of your means too. You too curb your greed. Listen, you poor, to the same apostle, "There is great gain," he says, "in godliness with contentment." You have the world in common with the rich. You don't have a house in common with the rich, but you do have the sky, you do have the light in common with them. Just look for a sufficiency, look for what is enough, not for more than that. Anything more is a weighing down, not a lifting up of the spirit; a burden, not a reward. Sermons 85.6.[14]

6:7 Bringing and Taking Nothing

Assisting a Thief. Anonymous: Abba Macarius, when in Egypt, found a man who had brought a beast to his cell and was stealing his possessions. As though he was a traveler who did not live there, he went up to the thief and helped him to load the beast, and peaceably led him on his way, saying to himself, "We brought nothing into this world,[15] but the Lord gave; as he willed, so it is done. Blessed be the Lord in all things." Sayings of the Fathers 16.6.[16]

Not Stung by Losses. Chrysostom: For there is no one free, save only one who lives for Christ. He stands superior to all troubles. And if he does not choose to injure himself, no one else will be able to do this, for he is impregnable. He is not stung by the loss of wealth, for he has learned that we "brought nothing into this world, neither can we carry anything out." He is not caught by the longings of ambition or glory, for he has learned that our citizenship is in heaven.[17] No one annoys him by abuse or provokes him by blows. There is only one calamity for a Christian: disobedience to God. All the other things, such as loss of property, exile, peril of life, one does not even reckon to be a grievance at all. And that which all dread, departure

hence to the other world—this is to him sweeter than life itself. Letters to the Fallen Theodore 2.5.[18]

Detachment. Augustine: But the world retains its hold on us. On all sides its charms decoy us. We like lots of money, we like splendid honors, we like power to overawe others. We like all these things, but let's listen to the apostle, "We brought nothing into this world, neither can we take anything out." Honor should be looking for you, not you for it. You, after all, should sit down in the humbler place, so he that invited you may make you go up to a more honored place. But if he doesn't wish to, eat where you are sitting, because you brought nothing into this world. Sermons 39.2.[19]

Disordered Desire. Augustine: We neither take nor snatch anything away with us. What if we could take something—wouldn't we be devouring people alive? What is this monstrously avid appetite, when even huge beasts know their limits? The time they pounce on something, you see, is when they are hungry; but when they feel satisfied, they spare their prey. It is only the avarice and greed of the rich that is forever insatiable. Sermons 367.1.[20]

6:8 If We Have Food and Clothing

The Apostolic Way of Life. Chrysostom: For it is not by beautifying herself, or by living a life of luxury, or by demanding from her husband money, or by being extravagant and lavish that a good wife will be able to win him over. When she removes herself from all present concerns and imprints upon herself the apostolic way of life, when she displays great modesty, decorum, disdain for money and forbearance, then she will be able to capture him. When she

---

[14]WSA 3/3:394. [15]1 Tim 6:7, but also Job 1:21. [16]LCC 12:177. [17]Cf. Phil 3:20. [18]NPNF 1 9:115*. [19]WSA 3/2:217. [20]WSA 3/10:296.

says, "If we have food and clothing, we have all that we need," when she practices this philosophy in her actions and, laughing at physical death, calls this life nothing, when she considers along with the prophet every glory of this life to be as the flower of the field,[21] then she will capture him. On Virginity 47.1.[22]

Not for Self-Exaltation. Chrysostom: And observe also their laws,[23] how moderate and freed from all vainglory. Thus: "Having," says he, "food and covering, let us be content." Not like him of Sinope [Diogenes the Cynic], who clothed in rags and living in a cask to no good, astonished many but profited none. Paul did none of these things. For neither had he an eye to ostentation, but was both clothed in ordinary apparel with all decency, and lived in a house continually, and displayed all exactness in the practice of all other virtue. These things the cynic despised, living impurely and publicly disgracing himself, and dragged away by his mad passion for glory. Homilies on First Corinthians 35.4.[24]

The Paradox of Faith. Cyril of Jerusalem: For those who in appearance are rich, though they have many possessions, are yet poor in soul. The more they amass, the more they pine with longing for what they lack. But the believer, paradoxically, is rich even when poor. Knowing that we have need only of raiment and food and being content with these, he has trampled riches underfoot. Catechetical Lectures 5.2.[25]

Touching the Ground. Jerome: Let us now speak in particular about the interior man. A wheel, as you know, rests upon the ground with a very slight base. Nor does it merely rest; it rolls along; it does not stand still but barely touches the ground and passes on. Further, when it rolls onward, it always mounts higher. So the saintly man, because he has a human body, has to give some thought to earthly mat-

ters. When it comes to food and clothing and other such things, he is content with what he has, and merely touching the ground with them, hastens on to higher things. Homilies on the Psalms 10.[26]

Daily Bread. Augustine: "Give us today our daily bread."[27] It can be taken quite simply that we pour out this prayer for our daily sustenance, that we may have plenty of it; and if we don't have plenty, that we may not lack it entirely. He called it "daily," "for as long as it is called 'today.' "[28] Daily we live, daily we get up, daily we take our fill, daily we get hungry. May he give us our daily bread. Sermons 58.5.[29]

Moderation. Basil the Great: But, if a man would also have mercy upon his body as being a possession necessary to the soul and its co-operator in carrying on life on earth, he will occupy himself with its needs only so far as is required to preserve it and keep it vigorous by moderate care in the service of the soul. He will by no means allow it to become unmanageable through satiety. On Detachment, Homily 21.[30]

Victory Over Covetousness. John Cassian: This then is the perfect victory over covetousness. It is not to allow a gleam from the very smallest scrap of it to remain in our heart, as we know that we shall have no further power of quenching it if we cherish even the tiniest bit of a spark of it in us. And we can better preserve this virtue unimpaired if we remain in a monastery, and as the apostle says, having food and clothing, are therewith content. Institutes 7.28-29.[31]

---

[21]Cf. Is 40:6. [22]COV 72-73. [23]Chrysostom is commenting on 1 Corinthians 14:19 and St. Paul's emphasis on the usefulness, rather than show, of truly spiritual things. [24]NPNF 1 12:212*. [25]FC 61:140. [26]FC 48:75. [27]Mt 6:11. [28]Heb 3:13. [29]WSA 3/3:120. [30]FC 9:495. [31]NPNF 2 11:256*.

6:9a Those Who Desire to Be Rich

Anxious Fear. Cyprian: You are afraid that your wealth may fail. You may have begun to do some good generously from it, yet you do not know, in your wretchedness, that your life itself may fail, and your salvation as well. While you are anxious lest any of your possessions be diminished, you do not take notice that you yourself, a lover of mammon rather than of your soul, are being diminished. While you are afraid lest for your own sake you lose your estate, you yourself are perishing for the sake of your estate. Works and Almsgiving 10.[32]

See the Consequences. Chrysostom: Do you see the skill of physicians, who besides health are supplying you also with the riches of wisdom? Sit down therefore with them, and learn from them the nature of your disease. For instance, do you love wealth and greedy gain, like the fevered love water? Listen to their admonitions. For it is just as the physician says to you, If you wish only to gratify your desire, you will perish and undergo this or that consequence. In the same way Paul wrote, "They that will be rich, fall into temptation, and a snare of the devil, and into foolish and hurtful lusts, which drown men in destruction and perdition." Homilies on Matthew 74.4.[33]

6:9b Falling into a Snare

The Worm of Avarice. Valerian: Therefore, dearly beloved, the rust is that worm which alone possesses the recesses of the human heart: the worm of envy and of avarice. But the thief is the devil. Believe this. To lay his plots against good deeds, he flatters us with the pomp of the world. To keep a man from sharing in the heavenly kingdom, he puts gold in his hands, silver before his eyes, gems about his neck. In this way he nourishes pride and by the goad of covetousness enkindles the desires of the flesh. Homilies 7.3.[34]

6:9c Hurtful Desires That Plunge People into Ruin

Unworthy Desire Is the Issue. Augustine: He did not say: Those who *are* rich. He said: Those who *seek to become* rich. . . . The name of riches is, as it were, sweet-sounding to the ear. But, "many vain and harmful desires"— does that sound sweet? To be "involved in many troubles"—does that sound sweet? Do not be so misled by one false good that you will thereby cling to many real evils. Sermons 11.3.[35]

Do Not Consent to Desire That Leads to Death. Augustine: See what a fight we have with our dead sins, as that active soldier of Christ and faithful teacher of the church shows. For how is sin dead when it works many things in us while we struggle against it? What are these many things except foolish and harmful desires which plunge into death and destruction those who consent to them? And to bear them patiently and not to consent to them is a struggle, a conflict, a battle. Against Julian 2.9.32.[36]

6:10 The Root of All Evils

The Just Person. Clement of Alexandria: Poverty of heart is the true wealth, and the true nobility is not that founded on riches but that which comes from a contempt for riches. It is disgraceful to boast about one's possessions. Not to be concerned about them any longer very clearly proves the just man. Christ the Educator 2.3.39.[37]

Virtue Its Own Reward. Ambrose: How happy is the man who has been able to cut out the root of vices, avarice. Surely he will not dread this balance. Avarice generally dulls men's senses and corrupts their judgments, so that

---

[32]FC 36:236-37. [33]NPNF 1 10:448-49*. [34]FC 17:346. [35]FC 11:359;* see 11:307 n. 1 for sermon numbering. [36]FC 35:95. [37]FC 23:129.

they think piety a gain, and money a sort of reward for sagacity. But great is the reward of piety and the gaining of sobriety. The possession of these virtues is sufficient. LETTERS 15.[38]

ENOUGH IS ENOUGH. AMBROSE: Therefore the man of good counsel says, "I have learned in whatever state I am to be content."[39] For he knew that the root of all evils is the love of money. Therefore he was content with what he had, without seeking for what was another's. Sufficient for me, he says, is what I have. Whether I have little or much, to me it is much. DUTIES OF THE CLERGY 2.17.89.[40]

LOVE OF MONEY LEADS TO BAD LIVING AND BAD FAITH. CHRYSOSTOM: What evils does it not cause! What fraudulent practices, what robberies! What miseries, enmities, contentions, battles! Does it not stretch forth its hand even to the dead, even to fathers and brothers? Do not they who are possessed by this passion violate the laws of nature and the commandments of God? In short everything? Is it not this that renders our courts of justice necessary? Take away therefore the love of money, and you put an end to war, to battle, to enmity, to strife and contention. HOMILIES ON 1 TIMOTHY 17.[41]

FAITH DAMAGED BY AVARICE. CHRYSOSTOM: In many places[42] Paul covertly signifies this point: a corrupt life is the parent of evil doctrines. "The love of money is the root of all kinds of evil, which some reaching after, have been led astray from the faith." Indeed, many of those who are conscious of wickedness and would prefer not to pay its penalty are by this fear damaged also in their faith concerning the resurrection. This can happen even when they on a daily basis are virtuously desiring to behold the resurrection. HOMILIES ON FIRST CORINTHIANS 40.3.[43]

POSSESSING NOTHING AS IF EVERYTHING. CHRYSOSTOM: The man who possesses nothing

as if he had everything disdains all. He is very outspoken with officials, and rulers, and the sovereign. For by despising possessions and advancing methodically, he will scorn even death with ease. Since he is above these things, he will speak openly with everyone and tremble with fear before no one. But the man who has devoted himself to money is a slave to it and also to his reputation, honor, the present life, in short, to all human concerns. Consequently, Paul has called it the root of all evil. ON VIRGINITY 81.[44]

SOME PHANTOM OF GOOD. GREGORY OF NYSSA: The tree, then, from which comes this fruit of mixed knowledge is among those things which are forbidden. Its fruit is combined of opposite qualities, and therefore for this reason perhaps has the serpent to commend it. For the evil is not exposed in its nakedness, thereby appearing in its own proper nature; for wickedness would surely fail of its effect were it not decked with some fair color to entice to the desire of it him whom it deceives. But now the nature of evil is in a manner mixed and thus keeps destruction like some snare concealed in its depths and displays some phantom of good in the deceitfulness of its exterior. The beauty of the substance seems good to those who love money. ON THE MAKING OF MAN 20.2.[45]

DISORDERED LOVE. AUGUSTINE: For when the soul loves its own power, it slips from the common whole to its own particular part. Had it followed God as its ruler in the universal creature, it could have been most excellently governed by his laws. But in that apostatizing pride, which is called "the beginning of sin,"[46] it sought for something more than the whole; and while it struggled to govern it by its own laws, it was

---

[38]FC 26:83. [39]Phil 4:11. [40]NPNF 2 10:57. [41]NPNF 1 13:469. [42]Chrysostom is commenting on 1 Corinthians 15:34. [43]NPNF 1 12:247*. [44]COV 122. [45]NPNF 2 5:410*. [46]Sir 10:15.

thrust into caring for a part, since there is nothing more than the whole. So by desiring something more, it becomes less, and for this reason covetousness is called "the root of all evils." ON THE TRINITY 12.9.14.[47]

GREED AND CHARITY. AUGUSTINE: So love God, and love your neighbor as yourself. I mean, I can see that you love yourself, because you love God. Charity is the root of all good works. Just as greed, after all, is the root of all evil, so charity is the root of all good things. SERMONS 179A.5.[48]

---

[47]FC 45:356. [48]WSA 3/5:310.

6:11-16 THE BATTLE OF FAITH

[11]*But as for you, man of God, shun all this; aim at righteousness, godliness, faith, love, steadfastness, gentleness.* [12]*Fight the good fight of the faith; take hold of the eternal life to which you were called when you made the good confession in the presence of many witnesses.* [13]*In the presence of God who gives life to all things, and of Christ Jesus who in his testimony before Pontius Pilate made the good confession,* [14]*I charge you to keep the commandment unstained and free from reproach until the appearing of our Lord Jesus Christ;* [15]*and this will be made manifest at the proper time by the blessed and only Sovereign, the King of kings and Lord of lords,* [16]*who alone has immortality and dwells in unapproachable light, whom no man has ever seen or can see. To him be honor and eternal dominion. Amen.*

OVERVIEW: The life of the believer is directed toward future rewards, not present pleasures. For such a person rejects the love of money, stands fast in the profession of faith, refuses to be intimidated by earthly powers and places all hope in God who is incomprehensible in his majesty (CHRYSOSTOM). The essence of Christian living is the struggle for the truth of faith, a struggle in which the rejection of earthly pleasures is uppermost (PELAGIUS). Carefully attend to those stirrings in the soul that predominate in prayer (ISAAC OF NINEVEH). Do not let other interests divert you from the central combat (ATHANASIUS, CHRYSOSTOM, AMBROSE). You are about to enter a noble contest in which the Holy Spirit is your trainer, whose crown is eternity, whose prize is citizenship in heaven (TERTUL-

LIAN). One does not first set out to become a martyr but holds fast to the good confession by deeds, knowing that it will be confirmed by the angels (ORIGEN).

God is alive and immortal in a more complete way than any creature or soul is alive and immortal (ORIGEN, AMBROSE, GREGORY OF NYSSA, AUGUSTINE). The soul images God's incorruptibility (METHODIUS). Charity does not most love what is corruptible (ORIGEN). Recall your baptismal confession (JOHN OF DAMASCUS) and the confession of the saints you have known (BASIL). The one who is King of kings is the same one who voluntarily lowers his rank to become a Father to orphans and a Judge to widows (GREGORY OF NAZIANZUS, CHRYSOSTOM). Seek to behold in mental contemplation the One whom you entreat, so as to realize what sort of person you should be in offering yourself prostrate before him (Cassiodorus). It was the Son who gave visibility to the invisible Father (Tertullian). God is seen not in his substance (Augustine, Pseudo-Dionysius) but in manifestation in the flesh of Christ (Chrysostom, Augustine).

God is beyond our comprehension (Chrysostom). Yet the inaccessible light in which God dwells shines upon us (Ambrose) in the life of love (Augustine). God's light is said to be inaccessible in its unique and almighty nature, but when the grace of God pours forth, we both approach him and obtain blessed enlightenment (Cassiodorus).

6:11a *Man of God*

Close to Spiritual Things. Isaac of Nineveh: Strive to discover stirrings that are good during the time of prayer, as the wise do. These consist in reflection on the Spirit's insights and sagacious thought, and consideration during the time of prayer of how to please the will of the Maker of all. This is the final end of all virtue and of all prayer. When in these matters you receive the power that stems from grace to be bound firmly to their continual stirrings, you will become a "man of God" and will be close to spiritual things. Instructions for Monks, second part.[1]

6:11 *Shun All This*

Freedom of the Heart. Augustine: "As for you, man of God, flee from these things." You see, he didn't just say, "Leave and forsake," but "Flee from," as from an enemy. You were trying to flee with gold; flee from gold instead. Let your heart flee from it, and your use of it need have no worries. Do without greed; don't do without concern for others. There's something you can do with gold, if you're its master, not its slave. If you're the master of gold, you can do good with it; if you're its slave, it can do evil with you. Sermons 177.3.[2]

6:12a *Fight the Good Fight*

Do Not Be Diverted. Ambrose: Let godliness move you to justice, continence, gentleness, that you may avoid childish acts, and that rooted and grounded in grace you may fight the good fight of faith. Do not entangle yourself in the affairs of this life, for you are fighting for God.[3] For he who fights for the emperor is forbidden by human laws to enter upon lawsuits or do any legal business or sell merchandise. How much more ought he who enters upon the warfare of faith to keep away from every kind of business. Let him be satisfied with the produce of his own little bit of land, if he has it. If he has not that, let him be content with the pay he will get for his service. Duties of the Clergy 1.36.185.[4]

Suffering Persecution. Athanasius: In another place the apostle says, "And all those who will live godly lives in Christ Jesus will suffer persecution."[5] Then, to help prevent people from renouncing godliness when they are persecuted, he urges them to cling to the faith. "You, therefore, continue in the things you have learned and been assured of."[6] Just as brothers become strongly knit together when one helps another, so faith and godliness, coming from the same family, cohere together. A person who gives his attention to one of the two is strengthened by the other. Consequently, wishing Timothy to live godly to the end and to fight the battle in faith, St. Paul says, "Fight the good fight of faith, and lay hold on eternal life." Festal Letters 9.[7]

6:12b *When You Made the Good Confession*

---

[1]SFPSL 296-97*. [2]WSA 3/5:281. [3]2 Tim 2:4. [4]NPNF 2 10:31*. [5]2 Tim 3:12. [6]2 Tim 3:14. [7]ARL 156.

Faithfulness to the Good Confession.
Origen: For the angels, as it were, have charge over our souls, to whom "while we are still children we are committed," as it were, "to tutors and governors until the time appointed by the father."[8] And they, therefore, now say about the progress of each of us, "Now I know that you fear God."[9] Suppose, for example, I intend to be a martyr. An angel could not say to me on this basis, "Now I know that you fear God," for an intention of the mind is known to God alone. But if I shall undertake the struggles, if I shall utter a "good confession," if I shall bear calmly all things which are inflicted. Then an angel can say, as if confirming and strengthening me, "Now I know that you fear God." Homilies on Genesis 8.8.[10]

The Christian Athlete.
Tertullian: In like manner, O blessed, consider whatever is hard in your present situation as an exercise of your powers of mind and body. You are about to enter a noble contest in which the living God acts the part of superintendent and the Holy Spirit is your trainer, a contest whose crown is eternity, whose prize is angelic nature, citizenship in heaven for ever and ever. To the Martyrs 3.3.[11]

Maintain Your Original Vows.
Basil the Great: Recall your glorious profession which you made before God, the angels and men. Remember the august company, the holy chorus of virgins, the assembly of the Lord and the church of saints. Call to mind also your grandmother, old in Christ but still young and strong in virtue, and your mother, vying with her in the Lord and striving by new and unusual toils to destroy former habits. Remember also your sister, who is likewise both imitating and aspiring to surpass them, and who by the advantage of her virginity is outstripping the virtuous actions of her elders and is industriously summoning, both by word and by life, you her sister, as she thought, to a contest of like eagerness. Recall

these, and also the angelic chorus singing with them to God, the spiritual life in the flesh and the heavenly life on earth. Letters 46, To a Fallen Virgin.[12]

6:14 Free from Reproach

Spiritual Combat.
Chrysostom: There is need not only of profession but of patience also to persevere in that profession, and of vehement contention, and of numberless toils, that you be not overthrown. . . . It is necessary therefore to be self-collected and well belted in on every side. All around appear pleasures attracting the eyes of the soul. Those of beauty, of wealth, of luxury, of indolence, of glory, of revenge, of power, of dominion, and these are all fair and lovely in appearance, and able to captivate those who are unsteady and who do not love the truth. Homilies on 1 Timothy 17.[13]

6:15a The Blessed and Only Sovereign

The Sovereign Son Inseparable from the Father.
Ambrose: When I speak of the Father, I do not make separation of the Son, because the Son is in the bosom and the solitude of the Father.[14] When I speak of the Son alone, I also associate the Father, even as the Son also associated him, saying, "Behold the hour is coming for you to leave me alone. But I am not alone, because the Father is with me."[15] In this way is the Father called "the blessed and only Sovereign"—in such a way that the Son, who is always in the Father, is not separated from him. The Prayer of Job and David 4.15.[16]

6:15b King of Kings and Lord of Lords

A King to Kings, Yet Lowly.
Chrysostom: When someone sees resplendent lords of rank,

---

[8]Gal 4:2-3. [9]Gen 22:12. [10]FC 71:144. [11]FC 40:23. [12]FC 13:120-21. [13]NPNF 1 13:469. [14]Jn 1:18. [15]Jn 16:32. [16]FC 65:400.

kings, leaders and all those who appear prominent in wealth, to them he speaks in fearful words. Their dynasties are advantaged by his fear. Yet "now, kings, understand; be instructed, all you who judge the earth; serve the Lord with fear and rejoice in him with trembling,"[17] because "he is the King of kings and the Lord of lords." Wherever the mighty rules, God threatens with the fear of his kingdom. Yet wherever the worthless are humbled, God offers the medicine of his clemency. For this God is a great King to those who reign and a Lord to those who exercise lordship. Again, the very same one lowers his rank and is found, according to holy Scripture, to be a Father to orphans and a Judge to widows, a King to kings, a Leader to leaders, a Lord to lords. ON REPENTANCE AND ALMSGIVING 7.3.9.[18]

THE ECONOMY OF TITLES. GREGORY OF NAZIANZUS: God's other titles fall into two distinct groups. The first group belongs to his power, the second to his providential ordering of the world, a twofold providential ordering— involving, and not involving, incarnation. Clear cases of titles which belong to his power are . . . "King" of "rulers" and "Lord of the masters." . . . For since we are controlled by three conditions—fear of punishment, hope for salvation and glory too, and the practice of the virtues which result in these last—the name which mentions retribution deals with fear. The one which mentions salvation with hope, and that which refers to virtues, disciplines us to practice them. The intention is that by, as it were, carrying God inside him, one may have some success here and press on all the harder to perfection, toward that affinity with God which comes from the virtues. ORATIONS 30.19.[19]

TO BEHOLD IN MENTAL CONTEMPLATION. CASSIODORUS: Prayer itself must come from a humble, meek, pure heart. It must confess its sins without making excuses. In the course of bitter tears it will show trust in the most sweet

pity of the Lord. It must not seek earthly aims but desire heavenly ones. It must be sequestered from desires of the body and attach itself solely to the divine. In short, it must be wholly spiritual, bestowing nothing but tears on the flesh. Insofar as it is lawful, seek to behold in mental contemplation him whom you entreat and then you realize what sort of person you should be in offering yourself prostrate before him. He is, as Paul says, "the blessed and only Mighty, the King of kings and Lord of lords." EXPLANATION OF THE PSALMS 141, CONCLUSION.[20]

BAPTISMAL FAITH. JOHN OF DAMASCUS: He, the framer of all creation and maker of our race, became man for our sake, and coming from a holy Virgin's womb, on earth conversed with men. For us ungrateful servants the master endured death, even the death of the cross, that the tyranny of sin might be destroyed, that the former condemnation might be abolished, that the gates of heaven might be open to us again. In this way he has exalted our nature, and set it on the throne of glory, and granted to them that love him an everlasting kingdom and joys beyond all that tongue can tell or ear can hear. He is the mighty and the only potentate, King of kings and Lord of lords, whose might is invincible and whose lordship is beyond comparison. He alone is holy and dwells in holiness, who with the Father and the Holy Spirit is glorified. Into this faith I have been baptized. BARLAAM AND IOASAPH 24.211.[21]

6:16a Who Alone Has Immortality

GOD'S IMMORTALITY UNIQUE. ORIGEN: To be fully alive belongs to God, more fully than to any creature. The apostle considered the superiority of the life of God to be beyond comparison. It is with this in mind that Scripture says

---

[17]Ps 2:10. [18]FC 96:93. [19]FGFR 274-75. [20]ACW 53:404-5. [21]JDBI 353.

"Surely as I live, all the earth will be filled with the glory of the Lord."[22] This is God, "Who alone has immortality," because none of the living beings with God has the life whose aliveness is absolutely unchangeable and immutable. Commentary on John 2.123.[23]

Shared with the Son. Ambrose: How could the Son not have immortality who has life in himself? He has it in his nature. He has it in his essential Being. God has it not as a temporal grace but owing to his eternal Godhead. He has it not by way of a gift as a servant but by peculiar right of his generation, as the coeternal Son. He has life in the same way that the Father has life. Of the Christian Faith 5.2.35.[24]

The Son Is the Immortality. Gregory of Nyssa: But we, even when we are told that God "only has immortality," we understand by "immortality" the Son. For life is immortality, and the Lord is that life, who said, "I am the Life."[25] And if he is said to dwell "in the light that no man can approach," again we make no difficulty in understanding that the true Light, unapproachable by falsehood, is the Only-begotten, in whom we learn from the Truth itself that the Father is.[26] Are we to think of the Only-begotten in a manner worthy of the Godhead, or to call him, as heresy prescribes, perishable and temporary? Against Eunomius 2.4.[27]

The Unchangeable Is Immortal. Augustine: Already you have told me, O Lord, by means of a loud voice in my interior ear, that you are eternal, alone possessing immortality, since you change in relation neither to any form nor to motion. Your will is not altered in regard to periods of time, because no will is immortal if it is now one way and now another. In your sight this is clear to me. May it become more and more clear, I pray, and may I continue to live soberly under your protecting wings, within the influence of this revelation. Confessions 12.11.11.[28]

The Soul Only Relatively Immortal. Augustine: I am doing the right thing in taking my time over this question [about the origin of the soul], because I have no doubt at all that the soul is immortal, not as God is, "Who only has immortality," but in a certain way according to its own nature, and that it is a created being, not the substance of the Creator: this I hold most firmly, as well as all other truths about the nature of the soul. Letters 143.1.7.[29]

God's Immortality Distinguished from the Soul's. Augustine: So if God alone has immortality, is the soul mortal? That's why I said the soul is immortal after its own fashion. You see, it can also die. Your graces must try to understand, and then the problem will be solved. I make bold to say, the soul can die, can be killed. Certainly it's immortal. So there you are; I make bold to say it is both immortal in one sense and capable of being killed in another sense. And that's why I said there is a kind of immortality, that is to say, an absolute and total unchangeableness, which God alone has, as it says of him, "Who alone has immortality." Sermons 65.4.[30]

6:16b Dwells in Unapproachable Light

Charity Does Not Love the Corruptible. Origen: We must understand, therefore, that this charity, which God is, in whoever it exists loves nothing earthly, nothing material, nothing corruptible. It is against its nature to love anything corruptible, seeing that it is itself the fount of incorruption. For, because God, "who only has immortality and inhabits light inaccessible," is charity, it is charity alone that possesses immortality. Commentary on the Song of Songs, Prologue.[31]

---

[22]Num 14:28. [23]FC 80:127. [24]NPNF 2 10:288-89*. [25]Jn 14:6. [26]Cf. Jn 14:11. [27]NPNF 2 5:105. [28]FC 21:376. [29]FC 20:155. [30]WSA 3/3:194*. [31]ACW 26:33.

THE SOUL IMAGES GOD'S INCORRUPTIBILITY.
METHODIUS: For the unbegotten and incorporeal beauty, which neither begins nor is corruptible but is unchangeable and grows not old and is in need of nothing, he resting in himself and in the very light which is in unspeakable and inapproachable places, embracing all things in the circumference of his power, creating and arranging, made the soul after the image of his image. Therefore, also, it is reasonable and immortal. THE BANQUET OF THE TEN VIRGINS 6.1.[32]

BEYOND COMPREHENSION. CHRYSOSTOM: And pay heed to the accuracy with which Paul speaks. He did not say, "Who is an unapproachable light" but "Who dwells in unapproachable light." Why? So that you may learn that if the dwelling is unapproachable, so much more so is the God that dwells in it. But Paul did not say this to make you suspect that there is a house or place surrounding God. Rather, he wished you to have a deeper and superior knowledge that God is beyond our comprehension. . . . A thing is unapproachable which, from the start, cannot be investigated nor can anyone come near to it. We call the sea incomprehensible because, even when divers lower themselves into its waters and go down to a great depth, they cannot find the bottom. We call that thing unapproachable which, from the start, cannot be searched out or investigated. ON THE INCOMPREHENSIBLE NATURE OF GOD 3.2.[33]

CREATION BY MEANS OF LIGHT. AMBROSE: There would be no purpose in the world if it were not seen. In fact, God himself was in the light, because he "dwells in light inaccessible," and he "was the true light that enlightens every man who comes into the world."[34] But he wishes the light to be such as might be perceived by mortal eyes. The person who desires to erect a house as a fitting habitation for the head of a family determines first how it may receive light abundantly before he lays the foundation. This is the first requisite. If this is lacking, the whole house is without beauty and is uninhabitable. It is light which sets off the other beautiful objects in the house. SIX DAYS OF CREATION 1.9.33.[35]

GOD IS LIGHT. GREGORY OF NAZIANZUS: God is light: the highest, the unapproachable, the ineffable, that can neither be conceived in the mind nor uttered with the lips, that gives life to every reasoning creature. He is in the world of thought what the sun is in the world of sense; presenting himself to our minds in proportion as we are cleansed; and loved in proportion as he is presented to our mind; and again, conceived in proportion as we love him; himself contemplating and comprehending himself and pouring himself out on what is external to him. That light, I mean, which is contemplated in the Father and the Son and the Holy Ghost, whose riches is their unity of nature and the one outleaping of their brightness. ORATIONS 40.5.[36]

SEEN WITH THE EYES OF THE HEART. AUGUSTINE: If you ask whether he can also be seen at any time as he is, I answer that this was promised to his sons, of whom it is said, "We know that when he shall appear, we shall be like him, because we shall see him as he is."[37] If you ask by what means we shall see him, I answer: as the angels see, for we shall then be equal to them,[38] as the angels see those things which are called visible; but no one has ever seen God nor can see him, because "he inhabits light inaccessible," and his nature is invisible as it is immortal. LETTERS 147.15.37.[39]

CHARITY THE EYES OF THE HEART. AUGUSTINE: This, then, is charity, however small a thing it appears to us, as it inheres in our will; "it is not seen in any locality, nor sought by bodily eyes, nor limited by our sight, nor held by touch,

---

[32]ANF 6:329. [33]FC 72:100. [34]Jn 1:9. [35]FC 42:38. [36]NPNF 2 7:361. [37]1 Jn 3:2. [38]Cf. Mt 18:10; Lk 20:36. [39]FC 20:204-5.

nor heard by its utterance, nor perceived in its approach."[40] How much more true this is of God, of whom charity is the pledge within us! If our interior man is an image of him—insignificant, indeed—not begotten of him but created by him, and, although it is still renewed day by day,[41] it now dwells in such light that no faculty of corporeal sight comes near to it, and if those things which we perceive with the eyes of the heart by means of that light are distinguished from each other and separated by no intervals of space, how much more is this true of God, who inhabits light inaccessible to the bodily senses, to whom there can be no approach except for the clean of heart! LETTERS 147.18.44.[42]

ENLIGHTENED BY THE LIGHT. CASSIODORUS: Since Paul says, "Only he that has immortality and inhabits inaccessible light," how can the psalmist say here, "Come to him, and be enlightened?[43] But the problem is solved by this brief statement of the truth: his light is said to be inaccessible when the unique and almighty nature of its substance is described; but when the grace of the sacred Godhead pours forth, we both approach him and obtain blessed enlightenment. EXPLANATION OF THE PSALMS 33.6.[44]

6:16c *Whom No One Has Ever Seen or Can See*

GOD INVISIBLE AND GOD VISIBLE. TERTULLIAN: There is a certain emphatic saying by John, "No man has seen God at any time";[45] meaning, of course, at any previous time. But he has indeed taken away all question of time, by saying that God has never been seen. The apostle confirms this statement. For, speaking of God, he says, "Whom no man has seen, nor can see," because the man indeed would die who should see him.[46] But the very same apostles testify that they had both seen and "handled" Christ.[47] Now, if Christ is himself both the Father and the Son,[48] how can he be both the

Visible and the Invisible? . . . It is evident that he was always seen from the beginning, who became visible in the end; and that he, on the contrary, was not seen in the end who had never been visible from the beginning; and that accordingly there are two—the Visible and the Invisible. It was the Son, therefore, who was always seen. . . .For the Father acts by mind and thought, while the Son, who is in the Father's mind and thought, gives effect and form to what he sees. AGAINST PRAXEAS 15.[49]

GOD IS SEEN IN CONTEMPLATION. CHRYSOSTOM: But if Paul said elsewhere, "God was manifested in the flesh,"[50] do not wonder, because the manifestation took place in the flesh, not in his substance. Furthermore, Paul also testified here that God himself was invisible, not only to men but also to the powers above. Having said "was manifested in the flesh," he added, "he appeared to angels." Thus he became visible to the angels as well, at the time when he put on the flesh. . . . Similarly, when he said, "Blessed are the pure in heart, for they shall see God,"[51] he was speaking of mental vision—which is within our power—and also of thought about God, so, likewise, it may be said of the angels that by reason of their pure and constant nature, they continually think of nothing else but God. . . . Therefore, just as he has been seen by many, in whatever way vision of him was possible for them, but no one has ever beheld his essence, so also we all now know God, but no one knows his substance, whatever it is, except only he who has been begotten from him. HOMILIES ON JOHN 15.1-2.[52]

GOD IS SEEN IN THE MIND AND HEART. AU-

---

[40]Augustine is citing his own statement from chapter eighteen of this same epistle. [41]2 Cor 4:16. [42]FC 20:212. [43]Ps 34:5. [44]ACW 51:327*. [45]Jn 1:18. [46]Cf. Ex 33:20. [47]1 Jn 1:1. [48]Tertullian is attacking the modalist heresy, in which the three persons of the Trinity are viewed as mere "modes" of the one God, that is, as lacking proper individuality. [49]ANF 3:610-11*. [50]1 Tim 3:16. [51]Mt 5:8. [52]FC 33:144-45.

gustine: God, Father Son and Holy Spirit, is in his own proper nature invisible. But he has appeared when he wished and to whom he wished; not as he is but in whatever way he wished, being served after all by all creation. If your mind, though it is invisible in your body, can appear by uttering your voice, and the voice in which your mind appears when you speak is not the substance of your mind, it means that mind is one thing and voice another, and yet mind becomes apparent in a thing which in itself is not. So too God, if he appeared in fire, is all the same not fire; if he appeared in smoke, still he isn't smoke; if he appeared in a sound, he isn't a sound. These things are not God, but they indicate God. If we bear this in mind, we may safely believe that it could have been the Son who appeared to Moses and was called both Lord and angel of the Lord. Sermons 7.4.[53]

So Bright That It Is Dark. Pseudo-Dionysius: The divine darkness is that "unapproachable light" where God is said to live. And if it is invisible because of a superabundant clarity, if it cannot be approached because of the outpouring of its transcendent gift of light, yet it is here that is found everyone worthy to know God and to look upon him. And such a one, precisely because he neither sees him nor knows him, truly arrives at that which is beyond all seeing and all knowledge. Letters 5.[54]

[53]WSA 3/1:235. [54]SDF 265.

6:17-21 KEEP THE TRUST

[17]*As for the rich in this world, charge them not to be haughty, nor to set their hopes on uncertain riches but on God who richly furnishes us with everything to enjoy.* [18]*They are to do good, to be rich in good deeds, liberal and generous,* [19]*thus laying up for themselves a good foundation for the future, so that they may take hold of the life which is life indeed.*

[20]*O Timothy, guard what has been entrusted to you. Avoid the godless chatter and contradictions of what is falsely called knowledge,* [21]*for by professing it some have missed the mark as regards the faith.*

Grace be with you.

Overview: Riches are inherently unstable, whereas eternal life is essentially enduring. The only way to this eternal life is through faith that leads to virtue and not by the fleeting esoteric knowledge that some claim to possess (Chrysostom). If you should attempt to throw over wealth a thousand chains, it will find a route of running away, dragging the chains after it (Chrysostom). Riches make humility all the harder (Augustine). Riches are like a disease (Augustine) or like a gnawing worm (Caesarius). Nothing is ours except that which is possessed by the heart, which clings to the soul and can never be taken away by anyone (John Cassian).

Timothy's task is to remain faithful to the teachings entrusted to him by his master, Paul (Tertullian, Ambrosiaster). The greatest gifts

God gives are held in common (Chrysostom). The rich stand in more uncertainty than the poor, experiencing frequent vulnerabilities (Chrysostom, Augustine). Those who give generously enjoy great gains to compensate them for light losses (Augustine, Leo, Caesarius). Without this comfort there is more grief than consolation to be found in earthly comforts, whatever they may be (Augustine).

The faith once delivered to the saints is the same faith held universally in all cultures by all believers of all times and places (Vincent). The deposit is variously interpreted as the public teaching of the kerygma (Tertullian) or the divine image in the soul (Origen) or the rule of faith (Nicetas). The deposit is that which is committed to you, not that which is invented by you; not of private assumption but of public tradition (Leo, Vincent). Heresy took firmer form only after the first generation of apostles died (Eusebius).

6:17a Not to Be Haughty

Wealth a Faithless Slave. Chrysostom: For nothing is so faithless as wealth; of which I have often said, and will not cease to say, that it is a runaway, thankless servant, having no fidelity. If you should throw over him the thousand chains, he will make off dragging his chains after him. Frequently, indeed, have those who possessed wealth shut him up with bars and doors, placing their slaves round about for guards. But he has overpersuaded these very servants and has fled away together with his guards, dragging his keepers after him as if in a manacle, so little security was there in this custody. Homilies Concerning the Statues 2.4.[1]

Humility Is the Key. Augustine: Praise to the rich if they remain humble. Praise the rich for being poor. The one who writes to Timothy wants them to be like that, when he says, "Order the rich of this world not to be haughty in mind." I know what I am saying: give them these

orders. The riches they have are whispering persuasively to them to be proud; the riches they have make it very hard for them to be humble. Sermons 14.2.[2]

The Disease of Riches. Augustine: It wasn't riches he was in dread of, but the disease of riches. The disease of riches is great pride. A grand spirit it is indeed, that in the midst of riches is not prone to this disease, a spirit greater than its riches, surpassing them not by desiring but by despising them. Sermons 36.2.[3]

Riches a Thing Indifferent. John Cassian: Riches are understood in a threefold way in holy Scripture—that is, as bad, good and indifferent. . . . The indifferent are those which can be either good or bad, since they can tend either way depending on the desire and the character of those who use them. The blessed apostle says with regard to these, "Charge the rich of this world not to be haughty or to hope in uncertain riches but in God, who gives us everything abundantly to enjoy, to do good, to give freely, to share, to store up for themselves a good foundation in the future, so that they may seize the true life." . . . When we abandon the visible riches of this world, then, we reject not our own but others' wealth, even though we boast either of having acquired it by our own labor or of having inherited it from our ancestors. For, as I have said, nothing is ours except this one thing, which is possessed by the heart, which clings to the soul and which can never be taken away by anyone. Conferences 3.9.1, 3; 10.1.[4]

The Gnawing Worm. Caesarius of Arles: Pride is the first worm of riches; it is a harmful gnawing worm which gnaws at everything and reduces it to ashes. "Charge the rich of this

---

[1]NPNF 1 9:348. [2]WSA 3/1:317. [3]WSA 3/2:174-75. [4]ACW 57:128-29.

world not to be proud, or to trust in the uncertainty of riches," lest perhaps one goes to sleep as a rich man and arises a poor man. SERMONS 153.3.[5]

6:17b God Richly Furnishes Us with Everything

DIVINE LIBERALITY. CHRYSOSTOM: The rich man stands in more uncertainty than the poor man, experiencing, as he does, frequent and diversified changes. What is the sense of this phrase: "Hope in God who richly furnishes us with everything to enjoy"? God gives all things with liberality that are more necessary than riches: the air, the water, the fire, the sun—all things of this kind. The rich man is not able to say that he enjoys more of the sunbeams than the poor man. He is not able to say that he breathes more plenteous air. These are offered to all alike. It is the greater and more necessary blessings, and those which maintain our life, that God has given to all in common. The smaller and less valuable (I speak of money) are not thus common. HOMILIES CONCERNING THE STATUES 2.6.[6]

6:18 To Be Rich in Good Deeds, Liberal and Generous

THE JOY OF GIVING. AUGUSTINE: Those who have given liberally of their riches[7] have had great gains to compensate them for light losses. Their joy at what they assured for themselves more securely by readiness to give outweighed their sadness at the surrender of possessions they more easily lost because they clung to them fearfully. Reluctance to remove their goods from this world exposed them to the risk of loss. There were those who accepted the Lord's advice: "Do not store your treasures on earth, where moth and rust destroy, and where thieves break in and steal. Pile up treasure in heaven, where no thief comes near and no moth destroys. For where your treasure is, there your

heart will be also."[8] Such people proved in the time of tribulation how wise they were in not despising the finest of advisers and the most faithful and unconquerable guardian of treasure. THE CITY OF GOD 1.10.2.[9]

VIRTUE FOR THE WEALTHY. CAESARIUS OF ARLES: Whenever we talk about contempt for riches, some rich man replies to me: I have learned not to hope in the uncertainty of riches; I do not want to be rich, lest I fall into temptation; but since I am rich already, what am I to do with the possessions which I now happen to have? The apostle continues, "Let them give readily, sharing with others." What does it mean to share with others? To share your possessions with the man who does not have any. Therefore, if you begin to share with others, you will not be that plunderer and robber who broods over the wants of the poor as over the property of another. SERMONS 182.2.[10]

THE COST OF THE KINGDOM. LEO THE GREAT: Let those who want Christ to spare them have compassion for the poor. Let those who desire a bond with the fellowship of the blessed be "readily disposed" toward nourishing the wretched. No human being should be considered worthless by another. The nature which the Creator of the universe made his own should not be looked down upon in anyone. SERMONS 9.2.[11]

6:19 The Life That Is Life Indeed

THIS TRUE LIFE. AUGUSTINE: Through love of this true life you ought to consider yourself desolate in this world, no matter what happiness you enjoy. That is the true life in comparison with

---

[5]FC 47:338. [6]NPNF 1 9:351*. [7]Augustine is praising those Christians who had the foresight and charity to give away their wealth to the poor at the time of the Vandal sack of Rome in 410. [8]Mt 6:19-20. [9]CG 18. [10]FC 47:468. [11]FC 93:40.

which this other, which is so much loved, is not to be called life, however pleasant and prolonged it may be. Similarly, that is the true comfort which God promised by the prophet saying, "I will give them true comfort, peace upon peace."[12] Without this comfort there is more grief than consolation to be found in earthly comforts, whatever they may be. LETTERS 130.2.3.[13]

6:20a *Guard What Has Been Entrusted to You*

THE PUBLIC TEACHING. TERTULLIAN: Nothing that was proclaimed before many witnesses could be kept secret. Nor can they [the Gnostic heretics] interpret as evidence of some hidden gospel[14] Paul's desire that Timothy should entrust "these things to faithful men, fit to teach others." "These things" meant the things of which he was then writing. To refer to things hidden in their minds he would have said "those," as of something absent, not "these."[15] PRESCRIPTIONS AGAINST HERETICS 25.[16]

THE DEPOSIT OF THE DIVINE IMAGE IN THE SOUL. ORIGEN: What is "the deposit" that each one of the faithful receives? For my part I think that we receive our soul itself and the body as a deposit from God. And do you want to see another greater "deposit" that you received from God? God entrusted "his own image and likeness"[17] to your own soul. That deposit, therefore, must be restored by you just as intact as it was received by you. For if you are merciful, "as your Father in heaven is merciful,"[18] the image of God is in you and you preserve the "deposit" intact. If you are perfect, "as your Father in heaven is perfect,"[19] the deposit of God's image remains in you. In like manner, in all other things, if you are pious, if you are just, if you are holy, if you are "pure in heart,"[20] and if all things which are present in God through nature remain in you by imitation, "the deposit" of the divine image is safe within you. HOMILIES ON LEVITICUS 4.3.[21]

CORRECT BELIEF ABOUT CHRIST. CYRIL OF JERUSALEM: I have many other testimonies from holy Scripture to the fact that the kingdom of Christ endures throughout all ages. But I will content myself with what I have said, because the day wears on. And do you, my hearers, worship him alone as king, and flee every misguided heresy. . . . Flee the false Christ, and look for the true. You have been taught the way to be among those on his right hand at the judgment. Retain "that which is committed to you" concerning Christ, and be adorned with good works. So you will stand with a good courage before the Judge and thereafter inherit the kingdom of heaven. CATECHETICAL LECTURES 15.33.[22]

FAITH IN THE TRINITY. NICETAS OF REMESIANA: Make strong in your hearts, my brothers, this faith in the Trinity, believing in one God the Father Almighty and in his Son, Jesus Christ our Lord, and in the Holy Spirit, the true light and sanctifier of souls, who is the pledge of our inheritance, who will lead us, if we will but follow, into all truth and will make us one with the citizens of heaven. This rule of faith the apostles received from the Lord. . . . May this faith remain in you. O beloved, "keep that which is committed to your trust, avoiding profane novelties of words and oppositions of knowledge falsely so called." EXPLANATION OF THE CREED 8.[23]

THE MESSAGE OF GRACE. JEROME: The apostle labors, and, although he has lived blameless, according to the justice that is from the law, he counts everything as worthless for Christ, that he may be found in Christ, not having his own justice which is from the law but that which is

---

[12]Is 57:18-19 (LXX). [13]FC 18:378. [14]That Gnostic teachers did often make such claims is seen, for example, in the opening words of the Gospel of Thomas: "These are the secret words which Jesus the Living spoke and [which] Didymus Thomas wrote." [15]See also 2 Tim 1:14; 1 Tim 1:18; 6:13-14; 2 Tim 2:2. [16]LCC 5:48. [17]Gen 1:26-27. [18]Lk 6:36. [19]Mt 5:48. [20]Mt 5:8. [21]FC 83:72. [22]LCC 4:167. [23]FC 7:48.

from the faith of Christ, from God. . . . Therefore, we are saved, not by the power of the free will but by the mercy of God. And, lest you think that the truth of faith can be subverted by vain argumentations which raise questions in the minds of the hearers, the same apostle writes to Timothy, "O Timothy, guard the trust and keep free from profane novelties in speech and the contradictions of so-called knowledge, which some have promised and have fallen away from the faith." For the goodness and mercy of our Savior have saved us, not by reason of good works that we did ourselves but according to his mercy, in order that, justified by his grace, we may be heirs in the hope of life everlasting.[24] AGAINST THE PELAGIANS 2.10.[25]

THE PUBLIC LEGACY. LEO THE GREAT: What is meant by "the deposit"? That which is committed to you, not that which is invented by you. That which you have received, not that which you have devised. A thing not of wit but of learning; not of private assumption but of public tradition; a thing brought to you, not brought forth by you; wherein you must not be an author but a keeper; not a leader but a follower. Keep the deposit. SERMONS 85.3.[26]

THE HEAVENLY HIERARCHY. PSEUDO-DIONYSIUS: And you, my child, must follow the recommendations of our hierarchic tradition. Listen carefully to the things sacredly said and be inspired by them in an initiation into inspired things. Keep these holy truths a secret in your hidden mind. Guard their unity safe from the multiplicity of what is profane, for, as Scripture says, you must not throw before swine that pure, shining and splendid harmony of the conceptual pearls. THE CELESTIAL HIERARCHY 2.5.[27]

6:20b Godless Chatter Falsely Called Knowledge

FALSE GNOSIS. CLEMENT OF ALEXANDRIA:

Pride and opinionated views have corrupted philosophy. In the same way, false knowledge, though it bears the same name, has corrupted true knowledge. The apostle writes of it, saying, "Timothy, guard what has been entrusted to you. Avoid the godless chatter and contradictions of what is falsely called knowledge, for by professing it some have missed the mark as regards the faith." Because this verse exposes them, the heretics regard the letters to Timothy as inauthentic. Well, if the Lord is "truth" and "the wisdom and power of God,"[28] as in fact he is, it would be demonstrated that the true knower is the one who has come to know Son and his Father through him. STROMATA 2.11.52.5-7.[29]

GOING INTO THE WAY OF THE GENTILES. ORIGEN: To go into the way of the Gentiles[30] is to adopt some Gentile teaching which is foreign to the "Israel of God"[31] and to walk according to it. And to enter a city of the Samaritans[32] is to be engaged in some knowledge falsely so-called of those who claim to devote themselves to the words of the law or the prophets or the Gospels or the apostles. COMMENTARY ON JOHN 13.343.[33]

VARIETIES OF INTERPRETATION FROM THE BEGINNING. ORIGEN: Celsus also says that "they were of one mind," not seeing even here that from the outset there were disagreements among the believers about the interpretation of the books regarded as divine. . . . In the epistles of Paul, who was contemporary with those who had seen Jesus, there are some statements to be found which concern certain disputes about the resurrection, and about the view that it had already occurred, and about the question whether the day of the Lord was already present or not.[34] Moreover, the words "Turning away from the profane babblings and oppositions of

---

[24]Tit 3:4-7. [25]FC 53:309-10. [26]NPNF 2 12:198*. [27]PSD 153. [28]Jn 4:16; 2 Cor 1:24. [29]FC 85:194. [30]Cf. Mt 10:5. [31]Gal 6:16. [32]Cf. Mt 10:5. [33]FC 89:142. [34]Cf. 1 Cor 15:12; 2 Tim 2:18; 1 Thess 5:2.

the knowledge falsely so-called, which some have professed and made shipwreck concerning the faith"[35] show that from the beginning there were certain varieties of interpretation. AGAINST CELSUS 3.11.[36]

THE FIRST RISE OF HERESY. EUSEBIUS OF CAESAREA: Besides this, the same man [Hegesippus], when relating the events of these times, adds that until then the church had remained a pure and undefiled virgin, since those who attempted to corrupt the sound rule of the Savior's preaching, if any did exist, until then lurked somewhere in obscure darkness. But when the sacred band of the apostles had received an end of life in various ways, and the generation of those who were deemed worthy to hear the divine wisdom with their own ears had passed away, then the league of godless error took its beginnings because of the deceit of heretical teachers who, since none of the apostles still remained, attempted henceforth barefacedly to proclaim in opposition to the preaching of truth "the knowledge falsely so-called." ECCLESIASTICAL HISTORY 3.32.[37]

COMBATING THE DENIAL OF THE HOLY SPIRIT'S DEITY. BASIL THE GREAT: But we must proceed to attack our opponents, in the endeavor to confute those "oppositions" advanced against us which are derived from "knowledge falsely so-called." It is not permissible, they assert, for the Holy Spirit to be ranked with the Father and the Son, on account of the difference of his nature and the inferiority of his dignity. Against them it is right to reply in the words of the apostles, "We ought to obey God rather than men.[38] ON THE HOLY SPIRIT 10.24.[39]

FALSE SPIRITUALITY. JOHN CASSIAN: The psalmist also declares that this is the sequence we must follow. He says, "Blessed are those who are unsullied upon their journey, who walk in the law of the Lord. Blessed are those who pay heed to his witness."[40] . . . In this way he shows clearly that no one can manage to engage in the correct scrutiny of God's Word unless in his daily life he proceeds unstained along the road of Christ. Therefore those whom you have mentioned cannot possess this knowledge if they are unclean. What they have is a false so-called lore, the kind about which the apostle has this to say, "O Timothy, guard what has been given to you. In all that you say avoid profane novelties and the claims of a falsely named knowledge." CONFERENCES 14.16.[41]

THE CATHOLIC FAITH IS ANCIENT TRUTH. VINCENT OF LÉRINS: "Avoiding," he says, "profane novelties of words."[42] Are there really people who can listen to such adjurations and then remain in such hardened and shameless stubbornness, such stony impudence, such adamant consistency, as not to yield to the mighty weight of these divine words and to weaken under such a load, as not to be shattered by these hammer strokes, as not to be crushed by such powerful thunderbolts? "Avoiding," he says, "profane novelties of words." He did not say "antiquities" or "the old traditions." No, he clearly shows the positive implications of this negative statement: Novelty is to be avoided, hence, antiquity has to be respected; novelty is profane, hence, the old tradition is sacred. COMMONITORIES 21.[43]

CATHOLIC TRUTH DOES NOT CHANGE. VINCENT OF LÉRINS: What does "avoiding" mean? "If anyone comes to you and does not bring this doctrine."[44] Of course, this means the catholic and universal doctrine, which remains one and the same through all successive ages in the uncorrupted tradition of truth and which will remain so without end for ever and ever. COMMONITORIES 24.[45]

---

[35]1 Tim 6:20 and 1:19 conflated. [36]OAC 134-35. [37]FC 19:192. [38]Acts 5:29. [39]NPNF 2 8:16. [40]Ps 118:1-2. [41]JCC 170. [42]Vincent's Latin text of 1 Timothy 6:20 was based on an underlying Greek text that read *kainophonias* ("novelties") instead of the generally accepted reading *kenophonias* ("empty words"). [43]FC 7:306. [44]2 Jn 10. [45]FC 7:313.

THE SECOND EPISTLE TO TIMOTHY

ARGUMENT: Paul writes in order to offer consolation in the midst of the practical cares of Timothy's ministry and as a consolation for their separation from one another. Timothy is in need also of continuing support in the struggle with heresy. Paul knows that his own death is approaching (CHRYSOSTOM). There is a lengthy period of time between the first and second letters to Timothy, since Paul is no longer at Ephesus and is on the verge of martyrdom. He now writes from Rome at a point between his first and second imprisonments, as 2 Timothy 4:12 suggests. While it is clear from 1 Timothy 3:14 that Paul still expects to join Timothy, in 2 Timothy 4:6, 9, it is also clear that by now this expectation no longer exists (THEODORE). In 1 Timothy Paul had laid out the order of good teaching and good administration for Timothy. Now he focuses on the promise of the gospel and the blessings to come in eternity (SEVERIAN). Paul is particularly concerned here to encourage Timothy and others as they face difficult contests with heresy and to guard them against certain dangers (THEODORET). Paul's purpose is to refresh Timothy for faithful witness to the hope contained in the gospel (AMBROSIASTER).

1:1-7 SALUTATION AND OPENING ADMONITION

¹*Paul, an apostle of Christ Jesus by the will of God according to the promise of the life which is in Christ Jesus,*

²*To Timothy, my beloved child:*

Grace, mercy, and peace from God the Father and Christ Jesus our Lord.

³*I thank God whom I serve with a clear conscience, as did my fathers, when I remember you constantly in my prayers.* ⁴*As I remember your tears, I long night and day to see you, that I may be filled with joy.* ⁵*I am reminded of your sincere faith, a faith that dwelt first in your grandmother Lois and your mother Eunice and now, I am sure, dwells in you.* ⁶*Hence I remind you to*

rekindle the gift of God that is within you through the laying on of my hands; [7]for God did not give us a spirit of timidity but a spirit of power and love and self-control.

OVERVIEW: Paul opens with deep affection for Timothy and with an emphasis on the fervency of his desire to see his spiritual son (CHRYSOSTOM). Paul launches his teaching in this epistle with the reminder that the Christian faith acquires credibility only as Christians faithfully live in the present the future life of eternity (CHRYSOSTOM, THEODORE). Paul writes to stabilize Timothy in the face of dangers, so that his faith might be steadfast and true (THEODORET). Paul reminds Timothy that steadfastness in faith always involves the rekindling of that which we have been given by those who came before us (AMBROSIASTER). Paul encourages Timothy to zeal and perseverance in his faith, since he himself has always operated in this fashion, even when he was misguided as a Jew (ORIGEN, AMBROSIASTER, CHRYSOSTOM, PELAGIUS). Timothy is addressed as Paul's spiritual son, his son by faith (CHRYSOSTOM, THEODORET, CASSIODORUS). Timothy's unfeigned faith had dwelt first in his grandmother and mother (CHRYSOSTOM). For the praises of our ancestors, when we share in them, redound also to us (CHRYSOSTOM, THEODORET). Timothy is urged to renew the spirit of his ordination (AMBROSIASTER). By sloth and carelessness grace may be quenched, and by watchfulness and diligence it may be kept alive (CHRYSOSTOM). We are called to pass beyond the fear of punishment to the fullest freedom of love and to the confidence that belongs to the friends and sons of God (JOHN CASSIAN). Facing dangers in this life make us ready for eternal life, where there are no dangers (CHRYSOSTOM).

1:1 *The Promise of Life in Christ Jesus*

TRUE CONSOLATION. CHRYSOSTOM: From the outset Paul lifts up Timothy's mind: Do not tell me of dangers in this life. They make us ready for eternal life, where there are no dangers, grief or mourning. God has not made us apostles that we might meet dangers but to be prepared to suffer and die. But Paul did not recount to him his own troubles, as this would merely increase his grief. Rather Paul begins immediately with offering comfort, saying, "According to the promise of life which is in Jesus Christ." But if it is a "promise," do not seek it here. For "hope that is seen is not hope."[1] HOMILIES ON 2 TIMOTHY 1.[2]

1:2 *Timothy, My Beloved Child*

A SON IN VIRTUE. CHRYSOSTOM: Those born of us physically are not loved purely on account of their virtue but out of the force of natural affection. But those born of us of faith are loved on account of nothing but their virtue [in Christ], for what else can it be? HOMILIES ON 2 TIMOTHY 1.[3]

A SPIRITUAL SON. THEODORET OF CYR: Timothy's sonship to Paul is that of the soul, not that generated by nature, and is based on the spiritual promise of life. INTERPRETATION OF THE SECOND LETTER TO TIMOTHY.[4]

A SON BY FAITH. CASSIODORUS: When writing to Timothy he put at the head of the letter, "To my dearly beloved son," for he had begotten him, not in body but in faith. EXPLANATION OF THE PSALMS 101.29.[5]

1:3a *Serving God with a Clear Conscience*

PAUL'S BLAMELESSNESS. CHRYSOSTOM: Paul

---

[1]Rom 8:24. [2]NPNF 1 13:475*. [3]NPNF 1 13:476*. Chrysostom expresses a similar idea with the help of this verse in *Homilies on the Statues* 1.8 (NPNF 1 9:333). [4]PG 82:831B/832B. [5]ACW 53:17.

speaks of his blameless life, for he everywhere calls his life his conscience. Even when he was a persecutor, he understood himself as sustaining a good conscience in what he sought. Hence he says, "I obtained mercy, because I did it ignorantly in unbelief,"[6] all but saying, "Do not suspect that it was done of wickedness." Here he commends his own disposition, that he not appear insincere in his love. What he is, in effect, saying is: "I am not false. I do not think one thing and profess another." Homilies on 2 Timothy 1.[7]

1:3b As Did My Fathers

THE SAME GOD OF JEWS AND CHRISTIANS. ORIGEN: We grant that there are some among us who may deny that the God of the Jews is truly God. Yet that is no reason to criticize those who prove from the same Scriptures that there is one and the same God for Jews and Gentiles. So also Paul, who came to Christianity from the Jews, says clearly, "I thank my God whom I serve from my forefathers in a pure conscience." AGAINST CELSUS 5.61.[8]

LEARNING TO LONG FOR TRUE RELIGION. CHRYSOSTOM: How then, you will say, were unclean persons considered worthy of the gospel? Because they wished and longed for it. Among these, some, though in error, were attracted to him because they were not made unclean through disordered loves. Then there are others who were not rejected because they sought God of their own accord. In these ways, many even from their ancestors have received the true religion. HOMILIES ON FIRST CORINTHIANS 8.2.[9]

PAUL'S ROOTS. AMBROSIASTER: When Paul persecuted the church, he did it for the love of God, not out of malevolence. In this way he served God "in his ancestors" and "from his ancestors," as Levi was served in Abraham, when he gave and accepted tithes from Melchizedek. COMMENTARY ON THE SECOND LETTER TO TIMOTHY.[10]

PAUL'S ZEAL FOR THE LAW. PELAGIUS: Paul says, My whole origin steered me to the worship of God. I devastated the church of Christ not from malevolence but from zeal for the law. PELAGIUS'S COMMENTARY ON THE SECOND LETTER TO TIMOTHY.[11]

1:5a Your Sincere Faith

TIMOTHY OF MIXED PARENTAGE. CHRYSOSTOM: For Timothy, Scripture says, "was the son of a certain woman which was a Jewess, and believed."[12] How a Jewess? How believing? Because she was not of the Gentiles, "but on account of his father, who was a Greek, and of the Jews that were in those quarters, he took and circumcised him." Thus, as these mixtures of Jews and Gentiles took place, the law began gradually to be dissolved. HOMILIES ON 2 TIMOTHY 1.[13]

YOUR UNFEIGNED FAITH. CHRYSOSTOM: Great was the grace of Timothy. When Barnabas departed, Paul found another equivalent to him. Of him he says, "Remembering your tears and your unfeigned faith, which dwelt first in thy grandmother Lois and in thy mother Eunice." His father continued to be a Gentile. HOMILIES ON ACTS 34.[14]

1:5b And Dwells in You

THE BURDEN AND THE POWER OF EXAMPLE. CHRYSOSTOM: For the praises of our ancestors, when we share in them, redound also to us. Otherwise, they avail nothing but rather condemn us. HOMILIES ON 2 TIMOTHY 1.[15]

EFFECTIVE DOMESTIC EXAMPLE. THEODORET OF CYR: Commenting on Timothy's Jewish back-

---

[6]1 Tim 1:13. [7]NPNF 1 13:476. [8]OAS 311. Origen expresses the same idea with this verse in *On First Principles* 2.4.2 (OFP 97). [9]NPNF 1 12:45. [10]CSEL 81 3:296. [11]PETE 506-7. [12]Acts 16:1. [13]NPNF 1 13:476-77. [14]NPNF 1 11:216. [15]NPNF 1 13:477.

ground, Paul mentions Timothy's parentage in order to confirm Timothy in faith. Nothing helps so much as a domestic example. Interpretation of the Second Letter to Timothy.[16]

1:6 The Gift of God Within You

Renew the Freshness. Ambrosiaster: Paul urges Timothy to nurture his spirit with eagerness of mind, rejoicing in his faith, just as he once rejoiced in the newness of his ordination. Commentary on the Second Letter to Timothy.[17]

Fire and Fuel. Chrysostom: For it requires much zeal to stir up the gift of God. As fire requires fuel, so grace requires our alacrity, that it may be ever fervent. . . . For it is in our power to kindle or extinguish this grace. . . . For by sloth and carelessness it is quenched, and by watchfulness and diligence it is kept alive. For it is in you indeed, but you must render it more vehement, that is, fill it with confidence, with joy and delight. Stand manfully. Homilies on 2 Timothy 1.[18]

1:7a Not a Spirit of Timidity

Love, Not Fear. Theodoret of Cyr: Grace was given to us so that we might not be afraid but love all the more steadily. Interpretation of the Second Letter to Timothy.[19]

No Longer Servile Fear. John Cassian: Therefore there are two degrees of fear. The one is for beginners—that is, for those who are still under the yoke and under servile dread. In regard to this it is said, "The slave shall fear his master."[20] And in the Gospel, "I no longer call you servants, because a servant does not know what his master is doing."[21] And consequently he says,

"The slave does not remain in the house forever; the son remains forever."[22] For he is instructing us to pass from the fear of punishment to the fullest freedom of love and to the confidence of the friends and sons of God. And the blessed apostle, who had long since passed beyond the degree of servile fear, thanks to the power of the Lord's love, disdains lower things and professes that he has been endowed with greater goods. Conferences 11.13.3-5.[23]

1:7b A Spirit of Power, Love and Self-Control

The Spirit Is Power. Chrysostom: For the Spirit that makes us cry, "Abba, Father," inspires us with love both toward him and toward our neighbor, that we may love one another. For love arises from power and not from fearing. Homilies on 2 Timothy 1.[24]

Receiving the Spirit of Wisdom. Augustine: Just as a man would not have wisdom, understanding, counsel, fortitude, knowledge, piety and fear of God unless, according to the prophet's words, he had received "the spirit of wisdom and of understanding, of counsel and of fortitude, of knowledge and of godliness, and of fear of God,"[25] and just as he would not have power and love and sobriety, except by receiving the Spirit of whom the apostle speaks, "We have not received the spirit of fear but of power and love and sobriety," so also he would not have faith unless he received the spirit of faith. Letters 194.4.17.[26]

---

[16]PG 82:833B/834B. [17]CSEL 81 3:297. [18]NPNF 1 13:477*. [19]PG 82:833C/834C. [20]Mal 1:6. [21]Jn 15:14. [22]Jn 8:35. [23]ACW 57:420-21. [24]NPNF 1 13:477*. [25]Is 11:2-3. [26]FC 30:310-11.

1:8-18 DO NOT BE ASHAMED OF THE GOSPEL

⁸*Do not be ashamed then of testifying to our Lord, nor of me his prisoner, but share in suffering for the gospel in the power of God, ⁹who saved us and called us with a holy calling, not in virtue of our works but in virtue of his own purpose and the grace which he gave us in Christ Jesus ages ago, ¹⁰and now has manifested through the appearing of our Savior Christ Jesus, who abolished death and brought life and immortality to light through the gospel. ¹¹For this gospel I was appointed a preacher and apostle and teacher, ¹²and therefore I suffer as I do. But I am not ashamed, for I know whom I have believed, and I am sure that he is able to guard until that Day what has been entrusted to me.ᵃ ¹³Follow the pattern of the sound words which you have heard from me, in the faith and love which are in Christ Jesus; ¹⁴guard the truth that has been entrusted to you by the Holy Spirit who dwells within us.*

¹⁵You are aware that all who are in Asia turned away from me, and among them Phygelus and Hermogenes. ¹⁶May the Lord grant mercy to the household of Onesiphorus, for he often refreshed me; he was not ashamed of my chains, ¹⁷but when he arrived in Rome he searched for me eagerly and found me—¹⁸may the Lord grant him to find mercy from the Lord on that Day—and you well know all the service he rendered at Ephesus.

a Or what I have entrusted to him

OVERVIEW: Paul urges Timothy to accept without curious questioning the divine mysteries that have been entrusted to him, recognizing that God's free grace calls for human co-operation. Paul has handed on the precious teaching to Timothy, so that by their relationship Timothy may be refreshed in brotherly affection as Paul had been by Onesiphorus (CHRYSOSTOM). Timothy must realize that he and Paul enjoy communion as fellow believers, and communion with the Lord himself, through their sufferings, so that, through the Spirit entrusted to them, they may already taste the joys of the life to come (THEODORE). In the incarnate life of the Son, Jesus hands on to us the mystery of his passion and death, so that we may share in the power of this saving event, which has been prepared from all eternity and bequeathed to us by the Spirit (THEODORET).

God becomes visible in the sufferings and hu-

mility of the faithful disciple. This manifestation is the power of grace at work in believers, assuring them of the free gift of salvation (AMBROSIASTER). In themselves death and imprisonment are matters of shame, but when the end time mystery is viewed rightly, they will appear full of dignity (CHRYSOSTOM). God foreknew those who would be reborn in response to the offer of grace (PELAGIUS). Subsequent grace assists humanity's good purpose, but the purpose itself would not exist if grace did not precede (AUGUSTINE). This grace, of which we were all unworthy (AMBROSIASTER), was prepared even before we came into being (ATHANASIUS, THEODORE, THEODORET). Christ is lamb and lion both in his suffering and his resurrection (AUGUSTINE). We now commend to God's keeping those things which we pray he will preserve, especially our faith (AUGUSTINE). Follow this pattern of sound words (CHRYSOSTOM), we are to let no weeds of heresy invade the heavenly seed of the truth committed to us (John of Damascus). If we offer glory to God in the Spirit, we mean that the Spirit enables us to fulfill the requirements of true religion (Basil).

1:8 Do Not Be Ashamed of Testifying to Our Lord

Glory in the Economy of the Cross. Chrysostom: Observe . . . how Marcion, and Manes, and Valentinus, and others who introduced their heresies and pernicious doctrines into the church of God, measuring divine things by human reasonings, became ashamed of the divine economy. Yet it was not a subject for shame but rather for glorying; I speak of the cross of Christ. . . . For in themselves death and imprisonment and chains are matters of shame and reproach. But when the cause is added before us and the mystery viewed aright, they will appear full of dignity and a matter for boasting. For it was that death on the cross that saved the world when it was perishing. That death connected earth with heaven; that death destroyed the power of the devil and made men angels and sons of God; that death raised our nature to the kingly throne. Those chains enabled the conversion of many. Homilies on 2 Timothy 2.[1]

1:9a He Called Us with a Holy Calling

Relative Worthiness. Ambrosiaster: When Paul says that we are not called according to our works, he means that all who are called are sinners, though by comparison with others some were found to be more worthy. With regard to God's own grace, however, all were totally unworthy. Commentary on the Second Letter to Timothy.[2]

1:9b Not Our Works but God's Purpose

Co-operating Grace. Chrysostom: If then he is mighty in calling us, and good, in that he has

done it of grace and not of debt, we ought not to fear. For he who, when we should have perished, saved us, though enemies, by grace, will he not much more co-operate with us, when he sees us working? "Not according to our own works," he says, "but according to his own purpose and grace," that is, no one compelling, no one counseling him, but of his own purpose, from the impulse of his own goodness, he saved us. This is the meaning of "according to his own purpose." Homilies on 2 Timothy 2.[3]

The Elect Foreknown. Pelagius: God foreknew those who would be reborn in response to the offer of grace. Pelagius's Commentary on the Second Letter to Timothy.[4]

Preceding Grace. Augustine: Why, then, is it that, in what follows, where they mention what the Pelagians themselves think, they say they confess that "grace also assists the good purpose of every one, but that yet it does not infuse the desire of virtue into a reluctant heart"? They say this as if man of himself, without God's assistance, has a good purpose and a desire of virtue, hence this preceding merit is supposedly worthy of being assisted by the subsequent grace of God. For they think perhaps that the apostle thus said, "For we know that he works all things for good to them that love God, to them who are called according to the purpose,"[5] so as to wish the purpose of man to be understood. This purpose is then viewed as a good merit that the mercy of the God who calls might follow. They are ignorant that it is said, "Who are called according to the purpose," so that this may be understood as the purpose of God, not man. Thus those whom he foreknew and predestinated as conformed to the image of his Son, he elected before the founda-

---

[1]NPNF 1 13:479-80. [2]CSEL 81 3:299. [3]NPNF 1 13:480*. [4]PETE 508, an example of a received Pelagian text that seems very non-Pelagian. See the introduction for a review of the uncertain transmission of the original text by Pelagius. [5]Rom 8:28.

tion of the world. . . . This then is the purpose of God, in relation to which it is said, "He works together all things for good for those who are called according to his own purpose." Indeed subsequent grace assists man's good purpose, but the purpose itself would not exist if grace did not precede. AGAINST TWO LETTERS OF THE PELAGIANS 2.10.22.[6]

1:9c The Grace Given Us in Christ Jesus

THE ECONOMY OF THE FLESH. ATHANASIUS: Here again allusion is made to the economy according to the flesh. For the grace which came to us from the Savior appeared, as the apostle says, just now, and has come when he sojourned among us. Yet this grace has been prepared even before we came into being. . . . The God of all then created us by his own Word, and knowing our destinies better than we, God foresaw that even though we were made "good," we should be transgressors of the commandment and be thrust out of paradise for disobedience. Being loving and kind, he prepared beforehand in his own Word, by whom also he created us, the economy of our salvation. Though by the serpent's deceit we fell from him, we would not remain wholly dead, but having in the Word the redemption and salvation which was earlier prepared for us, we might rise again and abide immortal. AGAINST THE ARIANS 2.75.[7]

1:10a Now Manifested Through the Appearing

OLD, YET NEW. THEODORE OF MOPSUESTIA: The gospel is ancient in the will of the Giver, even if new in the chain of events. God has demonstrated his eternal will in Christ. COMMENTARY ON 2 TIMOTHY.[8]

FULFILLMENT. THEODORET OF CYR: Indeed, the God of all pre-formed these things from the beginning and before the ages. Now he has brought about a conclusion to all that was

decreed. The incarnation is that in which the eternity of the Son is finally manifested. INTERPRETATION OF THE SECOND LETTER TO TIMOTHY.[9]

1:10b Our Savior Abolished Death and Brought Life

NO LONGER DYING. ATHANASIUS: "From Adam to Moses death reigned";[10] but the presence of the Word abolished death. No longer in Adam are we all dying.[11] In Christ we are all reviving. AGAINST THE ARIANS 1.59.8.[12]

LAMB AND LION. AUGUSTINE: Is he not at the same time a lamb and a lion in both his suffering and his resurrection? Let us discern the lamb in the suffering. "He was," as we just reminded you, "mute as a lamb before its shearer, and he opened not his mouth."[13] Let us discern the lion in the suffering. Jacob has said, "Thou hast risen: resting thou hast slept as a lion.[14] Let us discern the lamb in the resurrection. When the Apocalypse is speaking of the everlasting glory of virgins, it says, "They follow the lamb wherever he goes."[15] Let us discern the lion in the resurrection. The Apocalypse also says, "The lion of the tribe of Judah has overcome to open the scroll."[16] Why is he a lamb in his suffering? Because, although he was innocent, he suffered death.[17] Why is he a lion in his suffering? Because he slew death when he himself was slain. Why is he a lamb in his resurrection? Because his innocence is everlasting.[18] Why is he a lion in his resurrection? Because his power is everlasting.[19] SERMONS 4.1.[20]

1:12a I Know Whom I Have Believed

WE COMMEND OUR FAITH TO GOD'S KEEP-

---

[6]NPNF 1 5:401*. [7]NPNF 2 4:389*. [8]TEM 2:199. [9]PG 82:835A/ 836A. [10]Cf. Rom 5:14. [11]1 Cor 15:22. [12]NPNF 2 4:341*. [13]Is 53:7. [14]Gen 49:9. [15]Rev 14:4. [16]Rev 5:5. [17]Jas 5:6. [18]Cf. Heb 7:26. [19]Cf. Heb 1:20; Rev 5:13. [20]FC 11:308.

ing. Augustine: Paul says [elsewhere], "I have kept the faith,"[21] but the same apostle also says, "For I know whom I have believed, and I am certain that he is able to keep that which I have deposited with him against that day." "That which I have deposited with him" means: What I have commended to him, for some [Latin] copies do not have the word *depositum* but *commendatum,* which is clearer. Now what do we commend to God's keeping save those things which we pray he will preserve? Is not our very faith among these? For what did the Lord commend for the apostle Peter, by his prayer for him, when he said to him, "I have prayed for you, Peter, that your faith shall not fail"?[22] This means that God would preserve his faith and that it would not fail by giving way to temptation. Proceedings of Pelagius 14.35.[23]

1:12b *To Guard Until That Day*

The Deposit. Theodore of Mopsuestia: The "deposit" is the pledge[24] of the Spirit given to Paul that he may be preserved. Commentary on 2 Timothy.[25]

The Power of the Spirit. Theodoret of Cyr: The "deposit" is the power and grace offered to Paul by the Spirit for serving the Lord. Interpretation of the Second Letter to Timothy.[26]

1:12c *What Has Been Entrusted to Me*

The Faith Preached or the Faithful People. Chrysostom: What is "that which has been entrusted to me"?[27] The faith, the preaching of the gospel. God, who committed this to us, will preserve it unimpaired. I suffer everything, that I may not be despoiled of this treasure. I am not ashamed of these things, so long as the faith is preserved uninjured. Or by "that which is entrusted to me" he may be referring to the faithful people who God has committed to him. Homilies on 2 Timothy 2.[28]

1:13 *The Pattern of the Sound Words*

An Impressed Image. Chrysostom: After the manner of artists, Paul is saying, I have impressed on you the image of virtue, fixing in your soul a sort of rule and model and outline of all things pleasing to God. Hold fast to these things, whether you are meditating on any matter of faith or love or of a sound mind. Form your ideas from this pattern in the future. Homilies on 2 Timothy 3.[29]

1:14a *The Truth Entrusted to You*

Preserve the Heavenly Seed. John of Damascus: Before all things, keep that truth which is committed to your trust, the holy Word of faith by which you have been taught and instructed. And let no weeds of heresy grow up among you, but preserve the heavenly seed pure and sincere, that it may yield a great harvest to the master, when he comes to demand account of our lives. He shall reward us according to our deeds, when the righteous shall shine forth as the sun, but darkness and everlasting shame shall cover the sinners. Barlaam and Ioasaph 36.335.[30]

1:14b *The Holy Spirit Dwells Within Us*

The Spirit in Me. Basil the Great: If we offer glory to God in the Spirit, we mean that the Spirit enables us to fulfill the requirements of true religion. According to this usage, then, we say we are in the Spirit, but it is not objectionable for someone to testify, "the Spirit of God is in me, and I offer glory because his grace has given me the wisdom to do so." The

---

[21]2 Tim 4:7. [22]Lk 22:32. [23]FC 86:148. [24]Or earnest, or down payment. [25]TEM 2: 200 (Greek). [26]PG 82:835C/836C. [27]The Greek term *parathēkē* may refer to either what Paul has committed to God or what God has committed to Paul. [28]NPNF 1 13:481. [29]NPNF 1 13:484*. [30]JDBI 559*.

words of Paul are appropriate: "I think that I have the Spirit of God,"[31] and "guard the truth that has been entrusted to you by the Holy Spirit who dwells within us." ON THE HOLY SPIRIT 26.63.[32]

1:15 All Who Are in Asia Turned Away from Me

MOST TURNED ASIDE. CHRYSOSTOM: It seems that there were then in Rome many persons from the regions of Asia. "But no one stood by me," he says. No one acknowledged me. All were alienated. Take note of what his soul loves. He only mentions their conduct. He does not curse them, but he praises him who showed kindness to him and invokes a thousand blessings upon him, without any curse on them. HOMILIES ON 2 TIMOTHY 3.[33]

HIS CONCERN FOR TIMOTHY. THEODORET OF CYR: Paul was then at Rome. Many had wandered away, some for money, others for other reasons. Some of the Asian converts abandoned Paul there on account of the fear of Nero. Paul is afraid that they might be a problem to Timothy, and he wants him to be aware of them. INTERPRETATION OF THE SECOND LETTER TO TIMOTHY.[34]

1:16 Grant Mercy to the Household of Onesiphorus

ENCOURAGING FELLOW COMBATANTS. CHRYSOSTOM: Such ought the faithful to be—like Onesiphorus. Neither fear nor threats nor disgrace should deter them from assisting one another, standing by them and succoring them as in war. For they do not so much benefit those who are in danger, as themselves, by the service they render to them, making themselves partakers of the crowns due to them. . . . For as in the service of kings, not only those who fight the battle but those who guard the baggage share in the honor. Even more, they frequently even have an equal portion of the spoils, though they have not soaked their hands in blood, nor stood in array, nor even seen the ranks of the enemy. So it is in these conflicts. For he who relieves the combatant, when wasted with hunger, who stands by him, encouraging him by words and rendering him every service, is not inferior to the combatant. HOMILIES ON 2 TIMOTHY 3.[35]

---

[31]1 Cor 7:40. [32]OHS 96. [33]NPNF 1 13:484. [34]PG 82:837A/838A. [35]NPNF 1 13:484-85*.

2:1-13 EXHORTATION TO STEADFASTNESS

[1]*You then, my son, be strong in the grace that is in Christ Jesus,* [2]*and what you have heard from me before many witnesses entrust to faithful men who will be able to teach others also.* [3]*Share in suffering as a good soldier of Christ Jesus.* [4]*No soldier on service gets entangled in civilian pursuits, since his aim is to satisfy the one who enlisted him.* [5]*An athlete is not crowned unless he competes according to the rules.* [6]*It is the hard-working farmer who ought to have the first share of the crops.* [7]*Think over what I say, for the Lord will grant you understanding in everything.*

⁸*Remember Jesus Christ, risen from the dead, descended from David, as preached in my gospel, ⁹the gospel for which I am suffering and wearing fetters like a criminal. But the word of God is not fettered. ¹⁰Therefore I endure everything for the sake of the elect, that they also may obtain salvation in Christ Jesus with its eternal glory. ¹¹The saying is sure:*

If we have died with him, we shall also live with him;

¹²*if we endure, we shall also reign with him;*

if we deny him, he also will deny us;

¹³*if we are faithless, he remains faithful—*
for he cannot deny himself.

OVERVIEW: Paul appeals to the intimacy of the relationship between himself and Timothy, that it might become a source of strength in the fight to remain steadfast in suffering and in faithful witness to the truth of the gospel. Various analogies and inducements are evoked to stimulate Timothy to his best efforts (CHRYSOSTOM). What is at stake here is the rigor and self-discipline that Timothy must embrace in order to be true to his commission as well as to the strict truth of his message. This will reflect a firm emphasis on the "assumed body" of Jesus in his humanity as the source of our salvation (THEODORE). The strict, quasi-military discipline of the preacher and teacher is indispensable to the preacher's effective work, as is the free and orthodox proclamation of the incarnation as the means of salvation (THEODORET). The difficult and often unpopular position of the faithful preacher requires strict abstinence from worldly pleasures and a firm loyalty to the gospel (AMBROSIASTER).

It is clear that the whole thrust of the gospel, anticipated in the prophets, is toward the resurrection of the flesh, a resurrection anticipated by our discipline and faithfulness in the present body (PELAGIUS). If the apostle endures hardship without demoralization, much more ought the pastor to follow him in this (CHRYSOSTOM). The Scriptures are to be delivered over only to the faithful who desire to live a holy life, not to the unbelieving who will distort them (HIPPOLYTUS). The soldiers of Christ, subject to strict discipline (TERTULLIAN), form a fortification for truth (ORIGEN). Enduring hardship is a part of what it means to be a soldier (CHRYSOSTOM). The soldier's sustenance is provided by the king (BASIL), in this case for an eternal kingdom (AUGUSTINE). He does not sleep on an ivory bed (CHRYSOSTOM). He gives satisfaction to the One in whose ranks he serves (IGNATIUS). He lets nothing else interfere (AMBROSIASTER, AMBROSE, JEROME, LEO). He must first examine the rules of the contest (JOHN CASSIAN). The costs are high (JEROME). It means nothing if he has no opponent (GREGORY OF NYSSA). He needs a good coach (BASIL). The soul is being tested as gold by fire (ORIGEN).

The word Timothy heard Paul proclaim was not spoken in secret but before many witnesses (TERTULLIAN, CHRYSOSTOM, PELAGIUS), and even in the presence of angels (BASIL). The benefits that God's condescension has conferred upon us are of such a radical gratuitous nature that we are embarrassed to ascribe them to God (CHRYSOSTOM). The crucifixion and resurrection faith distinguish Christianity from its counterfeits (AUGUSTINE, THEODORE, THEODORET). In attesting this faith, our hands may be bound but not our tongue. Nothing can bind the tongue but cowardice and unbelief (CHRYSOSTOM). As partakers in his suffering, we rise up in his resurrection (APHRAHAT, BASIL). This we celebrate in Holy Week and Easter (AUGUSTINE). The soul is renewed who hastens to the Word (AMBROSE). Christ reigns by nature; we reign with him by grace (AMBROSE). The narrow path is unattractive by nature but becomes easy when we choose to follow it, because of our hope for the future (CHRYSOSTOM). Christ is the pattern of our patience (LEO). That he can do nothing of himself means nothing else than that he can do nothing in opposition to his Father, nothing different, nothing foreign (CHRYSOSTOM). God remains all-powerful precisely in what he, from one point of view, "cannot" do—lie, die or be unjust (AUGUSTINE).

2:1 Be Strong in Grace

AS WITH ME, SO WITH YOU. CHRYSOSTOM: The young sailor at sea is inspired with great confidence if the master of the ship has been preserved in a shipwreck. For he will not consider that it is from the master's inexperience that he is exposed to the storm, but from the nature of things, and this has no little effect upon his mind. In war also the captain, who sees his general wounded and recovered again, is much encouraged. And thus it produces some consolation to the faithful that the apostle should have been exposed to great sufferings and not been rendered weak by the utmost of them. . . . For if I, Paul, endure these things, much more ought you to bear them. If the master much, more the disciple. And this exhortation he introduces with much affection, calling him "son," and not only so, but "my son." If you are a son, he implies, imitate your father. HOMILIES ON 2 TIMOTHY 4.[1]

2:2a What You Have Heard from Me

PAUL HAS TESTIFIED BEFORE MANY WITNESSES. TERTULLIAN: Now what is this commandment, and what is this charge?[2] From the preceding and the succeeding contexts, it will be manifest that there is no mysterious hint darkly suggested in this expression about some farfetched doctrine. A warning is rather being given against receiving any other doctrine than that which Timothy had heard from Paul, as I take it,

publicly: "Before many witnesses" is his phrase. ON PRESCRIPTION AGAINST HERETICS 25.[3]

NOT IN SECRET. CHRYSOSTOM: As if he had said: You have not heard in secret, nor apart, but in the presence of many, with all openness of speech. HOMILIES ON 2 TIMOTHY 4.[4]

THE ANGELS ALSO ARE WITNESSES. BASIL THE GREAT: One does not speak of the Spirit and of angels as if they were equals. The Spirit is the Lord of life. The angels are our helpers, our fellow servants, faithful witnesses of the truth. It is customary for the saints to deliver God's commandments in the presence of witnesses. St. Paul says to Timothy: "what you have heard from me before many witnesses entrust to faithful men." He asks the angels to testify with him, because he knows that angels will be present when the Lord comes in the glory of his father to judge the world in righteousness. ON THE HOLY SPIRIT 13.29.[5]

BEFORE OR WITH MANY WITNESSES. PELAGIUS: Either "with many persons present I gave you mandates such as you should teach," or "what I said I have confirmed with many examples and testimonies from the prophets." PELAGIUS'S COMMENTARY ON THE SECOND LETTER TO TIMOTHY.[6]

2:2b Entrust to Faithful People

DO NOT DELIVER SCRIPTURE TO UNBELIEVERS. HIPPOLYTUS: [Only] see that you do not give these scriptural teachings over to unbelieving and blasphemous tongues, for that is a danger greatly to be avoided. But impart them to pious and faithful men who desire to live in a holy way and righteously with fear. For it is not to no purpose that the blessed apostle exhorts Timothy,

---

[1]NPNF 1 13:487-88.* [2]Tertullian has just cited all of the verses that mention the *parathēkē*, or "charge" (1 Tim 1:18; 6:13, 20; 2 Tim 1:14; 2:2. [3]ANF 3:255*. [4]NPNF 1 13:488*. [5]OHS 50-51. [6]PETE 511.

and says, "O Timothy, keep that which is committed to your trust, avoiding profane and vain babblings and oppositions of science falsely so called; which some professing have erred concerning the faith."[7] And again, "You therefore, my son, be strong in the grace that is in Christ Jesus. And the things that you have heard from me in many exhortations,[8] the same you should commit to faithful men, who shall be able to teach others also." The blessed apostle delivered these things with a pious caution, aware that they could be easily known and distorted by anyone who does not have faith.[9] How much greater will be our danger, if, rashly and without thought, we commit the revelations of God to profane and unworthy men. TREATISE ON CHRIST AND ANTICHRIST 1.[10]

2:3 A Good Soldier of Christ Jesus

CALL TO MILITARY DISCIPLINE. TERTULLIAN: I am aware of the excuses by which we color our insatiable carnal appetites. Our pretexts are: the necessities of props to lean on; a house to be managed; a family to be governed; chests and keys to be guarded; the wool-spinning to be dispensed; food to be attended to; cares to be generally lessened. Of course, the houses of none but married men fare well! The families of celibates, the estates of eunuchs, the fortunes of military men or of such as travel without wives have gone to rack and ruin! For are not we, too, soldiers? Soldiers, indeed, subject to all the stricter discipline, since we are subject to so great a General? ON EXHORTATION TO CHASTITY 12.[11]

KEEP THE FORT. ORIGEN: The true soldiers of Christ must, in every way, form a fortification for truth and nowhere permit an opening for persuasive falsehood, so far as they are able. COMMENTARY ON JOHN 6.32.[12]

ENDURE HARDNESS. CHRYSOSTOM: "You therefore must endure rough times as a good soldier of Jesus Christ." . . . Observe the kings on

earth, how great an honor it is esteemed to serve under them. If therefore the soldier of the king ought to endure hardness, not to endure hardness is not the part of any soldier. HOMILIES ON 2 TIMOTHY 4.[13]

2:4a No Soldier Entangled in Civilian Pursuits

TWO MASTERS IMPOSSIBLE. AMBROSIASTER: No one can serve two masters. Since business affairs often involve the exercise of greed, the faithful churchman must be separate from these. COMMENTARY ON THE SECOND LETTER TO TIMOTHY.[14]

NO PROPERTY MANAGEMENT. JEROME: How can the clergy be managers and stewards of other men's households and estates when they are bidden to disregard even their own interests? LETTERS 52.16.[15]

THE SOLDIER OF VIRTUE. CHRYSOSTOM: You are a spiritual soldier. This kind of soldier does not sleep on an ivory bed but on the ground. He is not anointed with perfumed oils. These are the concern of those corrupt men who dally with courtesans, of those who act on the stage, of those who live carelessly. You must not smell of perfumes but of virtue. ON LAZARUS AND THE RICH MAN 1.[16]

NO THOUGHT OF TOMORROW. AUGUSTINE: We are not anxious about the necessities of life, because, when we can perform these labors, he feeds and clothes us as men in general are fed and clothed. When, however, we are not able to work, then he feeds and clothes us just as the birds are

---

[7]1 Tim 6:20-21. [8]Hippolytus has here a Greek text apparently unique to himself: *parakleseon* ("exhortations") rather than the standard *martyrōn* ("witnesses"). [9]2 Thess 3:2. [10]ANF 5:204*. [11]ANF 4:56. [12]FC 80:177. [13]NPNF 1 13:488*. [14]CSEL 81 3:302-3. [15]LCC 5:329. [16]OWP 26.

fed and the lilies clothed, since we are of more value than they. Therefore, in this warfare of ours, we give no thought to the morrow, because it is not by temporal concerns pertaining to the morrow but by eternal matters, the concern of the everlasting today, that we have proved ourselves to him whom we cannot please if we are entangled in worldly affairs. THE WORK OF MONKS 27.35.[17]

SOCIALLY UNENCUMBERED. LEO THE GREAT: He who is enrolled in God's army must not be bound to others, lest any obligatory ties call him away from the Lord's camp, where his name is inscribed. LETTERS 4.[18]

2:4b *Satisfying the One Who Enlisted Us*

IN SERVICE TOGETHER. IGNATIUS: Pay attention to the bishop so that God will pay attention to you. I give my life as a sacrifice (poor as it is) for those who are obedient to the bishop, the presbyters and the deacons. Along with them may I get my share of God's reward! Share your hard training together—wrestle together, run together, suffer together, retire together, get up together, as God's stewards, assessors and assistants. Give satisfaction to him in whose ranks you serve and from whom you get your pay. Let none of you be a deserter. Let your baptism be your arms; your faith, your helmet; your love, your spear; your endurance, your armor.[19] LETTER TO POLYCARP 6.1-2.[20]

TO BE HOLY. ORIGEN: If you have understood how either an animal or a vessel or a garment is called holy, understand too that a person is also called holy by these observances and laws. For if anyone should devote himself to God, if anyone should not entangle himself in secular affairs, "in order to please him who appointed him," if anyone was separated and set apart from the rest of men who live carnally and are bound with mundane affairs and does not seek things which are upon the earth but which are in heaven,[21] that

person is deservedly called holy. HOMILIES ON LEVITICUS 11.4.[22]

IN THE KING'S CARE. BASIL THE GREAT: Where is Christ, the King? In heaven, to be sure. In this direction it behooves you, soldier of Christ, to direct your course. Forget all earthly delights. A soldier does not build a house. He does not aspire to the possession of lands. He does not concern himself with devious, coin-purveying trade. . . . The soldier enjoys a sustenance provided by the king. He need not furnish his own nor vex himself in this regard. AN INTRODUCTION TO THE ASCETICAL LIFE.[23]

CLERICAL DISCIPLINE. MAXIMUS OF TURIN: Clerics do not seem to be on military service in the world, yet they are nonetheless soldiers for God and the Lord. As the apostle says, No one soldiering for God involves himself in secular affairs. We seem, I say, not to be soldiers in our loose and flowing tunics, but we have our military belt, by which we are bound to an interior purity. SERMONS 26.4.[24]

2:5a *An Athlete Is Not Crowned*

THE WORLD AN ARENA. AMBROSE: What is the world but an arena full of fighting? Therefore the Lord says in the Apocalypse, "To the victor I shall give the crown of life,"[25] and Paul says, "I have fought the good fight,"[26] and elsewhere, "No one is crowned unless he has competed according to the rules." He who initiated the contest is actually almighty God. When one initiates a contest in this world, does he not prepare all that is necessary for the contest, and only after he has made ready the wreaths for rewards call those who are to contend for the crown, so that the winner may not meet with delay but depart after being given

---

[17]FC 16:383. [18]FC 34:24. [19]Cf. Eph 6:11-17. [20]LCC 1:119. [21]Cf. Col 3:1-2. [22]FC 83:209. [23]FC 9:9. [24]ACW 50:65. [25]Rev 2:10. [26]2 Tim 4:7.

his reward? The rewards of man are the fruits of the earth and the lights of heaven. The former are for his use in the present life; the latter, for his hope of life eternal. Like an athlete, then, he comes last into the arena. . . . It is he who poises the blow, it is Christ who strikes; he lifts his heel, Christ directs it to the wound. . . . In preaching Christ he deals wounds to all those spiritual evils which are his enemies. Not undeservedly, then, does man enter the stadium last, and a crown is prepared for him so that heaven might go before him as being his reward. LETTERS 49.[27]

2:5b Competing According to the Rules

MORTAL LIFE ITSELF THE CONTEST. ORIGEN: We who are concerned with the business of our Creator will live according to the laws of God. We have no desire to serve the laws of sin. . . . If necessary, we will also partake of the joys of this life and endure the appointed evils as trials of the soul. . . . In them the soul of the man who is being tested, like gold in the fire, is either convicted of failure or is manifested as reliable. . . . Moreover, no one is crowned unless he strives lawfully even here upon earth with the body of humiliation. AGAINST CELSUS 8.56.[28]

DO ALL THAT IS FITTING. CHRYSOSTOM: What is meant by "lawfully"? It is not enough that he enters into the lists, that he is anointed, and even engages, unless he comply with all the laws of the exercise. This includes those that pertain to diet, to temperance and sobriety, and all the rules of the wrestling school. Unless, in short, he goes through all that is befitting for a wrestler, he is not crowned. HOMILIES ON 2 TIMOTHY 4.[29]

THE ATHLETIC ANALOGY. CHRYSOSTOM: You say that her clothes are shabby, but virginity resides not in clothing nor in one's complexion but in the body and soul. Is it not strange that we have different standards? We will not judge the philosopher by his hair or his staff or his tunic but by his way of life, his character and soul. The

soldier too we will not approve for his mantle or belt but for his strength and manliness. Yet the virgin, who represents a state so admirable and superior to all others, we will simply and offhandedly assume practices her virtue because of the squalor of her hair, her dejected look and gray cloak. We do not strip her soul bare and scrutinize closely its inner state. But he who has drawn up the rules for this contest does not permit this. He orders that those who have entered not be judged by their clothing but by the convictions of their souls. "Athletes," Paul says, "deny themselves all sorts of things,"[30] anything that would trouble the health of the soul. "If one takes part in an athletic contest, he cannot receive the winner's crown unless he has kept the rules." What, then, are the laws of this contest? Hear again his words, or rather Christ himself, who has established the contest: "The virgin is concerned with things of the Lord, in pursuit of holiness in body and spirit."[31] ON VIRGINITY 7.1-2.[32]

EXPECT A RIGOROUS LIFE. CHRYSOSTOM: In a word, it is absolutely necessary for one who hopes to please God and to be acceptable and pure, not to pursue a relaxed and slippery and dissolute life, but a laborious life, groaning with much toil and sweat. For no one is crowned, Paul says, "unless he competes according to the rules." ON LAZARUS AND THE RICH MAN 3.[33]

YOU NEED A GOOD COACH. BASIL THE GREAT: But, if you place yourself in the hands of a man rich in virtue, you will become the heir of the good qualities he possesses and you will be supremely blessed with God and men. On the other hand, if, to spare the body, you seek a master who will condescend or, rather, degrade himself to the level of your vices, all in vain did you endure the struggle of renunciation, since you have surrendered yourself to a life of gratifying

---

[27]FC 26:255-56. [28]OAC 494. [29]NPNF 1 13:488*. [30]1 Cor 9:25. [31]1 Cor 7:34. [32]COV 9. [33]OWP 75.

your passions by choosing a blind guide who will lead you into the pit. ON RENUNCIATION OF THE WORLD.[34]

THE NECESSITY OF THE OPPONENT. GREGORY OF NYSSA: How can there be a lawful contest if there is no opponent? If there is no opponent, there is no crown. Victory does not exist by itself, without there being a defeated party. ON PERFECTION.[35]

THE COST OF THE CONTEST. JEROME: Christ's athlete is not crowned unless he has competed according to the rules, unless he has accepted and sustained the challenge, unless his face is black and blue from the fray and bathed in blood. It is the discolored bruises that deserve a crown, and suffering and pain that merit joy. HOMILIES 43.1.[36]

LOOK FIRST AT THE RULES OF THE CONTEST. JOHN CASSIAN: One who wants to extinguish the natural desires of the flesh should first hasten to overcome those vices whose ground is contrary to our nature. For if we desire to test out the force of the apostle's counsel, we ought first to learn what are the laws and what the discipline of the world's contest. This is so that finally by a comparison with these, we may be able to know what the blessed apostle meant to teach to us who are striving in the spiritual contest. INSTITUTES 5.12.[37]

2:8 Remember Jesus Christ

THE DIVINE CONDESCENSION. CHRYSOSTOM: Why is this mentioned? It is directed chiefly against the heretics, at the same time to encourage Timothy, by underscoring the divine blessings accompanying sufferings, since Christ, our Master, himself overcame death by suffering. . . . For upon this point many had already begun to subvert God's providence, being ashamed at the immensity of God's love for humanity. For of such a nature are the benefits which God has

conferred upon us that we were embarrassed to as-cribe them to God and could not believe he had so far condescended. HOMILIES ON 2 TIMOTHY 4.[38]

THE REALITY OF INCARNATION. THEODORE OF MOPSUESTIA: Some were teaching that it was merely the "assumed body" which came from the seed of David. Paul taught this to combat Simon's Docetic heresy, by which the resurrection is emptied of meaning. COMMENTARY ON 2 TIMOTHY.[39]

COUNTERING HERESY. THEODORET OF CYR: Paul discusses here only the human nature of Christ because he is responding to Simon's heresy, where the true enfleshment of the Savior is denied. INTERPRETATION OF THE SECOND LETTER TO TIMOTHY.[40]

THE CENTRALITY OF RESURRECTION. AUGUSTINE: Let us believe in Christ crucified; but in him as the one who rose again on the third day. That's the faith that distinguishes us from them, distinguishes us from the pagans, distinguishes us from the Jews—the faith by which we believe that Jesus Christ has risen from the dead. The apostle says to Timothy, "Remember that Jesus Christ has risen from the dead, of the seed of David, according to my gospel." And again the same apostle, "Because if you believe in your heart," he says, "that Jesus is Lord, and confess with your lips that God raised him from the dead, you will be saved."[41] This is the salvation, the well-being, the safety and the soundness, which I discussed yesterday. Whoever believes and is baptized will be saved.[42] I know that you believe; you will be saved. Hold firmly in your hearts, profess

---

[34]FC 9:20. [35]FC 58:121*. There is a chance that Gregory had before him as he wrote this passage Origen *Homilies on Genesis* 1.10 (FC 71:59), where the latter writer developed the same train of thought, using 2 Timothy 2:5. [36]FC 48:325. [37]NPNF 2 11:237*. [38]NPNF 1 13:489. [39]TEM 2:205-6. [40]PG 82:839C/840C. [41]Rom 10:9. [42]Mk 16:16.

it with your lips, that Christ has risen from the dead. SERMONS 234.3.[43]

2:9a The Gospel for Which I Am Suffering

PAUL TAUGHT FROM PRISON. CHRYSOSTOM: For just as it is not possible to bind a sunbeam or to shut it up within the house, so neither can the preaching of the word be bound. And what was much more, when the teacher was bound, the word flew abroad. He inhabited the prison, and yet his teaching winged its way everywhere throughout the world! HOMILIES CONCERNING THE STATUES 16.5.[44]

MORE CONSOLATION. CHRYSOSTOM: Out of his own story he once again brings consolation and encouragement. He prepares his hearer's mind in two phases: First that he should be ready to endure hard times. Second, he does this for a useful purpose, gaining though he suffers harm. HOMILIES ON 2 TIMOTHY 4.[45]

2:9b The Word of God Is Not Fettered

TONGUES UNBOUND. CHRYSOSTOM: But now God has made us such that nothing can subdue us. For our hands are bound but not our tongue, since nothing can bind the tongue but cowardice and unbelief. Where these are not, though you fasten chains upon us, the preaching of the gospel is not bound. HOMILIES ON 2 TIMOTHY 4.[46]

LIGHT AMID STORMS. CHRYSOSTOM: Any cloud passing over our skies may from time to time make us gloomy. But Paul's heart had no such storms sweeping over it. Or better, there did sweep over him, and often, many storms, but his day was not darkened. Rather in the midst of the temptations and dangers the light shone out. Thus when bound with his chain he kept exclaiming, "The word of God is not bound." Thus continually by means of that tongue the Word was sending forth its rays. HOMILIES ON FIRST CORINTHIANS 13.4.[47]

THE SOUL DRAWN TO THE WORD. AMBROSE: On this account also it is said to the soul, "Your youth shall be renewed like the eagle's."[48] For the psalmist spoke to the soul and said, "Bless the Lord, O my soul."[49] And therefore the soul hastens to the Word and asks that she be drawn to him, so that she may not, perhaps, be left behind, for "the Word of God runs and is not bound." ISAAC, OR THE SOUL 3.10.[50]

2:10 They Also May Obtain Salvation

FOR OTHERS. CHRYSOSTOM: Behold another incentive. I endure these things, he says, not for myself but for the salvation of others. It was in my power to have lived free from danger; to have suffered none of these things, if I had consulted my own interest. On what account then do I suffer these things? For the good of others, that others may obtain eternal life. HOMILIES ON 2 TIMOTHY 4.[51]

2:11 Dying and Living with Christ

FALLING, WE RISE. ORIGEN: The Savior, too, first granted you this very thing—that you should fall. You were a Gentile. Let the Gentile in you fall. You loved prostitutes. Let the lover of prostitutes in you perish first. You were a sinner. Let the sinner in you fall. Then you can rise again and say, "If we have died with him, we shall also live with him," and, "If we have been made like him in death, we shall also be like him in resurrection."[52] HOMILIES ON LUKE 17.3.[53]

IN BAPTISM AND IN LIVING. CHRYSOSTOM: But how are we "dead with him"? This death refers to both that in the Laver[54] and that in sufferings. HOMILIES ON 2 TIMOTHY 5.[55]

---

[43]WSA 3/7.37. [44]NPNF 1 9:450*. [45]NPNF 1 13:489*. [46]NPNF 1 13:489. [47]NPNF 1 12:75. [48]Ps 103:5. [49]Ps 103:1. [50]FC 65:17. [51]NPNF 1 13:489. [52]Rom 6:5. [53]FC 94:72. [54]The cleansing of baptism. [55]NPNF 1 13:492.

MADE KING, PRIEST AND PROPHET IN BAPTISM. CHRYSOSTOM: So also you are yourself made *king* and *priest* and *prophet* in the washing of baptism. You are a king by having dashed to earth all the deeds of wickedness and slain your sins. You are a priest in that you offer yourself to God, having sacrificed your body and being yourself slain also, "for if we died with him," says he, "we shall also live with him." You are a prophet, knowing what shall be, being inspired of God and sealed. HOMILIES ON SECOND CORINTHIANS 4.[56]

CHRIST REIGNS BY NATURE, WE BY GRACE. AMBROSE: The apostle says that even we shall reign together with Christ in the kingdom of Christ. "If we are dead with him, we shall also live with him; if we endure, we shall also reign with him." But we by adoption, he by power; we live by grace, he by nature. OF THE HOLY SPIRIT 3.20.157-58.[57]

HIS SIGN UPON OUR BODIES. APHRAHAT: Let us honor the spirit of Christ, that we may receive grace from him. Let us be strangers to the world,[58] even as Christ was not of it. Let us be humble and mild, that we may inherit the land of life. Let us be unflagging in his service, that he may cause us to serve in the abode of the saints. Let us pray his prayer in purity, that it may have access to the Lord of majesty. Let us be partakers in his suffering, so that we may also rise up in his resurrection. Let us bear his sign upon our bodies, that we may be delivered from the wrath to come. SELECT DEMONSTRATIONS 6.1.[59]

THE BAPTISMAL ASSURANCE. BASIL THE GREAT: Having been planted with him in the likeness of his death, we will assuredly be raised up together with Christ (for the planting implies this eventuality). But in the present life, we are formed in the inner man according to the measure of the incarnation in newness of life and obedience unto death, fully persuaded of the truth of his words, so that we may become worthy to say

with truth, "And I live, now not I, but Christ lives in me."[60] That this obtains also for the future life. The same apostle has strongly affirmed this in these words: "For if we be dead with him, we shall also live with him. If we suffer, we shall also reign with him." CONCERNING BAPTISM.[61]

PASSION AND RESURRECTION. AUGUSTINE: We ought to be humble of heart out of the sincerest devotion during the whole time of this wandering exile, in which we are living in the midst of trials and temptations. If so, how much more should we be so during these days, when as well as spending this time of humility by living it, we are also signifying it by our liturgical celebration of it. The lowliness of Christ has taught us to be lowly, because by dying he yielded to the godless. Christ's highness makes us exalted, because by rising again he has led the way for the godly. . . . We celebrate one of these things now, when his passion is, so to say, drawing near. We celebrate the other after Easter with appropriate devotion, when his resurrection, so to say, has been accomplished. SERMONS 206.1.[62]

HIS PASSION IN THE FLESH, IMPASSIBILITY AS GOD. NICETAS OF REMESIANA: We must believe both his passion according to the flesh and his impassibility inasmuch as he was God. . . . Let us confess our oneness with Christ, lest we be separated from him. In the words of the apostle, "If we have died with him, we shall also live with him." INSTRUCTION ON FAITH 7.[63]

2:12 Enduring and Reigning with Him

THE NARROW PATH MADE EASY. CHRYSOSTOM: Accordingly, I beseech you, let us so perform all our actions that we may not fail to obtain such glory as this. To obtain it is by no

---

[56]NPNF 1 12:293*. [57]NPNF 2 10:157*. [58]Cf. Mt 25:31. [59]NPNF 2 13:362-63. [60]Gal 2:20. [61]FC 9:370*. [62]WSA 3/6:106*. [63]FC 7:20-21.

means difficult, if we desire it, or arduous, if we apply ourselves to it. For, "If we endure, we shall also reign." What is the meaning of "If we endure"? If we patiently bear tribulations and persecutions; if we walk the narrow path. The narrow path is unattractive by nature but becomes easy when we choose to follow it, because of our hope for the future. HOMILIES ON JOHN 87.3.[64]

THE PATTERN OF OUR PATIENCE. LEO THE GREAT: In him therefore is our hope of eternal life, and in him also is the pattern of our patience. "If we suffer with him, we shall also reign with him," since, as the apostle says, "those who claim that they remain in Christ ought themselves to walk just as Christ walked."[65] Otherwise we are appearing under the likeness of a false profession if we do not follow the commands of him in whose name we glory. And these would indeed not be burdensome to us and would free us from all dangers, if we would only love what he commands us to love. SERMONS 90.2.[66]

2:13a He Remains Faithful

INEFFABLE STRENGTH. CHRYSOSTOM: Therefore, "He can do nothing of himself"[67] means nothing else than that he can do nothing in opposition to his Father, nothing different, nothing foreign. This is an attribute especially belonging to one who is giving proof of his equality with the Father and of complete agreement as well. But why does he not say, "He does nothing in opposition" instead of "He cannot"? It was in order that he might show from this once more that his equality is undeviating and complete. This statement does not imply any weakness in him but testifies to his great power. Besides, Paul says elsewhere of the Father, "That by two unchangeable things, in which it is impossible for God to deceive"; and again, "If we disown him, he remains faithful, for he cannot disown himself." Now this word "cannot" is not, of course, indicative of weakness but of strength;

indeed, ineffable strength. HOMILIES ON JOHN 38.3.[68]

GOD REMAINS FAITHFUL. ATHANASIUS: Now the so-called gods of the Greeks, unworthy of the name, are faithful neither in their essence nor in their promises. They do not abide everywhere. The local deities come to nought in the course of time and undergo a natural dissolution. . . . But the God of all, being one really and indeed and true, is faithful, who is ever the same. . . . He is ever the same and unchanging, deceiving neither in his essence nor in his promise. As again says the apostle writing to the Thessalonians, "Faithful is he who calls you, who also will do it";[69] for in doing what he promises, he is faithful to his words. And he thus writes to the Hebrews[70] as to the word's meaning "unchangeable": "If we believe not, yet he abides faithful; he cannot deny himself." AGAINST THE ARIANS 2.10.[71]

2:13b For He Cannot Deny Himself

WHY GOD CANNOT DENY HIMSELF. AUGUSTINE: The only thing the Almighty cannot do is what he does not will, in case anybody should consider it was very rash of me to say that the Almighty "cannot" do something. The blessed apostle said it too, "If we do not believe, he remains faithful, for he cannot deny himself." But it is because he does not wish to that he cannot do it, because he cannot even have the will to. Justice, after all, cannot have the will to do what is unjust, or wisdom will what is foolish, or truth will what is false. SERMONS 214.4.[72]

IS GOD ALL-POWERFUL IN WHAT HE "CANNOT" DO? AUGUSTINE: God is all-powerful, and, since he is all-powerful, he cannot die, he cannot

---

[64]FC 41:465. [65]1 Jn 2:6. [66]FC 93:380*. [67]Jn 5:19. [68]FC 33:378-79. [69]1 Thess 5:24. [70]The reference is to Hebrews 13:8, mentioned a little further on in the passage. [71]NPNF 2 4:353*. [72]WSA 3/6:152.

be deceived, he cannot lie, and, as the apostle says, "he cannot disown himself." Very much he cannot do, yet he is all-powerful. It is because he cannot do these things for the very reason that he is all-powerful. If he could die, he would not be all-powerful. If he could lie, if he could be deceived, if he could deceive, if it were possible for him to do an injustice, he would not be omnipotent. If it were in him to do any of this,

such acts would not be worthy of the Almighty. Absolutely omnipotent, our Father cannot sin. On the Creed 1.2.[73]

---

[73]FC 27:290. Augustine uses a similar logic to make the point that with God, by comparison with human beings, it is "not possible to sin," in *On Nature and Grace* 49.57 (FC 86:64-65).

2:14-26 EXHORTATION TO SIMPLICITY OF FAITH

[14]*Remind them of this, and charge them before the Lord[b] to avoid disputing about words, which does no good, but only ruins the hearers.* [15]*Do your best to present yourself to God as one approved, a workman who has no need to be ashamed, rightly handling the word of truth.* [16]*Avoid such godless chatter, for it will lead people into more and more ungodliness,* [17]*and their talk will eat its way like gangrene. Among them are Hymenaeus and Philetus,* [18]*who have swerved from the truth by holding that the resurrection is past already. They are upsetting the faith of some.* [19]*But God's firm foundation stands, bearing this seal: "The Lord knows those who are his," and, "Let every one who names the name of the Lord depart from iniquity."* [20]*In a great house there are not only vessels of gold and silver but also of wood and earthenware, and some for noble use, some for ignoble.* [21]*If any one purifies himself from what is ignoble, then he will be a vessel for noble use, consecrated and useful to the master of the house, ready for any good work.* [22]*So shun youthful passions and aim at righteousness, faith, love, and peace, along with those who call upon the Lord from a pure heart.* [23]*Have nothing to do with stupid, senseless controversies; you know that they breed quarrels.* [24]*And the Lord's servant must not be quarrelsome but kindly to every one, an apt teacher, forbearing,* [25]*correcting his opponents with gentleness. God may perhaps grant that they will repent and come to know the truth,* [26]*and they may escape from the snare of the devil, after being captured by him to do his will.[c]*

b Other ancient authorities read *God*   c Or *by him, to do his* (that is, God's) *will*

Overview: Paul exhorts Timothy to hold the faith in its essentials, especially faith in the coming resurrection and final judgment, that he may cling not only to right belief but also to right practice, so that by his own choice he may be a vessel fit for salvation (Chrysostom). What Timothy must remember is that when the teaching about the resurrection of the dead is correctly understood, it points to a future and spiritual life, which true believers know and practice in the present and which distinguishes them from false brethren (Theodore). Timothy is urged to interpret Scripture rightly in both teaching and practice, that his hearers may be taught an understanding of the incarnation that cuts through all of the obscurities of the heretics and that will lead believers to salvation (Theodoret). Paul makes it clear that the church itself is a mixed body, made up of persons at various stages of belief and practice. What matters is that official teachers stress the centrality of the resurrection yet to come and the life of freely chosen and virtuous faithfulness that looks toward the resurrection (Ambrosiaster).

The world itself is made up of all sorts and conditions of persons holding a great diversity of beliefs. The church, however, is pure, holding to right belief and practice and always exhorting its members to the faithful living of what they profess (Pelagius). Nothing is better said than that which is said truthfully (Augustine). One wins not with words but deeds (Pelagius). An audience of one is sufficient (Clement of Alexandria). Cut off what is spurious in Scripture interpretation (Chrysostom). Those who wish to change the gospel pour venom into our hearts (Cyprian), spreading like gangrene (Athanasius, Pelagius). They creep in low to the ground, take hold softly, squeeze gently and kill undetected (Leo). We pray that such deceptions may become circumscribed by a definite limit and boundary (Basil). The resurrection is heretically misunderstood by some as merely the natural procreation of children (Ambrosiaster, Theodore, Theodoret), as having happened already to Israel in Ezekiel's time (Pelagius) or reduced merely to the faith of the disciples (Augustine). If the resurrection is past, then the

wicked have unjustly remained unpunished (Chrysostom). The faith of the elect that works through charity either does not ever fail, or, if it fails in some, the loss is repaired before death (Augustine). The Lord knows those who are his because he has been made one with them and has given them a share of his own life (Origen).

Meanwhile, cheap faith is blown away by every wind of temptation (Tertullian). The abundance of bad people in the world is the big heap of dregs needed for refining the good, as in an olive press (Augustine, Bede). God does not recognize those who are not because they have not recognized him who is (Ambrose). If anyone is living an ungodly life, he or she is not of the elect, the foundation (Athanasius, Chrysostom, Augustine, Fulgentius). Correction must be made with gentleness (Basil, Chrysostom). Repentance is enabled by grace (Augustine). Neither consent to evil so as to approve of it nor be negligent so as not to reprove it, nor proud so as to reprove in a tone of insult (Augustine).

We are not to withdraw from the church just because it has tares in it but to become wheat ourselves (Cyprian). Various Fathers view the house either as the world (Theodoret, Pelagius), or the church (Ambrosiaster, Theodore, Basil, Augustine). There are all kinds in the church as there were in the ark (Jerome).

2:14 Avoid Disputing About Words

Don't Play to the Stands. Clement of Alexandria: You must not "make your phylacteries broad"[1] in eagerness for empty repute. The Christian Knower is satisfied with finding an audience of one. Stromata 1.49.1.[2]

Keep It Basic. Pelagius: Do not manipulate Scripture testimonies. This kind of argument

---

[1]Mt 23:5. [2]FC 85:58-59.

does not edify but does damage to one's hearers, who come to think that a certain sharpness and subtlety of mind is everything. Or: Don't try to win with words but with deeds. PELAGIUS'S COMMENTARY ON THE SECOND LETTER TO TIMOTHY.[3]

SUBSTANCE RATHER THAN VERBIAGE. AUGUSTINE: A good teacher chooses a good life in such a way that he does not also neglect good repute but provides "what may be good not only before God but also before men"[4] insofar as he is able by fearing God and caring for men. In his speech itself he should prefer to please more with the meanings expressed than with the words used to speak them. Nor should he think that anything may be said better than that which is said truthfully. Nor should the teacher serve the words but the words the teacher. ON CHRISTIAN DOCTRINE 4.28.61.[5]

2:15a Present Yourself as a Workman Approved

GOD'S WORK AND OURS. ORIGEN: But it is God's work to dwell invisibly by his spirit and by the Spirit of Christ in those whom he judges it right to dwell. Whereas it is our task, since we try to confirm faith by arguments and treatises, to do all in our power that we may be called "workmen who need not to be ashamed, handling rightly the word of truth." AGAINST CELSUS 5.1.[6]

2:15b Rightly Handling the Word of Truth

NO ADDITIONS. CHRYSOSTOM: This he has well said. For many distort the text of Scripture and pervert it in every way, and many additions are made to it. He has not said "directing" but "rightly dividing," that is, cutting away what is spurious, with much vehemence assailing it and extirpating it. With the sword of the Spirit cut off from your preaching, as from a thong, whatever is superfluous and foreign to it. HOMILIES ON 2 TIMOTHY 5.[7]

TEACHING CORRECTLY. THEODORE OF MOPSUESTIA: Paul's intent here is to urge Timothy to teach with a correct purpose, so that the word is not undermined. COMMENTARY ON 2 TIMOTHY.[8]

PLOW STRAIGHT FURROWS. THEODORET OF CYR: Good teachers are like farmers who plow straight furrows, thus presenting the rule of Scripture in a correct manner. INTERPRETATION OF THE SECOND LETTER TO TIMOTHY.[9]

TEACH THOSE WHO WISH TO HEAR. AMBROSIASTER: To teach the word of truth rightly is to speak it to men who wish to hear it and are peaceful in their hearing. COMMENTARY ON THE SECOND LETTER TO TIMOTHY.[10]

CONFIRMING THE WORD. PELAGIUS: It is correct living that confirms the word and that interprets it rightly. PELAGIUS'S COMMENTARY ON THE SECOND LETTER TO TIMOTHY.[11]

2:17 Their Talk Will Eat Its Way Like Gangrene

FALSE BISHOPS. CYPRIAN: From such men come those who, without divine appointment, set themselves over their rash associates, make themselves prelates without any lawful ordination and call themselves bishops though no one gives them a bishopric. The Holy Spirit portrays them in the Psalms "sitting in the seat of pestilence,"[12] plagues and blights to faith, snake-mouthed traitors, scheming to pervert truth, spewing deadly poisons from their pestiferous tongues. Their words "spread like a canker." Their teaching pours fatal venom into men's hearts and breasts. ON THE UNITY OF THE CATHOLIC CHURCH 10.[13]

ARIAN HERETICS. ATHANASIUS: And what

---

[3]PETE 513. [4]2 Cor 8:21. [5]ACD 165. [6]OAC 264. [7]NPNF 1 13:493. [8]TEM 2:208. [9]PG 82:841C/842C. [10]CSEL 81 3:306. [11]PETE 514. [12]Ps 1:1. [13]LCC 5:130-31.

they now write proceeds not from any regard for the truth, as I said before, but rather they do it as in mockery and by a subterfuge, for the purpose of deceiving others. They hope that by sending about their letters they may engage the ears of the people to listen to these notions and so put off the time when they will be brought to trial. By concealing their impiety from observation, they try to make room to extend their heresy, which, "like a gangrene," eats its way everywhere. To THE BISHOPS OF EGYPT 1.5.[14]

BOUNDARIES MUST BE SET. BASIL THE GREAT: "Let the wickedness of sinners be brought to nought."[15] He who says this prayer is obviously a disciple of the evangelical precepts. He prays for those who treat him maliciously, asking that the wickedness of the sinners be circumscribed by a definite limit and boundary. Just as if someone, when praying for those who are suffering in body, would say, "Let the disease of those who are suffering come to an end." In order that the sin slowly creeping farther may not spread like cancer, since he loves his enemy and wishes to do good to those who hate him, and for this reason prays for those who treat him maliciously, he begs of God that the further outpouring of sin may cease and have definite bounds. HOMILIES 11.6.[16]

A PHYSICAL ANALOGY. PELAGIUS: That kind of wound is called a suppurating sore, which begins in the female breasts and then grows quickly into the abdominal region. When it finally becomes a poison that permeates the heart, there is no remedy. In just such a way the discussions of heretics are to be avoided, lest through the ears they reach the mind with an irremediable wound. PELAGIUS'S COMMENTARY ON THE SECOND LETTER TO TIMOTHY.[17]

LIKE A CRAB. LEO THE GREAT: To deceive the first human beings, the devil claimed the serpent as his tool.[18] So to seduce the hearts of orthodox, he armed the tongues of these with the poison of

his falsehood. With pastoral care, however, we oppose these snares, dearly beloved, to the extent that the Lord helps us. To prevent any of the holy flock from perishing, we advise you with fatherly admonitions to turn away from "wicked lips and treacherous tongue," from which the prophet asks that his soul "be kept free,"[19] since "their talk crawls like a crab," as the blessed apostle said. They creep in low to the ground, take hold softly, squeeze gently and kill undetected. SERMONS 16.3.[20]

2:18 Holding That the Resurrection Is Past

THE IMMATERIALITY OF GNOSTIC RESURRECTION TEACHING. TERTULLIAN: Similarly Paul touches those who said that the resurrection had already happened. The Valentinians affirm this of themselves.[21] PRESCRIPTIONS AGAINST HERETICS 33.[22]

REDUCING RESURRECTION TO PROCREATION. AMBROSIASTER: These heretics deny that Christians shall rise in a future life and insist that the resurrection happens in the natural birth of children. COMMENTARY ON THE SECOND LETTER TO TIMOTHY.[23]

THEN NO GLORY AND NO JUDGMENT. CHRYSOSTOM: If the resurrection is already past, not only do we suffer loss in being deprived of that great glory, but because judgment is taken away and retribution also. For if the resurrection is

---

[14]NPNF 2 4:226*. [15]Ps 7:10. [16]FC 46:174-75. [17]PETE 514. [18]Gen 3:1. [19]Ps 120:2. [20]FC 93:60. [21]Tertullian expresses a similar thought about the Valentinian Gnostics in *Resurrection of the Flesh* 19, where he claims that they taught that resurrection happens in baptism. Irenaeus *Against Heresies* 2.48.2 claims that they taught resurrection to happen in the acquisition of truth (references cited in LCC 5:54 n. 72). For discussion of this aspect of Valentinian teaching, see Kurt Rudolph, *Gnosis: The Nature and History of Gnosticism*, trans. Robert McLachlan Wilson (New York: Harper & Row, 1983), pp. 189ff., where it is clear that such realized eschatology follows from the Gnostic commitment to the immateriality of the resurrection body. [22]LCC 5:54. [23]CSEL 81 3:307.

past, retribution also is past. The good therefore have reaped persecutions and afflictions, and the wicked have not been punished. On the contrary, they live in great pleasure. It would be better to say that there is no resurrection than that it is already past. HOMILIES ON 2 TIMOTHY 5.[24]

CORRECT ESCHATOLOGY. ATHANASIUS: Hymenaeus and Alexander and their fellows[25] were confused about time—ahead of time—when they said that the resurrection had already occurred. The Galatians misunderstood the dispensations by making so much of circumcision now. DISCOURSES AGAINST THE ARIANS 1.13.54.[26]

RESURRECTION MISUNDERSTOOD AS PROCREATION. THEODORE OF MOPSUESTIA: The heretical teaching about the resurrection is that it happens in the process of natural procreation, by which our children succeed us. COMMENTARY ON 2 TIMOTHY.[27]

NATURAL SUCCESSIONS. THEODORET OF CYR: The successions that happen through the procreation of children they unhappily call the resurrection. INTERPRETATION OF THE SECOND LETTER TO TIMOTHY.[28]

EZEKIEL'S REVIVIFIED BONES. PELAGIUS: The resurrection has happened, according to them, either in children or in Ezekiel's reference to the revivified bones of the people of Israel in captivity. PELAGIUS'S COMMENTARY ON THE SECOND LETTER TO TIMOTHY.[29]

WHETHER THE RESURRECTION TOOK PLACE IN FAITH. AUGUSTINE: Therefore, all who have established a sect of some religion, even a false one, wishing that they be believed, have not been able to deny this resurrection of human souls. All have agreed on that, but many have denied the resurrection of the flesh and have said that resurrection has already taken place in faith. . . . They said that resurrection had already taken place but

in such a way that another was not to be hoped for; and they reproached those who hoped for the resurrection of the flesh, as though the resurrection which had been promised was already fulfilled in the human soul by believing. TRACTATES ON JOHN 19.14.[30]

2:19a God's Firm Foundation Stands

THE ELECT. AUGUSTINE: It is the elect who are meant in the letter to Timothy, where, after mention of the attempts of Hymenaeus and Philetus to undermine the faith, the text goes on, "But the sure foundation of God stands firm, bearing this seal: 'The Lord knows who are his.'" The faith of these latter, which works through charity, either does not ever fail, or, if it fail in some, the loss is repaired before death, the sin that intervened is blotted out and perseverance to the end is granted. On the other hand, those who are not to persevere to the end, those who are to fall from Christian faith and conduct, in such a way that the end of this life will find them thus fallen— these men are certainly not to be counted in the number of the elect, not even at the time during which they are living in goodness and piety. ADMONITION AND GRACE 7.16.[31]

2:19b The Lord Knows Those Who Are His

ONLY GOD KNOWS. TERTULLIAN: You are human, and so you know other people only from the outside. You think as you see, and you see only what your eyes let you see. But "the eyes of the Lord are lofty."[32] "Man looks on the outward appearance, God looks on the heart."[33] So "the

---

[24]NPNF 1 13:493. [25]2 Tim 2:17-18; 1 Tim 1:20. [26]NPNF 2 4:338*. [27]TEM 2:209. [28]PG 82:843A/844A. [29]PETE 514-15. [30]FC 79:154-55. The critique of Rudolf Bultmann's teaching that the resurrection has already occurred in the faith of the disciples, not in history as flesh and not in the end time as flesh, is thereby anticipated by Augustine. [31]FC 2:263. Augustine expresses the same idea with this text from 2 Timothy at *The City of God* 20.8 (FC 24:268). [32]4 Esdr 8:20. [33]1 Sam 16:7.

Lord knows those who are his." He roots up the plant which he has not planted in his garden. He shows the last to be first. He carries a fan in his hand to purge his floor. Let the chaff of cheap faith fly away as it pleases before every wind of temptation. So much the purer is the heap of wheat which the Lord will gather into his barn. PRESCRIPTIONS AGAINST HERETICS 3.[34]

THE "KNOWING" AND "NOT KNOWING" OF GOD. ORIGEN: God ignores those who are alienated from him.... We say these things, however, not thinking anything blasphemous about God ... not ascribing ignorance to him, but thus we understand that these whose activity is considered unworthy of God are also considered to be unworthy of knowledge of God. For God does not deign to know him who has turned away from him and does not know him. HOMILIES ON GENESIS 4.6.[35]

NOT TO BE SNATCHED AWAY. ORIGEN: Those who have been made one with and united with something know that with which they have been made one and have been united. Yet before such unity and participation, even if they objectively grasp something of the explanations given about a thing, they still do not know it.... For, in our view, the Lord has known those who are his because he has been made one with them and has given them a share of his own divinity and has taken them up, as the language of the Gospel says, into his own hand, since those who have believed in the Savior are in the Father's hand. For this reason also, unless they fall from his hand—thereby removing themselves from the hand of God, they will not be snatched away, for no one snatches anyone from the Father's hand. COMMENTARY ON JOHN 19.22, 25.[36]

GOD DRAWS HIS SAINTS TO HIMSELF. AMBROSE: The Lord considered and knew who were his, and he drew his saints to himself. And those whom he did not choose he did not draw to himself. LETTERS 59.[37]

THOSE WHO ARE NOT. AMBROSE: And if there is some disturbance here, lift up the footstep of your spirit to the things which are to be, and you will discover that the wicked whom you believed to be here will not be there. For one who is nothing is not. Indeed, "the Lord knows those who are his." He does not recognize those who are not, because they have not recognized him who is. THE PRAYER OF JOB AND DAVID 7.22.[38]

GOD WILL SEPARATE GOLD FROM STRAW. AUGUSTINE: The abundance of bad people in the world is the big heap of stuff needed for refining the good. Although the good can't be seen, mixed up in the vast multitude of the bad, the Lord knows who are his own. Under the hand of such a great craftsman, the speck of gold cannot get lost in the huge pile of straw. How much straw is there, how little gold! But have no fear: the craftsman is so great that he can refine it and cannot lose it. SERMONS 15.5.[39]

THE OLIVE PRESS. AUGUSTINE: Something is always going on in this olive press. The world is the press; there is no end to its pressures. Be oil, not dregs. Let each of you be converted to God and change your manner of life. The oil goes by hidden channels to its own secluded vats. Others sin, mock, blaspheme, make loud accusations in the streets—the dregs are oozing out. Yet the Lord of the press does not cease from operating it through his workmen, the holy angels. He knows his oil; he knows how much it can take, the exact pressure needed to squeeze it out. "The Lord knows," you see, "who are his own." Avoid the dregs. They are murky, out in the open for all to see. SERMONS 19.6.[40]

---

[34]LCC 5:32-33. [35]FC 71:110. [36]FC 89:172-73. [37]FC 26:340. [38]FC 65:381-82. [39]WSA 3/1:326. Second Timothy 2:19 is a very popular text with Augustine as a support for his doctrine of election. [40]WSA 3/1:384.

MYSTICAL CHOOSING. THE VENERABLE BEDE: This statement of the Lord[41] . . . can also be understood mystically with regard to the choosing of the spiritual Israel, that is, the Christian people, since the Lord mercifully deigned to see them when they did not yet see him, when they had not yet been called by his apostles to the grace of faith, but they were still concealed under the covering of oppressing sin. . . . And sometimes in the Scriptures, to be sure, the fig tree suggests the sweetness of divine love. . . . Those placed under it can be his elect even when they do not yet recognize the grace of their election—just as the Lord saw Nathanael when he was situated under the fig tree though Nathanael did not see him. For the Lord knows who are his, and the very name *Nathanael* is most suitably appropriate to their salvation. For Nathanael is interpreted "gift of God." HOMILIES ON THE GOSPELS 1.17.[42]

2:19c Departing from Iniquity

FAITH AND GODLINESS INTERTWINED. ATHANASIUS: Faith and godliness, you see, are so closely allied that they can be considered sisters. Anyone who believes in the Lord is godly, and the person who is godly believes all the more. On the other hand, one who is in a state of wrong relationships will certainly wander from the faith, and one who falls from godliness falls from the true faith. Paul, recognizing this, advised his disciples: "Avoid profane conversations, for they lead people further into ungodliness." That is why the Ario-maniacs,[43] being enemies of Christ, have left the church. They have dug a pit of unbelief into which they themselves have fallen. . . . The apostle Paul's words against Philetus and Hymenaeus stand as a warning against ungodliness such as that of the Arians: "God's foundation is firm, bearing this seed: 'The Lord knows his own people' and 'Let everyone who names the name of the Lord depart from iniquity.'" FESTAL LETTERS 9.[44]

THE STONE AND THE SOUL. CHRYSOSTOM: These are the distinguishing marks of the foundation. A foundation is firm. The letters are inscribed upon the stone so that the letters may be seen. But these letters are shown by works, "Having," he says, "this seal fixed thereon, let every one that names the name of the Lord depart from iniquity." Thus if any one is unrighteous, he is not of the foundation. So it belongs to the seal not to do wrong. HOMILIES ON 2 TIMOTHY 5.[45]

PERSEVERE IN RIGHTEOUSNESS. AUGUSTINE: And we know that the apostle said of the vessels placed in the great house, "If a man therefore purge himself from these, he shall be a vessel unto honor, sanctified and ready for the Master's use, and prepared for every good work."[46] But in what manner each man ought to purge himself from these he shows a little above, saying, "Let everyone that names the name of Christ depart from iniquity." This is so that he may not in the last day be blown away with the chaff from the threshing floor. Nor may he be separated at the last by hearing the command, "Depart from me, you that work iniquity."[47] ON BAPTISM, AGAINST THE DONATISTS. 4.14.21.[48]

REPENT NOW. FULGENTIUS OF RUSPE: He therefore will attain life who keeps the commandments. But who keeps the divine commandments except the one who, converted to God before the end of this present life, has departed from his earlier sins? So the blessed Peter[49] warns us, "Let everyone who calls upon the name of the Lord avoid evil." He said this, knowing that penance is done fruitfully in this present world in which forgiveness is given to penitents. But in the future

---

[41]Bede refers to John 1:48 with Jesus' statement to Nathanael, "Before Philip called you, when you were under the fig tree, I saw you." [42]*HOG* 1:173. [43]Fanatic Arians. [44]ARL 155-57*. [45]NPNF 1 13:494*. [46]2 Tim 2:21. [47]Mt 7:23. [48]NPNF 1 4:456*. [49]Fulgentius's memory has failed him here.

world the penitence of the wicked will bear no fruit because there will be no conversion of the wicked. They will be sent into the exterior darkness where there will be wailing and the gnashing of teeth. On the Forgiveness of Sins 7.2.[50]

2:20a Vessels of Gold and Silver, Wood and Earthenware

God's Arrangement. Origen: God who from the beginning felt it just to arrange his creation according to merit gathered the diversities of minds into the harmony of a single world, so as to furnish, as it were, out of these diverse vessels or souls or minds one house. In this house there must be "not only vessels of gold and silver, but also of wood and of earth, and some unto honor and some unto dishonor." On First Principles 2.9.6.[51]

Differing Levels of Maturity. Ambrosiaster: Paul indicates that the church has diverse members, who are at differing levels of maturity. The heretic Novatian believes that this passage applies to the world, since he defends the general truth and holiness of his church. But this is wrong. Commentary on the Second Letter to Timothy.[52]

Chrysostom: As in a great house it is likely there should be a great difference of vessels, so here also, in the whole world. He speaks here not of the church only but of the world at large. For do not think, I pray, that he means it of the church. For there he would not have any vessels of wood or of earth but all of gold or silver, which is the body of Christ, which is that "pure virgin, without spot, or wrinkle, or any such thing."[53] Homilies on 2 Timothy 6.[54]

Gold, Silver and Wood Distinguished. Theodoret of Cyr: Paul applies the image of the great house to the world, where the golden vessels are persons of faith and virtue, the silver those who embrace civil life virtuously and righ-

teously and the wooden those who live irreverent and disgraceful lives. Interpretation of the Second Letter to Timothy.[55]

Whether the Church Is Pure. Pelagius: The house described by Paul cannot be the church, which is pure, but must be the world with its mixture of wheat and tares. Pelagius's Commentary on the Second Letter to Timothy.[56]

Become Wheat. Cyprian: For although there seem to be tares in the church, yet neither our faith nor our love ought to be hindered, so that, because we see that there are tares in the church, we ourselves should withdraw from the church. We must labor only that we may become wheat, so that when the wheat has begun to be gathered into the barns of the Lord, we may receive the reward for our work and labor. Letters 54.3.[57]

Judgment Belongs to God. Cyprian: Then, finally, what a great swelling of avarice it is, what a great forgetfulness of humility and meekness, what a great boasting of his own arrogance that anyone should either dare or think he is able to do what the Lord did not allow to the apostles, that he should think that he can discern the tares from the grain, or, as if it were granted to him to bear the spade and to purge the threshing floor, he should attempt to separate the chaff from the wheat and, although the apostle says, "But in a great house there are vessels not only of gold and silver but of wood and clay," he should seem to chose the gold and silver vessels and to despise, indeed, to cast away, to condemn those of wood and clay. It is only in the day of the Lord that wooden vessels are to be

---

[50]FC 95:156*. [51]OFP 134. [52]CSEL 81 3:308-9. Novatian is not generally regarded as heretical except in his ecclesiology, which taught the perfection of the church in this life. As a result, he read this passage differently. The Fathers disagreed on whether the passage refers to the church or the world. [53]Eph 5:27. [54]NPNF 1 13:496*. [55]PG 82:843C/844C. [56]PETE 515. [57]FC 51:132.

burned by the fire of divine flame, and those of clay are to be broken by him to whom is given the rod of iron. Letters 70.25.[58]

Not All Equal. Theodore of Mopsuestia: Here the house is the church, where different persons are not at all equal, yet each serves his or her use. Commentary on 2 Timothy.[59]

Various Vessels in the Church. Basil the Great: Every one of us, indeed, who is instructed in the holy Scripture is the administrator of some one of those gifts which, according to the gospel, have been apportioned to us. In this great household of the church not only are there vessels of every kind—gold, silver, wooden and earthen—but also a great variety of pursuits. Homily on the Words: "Give Heed to Thyself."[60]

A Mixed Body. Augustine: Cyprian argued against those who, under the pretext of avoiding the society of wicked men, had severed themselves from the unity of the church. By the great house of which the apostle spoke—in which there were not only vessels of gold and of silver but also of wood and of earth—Paul understood nothing else but the church. In the church there should be good and bad, till at the last day it should be cleansed as a threshing floor by the winnowing fan. On Baptism, Against the Donatists 4.12.18.[61]

The Cockle Scattered in the Field. Augustine: That law of charity was pronounced by the lips of the Lord Christ, for those parables are his about the cockle scattered through the world in the unity of the field until the time of the harvest and about the bad fishes which are to be left in the same net until the time for landing on the shore.[62] Letters 108.3.11.[63]

All Kinds in the Ark. Jerome: Noah's ark was a type of the church. . . . As in the ark there were all kinds of animals, so also in the church there are men of all races and characters. As in

the one there was the leopard with the kids, the wolf with the lambs, so in the other there are found the righteous and sinners, that is, vessels of gold and silver with those of wood and earth. Dialogue Against the Luciferians 22.[64]

2:20b Noble and Ignoble Use

Number and Beyond Number. Augustine: But in the Christian community, as far as sharing and communion in the sacraments goes, they have been multiplied beyond number.[65] So number is one thing; beyond number is something else. Number is those of whom the apostle says, The Lord knows who are his. There are some beyond number, though, because in a great house there are not only vessels of gold and silver but also ones of wood and earthenware; some for noble, others for ignoble use. Number, then, applies to vessels for noble use; beyond number are vessels for ignoble use. Sermons 15.2.[66]

For Noble Use. Abba Poemen: A brother asked Abba Poemen saying, "Why do the demons persuade my soul to look up to him who is superior to me and make me despise him who is my inferior?" The old man replied, "About that, the apostle has this to say: 'In a great house there are not only vessels of gold and silver but also of wood and earthenware; and if anyone purifies himself from what is ignoble, then he will be a vessel for noble use, consecrated and useful to the master of the house, ready for any good work.'" Sayings of the Fathers 100.[67]

---

[58]FC 51:150. [59]TEM 2:210. [60]FC 9:436-37. [61]NPNF 1 4:455. Augustine is referring to Cyprian Letters 70.25. Later, in Retractations 2.44 (FC 60:156-58), Augustine comments on his work On Baptism and modifies his interpretation of 2 Timothy 2:20-21, originally taken from Cyprian, to argue that the gold and silver vessels, and the wooden and earthenware vessels, severally contain members both for noble and ignoble use—a view he derived from the Donatist Tyconius. The interested reader should consult the editorial notes at FC 60:157-58 and FC 18:104, the latter on Letters 93. [62]Cf. Mt 13:24-43, 47-50. [63]FC 18:224. [64]NPNF 2 6:331. [65]Ps 40:5. [66]WSA 3/1:323. [67]SDF 181.

2:21 *Purifying Oneself*

Prepared for the Future. Origen: Whoever purges himself when placed in this life will be prepared for every good work in the future. On First Principles 2.9.8.[68]

Freedom for Fit Use. Basil the Great: The infinite God, remaining changeless, assumed flesh and fought with death, freeing us from suffering by his own suffering! . . . He himself has bound the strong man and plundered his goods[69]—that is, us, who had been abased in every manner of evil—and made us vessels fit for the Master's use, the use of our free will being made ready for any good work.[70] On the Holy Spirit 8.18.[71]

Cleansing Oneself. John of Damascus: It is clear that this cleansing is done freely, for he says, "if any man shall cleanse himself," the converse of which rejoins that, if he does not cleanse himself, he will be a vessel unto dishonor, of no use to the Lord and only fit to be broken. Orthodox Faith 4.19.[72]

2:24 *Not Quarrelsome*

Be Teachable. Cyprian: But it happens by the practice of presumption and of insolence that each one defends more his own depraved and false views than he consents to the rights and truths of another. Foreseeing this matter, the blessed apostle Paul writes to Timothy and warns that the bishop ought not to be quarrelsome or contentious but gentle and teachable. One who is meek and mild in the patience of learning is teachable. For bishops ought not only to teach but also to learn because he who grows daily and profits by learning better things teaches better. Letters 74.10.[73]

Peacemakers. Augustine: Since there are so many deceptions and errors of wicked and perverse men clamoring against wisdom, how great is the need of a clean and single eye in order to find the path to wisdom! To escape all of these is the same as to reach the utmost security of peace and the unchangeable abode of wisdom. The noise of wranglers is of little account unless a man becomes a hindrance even to himself. But this can be seen only by a few, and there is great danger that no one may see it in the midst of contention and strife. . . . Therefore, "Blessed are the peacemakers, for they shall be called the children of God."[74] Sermon on the Mount 2.25.86.[75]

2:25a *Correcting with Gentleness*

Anger No Excuse. Chrysostom: Therefore, let us not be provoked with these men, let us not use anger as an excuse, but let us talk with them gently and with kindness. Nothing is more forceful and effective than treatment which is gentle and kind. This is why Paul told us to hold fast to such conduct with all the earnestness of our hearts when he said, "The servant of the Lord must not be quarrelsome but must be kindly toward all." He did not say "only to your brothers" but "toward all." And again, when he said, "Let your gentleness be known,"[76] he did not say "to your brothers" but "to all men." What good does it do you, he means, if you love those who love you. On the Incomprehensible Nature of God 1.7.[77]

Avoid the Tone of Insult. Augustine: But then in the correction and repression of other men's sins, one must take heed that in rebuking another he does not lift up himself. The sentence of the apostle must be remembered: "Let one who thinks he stands, take heed lest he

---

[68]OFP 136. [69]Mt 12:21. [70]The translation of this last phrase from Basil's Greek text is problematic, as pointed out by the editor at NPNF 2 8:12, ad loc., where it means literally "that which is within our control," that is, we are free to do that which is within the power of human willing. [71]OHS 36-37. [72]FC 37:384. [73]FC 51:292-93. [74]Mt 5:9. [75]FC 11:197. [76]Phil 4:5. [77]FC 72:68.

fall."[78] Let the voice of chiding sound outwardly in tones of terror, let the spirit of love and gentleness be maintained within. . . . So then you must neither consent to evil, so as to approve of it, nor be negligent, so as not to reprove it, nor be proud, so as to reprove it in a tone of insult. SERMONS ON NEW TESTAMENT LESSONS 38.20.[79]

WISE ADMONISHMENT. BASIL THE GREAT: The superior should not administer a rebuke to wrongdoers when his own passions are aroused. By admonishing a brother with anger and indignation, he does not free him from his faults but involves himself in the error. . . . Nor should he become vehemently angry even when he himself is treated with contempt. When he sees such treatment inflicted upon another, he should again show himself indulgent toward the sinner; but more than that, he ought, in the latter case, to manifest displeasure at the wrong done. THE LONG RULES, Q.50.R.[80]

2:25b God May Grant That They Will Repent

THE HEROIC SPIRIT OF THE PASTOR. CHRYSOSTOM: The shepherd of sheep has the flock following him wherever he leads; or if some turn aside from the direct path and leave the good pasture to graze in barren and precipitous places, it is enough for him to call more loudly, lead them back again and restore to the flock those that were separated. But if a man wanders away from the right path, the shepherd needs a lot of concentration, perseverance and patience. He cannot drag by force or constrain by fear but must by persuasion lead him back to the true beginning from which he has fallen away. He needs, therefore, a heroic spirit, not to grow despondent or neglect the salvation of wanderers but to keep on thinking and saying, "God perhaps may give them the knowledge of the truth and they may be freed from the snare of the devil." ON THE PRIESTHOOD 2.4.[81]

MERCY PRECEDES REPENTANCE. AUGUSTINE: Now, penance itself is often omitted because of weakness, even when in church custom there is an adequate reason why it should be performed. For shame is the fear of displeasing men, when one loves good opinion more than he regards judgment, which would make him humble in penitence. Thus not only for one to repent but also in order that he may be enabled to do so, the mercy of God is prerequisite. Otherwise, the apostle would not say of some, "In case God gives them repentance." ENCHIRIDION 82.22.[82]

GOD GRANTS REPENTANCE. AUGUSTINE: Let Pelagius confess that pardon is granted to the repentant according to the grace and mercy of God, not according to his merits. It is that very repentance which the apostle called the gift of God when he said of certain ones, "Lest God perhaps may grant them repentance." LETTERS 186.9.33.[83]

---

[78]1 Cor 10:12. [79]NPNF 1 6:385-86*. [80]FC 9:327*. [81]COP 58*. [82]LCC 7:389. [83]FC 30:215.

3:1-9 THE CHARACTER OF HERETICS

¹*But understand this, that in the last days there will come times of stress.* ²*For men will be lovers of self, lovers of money, proud, arrogant, abusive, disobedient to their parents, ungrateful, unholy,* ³*inhuman, implacable, slanderers, profligates, fierce, haters of good,* ⁴*treacherous, reckless, swollen with conceit, lovers of pleasure rather than lovers of God,* ⁵*holding the form of religion but denying the power of it. Avoid such people.* ⁶*For among them are those who make their way into households and capture weak women, burdened with sins and swayed by various impulses,* ⁷*who will listen to anybody and can never arrive at a knowledge of the truth.* ⁸*As Jannes and Jambres opposed Moses, so these men also oppose the truth, men of corrupt mind and counterfeit faith;* ⁹*but they will not get very far, for their folly will be plain to all, as was that of those two men.*

OVERVIEW: Inevitably, unfaithfulness is displayed by some, as pride rears its head particularly in the form of a greedy, worldly lovelessness. This kind of deceit, or false faith, has been present from of old and especially victimizes weak and needy women in this present time (CHRYSOSTOM). The evil of our times is the evil in people's hearts, an evil that leads them to be false, proud and grandiose (THEODORE). The present time of heresy and unfaithfulness is that foretold by Paul, but these heretics, while they may increase in number, will ultimately fail and their deceit will become manifest (THEODORET). The Fathers discuss whether these are the last days (TERTULLIAN, CYPRIAN) or whether these evils are typical of the trials of the righteous of all times (CHRYSOSTOM). The last days were also felt to be coming in earlier times (AUGUSTINE). In any event, in our time modesty seems to have become obsolete (TERTULLIAN). No one fears future judgment (CAESARIUS). The mad fury of discord rends the church, destroys faith, disturbs peace, puts love to flight and profanes religion (CYPRIAN). The only progress heretics make is in impiety, for they cannot simulate genuine piety for very long (THEODORET). We are not to follow that worst of all teachers, our own self-confidence (JEROME). Lacking works, faith is like an impotent cartoon (CHRYSOSTOM) as if one is called a virgin without being one (PSEUDO-CLEMENT). People who love themselves by leaving God out of their lives do not even remain in themselves but go away from themselves (AUGUSTINE). God is so immeasurable that, even though he has been found, he may still be sought (AUGUSTINE).

3:1 *There Will Come Times of Stress*

SURROUNDED BY CORRUPTION. TERTULLIAN: The conquering power of evil is on the increase. This is characteristic of the last times. Innocent babies are now not even allowed to be born, so corrupted are the moral standards. Or if born, no one educates them, so desolate are studies. Or if trained, no one enforces the training, so impotent are the laws. In fact, the case for modesty which we are now beginning to treat, has in our time become an obsolete subject. So much is this so that modesty is considered to be not the renunciation of the appetites but merely in their mild constraint. People these days are thought to be chaste if they are not too chaste. On Modesty 7.1.[1]

These Are the Last Days. Cyprian: The Lord's teaching required both unity and love. They embraced all the prophets and the law in two commandments. But what sort of unity, what sort of love, is preserved or contemplated by the mad fury of discord that rends the church, destroys faith, disturbs peace, scatters charity, profanes religion? This evil began long ago, my brothers in the faith. Now its cruel havoc has increased, now the poisonous plague of heretical perversity and schism is beginning to spring up and put out new shoots. So it must be at the end of the world, as the Holy Spirit forewarns and foretells through the apostle. Unity of the Catholic Church 15-16.[2]

Troubles Are Perennial for the Righteous. Chrysostom: He had said in the former epistle that "the Spirit speaks expressly, that in the latter times some shall depart from the faith."[3] And elsewhere in this epistle he foretells that something of this kind will afterwards happen; and here again he does the same thing: "This know, that in the last days perilous times shall come." And this he pronounces not only from the future but from the past: "As Jannes and Jambres withstood Moses." And again from reasoning: "In a great house there are not only vessels of gold and silver." But why does he do this? In order that Timothy may not be troubled, nor any one of us, when there are evil men. If there were such in the time of Moses and will be in later times, it is no wonder that there are such in our times. Homilies on 2 Timothy 7.[4]

Whether the Last Days Were Also Felt in Earlier Times. Augustine: We do not think that in this passage he used his verbs in the present tense for the future, because, in fact, he was warning his correspondent to avoid these persons. Yet he had a purpose in

saying: "In the last times shall come on dangerous days." He demonstrates that the times will be dangerous by prophesying that evil men will become more numerous as the end draws near. They are already numerous at present. But what does that signify if they will be even more numerous after us and most numerous of all when the end itself is imminent, although it is not known how far off it is? Indeed, those last days were spoken of even in the first days of the apostles when the Lord's ascension into heaven was a recent happening. . . . So there were last days even then! How much more now is this so, even if there remained as many days to the end as have already passed from the ascension of the Lord to this day, or even if there remain more or less days to come! Letters 199.8.23-24.[5]

Holy Fear Lacking. Caesarius of Arles: We see his prediction[6] verified to such an extent, dearly beloved, that there is no more fidelity in the fear of God, in laws of justice, in charity or in good works. Blessed Paul foretold this. . . . Therefore, let us consider, dearly beloved, whether almost the whole world is not filled with these vices. Why? We reply: Because no one has any fear of the future or trembles within himself over the day of the Lord and God's wrath, the punishment prepared for unbelievers and the eternal torments to come for the unfaithful. Sermons 71.3.[7]

3:2 People Will Be Lovers of Self

Arrogant Self-Assertion. Clement of Alexandria: The Lord says, "My teaching is not mine but my father's, and he sent me."[8] About the robbers he says, "Anyone who speaks on his own authority is seeking his own glory."[9] Yet are the Greeks: "Lovers of self, arrogant." In calling them

---

[1]ANF 4:74*. [2]LCC 5:135. [3]1 Tim 4:1-2. [4]NPNF 1 13:500. [5]FC 30:374-75. [6]Lk 18:8. [7]FC 31:336-37. [8]Jn 7:16. [9]Jn 7:18.

wise, Scripture is not attacking the real sages but those masquerading as sages. STROMATA 1.17.3-7.[10]

GOOD AND BAD LOVE OF SELF. AUGUSTINE: There isn't anyone, after all, who doesn't love himself. But we have to look for the right sort of love and avoid the wrong sort. You see, anyone who loves himself by leaving God out of his life and leaves God out of his life by loving himself, doesn't even remain in himself but goes away from himself. . . . Listen to the apostle giving his support to this understanding of the matter. "In the last days," he says, "dangerous times will loom up." What are the dangerous times? "There will be people loving themselves." That's the core of the evil. So let's see if they remain in themselves by loving themselves; let's see, let's hear what comes next: "There will be people, he says, loving themselves, lovers of money." Where are you now, you that were busy loving yourself? Obviously, you're outside. Are you, I'm asking you, are you money? Obviously, after loving yourself by neglecting God, by loving money you have even abandoned yourself. SERMONS 330.3.[11]

LOVING BADLY. AUGUSTINE: Since I have already given an example of love [amor] used in a good sense, someone may want an example of the same word used in a bad sense. If so, let him read the text, "Men will be lovers [amantes] of self, covetous [amatores pecuniae]." THE CITY OF GOD 14.7.2.[12]

3:3 Profligates

THE GREATEST OF EVILS. BASIL THE GREAT: The apostle also showed how much incontinency is to be dreaded by including it among the signs of apostasy, when he said, "In the last days shall come dangerous times. Men shall be lovers of themselves." Then, after enumerating several forms of iniquity, he adds, "slanderers, incontinent."[13] Also, for selling his birthright for one portion of food, Esau was charged with incontinency as the greatest of evils.[14] The first disobedience befell men as a consequence of incontinency. THE LONG RULES, Q.16.R.[15]

3:5 Holding the Form of Religion But Denying Its Power

VIRGINITY KNOWN BY ITS BEHAVIOR. PSEUDO-CLEMENT: Virgins are a beautiful pattern to believers and to those who shall believe. But the name alone, indeed, without works, does not introduce one into the kingdom of heaven. Only if one is truly a believer can one be saved. But if one is called a believer yet does not evidence his belief through works, he cannot possibly be a believer. . . . Similarly, merely because a person is called a virgin, if he remains destitute of the excellent and comely behavior suitable to virginity, he is no virgin and cannot possibly be saved. ON VIRGINITY 1.3.[16]

LIKE A PAINTED FIGURE. CHRYSOSTOM: Faith without works is fitly called a mere form without power. For as a fair and ruddy body, when it has no strength, is like a painted figure, so is a right faith apart from works. For let us suppose anyone to be "covetous, a traitor, heady" and yet believes correctly. Of what advantage is it, if he lacks all the qualities fitting to a Christian, if he does not the works that characterize godliness but outdoes the Greeks in impiety? What good when he becomes a mischief to those with whom he associates or when he causes God to be blasphemed and the doctrine to be slandered by his evil deeds? HOMILIES ON 2 TIMOTHY 8.[17]

THE POWER OF GODLINESS. AUGUSTINE: You heard just now, when that reading was read, that Simon Magus was baptized and yet did not lay aside his evil mind. He had the form of the sac-

---

[10]FC 85:89. [11]WSA 3/9:186. [12]FC 14:360. [13]2 Tim 3:3. [14]Gen 25:33. [15]FC 9:269. [16]ANF 8:55*. [17]NPNF 1 13:505*.

rament, but the power of the sacrament he did not have. Listen to what the apostle says about the godless, "having," he says, "the form of godliness, while refusing its power." What is the form of godliness? The visible sacrament. What is the power of godliness? Invisible charity. SERMONS 229U.[18]

THE MAINSTAY OF SALVATION. AUGUSTINE: Shut out the evil love of the world so that you may be filled with the love of God. You are a vessel, but you are still full. Pour out what you have that you may receive what you have not. . . . It is good for us not to love the world in order that the sacraments may not remain in us for our damnation rather than as the mainstays of our salvation. The mainstay of salvation is to have the root of love, to have the power of godliness, not the external form alone. TRACTATES ON THE EPISTLE OF JOHN 2.2.9.[19]

3:6 Weak Women, Burdened with Sins

THE ARROGANCE OF THE VALENTINIAN GNOSTICS. IRENAEUS: Some of the disciples of Marcus[20] wandered about among the faithful, deceived many silly women and defiled them. They boasted of being so perfect that no one was able to come up to the greatness of their knowledge. No one, not even Peter or Paul, or any other of the apostles. They imagined that they knew more than all others and alone imbibed the greatness of the knowledge and the unspeakable Power. They thought of themselves as on a height above all Power, and so they felt free to do all things without fear of anyone in regard to anything. AGAINST THE HERESIES 13.6.[21]

FALSE ASCETICS. JEROME: Avoid men, also, when you see them loaded with chains and wearing their hair long like women, contrary to the apostle's precept,[22] not to speak of beards like those of goats, black cloaks and bare feet braving the cold. All these things are tokens of

the devil. Such a one was Antimus, who Rome groaned over some time ago. And Sophronius is a still more recent instance. Such persons, when they have once gained admission to the houses of the highborn, and have deceived "silly women laden with sins, ever learning and never able to come to the knowledge of the truth," feign a sad face and pretend to make long fasts while at night they would feast in secret. LETTERS 22.28.[23]

3:7 Who Never Arrive at a Knowledge of the Truth

SEEKING AND FINDING. AUGUSTINE: Let us direct the mind's gaze and, with the Lord's help, let us search out God. The word of the divine canticle is, "Seek God and your soul will live."[24] Let us seek him who is to be found, and in doing so let us seek him who has been found. He has been hidden so that he may be sought for and found. He is immeasurable so that, even though he has been found, he may still be sought for. . . . Therefore it was not thus said, "Seek his face always," as about certain men: "always learning and never attaining to a knowledge of the truth," but rather as that one says, "When a man ends, then he is beginning."[25] TRACTATES ON JOHN 63.1.[26]

DEFERRING TO PROPER AUTHORITY. JEROME: It is a good thing . . . to defer to one's betters, to obey those set over one, to learn not only from the Scriptures but from the example of others how one ought to order one's life, and not to follow that worst of teachers, one's own self-confidence. Of women who are thus presumptuous the apostle says that they "are carried about with

---

[18]*WSA* 3/6:337*. [19]FC 92:151. Augustine expresses a similar idea with this verse at *Reply to Faustus the Manichaean* 19.12 (NPNF 1 4:243-44). [20]Follower of the Gnostic Valentinus. [21]ACW 55:58. [22]Cf. 1 Cor 11:14. [23]NPNF 2 6:34. [24]Ps 69:33. [25]Sir 18:6. [26]FC 90:42-43.

every wind of doctrine,"[27] "ever learning and never able to come to the knowledge of the truth." LETTERS 130.17.[28]

3:8 As Jannes and Jambres Opposed Moses

AN UNKNOWN TRADITION. CHRYSOSTOM: Who are these? The magicians in the time of Moses. But how is it their names are nowhere else introduced? Either they were handed down by tradition or it is probable that Paul knew them by inspiration. HOMILIES ON 2 TIMOTHY 8.[29]

PAUL'S SOURCE UNKNOWN. THEODORE OF MOPSUESTIA: A great deal of foolishness has been written about how Paul could have known the names of these two men who resisted Moses. Particularly absurd is the notion that he had access to some information or writing now lost to us. COMMENTARY ON 2 TIMOTHY.[30]

FROM UNWRITTEN TRADITION? THEODORET OF CYR: Paul takes the story of Jannes and Jambres not from holy Scripture but from an unwritten Jewish tradition. INTERPRETATION OF THE SECOND LETTER TO TIMOTHY.[31]

THE PRIDE OF SELF-RIGHTEOUSNESS. AUGUSTINE: Do they not resist this truth, men corrupted in mind, reprobates concerning the faith, who respond and speak iniquity, saying, "We have it from God that we are men but from our own selves that we are just"? What are you [Pelagians] saying? You deceive your own selves, not protecting but jettisoning free will, from the height of haughtiness through empty expanses of presumption into the depths of a drowning deep in the sea. Without doubt it is your pronouncement that man of himself does justice. This is the height of your presumption. TRACTATES ON JOHN 81.2.[32]

SACRILEGE, VICE AND CRIME. FULGENTIUS OF RUSPE: The sins of the wicked come about in three ways. Either they are bound up with sacrileges or vices or crimes. For they commit *sacrilege* when they do not believe rightly concerning God and depart from the true faith either because of fear of temporal misfortunes or desire for temporal advantages or by blindness or perversity of heart alone. They sin by *vice* when unrestrained or obscene in themselves; they live in a shameful fashion. Then they sin by *crimes* when they cruelly harm others, either by damages or some kind of oppression. The blessed apostle calls both of them reprobate whether sinning capitally in faith or in works, saying about those who contradict the true faith, "Just as Jannes and Jambres opposed Moses, so they also oppose the truth, people of depraved mind, unqualified in the faith." LETTER TO SCARILA 10.37.[33]

3:9 But They Will Not Get Far

WHO WOULD DIE FOR A DECEIT? CHRYSOSTOM: For if errors flourish at first, they do not continue to the end, for so it is with things that are not fair by nature but fair in appearance. They flourish for a time and then are detected and come to nothing. But this does not happen to our teaching. Of this you are a witness. For in our doctrines there is no deceit. For who would choose to die for a deceit? HOMILIES ON 2 TIMOTHY 8.[34]

PSEUDO-PROSPERITY. THEODORE OF MOPSUESTIA: The growth that the heretics enjoy will only be in numbers, not in depth or substance. COMMENTARY ON 2 TIMOTHY.[35]

PROGRESS IN IMPIETY. THEODORET OF CYR: The only progress which heretics will make is in impiety, for they cannot simulate genuine piety

---

[27]Eph 4:14. [28]NPNF 2 6:270. [29]NPNF 1 13:505. [30]TEM 2:218. [31]PG 82:847B/848B. [32]FC 90:121. [33]FC 95:458. [34]NPNF 1 13:506. [35]TEM 2:218-19 (Greek).

for very long. INTERPRETATION OF THE SECOND LETTER TO TIMOTHY.[36]

EVENTUAL REVERSAL. AUGUSTINE: For those whom the Manichaeans lead astray are Christians who have already been born of the gospel, whose profession has been misled by the heretics. They make riches with inconsiderate haste but without good judgment. They do not consider that the followers whom they gather as their riches are taken from the genuine original Christian society and deprived of its benefits. . . . This recalls what the prophet said of the partridge, which gathers what it has not brought forth, "In the midst of his days they shall leave him, and in the end he shall be a fool."[37] In other words, he who at first misled people by a promising display of superior wisdom shall be a fool, that is, shall be seen to be a fool. He will be seen when his folly is manifest to all, and those to whom he was at first a wise man he will then be a fool. REPLY TO FAUSTUS THE MANICHAEAN 13.12.[38]

---

[36]PG 82:847B/848B. [37]Jer 17:11. [38]NPNF 1 4:204*.

3:10—4:8 THE COST OF FAITHFULNESS

[10]Now you have observed my teaching, my conduct, my aim in life, my faith, my patience, my love, my steadfastness, [11]my persecutions, my sufferings, what befell me at Antioch, at Iconium, and at Lystra, what persecutions I endured; yet from them all the Lord rescued me. [12]Indeed all who desire to live a godly life in Christ Jesus will be persecuted, [13]while evil men and impostors will go on from bad to worse, deceivers and deceived. [14]But as for you, continue in what you have learned and have firmly believed, knowing from whom you learned it [15]and how from childhood you have been acquainted with the sacred writings which are able to instruct you for salvation through faith in Christ Jesus. [16]All scripture is inspired by God and[d] profitable for teaching, for reproof, for correction, and for training in righteousness, [17]that the man of God may be complete, equipped for every good work.

4 I charge you in the presence of God and of Christ Jesus who is to judge the living and the dead, and by his appearing and his kingdom: [2]preach the word, be urgent in season and out of season, convince, rebuke, and exhort, be unfailing in patience and in teaching. [3]For the time is coming when people will not endure sound teaching, but having itching ears they will accumulate for themselves teachers to suit their own likings, [4]and will turn away from listening to the truth and wander into myths. [5]As for you, always be steady, endure suffering, do the work of an evangelist, fulfil your ministry.

[6]For I am already on the point of being sacrificed; the time of my departure has come. [7]I have fought the good fight, I have finished the race, I have kept the faith. [8]Henceforth there is laid up

for me the crown of righteousness, which the Lord, the righteous judge, will award to me on that Day, and not only to me but also to all who have loved his appearing.

d Or Every scripture inspired by God is also

OVERVIEW: Paul knew that his death was at hand (EUSEBIUS). He would endure death in the confession of Christ as a libation of wine is poured out on behalf of honoring God (THEODORE, THEODORET). The dogged pursuit of virtue lies at the very center of the Christian life, with all of its necessary self-denial and with the suffering that must inevitably come. Scripture is our constant reminder that we must not be overcome by weakness but must be strong in the wisdom of Christ. Thus we must always persist in the teaching that rejects false doctrine and its imbalanced ways (CHRYSOSTOM).

Writing from a prison cell, Paul recalls some of the sufferings that he and Timothy experienced together, so that Timothy will be consoled and strengthened for the refutation of heresy and for the exercise of that discipline, contained in Scripture, which is required for convicting sin, correcting the penitent and bringing persons to righteousness. In Paul's sacrifice Timothy can see what it means to honor God in faithfulness (THEODORE). Paul's intention is to recall Timothy to the presence of divine help in the adversities and struggles of ministry, so that he will be firm in teaching the truth of Christ. He calls Timothy to the work of proclaiming the word always, offering him the example of his own steadfastness and humility (THEODORET).

Anyone who pursues the course of virtue should not expect to avoid grief, tribulation and temptations (ORIGEN, CHRYSOSTOM, THEODORET, AUGUSTINE, CAESARIUS). Yet it is possible for even what is unendurable by nature to become light when we accept it with eagerness (CHRYSOSTOM). The faithful are comforted by the sufferings of the saints, prophets, apostles and martyrs (THEODORET). The reward comes after the battle, not before or during (CAESARIUS).

Persecution is not only that which is done by the sword or fire but also by barbs of slanderous tongues (LEO). All who live in Christ will suffer persecution (ISAAC OF NINEVEH, BEDE). One cannot be wrestling and feasting at the same time (CHRYSOSTOM).

Learn what you have to teach (JEROME). Do not lead astray one who can be corrected (ANONYMOUS) or follow those drunk with illusions (ATHANASIUS). Some things God does, and other things God permits. All evil things are done by our wills alone, all good things by our will conjointly with God's grace (CHRYSOSTOM). The mind and mouth of the priest of Christ should be in harmony (JEROME). The force of what is said is wasted when it is enfeebled in the hearts of the hearers by a careless and offensive torrent of words (GREGORY THE GREAT). When we have gone wrong because we haven't understood Scripture, we don't make out Scripture to be wrong, but it continues to stand upright for us that we may return to it for correction (AUGUSTINE). The soul refreshed by Scripture bears fruit in due season (JOHN OF DAMASCUS). Admonition is best given with comfort in the spirit of meekness (AMBROSE, CHRYSOSTOM).

The martyrs carried to heaven no treasure that could be plundered, but the riches of patience, courage and love (CHRYSOSTOM, NEMESIUS). The confidence shown by the faithful toward the future does not lie in their own power but in God's generosity (CASSIODORUS). They trust in his judgment and mercy (AMBROSE). Whether the Lord comes sooner or later than expected, his coming is loved with faithful charity (AUGUSTINE). Eternal rest is not given in payment for a debt owed for works but as a grace of the generous God for those who have hoped in him (BASIL).

3:10 My Teaching, My Conduct

NOT JUST IN WORDS. CHRYSOSTOM: I did not say these things, he says, and not do them. I was not a philosopher in words only. HOMILIES ON 2 TIMOTHY 8.[1]

3:11 Rescued from Persecutions

CONSOLATION. CHRYSOSTOM: Two consolations appear here, says Paul: I displayed sufficient steadfastness, and in doing so was not forsaken. It cannot be said that God abandoned me. Rather he rendered my crown more radiant. HOMILIES ON 2 TIMOTHY 8.[2]

RECALLING DIVINE HELP. THEODORET OF CYR: Paul's point in recalling these events is to show the divine help, thus adding spirit to the disciple. INTERPRETATION OF THE SECOND LETTER TO TIMOTHY.[3]

3:12 The Godly Will Be Persecuted

THE NATURE OF SPIRITUAL GROWTH. ORIGEN: When you flee Egypt, you come to these steep ascents of work and faith. You face a tower, a sea and waves. The way of life is not pursued without the waves of temptation. The apostle says, "All who wish to live piously in Christ will suffer persecution." Job also, no less, declares, "Our life upon earth is a temptation."[4] HOMILIES ON EXODUS 5.3.[5]

INEVITABLE STRUGGLE. CHRYSOSTOM: Here he calls afflictions and sorrows "persecutions." Anyone who pursues the course of virtue should not expect to avoid grief, tribulation and temptations. HOMILIES ON 2 TIMOTHY 8.[6]

WORTHY TO BE DISHONORED. CHRYSOSTOM: If the road is narrow and difficult, how can it be that "My yoke is easy and my burden is light"?[7] He says difficult because of the nature of the trials but easy because of the willingness of the travelers. It is possible for even what is unendurable by nature to become light when we accept it with eagerness. Remember that the apostles who had been scourged returned rejoicing that they had been found worthy to be dishonored for the name of the Lord.[8] ON LAZARUS AND THE RICH MAN 3.[9]

COMFORTED BY SUFFERING. THEODORET OF CYR: Many are the devices secretly plotted against me and through me patched up against the faith of apostles. I am however comforted by the sufferings of the saints, prophets, apostles, martyrs and men famous in the churches in the word of grace and besides these by the promises of our God and Savior. For in the present life he has promised us nothing pleasant or delightful, but rather trouble, toil, and peril and attacks of enemies. LETTERS 109.[10]

FAITH AND PRACTICE TOGETHER. ATHANASIUS: In another place the apostle says, "And all those who will live godly lives in Christ Jesus will suffer persecution." Then, to help prevent people from renouncing godliness when they are persecuted, he urges them to cling to the faith. "You, therefore, continue in the things you have learned and been assured of."[11] Just as brothers become strongly knit together when one helps another, so faith and godliness, coming from the same family, cohere together. A person who gives his attention to one of the two is strengthened by the other. FESTAL LETTERS 9.[12]

ONE WAY OR THE OTHER. AUGUSTINE: Persecution, therefore, will never be lacking. For, when our enemies from without leave off raging and there ensues a span of tranquillity—even of genuine tranquillity and great consolation at least to the weak—we are not without enemies within,

---

[1]NPNF 1 13:506. [2]NPNF 1 13:506*. [3]PG 82:847D/848D. [4]Job 7:1. [5]FC 71:280. [6]NPNF 1 13:506. [7]Mt 11:30. [8]Cf. Acts 5:41. [9]OWP 67-68. [10]NPNF 2 3:289*. [11]2 Tim 3:14. [12]ARL 156.

the many whose scandalous lives wound the hearts of the devout. . . . So it is that those who want to live piously in Christ must suffer the spiritual persecution of these and other aberrations in thought and morals, even when they are free from physical violence and vexation. THE CITY OF GOD 18.51.2.[13]

PREPARE FOR TRIALS. AUGUSTINE: What sort of people, though, are those who, being afraid to offend the ones they are talking to, not only don't prepare them for the trials that are looming ahead but even promise them a well-being in this world which God himself hasn't promised to the world? He foretells distress upon distress coming upon the world right up to the end, and do you wish the Christian to be exempt from these distresses? Precisely because he's Christian, he is going to suffer more in this world. SERMONS 46.11.[14]

CONSTANT VIGILANCE. CAESARIUS OF ARLES: "All who want to live piously in Christ suffer persecution," says the apostle. They are under attack from the enemy. For this reason, with Christ's help, everyone who travels the journey of this life should be armed unceasingly and always stand in camp. So if you want to be constantly vigilant so that you may know you serve in the Lord's camp, observe what the same apostle says, "No one serving as God's soldier entangles himself in worldly affairs, that he may please him whose approval he has secured." SERMONS 103.1.[15]

THE REWARD COMES AFTER THE BATTLE. CAESARIUS OF ARLES: Do not seek on the journey what is being kept for you in your fatherland. Because it is necessary for you to fight against the devil every day under the leadership of Christ, do not seek in the midst of battle the reward which is being saved for you in the kingdom. During the fight you ought not to look for what is being kept for you when victory has been attained. Rather pay attention to what the apostle says, "Anyone who wants to

live a godly life in Christ can expect to be persecuted," and again, "We must undergo many trials if we are to enter the reign of God."[16] Sermons 215.3.[17]

A SEEMING CONTRADICTION. JOHN CASSIAN: Abba Germanus said: "Since you have given us the remedies for every illusion, and since the diabolical snares that used to trouble us have been disclosed to us by your teaching and by the Lord's gift, we beseech you likewise to explain to us completely this phrase from the Gospel, 'My yoke is easy and my burden is light.'"[18] For it seems quite contrary to the words of the prophet, which say, "On account of the words of your lips I have kept to hard ways."[19] Indeed, even the apostle says, "All who wish to live devoutly in Christ suffer persecution." Whatever is hard and has reference to persecution, however, can be neither light nor easy." Abba Abraham said, "We shall demonstrate by the easy proof of experience itself that the words of our Lord and Savior are most true, if we set out on the path of perfection in lawful manner and in accordance with the will of Christ. . . . For what can be heavy or hard to the person who has taken up Christ's yoke with his whole mind, is established in true humility, reflects constantly upon the Lord's suffering and rejoices in all the hardships that come upon him?" CONFERENCES 23-24.[20]

EVERY VIRTUE A CROSS. ISAAC OF NINEVEH: And the blessed Mark the Monk has said, "Every virtue on being achieved is called a cross, when it fulfills the Spirit's commandment." That is why all those who wish in the fear of the Lord to live in Jesus Christ will suffer persecution. HOMILIES 72.[21]

PERSECUTION COMES IN ALL SHAPES AND

---

[13]FC 24:172-73. [14]WSA 3/2:269*. [15]FC 47:108-9. [16]Acts 14:22. [17]FC 66:115. [18]Mt 11:30. [19]Ps 17:4-5. [20]ACW 57:842-43*. [21]AHSIS 355.

SIZES. LEO THE GREAT: I am amazed that your charity is so overcome with tribulation from scandals, no matter from what occasion they arise, that you say you desire to be freed from the labors of your bishopric and prefer to live in silence and leisure rather than continue handling those problems which were entrusted to you. But, as the Lord said, "Blessed is he that perseveres to the end."[22] From what will this blessed perseverance come if not from the virtue of patience? For, according to the teaching of the apostle, "All who want to live piously in Christ will suffer persecution." Persecution is to be reckoned not only as that which is done against Christian piety by the sword or fire or by any torments whatever, for the ravages of persecution are also inflicted by differences of character, the perversity of the disobedient and the barbs of slanderous tongues. LETTERS 167.1.[23]

THE GLORY OF HIS WITNESS. THE VENERABLE BEDE: Paul permeated the corpus of his writings, which is made up of fourteen letters, with the aroma of Christ alone, if I may speak of Christ in this way. Whatever you read there either reveals the hidden mysteries of the faith, or shows the results of good works, or promises the joys of the heavenly kingdom, or lays bare the tribulations he sustained in preaching these things, or relates the divine consolation he received in the midst of his tribulations or suggests by a general exhortation that all "those who wish to live a good life in Christ" will not lack persecutions. . . . He knew most clearly and foretold with an unrestrained voice that his being killed for the Lord's sake was nothing else but a most acceptable and pure sacrificial offering made to the Lord. Therefore Paul too glorified God, as did the rest of the apostles, for they too loved Christ with a pure heart and took care of Christ's sheep with a sincere intent. HOMILIES ON THE GOSPELS 2.22.[24]

3:13a From Bad to Worse

UNENDING STRIFE. CHRYSOSTOM: Do not allow yourself to be distressed, he says, if some people prosper, while you are in the midst of suffering. Such is the nature of the case. From my own instance you may learn that it is impossible for man, in his warfare with the wicked, not to be exposed to tribulation. One cannot be in combat and live luxuriously. One cannot be wrestling and feasting. HOMILIES ON 2 TIMOTHY 8.[25]

DO NOT REMAIN STATIONARY. AUGUSTINE: Make progress, make progress in well-doing, for, according to the apostle, there are certain people who go from bad to worse. If you are progressing, you are advancing. Progress in well-doing, progress in good faith, progress in good deeds. Keep singing. Keep advancing. Do not wander. Do not return. Do not remain stationary. SERMONS 256.[26]

3:13b Deceivers and Deceived

DO NOT FOLLOW THOSE DRUNK WITH ILLUSIONS. ATHANASIUS: These ignorant men are drunk, not with wine but with their own wickedness. They make a profession of priesthood and glory in their threats. Do not believe them. When we are tried, let us humble ourselves, not being made captive by them. . . . So we, when we are tried by these things, must not become separated from the love of God. FESTAL LETTERS 13.7.[27]

DO NOT LEAD ASTRAY ONE WHO CAN BE CORRECTED. ANONYMOUS: Suppose a counselor reprimands a brother under his care, instructing him in the fear of God and desiring to correct his error. Yet suppose another intervenes and wishes to defend the offender, so as to turn his heart astray again. One who thus intervenes sins against his own soul, because he led astray the person who could have been corrected. He threw

---

[22]Mt 10:42; 24:13. [23]FC 34:289-90. [24]HOG 2:226-27. [25]NPNF 1 13:506*. [26]FC 38:362*. [27]NPNF 2 4:541*.

to the ground the one who was rising. He deceived with evil persuasion the one who was tending to better things. Going astray himself, he led others astray too. The Testament of Horiesios 24.[28]

3:14 Continue in What You Have Learned

Mind and Mouth at One. Jerome: Read the divine Scriptures constantly. Never, indeed, let the sacred volume be out of your hand. Learn what you have to teach.... Do not let your deeds belie your words, lest when you speak in church someone may mentally reply, "Why do you not practice what you preach?" He is a fine and dainty master who, with his stomach full, reads us a homily on fasting. Let the robber accuse others of covetousness if he will. The mind and mouth of a priest of Christ should be at one. Letters 52.7.[29]

Whether God Makes Medicines Effective. Augustine: It may happen that even with the assistance of holy men, or even if the holy angels themselves take part, no one rightly learns those things which pertain to life with God unless he is made by God docile to God.... Medicines for the body which are administered to men by men do not help unless health is conferred by God, who can cure them without medicines. Yet they are nevertheless applied even though they are useless without his aid. And if they are applied courteously, they are considered to be among works of mercy or kindness. In the same way, the benefits of teaching profit the mind when they are applied by men where assistance is granted by God, who could have given the gospel to man even though it came not from men nor through a man.[30] On Christian Doctrine 4.16.33.[31]

3:15 The Sacred Writings Are Able to Instruct You

True Wisdom. Chrysostom: For he who knows the Scriptures as he ought is not offended at anything that happens. He endures all things patiently, referring them partly to faith and to the incomprehensible nature of the divine dispensation, and partly knowing reasons for them and finding examples in the Scriptures.... Know this, however, that God dispenses all things, that he provides for all, that we are free agents, that some things he works and some things he permits. Indeed, God wills nothing evil to be done, for all things are not done by his will but some by ours also. All evil things are done by ours alone, all good things by our will conjointly with his influence. Thus, nothing is without his knowledge. Therefore he works all things. You then knowing this can reckon what things are good, what are evil and what are indifferent. Homilies on 2 Timothy 8.[32]

Reasons to Remain Steadfast. Theodore of Mopsuestia: Paul here lays out four reasons why Timothy ought to be steadfast, if he will recall them: first, because of the teacher from whom he learned; second, the time when he learned it; third, the source from which the teaching came; and finally, the sublime purpose for which he learned it. Commentary on 2 Timothy.[33]

3:16 All Scripture Inspired by God and Profitable

A Lifetime of Study. Aphrahat: For if the days of a man should be as many as all the days of the world from Adam to the end of the ages and he should sit and meditate upon the holy Scriptures, he would not comprehend all the force of the depth of the words. And man cannot rise up to the wisdom of God. Demonstrations 22.26.[34]

---

[28]PK 3:188-89. [29]LCC 5:322. [30]Cf. Gal 1:1. [31]ACD 142. [32]NPNF 1 13:507*. [33]TEM 2:221-22. [34]NPNF 2 13:411.

Profitable for Correction. Chrysostom: By Scripture we may disprove what is false, be corrected, be brought to a right understanding, and be comforted and consoled. Homilies on 2 Timothy 9.[35]

Scriptures Teach Righteousness. Theodore of Mopsuestia: The usefulness of Scripture lies in its detailing of what one ought to do, either to convict sinners or to clarify what correction is necessary for penitents or to teach what can bring persons to righteousness. Commentary on 2 Timothy.[36]

Reliability of Scripture. Anonymous: Indeed the words of Scripture, the very breath of God, are true and very dependable,[37] whether concerning favors or punishments. The Regulations of Horiesios 52.[38]

The Profit of Scripture. Gregory of Nyssa: The Scripture is "given by inspiration of God," as the apostle says. The Scripture is of the Holy Spirit, and its intention is the profit of men. For "every Scripture," he says, "is given by inspiration of God and is profitable. "The profit is varied and multiform, as the apostle says—"for doctrine, for reproof, for correction, for instruction in righteousness." Such a gift as this, however, is not within any man's reach to lay hold of. Rather, the divine intention lies hidden under the body of the Scripture, as it were under a veil, some legislative enactment or some historical narrative being cast over the truths that are contemplated by the mind. Against Eunomius 3.7.1.[39]

Absolutely Dependable. Augustine: The Scriptures are holy, they are truthful, they are blameless. . . . So we have no grounds at all for blaming Scripture if we happen to deviate in any way, because we haven't understood it. When we do understand it, we are right. But when we are wrong because we haven't understood it, we leave it in the right. When we have gone wrong, we don't make out Scripture to be wrong, but it con-

tinues to stand up straight and right, so that we may return to it for correction. Sermons 23.3.[40]

The Soul Refreshed by Scripture. John of Damascus: To search the sacred Scripture is very good and most profitable for the soul. For, "like a tree which is planted near the running waters,"[41] so does the soul watered by sacred Scripture also grow hearty and bear fruit in due season. This is the orthodox faith. It is adorned with its evergreen leaves, with actions pleasing to God. Orthodox Faith 4.17.[42]

3:17 Equipped for Every Good Work

Depend upon Scriptures. Chrysostom: This is why the exhortation of the Scripture is given: that the man of God may be rendered complete by it. Without this he cannot grow to maturity. You have the Scriptures, he says, in place of me. If you would learn anything, you may learn it from them. Homilies on 2 Timothy 9.[43]

Uninterrupted Converse. Athanasius: Here is why meditation on the law is necessary, my beloved, along with an uninterrupted conversion with virtue: "that the saint may lack nothing but be perfect to every good work." For by these things comes the promise of eternal life, as Paul wrote to Timothy, calling constant meditation exercise, and saying, "Exercise yourself unto godliness." Festal Letters 11.7.[44]

4:1 By His Appearing and His Kingdom

The General Resurrection and Judgment. Fulgentius of Ruspe: Concerning the coming judgment of human beings, living and dead, the blessed Paul says this, "I bear witness in the presence of God and of Christ Jesus, who

---

[35]NPNF 1 13:510. [36]TEM 2:222. [37]2 Tim 1:15; 4:9. [38]PK 2:216. [39]NPNF 2 5:192*. [40]WSA 3/2:57. [41]Ps 1:3. [42]FC 37:373-74*. [43]NPNF 1 13:510*. [44]NPNF 2 4:535.

will judge the living and the dead, and by his appearing and his kingly power." At his coming, from the body of the first man which God fashioned from the earth, up until the bodies of all human beings which began to live when they were infused with a soul, all will be raised by him by whose action they were created. In the resurrection, individual bodies will be restored to their individual souls, which they began to have in the wombs of their mothers, in order that they might begin to live—in order that, in the examination of the just judge, souls might receive in their very same individual bodies their reward, of the kingdom or of punishment, in those bodies in which they had led a good or evil life in this world. To PETER ON THE FAITH 35.[45]

4:2a Preach, Convince, Rebuke, Exhort

ADMONITION AND CONSOLATION BELONG TOGETHER. CHRYSOSTOM: Whether you are in danger, in prison, in chains or going to your death, at that very time do not hesitate to admonish. Do not withhold your admonition. For it is then most seasonable, when your rebuke will be most successful, when the circumstance is at hand. "Exhort," he says. After the manner of physicians, having shown the wound, he makes the incision, he applies the remedy. If you omit either of these, the other becomes useless. If you rebuke without convicting, you will seem to be rash, and no one will tolerate it. After the matter is proved, one will submit to rebuke. But before this, he will be headstrong. If you convict and rebuke, but vehemently, but do not apply exhortation, all your labor will be lost. For conviction is intolerable in itself if consolation is not mingled with it. HOMILIES ON 2 TIMOTHY 9.[46]

DISTINGUISHING REPROOF, REBUKE AND EXHORTATION. THEODORE OF MOPSUESTIA: "Reprove" applies to those who persist in their sin, that they might be led to understand it as sin. "Rebuke" is aimed at those actually engaging in sin. "Exhort" is directed to those who might be

led back to their former state after penitence. COMMENTARY ON 2 TIMOTHY.[47]

BITTER GALL OR SWEET WINE. AMBROSE: Accordingly, the apostle says, "What do you wish? Shall I come to you with a rod, or in love and a spirit of meekness?"[48] He mentioned a rod first, striking those who were astray as with an almond rod, that he might afterwards comfort them with the spirit of meekness. So the man whom the rod deprived of the heavenly sacraments was restored by meekness.[49] He gave similar instructions to his disciple also, saying, "Reprove, exhort, rebuke," two stern words and one gentle, but stern only that he might soften them. To bodies sick with excess of gall, bitter food and drink taste sweet and, on the other hand, sweet dishes taste bitter. Similarly when the mind is wounded, it sickens under the attentions of an unctuous flattery and is again tempered by the bitterness of correction. LETTERS 41.4.[50]

A JUDICIOUS TIMING. BENEDICT OF NURSIA: In his teaching the abbot is ever to observe this rule of the apostle: "Reprove, beseech, correct." This consists in a judicious timing: to mix gentleness with sternness—at one time to show the severity of a master, at another the tenderness of a father. Use rigor with the irregular and the turbulent, but win to better things the obedient, mild and patient. RULE OF ST. BENEDICT 2.[51]

4:2b Be Urgent In and Out of Season

A RIGHT TIME. ATHANASIUS: It is our duty and obligation to remember and heed the special day of Easter Sunday every year. St. Paul taught his disciple Timothy to be aware of dates, saying, "Stand ready in season and out of season." Paul wrote that, of course, so that Timothy would do

---

[45]FC 95:82. [46]NPNF 1 13:510*. [47]TEM 2:223. [48]1 Cor 4:21. [49]2 Cor 2:10. [50]LCC 5:241*. [51]LCC 12:295.

things when they were supposed to be done and avoid the blame for doing things at the wrong time. FESTAL LETTERS 1.1.[52]

BE TIMELY! CHRYSOSTOM: Let it always be your season, not merely in peace and security and when sitting in the church. HOMILIES ON 2 TIMOTHY 9.[53]

LET INSTRUCTION BE ALWAYS AVAILABLE. CHRYSOSTOM: Therefore, let food, and bathing, and banqueting, and the other necessities of life have a definite time. But let instruction about the love of truth from above have no set hour— let all the time belong to it. "In season, out of season, reprove, entreat, rebuke," Scripture says. And the prophet, "On his law he will meditate day and night."[54] And Moses too asked the Jews to do this continually. HOMILIES ON JOHN 18.4.[55]

EVERY TIME OPPORTUNE. THEODORE OF MOPSUESTIA: Every occasion constitutes an opportune time for preaching. COMMENTARY ON 2 TIMOTHY.[56]

HELPED AT THE RIGHT MOMENT. SEVERIAN OF GABALA: The opportune time for preaching and teaching is when the sinner needs the prophylaxis that will lead him to repentance. The sinner will be helped at exactly the right moment between the intention to sin and the commission of sin and will turn to penitence instead. PAULINE COMMENTARY FROM THE GREEK CHURCH.[57]

TEACH BOLDLY. THEODORET OF CYR: Every occasion is appropriate for teaching, so long as this is done boldly and with forethought. INTERPRETATION OF THE SECOND LETTER TO TIMOTHY.[58]

PREACHING ALWAYS FITTING. PELAGIUS: Preaching is always appropriate, whether to those who hear willingly or not. PELAGIUS'S

COMMENTARY ON THE SECOND LETTER TO TIMOTHY.[59]

NECESSARY AND TIMELY SPEECH. AUGUSTINE: I know that it is written, "In the multitude of words you shall not avoid sin."[60] But would that I were to speak only by preaching your word and by praising you, Lord! Not only would I avoid sin, but I would obtain a good reward, no matter how many words I spoke in this way. For the blessed Paul would not command a sin to his own true son in the faith, to whom he wrote, "Preach the word, be urgent in season, out of season." For are we to say that a man did not speak many words, who not only in season but also out of season did not keep silent, O Lord, respecting your word? But they were not many, therefore, because they were only what was necessary. ON THE TRINITY 15.28.51.[61]

THE GOLDEN MEAN. GREGORY THE GREAT: Pastoral guides must also see to it with careful concern that not only should nothing evil proceed from their lips but that not even what is proper be said in excess or in a slovenly manner. Often the force of what is said is wasted when it is enfeebled in the hearts of the hearers by a careless and offensive torrent of words. Indeed, this sort of loquacity defiles the speaker himself, inasmuch as it takes no notice of the practical needs of the hearer. . . . Thus Paul also, admonishing his disciple to be constant in preaching, said: I charge you before God and Jesus Christ, who shall judge the living and the dead, by his coming and his kingdom: preach the word, be instant in season, out of season. When he was about to say "out of season," he premised it with "in season," for if being in season is not com-

---

[52]ARL 48. [53]NPNF 1 13:510. [54]Ps 1:2. [55]FC 33:183. [56]TEM 2:223. [57]NTA 15:343-44. [58]PG 82:851A/852A. [59]PETE 521. Augustine *Sermons* 46.14 (*WSA* 3/2:272) and Caesarius of Arles *Sermons* 1.3; 4.2 (FC 31:5, 29) offer the same interpretation. [60]Prov 10:19. [61]FC 45:524*.

bined with being out of season, the preaching destroys itself in the mind of the hearer by its worthlessness. PASTORAL CARE 2.4.[62]

4:3-4 Having Itching Ears

POOR TEACHING, BAD DIGESTION. ORIGEN: You can understand the desire of the prodigal son to be sated with pods in this way.[63] When rational nature exists in irrationality, it simply desires. If it does not get more convincing reasons, then it accepts any reason at all. Since the pods taste sweet and make the body fat, they do not bind the bowels. They are the specious words of lovers of matter and the body, who say that pleasure is a good, "itching at their ears and running after myths." FRAGMENT ON LUKE 216.[64]

SUPERFLUOUS TEACHING. GREGORY OF NAZIANZUS: For there are certain persons who have not only their ears and their tongues but even, as I now perceive, their hands too, itching for words. They delight in profane babblings, and oppositions of science falsely so called,[65] and strifes about words,[66] which tend to no profit. Paul is the preacher and establisher of the "Word cut short."[67] The teacher of the fishermen calls to question all that is excessive or superfluous in discourse. ORATIONS 27.1.[68]

PLEASING TEACHING. HILARY OF POITIERS: The apostle was cognizant of these sinful tendencies of the will, and besides his numerous admonitions to defend the faith and to preach the word, he said in his epistle to Timothy: "There will come a time when they will not endure the sound doctrine; but having itching ears, will heap up to themselves teachers according to their lusts, and they will turn away from hearing the truth and turn aside rather to fables." When they will no longer endure sound doctrine in their eagerness for godlessness, they will gather teachers together for these things which they desire. They will compile a doctrine that fits in with their desires, since they are no longer eager to be

taught. They want to bring together teachers for that which they already desire in order that this large number of teachers whom they have sought and assembled may satisfy the doctrines of their own passionate desires. ON THE TRINITY 10.2.[69]

ESOTERIC TEACHING. AUGUSTINE: All the most foolish heretics who want themselves to be called Christians try to color the impertinencies of their inventions. At this human sensibility especially shudders, with the occasion of the sentence of the Gospel where the Lord says, "I have yet many things to say to you, but you cannot bear them now."[70] These were the very things that at that time the disciples could not bear, and the Holy Spirit taught such things as an unclean spirit pales to teach and preach openly, by whatever impertinence he may be moved. These are the ones that the apostle foresees in the Holy Spirit and says, "For there will be a time when they will not endure sound doctrine, but, according to their own desires, they will heap to themselves teachers, itching to hear, and will indeed turn away their hearing from the truth but will be turned to fables." TRACTATES ON JOHN 97.3-4.[71]

4:6 On the Point of Being Sacrificed

HIS MARTYRDOM AT HAND. EUSEBIUS OF CAESAREA: He did not add next something like "he will deliver me out of the mouth of the lion," for he saw in the spirit that his death was all but at hand. So he adds to his words, "And I was delivered out of the mouth of the lion." He says: "The Lord will deliver me from every evil work and will preserve me unto his heavenly kingdom,"[72] indicating his speedy martyrdom, which he foretells even more clearly in the same writing,

---

[62]ACW 11:54-55*. [63]Origen is commenting on Luke 15:16 and the plight of the prodigal son. [64]FC 94:214*. [65]1 Tim 6:20. [66]1 Tim 6:4. [67]Rom 9:28. [68]NPNF 2 7:285*. [69]FC 25:400. [70]Jn 16:12. [71]FC 90:203-4. [72]2 Tim 4:18.

when he says, "For I am even now ready to be sacrificed, and the time of my dissolution is at hand." ECCLESIASTICAL HISTORY 2.22.[73]

BEING POURED OUT. THEODORE OF MOPSUESTIA: Paul does not say *libor* but *delibor*, that is, enduring death in the confession of Christ as a libation of wine is poured out on behalf of honoring God. COMMENTARY ON 2 TIMOTHY.[74]

A LIBATION. THEODORET OF CYR: Paul calls his destruction a libation, as if his blood were poured out for the sake of true religion. INTERPRETATION OF THE SECOND LETTER TO TIMOTHY.[75]

AN IMMOLATION. AUGUSTINE: Let me say something about this; I am helped, you see, by their words, which have gone out to the ends of the whole wide world. Notice first of all his holy act of pouring himself out. He said he was being immolated, not that he was dying. It is not because one who is immolated doesn't die but that not everyone who dies is immolated. So being immolated he is dying for God. The word is taken from sacrifice. Everything that is sacrificed is slaughtered for God. SERMONS 299.3.[76]

THE CROWN OF GRACE. AUGUSTINE: Hear Paul the apostle first acknowledging grace and afterwards seeking what was owed. What is the acknowledgment of grace in Paul? He "was before a blasphemer and a persecutor and contumelious," he says, "but I obtained mercy."[77] He said that he was unworthy to obtain it, but that he obtained it not by his own merits but by the mercy of God. Hear him now ready to receive what is owed, he who had first accepted unmerited grace. He says, "For I am even now ready to be sacrificed, and the time of my dissolution is at hand. I have fought the good fight, I have finished the course, I have kept the faith. As to the rest, there is laid up for me a crown of justice." Now he demands what is owed. Now he exacts what is to be paid. For look at the following words: "Which the Lord, the just judge, will render to me in that

day." TRACTATES ON JOHN 3.10.[78]

4:7 I Have Kept the Faith

CONSOLATION. CHRYSOSTOM: He is desirous to console the despondency of his disciple and therefore bids him be of good cheer, since he was going to his crown, having finished all his work and obtained a glorious end. . . . As a father whose son was sitting nearby, bewailing his orphan state, might console him, saying, Weep not, my son; we have lived a good life, we have arrived at old age, and now we leave you. . . . These things then he wrote to console Timothy. Indeed the whole epistle is full of consolation and is a sort of testament. HOMILIES ON 2 TIMOTHY 9.[79]

A STRIVING GROUND FOR VIRTUE. NEMESIUS OF EMESA: If anyone should think it out of all reason that a godly man should suffer grievously so that someone else should be put right, let him reflect that this life is a contest and a striving ground for virtue. The victors' chaplets are splendid in exact proportion, therefore, to the pains with which they are won. That is why Paul was allowed to fall into countless afflictions. The purpose was that the crown of victory which he should bear off might be the greater. OF THE NATURE OF MAN 44.69.[80]

ONLY AT THE END. AMBROSE: For in a contest there is much labor needed. After the contest victory falls to some, to others disgrace. Is the palm ever given or the crown granted before the course is finished? Paul writes well when he says, "I have fought a good fight, I have finished my course, I have kept the faith; henceforth there is laid up for me a crown of righteousness, which the Lord, the

---

[73]FC 19:124. [74]TEM 2:225. [75]PG 82:851C/852C. [76]WSA 3/8:230. [77]1 Tim 1:13. [78]FC 78:83-84. For a similar interpretation, see Augustine *On Grace and Free Will* 6.14 (FC 59:266). [79]NPNF 1 13:511. [80]LCC 4:449.

righteous judge, shall give me at that day; and not to me only, but to all who love his appearing." DUTIES OF THE CLERGY 1.15.58.[81]

ONLY BY HOPE. BASIL THE GREAT: "Turn, O my soul, into your rest: for the Lord has been bountiful to you."[82] The brave contestant applies to himself the consoling words, very much like to Paul, when he says: "I have fought the good fight, I have finished the course, I have kept the faith. For the rest, there is laid up for me a crown of justice." These things the prophet also says to himself: Since you have fulfilled sufficiently the course of this life, turn then to your rest, "for the Lord has been bountiful to you." For, eternal rest lies before those who have struggled through the present life observant of the laws, a rest not given in payment for a debt owed for their works but provided as a grace of the munificent God for those who have hoped in him. HOMILIES 22.[83]

JUST IN COMPARISON WITH MEN, NOT GOD. JEROME: For I am of the opinion that no creature can be perfect according to true and consummate justice. Moreover, no one denies that one individual differs from another individual. I know that there are different measures of justice among men, that one individual is greater or lesser than another individual and that individuals who are not just in comparison with other individuals can still be called just according to their own standard and measure. The apostle Paul, the chosen vessel, who labored more abundantly than all of the apostles, was certainly just when he wrote to Timothy: "I have fought the good fight, I have finished the course, I have kept the faith. For the rest, there is laid up for me a crown of justice, which the Lord, the just judge, will give to me in that day; yet not to me only, but also to those who love his coming." Timothy, who was his disciple and follower, who was guided by him in the way of life that he was to follow and the course he was to pursue in the acquisition of virtues, was also a just man. Are we to suppose for a moment that both of them possessed the one and the same

measure of justice? Or that he who labored more abundantly than all of them does not have greater excellence? AGAINST THE PELAGIANS 1.16.[84]

ONLY BY GRACE. AUGUSTINE: There is, of course, the passage where he speaks of immortality after good works, as if he really demands it as his due, for he says: "I have fought the good fight, I have finished the course, I have kept the faith. Henceforth there is laid up for me the crown of righteousness, which the Lord, the righteous judge, shall render to me at that day." Do you think, perhaps, that because he said "shall render" he meant that it was his due? But when "he ascended on high and took captivity captive," he did not render but "gave gifts to men."[85] How could the apostle speak presumptuously as of a debt being paid back to him, unless he had first received grace which was not due to him, being justified by which, he fought the good fight? To SIMPLICIAN—ON VARIOUS QUESTIONS 1.2.3.[86]

PRAYER THE PRIMARY ARENA. CASSIODORUS: As someone has said, you will scarcely ever find that when a person prays, some empty and external reflection does not impede him, causing the attention which the mind directs on God to be sidetracked and interrupted. So it is a great and most wholesome struggle to concentrate on prayer once begun, and with God's help to show lively resistance to the temptations of the enemy, so that our minds may with unflagging attention strain to be ever fastened on God. Then we can deservedly recite Paul's words: I have fought a good fight, I have finished my course, I have kept the faith. EXPLANATION OF THE PSALMS 101.1.[87]

4:8 *The Crown of Righteousness*

---

[81]NPNF 2 10:11. [82]Ps 114:7. [83]FC 46:356-57. [84]FC 53:254-55. [85]Eph 4:8. [86]LCC 6:388. Augustine frequently interpreted 2 Timothy 4:7-8 in this way in the sermons and also in the later tractates, for example, *On Grace and Free Will* 7.16 (NPNF 1 5:450) and *Proceedings of Pelagius* 14.35 (FC 86:147-48). [87]ACW 53:1.

REJOICE! CHRYSOSTOM: You should not grieve that I shall depart, to be invested with that crown which will by Christ be placed upon my head. But if I continued here, truly you might rather grieve and fear lest I should fail and perish. HOMILIES ON 1 TIMOTHY 9.[88]

THE MARTYR'S STRUGGLE. CHRYSOSTOM: The martyr's own struggles surpass our mortal nature. The prizes they won go beyond our powers and understanding. They laughed at the life lived on earth. They trampled underfoot the punishment of the rack. They scorned death and took wing to heaven. They escaped from the storms of temporal things and sailed into a calm harbor. They brought with them no gold or silver or expensive garments. They carried along no treasure which could be plundered but the riches of patience, courage and love. Now they belong to Paul's choral band while they still await their crowns, because they have escaped henceforth the uncertainty of the future. AGAINST PAGANS AND JEWS 6.7.[89]

THE JUST JUDGE. THEODORET OF CYR: He calls the "crown of righteousness" that which has been prepared for the righteous, which is given by a just sentence. When? On that day. By whom? By the just judge. I have known him as just; I have known him as the judge. I trust in his judgment. I look for a sentence. In this way Paul offers consolation to all children of faith. INTERPRETATION OF THE SECOND LETTER TO TIMOTHY.[90]

THE FINAL DISPENSATION. AMBROSE: While we await the fullness of time, the souls await their due reward. Some await punishment and others glory. And yet in the meantime the one group is not without harm nor the other without gain. For the former will be dismayed upon seeing that the reward of glory has been stored up for those who keep the law of God, that the chambers of those souls are being preserved by the angels, that shame and ruin will be the punishments of their negligence and rebellion, so that they may gaze on the glory of the Most High and blush to come into his sight, for they have profaned his commandments. DEATH AS A GOOD 10.47.[91]

LOOKING FOR THE CROWN. AUGUSTINE: I have received the letter of your Reverence[92] in which you urge on us the great good of loving and longing for the coming of our Savior. In this you act like the good servant of the master of the household who is eager for his lord's gain and who wishes to have many sharers in the love which burns so brightly and constantly in you. Examining, therefore, the passage you quoted from the apostle where he said that the Lord would render a crown of justice not only to him but to all who love his coming, we live as uprightly as he and we pass through this world as pilgrims while our heart constantly expands with this love, and whether he comes sooner or later than he is expected, his coming is loved with faithful charity and longed for with pious affection. LETTERS 199.1.1.[93]

GOD'S GENEROSITY THE KEY. CASSIODORUS: The holy man demands judgment because he is certain of the Lord's mercy. As Paul has it: "As to the rest, there is laid up for me a crown of justice, which the Lord, the just Judge, will render to me in that day." He walks in his innocence because . . . he puts his trust in the Lord. The presumption he shows is not in his own powers but in God's generosity. EXPLANATION OF THE PSALMS 25.1.[94]

---

[88]NPNF 1 13:512*. [89]FC 68:148-49. [90]PG 82:853A/854A. [91]FC 65:103-4. [92]Augustine addresses Bishop Hesychius. [93]FC 30:356-57. [94]ACW 51:257.

4:9-22 PERSONAL INSTRUCTIONS AND FINAL GREETINGS

⁹*Do your best to come to me soon.* ¹⁰*For Demas, in love with this present world, has deserted me and gone to Thessalonica; Crescens has gone to Galatia,ᵉ Titus to Dalmatia.* ¹¹*Luke alone is with me. Get Mark and bring him with you; for he is very useful in serving me.* ¹²*Tychicus I have sent to Ephesus.* ¹³*When you come, bring the cloak that I left with Carpus at Troas, also the books, and above all the parchments.* ¹⁴*Alexander the coppersmith did me great harm; the Lord will requite him for his deeds.* ¹⁵*Beware of him yourself, for he strongly opposed our message.* ¹⁶*At my first defense no one took my part; all deserted me. May it not be charged against them!* ¹⁷*But the Lord stood by me and gave me strength to proclaim the message fully, that all the Gentiles might hear it. So I was rescued from the lion's mouth.* ¹⁸*The Lord will rescue me from every evil and save me for his heavenly kingdom. To him be the glory for ever and ever. Amen.*

¹⁹*Greet Prisca and Aquila, and the household of Onesiphorus.* ²⁰*Erastus remained at Corinth; Trophimus I left ill at Miletus.* ²¹*Do your best to come before winter. Eubulus sends greetings to you, as do Pudens and Linus and Claudia and all the brethren.*

²²*The Lord be with your spirit. Grace be with you.*

e Other ancient authorities read *Gaul*

OVERVIEW: While Paul was being held in Nero's prison, he was composing this second epistle to Timothy, indicating that his first defense had taken place and that martyrdom was at hand (EUSEBIUS). Amid defections of some colleagues, Paul is alone in his prison in Rome, wishing to see Timothy soon. He asks Timothy to bring his books and parchments and cloak (AMBROSIASTER, CHRYSOSTOM, THEODORE) and warns him to avoid Alexander, a dangerous man (CHRYSOSTOM). He describes his lonely preliminary trial at Rome. He conveys greetings and gives news of his close associates in ministry, especially recounting the importance of the ministry of women (CHRYSOSTOM).

Paul concludes with words of encouragement for Timothy as sufferings inevitably come and as Timothy will have to learn to rely increasingly, in the face of his human weakness, on fresh measures of divine grace for his sustenance (CHRYSOSTOM). Paul is preoccupied with the practical arrangements and details that will govern the continuing mission by his disciples, so that he himself may have the assistance that he needs and so that the others may receive guidance (THEODORE, THEODORET, AMBROSIASTER).

4:9 Come to Me Soon

PAUL NOT ARROGANT. CHRYSOSTOM: It is worthwhile to raise the question of why Paul calls Timothy to come to him, when it is Paul who has the responsibility of caring for the church, indeed for a whole people. Paul does not do this out of arrogance. Paul was in fact ready to come to Timothy, as he says, "If I am delayed, you may know how one ought to behave in the household of

God."[1] But necessity constrained him. He was no longer the master of his own movements. He was in prison and had been confined by Nero and was all but on the point of death. That he might not die before he saw his disciple, he therefore sends for him, desiring to see him before he dies and perhaps to turn over heavy responsibilities to him. HOMILIES ON 2 TIMOTHY 10.[2]

4:10a Demas, in Love with This World

TO CONFIRM US. CHRYSOSTOM: Demas, having loved his own ease and security away from danger, has chosen rather to live luxuriously at home, rather than suffer hardships with Paul and share his present dangers. Paul has indeed blamed him, but only in order to confirm us, that we may not sink to self-indulgent weakness in declining toils and dangers, for this would amount to "having loved this present world." HOMILIES ON 2 TIMOTHY 10.[3]

THE FUTURE WORLD OUR HOPE. POLYCARP: Now I exhort all of you to be obedient to the word of righteousness[4] and to exercise all patient endurance, such as you have seen with your very eyes, not only in the blessed Ignatius and Zosimus and Rufus but also in others who were of your membership, and in Paul himself and the rest of the apostles; being persuaded that all these "did not run in vain"[5] but in faith and righteousness, and that they are now in their deserved place with the Lord, in whose suffering they also shared. For they "loved not this present world" but him who died on our behalf and was raised by God for our sakes. LETTER OF POLYCARP 8.[6]

4:10b Crescens Gone to Galatia

WHICH GALATIA? THEODORE OF MOPSUESTIA: He calls "Galatia" what we now call Gaul; for so all of the older peoples called this place, as anyone can recognize from many sources, especially from the Jewish history written by Josephus. For those people who are now called Galatians are so designated in the old narratives that trace their movement from those regions to various places. COMMENTARY ON 2 TIMOTHY.[7]

4:11 Bring Mark with You

ALWAYS FOCUSED ON THE GOSPEL. CHRYSOSTOM: It was not for his own relief but for the ministry of the gospel that Paul wanted Mark with him. For though he was imprisoned, he never ceased to preach. For the same reason he sent for Timothy, not for his own comfort but for the work of the gospel, so that his death would not disturb the faithful. HOMILIES ON 2 TIMOTHY 10.[8]

4:13 Bring the Coat and the Books

BRING THE COAT. CHRYSOSTOM: This *phailonēn* may mean a garment, or, as some say, a bag, in which the books were contained. HOMILIES ON 2 TIMOTHY 10.[9]

A GARMENT. THEODORE OF MOPSUESTIA: The view that this *paenula*[10] is some other kind of book, rather than just a garment, is ridiculous. COMMENTARY ON 2 TIMOTHY.[11]

THE DRESS OF A ROMAN CITIZEN. AMBROSIASTER: The *paenula* is the distinctive dress of a Roman citizen, thus a garment that Paul would have needed on his journeys to identify him as such. COMMENTARY ON THE SECOND LETTER TO TIMOTHY.[12]

THE PATRIMONY OF BOOKS. CHRYSOSTOM: What had he to do with books, who was about to depart and go to God? He needed them much,

---

[1] Tim 3:15. [2] NPNF 1 13:513*. [3] NPNF 1 13:513*. [4] Heb 5:13. [5] Phil 2:16; cf. Gal 2:2. [6] LCC 1:135. [7] TEM 2:227 (Greek). [8] NPNF 1 13:513*. [9] NPNF 1 13:513-14. [10] *Paenula* is the Latin spelling of *phailonēn*. [11] TEM 2:228. [12] CSEL 81 3:317.

that he might deposit them in the hands of the faithful, who would retain them in place of his own teaching. HOMILIES ON 2 TIMOTHY 10.[13]

BOOKS AND PARCHMENTS. THEODORE OF MOPSUESTIA: Paul makes a distinction here between the parchment *volumina*, which are in the form of scrolls, and the regular *libros*, which are in book or codex form. COMMENTARY ON 2 TIMOTHY.[14]

4:14 *Alexander the Coppersmith*

CALL TO FORTITUDE. CHRYSOSTOM: Here again he makes mention of his trial, not wishing merely to censure and accuse the man but to prepare his disciple for the conflicts, that he might bear them firmly. Though they be mean and contemptible persons, and without honor, who cause these trials, they ought all, he says, to be borne with fortitude. HOMILIES ON 2 TIMOTHY 10.[15]

4:16 *No One Took My Part*

PAUL SPARES HIS BETRAYERS. CHRYSOSTOM: If in time of war someone abandons a companion who is exposed to danger and shrinks back from the confrontation with the enemy, he would be justly condemned by the others for this gross betrayal. It is even more true with those who work for the gospel. But he then moves on to give encouragement to his disciple in what follows. HOMILIES ON 2 TIMOTHY 10.[16]

OUR DEBT TO PAUL. AUGUSTINE: For we owe "fruits" to those who minister spiritual doctrine to us through their understanding of the divine mysteries. We owe these to them as men. We owe these fruits also to "the living souls" since they offer themselves as examples for us in their own continence. CONFESSIONS 13.25.38.[17]

4:17 *Rescued from the Lion's Mouth*

WRITTEN FROM NERO'S PRISON. EUSEBIUS OF CAESAREA: Story has it that the apostle, after defending himself, was again sent upon the ministry of preaching and coming a second time to the same city met death by martyrdom under Nero. While he was being held in prison, he composed the second epistle to Timothy, at the same time indicating that his first defense had taken place and that martyrdom was at hand. ECCLESIASTICAL HISTORY 2.22.[18]

THE LION IS NERO. CHRYSOSTOM: He had fallen into the very jaws of the lion. For he calls Nero a lion from his ferocity and the violent and daring character of his government. HOMILIES ON 2 TIMOTHY 10.[19]

THE ONE WHO DEVOURS SOULS. ANONYMOUS: And again Paul, giving thanks to the Lord for his own salvation, says, "I was rescued from the lion's mouth, meaning the one who roars to devour souls."[20] For he is full of wiles and at times he makes a lie appear as truth. THE FIRST GREEK LIFE OF PACHOMIUS 135.[21]

4:20 *Trophimus Ill*

DIVINE PERMISSION. CHRYSOSTOM: The apostles could not do everything. They did not dispense miraculous gifts upon all occasions, lest more should be ascribed to them than was right. . . . For many things were permitted by God that the weakness of human nature might be manifested. HOMILIES ON 2 TIMOTHY 10.[22]

4:21 *Claudia*

MANY WOMEN SUFFERED MARTYRDOM. CHRYSOSTOM: You see how zealous for the faith

[13]NPNF 1 13:514. [14]TEM 2:228-29 (Greek). [15]NPNF 1 13:514. [16]NPNF 1 13:514*. [17]LCC 7:324. Augustine is commenting allegorically on Genesis 1:29, in order to make the point that the "fruits" that God bestows on humankind are also the works of mercy that we do, and that we owe, to those who preach the gospel. [18]FC 19:123. [19]NPNF 1 13:514. [20]1 Pet 5:8. [21]PK 1:394. [22]NPNF 1 13:515.

the women were, how ardent! Such was Priscilla and this Claudia, already crucified, already prepared for the battle! But why, when there were so many faithful, does he mention only these women? Clearly because they in purpose had already withdrawn from worldly affairs and were illustrious above others. . . . Such holy women are not prone to be discouraged by impediments in the affairs of this life. This is a work of divine grace given to this sex. A woman undertakes no small share of the whole administration, being the keeper of the house. And without her not even political affairs could be properly conducted.

For if their domestic concerns were in a state of confusion or disorder, those who are engaged in public affairs would be kept at home and political business would be ill managed. So that neither in these matters, as neither in spiritual, is she inferior. For she is able, if so inclined, to endure a thousand deaths. Accordingly many women have suffered martyrdom. HOMILIES ON 2 TIMOTHY 10.[23]

---

[23]NPNF 1 13:516.

THE EPISTLE TO TITUS

ARGUMENT: Paul's intention is to write a letter of encouragement, so that believers will persevere in virtue and so that they may be protected from Judaizing tendencies (CHRYSOSTOM). Having evangelized the Cretans, Paul, after dispatching Timothy to Ephesus, turns over the mission in Crete to Titus, who needs instruction on matters of organization and guidance in countering the arguments of the Jews (THEODORE). More specifically, it is particular instruction about the importance of the incarnation that Paul intends as Titus's mainstay (THEODORET). Paul's instructions to Titus the bishop are intended to make him appropriately careful about ordinations, since there are many who seek this by pretending that they are worthy (AMBROSIASTER). Despite objection by some heretics to the authority of this letter, it must be accepted as ancient and genuine (JEROME).

1:1-4 GREETINGS

¹*Paul, a servant*ᵃ *of God and an apostle of Jesus Christ, to further the faith of God's elect and their knowledge of the truth which accords with godliness,* ²*in hope of eternal life which God, who never lies, promised ages ago* ³*and at the proper time manifested in his word through the preaching with which I have been entrusted by command of God our Savior;*

⁴*To Titus, my true child in a common faith:*

Grace and peace from God the Father and Christ Jesus our Savior.

a Or *slave*

OVERVIEW: Paul describes his great confidence in Titus and emphasizes the central importance of reliance on God's grace as it builds on and transforms the human striving for godliness (CHRYSOSTOM). Paul's apostleship is for the sake of those whom God has chosen to receive his goodness and to know the truth of eternal life. The natural drift of the letter is toward Paul's spiritual relationship with Titus and the instructions to follow. Paul hands on to Titus faith in the coequal Father and Son, a reality from all eternity and a belief essential to the success of his mission (THEODORET).

As servant and apostle, Paul occupies a position of great honor, one to which God has chosen him on the basis of spiritual virtues and which requires Paul to proclaim the fatherhood of God in all creation, a fatherhood that manifests the essential immortality of God, far above that of the angels (JEROME). Paul's entrustment to apostolic leadership of the elect (JEROME) was not due to his own achievements but to grace (CHRYSOSTOM). God existed before time (AUGUSTINE). Nothing is impossible to God except to lie (CLEMENT OF ROME). God has no difficulty knowing the future, since God exists in an entirely different relation to time than we do (AMBROSE, AUGUSTINE). The excellence of a herald consists in boldly proclaiming to all what has really happened, not in adding or taking away anything. Commands are not left to our choice (CHRYSOSTOM). The sonship of Titus is in relation to a common faith into which both Paul and Titus have been born—a sonship by choice rather than natural birth (CHRYSOSTOM, THEODORET).

1:1a *A Servant of God, an Apostle of Jesus Christ*

APOSTOLIC DIGNITY ESTABLISHED. JEROME: When he says, "An apostle of Jesus Christ," it seems to be as if he had said, "commanding officer of the praetorian guard of Augustus Caesar, master of the army for Tiberius Caesar." Just as secular judges are seen as more noble in accordance with the kings whom they serve and are assigned a name from the dignity by which they are elevated, so by establishing his great dignity among Christians as an apostle, he has designated himself with the title of apostle of Christ, that he might strike awe into his readers

by the authority of the name. Thereby he indicates that all who believe in Christ are to be in submission to him. COMMENTARY ON TITUS.[1]

FATHER AND SON TOGETHER. THEODORET OF CYR: The opening of every one of his letters is distinguished by the divine apostle with this address. At one time it is "Paul a servant of Jesus Christ called to be an apostle."[2] At another "Paul called to be an apostle of Jesus Christ."[3] At another "Paul a servant of God and an apostle of Jesus Christ." And suiting his benediction to his salutation he deduces it from the same source and links the title of the Son with God the Father, saying "grace to you and peace from God our Father and the Lord Jesus Christ."[4] LETTERS 146.[5]

1:1b *To Further the Faith of God's Elect*

ELECTED TO GUARDIANSHIP BY GRACE. CHRYSOSTOM: I think Paul's meaning is this: I was entrusted with God's elect, not for any achievements of mine. It was not from my toils and labors that I received this dignity. It was wholly the effect of the goodness of the One who entrusted it to me. Yet that this grace may not seem without reason, . . . he adds: "and the acknowledging of the truth that is after godliness." For it was for this acknowledgment that I was entrusted. It was of his grace that all this was entrusted to me. God was the author of all this. HOMILIES ON TITUS 1.[6]

1:2a *In Hope of Eternal Life*

THE ETERNITY OF THE SON. HILARY OF POITIERS: Since the periods of time, therefore, come within the scope of our knowledge or speculations, we pass judgment upon them according to the understanding of human reasoning. In

---

[1]PL 26:592AB. [2]Rom 1:1. [3]1 Cor 1:1. [4]Rom 1:7. [5]NPNF 2 3:317. [6]NPNF 1 13:520.

this way we believe ourselves justified in saying about anything: "It has not been before it is born." The times that have already past always come before the origin of everything. Since in the things of God, that is, in the birth of God, everything is before the eternal time, then we cannot say of him: "Before he was born." Nor can we say that he to whom the eternal promise was made before the eternal time has the "hope of life everlasting," according to the statement of the apostle, which the God who does not lie has promised to him before the eternal time, nor can we say that at one time he had not been. We cannot assume that he whom we must confess as being before the eternal time has had his beginning after something. ON THE TRINITY 12.27.[7]

WHETHER GOD EXISTED BEFORE TIME.
AUGUSTINE: I confess that I do not know what ages passed before the human race was created, yet I am perfectly sure that no one creature is coeternal with the Creator. Curiously enough, the apostle uses the expression *tempora aeterna*[8] in reference not to the future but to the past. Thus he says: "in the hope of eternal life which God, who does not lie, promised before the eternal times, he has in due times manifested, his word." He seems to be saying that time stretches backward eternally; yet time is not coeternal with God, since not only did God exist "before eternal times" but he promised eternal life which he manifested in his own time, that is, in due time. Now, what he promised was his Word. For the Word is eternal life. But how did he make this promise, since it was made to those who certainly did not exist before the "eternal times"? The meaning, then, must be that what was to take place in its own time was already predestined and determined in his eternity and in his coeternal Word. THE CITY OF GOD 12.16.[9]

1:2b God Who Never Lies

NOTHING IMPOSSIBLE TO GOD EXCEPT TO LIE. CLEMENT OF ROME: Having then this hope

[in the resurrection], let our souls be bound to him who is faithful in his promises and just in his judgments. He who has commanded us not to lie shall much more himself not lie; for nothing is impossible with God, except to lie. FIRST LETTER OF CLEMENT 27.[10]

GOD HAS NO DOUBT ABOUT THE FUTURE.
AMBROSE: But God can neither be in doubt, nor can he be deceived. For he only is in doubt who is ignorant of the future. One who has predicted one thing while something else has happened is deceived about the future. Not so with God. What is plainer than the fact that Scripture states the Father to have said one thing of the Son and that the same Scripture proves another thing to have taken place? The Son was beaten, he was mocked, was crucified and died. He suffered much worse things in the flesh than those servants[11] who had been appointed before. Was the Father deceived? Was he ignorant of it? Was he unable to give help? The One who is the truth cannot make a mistake. It is written that "the ever-truthful God cannot lie." How could he who knows all be ignorant? What could he not do, who could do all? OF THE CHRISTIAN FAITH 5.17.215-16.[12]

1:3a The Preaching Entrusted to Me

BOLDNESS ESSENTIAL IN THE HERALD. CHRYSOSTOM: "Through the preaching," that is, openly and with all boldness, for this is the meaning of "preaching." For as a herald proclaims in the theater in the presence of all, so also we preach, adding nothing but declaring the things which we have heard. For the excellence of a herald consists in proclaiming to all what has really happened, not in adding or taking away anything. HOMILIES ON TITUS 1.[13]

---

[7]FC 25:520. [8]Promised from eternal times, or from ages ago. [9]FC 14:275-76. See also Augustine *Questions* 72 (FC 70:185-86). [10]ANF 9:237. [11]The prophets. [12]NPNF 2 10:311-12. [13]NPNF 1 13:521.

1:3b By Command of God Our Savior

Commands Not Left to Our Choice.
Chrysostom: If then it is a commandment, it is not at my disposal. I fulfill what is commanded. For of things to be done, some are in our power; others are not. For what he commands, that is not in our power; what he permits is left to our choice.... But commandments are not left to our choice, we must either perform them or be punished for not doing so. Homilies on Titus 1.[14]

1:4 Titus, My True Child in a Common Faith

The Common Faith. Chrysostom: After Paul had called Titus his own son and assumed the dignity of a father, hear how it is that he lessens and lowers that honor. He adds, "After the common faith"—that means: with respect to the faith I have no advantage over you. It is common to us both. You and I were together born by it. Why then does he call him son? Either wishing to express his affection for him, or his priority in the gospel, or to show that Titus had been enlightened by him. In a similar way he calls the faithful both children and brothers. They are brothers because they were born by the same faith. They are children, because it was by his hands. Homilies on Titus 1.[15]

This Sonship Is by Choice. Chrysostom: For in children by nature, the true and the spurious are determined by the father who begot and the mother who bore them. But it is not so in this case, but it depends on the disposition. For one who was a true son may become spurious, and a spurious son may become a true one. For it is not the force of nature but the power of choice on which it depends, whence it is subject to changes in time. Homilies on Titus 1.[16]

Distinguishing Natural and Spiritual Sons. Theodoret of Cyr: Natural generation does not operate by the assent of the one who is born, whereas the birth that comes from faith requires such assent. Although the one who preaches may sincerely believe, he who hears, unless he takes to himself what he learns with faith, cannot be called the son of the preacher. Interpretation of the Letter to Titus.[17]

---

[14]NPNF 1 13:521. [15]NPNF 1 13:521-22. [16]NPNF 1 13:521. [17]PG 82:859AB/860AB.

1:5-9 INSTALLATION OF PRESBYTERS

[5]*This is why I left you in Crete, that you might amend what was defective, and appoint elders in every town as I directed you, [6]if any man is blameless, the husband of one wife, and his children are believers and not open to the charge of being profligate or insubordinate. [7]For a bishop, as God's steward, must be blameless; he must not be arrogant or quick-tempered or a drunkard or violent or greedy for gain, [8]but hospitable, a lover of goodness, master of himself, upright, holy, and self-controlled; [9]he must hold firm to the sure word as taught, so that he may be able to give instruction in sound doctrine and also to confute those who contradict it.*

OVERVIEW: Paul lays out the ethical and moral requirements for anyone who would be suitable for the episcopal office by setting standards for domestic life, personal habits and faithfulness in ministry (CHRYSOSTOM, THEODORE, THEODORET, JEROME). By Jerome's time, church governance had gone through a change from a council of presbyters to the election of a presiding elder or bishop (JEROME). Earlier the bishop and the elder were interchangeable terms; later they were distinguished (THEODORE, THEODORET). Pastors are ordained to teach (THEODORE), holding the presidency of a single church (CHRYSOSTOM). A bishop should have an exemplary moral character (JEROME). He must not have committed any crime within the civil order (AUGUSTINE). A bishop must be content with the wife he had when he came to ordination (APOSTOLIC CONSTITUTIONS). If bishops can marry, marriage itself is not condemned, as some heretics claim (CHRYSOSTOM, AMBROSE). Monogamy is thereby taught by example (JEROME). The bishop's care of his own children is a valid measure of his ability to care for others (CHRYSOSTOM). Yet even well-taught children may go astray (THEODORE, JEROME). The bishop must not be intemperate or acrimonious (CHRYSOSTOM, THEODORET, JEROME). A bishop must be capable of refuting adversaries (ORIGEN) on the basis of careful Scripture study, a good mind and a general education (CHRYSOSTOM, JEROME, AUGUSTINE). An inept teacher is not qualified (CHRYSOSTOM).

1:5 Appoint Elders in Every Town

BRINGING ONE CHURCH INTO GOOD ORDER. CHRYSOSTOM: Here he is speaking of *episkopoi* [bishops].... He did not wish the whole island to be entrusted to one elder, but that each one should have his own charge and care, for thus he would have less labor himself, and those under his rule would receive greater attention. The teacher would not then be required to hold the presidency of many churches but was left to be occupied with one only, and to bring that into order. HOMILIES ON TITUS 2.[1]

ORDINATION TO TEACH. THEODORE OF MOPSUESTIA: Paul emphasizes that correct teaching must accompany these ordinations. He mentions only presbyters, since theirs is the most general office. COMMENTARY ON TITUS.[2]

HOW CHURCH GOVERNANCE CHANGED. JEROME: Paul is speaking here to bishops who have the power of placing presbyters in the individual towns, so that they would hear clearly by what kind of rule correct church order should be maintained.... Originally the churches were governed by a common council of the presbyters. But after one of their number began to think that those whom he had baptized were his and not Christ's, it was universally decreed that one of the presbyters should be elected to preside over the others, to whom the care of the whole church should pertain, that the seeds of schism might be alleviated. COMMENTARY ON TITUS.[3]

PRESBYTER AND BISHOP WERE THE SAME. JEROME: And lest any should in a spirit of contention argue that there must then have been more bishops than one in a single church, there is the following passage which clearly proves a bishop and a presbyter to be the same. Writing to Titus the apostle says: "For this cause I left you in Crete, that you should set in order the things that are wanting, and appoint presbyters in every city, as I had instructed you: if any be blameless, the husband of one wife, having believing children not accused of wantonness or unruly. For a bishop must be blameless as the steward of God." ... When subsequently one was chosen to preside over the rest, this was done to remedy schism and to prevent each individual from rending the church of Christ by drawing it to himself. LETTERS 146.1.[4]

---

[1]NPNF 1 13:524. [2]TEM 2:237. [3]PL 26:596B-597AB. [4]LCC 5:386-87.

1:6a If Anyone Is Blameless

Freedom from Crime. Augustine: The first freedom, then, is to be without crimes. And so when the apostle Paul chose either priests or deacons to be ordained, and when anyone is to be ordained to take charge of a church, he does not say, If anyone is without sin. For if he were to say this, every person would be rejected, no one would be ordained. But he says, "if anyone is without crime,"[5] such as homicide, adultery and uncleanness of fornication, theft, fraud, sacrilege, and other things of this sort. Tractates on John 41.10.1.[6]

Blameless Comprehends All Virtues. Jerome: "A bishop then must be blameless." The same thing that he says to Titus, "if any be blameless." All the virtues are comprehended in this one word; thus he seems to require an impossible perfection. For if every sin, every idle word, is deserving of blame, who is there in this world that is sinless and blameless? Still he who is chosen to be shepherd of the church must be one compared with whom other men are rightly regarded as but a flock of sheep. Letters 69.8.[7]

1:6b The Husband of One Wife

Monogamy the Rule. Tertullian: Should we not rather recognize, from among the store of primitive scriptural precedents, those that correspond with the gospel order of things respecting discipline? By this means we convey to the new community the typical requirements of antiquity. In the old law I find the pruning knife applied to the license of repeated marriage. . . . Among us the prescript is more fully and more carefully laid down, that they who are chosen into the sacerdotal order must be men of one marriage. This rule is so rigidly observed that I remember some removed from their office for bigamy. On Exhortation to Chastity 7.[8]

Married No More Than Once. Anony-mous: We have already said that a bishop, a presbyter and a deacon, when they are constituted, must be married but once, whether their wives are alive or whether they are dead. It is not lawful for them, if they are unmarried when they are ordained, to be married afterwards; or if they are married at that time, to marry a second time, but to be content with that wife which they had when they came to ordination. Constitutions of the Holy Apostles 6.3.17.[9]

Bishop Not Excluded from Marriage. Ambrose: I have put down the faults which I have been taught to avoid. But it is the apostle who is the teacher of virtues. He teaches a bishop . . . to be "the husband of one wife." The bishop is thereby not excluded from marriage altogether . . . but rather encouraged by chastity in marriage to preserve the grace of his baptism. . . . There are many who argue that "husband of one wife" is said of marriage after baptism, on the ground that the fault which would constitute an impediment has been washed away in baptism. . . . But where there has been a second marriage, it is not dissolved. Sin is washed away in baptism, law is not. Letters 63.62-63.[10]

Marriage Honorable. Chrysostom: Paul says this to stop the mouths of those heretics who condemned marriage. He shows that it is not an unholy thing in itself, but so far honorable that a married man might ascend the holy throne. And at the same time he wishes to reprove the wanton, not permitting their admission into this high office those who contracted a second marriage. Homilies on Titus 2.[11]

Teaching Monogamy by Example. Jerome: It is not that every monogamous man is better

---

[5]1 Tim 3:10. [6]FC 88:145. See also Augustine *On Man's Perfection in Righteousness* 17.38 (NPNF 1 5:173) and *Against Two Letters of the Pelagians* 1.28.14 (NPNF 1 5:386). [7]NPNF 1 6:147*. See also Jerome *Against the Pelagians* 22 (FC 53:264-65). [8]ANF 4:54*. [9]ANF 7:457. [10]LCC 5:274. [11]NPNF 1 13:524*.

than every man who has been married twice. Rather, it is that the bishop must teach monogamy and, best of all, continence, by example. Indeed, some monogamous men are less continent than some who have been married twice and widowed. COMMENTARY ON TITUS.[12]

1:6c His Children Are Believers

HIS CARE FOR HIS OWN CHILDREN. CHRYSOSTOM: We should observe what care he bestows upon children. For he who cannot be the instructor of his own children, how could he be the teacher of others? . . . For if he was unable to restrain them, it is a great proof of his weakness. And if he was unconcerned, his want of affection is much to be blamed. He then who neglects his own children, how shall he take care of others'? HOMILIES ON TITUS 2.[13]

WELL-TAUGHT CHILDREN MAY GO ASTRAY. JEROME: Parents should not be faulted if, having taught their children well, these turn out badly later. Indeed, if anyone had taught his sons well, it was Isaac, who must be viewed as setting even Esau on a firm foundation. But Esau turned out to be profligate and worldly, when he sold his birthright for a single meal.[14] Samuel also, though he invoked God and God heard him, and he obtained rain at the time of the winter harvest,[15] had sons who declined into greed. COMMENTARY ON TITUS.[16]

1:6d Not Profligate or Insubordinate

RULING HIS OWN HOUSE WELL. JEROME: "One that rules well his own house." That is, not by increasing riches, not by providing regal banquets, not by having a pile of finely wrought plates, not by slowly steaming pheasants so that the heat may reach the bones without melting the flesh upon them. No, he does this rather by first requiring of his own household the conduct which he has to inculcate in others. LETTERS 69.9.[17]

ARE THERE EXCEPTIONS? THEODORE OF MOPSUESTIA: Paul does not measure the virtue of fathers by the depravity of their children, nor did the misbehavior of his sons make Samuel unworthy of the priesthood; Paul wishes only to show the likely intentions of the father from what has been created in the sons. COMMENTARY ON TITUS.[18]

1:7a A Bishop

SAME IN DIGNITY AS PRESBYTERS. THEODORE OF MOPSUESTIA: Paul here shows that at this time "elders" and "bishops" were interchangeable and that some were put in charge of towns, some of whole regions. These latter became the bishops of later times. COMMENTARY ON TITUS.[19]

FEWER BISHOPS THAN PRESBYTERS. THEODORET OF CYR: Here it is clear that he calls presbyters bishops. In the same community it was the custom that there would be more presbyters than bishops. INTERPRETATION OF THE LETTER TO TITUS.[20]

1:7b Not Violent

NO STRIKER. CHRYSOSTOM: The teacher is the physician of souls. But the physician does not strike. Rather he heals and restores any who might strike him. HOMILIES ON TITUS 2.[21]

NOT ACRIMONIOUS. THEODORE OF MOPSUESTIA: He is not given to useless discord. COMMENTARY ON TITUS.[22]

NOT INTEMPERATE. JEROME: He does not raise a hand easily for striking. COMMENTARY ON TITUS.[23]

---

[12]PL 26:598C. [13]NPNF 1 13:524-25. [14]Gen 25:33. [15]1 Sam 12:18 [16]PL 26:599BC. [17]NPNF 1 6:148*. [18]TEM 2:239. [19]TEM 2:237. [20]PG 82:859C/860C. [21]NPNF 1 13:525. [22]TEM 2:240. [23]PL 26:601D

1:7c Not Greedy for Gain

NOT FOND OF SORDID GAIN. JEROME: That a priest must avoid covetousness even Samuel teaches when he proves before all the people that he has taken nothing from anyone.[24] And the same lesson is taught by the poverty of the apostles who used to receive sustenance and refreshment from their brothers and to boast that they neither had nor wished to have anything besides food and clothing.[25] What the epistle to Timothy calls covetousness Titus openly censures as the desire for filthy lucre. LETTERS 69.9.[26]

1:9 Able to Give Instruction

CAPABLE OF REFUTING ADVERSARIES. ORIGEN: When Paul describes the character of those who are called bishops and portrays what sort of a man a bishop ought to be, he instructs that he should be a teacher. He must be "able also to refute the adversaries," that by his wisdom he may restrain those who speak vainly and deceive souls. He prefers for the episcopate a man once married rather than one twice married, and a man unblamable rather than blameable, and a sober man rather than one not of this character, and a prudent man rather than one imprudent, and an orderly man rather than one even slightly disorderly. In the same way he most wishes that the one who is to be selected as bishop should be a teacher and capable of "refuting adversaries." AGAINST CELSUS 3.48.[27]

DO NOT WELCOME INEPTNESS IN A BISHOP. CHRYSOSTOM: "For the bishop," he says, "must hold to the faithful word which is according to the teaching, that he may be able to convict even the gainsayers." How, then, if he is inexperienced at speaking, as they say, will he be able to convict the objectors and to stop their mouths? If it is permissible to welcome such inexperience in the episcopacy, then why should any church leader bother to read books and study the Scrip-

tures? This is all just a pretense and excuse and a pretext for carelessness and indolence. ON THE PRIESTHOOD 4.8.[28]

A STRONG MIND REQUIRED. CHRYSOSTOM: There is need not of pomp of words but of strong minds, of skill in the Scriptures and of powerful thoughts. Do you not see that Paul put to flight the whole world, that he was more powerful than Plato and all the rest? HOMILIES ON TITUS 2.[29]

SCRIPTURAL KNOWLEDGE REQUIRED. JEROME: To Titus he gives commandment that among a bishop's other virtues [which he briefly describes] he should be careful to seek a knowledge of the Scriptures. A bishop, he says, must hold fast "the faithful word as he has been taught that he may be able by sound doctrine both to exhort and to convince the gainsayers." In fact, want of education in a clergyman prevents him from doing good to any one but himself. Even if the virtue of his life may build up Christ's church, he does it an injury as great by failing to resist those who are trying to pull it down. LETTERS 53.3.[30]

THE ABSURDITY OF NEGLECTING EDUCATION. AUGUSTINE: If anyone says, however, that if teachers are made learned by the Holy Spirit then they do not need to be taught by educators what they should say or how they should say it, he should also say that we should not pray because the Lord says, "for your Father knows what is needful for you, before you ask him."[31] With such a false premise one might argue that the apostle Paul should not have taught Timothy and Titus what or how they should teach others. One upon whom is imposed the personage of a teacher in the church should have these three apostolic epistles before his eyes. Do we

---

[24]1 Sam 12:3-5. [25]1 Tim 6:8. [26]NPNF 1 6:148*. [27]OAC 161-62. [28]COP 124. [29]NPNF 1 13:525. [30]NPNF 1 6:97*. [31]Mt 6:8.

not read in the first epistle to Timothy . . . and in the second epistle is it not said . . . again, does he not say to Titus that a bishop should persevere in "that faithful word which is according to doctrine, that he may be able to exhort in sound doctrine and to convince the gainsayers"? ON CHRISTIAN DOCTRINE 4.16.33.[32]

[32]ACD 141.

1:10-16 THE ACTIVITY OF HERETICS

[10]*For there are many insubordinate men, empty talkers and deceivers, especially the circumcision party;* [11]*they must be silenced, since they are upsetting whole families by teaching for base gain what they have no right to teach.* [12]*One of themselves, a prophet of their own, said, "Cretans are always liars, evil beasts, lazy gluttons."* [13]*This testimony is true. Therefore rebuke them sharply, that they may be sound in the faith,* [14]*instead of giving heed to Jewish myths or to commands of men who reject the truth.* [15]*To the pure all things are pure, but to the corrupt and unbelieving nothing is pure; their very minds and consciences are corrupted.* [16]*They profess to know God, but they deny him by their deeds; they are detestable, disobedient, unfit for any good deed.*

OVERVIEW: The unwillingness of these heretics to submit to authority and their love of money make them unworthy of office. Their deeds are in keeping with traditional Cretan misbehavior and play into Jewish fables and superstitions (CHRYSOSTOM). Paul says these things to Titus to remind him that the heresies he will be fighting are forms of Jewish subversion of the gospel and Gentile perversion of it (THEODORE). What is at stake here is the distortion of their own law by Jewish teachers in a way that appeals to the inconstancy and waywardness of the Cretans, disguising from them the fact that the time of the observance of the literal law is past (THEODORET). It is clear that Paul is equipping Titus for the struggle with outright Judaizing of the gospel, in which the interpretation of the law is turned into a matter of outward observances and nothing else (AMBROSIASTER). These false teachers create an atmosphere of deceit in which Hebrew and Gentile elements are mixed into a duplicitous stew, which is then served up to the gullible and deceitful Cretans (JEROME).

1:11 They Must Be Silenced

FALSE BRETHREN. AMBROSIASTER: Reborn in Christ, they are still not pure Christians; they wish for the law to be partly venerated, for Christ to be partly venerated, all of this as if to profit from the Jews. COMMENTARY ON THE LETTER TO TITUS.[1]

THE BISHOP MUST SPEAK OUT. AUGUSTINE: But I, pierced with such grief as I am, what can I do except speak? Or do they do such things and

[1]CSEL 81 3:325.

then say to me: "Be silent"? May the Lord preserve me from such cowardice that I should hold my peace through fear of their wrath, when he commands me through his apostle, saying that "they ought to be reproved" by the bishop for "teaching the things which they ought not." . . . For when God commands that we speak and preach the word and that we refute and condemn "in season and out of season"[2] those who "teach the things which they ought not"—as I can prove by the words of the Lord and the apostles—let no man think that I can be enjoined to silence in these matters. LETTERS 34.4, 35.3.[3]

1:12 A Prophet of Their Own

THE PAGANS CRITICIZE THE ABSURDITY OF THEIR OWN GODS. ATHENAGORAS: What wonder, too, that others, such as Heracles and Perseus, should be called gods on the ground of their strength? And yet others, as Asclepius, on the ground of their skill? Either their subjects accorded them this honor or else the rulers themselves seized it. Some got the title from fear, others from reverence. . . . And those who lived later accepted these deifications uncritically.

> The Cretans always lie; for they, O King,
> Have built your tomb, and you are not yet
> dead.

While you, Callimachus, believe in the birth of Zeus, you disbelieve in his tomb. While you imagine you are hiding the truth, you actually proclaim, even to those who do not realize it, that Zeus is dead. A PLEA REGARDING CHRISTIANS 30.[4]

WHO IS BEING QUOTED, AND WHY? CHRYSOSTOM: It was Epimenides who said this, himself a Cretan, and the reason he was moved to say it is necessary to mention. It is this. The Cretans have a tomb of Jupiter, with this inscription. "Here lieth Zan, whom they call Jove." On account of this inscription, then, the poet ridi-

culing the Cretans as liars, as he proceeds, introduces, to increase the ridicule, this passage.

> For even a tomb, O King, of thee
> They made, who never diedst, but aye shalt be.

If then this testimony is true, observe what a difficulty! For if the poet is true who said that they spoke falsely, in asserting that Jupiter could die, as the apostle says, it is a fearful thing! Attend, beloved, with much exactness. The poet said that the Cretans were liars for saying that Jupiter was dead. The apostle confirmed his testimony: so, according to the apostle, Jupiter is immortal: For he says, "this witness is true"! What shall we say then? Or rather how shall we solve this? The apostle has not said this but simply and plainly applied this testimony to their habit of falsehood. . . . And as to the question, why does he cite the testimonies of the Greeks? It is because we put them most to confusion when we bring our testimonies and accusations from their own writers, when we make those their accusers, who are admired among themselves. . . . And from what writers should he address them? From the Prophets? They would not have believed them. Since with the Jews too he does not argue from the Gospels, but from the Prophets. HOMILIES ON TITUS 3.[5]

THEODORE OF MOPSUESTIA: Having criticized the dangers that arise from Christians of Jewish background, Paul now does the same with Gentile believers. "Of their own" does not refer to the Jews but to a poet or prophet of Gentile background, even one of the Cretans. He wished to criticize the Cretans because they believed they could show the tomb of Jove, even though Jove existed not as a man (as the poet thought) but as a god. COMMENTARY ON TITUS.[6]

---

[2]2 Tim 4:2. [3]FC 12:133, 137. [4]LCC 1:334. Compare Origen *Against Celsus* 3.43 and Chadwick's note (OAC 157 n. 2) for a different use of this poetic text from Callimachus, which was a staple of the antitheistic arguments of the Skeptics. [5]NPNF 1 13:528. [6]TEM 2:242-43.

THEODORET OF CYR: The quote is from Calli-machus, who is not a Jewish prophet but a pagan poet. He calls the Cretans liars on account of a tomb of Jove. Paul is not here offering fables but insisting on the inconsistency of the Cretans, for it is true that the one they call Jove is in another place dead and they have built him a tomb. INTERPRETATION OF THE LETTER TO TITUS.[7]

JEROME: "One of their own prophets" refers to the "men of the circumcision" in the preceding verse. But since the saying is not found in Hebrew Scripture, it must be that the saying is spoken in a duplicitous way, that is, it is a Cretan prophet who speaks, but disguised as a Hebrew in order to be more believable. This is all part of the deceitful atmosphere created by these teachers. COMMENTARY ON TITUS.[8]

JEROME: You ask me at the close of your letter why it is that sometimes in my writings I quote examples from secular literature and thus defile the purity of the church with the foulness of heathenism. . . . For who is there who does not know that both in Moses and the prophets there are passages cited from Gentile books and that Solomon proposed questions to the philosophers of Tyre and answered others put to him by them. . . . The apostle Paul also, in writing to Titus, has used a line of the poet Epimenides: "The Cretans are always liars, evil beasts, slow bellies." Half of this line was afterward adopted by Callimachus. LETTERS 70. 2.[9]

THE HOLY USE OF THE UNHOLY. ATHANA-SIUS: But the heretic, though he use scriptural terms, yet, as being equally dangerous and depraved, shall be asked in the words of the Spirit, "Why do you preach my laws and take my covenant in your mouth?"[10] Thus, the devil, though speaking from the Scriptures, is silenced by the Savior. The blessed Paul, though he speaks from profane writers, "The Cretans are always liars," and "We are his offspring," and "Evil communications corrupt good manners,"

yet has a religious meaning, as being holy—is "doctor of the nations, in faith and verity," as having "the mind of Christ."[11] COUNCILS OF ARIMINUM AND SELEUCIA 3.39.[12]

THE FALSE USE OF WHAT IS TRUE. AUGUS-TINE: If you were to hear, even from one who was profane, the prayer of the priest couched in words suitable to the mysteries of the gospel, can you possibly say to him, "Your prayer is not true," though he himself may be not only a false priest but not a priest at all? The apostle Paul said that certain testimony of a Cretan prophet (he knew not which) was true, though he was not reckoned among the prophets of God. . . . If, therefore, the apostle himself bore witness to the testimony of some obscure prophet of a for-eign race because he found it to be true, why do not we, when we find in any one what belongs to Christ and is true even though the man with whom it may be found is deceitful and perverse? Why do we not in such a case make a distinction between the fault which is found in the man and the truth which he has not of his own but of God? THE LETTERS OF PETILIAN THE DONA-TIST 2.30.69.[13]

1:14 Jewish Fables

SPIRITUAL VERSUS LITERAL INTERPRETA-TION. ORIGEN: Let us see, however, what sort of rule of interpretation the apostle Paul taught us about these matters. Writing to the Corin-thians he says in a certain passage, "For we know that our fathers were all under the cloud, and all were baptized in Moses in the cloud and in the sea, and all ate the same spiritual food and all drank the same spiritual drink. And

[7]PG 82:861B/862B. [8]PL 26:605D-606A. [9]NPNF 1 6:149. [10]Ps 50:16. [11]Acts 17:28; 1 Cor 15:33; 1 Tim 2:7; 1 Cor 2:16. [12]NPNF 2 4:471*. The same idea is already found in Origen Homilies on Luke 31.3 (FC 94:126-27) and Homilies on Leviticus 5.5 (FC 83:103-4). [13]NPNF 1 4:547. Compare Augustine Reply to Faustus the Man-ichaean 19.1 (NPNF 1 4:239-40).

they drank of the spiritual rock which followed them, and the rock was Christ."[14] Do you see how much Paul's teaching differs from the literal meaning? What the Jews supposed to be a crossing of the sea, Paul calls a baptism. What they supposed to be a cloud, Paul asserts is the Holy Spirit. . . . What then are we to do who received such instructions about interpretation from Paul, a teacher of the church? Does it not seem right that we apply this kind of rule which was delivered to us in a similar way in other passages? Or as some wish, forsaking these things which such a great apostle taught, should we turn again to "Jewish fables"? Homilies on Exodus 5.1.[15]

Origen: But the apostles, who were about to say, "If you are circumcised, Christ will profit you nothing,"[16] and who were also about to say, "Let no one judge you in food, or in drink, or in participation of a feast day, or in new moons, or sabbaths, which are shadows of what will be,"[17] they are prohibited from having two tunics so that they might inwardly and completely repudiate observances of this kind according to the letter of the law and not concern the disciples "with Jewish myths" and "place a yoke on them which neither they nor their fathers would have been able to bear."[18] But one is sufficient for them, and this one "inward." For they do not want this tunic of the law that is external but that which comes from above. For Jesus permits them to have one, and that one is "interior." Homilies on Leviticus 3.5.[19]

Confusing Past and Present, False and True. Chrysostom: The Jewish tenets were fables in two ways, because they were imitations and because the thing was past its season, for such things become fables at last. For when a thing ought not to be done, and being done, is injurious, it is a fable even as it is useless. Homilies on Titus 3.[20]

Theodoret of Cyr: Paul uses the term "Jewish fables" not to describe the law but the interpretation of the law put forward by the Jews. The Lord accuses them of this very thing when he says, "Why do you transgress the law for the sake of your own traditions?"[21] Interpretation of the Letter to Titus.[22]

1:15 To the Pure, to the Corrupt

Disposition Is the Key. Chrysostom: Things then are not clean or unclean from their own nature but from the disposition of him who partakes of them. Homilies on Titus 3.[23]

Severian of Gabala: God has made all things pure. If anything is unclean, the use to which it is put makes it so. Pauline Commentary from the Greek Church.[24]

Ambrosiaster: Everything created by God is good; for those who do not know this, they become impure. Commentary on the Letter to Titus.[25]

Augustine: Therefore, if a man offers sacrifice to God, and a good man receive it at his hands, the sacrifice is to each man of such character as he himself has shown himself to be, since we find it also written that "unto the pure all things are pure." The Letters of Petilian the Donatist 2.52.120.[26]

Augustine: With all this, no one is pressed to endure hardships for which he is unfit. Nothing is imposed on anyone against his will, nor is he condemned by the rest because he confesses himself too feeble to imitate them. They bear in mind how strongly Scripture enjoins charity on all. . . . Accordingly, all their endeavors are con-

---

[14]1 Cor 10:1-4. [15]FC 71:276. [16]Gal 5:2. [17]Col 2:16. [18]Acts 15:10. [19]FC 83:122. [20]NPNF 1 13:529. [21]Mt 15:13. [22]PG 82:861C/862C. [23]NPNF 1 13:529. [24]NTA 15:344-45. [25]CSEL 81 3:327. [26]NPNF 1 4:561.

cerned not about the rejection of kinds of food as polluted but about the subjugation of inordinate desire and the maintenance of brotherly love. The Morals of the Catholic Church 1.33.71.[27]

Jerome: This is entirely directed against the Jewish distinction of clean and unclean, which was maintained on a mistaken view of abolished laws. Commentary on Titus.[28]

Gregory the Great: For, as in the Old Testament outward acts were attended to, so in the New Testament it is not so much what is done outwardly as what is thought inwardly that is regarded with close attention, that it may be punished with searching judgment. Letters 64.[29]

Food Laws and the Future. Augustine: The Jews, you see, had accepted that there were certain animals which they could not eat, and others from which they must abstain. The apostle Paul makes it clear that they received this law as a symbolic sign of future realities. Sermons 149.3.[30]

A Proper Asceticism. Augustine: But now, when you abstain for the sake of chastising the body from various kinds of food that are in themselves quite permissible, remember that "to the pure all things are pure"; don't regard anything as impure except what unbelief has defiled; "for to the impure and unbelievers," the apostle says, nothing is pure.[31] But naturally, when the faithful are reducing their bodies to slavery, whatever is deducted from bodily pleasure is credited to spiritual health. Sermons 208.1.[32]

Humility. Poemen: "If a man has attained to that which the apostle speaks of 'to the pure, everything is pure,' he sees himself less than all creatures." The brother said, "How can I deem myself less than a murderer?" The old man said, "When a man has really comprehended this say-

ing, if he sees a man committing a murder he says, 'He has only committed this one sin, but I commit sin every day.'" Sayings of the Fathers 97.[33]

Nothing Natural Unclean. Athanasius: All things made by God are beautiful and pure, for the Word of God has made nothing useless or impure. . . . But since the devil's darts are varied and subtle, he contrives to trouble those who are of simpler mind, and tries to hinder the ordinary exercises of the brethren, scattering secretly among them thoughts of uncleanness and defilement. Come, let us briefly dispel the error of the evil one by the grace of the Savior and confirm the mind of the simple. . . . For tell me, beloved and most pious friend, what sin or uncleanness there is in any natural secretion— as though a man were minded to make a culpable matter of the cleanings of the nose or the sputa from the mouth? And we may add also the secretions of the belly, such as are of a physical necessity of animal life. Moreover if we believe man to be, as the divine Scriptures say, a work of God's hands, how could any defiled work proceed from a pure Power? . . . But when any bodily excretion takes place independently of will, then we experience this, like other things, by a necessity of nature. Letters to Amun 48.[34]

The True Humanity of Jesus. Augustine: Those likewise are to be detested who deny that our Lord Jesus Christ had Mary as his mother on earth. That dispensation did honor to both sexes male and female and showed that both had a part in God's care; not only that which he assumed but that also through which he assumed it, being a man born of a woman. . . . Nor should our faith be lessened by any reference to "a woman's internal organs," as if it might appear

[27]NPNF 1 4:61. [28]PL 26:611B. [29]NPNF 2 13:79. [30]WSA 3/5:19. [31]See also Rom 14:20. [32]WSA 3/6:112. [33]SDF 180. [34]NPNF 2 4:556.

that we must reject any such generation of our Lord because sordid people think that sordid. "The foolishness of God is wiser than men";[35] and "to the pure all things are pure." FAITH AND THE CREED 4.9-10.[36]

1:16 They Deny Him by Their Deeds

THE EVIL WILL. CHRYSOSTOM: But he that has a weak soul makes everything unclean, and if there be set abroad a scrupulous inquiry into what is clean or unclean, he will touch nothing. . . . Yet Paul says not so; he turns the whole matter upon themselves. For nothing is unclean, he says, but themselves, their mind and their conscience; and nothing is more unclean than these; but an evil will is unclean. HOMILIES ON TITUS 3.[37]

JEROME: Some think that this verse applies only to those who deny the faith during a persecution, but the apostle contends that all perverse behavior denies God. COMMENTARY ON TITUS.[38]

WHAT IS DENIED BY DEEDS CAN BE SAID BY DEEDS. AUGUSTINE: All the heresies . . . they all say, "Jesus is Lord." And he's not, of course, going to eliminate from the kingdom of heaven those whom he finds to be in the Holy Spirit; and yet he did say, "Not everyone who says to me, Lord, Lord, will enter into the kingdom of heaven."[39] But: "Nobody can say: Jesus is Lord, except in the Holy Spirit";[40] nobody at all, evidently; but in the sense in which it was meant, that is in deeds. . . . The same apostle, you see, also says of some people, "They claim to know the Lord but deny it by their deeds." As it can be denied by deeds, so it can be said by deeds. SERMONS 269.4.[41]

QUALITY IS REVEALED. LEO THE GREAT: Our peace also has its dangers, dearly beloved. In vain do people feel secure as a result of freedom for their faith if they do not resist the desires of vice. By the quality of works is the human heart made known, and outward actions disclose the beauty of souls. There are some, as the apostle says, who "profess to know God but deny him through their deeds." Truly the guilt of denial is incurred when the ears have heard what is good but the conscience does not hold on to it. The frailty of the human condition easily slides into sin. SERMONS 37.4.[42]

---

[35]1 Cor 1:25. [36]LCC 6:358-59. See also Augustine *The City of God* 12.5.5 (FC 45:346-47) and *Sermons* 12.2 (*WSA* 3/1:303-4). [37]NPNF 1 13:530. [38]PL 26:611D. [39]Mt 7:21. [40]1 Cor 12:3. [41]*WSA* 3/7:286. See also Augustine *Tractates on John* 3.8 (FC 92:166-67); 74.4 (FC 90:89). [42]FC 93:158.

2:1-10 INSTRUCTIONS FOR MEN, WOMEN AND SLAVES

¹*But as for you, teach what befits sound doctrine.* ²*Bid the older men be temperate, serious, sensible, sound in faith, in love, and in steadfastness.* ³*Bid the older women likewise to be reverent in behavior, not to be slanderers or slaves to drink; they are to teach what is good,* ⁴*and so train the young women to love their husbands and children,* ⁵*to be sensible, chaste, domestic, kind, and submissive to their husbands, that the word of God may not be discredited.* ⁶*Likewise urge the younger men to control themselves.* ⁷*Show yourself in all respects a model of good deeds, and in your teaching show in-*

tegrity, gravity, [8]and sound speech that cannot be censured, so that an opponent may be put to shame, having nothing evil to say of us. [9]Bid slaves to be submissive to their masters and to give satisfaction in every respect; they are not to be refractory, [10]nor to pilfer, but to show entire and true fidelity, so that in everything they may adorn the doctrine of God our Savior.

OVERVIEW: Paul has made it clear that purity is a matter of the heart, that the pure person will venture in all things, the impure in none. Physical acts become unclean only as they contaminate the soul with impure desires. All of this is seen in the doctrine and virtue that Paul urges Titus to teach. Such virtue will win the respect of unbelievers (CHRYSOSTOM). It is the moral rigor and seriousness of believers, their good order and uprightness, that mark doctrine as true (THEODORE). Paul lays out more of the practical aspects of Christian living in order to show how sound doctrine translates into sound living and the practical appropriation of salvation (HILARY OF POITIERS). When the soul is unclean, it thinks all things unclean (CHRYSOSTOM).

Be attentive both to good conscience and reputation (AUGUSTINE). Paul wanted church leaders to possess learning, the consciousness of the true faith and a knowledge of argument that would withstand godless objections (HILARY). Christ gave the same price for both slave and master (AUGUSTINE). If observers see a slave who has been taught the philosophy of Christ displaying more self-command than their own philosophers, they will in every way admire the power of the gospel (CHRYSOSTOM). Women are to be decently adorned, reverent and dignified (ORIGEN, JEROME, THEODORE).

2:1 Sound Doctrine

CLEAN AND UNCLEAN. CHRYSOSTOM: When the soul is unclean, it thinks all things unclean. Therefore scrupulous observances are no mark of purity, but it is the part of purity to be bold in all things.... What then is unclean? Sin, malice, covetousness, wickedness. HOMILIES ON TITUS 3.[1]

2:3a Bid Older Women to Be Reverent

OFFICEHOLDERS? THEODORE OF MOPSUESTIA: These are elders in age only, though some have taken the position that the women held an office analogous to that of male presbyters. COMMENTARY ON TITUS.[2]

2:3b Not Slaves to Drink

THE MOTHER OF VICE. ORIGEN: Therefore, he wants those for whom "the Lord is their portion" to be sober, to fast, to be vigilant at all times, but especially when they are present at the altar to pray to the Lord and to offer sacrifices in his presence. These commands preserve their force. They ought to be maintained in strict observance. The apostle confirms these as laws of the new covenant. In the same way, setting up the rules of life for the priests or the chief priests to this, he tells them that they ought not to be enslaved "to much wine" but to be "sober."[3] Sobriety is the mother of virtues, drunkenness the mother of vices. HOMILIES ON LEVITICUS 7.4.[4]

2:3 Reverent in Behavior

HOLY DECORUM. JEROME: The women are, like the older men, to be honest, sober, chaste, strong in faith and charity and patience. They are also to bear themselves in a way proper for their sex, to maintain a holy manner in bodily movements, facial expressions, words, silence, and whatever tends to the dignity of a holy

[1]NPNF 1 13:530. [2]TEM 2:246 (partly in Greek). [3]Tit 1:7-8; 2:2-3 [4]FC 83:130.

decorum. COMMENTARY ON TITUS.[5]

PROPERLY DRESSED. THEODORE OF MOPSUES-TIA: The women are to be decently adorned, reverent and dignified. COMMENTARY ON TITUS.[6]

2:4 Young Women to Love Their Husbands

IN HARMONY. CHRYSOSTOM: This is the chief point of all that is good in a household: "that a man and his wife agree together."[7] For where this exists, there will be nothing that is unpleasant. For where the head is in harmony with the body and there is no disagreement between them, how shall not all the other members be at peace? HOMILIES ON TITUS 4.[8]

2:7 A Model of Good Deeds

SOUND SPEECH. HILARY OF POITIERS: Finally, Paul instructed Titus, whom he addresses directly about attaining perfection in the practice of the true religion, in this admonition: "Show yourself in all respects a model of good deeds, and in your teaching show integrity, gravity and sound speech that cannot be censured, so that an opponent may be put to shame, having nothing evil to say of us." This teacher of the Gentiles and the chosen leader of the church, conscious of Christ who spoke and dwelt within him, knew that the plague of a deadly eloquence would rise up against him. . . . For this reason, he wished the bishop to possess learning, the consciousness of the faith and the knowledge of argument that would withstand godless lying and insane objections. ON THE TRINITY 8.1.[9]

CONSCIENCE AND REPUTATION. AUGUSTINE: As far as we are concerned, our consciences are all that matters. As far as you are concerned, our reputation among you ought not to be tarnished but influential for good. Mark what I've said, and make the distinction. There are two things, conscience and reputation; conscience for your-self, reputation for your neighbor. Those who, being clear in their consciences, neglect their reputations, are being cruel; especially if they find themselves in this position. The apostle writes about this to his disciple: "Showing yourself to all around you as an example of good works." SERMONS 355.1.[10]

EQUAL TREATMENT. ANONYMOUS: Therefore, O man, do not cease to recommend and to teach the things that are holy down to the last soul entrusted to you. And "present yourself as an example of good works." Be especially careful not to love one and hate another. Show an equal attitude to all, lest the one whom you love God might hate, and the one whom you hate God might love. THE TESTAMENT OF HORIESIOS 9.[11]

2:9-10 Bid Slaves to Show Fidelity

GOOD EVANGELISM. CHRYSOSTOM: For if you serve your master with good will, yet the occasion of this service proceeds from your fear of God, and he who with so great fear renders him service, shall receive the greater reward. For if he restrains not his hand or his unruly tongue, how shall the Gentile admire the doctrine that is among us? But if they see their slave, who has been taught the philosophy of Christ, displaying more self-command than their own philosophers and serving with all meekness and good will, he will in every way admire the power of the gospel. For the Greeks judge not of doctrines by the doctrine itself but make the life and the conduct the test of the doctrines. HOMILIES ON TITUS 4.[12]

---

[5]PL 26:615B. [6]TEM 2:24 (Greek). The Greek text of Titus translated in RSV as "reverent in behavior" means literally "priestly in adornment." Metaphorically this may mean "behaving in a holy way," but there may also be an allusion to women vested with an ecclesial stole, that is, deaconesses. This is the way in which Theodore takes it, though the dominant Western tradition disagreed. Cf. the note in Swete, 246-47, ad loc. [7]Sir 25:1. [8]NPNF 1 13:532. [9]FC 25:274. [10]WSA 3/10:165. [11]PK 3:176.

CHRIST GAVE THE SAME PRICE FOR SLAVE AND MASTER. AUGUSTINE: A bishopric necessarily pertains to him who is the head of the household. It is a superintendence of the faith of the members of the household, lest any fall into heresy. It extends to the wife, to a son or a daughter; it extends also to a slave, for he has also been redeemed at so great a price. The apostolic teaching assumes the placement of the master above the slave and the slave beneath the master,[13] but Christ has given the same price for each of them. Do not neglect even the lowliest among your household. SERMONS 94.[14]

[12]NPNF 1 13:533*. [13]Cf. Eph 6:5. [14]FC 11:294.

2:11-15 THE WORK OF GRACE

[11]*For the grace of God has appeared for the salvation of all men,* [12]*training us to renounce irreligion and worldly passions, and to live sober, upright, and godly lives in this world,* [13]*awaiting our blessed hope, the appearing of the glory of our great God and Savior*[c] *Jesus Christ,* [14]*who gave himself for us to redeem us from all iniquity and to purify for himself a people of his own who are zealous for good deeds.*

[15]*Declare these things; exhort and reprove with all authority. Let no one disregard you.*

c Or of the great God and our Savior

OVERVIEW: The work of grace is first to offer the forgiveness of sins and then to instill virtue by delivering us from the power of worldly things, and so that we may await with the joy the second coming of Christ (CHRYSOSTOM). Christ has demonstrated for us the right way, that now we may live life piously and moderately (THEODORET). Paul intends to show that all believers share the same faith, that all are one in Christ Jesus (JEROME). He gave himself to us in the flesh (ATHANASIUS) as both Savior and God (THEODORET). He for our sake became as we are, and yet he is above us insofar as he is understood as God (CYRIL OF ALEXANDRIA). We acknowledge with thanksgiving Jesus' first coming and look for a second coming, with glory at the last day (CYRIL OF JERUSALEM, CHRYSOSTOM). Animal sacrifices have disappeared (GREGORY OF NYSSA). The prophetic expectations have been fulfilled (CHRYSOSTOM). We celebrate the Christmas feast with joy (LEO). Not everyone is given the grace to work miracles, but to live piously and preserve charity toward all with God's help is possible for everyone (AUGUSTINE, FULGENTIUS). We fast with hope (AUGUSTINE). What is truly blessed is Goodness itself toward which all things look, which all things desire (BASIL). This blessedness is anticipated in chaste living in this life (GREGORY OF NYSSA). The measure of God's love to each one of us is as great as to the whole world (CHRYSOSTOM). Despite scandals, the church shines forth in its stronger members (AUGUSTINE). Some sins are to be admonished by simple command, not by cajoling (CHRYSOSTOM).

2:11a *The Grace of God Has Appeared*

This Wonderful and Noble Economy.
Cyril of Alexandria: We say, therefore, that he came forth from a woman, and in the likeness of sinful flesh, he who for our sake became as we are and yet is above us insofar as he is understood as God. . . . The same was at once God and man. I cannot understand how these people pillage this wonderful and noble economy of the Only-Begotten. They connect a man to him in terms of a relationship adorned with external honors and radiant in a glory which is not his, for then he is not truly God. They treat him as someone who has fellowship and participation with God, and is thus a falsely-named son, a saved savior, a redeemed redeemer; all of which contradicts what the blessed Paul wrote. On the Unity of Christ.[1]

Two Comings. Cyril of Jerusalem: For Paul has also shown us that there are these two comings, in his epistle to Titus where he says, "The grace of God our Savior has appeared unto all men, teaching us that, denying ungodliness and worldly lusts, we should live soberly, righteously and godly in this present world; looking for that blessed hope and the glorious appearing of the great God and our Savior Jesus Christ." You note how he acknowledges with thanksgiving the first coming and that we look for a second. . . . So our Lord Jesus Christ comes from heaven and comes with glory at the last day to bring this world to its close. Catechetical Lectures 15.2-3.[2]

Grace and Justice. Chrysostom: He speaks here of two appearings: the first of grace, the second of retribution and justice. Homilies on Titus 5.[3]

Sacrifices Disappeared Like Smoke.
Gregory of Nyssa: Who does not know that the deceit of demons filled every corner of the world and held sway over human life by the madness of idolatry? Who does not realize that every people on earth was accustomed to worship demons under the form of idols, by sacrificing living victims and making foul offerings on their altars? But as the apostle says, from the moment that God's saving grace appeared among men and dwelt in human nature, all this vanished into nothing, like smoke. Address on Religious Instruction 18.[4]

The Christmas Feast. Leo the Great: It is, therefore, with an unmistakable tenderness that so great a wealth of divine goodness has been poured out on us, dearly beloved. Not only has the usefulness of foregoing examples served for calling us to eternity, but the Truth himself has even "appeared" in a visible body. We ought, then, to celebrate this day of the Lord's birth with no listless and worldly joy. Sermons 23.5.[5]

2:11b For the Salvation of All People

Zephaniah's Promise Fulfilled. Chrysostom: You hear that the prophets foretold and predicted that men will no longer be bound to come from all over the earth to offer sacrifice in one city or in one place but that each one will sit in his own home and pay service and honor to God. What time other than the present could you mention as fulfilling these prophecies? At any rate listen to how the Gospels and the apostle Paul agree with Zephaniah. The prophet said: "The Lord shall appear";[6] Paul said: "The grace of God has appeared for the salvation of all people." Zephaniah said: "To all nations"; Paul said: "To all people." Zephaniah said: "He will make their gods waste away"; Paul said: "training us to renounce irreligion and worldly passions and to live sober, upright and godly lives in this world." Discourses Against Judaizing Christians 5.12.9.[7]

---

[1]OUC 89-90. [2]LCC 4:148-49*. [3]NPNF 1 13:536. [4]LCC 3:295. [5]FC 93:91. [6]Zeph 2:11. [7]FC 68:143.

2:12 To Renounce Irreligion and Worldly Passions

TRUE RENUNCIATION. CHRYSOSTOM: Worldly passions are directed toward things that perish with the present life. Let us then have nothing to do with these. HOMILIES ON TITUS 5.[8]

FASTING AND HOPE. AUGUSTINE: But there is a great and general fasting, which is perfect fasting, to abstain from the iniquities and illicit pleasures of the world: "that, denying ungodliness and worldly desires, we may live soberly and justly and godly in this world." What reward does the apostle add to this fasting? He continues and says, "Looking for that blessed hope and the manifestation of the glory of the blessed God and Savior, Jesus Christ." Therefore, in this world we celebrate, so to speak, a Lent of abstinence when we live well, when we abstain from iniquities and illicit pleasures. But because this abstinence will not be without a wage, we look for "that blessed hope." In that hope, when reality shall have come to pass from hope, we shall receive a *denarius* as a wage.[9] TRACTATES ON JOHN 17.4.[10]

BUT ONLY BY GRACE. AUGUSTINE: Paul must receive, embrace and observe, without any reserve, those commandments of the law which help to form the character of the faithful, such as that "denying ungodliness and worldly desires, we should live soberly and justly and godly in this world" and "Thou shalt not covet," chosen by the apostle as the part of the law worthy of the greatest commendation; and also the commandments about loving God and our neighbor, as set forth in the law without any figure or mystery. . . . But whatever progress he makes in them he must not attribute it to himself but to "the grace of God by Jesus Christ our Lord." LETTERS 196.2.8.[11]

FULGENTIUS OF RUSPE: The apostle Paul exclaims in a similar way: "Be imitators of God

as his dear children."[12] What will we reply to these words, brethren, or what excuse will we be able to have? If someone tells you that you should imitate the powers which our Lord exercised, there is a reasonable excuse for you, because not everyone is given the grace to exercise those powers and to work miracles. But to live piously and chastely, to preserve charity with all men,[13] with God's help is possible for everyone. SERMONS 223.2.[14]

2:13a Our Blessed Hope

LIFE WITH GOD THE GOAL. BASIL THE GREAT: Therefore, the common Director of our lives, the great Teacher, the Spirit of truth, wisely and cleverly set forth the rewards, in order that, rising above the present labors, we might press on in spirit to the enjoyment of eternal blessings. "Blessed is the man who has not walked in the counsel of the ungodly."[15] What is most truly good, therefore, is principally and primarily the most blessed. And that is God. So Paul also, when about to make mention of Christ, said: "according to the manifestation of our blessed God and Savior Jesus Christ." For, truly blessed is Goodness itself toward which all things look, which all things desire, an unchangeable nature, lordly dignity, calm existence; a happy way of life, in which there is no alteration, which no change touches; a flowing fount, abundant grace, inexhaustible treasure. HOMILIES ON THE PSALMS 10.3.[16]

GRACED WAITING. GREGORY OF NYSSA: In fact, the life of virginity seems to be an actual refraction of the blessedness in the world to come, showing as it does in itself so many signs of the presence of those expected blessings

---

[8]NPNF 1 13:536. [9]Cf. Mt 20:9-10. [10]FC 79:112. [11]FC 30:338. Augustine makes a similar use of Titus 2:12 in *Predestination of the Saints* 3.7 (FC 86:223-24). [12]Eph 5:1. [13]See also Rom 12:18. [14]FC 66:145. [15]Ps 1:1. [16]FC 46:155.

which are reserved for us there. That the truth of this statement may be grasped we will verify in this way: It is so, first, because a man who has thus died once for all to sin lives for the future to God. This man brings forth no more fruit unto death. Having so far as in him lies made an end of this life according to the flesh, he awaits the expected blessing of the manifestation of the great God. He refrains from putting any distance between himself and this coming of God by an intervening posterity. The second reason is that he enjoys even in this present life a certain exquisite glory of all the blessed results of our resurrection. For the Lord has announced that the life after our resurrection shall be as that of the angels. On Virginity 13.[17]

2:13b Our Great God and Savior

Father and Son the Same God. Chrysostom: And Paul said: "from whom is the Christ according to the flesh, who is over all things, God blessed forever, Amen."[18] And again: "No fornicator or covetous one has an inheritance in the kingdom of Christ and God."[19] And still again: "through the appearance of our great God and Savior Jesus Christ." And John calls him by the same name of God when he says: "In the beginning was the Word, and the Word was with God; and the Word was God."[20] On the Incomprehensible Nature of God 5.2.[21]

Both Savior and God. Theodoret of Cyr: Here he says that he who according to the flesh derived his descent from the Jews is eternal God and is praised by the right minded as Lord of all created things. The same teaching is given us in the apostle's words to the excellent Titus: "Looking for that blessed hope and the glorious appearing of the great God and Savior Jesus Christ." Here he calls the same one both Savior and great God and Jesus Christ. Letters 146.[22]

2:14a Who Gave Himself for Us

He Offered His Real Flesh. Athanasius: How could he have given himself if he had not worn flesh? He offered his flesh and gave himself for us, in order that undergoing death in it, "He might bring to nothing the one who held the power of death, that is, the devil."[23] For this reason we continually give thanks in the name of Jesus Christ. We do not bring to nothing the grace which came to us through him. For the coming of the Savior in the flesh has been the ransom and salvation of all creation. Letter to Adelphus 60.6.[24]

2:14b A People of His Own

For One and All At the Same Time. Chrysostom: "That he might purify unto himself a people of his own." Considering the desperate condition of human nature and the ineffably tender solicitude of Christ, in what he delivered us from and what he freely gave us, and kindled by the yearning of affection towards him, this is a remarkably tender expression. Thus the prophets often appropriate to themselves him who is God of all, as in the words, "O God, you are my God, early will I seek you."[25] Moreover, this language teaches that each individual justly owes a great debt of gratitude to Christ, as if he had come for that person's sake alone. For he would not have grudged this his condescension even if it were only for one person. The measure of his love to each is as great as to the whole world. Commentary on Galatians, Galatians 2:20.[26]

Church Within the Church. Augustine: The faithful who are holy and good may be few in comparison with the larger number of the wicked, but . . . "many shall come from the east

[17]NPNF 2 5:360*. [18]Rom 9:5. [19]Eph 5:5. [20]Jn 1:1. [21]FC 72:145. Chrysostom uses Titus 2:13 in a similar way in *Homilies on John* 4 (FC 33:50-51). [22]NPNF 2 3:319. [23]Heb 2:14. [24]NPNF 2 4:577. [25]Ps 63:1. [26]NPNF 1 13:23*.

and the west and shall sit down with Abraham and Isaac and Jacob in the kingdom of heaven."[27] God shows to himself "a numerous people, zealous for good works." . . . Even when sometimes darkened and, as it were, clouded over by a great number of scandals . . . still this people shines forth in her strongest members. LETTERS 93.9.30.[28]

A PECULIAR PEOPLE. JEROME: He gave himself for us that he might make a *periousion* people (for thus is the term in Greek for "peculiar") and that he might make them the emulator of good works. Though I have often pondered this term *periousion* and have sought after clues to its meaning in secular writers, I have come up with nothing. Thus, I have come to see that the apostle's reference is primarily to the Old Testament. . . . It carries the meaning of "emulator of good works" through the special status conferred by the blood of Christ. COMMENTARY ON TITUS.[29]

2:15 Exhort and Reprove

SOME SINS ADMONISHED BY COMMAND. CHRYSOSTOM: Where the manners of this people were more stubborn, he orders them to be admonished more roughly, and with all authority. For there are some sins which ought to be prevented by command. We may with persuasion advise men to despise riches, to be meek and the like. But the adulterer, the fornicator, the defrauder ought to be brought to a better course by command. HOMILIES ON TITUS 5.[30]

---

[27]Mt 8:11. [28]FC 18:86. [29]PG 26:622CD-623AB. In a famous discussion, Jerome carries this analysis further by linking up *periousios* with the term *epiousios*, the term in the Lord's Prayer for "daily" in "daily bread." The conclusion that Jerome comes to, based partly on the common etymology of the two terms, is that *epiousios* refers to heavenly bread, which is Christ, who is the means by which Christians become a peculiar, *periousios* people. [30]NPNF 1 13:537.

3:1-8 ADMONITIONS TO OBEDIENCE

[1]*Remind them to be submissive to rulers and authorities, to be obedient, to be ready for any honest work, [2]to speak evil of no one, to avoid quarreling, to be gentle, and to show perfect courtesy toward all men. [3]For we ourselves were once foolish, disobedient, led astray, slaves to various passions and pleasures, passing our days in malice and envy, hated by men and hating one another; [4]but when the goodness and loving kindness of God our Savior appeared, [5]he saved us, not because of deeds done by us in righteousness, but in virtue of his own mercy, by the washing of regeneration and renewal in the Holy Spirit, [6]which he poured out upon us richly through Jesus Christ our Savior, [7]so that we might be justified by his grace and become heirs in hope of eternal life. [8]The saying is sure.*

OVERVIEW: Paul calls us to be humble and self-effacing, always thereby manifesting the new life given in baptism (CHRYSOSTOM). We are enjoined to be properly respectful of earthly authority and in all our relationships to show forth that already accomplished participation in immortality that is ours through Christ's death and resurrection and that is given in baptism (THEODORE).

Be subject to governing authorities (APOSTOLIC CONSTITUTIONS) yet without idolatry (TERTULLIAN). At some point it may be necessary to say that it is better to obey God than humans (JEROME). We honor earthly governance in relation to the King of kings (JOHN OF DAMASCUS). Both Jews and Gentiles have been deceitful and foolish (ORIGEN). We should be gently disposed toward all and not search too closely at evil doing (CHRYSOSTOM). Even if his saving work seems to us delayed, he in his own time by a wise providence (LEO) redeems us as Bridegroom and heals us as Physician (BASIL). The infinite God, while remaining in himself changeless, assumed flesh and fought with death, freeing us from suffering by his own suffering (BASIL). It is not by our works but by his inscrutable will that God saves us and draws us toward the love of all things (AUGUSTINE). God has not repaired the old nature in us but made us anew (CHRYSOSTOM). The symbols of baptism and Eucharist come from the side of Christ, from his blood mixed with water (CHRYSOSTOM). Anyone who is baptized with the Holy Spirit is the one referred to as born again through water and the Holy Spirit (AMBROSE). We are saved by hope in the regenerative work of the Spirit in baptism (AUGUSTINE).

3:1 Submissive to Rulers and Authorities

BE GOOD CITIZENS. ANONYMOUS: Be subject to all governmental power and dominion in things which are pleasing to God, as to the ministers of God and the punishers of the ungodly.[1] Render all the fear that is due to them, all offerings, all customs, all honor, gifts and taxes.[2] For this is God's command, that you owe nothing to anyone but the pledge of love, which God has commanded by Christ.[3] CONSTITUTIONS OF THE HOLY APOSTLES 4.13.[4]

SUBJECT TO MAGISTRATES YET WITHOUT IDOLATRY. TERTULLIAN: Therefore, with regard to the honors due to kings or emperors, we have a sufficient rule, that it is fitting to be in all obedience, according to the apostle's instruction, "subject to magistrates, and princes and powers." But this must be within the limits of discipline, so long as we keep ourselves separate from idolatry. ON IDOLATRY 15.[5]

OBEY GOD. JEROME: If what the emperor or leader orders is good, follow the will of him who orders. But if it is evil and is contrary to God, answer to it from the words of the Acts of the Apostles, "it is more important to obey God than men."[6] COMMENTARY ON TITUS.[7]

THE ANALOGY BETWEEN CIVIL AND DIVINE GOVERNANCE. JOHN OF DAMASCUS: If men honor emperors, who are often corrupt and impious sinners, as well as those appointed by them to rule over provinces, who often are greedy and violent, in obedience to the words of the divine apostle, "Be submissive to rulers and authorities" and "Pay all of them their dues, honor to whom honor is due; respect to whom respect is due"[8] and "Render therefore to Caesar the things that are Caesar's and to God the things that are God's"[9]—if we do all this, how much more ought we to worship the King of kings? ON DIVINE IMAGES 3.41.[10]

3:3 For We Were Once Foolish

THE BLINDNESS OF JEWS AS WELL AS GENTILES. ORIGEN: Paul, the apostle from Israel, came to us as one "blameless according to the justice in the law."[11] Yet he says "we ourselves," those from Israel, "were then deceitful, foolish." So not only those from the pagan nations were "deceit-

---

[1]Cf. 1 Pet 2:13. [2]Cf. Rom 13:1, 4, 7. [3]Cf. Rom 13:8. [4]ANF 7:436*. [5]ANF 3:71*. [6]Acts 5:29. [7]PL 26:626CD. [8]Rom 13:7. [9]Mt 22:21. [10]JDDI 88-89. [11]Phil 3:6.

ful," nor only sinners, but we "also," who have been taught by the law, were such before the coming of Christ. Homilies on Jeremiah 5.2.[12]

Humbly Consider Your Own Former Life. Chrysostom: Therefore we ought to be gently disposed to all. For he who was formerly in such a state and has been delivered from it ought not to reproach others but to pray, to be thankful to him who has granted both to him and them deliverance from such evils. Let no one boast. All have sinned. If then, doing well yourself, you are inclined to revile others, consider your own former life and the uncertainty of the future, and restrain your anger. Homilies on Titus 5.[13]

Not Searching Too Closely at Evil Doing. Chrysostom: One who breaks down the wall and steals something from within is not the only burglar, but also he who corrupts justice and wrongfully takes something from his neighbor. Let us not, then, overlook our own faults and sit in judgment on those of others. When it is the time for mercy, let us not search too closely into evil doing, but, keeping in mind what we ourselves have been previously like, let us now become gentle and merciful. Homilies on John 60.5.[14]

The Old Man. Augustine: Paul could be fulfilling the open works of the law, either by fear of man or God, and yet have evil affections within himself. . . . Knowing himself to be such in his internal affections, before the grace of God which is in Jesus Christ our Lord, the apostle elsewhere confesses this very plainly. . . . "For we ourselves also were sometimes foolish and unbelieving, erring, serving various lusts and pleasures, living in malice and envy, hateful, and holding one another in hatred." Such was Saul even when he says that he was touching the righteousness which is in the law, without reproach. Against Two Letters of the Pelagians 1.9.15.[15]

3:4 The Goodness of God Our Savior

Bridegroom and Physician. Basil the Great: Every kind of help comes to our souls through Christ. Various appropriate titles have been devised for each particular kind of care. When he presents a blameless soul to himself, a soul which like a pure virgin has neither spot nor wrinkle, he is called Bridegroom. But when he receives someone paralyzed by the devil's evil strokes and heals the heavy burden of his sins, he is called Physician. Because he cares for us, will this make us think less of him? Or will we not be struck with amazement at our Savior's mighty power and love for mankind,[16] who patiently endured to suffer our infirmities with us and condescended to our weakness? No heaven, or earth, or the great oceans, or all creatures living in the waters and on dry land, or plants, stars, air, or seasons or the vast expanse of the universe can illustrate the surpassing greatness of God's might so well as he has himself. The infinite God, remaining changeless, assumed flesh and fought with death, freeing us from suffering by his own suffering! On the Holy Spirit 8.18.[17]

Wise Providence. Leo the Great: By the delay of his saving work, he has made us better disposed to accept his calling. In this is shown the "goodness and kindness of God." By this means, what had been foretold through so many ages by numerous signs, numerous words and numerous mysteries would no longer be open to doubt in these days of the gospel. That way, the birth of the Savior—which was to exceed all wonders and the whole measure of human intelligence— would engender in us a faith all the more steadfast, the more often and the earlier it had been proclaimed beforehand. Sermons 23.4.[18]

---

[12]FC 97:41. [13]NPNF 1 13:537. [14]FC 41:148*. [15]NPNF 1 5:382. [16]On this theme of *philanthropia* ("love of humankind") compare Clement of Alexandria *Stromateis* 2.9.41 (FC 85:187). [17]OHS 36. [18]FC 93:90.

3:5a *In Virtue of His Own Mercy*

**THE LENGTH, BREADTH, DEPTH AND HEIGHT
OF LOVE.** AUGUSTINE: For this reason, charity,
which has more regard for the common good
than for its own, is said "not to seek the things
that are its own.". . . Hence, this charity is practiced now in the good works of love, by which it
reaches out to give aid in whatever direction it
can, and this is its breadth. It bears adversity
with longsuffering, and perseveres in what it
holds as true, and this is its length. But it does
all this in order to attain eternal life which is
promised to it on high, and this is its height.
This charity, indeed, is hidden in the place
where we are founded and, so to speak, rooted in
depth.[19] Hence we do not search into the reasons for God's will, by whose grace we are saved.
This has come "not by the works of justice which
we have done but according to his mercy." "For
of his own will he has begotten us by the word
of truth,"[20] and this will of his is hidden. LET-
TERS 140.25.62.[21]

3:5b *The Washing of Regeneration*

REBUILT FROM THE FOUNDATION. CHRYSOS-
TOM: Strange, isn't it, how we were so drowned
in wickedness that we could not be purified? We
needed a new birth! For this is implied by
"regeneration." For as when a house is in a ruinous state no one places props under it nor makes
any addition to the old building, but pulls it
down to its foundations and rebuilds it anew. So
in our case, God has not repaired us but made us
anew. HOMILIES ON TITUS 5.[22]

AS WATER AND BLOOD CAME FROM HIS SIDE.
CHRYSOSTOM: "There came out from his side
water and blood."[23] Beloved, do not pass this
mystery by without a thought. For I have still
another mystical explanation to give. I said that
there was a symbol of baptism and the mysteries
in that blood and water. It is from both of these
that the church is sprung "through the bath of

regeneration and renewal by the Holy Spirit,"
through baptism and the mysteries. But the
symbols of baptism and the mysteries, water and
blood, come from the side of Christ. It is from
his side, therefore, that Christ formed his
church, just as he formed Eve from the side of
Adam. BAPTISMAL INSTRUCTIONS 3.17.[24]

WASHED CLEAN. AUGUSTINE: If the forgiveness
of sins were not to be had in the church, there
would be no hope of a future life and eternal
liberation. We thank God, who gave his church
such a gift. Here you are; you are going to come
to the holy font, you will be washed in saving
baptism, you will be renewed in "the bath of
rebirth." You will be without any sin at all as you
come up from that bath. All the things that were
plaguing you in the past will be blotted out.
SERMONS 213.8.[25]

SAVED IN HOPE. AUGUSTINE: It is true we have
not yet risen as Christ has, but we are said to
have risen with him on account of the hope
which we have in him. So again he says:
"According to his mercy he saved us, by the
washing of regeneration." Evidently what we
obtain in the washing of regeneration is not the
salvation itself but the hope of it. And yet,
because this hope is certain, we are said to be
saved, as if the salvation were already bestowed.
REPLY TO FAUSTUS THE MANICHAEAN 11.7.[26]

3:5c *Renewal in the Holy Spirit*

BAPTIZED THROUGH THE HOLY SPIRIT.
AMBROSE: Who is the one who is born of the
Spirit and is made Spirit? It is one who is
renewed in the Spirit of his mind.[27] It is one who
is regenerated by water and the Holy Spirit. We
receive the hope of eternal life through the laver

---

[19]Cf. Eph 3:18. [20]Jas 1:18. [21]FC 20:110-11. [22]NPNF 1 13:538. [23]Jn
19:34. [24]ACW 31:62. [25]WSA 3/6:145. [26]NPNF 1 4:181. [27]Eph
4:23.

of regeneration and renewing of the Holy Spirit. And elsewhere the apostle Peter says: "You shall be baptized with the Holy Spirit."[28] For who is he that is baptized with the Holy Spirit but he who is born again through water and the Holy Spirit? Therefore the Lord said of the Holy Spirit, "Truly, truly, I say to you, except a man be born again by water and the Spirit, he cannot enter into the kingdom of God."[29] And therefore he declared that we are born of him into the kingdom of God by being born again by water and the Spirit. OF THE HOLY SPIRIT 3.10.[30]

CONDEMNED UNLESS DELIVERED. AUGUSTINE: Little children alone who have performed no deeds of their own, either good or bad, will be condemned solely because of original sin, unless the grace of the Savior has freed them from it through "the laver of regeneration." All others [are condemned], who have used their free will to add their own sins to original sin, but also for the deliberate acts of their own will.

This is so unless they are delivered from the power of darkness and translated to the kingdom of Christ by the grace of God.[31] LETTERS 215.1.1.[32]

WHETHER WE ARE SAVED BY BAPTISM. AUGUSTINE: For if anyone should ask of me whether we have been saved by baptism, I shall not be able to deny it, since the apostle says, "He saved us by the washing of regeneration and renewing of the Holy Spirit." But if he should ask whether by the same washing he has already in every way immediately saved us, I shall answer: It is not so. Because the same apostle also says, "For we are saved by hope."[33] AGAINST TWO LETTERS OF THE PELAGIANS 3.3.5.[34]

---

[28]Acts 9:16. [29]Jn 3:5. [30]NPNF 2 10:144*. [31]Cf. Col 1:13. [32]FC 32:63. [33]Rom 8:24. [34]NPNF 1 5:404.

3:8-15 FINAL ADMONITIONS, ASSIGNMENTS AND GREETINGS

[8]I desire you to insist on these things, so that those who have believed in God may be careful to apply themselves to good deeds;[d] these are excellent and profitable to men. [9]But avoid stupid controversies, genealogies, dissensions, and quarrels over the law, for they are unprofitable and futile. [10]As for a man who is factious, after admonishing him once or twice, have nothing more to do with him, [11]knowing that such a person is perverted and sinful; he is self-condemned.

[12]When I send Artemas or Tychicus to you, do your best to come to me at Nicopolis, for I have decided to spend the winter there. [13]Do your best to speed Zenas the lawyer and Apollos on their way; see that they lack nothing. [14]And let our people learn to apply themselves to good deeds,[d] so as to help cases of urgent need, and not to be unfruitful.

[15]All who are with me send greetings to you. Greet those who love us in the faith.

Grace be with you all.

d Or enter honorable occupations

Overview: In his parting instructions, Paul emphasizes that our response to God's gracious initiative must be that of virtuous living, so that all contentiousness is avoided and humility is the order of the day. All preaching derives its credibility precisely from this virtue. Finally it is embodied actions that touch the human heart that enable conversion (Chrysostom). Paul coaches Titus on the importance of diligence in what is fitting, so that heresy will be refuted by the very lives of the faithful (Athanasius, Ambrose). Follow the pattern of Matthew 18 in the discipline of the lapsed: admonition, community accountability, and excommunication only as a last resort (Basil). The heresies, being self-chosen, are self-condemned (Tertullian, Cyprian, Maximus).

3:9 Avoid Quarrels and Disputes

The Faithful Shepherd. Ambrose: Blessed is that servant [Paul] who can say: "I have fed you with milk and not with meat; for until now you were not able to bear it."[1] . . . Yet he—being so great a man and chosen by Christ for the care of his flock in order to strengthen the weak and to heal the sick—rejects immediately after a single admonition a heretic from the fold entrusted to him. This he does for fear that the taint of one erring sheep might infect the whole flock with a spreading sore. He further bids that foolish questions and contentions be avoided. Of the Christian Faith 5, Prologue 3-4.[2]

Do Not Sow on a Rock. Chrysostom: "Contentions," he means, with heretics. He would not have us labor to no purpose, where nothing is to be gained, for they end in nothing. For when a man is perverted and predetermined not to change his mind, whatever may happen, why should you labor in vain, sowing upon a rock, when you should spend your honorable toil upon your own people, in discoursing with them upon almsgiving and every other virtue? Homilies on Titus 6.[3]

3:10 Have Nothing More to Do with Him

Choose Your Battles! Chrysostom: He shows that they do not so much err from ignorance as they owe their ignorance to their indolence. Those who are contentious for the sake of money you will never persuade. They are only to be persuaded, so long as you keep paying out, and even so you will never satisfy their desires. . . . From such then, as being incorrigible, it is right to turn away. Homilies on 1 Timothy 17.[4]

Avoid the Rocks of Unbelief. Ambrose: This monster's cavern [of heresies], your sacred Majesty, is thick laid (as seafaring men do say it is) with hidden lairs, and all the surrounding neighborhood, where the rocks of unbelief echo to the howling of her black dogs, we must pass by with ears stopped up. For it is written: "Hedge your ears about with thorns"[5] and again: "Beware of dogs. Beware of evil workers";[6] and yet again: "One who is a heretic, avoid after the first reproof knowing that such a one is fallen and is in sin, being condemned of his own judgment." So then, like prudent pilots, let us set the sails of our faith for the course wherein we may pass by most safely and again follow the coasts of the Scriptures. Of the Christian Faith 1.6.47.[7]

Reprove Vain Teachings. Athanasius: Perhaps even thus being put to shame by the bad odor of their names, they [the heretics] may be enabled to grasp the depth of impiety into which they have fallen. It would be within our rights not to answer them at all, according to the apostolic advice: "One who is heretical, after a first and a second admonition refuse, knowing that such a one is perverted and sins, being self-condemned." This is even more the case, in that the

---

[1]1 Cor 3:2. [2]NPNF 2 10:284*. [3]NPNF 1 13:540*. [4]NPNF 1 13:468. [5]Sir 28:28. [6]Phil 3:2. [7]NPNF 2 10:208*.

prophet says about such men: "The fool shall utter foolishness, and his heart shall imagine vain things."[8] But since, like their leader, they too go about like lions seeking whom among the simple they shall devour,[9] we are compelled to write in reply to your piety, that the brethren being once again instructed by your admonition may still further reprove the vain teaching of those men. LETTER TO ADELPHUS 60.2.[10]

COMMUNITY DISCIPLINE. BASIL THE GREAT: If he who has been corrected for his first sins and has been deemed worthy of pardon again falls, he prepares for himself a more wrathful judgment.[11] He who after the first and second admonition remains in his fault should be re-ported to the superior, that perhaps he may be ashamed when further rebuked. But, if he does not even in this case correct himself, he must be cut off from the rest as a cause of scandal and be looked upon as a heathen and a publican.[12] LETTERS 22.[13]

3:11 He Is Self-Condemned

THE NATURE OF HERESY. TERTULLIAN: It is the same Paul who, in his epistle to the Galatians, counts "heresies" among "the sins of the flesh,"[14] who also intimates to Titus that "a man who is a heretic" must be "rejected after the first admonition." This is on the ground that "he that is perverted and commits sin as a self-condemned man." Indeed, in almost every epistle, when enjoining on us [the duty] of avoiding false doctrines, he sharply condemns heresies. Of these the practical effects are false doctrines, called in Greek *heresis*, a word used in the sense of that choice which a man makes when he either teaches them [to others] or takes up with them [for himself]. For this reason it is that he calls the heretic self-condemned, because he has himself chosen that in which he is condemned. ON PRESCRIPTION AGAINST HERETICS 6.[15]

HIMSELF TO BLAME. CYPRIAN: The church cannot be rent or divided against itself. It maintains the unity of a single, indivisible house. . . . All who are to live and escape the destruction of the world must be gathered into one house alone, the church. If any of the gathered goes outside, that is, if anyone who once obtained grace in the church nevertheless abandons the church, his blood will be upon his head. He will have himself to blame for his damnation. The apostle Paul explains this, directing us to avoid a heretic as perverted, sinful and self-condemned. LETTERS 69.4.[16]

SELF-EXCOMMUNICATED. MAXIMUS OF TURIN: For the heretic damns himself when he casts himself out of the Catholic church and under no compulsion leaves the gathering of the saints. He who separates himself from everyone by his own judgment shows what is merited from everyone. The heretic himself, I say, damns himself because, although all the wicked are cast out from the Christian assembly by the sentence of the bishop, the heretic departs himself, by the judgment of his own will, before anyone's subsequent wishes are expressed. SERMONS 58.3.[17]

3:13-14 Help Cases of Urgent Need

ACTIVE CHARITY. CHRYSOSTOM: Paul urges that they not wait for those who are needy to come to them but that they seek out those who need their assistance. Thus the considerate man shows his concern, and with great zeal he will perform his duty. For in doing good actions, it is not those who receive the kindness who are benefitted, so much as those who do the kindness that make gain and profit, for it gives them confidence toward God. HOMILIES ON TITUS 6.[18]

---

[8]Is 32:6 (LXX). [9]1 Pet 5:8. [10]NPNF 2 4:575*. [11]Heb 10:26-27. [12]Cf. Mt 18:17. [13]FC 13:59-60. [14]Gal 5:20. [15]ANF 3:245*. [16]LCC 5:152. [17]ACW 50:141*. [18]NPNF 1 13:541.

SERVING THE SERVANTS OF GOD. AUGUSTINE: Nevertheless, after the apostle had said in such instruction and advice: "Now such persons we charge and exhort in the Lord Jesus Christ that they work quietly and eat their own bread,"[19] he was mindful of such needs of the holy persons who, although they would obey his commands to work quietly and eat their own bread, would, for many reasons, lack some provision of such necessary commodities. Hence, with foresight he added immediately: "But you, brothers, do not grow tired of well-doing,"[20] so that those who had the means of furnishing sustenance to the servants of God would not grow careless in this respect. Furthermore, when in writing to Titus he said: "Help Zenas the lawyer and Apollos on their way, taking care that nothing be wanting to them." He continued thus, in order to show why nothing should be lacking in their regard: "And let the people also learn to excel in good works, in order to meet cases of necessity, that they may not be unfruitful." THE WORK OF MONKS 15.16.[21]

---

[19]2 Thess 3:12. [20]2 Thess 3:13. [21]FC 16:356.

THE EPISTLE
TO PHILEMON

ARGUMENT: In writing to Philemon, Paul addresses himself to a household of devout Christians, from whom Onesimus, the slave, has run away and from whom he has stolen. The apparent triviality of this letter disguises the fact that it displays the virtue and godly humanity of the apostle in concrete terms, it shows that wicked slaves should not be abandoned, and it implies that slavery as an institution is such that slaves ought not to be withdrawn from their masters (CHRYSOSTOM). Paul means to demonstrate the moderation with which those in ecclesiastical authority should treat brothers in the faith, this moderation coming through in his tone and humility. Finally, he clarifies the fact that men and women are spiritually equal but have different functions (THEODORE). The central thrust of Paul's message is that Onesimus, the runaway slave, is a man for whom Christ died and therefore is worthy of Philemon's tender care, whatever his crimes (THEODORET). Paul demonstrates in this short letter the humility of true holiness (PELAGIUS). While it is the case that some have doubted the Pauline authorship of this letter and others relegate it solely to the area of practice and not of doctrine, it is a valuable and authentic composition by the apostle, as even Marcion recognized (JEROME).

1-7 GREETINGS AND THANKSGIVINGS

¹Paul, a prisoner for Christ Jesus, and Timothy our brother,
To Philemon our beloved fellow worker ²and Apphia our sister and Archippus our fellow soldier, and the church in your house:
³Grace to you and peace from God our Father and the Lord Jesus Christ.
⁴I thank my God always when I remember you in my prayers, ⁵because I hear of your love and of the faith which you have toward the Lord Jesus and all the saints, ⁶and I pray that the sharing of your faith may promote the knowledge of all the good that is ours in Christ. ⁷For I

have derived much joy and comfort from your love, my brother, because the hearts of the saints have been refreshed through you.

OVERVIEW: In these opening comments Paul's humility is in the forefront as he attempts to quench Philemon's anger. Apphia is probably Philemon's wife. By addressing the church, Paul speaks to Philemon's household, including the slaves, thereby increasing compassion for Onesimus. Intentionally Paul offers praise and favors before asking for them (CHRYSOSTOM). Only here does Paul begin an epistle by designating himself a prisoner, in order to make it clear that he is not presuming upon his apostolic authority. He observes the social hierarchy in the order of address, Archippus being the son of Philemon and Apphia, and he reveals to Philemon in a wonderful way his knowledge of the latter's deep faith and goodness (THEODORE). As Paul speaks to Philemon and the others from his chains, he shows that such hardship is the price of faithfulness to an apostolic calling (THEODORET). The central emphasis in these verses is on Paul's deliberate eschewal of authority, in order that humility and gentleness will prevail with Philemon (PELAGIUS, JEROME).

1a *Paul, a Prisoner for Christ Jesus*

HIS CHAINS. CHRYSOSTOM: For if a chain for Christ's sake is not a shame but a boast, much more is slavery not to be considered a reproach. And Paul says this not to exalt himself but for a merciful purpose. He believes his chains demonstrate he can be trusted. He does not mention his chains for his own sake but that he may more readily obtain the favor from Philemon. HOMILIES ON PHILEMON 1.[1]

THEODORE OF MOPSUESTIA: The wearing of such chains would be a vile thing only if Paul refused them out of lack of concern for the salvation of others. COMMENTARY ON PHILEMON.[2]

JEROME: Paul has not used "prisoner of Jesus Christ" in any other epistle as a part of his name, though he has used it in Ephesians and in Philippians as a form of proclamation. Thus, I think it of more importance that he says he is a prisoner of Jesus Christ than an apostle. Indeed, the apostles gloried that they were worthy to suffer abuse for the name of Jesus Christ. Indeed, their chains carried an automatic authority. COMMENTARY ON PHILEMON.[3]

THE GLORY OF SUCH IMPRISONMENT. AMBROSE: How many masters he has who runs from the one Lord. But let us not run from him. Who will run away from him whom they follow bound in chains, but willing chains, which loose and do not bind? Those who are bound with these chains boast and say: "Paul, a prisoner of Christ Jesus, and Timothy." It is more glorious for us to be bound by him than to be set free and loosed from others. LETTERS 59.[4]

TRUE HUMILITY, JUST PRIDE. CHRYSOSTOM: Great is Paul's self-designation. He mentions no title of principality and power but speaks of bonds and chains! Truly great indeed! Although many other things made him illustrious . . . yet he sets down none of these but mentions the chain instead of all, for this made him more conspicuous and illustrious than these other things. . . . But it is customary with those who love, to glory more in the things which they suffer for those who are beloved, than in the benefits they receive from them. A king is not so proud of his diadem, as was Paul, who gloried in his chains. HOMILIES CONCERNING THE STATUES 16.3.[5]

---

[1]NPNF 1 13:547*. [2]TEM 2:267. [3]PL 26:641AB. [4]FC 26:357. Ambrose makes a similar use of this text in *Six Days of Creation* 3.53 (FC 42: 108-9). [5]NPNF 1 9:447*.

1b *Philemon, Beloved Fellow Worker*

PROOF OF AFFECTION. CHRYSOSTOM: If "beloved," then his confidence is not boldness nor conceit but proof of deep affection. If Philemon is a "fellow laborer," then not only may he be instructed in such a matter, but he ought to acknowledge it as a favor. For Philemon is bringing blessing upon himself, and he is building up the same work [i.e., of spreading the gospel and bringing others to faith]. So that apart from any request, Paul says, you have another reason for granting the favor. For if he is profitable to the gospel and you are anxious to promote the gospel, then you should be the one pleading with me, rather than me with you. HOMILIES ON PHILEMON 1.[6]

2a *Apphia Our Sister*

HER EXACT STATUS? CHRYSOSTOM: It seems to me that she was his partner in life. Observe the humility of Paul. He both joins Timothy with him in his request and asks not only the husband but the wife also, to whom Paul may be a friend as well. HOMILIES ON PHILEMON 1.[7]

THEODORE OF MOPSUESTIA: Paul makes a point of greeting Philemon and Apphia equally. He wishes to indicate thereby that in no way is there a difference of faith or strength of faith between men and women. COMMENTARY ON PHILEMON.[8]

PELAGIUS: Apphia is believed to be either Philemon's sister or spouse. PELAGIUS'S COMMENTARY ON THE LETTER TO PHILEMON.[9]

2b *Archippus Our Fellow Soldier*

SPECULATIONS ON ARCHIPPUS. CHRYSOSTOM: It seems to me too, that he, whom he joins with him in this request, was also one of the clergy. HOMILIES ON PHILEMON 1.[10]

THEODORE OF MOPSUESTIA: Archippus was

their son. COMMENTARY ON PHILEMON.[11]

JEROME: I think that Archippus was the bishop of the church at Colossae. COMMENTARY ON PHILEMON.[12]

PELAGIUS: Archippus is a deacon of the church, as suggested in Colossians 4:17. PELAGIUS'S COMMENTARY ON THE LETTER TO PHILEMON.[13]

2c *The Church in Your House*

WHO IS INCLUDED? CHRYSOSTOM: Here Paul has not omitted even the slaves. For he knew that often even the words of slaves have power to turn around their master. This is especially true when his request was in behalf of a slave. HOMILIES ON PHILEMON 1.[14]

THEODORE OF MOPSUESTIA: While keeping the social order here, Paul does not call some indiscriminate multitude "the church," but only those who are bound together in faith. This bond sets the frame for Paul's appeal in the letter. COMMENTARY ON PHILEMON.[15]

4 *I Remember You in My Prayers*

ASKING IN HUMILITY. CHRYSOSTOM: For if others obtain the things they ask, much more Paul. If as an esteemed figure of authority, he was worthy to obtain, much more when he comes in all humility and asks a thing not pertaining to himself but in behalf of another. HOMILIES ON PHILEMON 2.[16]

JEROME: Now Paul shifts to his own voice alone [i.e., not speaking for Timothy and himself] and speaks solely to Philemon. COMMENTARY ON PHILEMON.[17]

---

[6]NPNF 1 13:547*. [7]NPNF 1 13:547*. [8]TEM 2:269 (Greek). [9]PETE 536. [10]NPNF 1 13:547. [11]TEM 2:270 (Greek). [12]PL 26:642B. [13]PETE 536. [14]NPNF 1 13:547*. [15]TEM 2:271. [16]NPNF 1 13:550* [17]PL 26:644D.

5 Of the Faith You Have

A DISTINCTION? JEROME: If the question is asked—"How can we have the same faith in Christ Jesus and toward all the saints?"—the answer is that you have love in Christ Jesus and toward the saints, and you have the same faith in Christ Jesus and toward the saints by a shared property. . . . It is because the same holiness is shared by the Lord and by his servants, as Old Testament usage shows. As long as we believe in the holiness of God, we shall see it in his true servants as well.

COMMENTARY ON PHILEMON.[18]

7 I Have Derived Much Joy and Comfort

KINDNESSES BESTOWED. CHRYSOSTOM: Nothing so shames us into giving as to bring forward the kindnesses bestowed on others, and particularly when the intercessor is more entitled to respect than they. HOMILIES ON PHILEMON 2.[19]

---

[18]PL 26:645A. [19]NPNF 1 13:550

8-20 INTERCESSION FOR ONESIMUS

[8]*Accordingly, though I am bold enough in Christ to command you to do what is required,* [9]*yet for love's sake I prefer to appeal to you—I, Paul, an ambassador*[a] *and now a prisoner also for Christ Jesus—*[10]*I appeal to you for my child, Onesimus, whose father I have become in my imprisonment.* [11]*(Formerly he was useless to you, but now he is indeed useful*[b] *to you and to me.)* [12]*I am sending him back to you, sending my very heart.* [13]*I would have been glad to keep him with me, in order that he might serve me on your behalf during my imprisonment for the gospel;* [14]*but I preferred to do nothing without your consent in order that your goodness might not be by compulsion but of your own free will.*

[15]*Perhaps this is why he was parted from you for a while, that you might have him back for ever,* [16]*no longer as a slave but more than a slave, as a beloved brother, especially to me but how much more to you, both in the flesh and in the Lord.* [17]*So if you consider me your partner, receive him as you would receive me.* [18]*If he has wronged you at all, or owes you anything, charge that to my account.* [19]*I, Paul, write this with my own hand, I will repay it—to say nothing of your owing me even your own self.* [20]*Yes, brother, I want some benefit from you in the Lord. Refresh my heart in Christ.*

a Or an old man *b The name Onesimus means* useful *or (compare verse 20)* beneficial

---

OVERVIEW: Paul approaches his request cautiously and delicately, hoping to extinguish Philemon's anger and to shame him into compliance by the mention of the chains (CHRYSOS- TOM). Paul appeals to his chains and his age, always emphasizing Philemon's spiritual growth and highlighting what will be to his personal benefit as the Lord makes use of the whole situation (THEODORE). Everywhere Paul shows his deep humility and the power of the gospel to make the slave and the master equal as children of God (THEODORET). Paul's essential greatness comes through in this passage, where he showers Philemon with praise but also exhibits his love for and devotion to Onesimus as a son in the faith. It is this balance that keeps the spirit of the gospel at the center of the letter (JEROME). Paul's appeal is to the free willing of Philemon, that he rise to this occasion in pursuit of the holiness and virtue that are the call of the gospel (PELAGIUS).

8 Bold Enough in Christ to Command

SPEAKING FROM LOVE. CHRYSOSTOM: Observe how cautious he is, lest any of the things which were spoken even from exceeding love should so strike the hearer as to hurt him. HOMILIES ON PHILEMON 2.[1]

THEODORET OF CYR: Paul's appeal is out of humility, not glory. INTERPRETATION OF THE LETTER TO PHILEMON.[2]

AMBROSIASTER: Though Paul is writing to a layman, he nonetheless does not exert his apostolic authority in order to issue orders but respects Philemon as a faithful Christian and of the same age, one who is bound to Christ as he is. COMMENTARY ON PAUL'S EPISTLES.[3]

9 I Prefer to Appeal to You

THE BASIS OF THE APPEAL. CHRYSOSTOM: Paul appeals to Philemon on a number of grounds: the quality of his person, his age,[4] because he was old, and from what was more just than all, because he was also a "prisoner of Jesus Christ." HOMILIES ON PHILEMON 2.[5]

THEODORE OF MOPSUESTIA: Paul shows here what power his name alone has. COMMENTARY ON PHILEMON.[6]

10 I Appeal to You for Onesimus

A SPIRITUAL CHILD OF AFFLICTION. CHRYSOSTOM: For I would not have called him my son, Paul says, if he were not of great use and importance to me. What I called Timothy, that I also call Onesimus. Paul repeatedly shows his affection for Onesimus, reminding Philemon of Onesimus's recent birth in Christ. "I have begotten him in my bonds," he says, so that also on this account Onesimus was worthy to obtain much honor, because he was begotten in Paul's very conflicts, in his trials in the cause of Christ. HOMILIES ON PHILEMON 2.[7]

CHRYSOSTOM: And note, on the other hand, also Paul's fervency. He preached the gospel bound and scourged. Oh, that blessed chain, with what great effort did it labor that night, and what children did it birth! Yes, of them, too, may he say, "Whom I have begotten in my bonds." Observe how Paul glories. He will have the children born this way considered even more illustrious! Observe how transcendent is the glory of those bonds, in that they give luster not only to him that wore them but also to those who were on that occasion begotten by him. HOMILIES ON EPHESIANS 8.[8]

THEODORE OF MOPSUESTIA: Now Paul uses the name of Onesimus, but only after signaling the profound change that has occurred [i.e., Onesimus's conversion]. COMMENTARY ON PHILEMON.[9]

11 Useful to You and to Me

SPEAKING PRUDENTLY. CHRYSOSTOM: See how great is Paul's prudence, how he confesses

[1]NPNF 1 13:550*. [2]PG 82:873C/874C. [3]CSEL 81 3:338-39. [4]Chrysostom assumes that the Greek term *presbeutes*, translated "ambassador" in the RSV, refers to Paul's age and not to his status as an elder or honored figure in the church. [5]NPNF 1 13:551*. [6]TEM 2:276. [7]NPNF 1 13:551*. [8]NPNF 1 13:89*. [9]TEM 2:277.

the man's faults and thereby extinguishes Philemon's anger. . . . He has not said Onesimus will be useful to you, lest Philemon should refute this argument, but he has introduced his own person, that his hopes may seem worthy of trust. "But now," he says, "profitable to you and to me." For if Onesimus was profitable to Paul, who was quite strict, how more would he be so to his master. HOMILIES ON PHILEMON 2.[10]

THE GOSPEL FIRST. JEROME: I must stand in awe of the apostle's greatness of soul here, as a man whose mind burns for Christ. He is held in prison, he is constrained by chains, in physical misery, separated from dear ones, plunged into prison darkness, yet he does not feel the injury, he is not crucified with sadness. Rather, he knows nothing else than to ponder the gospel of Christ. COMMENTARY ON PHILEMON.[11]

BOTH MASTER AND SLAVE CHANGED. BASIL THE GREAT: All bound slaves who flee to religious communities for refuge should be admonished and sent back to their masters in better dispositions, after the example of St. Paul who, although he had begotten Onesimus through the gospel, sent him back to Philemon. He had convinced Onesimus that the yoke of slavery, borne in a manner pleasing to the Lord, would render him worthy of the kingdom of heaven. Paul not only urged Philemon to annul the threat against his servant, being mindful of the Lord's own words: "If you forgive men their offenses, your heavenly Father will forgive you also your offenses."[12] But also, in order that Philemon might be more kindly disposed toward Onesimus, Paul writes: "For perhaps he therefore departed for a season from you that you might receive him again forever; not as a servant, but instead of a servant, as a most dear brother." If, however, it should be the case of a wicked master who gives unlawful commands and forces the slave to transgress the command of our Master, the Lord Jesus Christ, then it is our duty to oppose him, so that the name of God not be blasphemed by that slave's performing an act displeasing to God. THE LONG RULES, Q.II.R.[13]

13 Glad to Keep Him with Me

CAREFUL GROUNDWORK. CHRYSOSTOM: Be careful to observe how much groundwork is necessary before Paul honorably brought Onesimus before his master. Observe how wisely he has done this. See for how much he makes Philemon answerable and how much he honors Onesimus. You have found, he says, a way by which you may through Onesimus repay your service to me. Here Paul shows that he has considered Philemon's advantage more than that of his slave and that he deeply respects him. HOMILIES ON PHILEMON 2.[14]

THEODORE OF MOPSUESTIA: Paul indicates that had he kept Onesimus, the result would have been that he could serve Paul as an extension of Philemon's service and thus have been a source of gain for Philemon. COMMENTARY ON PHILEMON.[15]

THEODORET OF CYR: The idea that Paul could have kept Onesimus with him to minister to him in Philemon's place shows the great power of the gospel: that the servant is made equal to the master. INTERPRETATION OF THE LETTER TO PHILEMON.[16]

14 Goodness Not by Compulsion

FREE WILL A REALITY. ORIGEN: God does not tyrannize but rules, and when he rules, he does not coerce but encourages and he wishes that those under him yield themselves willingly to his direction so that the good of someone may

---

[10]NPNF 1 13:551*. [11]PL 26:648C. [12]Mt 6:14. [13]FC 9:261-62*. [14]NPNF 1 13:551*. [15]TEM 2:279. [16]PG 82:875A/876A.

not be according to compulsion but according to his free will. This is what Paul with understanding was saying to Philemon in the letter to Philemon concerning Onesimus: "So that your good be not according to compulsion but according to free will." Thus, the God of the universe hypothetically might have produced a supposed good in us so that we would give alms from "compulsion" and we would be temperate from "compulsion," but he has not wished to do so. HOMILIES ON JEREMIAH 20.2.[17]

TWO GOOD EFFECTS. CHRYSOSTOM: This is a strategy that is particularly flattering to the person asked. The idea is that since the act proposed is a thing profitable in itself, it is brought forward in such a way as to win Philemon's concurrence. For two good effects are thus produced: the intercessor gains his point, and the other person is rendered more secure.[18] HOMILIES ON PHILEMON 2.[19]

JEROME: This verse answers the question of why God, in creating human beings, did not constitute them invariably good and upright. If, indeed, God is good not out of some impersonal necessity but because in his essence he freely wills his own goodness,[20] he should in making man have made him to the divine image and likeness, that is, that he be good willingly and not by necessity. COMMENTARY ON PHILEMON.[21]

AUGUSTINE: And addressing himself to Philemon, Paul says: "that your kindness may not be as it were of necessity, but voluntary." . . . Now wherever there is the express statement not to do this or that, and whenever the performance of the will is required to do or refrain from some action, in keeping with God's commandments, that is sufficient proof of the free choice of the will. Let no one, therefore, blame God in his heart whenever he sins, but let him impute the sin to himself. GRACE AND FREE WILL 2.4.[22]

PELAGIUS: It is to be noted that he wished no one to do anything good by necessity, lest that person lose the reward of freely choosing to do the right thing. PELAGIUS'S COMMENTARY ON THE LETTER TO PHILEMON.[23]

15 To Have Him Back Forever

ELICITING TENDERNESS. CHRYSOSTOM: Paul wisely said "perhaps," that the master may yield to his request. For since Onesimus's flight arose from wickedness and a corrupt mind and not from the intention to accomplish good, Paul has said, "perhaps." And he has not said, "therefore he fled," but "therefore he was separated," in order to elicit some tenderness on the part of Philemon.[24] HOMILIES ON PHILEMON 2.[25]

THEODORE OF MOPSUESTIA: Clearly Onesimus's flight has served to reverse the wickedness of his judgment. The "perhaps," however, makes Paul more persuasive [i.e., Paul puts this thought forward as a consideration for Philemon]. COMMENTARY ON PHILEMON.[26]

THEODORET OF CYR: Onesimus's flight has become the source of good things to him. INTERPRETATION OF THE LETTER TO PHILEMON.[27]

---

[17]FC 97:224. [18]In other words, Paul's skillful way of pleading Onesimus's case wins Philemon's approval in a way that is likely to produce good feeling for both him and Philemon. [19]NPNF 1 13:552. [20]God is good because pure goodness and divinity are inseparable, but Jerome wants to make the point that God's goodness is free, not mechanical and impersonal in a way that would make it seem automatic and thus not moral in the strict sense. [21]PL 26:649A. [22]FC 59:254-55*. [23]PETE 538*. [24]Chrysostom wishes to make the subtle point that Onesimus's intentions in running away from Philemon were wrong-headed but that God has used the occasion in a beneficent way. Paul's use of "perhaps" is therefore an attempt to draw out a concession from Philemon that the whole affair has worked to everyone's benefit, in that Philemon will now receive back a slave and a brother. This kind of interpretation is Chrysostom at his most subtle and most wise in giving pastoral care. [25]NPNF 1 13:551*. [26]TEM 2:280-81. [27]PG 82:875C/876C

JEROME: Sometimes the occasion of evil becomes the occasion of good, and God turns evil human plans to an upright end. . . . If indeed [Onesimus] had not fled his master, he never would have come to Rome where Paul was in prison in chains. If he had not seen Paul in chains, he would not have received faith in Christ. If he had not had faith in Christ, he never would have become Paul's son, so that he might be sent for the work of the gospel. . . . Paul says "perhaps" cautiously, hesitantly, with trepidation and not with certainty. If he had not said "perhaps," all slaves would need to flee in order to become apostles. COMMENTARY ON PHILEMON.[28]

16 More Than a Slave

FROM SLAVERY TO FREEDOM. CHRYSOSTOM: Shall I show you freedom arising from slavery? There was a certain Onesimus, a slave, a good-for-nothing runaway. He escaped and went to Paul. He obtained baptism, washed away his sins and remained at Paul's feet. . . . Do you see his nobility? Do you see a character that brings freedom? Slave and free are simply names. What is a slave? It is a mere name. How many masters lie drunken upon their beds, while slaves stand by sober? Whom shall I call a slave? The one who is sober, or the one who is drunk? The one who is the slave of a man, or the one who is the captive of passion? The former has his slavery on the outside; the latter wears his captivity on the inside. ON LAZARUS AND THE RICH MAN 6.[29]

17 If You Consider Me Your Partner

THE HEART OF THE MATTER. CHRYSOSTOM: No procedure is so apt to gain a hearing, as not to ask for everything at once. For we see Paul only introduces the heart of the matter after praising Philemon and with much preparation. After having said that Onesimus is "my son," that he is a partaker of the gospel, that he is "my very heart," that you receive him back "as a brother" and "regard him as a brother," then Paul has added "as myself." And Paul was not ashamed to do this. For he who was not ashamed to be called the servant of the faithful but confesses that he was such, much more would he not refuse this. HOMILIES ON PHILEMON 3.[30]

THEODORE OF MOPSUESTIA: Paul argues that what he desires of Philemon is consistent with the shared faith and shared condition of believers. The injunction to receive Onesimus as if he were Paul does not mean Philemon should receive him as an apostle but "as you would personally receive me." COMMENTARY ON PHILEMON.[31]

JEROME: Let him be received as an apostle and thus as Paul's companion. COMMENTARY ON PHILEMON.[32]

19 Owing Me Your Own Self

SPIRITUAL GRACE. CHRYSOSTOM: Paul writes at once movingly and with subtle spiritual grace. The idea is that since Paul did not refuse to extend his credit, [how ironic it would be] if Philemon should refuse to receive Onesimus! The mention of this deserved favor would both shame Philemon into compliance and bring Onesimus out of trouble.[33] HOMILIES ON PHILEMON 3.[34]

THEODORE OF MOPSUESTIA: Paul says, "I make this promise to you, since you yourself see the abundant rewards that God's mercy has in store

---

[28]PL 26:650AB. [29]OWP 15-16. [30]NPNF 1 13:554*. [31]TEM 2:282-83. [32]PL 26:650C. [33]The idea seems to be that Philemon owes Paul a debt, namely, the former's conversion to the gospel. Paul is extending his credit, paying a bond, to cover Onesimus's return to Philemon. With regard to Philemon, Paul is calling in a favor. If Philemon should refuse to pay him back, it would be an affront to Paul and would leave Onesimus stranded. [34]NPNF 1 13:555.

when you exercise goodness toward Onesimus. You ought to think on these things in the light of what you owe to me, though I ought not to refer to it." COMMENTARY ON PHILEMON.[35]

[35]TEM 2:283.

21-25 CONCLUSION AND GREETINGS

[21]*Confident of your obedience, I write to you, knowing that you will do even more than I say.* [22]*At the same time, prepare a guest room for me, for I am hoping through your prayers to be granted to you.*
[23]*Epaphras, my fellow prisoner in Christ Jesus, sends greetings to you,* [24]*and so do Mark, Aristarchus, Demas, and Luke, my fellow workers.*
[25]*The grace of the Lord Jesus Christ be with your spirit.*

OVERVIEW: Paul finishes with a renewed note of confidence, with a reminder of his imprisonment and suffering for the gospel and with a prayer for God's gracious mercy—the key to everything (CHRYSOSTOM). Paul shows something of the nature of his work as a missionary, for he presumes upon the future hospitality of his host, yet his request for accommodations is modest, and he makes it clear that he is dependent on the prayers of the whole church (JEROME).

21-22 Confident of Your Obedience

ALWAYS CONFIDENT. CHRYSOSTOM: What stone would not these words have softened? What wild beast would not these requests have rendered mild and prepared to receive him heartily? . . . What he had said at the beginning, "having confidence," that he also says here in the sealing up of his letter. . . . This also was the part of one who was exceedingly confident. It may also be the case that this statement too was in behalf of Onesimus. For he, not being a neutral personage but rather being intimately knowledgeable

about Paul's situation and special to the apostle, they might lay aside all remembrance of the wrong and might the rather grant the favor. HOMILIES ON PHILEMON 3.[1]

23 Epaphras, My Fellow Prisoners

ALSO FROM COLOSSAE. CHRYSOSTOM: Epaphras was sent by the Colossians, so that from this it appears that Philemon was also at Colossae. And Paul calls him his "fellow prisoner," showing that he was also in great tribulation, so that if not on his own account, yet on account of Epaphras, it was right that he should be heard. HOMILIES ON PHILEMON 3.[2]

JEROME: Concerning the identity of Epaphras, Paul's coprisoner, we accept a story. Some say that the apostle Paul's parents were from Giscala in Judea and that when the province was devastated by the Romans and the Jews scattered, they emigrated to Tarsus in Cilicia, where

[1]NPNF 1 13:555*. [2]NPNF 1 13:555*.

Paul was born. Here he inherited as a young man the personal status of his parents. Thus he could state: "They are Hebrews, but so am I; they are Israelites, so am I; they are Abraham's seed, so am I."[3] And again, "I am a Hebrew of the Hebrews."[4] These indicate that he felt himself more of a Jew than a citizen of Tarsus. Because this was so, we can guess that Epaphras was captured and imprisoned about the same time and that with his parents in Colossae, a city of Asia, he later received the word about Christ. COMMENTARY ON PHILEMON.[5]

25 The Grace of the Lord Jesus Christ

THE ONE THING NEEDFUL. CHRYSOSTOM: He has finished his epistle with a prayer. And indeed prayer is a great good, beneficial, and preserves our souls. But prayer is great when we act in line with our prayers and do not undermine by our behavior the very thing for which we pray. And you, too, therefore, when you go to the priest, and he says to you, "The Lord will have mercy on you, my son," do not trust in the word only but add works to your trust. Mercy is an excellent thing! Why, then, haven't you shown it to another? HOMILIES ON PHILEMON 3.[6]

---

[3]2 Cor 11:22. [4]Phil 3:5. [5]PL 26:653D. This tradition that Jerome relates about Paul's background is an important historical note that he probably derived from Origen's lost commentary on Philemon and shows every indication of being reliable (Jerome Murphy-O'Connor, *Paul: A Critical Life* [Oxford: Clarendon, 1996], 37-38). Origen probably included it at this point because of Paul's mention that Epaphras is a coprisoner with him. At Colossians 4:12 Epaphras is mentioned as a person dear to the Colossian church, and he functioned as Paul's emissary to that church. Paul is dropping a name that he knows has weight with the Colossian Christians, Philemon included. Origen seems, therefore, to have used this mention as an occasion for discussing Paul's distinguished background that, by virtue of his parentage, made him a Roman citizen and Epaphras's equal. Hence they were both citizens in a Roman prison awaiting trial, truly "coprisoners" in every sense. [6]NPNF 1 13:556*.

Early Christian Writers and the Documents Cited

The following table lists all the early Christian documents cited in this volume by author. Where available, Cetedoc and TLG digital references are listed.

Alexander of Alexandria
"Epistle on the Arian Heresy"

Ambrose

"Cain and Abel" (*De Cain et Abel*)	Cetedoc 0125
"Concerning Repentance" (*De paenitentia*)	Cetedoc 0156
"Concerning Widows" (*De viduis*)	Cetedoc 0146
"Consolation on the Death of Emperor Valentinian" (*De obitu Valentiniani*)	Cetedoc 0158
"Death as a Good" (*De bono mortis*)	Cetedoc 0129
"Duties of the Clergy" (*De officiis*)	Cetedoc 0144
"Flight from the World" (*De fuga saeculi*)	Cetedoc 0133
"Isaac, or The Soul" (*De Isaac vel anima*)	Cetedoc 0130
"Joseph" (*De Joseph patriarcha*)	Cetedoc 0131
"Letters" (*Epistulae*)	Cetedoc 0160
"Of the Christian Faith" (*De fide*)	Cetedoc 0150
"Of the Holy Spirit" (*De Spiritu Sancto*)	Cetedoc 0151
"On Belief in the Resurrection" (*De excessu fratris Satyri*)	Cetedoc 0157
"On the Death of His Brother Satyrus" (*De excessu fratris Satyri*)	Cetedoc 0157
"Paradise" (*De paradiso*)	Cetedoc 0124
"Six Days of Creation" (*Hexaemeron*)	Cetedoc 0123
"The Patriarchs" (*De patriarchis*)	Cetedoc 0132
"The Prayer of Job and David" (*De interpellatione Job et David*)	Cetedoc 0134

Ambrosiaster
"Commentary on Colossians"
"Commentary on First Thessalonians"
"Commentary on First Timothy"
"Commentary on Paul's Epistles"
"Commentary on Second Timothy"
"Commentary on the Letter to Titus"

Anonymous
"Book of Steps"
"Constitutions of the Holy Apostles"
"Letter to Diognetus" *(Epistula ad Diognetum)* TLG 1350.001
"The Bohairic Life of Pachomius"
"The Didache" *(Didache XII Apostolorum)* TLG 1311.001
"The First Greek Life of Pachomius"
"The Sayings of the Fathers"
"The Testament of Horiesios"

Aphrahat
"Demonstrations"
"Select Demonstrations"

Athanasius
"Against Pagans" or "Against the Heathen" *(Contra gentes)* TLG 2035.001
"Against the Arians" *(Apologia contra Arianos)* TLG 2035.005
"Councils of Ariminum of Seleucia" *(De synodis)* TLG 2035.010
"Defence of the the Nicene Definition" *(De decretis)* TLG 2035.003
"Festal Letters" *(Epistulae festales)* TLG 2035.x01*
"History of the Arians" *(Historia Arianorum)* TLG 2035.009
"Letter to Adelphus" *(Epistula ad Adelphium)* TLG 2035.050
"Letter to Amun" *(Epistula ad Amun)* TLG 2035.013
"Letter to Dracontius" *(Epistula ad Dracontium)* TLG 2035.040
"Letter to the Bishops of Egypt" *(Epistula ad episcopos Aegypti et Libyae)* TLG 2035.041
"On the Incarnation of the Word" *(De incarnatione Verbi)* TLG 2035.002

Athenagoras
"A Plea Regarding Christians" *(Legatio)* TLG 1205.001

Augustine
"Admonition and Grace" *(De correptione et gratia)* Cetedoc 0353
"Against Julian" *(Contra Julianum)* Cetedoc 0351
"Against the Manichees" *(De Genesi contra Manichaeos)* Cetedoc 0265
"Against Two Letters of the Pelagians" *(Contra duas epistulas Pelagianorum)* Cetedoc 0346
"Confessions" *(Confessionum)* Cetedoc 0251
"Eighty-three Different Question" *(De diversis quaestionibus LXXXIII)* Cetedoc 0289
"Enchiridion" *(Enchiridion de fide, spe et caritate)* Cetedoc 0295
"Faith and Creed" *(De fide et symbolo)* Cetedoc 0293
"Faith and Works" *(De fide et operibus)* Cetedoc 0294
"Grace and Free Will" *(De gratia et libero arbitrio)* Cetedoc 0352
"Holy Virginity" *(De sancta virginitate)* Cetedoc 0300
"Homilies on First John" *(In Johannis epistulam ad Parthos tractatus)* Cetedoc 0279
"Letters" *(Epistulae)* Cetedoc 0262
"On Baptism, Against the Donatists" *(De baptismo)* Cetedoc 0332

"On Christian Doctrine" (*De doctrina christiana*)	Cetedoc 0263
"On Man's Perfection in Righteousness" (*De perfectione justitiae hominis*)	Cetedoc 0347
"On Marriage and Concupiscence" (*De nuptiis et concupiscentia*)	Cetedoc 0350
"On Nature and Grace" (*De natura et gratia*)	Cetedoc 0344
"On Original Sin" (*De gratia Christi et de peccato originali*)	Cetedoc 0349
"On Rebuke and Grace" (*De correptione et gratia*)	Cetedoc 0353
"On the Creed" (*De symbolo ad catechumenos*)	Cetedoc 0309
"On the Grace of Christ" (*De gratia Christi et de peccato originali*)	Cetedoc 0349
"On the Psalms" (*Enarrationes in Psalmos*)	Cetedoc 0283
"On the Soul and Its Origin" (*De natura et origine animae*)	Cetedoc 0345
"On the Trinity" (*De Trinitate*)	Cetedoc 0329
"Predestination of the Saints" (*De praedestinatione sanctorum*)	Cetedoc 0354
"Proceedings of Pelagius" (*Contra duas epistulas Pelagianorum*)	Cetedoc 0346
"Reply to Faustus the Manichaean" (*Contra Faustum*)	Cetedoc 0321
"Retractations" (*Retractationum*)	Cetedoc 0250
"Sermon of the Mount" (*De sermone Domini in monte*)	Cetedoc 0274
"Sermons" (*Sermones*)	Cetedoc 0284
"The Christian Life" (*De disciplina christiana*)	Cetedoc 0310
"The City of God" (*De civitate Dei*)	Cetedoc 0313
"The Excellence of Widowhood" (*De bono viduitatis*)	Cetedoc 0301
"The Letters of Petilian, the Donatist" (*Contra litteras Petiliani*)	Cetedoc 0333
"The Morals of the Catholic Church" (*De moribus ecclesiae catholicae*)	Cetedoc 0261
"The Nature of the Good" (*De natura boni*)	Cetedoc 0323
"The Spirit and the Letter" (*De spiritu et littera*)	Cetedoc 0343
"The Way of Life of the Catholic Church" (*De moribus ecclesiae catholicae*)	Cetedoc 0261
"The Work of Monks" (*De opere monachorum*)	Cetedoc 0305
"To Simplician: On Various Questions" (*De diversis quaestionibus ad Simplicianum*)	Cetedoc 0290
"Tractates on John" (*In Johannis evangelium tractatus*)	Cetedoc 0278

Babai
"Letter to Cyriacus"

Basil the Great

"An Introduction to the Ascetical Life" (*Praevia institutio ascetica*)	TLG 2040.040
"Concerning Baptism" (*De baptismo libri duo*)	TLG 2040.052
"Concerning Faith" (*De fide*)	TLG 2040.031
"Hexameron" (*Homiliae in Hexaemeron*)	TLG 2040.001
"Homilies on the Psalms" (*Homiliae super Psalmos*)	TLG 2040.018
"Homily 10 - On Psalm 1" (*Homiliae super Psalmos*)	TLG 2040.018
"Homily 11 - On Psalm 7" (*Homiliae super Psalmos*)	TLG 2040.018
"Homily 16 - On Psalm 33" (*Homiliae super Psalmos*)	TLG 2040.018
"Homily 17 - On Psalm 44" (*Homiliae super Psalmos*)	TLG 2040.018
"Homily 22 - On Psalm 114" (*Homiliae super Psalmos*)	TLG 2040.018
"Homily on the Words: 'Give Heed to Thyself'" (*Homilia in illud: Attende tibi ipsi*)	TLG 2040.006
"Letters" (*Epistulae*)	TLG 2040.004

"On Detachment" (*Quod rebus mundanis adhaerendum non sit*)	TLG 2040.037
"On Renunciation of the World" (*Sermo asceticus et exhortatio de renuntiatione mundi*)	TLG 2040.041
"On the Holy Spirit" (*De Spiritu Sancto*)	TLG 2040.003
"Preface on the Judgment of God" (*Proemii de judicio Dei*)	TLG 2040.043
"The Long Rules" (*Regulae morales*)	TLG 2040.048

Bede the Venerable

"Homilies on the Gospels" (*Homeliarum evangelii libri II*)	Cetedoc 1367

Benedict of Nursia

"Rule" (*Regula*)	Cetedoc 1852

Caesarius of Arles

"Sermons" (*Sermones*)	Cetedoc 1008

Cassiodorus

"Commentary of the Psalms" (*Expositio Psalmorum*)	Cetedoc 0900

Clement of Alexandria

"Christ the Instructor" (*Paedagogus*)	TLG 0555.002
"Stromata" (*Stromata*)	TLG 0555.004

Clement of Rome

"The First Epistle of Clement" (*Epistula i ad Corinthios*)	TLG 1271.001

Cyprian

"Letters"
  "To Antonian"
  "To Cornelius"
  "To Maximus"
  "To Pompey"

"On the Unity of the Church" (*De ecclesiae catholicae unitate*)	Cetedoc 0041
"Works and Almsgiving" (*De opere et eleemosynis*)	Cetedoc 0047

Cyril of Alexandria

"Letters" (*Epistula i ad monachos Aegypti*)	TLG 4090.001*
"On the Unity of Christ" (*Quod unus sit Christus*)	TLG 4090.027*

Cyril of Jerusalem

"Catechetical Lectures"
"Lectures on the Mysteries"

Ephrem the Syrian

"Commentary on Tation's Diatessaron"
"Hymns on the Nativity"
"Three Homilies"

Eusebius of Caesarea
"Ecclesiastical History" (*Historia ecclesiastica*)   TLG 2018.002
"Proof of the Gospel" (*Demonstratio evangelica*)   TLG 2018.005

Fulgentius of Ruspe
"Letters" (*Epistulae*)   Cetedoc 0817
"Letter to Scarila" (*Liber ad Scarilam*)   Cetedoc 0822
"Letter to Victor" (*Liber ad Victorem*)   Cetedoc 0820
"On the Forgiveness of Sins" (*Ad Euthymium de remissione peccatorum*)   Cetedoc 0821
"To Peter on the Faith" (*De fide ad Petrum*)   Cetedoc 0826

Gregory of Nazianzus
"On His Brother S. Caesarius" (*Funebris in laudem Caesarii fratris oratio*)   TLG 2022.005
"Oration 27: Against the Eunomians" (*Adversus Eunomianos*)   TLG 2022.007
"Oration 30: On the Son" (*De filio*)   TLG 2022.010
"Oration 40: On Holy Baptism" (*In sanctum baptisma*)   TLG 2022.048
"Oration 42: The Last Farewell" (*Supremum vale*)   TLG 2022.050

Gregory of Nyssa
"Address on Religious Instruction" (*Oratio catechetica magna*)   TLG 2017.046
"Against Eunomius" (*Contra Eunomium*)   TLG 2017.030
"An Answer to Ablabius: That We Should Not Think of Saying There Are Three Gods" (*Ad Ablabium quod non sint tres dei*)   TLG 2017.003
"Letters" (*Epistulae*)   TLG 2017.033
"On Perfection" (*De perfectione*)   TLG 2017.026
"On the Christian Mode of Life" (*De instituto Christiano*)   TLG 2017.024
"On the Making of Man" (*De creatione hominis sermo primus*)   TLG 2017.034
"On the Soul and Resurrection" (*Dialogus de anima et resurrectione*)   TLG 2017.056
"On Virginity" (*De virginitate*)   TLG 2017.043

Gregory the Great
"Letters" (*Registrum epistularum*)   Cetedoc 1714
"Pastoral Care" (*Regula pastoralis*)   Cetedoc 1712

Hilary of Poitiers
"On the Trinity" (*De Trinitate*)   Cetedoc 0433

Hippolytus
"The Refutation of All Heresies" (*Refutatio omnium haeresium*)   TLG 2115.060*
"Treatise on Christ and Antichrist" (*De Antichristo*)   TLG 2115.003

Ignatius of Antioch
"Letter to Polycarp" (*Epistulae vii genuinae*)   TLG 1443.001
"To the Romans" (*Epistulae vii genuinae*)   TLG 1443.001

Irenaeus
"Against Heresies: Book I" *(Adversus haereses)*   TLG 1447.001
"Against Heresies: Book III" *(Adversus haereses)*   TLG 1447.002

Isaac of Nineveh
"An Epistle to Abba Symeon of Caesarea"
"Ascetical Homilies"
"Homilies"
"Instructions for Monks, Part 2"
"The First Syriac Epistle of St. Makarios of Egypt"

Jerome
"Against Jovinian" *(Adversus Jovinianum)*   Cetedoc 0610
"Against the Pelagians" *(Dialogi contra Pelagianos)*   Cetedoc 0615
"Commentary on Philemon" *(Commentarii in iv epistulas Paulinas)*   Cetedoc 0591
"Commentary on Titus" *(Commentarii in iv epistulas Paulinas)*   Cetedoc 0591
"Dialogue Against the Luciferians" *(Altercatio Luciferiani et Orthodoxi)*   Cetedoc 0608
"Homilies"
    (Prologus in libro Psalmorum)   Cetedoc 0591P
    (Tractatus lix in Psalmos)   Cetedoc 0592
    (Tractatuum in Psalmos series altera)   Cetedoc 0593
"On Obedience" *(Tractatus de oboedientia)*   Cetedoc 0605
"On Psalm 128" *(Tractatus lix in Psalmos)*   Cetedoc 0592
"Homilies on Mark" *(Tractatus in Marci evangelium)*   Cetedoc 0594
"Homilies on the Psalms" *(Commentarioli in Psalmos)*   Cetedoc 0582
"Letters" *(Epistulae)*   Cetedoc 0620
"Letter to Pammachius Against John of Jerusalem" *(Contra Joannem Hierosolymitanum)*   Cetedoc 0612

John Cassian
"Conferences" *(Collationes)*   Cetedoc 0512
"Institutes" *(De institutis coenobiorum)*   Cetedoc 0513

John Chrysostom
"Against Remarriage" *(De virginitate)*   TLG 2062.009
"Baptismal Instructions" *(Catechesis ad illuminandos)*   TLG 2062.382
"Commentary on Galatians" *(In epistulam ad Galatas commentarius)*   TLG 2062.158
"Concerning the Power of Demons" *(De diabolo tentatore)*   TLG 2062.026
"Discourses" *(De oratione)*   TLG 2062.322
"Homilies Concerning the Statues" *(Ad populum Antiochenum)*   TLG 2062.024
"Homilies on Colossians" *(In epistulam ad Colossenses)*   TLG 2062.161
"Homilies on Ephesians" *(In epistulam ad Ephesios)*   TLG 2062.159
"Homilies on First Corinthians" *(In epistulam i ad Corinthios)*   TLG 2062.156
"Homilies on First Thessalonians" *(In epistulam i ad Thessalonicenses)*   TLG 2062.162
"Homilies on First Timothy" *(In epistulam i ad Timotheum)*   TLG 2062.164
"Homilies on Genesis" *(In Genesim homiliae 1-67)*   TLG 2062.112

"Homilies on Hebrews" (*In epistulam ad Hebraeos*)	TLG 2062.168
"Homilies on John" (*In Joannem*)	TLG 2062.153
"Homilies on Matthew" (*In Matthaeum*)	TLG 2062.152
"Homilies on Philemon" (*In epistulam ad Philemonem*)	TLG 2062.167
"Homilies on Romans" (*In epistulam ad Romanos*)	TLG 2062.155
"Homilies on Second Corinthians" (*In epistulam ii ad Corinthios*)	TLG 2062.157
"Homilies on Second Thessalonians" (*In epistulam ii ad Thessalonicenses*)	TLG 2062.163
"Homilies on Second Timothy" (*In epistulam ii ad Timotheum*)	TLG 2062.165
"Homilies on S. Ignatius and S. Babylas, Eulogion for Ignatius" (*In sanctum Ignatium martyrem*)	TLG 2062.044
"Homilies on the Acts of the Apostles" (*In Acta apostolorum*)	TLG 2062.154
"Homilies on Titus" (*In epistulam ad Titum*)	TLG 2062.166
"Instructions to Catechumens" (*Catechesis ultima ad baptizandos*)	TLG 2062.381
"Letter to a Young Widow" (*Ad viduam juniorem*)	TLG 2062.010
"Letters to the Fallen Theodore" (*Ad Theodorum lapsum*)	TLG 2062.001
"On Lazarus and the Rich Man" (*De Lazaro et divite*)	TLG 2062.244
"On Repentance and Almsgiving" (*De eleemosyna*)	TLG 2062.075
"On the Incomprehensible Nature of God" (*De incomprehensibili Dei natura*)	TLG 2062.012
"On the Priesthood" (*De sacerdotio*)	TLG 2062.085 & TLG 2062.119
"On Virginity" (*De virginitate*)	TLG 2062.009

John of Damascus

"Barlaam and Ioasaph" (*Vita Barlaam et Joasaph*)	TLG 2934.066
"On Divine Images" (*Orationes de imaginibus tres*)	TLG 2934.005
"Orthodox Faith" (*Expositio fidei*)	TLG 2934.004

John the Elder
"Letters"

Justin Martyr

"Dialogue with Trypho, the Jew" (*Dialogus cum Tryphone*)	TLG 0645.003

Leo the Great

"Letters" (*Tractatus septem et nonaginta*)	Cetedoc 1657
"Sermons" (*Tractatus septem et nonaginta*)	Cetedoc 1657

Mark the Hermit
"On Baptism"

Maximus of Turin

"Sermons" (*Collectio sermonum*)	Cetedoc 0219a

Methodius

"The Banquet of the Ten Virgins" (*Symposium or Convivium decem virginum*)	TLG 2959.001*

Nemesius of Emesa
"Of the Nature of Man" (*De natura hominis*)   TLG 0743.001

Nicetas of Remesiana
"Explanation of the Creed"
"Instruction on Faith"
"Power of the Holy Spirit"

Novatian
"Jewish Foods" (*De cibis Judaicis*)   Cetedoc 0068
"The Trinity" (*De Trinitate*)   Cetedoc 0071

Origen
"Commentary of John" (*Commentarii in evangelium Joannis:*
   Lib. 1, 2, 4, 5, 6, 10, 13)   TLG 2042.005
"Commentary of John" (*Commentarii in evangelium Joannis: Lib. 19, 20, 28, 32*)   TLG 2042.079
"Commentary on the Song of Songs" (*In Canticum canticorum*)   TLG 2042.060
"Commentary on the Song of Songs" (*Scholia in Canticum canticorum*)   TLG 2042.076
"Exhortation to Martyrdom" (*Exhortatio ad martyrium*)   TLG 2042.007
"Fragment on Luke" (*Fragmenta in Lucam*)   TLG 2042.017
"Homilies on Exodus" (*Homiliae in Exodum*)   TLG 2042.023
"Homilies on Genesis" (*Homiliae in Genesim*)   TLG 2042.022
"Homilies on Jeremiah: Book 5" (*Homiliae in Jeremiam*)   TLG 2042.009
"Homilies on Jeremiah: Book 20" (*Homiliae in Jeremiam*)   TLG 2042.021
"Homilies on Leviticus" (*Homiliae in Leviticum*)   TLG 2042.024
"Homilies on Luke" (*Homiliae in Lucam*)   TLG 2042.016
"Homilies on Matthew" (*Commentarium in evangelium Matthaei: Lib. 10-11*)   TLG 2042.030
"Homilies on Matthew" (*Commentarium in evangelium Matthaei: Lib. 12-17*)   TLG 2042.029
"On First Principles" (*De principiis*)   TLG 2042.002
"On Prayer" (*De oratione*)   TLG 2042.008
"Origen Against Celsus" (*Contra Celsum*)   TLG 2042.001

Pelagius
"Pelagius's Commentary on Colossians"
"Pelagius's Commentary on Philemon"
"Pelagius's Commentary on the First Letter to the Thessalonians"
"Pelagius's Commentary on the First Letter to Timothy"
"Pelagius's Commentary on the Second Letter to the Thessalonians"
"Pelagius's Commentary on the Second Letter to Timothy"

Peter Chrysologus
"Sermons" (*Collectio sermonum*)   Cetedoc 0227

Philoxenus of Mabbug
"On the Indwelling of the Holy Spirit"

Polycarp of Smyrna
"The Epistle of Polycarp to the Philippians" *(Epistula ad Philippenses)*   TLG 1622.001

Prudentius
"Hymns"
   "Hymn Apotheosis" *(Liber apotheosis)*   Cetedoc 1439
   "Hymn Psychomachia" *(Psychomachia)*   Cetedoc 1441

Pseudo-Clement
"On Virginity"

Pseudo-Cyprian
"On the Discipline and Advantage of Chastity"

Pseudo-Dionysius
"Letters: 5" *(Ad Dorotheum ministrum)*   TLG 2798.010*
"Letters: 8" *(Ad Demophilum monachum)*   TLG 2798.013*
"The Celestial Hierarchy" *(De caelesti hierarchia)*   TLG 2798.001*
"The Divine Names" *(De divinis nominibus)*   TLG 2798.004*

Rufinus of Aquileia
"A Commentary on the Apostles' Creed" *(Expositio symboli)*   Cetedoc 0196
"Apology for Origen" *(De adulteratione librorum Origenis)*   Cetedoc 0198a
   (Prologus in apologeticum pamphili martyris pro Origene)   Cetedoc 0198b

Severian of Gabala
"Pauline Commentary from the Greek Church"
   "Fragments on the First Letter to the Thessalonians"
      (Fragmenta in epistulam i ad Thessalonicenses)   TLG 4139.046*
   "Fragments on the Letter to the Colossians"
      (Fragmenta in epistulam ad Colossenses)   TLG 4139.045*
   "Fragments on the Letter to Titus" *(Fragmenta in epistulam ad Titum)*   TLG 4139.050*
   "Fragments on the Second Letter to the Thessalonians"
      (Fragmenta in epistulam ii ad Thessalonicenses)   TLG 4139.047*
   "Fragments on the Second Letter to Timothy"
      (Fragmenta in epistulam ii ad Timotheum)   TLG 4139.049*

Tertullian
"Against Marcion" *(Adversus Marcionem)*   Cetedoc 0014
"Against Praxeas" *(Adversus Praxean)*   Cetedoc 0026
"Apology" *(Apologeticum)*   Cetedoc 0003
"On Baptism" *(De baptismo)*   Cetedoc 0008
"On Exhortation to Chastity" *(De exhortatione castitatis)*   Cetedoc 0020
"On Fasting" *(De jejunio adversus psychicos)*   Cetedoc 0029
"On Idolatry" *(De idololatria)*   Cetedoc 0023

"On Modesty" (De pudicitia)	Cetedoc 0030
"On Monogamy" (De monogamia)	Cetedoc 0028
"On Prayer" (De oratione)	Cetedoc 0007
"On Prescription Against Heretics" (De praescriptione haereticorum)	Cetedoc 0005
"On Repentance" (De paenitentia)	Cetedoc 0010
"On the Flesh of Christ" (De carne Christi)	Cetedoc 0018
"On the Resurrection of the Flesh" (De resurrectione mortuorum)	Cetedoc 0019
"To His Wife" (Ad uxorem)	Cetedoc 0012
"To the Martyrs" (Ad martyras)	Cetedoc 0001

Theodore of Mopsuestia
"Commentary on Colossians"
"Commentary on First Thessalonians"
"Commentary on First Timothy"
"Commentary on Philemon"
"Commentary on Second Thessalonians"
"Commentary on Second Timothy"
"Commentary on Titus"

Theodoret of Cyr
"Demonstrations by Syllogisms"

"Interpretation of the 14 Letters of St. Paul" (Interpretatio in xiv epistulas sancti Pauli)	TLG 4089.030
"Interpretation of the First Letter to the Thessalonians"	TLG 4089.030
"Interpretation of the First Letter to Timothy"	TLG 4089.030
"Interpretation of the Letter to Philemon"	TLG 4089.030
"Interpretation of the Letter to the Colossians"	TLG 4089.030
"Interpretation of the Letter to the Romans"	TLG 4089.030
"Interpretation of the Letter to Titus"	TLG 4089.030
"Interpretation of the Second Letter to the Thessalonians"	TLG 4089.030
"Interpretation of the Second Letter to Timothy"	TLG 4089.030
"Letters:78" (Epistulae: Collectio Sirmondiana, 1-95)	TLG 4089.006
"Letters: 109, 146" (Epistulae: Collectio Sirmondiana, 96-147)	TLG 4089.007

Valerian
"Homilies"

Vincent of Lérins
"Commonitories" (Commonitorium)	Cetedoc 0510

*At the time of publication these texts had not yet been included in the TLG database.

CHRONOLOGICAL LIST OF PERSONS & WRITINGS

The following chronology will assist readers in locating patristic writers, writings and recipients of letters referred to in this patristic commentary. Persons are arranged chronologically according to the terminal date of the years during which they flourished (fl.) or, where that cannot be determined, the date of death or approximate date of writing or influence. Writings are arranged according to the approximate date of composition.

Clement of Rome (pope), regn. 92-101?

Ignatius of Antioch, d. c. 110-112

Didache, c. 140

Shepherd of Hermas, c. 140/155

Marcion of Sinope, fl. 144, d. c. 154

Second Letter of Clement (so-called), c. 150

Polycarp of Smyrna, c. 69-155

Justin Martyr (of Flavia Neapolis in Palestine), c. 100/110-165, fl. c. 148-161

Montanist Oracles, c. latter half-2nd cent.

Theophilus of Antioch, late second century

Tatian the Syrian, c. 170

Athenagoras of Athens, c. 177

Irenaeus of Lyons, b. c. 135, fl. 180-199; d. c. 202

Clement of Alexandria, b. c. 150, fl. 190-215

Tertullian of Carthage, c. 155/160-225/250; fl. c. 197-222

Callistus of Rome (pope), regn. 217-222

Hippolytus of Rome, d. 235

Minucius Felix of Rome, fl. 218/235

Origen of Alexandria, b. 185, fl. c. 200-254

Novatian of Rome, fl. 235-258

Cyprian of Carthage, fl. 248-258

Dionysius the Great of Alexandria, fl. c. 247-265

Gregory Thaumaturgus (the Wonderworker), c. 213-270/275

Euthalius the Deacon, fourth century?

Victorinus of Petovium (Pettau), d. c. 304

Methodius of Olympus, d. c. 311

Lactantius (Africa), c. 250-325; fl. c. 304-321

Eusebius of Caesarea, b. c. 260/263; fl. c. 315-340

Aphrahat (Aphraates), c. 270-c. 345

Hegemonius (Pseudo-Archelaus), fl. c. 325-350

Cyril of Jerusalem, c. 315-386; fl. c. 348

Marius Victorinus, c. 280/285-c. 363; fl. 355-363

Acacius of Caesarea, d. 366

Macedonius of Constantinople, d. c. 362

Hilary of Poitiers, c. 315-367; fl. 350-367

Athanasius of Alexandria, c. 295-373; fl. 325-373

Ephrem the Syrian, b. c. 306; fl. 363-373

Macrina the Younger, c. 327-380

Basil the Great of Caesarea, b. c. 330; fl. 357-379

Gregory Nazianzen, b. 329/330, fl. 372-389

Gregory of Nyssa, c. 335-394

Amphilochius of Iconium, c. 340/345-post 394

Paulinus of Nola, 355-431; fl. 389-396

Ambrose of Milan, c. 333-397; fl. 374-397

Didymus the Blind, c. 313-398

Evagrius of Pontus, 345-399; fl. 382-399

Syriac *Book of Steps (Liber Graduum),* c. 400

Apostolic Constitutions, c. 400

Severian of Gabala, fl. c. 400

Prudentius, c. 348-after 405

John Chrysostom, 344/354-407; fl. 386-407
Jerome, c. 347-420
Maximus of Turin, d. 408/423
Pelagius, c. 350/354-c. 420/425
Palladius, c. 365-425; fl. 399-420
Theodore of Mopsuestia, c. 350-428
Honoratus of Arles, fl. 425, d. 429/430
Augustine of Hippo, 354-430; fl. 387-430
John Cassian, c. 360-432
Sixtus III of Rome (pope), regn. 432-440
Cyril of Alexandria, 375-444; fl. 412-444
Pseudo-Victor of Antioch, fifth century
Peter Chrysologus, c. 405-450
Leo the Great of Rome (pope), regn. 440-461
Theodoret of Cyr, 393-466; fl. 447-466
Basil of Selucia, fl. 440-468
Salvian the Presbyter of Marseilles, c. 400-c. 480
Euthymius (Palestine), 377-473

Gennadius of Constantinople, d. 471; fl. 458-471
Pseudo-Dionysius the Areopagite, c. 482-c. 532; fl c. 500
Symmachus of Rome (pope), regn. 498-514
Jacob of Sarug, 451-521
Philoxenus of Mabbug, c. 440-523
Fulgentius of Ruspe, c. 467-532
Caesarius of Arles, 470-542
Cyril of Scythopolis, b. 525; fl. c. 550
Oecumenius, sixth century
Gregory the Great (pope), 540-604; regn. 590-604
Isidore of Seville, c. 560-636
Sahdona (Martyrius), fl. 635-640
Isaac of Nineveh, d. c. 700
Bede the Venerable, 673-735
John of Damascus, c. 645-c. 749

Biographical Sketches & Short Descriptions of Select Anonymous Works

Alexander of Alexandria (fl. 312-328). Bishop of Alexandria and predecessor of Athanasius, upon whom he asserted considerable theological influence during the rise of Arianism. Alexander excommunicated Arius, whom he had appointed to the parish of Baucalis, in 319. His teaching regarding the eternal generation and divine substantial union of the Son with the Father was eventually confirmed at the Council of Nicea (325).

Ambrose of Milan (c. 333-397; fl. 374-397). Bishop of Milan and teacher of Augustine who defended the divinity of the Holy Spirit and the perpetual virginity of Mary.

Ambrosiaster (fl. c. 366-384). Name given by Erasmus to the author of a work once thought to have been composed by Ambrose.

Aphrahat (c. 270-350 fl. 337-345). "The Persian Sage" and first major Syriac writer whose work survives. He is also known by his Greek name Aphraates.

Apollinarius of Laodicea (310-c. 392). Bishop of Laodicea who was attacked by Gregory of Nazianzus, Gregory of Nyssa and Theodore for denying that Christ had a human mind.

Apostolic Constitutions (c. 381-394). Thought to be the work of the Arian bishop Julian of Neapolis. The work is divided into eight books, and is primarily a collection of and expansion on previous works such as the *Didache* (c. 140) and the *Apostolic Traditions*. Book 8 ends with eighty-five canons from various sources and is elsewhere known as the *Apostolic Canons*.

Arius (fl. c. 320). Heretic condemned at the Council of Nicaea (325) for refusing to accept that the Son was not a creature but was God by nature like the Father.

Athanasius of Alexandria (c. 295-373; fl. 325-373). Bishop of Alexandria from 328, though often in exile. He wrote his classic polemics against the Arians while most of the eastern bishops were against him.

Athenagoras (fl. 176-180). Early Christian philosopher and apologist from Athens, whose only authenticated writing, *A Plea Regarding Christians*, is addressed to the emperors Marcus Aurelius and Commodius, and defends Christians from the common accusations of atheism, incest and cannibalism.

Augustine of Hippo (354-430). Bishop of Hippo and a voluminous writer on philosophical, exegetical, theological and ecclesiological topics. He formulated the Western doctrines of predestination and original sin in his writings against the Pelagians.

Babai the Great (d. 628). Syriac monk who founded a monastery and school in his region of Beth Zabday and later served as third superior at the Great Convent of Mount Izla during a period of crisis in the Nestorian church.

Basil the Great (b. c. 330; fl. 357-379). One of the Cappadocian fathers, bishop of Caesarea and champion of the teaching on the Trinity propounded at Nicaea in 325. He was a great administrator and founded a monastic rule.

Basilides (fl. second century). Alexandrian heretic of the early second century who is said to have believed that souls migrate from body to body and that we do not sin if we lie to protect the body from martyrdom.

Bede the Venerable (c. 672/673-735). Born in Northumbria, at the age of seven he was put under the care of the Benedictine monks of Saints Peter and Paul at Jarrow and given a broad classical education in the monastic tradition. Considered one of the most learned men of his age, he is the author of *An Ecclesiastical History of the English People*.

Book of Steps (c. 400). Written by an anonymous Syriac author, this work consists of thirty homilies or discourses and which specifically deal with the more advanced stages of growth in the spiritual life.

Benedict of Nursia (c. 480-547). Considered the most important figure in the history of Western monasticism. Benedict founded many monasteries, the most notable found at Montecassino, but his lasting influence lay in his famous Rule. The Rule outlines the theological and inspirational foundation of the monastic ideal while also legislating the shape and organization of the coenobitic life.

Caesarius of Arles (c. 470-542). Bishop of Arles from 503 known primarily for his pastoral preaching.

Cassian, John (360-432). Author of a compilation of ascetic sayings highly influential in the development of Western monasticism.

Cassiodorus (c. 485-c. 540). Founder of Western monasticism whose writings include valuable histories and less valuable commentaries.

Chromatius (fl. 400). Friend of Rufinus and Jerome and author of tracts and sermons.

Clement of Alexandria (c. 150-215). A highly educated Christian convert from paganism, head of the catechetical school in Alexandria and pioneer of Christian scholarship. His major works, *Protrepticus, Paedagogus* and the *Stromata*, bring Christian doctrine face to face with the ideas and achievements of his time.

Clement of Rome (fl. c. 92-101). Pope whose *Epistle to the Corinthians* is one of the most important documents of subapostolic times.

Cyprian of Carthage (fl. 248-258). Martyred bishop of Carthage who maintained that those baptized by schismatics and heretics had no share in the blessings of the church.

Cyril of Alexandria (375-444; fl. 412-444). Patriarch of Alexandria whose strong espousal of the unity of Christ led to the condemnation of Nestorius in 431.

Cyril of Jerusalem (c. 315-386; fl. c. 348). Bishop of Jerusalem after 350 and author of *Catechetical Homilies*.

Didache (c. 140). Of unknown authorship, this text intertwines Jewish ethics with Christian liturgical practice to form a whole discourse on the "way of life." It exerted an enormous amount of influence in the patristic period and was especially used in the training of catechumen.

Didymus the Blind (c. 313-398). Alexandrian exegete who was much influenced by Origen and admired by Jerome.

Dionysius the Areopagite. The name of Dionysius the Areopagite was long given to the author of four mystical writings, probably from the late fifth century, which were the foundation of the apophatic school of mysticism in their denial that anything can be truly predicated of God.

Epiphanius of Salamis (c. 315-403). Bishop of Salamis in Cyprus, author of a refutation of eighty heresies (the *Panarion*) and instrumental in the condemnation of Origen.

Ephrem the Syrian (b. c. 306; fl. 363-373). Syrian writer of commentaries and devotional hymns which are sometimes regarded as the greatest specimens of Christian poetry prior to Dante.

Eunomius (d. 393). Bishop of Cyzicyus who was attacked by Basil and Gregory of Nyssa for maintaining that the Father and the Son were of different natures, one ingenerate, one generate.

Eusebius of Caesarea (c. 260/263-340). Bishop of Caesarea, partisan of the Emperor Constantine and first historian of the Christian church. He argued that the truth of the gospel had been foreshadowed in pagan writings but had to defend his own doctrine against suspicion of Arian sympathies.

Eusebius of Vercelli (fl. c. 360). Bishop of Vercelli who supported the trinitarian teaching of Nicaea (325) when it was being undermined by compromise in the West.

Faustinus (fl. 380). A priest in Rome and supporter of Lucifer and author of a treatise on the Trinity.

Filastrius (fl. 380). Bishop of Brescia and author of a compilation against all heresies.

Fulgentius of Ruspe (c. 467-532). Bishop of Ruspe and author of many orthodox sermons and tracts under the influence of Augustine.

Gaudentius of Brescia (fl. 395). Successor of Filastrius as bishop of Brescia and author of numerous tracts.

Gennadius of Constantinople (d. 471). Patriarch of Constantinople, author of numerous commentaries and an opponent of the Christology of Cyril of Alexandria.

Gnostics. Name now given generally to followers of Basilides, Marcion, Valentinus, Mani and others. The characteristic belief is that matter is a prison made for the spirit by an evil or ignorant creator, and that redemption depends on fate, not on free will.

Gregory of Elvira (fl. 359-385). Bishop of Elvira who wrote allegorical treatises in the style of Origen and defended the Nicene faith against the Arians.

Gregory of Nazianzus (b. 329/330; fl. 372-389). Bishop of Nazianzus and friend of Basil and Gregory of Nyssa. He is famous for maintaining the humanity of Christ as well as the orthodox doctrine of the Trinity.

Gregory of Nyssa (c. 335-394). Bishop of Nyssa and brother of Basil, he is famous for maintaining the equality in unity of the Father, Son and Holy Spirit.

Gregory the Great (c. 540-604). Pope from 590, the fourth and last of the Latin "Doctors of the Church." He was a prolific author and a powerful unifying force within the Latin Church, initiating the liturgical reform that brought about the Gregorian Sacramentary and Gregorian chant.

Hilary of Poitiers (c. 315-367). Bishop of Poitiers and called the "Athanasius of the West" because of his defense (against the Arians) of the common nature of Father and Son.

Hippolytus (fl. 222-245). Recent scholarship places Hippolytus in a Palestinian context, personally familiar with Origen. Though he is known mostly for *The Refutation of All Heresies*, he was primarily a commentator on Scripture (especially the Old Testament) and other sacred texts.

Ignatius of Antioch (c. 35-107/112). Bishop of Antioch who wrote several letters to local churches while being taken from Antioch to Rome to be martyred. In the letters, which warn against heresy, he stresses orthodox Christology, the centrality of the Eucharist and unique role of the bishop in preserving the unity of the church.

Irenaeus of Lyon (c. 135-c. 202). Bishop of Lyons who published the most famous and influential refutation of Gnostic thought.

Isaac of Nineveh (d. c. 700). Also known as Isaac the Syrian or Isaac Syrus, this monastic writer served for a short while as bishop of Nineveh before retiring to live a secluded monastic life. His writings on ascetic subjects survive in the form of numerous homilies.

Jerome (c. 347-420). Gifted exegete and exponent of a classical Latin style, now best known as the translator of the Latin Vulgate. He defended the perpetual virginity of Mary, attacked Origen and Pelagius and supported extreme ascetic practices.

John Chrysostom (344/354-407; fl. 386-407). Bishop of Constantinople who was famous for his orthodoxy, his eloquence and his attacks on Christian laxity in high places.

John of Damascus (c. 650-750). Arab monastic and theologian whose writings enjoyed great influence in both the Eastern and Western Churches. His most famous writing was the *Orthodox Faith*.

John the Elder (c. eighth century) A Syriac author who belonged to monastic circles of the

Church of the East and lived in the region of Mount Qardu (north Iraq). His most important writings are twenty-two homilies and a collection of fifty-one short letters in which he describes the mystical life as an anticipatory experience of the resurrection life, the fruit of the sacraments of baptism and the Eucharist.

Justin Martyr (c. 100/110-165, fl. c. 148-161). Palestinian philosopher who was converted to Christianity, "the only sure and worthy philosophy." He traveled to Rome where he wrote several apologies against both pagans and Jews, combining Greek philosophy and Christian theology; he was eventually martyred.

Leo the Great (regn. 440-461). Bishop of Rome whose *Tome to Flavian* helped to strike a balance between Nestorian and Cyrilline positions at the Council of Chalcedon in 451.

Letter to Diognetus (c. third century). The author of this letter is unknown, and the exact identity of its recipient, Diognetus, continues to elude patristic scholars. The letter is essentially a refutation of paganism and an exposition of the Christian life and faith.

Lucifer (fl. 370). Bishop of Cagliari and fanatical partisan of Athanasius. He and his followers entered into schism after refusing to acknowledge less orthodox bishops appointed by the Emperor Constantius.

Macrina the Younger (c. 327-380). The elder sister of Basil the Great and Gregory of Nyssa, she is known as `the Younger" to distinguish her from her paternal grandmother. She had a powerful influence on her younger brothers, especially on Gregory, who called her his teacher and relates her teaching in *On the Soul and the Resurrection*.

Manichaeans. A religious movement that originated circa 241 in Persia under the leadership of Mani but was apparently of complex Christian origin. It is said to have denied free will and the universal sovereignty of God, teaching that kingdoms of light and darkness are coeternal and that the redeemed are particles of a spiritual man of light held captive in the darkness of matter (*see* Gnostics).

Marcion (fl. 144). Heretic of the mid-second century who rejected the Old Testament and much of the New Testament, claiming that the Father of Jesus Christ was other than the Creator God (*see* Gnostics).

Marius Victorinus (b. c. 280/285; fl. c. 355-363). Grammarian who translated works of Platonists and, after his late conversion (c. 355), used them against the Arians.

Mark the Hermit (c. sixth century). Monk who lived near Tarsus and produced works on ascetic practices as well as christological issues.

Maximus of Turin (d. 408/423). Bishop of Turin who died during the reigns of Honorius and Theodosius the Younger (408-423). Over one hundred of his sermons survive.

Methodius of Olympus (fl. 290). Bishop of Olympus who celebrated virginity in a *Symposium* partly modeled on Plato's dialogue of that name.

Montanist Oracles. Montanism was an apocalyptic and strictly ascetic movement begun in the latter half of the second century by a certain Montanus in Phrygia, who, along with certain of his followers, uttered oracles they claimed were inspired by the Holy Spirit. Little of the authentic oracles remains and most of what is known of Montanism comes from the authors who wrote against the movement. Montanism was formally condemned as a heresy before by Asiatic synods.

Nemesius of Emesa (fl. late fourth century). Bishop of Emesa in Syria whose most important work, Of the Nature of Man, draws on several theological and philosophical sources and is the first exposition of a Christian anthropology.

Nestorius (b. 381; fl. 430). Patriarch of Constantinople 428-431 and credited with the foundation of the heresy which says that the divine and human natures were associated, rather than truly united, in the incarnation of Christ.

Nicetas of Remesiana (fl. second half of fourth century). Bishop of Remesiana in Serbia, whose works affirm the consubstantiality of the Son and the deity of the Holy Spirit.

Novatian of Rome (fl. 235-258). Roman theologian, otherwise orthodox, who formed a schismatic church after failing to become pope. His treatise on the Trinity states the classic western doctrine.

Oecumenius (sixth century). Called the Rhetor or the Philosopher, Oecumenius wrote the earliest extant Greek commentary on Revelation. Scholia by Oecumenius on some of John Chrysostom's commentaries on the Pauline Epistles are still extant.

Origen of Alexandria (b. 185; fl. c. 200-254). Influential exegete and systematic theologian. He was condemned (perhaps unfairly) for maintaining the preexistence of souls while denying the resurrection of the body, the literal truth of Scripture and the equality of the Father and the Son in the Trinity.

Pelagius (c. 354-c. 420). Christian teacher whose followers were condemned in 418 and 431 for maintaining that a Christian could be perfect and that salvation depended on free will.

Peter Chrysologus (c. 380-450). Latin archbishop of Ravenna whose teachings included arguments for the supremacy of the papacy and the relationship between grace and Christian living.

Philoxenus of Mabbug (c. 440-523). Bishop of Mabbug (Hierapolis) and a leading thinker in the early Syrian Orthodox Church. His extensive writings in Syriac include a set of thirteen *Discourses on the Christian Life*, several works on the incarnation and a number of exegetical works.

Poemen (c. fifth century) One-seventh of the sayings in the *Sayings of the Desert Fathers* are attributed to Poemen, which is Greek for shepherd. Poemen was a common title among early Egyptian desert ascetics, and it is unknown whether all the sayings come from one person.

Polycarp of Smyrna (c. 69-155). Bishop of Smyrna who vigorously fought heretics such as the Marcionites and Valentinians. He was the leading Christian figure in Roman Asia in the middle of the second century.

Prudentius (c. 348-c. 410). Aurelius Prudentius Clemens was a Latin poet and hymn-writer who devoted his later life to Christian writing. He wrote didactic poems on the theology of the incarnation, against the heretic Marcion and against the resurgence of paganism.

Quodvultdeus (fl. 430). Carthaginian deacon and friend of Augustine who endeavored to show at length how the New Testament fulfilled the Old Testament.

Rufinus of Aquileia (c. 345-411). Orthodox Christian thinker and historian who nonetheless translated Origen and defended him against the strictures of Jerome and Epiphanius.

Sabellius (fl. 200). Allegedly the author of the heresy which maintains that the Father and Son are a single person. The patripassian variant of this heresy states that the Father suffered on the cross.

Sahdona (fl. 635-640). Known in Greek as Martyrius, this Syriac author was bishop of Beth Garmai for a short time. His most important work is the deeply scriptural *Book of Perfection* which ranks as one of the masterpieces of Syriac monastic literature.

Second Letter of Clement (c. 150). The so-called *Second Letter of Clement* is the earliest surviving Christian sermon probably written by a Corinthian author, though some scholars have assigned it to a Roman or Alexandrian author.

Severian of Gabala (fl. c. 400). A contemporary of John Chrysostom, he was highly regarded preacher in Constantinople, particularly at the imperial court, and ultimately sided with Chrysostom's accusers. His sermons are dominated by antiheretical concerns.

Shepherd of Hermas (second century). Divided into five *Visions*, twelve *Mandates* and ten *Similitudes*, this Christian apocalypse was written by a former slave and named for the form of the second angel said to have granted him his visions. This work was highly esteemed for its moral value and was used as a textbook for catechumens in the early church.

Tertullian of Carthage (c. 155/160-225/250; fl. c. 197-222). Brilliant Carthaginian apologist and polemicist who laid the foundations of Christology and trinitarian orthodoxy in the West, though he himself was estranged from the main church by its laxity.

Theodore of Mopsuestia (c. 350-428). Bishop of Mopsuestia, founder of the Antiochene, or literalistic, school of exegesis. A great man in his day, he was later condemned as a precursor of Nestorius.

Theodoret of Cyr (c. 393-466). Bishop of Cyr (Cyrrhus), he was an opponent of Cyril, whose doctrine of Christ's person was finally vindicated in 451 at the Council of Chalcedon.

Valentinus (fl. c. 140). Alexandrian heretic of the mid-second century who taught that the material world was created by the transgression of God's Wisdom, or Sophia (*see* Gnostics).

Vincent of Lérins (d. 435). Monk who has exerted considerable influence through his writings on orthodox dogmatic theological method, as contrasted with the theological methodologies of the heresies.

Subject Index

abstinence, 43, 79
Adam, 18, 33, 160, 166. *See also*
  sin, Adam and Eve
admonition, 211, 270. *See also*
  correction
adoption, 14, 62, 117, 245
adversity, 63
affliction
  and death, 84
  enduring, 74, 86, 93-94,
    103, 189, 265
  expectation of, 75
  joy in, 61, 75
  judgment and, 104
  repayment of, 104
  See also persecution;
    prayer; reward; virtue
Africa, 4
ancestor, 231
angels
  and Christ, 18, 180
  guardian, 66
  and humans, 234
  and the law, 39
  limitation of, 2, 5, 8, 13,
    14, 21, 31, 113, 114, 239
  and wisdom, 179-80
  as witness, 239
  worship of, 38, 39, 40
Antichrist
  and Christ, 112
  and the day of judgment,
    109
  identity of the, xxix, 109,
    110, 111, 114
  nature of, 108
Antiochene, 90
antiquity, 181, 228
anxiety, 78, 240-41
Apocrypha, 188
Apollinaris, 158
apostle, 6, 26, 143, 207
Archippus, 311
Arian, Arianism, xxvii, 102,
  133, 182, 249, 253
ascension, 118

asceticism
  false, 41, 42, 261
  Paul on, xxx-xxxi
  Pelagius on, xxiv
  proper, xxxi, 184, 293
assistantship, 74
Asterius, 136
avarice, 214
baptism
  administration of, 205
  analogies of, 31-32, 120,
    135, 241
  and commandments, 99
  and the devil, 9
  and salvation, 7-8, 14, 17,
    62, 99, 245, 304, 305
  of water and blood, 304
  See also adoption; redemp-
    tion; regeneration;
    renewal; resurrection
belief, 62
bishops
  instructions to, 168-73,
    285, 289, 296
  and presbyters, 193-285
  qualities of, xxxi-xxxii,
    168-73, 256
blindness, 40
blood, 34
body
  care of the, 207, 213
  conditions of the, 33, 48,
    70, 79, 199
  and soul, 198, 199
  and spirit, 100
  See also flesh
bond, xxviii, 33, 34. *See also*
  Christ, Jesus, and the bond
Callimachus, 290, 291
calling, 234
celibacy, xxxii, 41, 183
Celsus, 108, 109, 153, 190
charity, 126-27, 134, 221-22,
  292-93, 307-8
  importance of, 82, 119
  spiritual, 67
  virtues of, xxiv, 199, 216,
    220, 260-61
  See also love
chastity, 42, 79, 184, 200
children, 51, 65, 305. *See also*
  family relations, children,
  parents and children
choice, freedom of, 6, 48
Christ, Jesus
  and adoption, 117
  appearances of, 12, 35
  ascension of, 20, 107, 118

body of, 22, 35, 36, 38, 88
and the bond, 33-35
and the church, 13, 17, 31
as the cornerstone, 136
and creation, xxvii, 14-16,
  30, 31
cross of, xxvii, 21, 36, 179,
  234
divinity of, xxvii, 12, 13,
  17, 19-21, 29-31, 35,
  157, 159, 298
as firstborn, xxvii, 12-14,
  18-19
and hell, 20
humanity of, xxviii, 12, 13,
  17-22, 30, 89, 109, 157-
  60, 243, 293
humility of, 110, 211
imitation of, 192, 211
incarnation of, xxvii,
  xxviii, 16, 235, 243
as judge, 86, 88, 89, 113,
  161, 269, 275
and knowledge, 17, 26, 27
lordship of, xxviii, xxxi, 40,
  161, 241, 226
as mediator, xxviii, 26,
  154, 157, 158, 159, 160
and mystery, 25, 26, 179
as only-begotten, 14, 298
as physician, 303
pre-existence of, 16
and reconciliation, 20-22,
  26, 30
resurrection of, xxviii, 36,
  235
return of, xxviii, xxix, 46,
  86, 104, 106, 108, 118,
  181, 275, 298
sacrifice of, 158, 298
and salvation, xxiv, xxvii,
  xxviii, xxix, 3, 5, 8, 19,
  32, 56, 144, 155-56, 190,
  227, 235, 244-45, 300
soldiers of, 240, 241
soul of, 159
suffering of, 24-25, 71, 79,
  235, 243
as sustainer, 16
tree of, 160
unity in, 27, 245, 297
and wisdom, 18, 26, 27
the Word, 11, 15, 112
See also angels; Antichrist;
  church; elect; humility;
  image; immortality;
  law; light; mystery;
  peace; providence; soul;

spirit; tree
Christian life, xxxiii, 57, 95, 98,
  242
  athletic analogy of, xxx,
    241-42
  and perfection, xxix, 88,
    100
  qualities of, xxix, 169, 189,
    225-26, 299
  and virtue xxiv, 264
  See also holiness; perfec-
    tion; purity
Christmas, 298
church, 177, 178, 179, 285
  and affliction, 24-25
  and Christ, 18, 166, 198,
    304
  and God, 19-20, 177
  membership, 17, 178, 255,
    300-301, 311
  and salvation, xxviii, xxx,
    3, 206
  unity of, 120, 177, 178,
    307
  universality of, 4, 18
  and use of resources, 196,
    203-4, 211
  See also Christ, Jesus, and
    the church
circumcision, 26, 31-32. *See
  also* Galatians
clergy, xxxi, 240. *See also* bishops; elders; pastor; presbyters
Colossians, 1, 2, 5, 42, 49-50,
  56
commandments, 45, 138
compassion, xxvi, 96, 97, 225.
  See also charity; love
confession, 114
contentment, 213
continence, 185-86, 287. *See
  also* self-control; virtue
correction, 96, 196, 205, 256-
  57, 270. *See also* admonition
covetousness, 213
creation, xxvii, 14-16, 186,
  187, 221, 254
  goodness of, xxxi, 186,
    187, 292, 294
Cretans, 290, 291
cross, 34, 35, 36, 163. *See also*
  Christ, Jesus, cross of
darkness, 92, 93, 223, 254
day of judgment, 27, 109
day of the Lord, 92, 108, 254
deacon, xxxii, 174-76
death, xxviii, 32, 83-87, 190